Treasury of the True Dharma Eye

Dōgen's *Shōbōgenzō*

Treasury of the True Dharma Eye
Dōgen's *Shōbōgenzō*

Volume II

The Seventy-five-Chapter Compilation

Part 2

Chapters 16–30

An annotated translation
by the Sōtō Zen Text Project

Sōtōshū Shūmuchō
Tokyo

University of Hawai'i Press
Honolulu

© 2023 by Sōtōshū Shūmuchō
The Administrative Headquarters of Sōtō Zen Buddhism
All rights reserved.
Printed in China

Treasury of the True Dharma Eye: Dōgen's *Shōbōgenzō*
Volume II: The Seventy-five-Chapter Compilation, Part 2, Chapters 16–30

Published in Japan by Sōtōshū Shūmuchō, Tokyo
ISBN: 978-4-911061-00-8

Published for the rest of the world by University of Hawai'i Press, Honolulu

Library of Congress Cataloging-in-Publication Data

Names: Dōgen, 1200–1253, author. | Sōtō Zen Text Project, translator.

Title: Treasury of the true dharma eye : Dōgen's Shōbōgenzō / an
annotated translation by the Sōtō Zen Text Project.

Other titles: Shōbō genzō. English

Description: Honolulu : University of Hawai'i Press, [2024] | Published in
Japan by Sōtōshū Shūmuchō, 2023. | Includes bibliographical
references and index. | Contents: v. 2. The seventy-five-chapter
compilation, part 2, chapters 16–30

Identifiers: LCCN 2024004760 (print) | LCCN 2024004761 (ebook) | ISBN
9780824899172 (v. 1 ; paperback) | ISBN 9780824899189 (v. 2 ; paperback)
| ISBN 9780824899196 (v. 3 ; paperback) | ISBN 9780824899202 (v. 4 ;
paperback) | ISBN 9780824899219 (v. 5 ; paperback) | ISBN 9780824899226
(v. 6 ; paperback) | ISBN 9780824899233 (v. 7 ; paperback) | ISBN
9780824899240 (v. 8 ; paperback) | ISBN 9780824899257 (paperback) | ISBN
9798880700264 (v. 1 ; pdf) | ISBN 9798880700271 (v. 2 ; pdf) | ISBN
9798880700288 (v. 3 ; pdf) | ISBN 9798880700295 (v. 4 ; pdf) | ISBN
9798880700301 (v. 5 ; pdf) | ISBN 9798880700318 (v. 6 ; pdf) | ISBN
9798880700325 (v. 7 ; pdf) | ISBN 9798880700332 (v. 8 ; pdf)

Subjects: LCSH: Sōtōshū—Doctrines—Early works to 1800.

Classification: LCC BQ9449.D653 E5 2024 (print) | LCC BQ9449.D653 (ebook)
| DDC 294.3/85—dc23/eng/20240318

LC record available at https://lccn.loc.gov/2024004760
LC ebook record available at https://lccn.loc.gov/2024004761

Cover art: Eihei Dōgen Zenji Gyōjōzu scroll, courtesy of Rev. Ōtani Tetsuo
Cover design by Urs App

University of Hawai'i Press books are printed on acid-free paper and meet the
guidelines for permanence and durability of the Council on Library Resources.
Printer-ready copy has been provided by Sōtōshū Shūmuchō

Contents

Volume II

The Seventy-five-Chapter Compilation

Part 2

Conventions iii

Abbreviations v

16A. Sustained Practice, Part 1 *Gyōji jō* 行持上 1

16B. Sustained Practice, Part 2 *Gyōji ge* 行持下 53

17. Such *Inmo* 恁麼 113

18. Avalokiteśvara *Kannon* 觀音 133

19. The Old Mirror *Kokyō* 古鏡 151

20. Sometimes *Uji* 有時 191

21. Prediction *Juki* 授記 211

22. Full Function *Zenki* 全機 237

23. The Moon *Tsuki* 都機 245

24. Painted Cake *Gabyō* 畫餅 259

25. Sound of the Stream, Form of the Mountain
    Keisei sanshoku 溪聲山色 277

26. Beyond the Buddha *Butsu kōjō ji* 佛向上事 305

27. Talking of a Dream within a Dream *Muchū setsumu* 夢中説夢 .. 329

28. Making a Bow and Getting the Marrow *Raihai tokuzui* 禮拜得髓 351

29. The Mountains and Waters Sūtra *Sansui kyō* 山水經 387

30. Sūtra Reading *Kankin* 看經 419

Conventions

This publication is an annotated translation, in seven volumes, of one hundred three texts of Dōgen's Japanese *Shōbōgenzō,* plus an additional volume containing an introduction, supplementary notes, appendices, and list of works cited. The translation is based on the edition of the *Shōbōgenzō* published in Kawamura Kōdō 河村孝道, ed., *Dōgen zenji zenshū* 道元禅師全集, vols. 1-2 (Tokyo: Shunjūsha, 1991, 1993), cited herein as DZZ.1 and DZZ.2; volume and page numbers of this edition are noted in braces at the corresponding locations in the translation.

The Japanese text accompanying the translation here follows the punctuation and *kanazukai* of the Kawamura edition; for ease of reference to premodern sources, Kawamura's modern Japanese kanji have been replaced with traditional forms. Also, for ease of reference, the sections into which the texts of the Kawamura edition are divided have been assigned numbers in square brackets by the translators. The translation of Kawamura's longer sections is sometimes broken into separate paragraphs, and transitions to new topics between sections are sometimes marked by a string of asterisks.

Though primarily written in Japanese, the *Shōbōgenzō* includes many passages of Chinese, ranging from long quotations of texts to short phrases inserted into the Japanese sentences. Since this inclusion of Chinese is a prominent linguistic feature of the original texts, the translation seeks to indicate such passages by the use of oblique font. The reader is warned that, given the ubiquity in the Japanese language of expressions adopted from Chinese, the identification of the shorter phrases as Chinese, rather than Japanese, is often rather arbitrary.

Much of the *Shōbōgenzō* is devoted to comment on material in other texts. The translation uses quotation marks to indicate terms and passages on which Dōgen is commenting. Here, again, the reader is warned that the distinction between use and mention can often be difficult to draw.

Sanskrit, Chinese, and Japanese terms appearing in the *Oxford English Dictionary* (3rd edition) are considered to have been adopted into English; other such terms are treated as foreign words and rendered in italics. Romanization of all such terms, whether treated as foreign or English, is given with diacritics.

DŌGEN'S *SHŌBŌGENZŌ* VOLUME II

With some exceptions, Chinese transliterations of Sanskrit terms are rendered as romanized Sanskrit. Indic proper nouns, whether transliterated or translated in the Chinese, are rendered as their presumed originals where possible; the reader is warned that some such reconstructions are unattested and speculative.

The proper noun "Zen" is used in reference to (a) the tradition that Dōgen calls the "buddhas and ancestors," and (b) the Japanese instantiation of that tradition; the Chinese name "Chan" is used in reference to the Chinese instantiation of the tradition.

Romanized readings of the Japanese text given in the notes follow wherever possible the ruby in Kawamura's text; readings not provided by Kawamura are based on *Zengaku daijiten* 禅学大辞典 (1978) and/or Katō Shūkō 加藤宗厚, *Shōbōgenzō yōgo sakuin* 正法眼藏用語索引 (1962).

Citations of T (*Taishō shinshū daizōkyō* 大正新脩大藏經) are from the *SAT Daizōkyō Text Database* (https://21dzk.l.u-tokyo.ac.jp/SAT). Citations of ZZ (*Dainihon zokuzōkyō* 大日本続藏經) are from the *CBETA Hanwen dazangjing* 漢文大藏經 (http://tripitaka.cbeta.org). Citations of KR are from *Kanripo* 漢リポ *Kanseki Repository* (https://www.kanripo.org).

The Kawamura edition provides colophons from several sources, some following the relevant chapter, some in the head notes of the chapter, some in the collation notes (*honbun kōi* 本文校異) for that chapter in the end matter of DZZ.1 and DZZ.2. For the convenience of the reader, this translation collects these colophons (and occasionally others omitted by Kawamura) at the end of each chapter. Colophons without attribution are assumed to have been written by Dōgen.

ABBREVIATIONS

C   Chinese language

DZZ   *Dōgen zenji zenshū* 道元禅師全集, Kagamishima Genryū 鏡島元隆 et al., compilers. 7 vols. Tokyo: Shunjūsha, 1988–1993.

ESST *Eihei Shōbōgenzō shūsho taisei* 永平正法眼蔵蒐書大成, Kawamura Kōdō 河村孝道, ed. 27 vols. Tokyo: Taishūkan Shoten, 1974-1982.

J   Japanese language

KR   Kanseki Repository (Kanseki Ripo 漢籍リポ). Online: https://www.kanripo.org

M   *Dai kanwa jiten* 大漢和辞典, Morohashi Tetsuji 諸橋轍次, ed. 13 vols. (plus 2-vol. supplement) Tokyo: Taishūkan Shoten, 1955-1960.

S   Sanskrit

SCZ   *Shōbōgenzō chūkai zensho* 正法眼藏註解全書, Jinbo Nyoten 神保如天 and Andō Bun'ei 安藤文英, eds. 11 vols. Reprint Tokyo: Nihon Bussho Kankōkai, 1956-1957.

SZ   *Sōtōshū zensho* 曹洞宗全書. 20 vols. Tokyo: Kōmeisha, 1929-1938.

T   *Taishō shinshū daizōkyō* 大正新脩大藏經, Takakusu Junjirō 高楠順次郎 and Watanabe Kaikyoku 渡邊海旭, eds. 100 vols. Tokyo: Daizōkyōkai, 1924–1935.

ZT   *Zengaku taikei* 禪學大系. 8 vols. Tokyo: Kokusho Kankōkai, 1952 (orig. publ. 1910-11).

ZTS   *Zengaku tenseki sōkan* 禅学典籍叢刊, Yanagida Seizan 柳田聖山 and Shiina Kōyū 椎名宏雄, eds. 12 vols. Kyoto: Rinsen Shoten, 1999-2001.

ZZ   *Dainihon zokuzōkyō* 大日本続藏經. 150 vols. Kyoto: Bussho Kankōkai, 1905-1912.

Treasury of the True Dharma Eye
Number 16A

Sustained Practice
Part 1

Gyōji

行持

Sustained Practice

Gyōji

Part 1

INTRODUCTION

This work, easily the longest in the *Shōbōgenzō*, consists of two parts. In the seventy-five-chapter *Shōbōgenzō*, they are numbered as chapter 16, Parts 1 (*jō* 上) and 2 (*ge* 下); in the sixty-chapter *Shōbōgenzō*, they are treated as two separate chapters, numbers 16 and 17. The ninety-five-chapter Honzan edition accords with the seventy-five-chapter compilation in treating the two parts as a single chapter, numbered 30. At the end of Part 2, both the sixty- and seventy-five-chapter manuscripts bear a colophon by Dōgen placing the composition in May of 1242, at Kōshōji, with a second colophon in the sixty-chapter witnesses by Dōgen's disciple Ejō recording the latter's copying of the work in early 1243. These notices are presumed to refer to both parts of the work.

The title term, *gyōji* 行持, which in other contexts, might better be rendered "to observe" or "to uphold" (as in "uphold" the Buddhist precepts), is translated here in keeping with the common interpretation of Dōgen's use in the sense "spiritual practice that is constant (or endures or is continuously maintained)." As this title suggests, then, our text is devoted to accounts of the spiritual practice of its author's predecessors. Part 1 opens with a panegyric on "sustained practice" — what Dōgen describes as "the way circling round without being cut off — aspiration for buddhahood, practice, bodhi, and nirvāṇa, without the slightest interval." This is not, he goes on to say, simply the individual's intentional practice: it is the sustained practice of the buddhas and ancestors manifested in us and, indeed, in the sun, moon, and stars. He then proceeds to recount edifying examples of such practice by some two dozen figures, including Buddha Śākyamuni and two of the early ancestors in India, as well as the example of Chinese emperors.

正法眼藏第十六
Treasury of the True Dharma Eye
Number 16

行持 上
Sustained Practice
Part 1

[16A:1] {1:145}

佛祖の大道、かならず無上の行持あり、道環して斷絶せず、發心・修行・菩提・涅槃、しばらくの間隙あらず、行持道環なり。このゆえに、みづからの強爲にあらず、他の強爲にあらず、不曾染汚の行持なり。この行持の功德、われを保任し、他を保任す。その宗旨は、わが行持、すなはち十方の匝地漫天、みなその功德をかうぶる。他もしらず、われもしらずといへども、しかあるなり。このゆえに、諸佛諸祖の行持によりて、われらが行持見成し、われらが大道通達するなり。われらが行持によりて、諸佛の行持見成し、諸佛の大道通達するなり。われらが行持によりて、この道環の功德あり。これによりて、佛佛祖祖、佛住し、佛非し、佛心し、佛成して、斷絶せざるなり。この行持によりて日月星辰あり、行持によりて大地虚空あり、行持によりて依正身心あり、行持によりて四大五蘊あり。行持、これ世人の愛處にあらざれども、諸人の實歸なるべし。過去・現在・未來の諸佛の行持によりて、過去・現在・未來の諸佛は現成するなり。その行持の功德、ときにかくれず、かるがゆえに發心・修行す。その功德、ときにあらはれず、かるがゆえに見聞・覺知せず。あらはれざれども、かくれずと參學すべし、隱顯・存没に染汚せられざるがゆえに。われを見成する行持、いまの當隱に、これいかたる緣起の諸法ありて行持すると不會なるは、行持の會取、さらに新條の特地にあらざるによりてなり。緣起は行持なり、行持は緣起せざるがゆえにと、功夫參學を審細にすべし。かの行持を見成する行持は、すなはちこれわれらがいまの行持なり。行持のいまは、自己の本有・元住にあらず。行持のいまは、自己に去來・出入するにあらず。いまといふ道は、行持よりさきにあるにはあらず、行持現成するをいまといふ。

In the great way of the buddhas and ancestors, there is always unsurpassed sustained practice: the way circling round without being cut off — bringing forth the mind [of bodhi], practice, bodhi, and nirvāṇa, without the slightest interval — sustained practice is the way circling round.[1] Therefore, it is not something we force ourselves to do or that others

---

1 **sustained practice** (*gyōji* 行持): A term appearing often in Dōgen's writing. While in other contexts, it might better be rendered "observance" (as in "to observe" the Buddhist precepts), the translation here reflects the common interpretation of Dōgen's use as "practice that is constant or enduring."

4   DŌGEN'S *SHŌBŌGENZŌ* VOLUME II

force us to do: it is sustained practice that has never defiled.[2] The merit of this sustained practice maintains the self and maintains the other.[3] The essential point here is that, in our practice, around the earth and throughout the heavens in the ten directions, everything receives its merit.[4] Although the other may not be aware of it, and we may not be aware of it, it is so.

Therefore, owing to the sustained practice of the buddhas and ancestors, our sustained practice is manifested, and our great way penetrates everywhere; owing to our sustained practice, the sustained practice of the buddhas is manifested, and the great way of the buddhas penetrates everywhere. Owing to our sustained practice, there is this virtue of the way circling round; owing to this, buddha after buddha and ancestor after ancestor do buddha-abiding, do buddha-denying, do buddha-minding, do buddha-attaining, and are not cut off.[5] Owing to this sustained practice, there are the sun, moon, and stars; owing to sustained practice, there are the whole earth and empty space; owing to sustained practice, there are secondary and primary recompense, body and mind; owing to sustained practice, there are the four elements and five aggregates.[6]

---

the way circling round (*dōkan* 道環): An unusual expression occurring several times in the *Shōbōgenzō*.

bringing forth the mind [of bodhi], practice, bodhi, and nirvāṇa (*hosshin shugyō bodai nehan* 發心修行菩提涅槃): A standard set of terms summarizing the spiritual path of the bodhisattva, from the initial aspiration for bodhi through final nirvāṇa; see Supplementary Notes, s.v. "Bring forth the mind."

2   **sustained practice that has never defiled** (*fuzō zenna no gyōji* 不曽染汚の行持): Likely reflecting the remark of Nanyue Huairang 南嶽懷讓 (677-744), recorded in the *shinji Shōbōgenzō* 眞字正法眼藏 (DZZ.5:178, case 101) and alluded to throughout the *Shōbōgenzō*, to the effect that he is "not defiled" (*fuzenna* 不染汚) by Buddhist practice and verification; see Supplementary Notes, s.v. "Not defiled."

3   **maintains the self and maintains the other** (*ware o hōnin shi, ta o hōnin su* われを保任し、他を保任す): Although this might be taken as a reference simply to "oneself and others," the context suggests a more metaphysical sense: "the self and the world."

4   **around the earth and throughout the heavens** (*sōchi manten* 匝地漫天): A fixed expression for "everywhere"; common in Chinese texts but not used elsewhere in the *Shōbōgenzō*.

5   **do buddha-abiding, do buddha-denying, do buddha-minding, do buddha-attaining** (*butsujū shi, buppi shi, busshin shi, butsujō shite* 佛住し、佛非し、佛心し、佛成して): An awkward attempt to render an odd string of four compound terms, each beginning with "buddha," used as verbs.

6   **secondary and primary recompense** (*eshō* 依正): A standard Buddhist term for the results of past karma reflected respectively in the circumstances into which one is born and the mental and physical makeup of the person; see Supplementary Notes, s.v. "Secondary and primary recompense."

16A. Sustained Practice, Part 1 *Gyōji* 行持

Although sustained practice is not what the worldly love, it should be people's real refuge.[7] Owing to the sustained practice of the buddhas of past, present, and future, the buddhas of past, present, and future appear. The merit of that sustained practice at times is not hidden; hence, we bring forth the mind and engage in the practice; at times, that merit is not apparent; hence we do not see, hear, perceive, or know it. Although it is not apparent, we should study it as not hidden; for it is not defiled by "hidden" or "apparent," "existing" or "vanishing." The sustained practice that manifests the self — that we do not understand, in its present hiddenness, from what conditioned dharmas the sustained practice occurs is due to the fact that the understanding of sustained practice is not some further new special state.[8] We should make concentrated effort and study in detail that conditioned arising is sustained practice, for sustained practice does not arise from conditions.[9] The sustained practice that manifests that sustained practice — this is precisely our present sustained practice. The present of sustained practice is not the original being or primal abode of the self; the present of sustained practice does not come to and go from, enter or exit, the self. It is not that the word "the present" exists prior to sustained practice: the manifestation of sustained practice is called "the present."

[16A:2] {1:146}

しかあればすなはち、一日の行持、これ諸佛の種子なり、諸佛の行持なり。この行持に諸佛見成せられ、行持せらるるを、行持せざるは、諸佛をいとひ、諸佛を供養せず、行持をいとひ、諸佛と同生同死せず、同學同參せざるなり。いまの華開・葉落、これ行持の見成なり。磨鏡・破鏡、それ行持にあらざるなし。このゆえに、行持をさしおかんと擬するは、行持を

---

four elements and five aggregates (*shidai goun* 四大五蘊): I.e., the four primary forms of matter (S. *mahābhūta*) — earth, water, fire, and wind, of which the physical world is composed; and the five "heaps" (S. *skandha*) — form, sensation, perception, formations, and consciousness — into which the psychophysical organism can be analyzed. See Supplementary Notes, s.v. "Four elements and five aggregates."

7 **Although sustained practice is not what the worldly love** (*gyōji kore sejin no aisho ni arazaredomo* 行持これ世人の愛處にあらざれども): Perhaps recalling a line, alluded to elsewhere in the *Shōbōgenzō*, from the poem *Caoan ge* 草庵歌, by Shitou Xiqian 石頭希遷 (700-790): "What the worldly love, I don't love" (*sejin aisho ga fu ai* 世人愛處我不愛). See Supplementary Notes, s.v. "*Reverend Shitou's Song of the Thatched Hut*."

8 **The sustained practice that manifests the self** (*ware o genjō suru gyōji* われを見成する行持): A convoluted sentence perhaps to be understood, "we do not understand what occurs to bring about the sustained practice that manifests the self, because the practice and our understanding of it are not separate from each other."

9 **conditioned arising is sustained practice, for sustained practice does not arise from conditions** (*engi wa gyōji nari, gyōji wa engi sezaru ga yue ni* 緣起は行持なり、行持は緣起せざるがゆえに): I.e., sustained practice is not conditioned; rather, conditioned phenomena arise from the practice.

6   DŌGEN'S *SHŌBŌGENZŌ* VOLUME II

のがれんとする邪心をかくさんがために、行持をさしおくも行持なるによ
りて、行持におもむかんとするは、なほこれ行持をこころざすににたれど
も、眞父の家郷に寶財をなげすてて、さらに他國跉跰の窮子となる。跉跰
のときの風水、たとひ身命を喪失せしめずといふとも、眞父の寶財なげす
つべきにあらず、眞父の法財なほ失誤するなり。このゆえに、行持はしば
らくも懈倦なき法なり。

This being the case, a single day's sustained practice is the seed of
the buddhas, is the sustained practice of the buddhas. The buddhas are
manifested and continuously practiced by this continuous practice; not
continuously to practice it is to hate the buddhas, is not to make offerings
to the buddhas, is to hate sustained practice, is not to be born together
and die together, not to study together and practice together, with the
buddhas. The present blooming of flowers and falling of leaves — these
are manifestations of sustained practice; polishing the mirror and breaking the mirror — they are nothing but sustained practice.[10] Therefore, for
those who think to set aside sustained practice, to think of setting aside
sustained practice in order to hide the wrong thought of escaping sustained practice is also sustained practice; hence, to try to move toward
sustained practice, while it may seem to be aiming for sustained practice,
is to become the impoverished son who, throwing away the wealth of the
household of his true father, wanders aimlessly through other lands.[11]
While it may be that the winds and waters during our wanderings do
not cause loss of life, we should not throw away the wealth of our true
father; it is to lose the dharma wealth of our true father.[12] Therefore,
sustained practice is a dharma not to be neglected even for a moment.

* * * * *

10 **polishing the mirror and breaking the mirror** (*makyō hakyō* 磨鏡・破鏡): Whether
Dōgen had specific sources in mind here is unclear. The metaphor of spiritual practice as
"polishing the mirror" (*makyō* 磨鏡) of the mind is not uncommon in Buddhist literature; in
Zen lore, it is perhaps best known as the theme of the famous poetry contest to choose the
Sixth Ancestor, in which Huineng questions the practice of polishing a mirror on which there
is no dust. See Supplementary Notes, s.v. "Bright mirror." "Breaking the mirror" (*hakyō* 破
鏡) as an act of abandoning one's presuppositions can be found in the popular expression
"break the mirror and I'll meet you" (*taha kyō rai yo ni shōken* 打破鏡來與爾相見).

11 **those who think to set aside sustained practice** (*gyōji o sashiokan to gi suru wa*
行持をさしおかんと擬するは): The logic of this complicated sentence would seem to
be that, since we are engaged in sustained practice even when we try to escape it, to try
intentionally to produce it is to go astray from it.

impoverished son (*gūji* 窮子): Reference to the famous parable in the *Lotus Sūtra*
(*Miaofa lianhua jing* 妙法蓮華經, T.262.9:16b25ff) of the man who wanders as a beggar,
unaware that he is the son of a rich man.

12 **winds and waters during our wanderings** (*reihei no toki no fūsui* 跉跰のときの
風水): The sentence could also be read as referring to the wanderings of the son in the
Lotus Sūtra story.

16A. Sustained Practice, Part 1 *Gyōji* 行持

[16A:3] {1:147}

慈父大師釋迦牟尼佛、十九歳の佛壽より、深山に行持して、三十歳の佛壽
にいたりて、大地有情同時成道の行持あり。八旬の佛壽にいたるまで、な
ほ山林に行持し、精藍に行持す。王宮にかへらず、國利を領せず。布僧伽
梨を衣持し、在世に一經するに、互換せず。一盂、在世に互換せず、一時
一日も獨處することなし。人天の閑供養を辭せず、外道の訕謗を忍辱す。
おほよそ一化は行持なり。淨衣乞食の佛儀、しかしながら行持にあらずと
いふことなし。

The compassionate father, the Great Master, Buddha Śākyamuni, after
a buddha's lifespan of nineteen years, engaged in sustained practice in
the deep mountains; and, upon reaching a buddha's lifespan of thirty
years, he had the sustained practice of *"attaining the way simultaneously
with the whole earth and sentient beings."*[13] Until he reached a buddha's
lifespan of eight decades, he engaged in sustained practice in the mountains and forests, or engaged in sustained practice in gardens and parks.[14]
He never returned to his palace and never availed himself of the priv-
ileges afforded by his country. He used as his robe a hemp *saṃghāṭī*
and never exchanged it throughout his entire stay in this world; his one
bowl, he never exchanged during his stay in this world; he never lived

---

13 **after a buddha's lifespan of nineteen years** (*jūkyū sai no butsuju yori* 十九歳の佛
壽より); **reaching a buddha's lifespan of thirty years** (*sanjissai no butsuju ni itarite* 三
十歳の佛壽にいたりて): This somewhat odd way of expressing the Buddha's age plays
on usage in scriptural discussions of the length of a buddha's life. The tradition that
Gautama left home at age nineteen and achieved awakening at age thirty is found in the
Jingde chuandeng lu 景德傳燈錄, T.2076.51:205b12-24; the more common version of
the Buddha's life has him leaving his father's palace at age twenty-nine and awakening
under the bodhi tree at age thirty-five. In his "Shōbōgenzō sansui kyō" 正法眼藏山水
經 as well, Dōgen gives the Buddha's period of training as twelve years, rather than the
usual six.

"attaining the way simultaneously with the whole earth and sentient beings" (*daichi ujō dōji jōdō* 大地有情同時成道): A reference to the Buddha's awakening under the
bodhi tree. The expression, which appears in several of Dōgen's texts, is from a line
that he cites in his "Shōbōgenzō hotsu bodai shin" 正法眼藏發菩提心 (DZZ.2:164; also
quoted at *Eihei kōroku* 永平廣錄, DZZ.3:28, no. 37):

釋迦牟尼佛言、明星出現時、我與大地有情、同時成道。

Buddha Śākyamuni said, "When the dawn star appeared, I, together with the whole
earth and sentient beings, simultaneously attained the way."

Although the passage appears in Chan texts from this period (see, e.g, *Jianzhong Jingguo xudeng lu* 建中靖國續燈錄, ZZ.136:36b17-18), it has not been located in any extant
sūtra. The translation here follows the usual reading of *daichi ujō* 大地有情 as a compound subject; the phrase could also be read, 'sentient beings of the whole earth."

14 **mountains and forests** (*sanrin* 山林); **gardens and parks** (*shōran* 精藍): Presumably, indicating the locations, respectively, of Gautama's practice before and after he
became a buddha. *Shōran* 精藍 (elsewhere translated "monastic complex") is an abbreviation of *shōja garan* 精舍伽藍, used to render S. *ārama, vihara*, etc.

DŌGEN'S *SHŌBŌGENZŌ* VOLUME II

in solitude for a single day or a single hour.[15] He did not refuse the idle offerings of humans and devas; he endured the calumny of followers of the other paths.[16] In sum, his entire ministry was sustained practice. The Buddha's deportment in regard to the pure robes and the begging of food was in every case nothing but sustained practice.

* * * * *

[16A:4]

第八祖摩訶迦葉尊者は、釋尊の嫡嗣なり。生前もはら十二頭陀を行持して、さらにおこたらず。十二頭陀といふは、

The Eighth Ancestor, Venerable Mahākāśyapa, was the legitimate heir of Śākya, the Honored One.[17] During his lifetime, he devoted himself wholly to the sustained practice of the twelve *dhūta*, never neglecting them.[18] The twelve *dhūta* are:

[16A:5]

一者不受人請、日行乞食。亦不受比丘僧一飯食分錢財。二者止宿山上、不宿人舍・郡縣・聚落。三者不得從人乞衣被。人與衣被亦不受。但取丘塚間死人所棄衣、補治衣之。四者止宿野田中樹下。五者一日一食。一名僧迦僧泥。六者晝夜不臥、但坐睡・經行。一名僧泥沙者偈。七者有三領衣、無有餘衣。亦不臥被中。八者在塚間、不在佛寺中、亦不在人間。目視死人骸骨、坐禪求道。九者但欲獨處、不欲見人、亦不欲與人共臥。十者先食果蓏、却食飯。食已不得復食果蓏。十一者但欲露臥、不在樹下・屋宿。十二者不食肉、亦不食醍醐。麻油不塗身。

---

15 **He used as his robe a hemp *saṃghāṭī*** (*fu sōgyari o eji shi* 布僧伽梨を衣持し): The *saṃghāṭī* is the most formal of the traditional three robes (*kesa* 袈裟; S. *kāṣāya*) of the monk, sewn in nine to twenty-five pieces. The term *fu* 布 can refer to hemp, linen, cotton, or other fabrics made from plant fiber (as opposed to silk or wool). See Supplementary Notes, s.v. "Robe of the Tathāgata."

he never lived in solitude (*dokusho suru koto nashi* 獨處することなし): I.e., he never had a place of his own.

16 **He did not refuse the idle offerings of humans and devas** (*ninten no kan kuyō o ji sezu* 人天の閑供養を辭せず): The term *kan kuyō* 閑供養 is generally understood to be "unnecessary offerings" — i.e., offerings not needed by the recipient but, of course, bringing merit to the donor.

17 **Eighth Ancestor, Venerable Mahākāśyapa** (*daihasso Makakashō sonja* 第八祖摩訶迦葉尊者): An unusual designation for Mahākāśyapa, traditionally treated as the first ancestor of the Zen lineage. The standard set of seven ancient buddhas ending with Buddha Śākyamuni is here treated as the first seven ancestors of Zen, thus making Śākyamuni's disciple Mahākāśyapa the eighth. See Supplementary Notes, s.v. "Seven buddhas."

18 **twelve *dhūta*** (*jūni zuda* 十二頭陀): A set of ascetic practices mentioned throughout Buddhist literature; the number is sometimes given as thirteen, and the members of the set vary somewhat with the source. The definitions of the twelve *dhūta* that follow in the next section are taken from the *Da biqiu sanqian weiyi* 大比丘三千威儀 (T.1470.24:919b6-18). Mahākāśyapa was described by the Buddha as the best of his disciples in the practice of the *dhūta*.

16A. Sustained Practice, Part 1 *Gyōji* 行持

1. Without accepting invitations from people, to make the daily rounds begging for food; also, not to accept money for a meal of the bhikṣu saṃgha.

2. To lodge in the mountains, not to lodge in people's residence, region, district, or village.

3. Not to beg clothing from people, also not to accept clothing from people; to obtain and mend the clothing of the dead discarded in the cemetery.

4. To lodge under a tree in a field or paddy.

5. To take one meal a day; this is termed sengjiasengni.[19]

6. Not to recline day or night, only to sleep while seated and to walk; this is termed sengnishazheyu.[20]

7. To possess three robes, not to possess other robes; also, not to sleep under a quilt.

8. To stay in a cemetery, not to stay in a Buddhist monastery, not to stay among people; to look upon the skeletons of the dead, sitting in meditation seeking the way.

9. To wish only solitude, not to wish to meet people or wish to sleep with people.

10. To eat fruit first and then eat rice, not to eat fruit after finishing the meal.

11. To wish only to sleep outdoors, not to stay under a tree or in a lodging.

12. Not to eat meat, not to eat ghee; not to anoint the body with sesame oil.

[16A:6] {1:148}

これを十二頭陀といふ。摩訶迦葉尊者、よく一生に不退不轉なり。如來の正法眼藏を正傳すといへども、この頭陀を退することなし。あるとき、佛言すらく、なんぢすでに年老なり、僧食を食すべし。摩訶迦葉尊者いはく、われもし如來の出世にあはずば、辟支佛となるべし、生前に山林に居すべし。さいはひに如來の出世にあふ、法のうるほひあり、しかありといふとも、つひに僧食を食すべからず。如來、稱讃しまします。

19　**this is termed *sengjiasengni*** (*sunkasunnai* 僧迦僧泥): This Chinese transliteration of an Indic word occurs only in the *Da biqiu sanqian weiyi* 大比丘三千威儀 (T.1470.24:919b11). It has been suggested that it is an error for *yigiasengni* 伊迦僧泥, intended to represent the Sanskrit *ekāsanika* ("having a single seat") — i.e., eating a day's provisions in a single sitting.

20　**This is termed *sengnishazheyu*** (*sunnaisashakyū* 僧泥沙者傴): Another Chinese transliteration found only in the *Dc biqiu sanqian weiyi* 大比丘三千威儀 (T.1470.24:919b12). Judging from the definition here, the Sanskrit original would appear to be *naiṣadika* or *naiṣadyika*, "one who sleeps in a sitting posture."

10 DŌGEN'S *SHŌBŌGENZŌ* VOLUME II

These are called the twelve *dhūta*. Throughout his life, Venerable Mahākāśyapa never regressed from them. While he may have received the direct transmission of the treasury of the true dharma eye of the Tathāgata, he never retreated from these *dhūta*.

Once the Buddha said to him, "You are advanced in years; you should eat the saṃgha food."[21]

Mahākāśyapa said, "Had I not encountered the appearance in the world of the Tathāgata, I would have become a *pratyeka-buddha* and lived in the mountains and forests for the rest of my life. Fortunately, I did encounter the appearance in the world of the Tathāgata and enjoy the benefits of the dharma. While this may be so, in the end, I cannot eat the saṃgha food."

The Tathāgata praised him.

[16A:7] {1:149}

あるいは迦葉、頭陀行持のゆえに、形體憔悴せり。衆、みて輕忽するがごとし。ときに如來、ねんごろに迦葉をめして、半座をゆづりまします。迦葉尊者、如來の座に坐す。しるべし摩訶迦葉は、佛會の上座なり。生前の行持、ことごとくあぐべからず。

Kāśyapa's body became emaciated due to his sustained practice of the *dhūta*. It seems the assembly looked on him with disdain. At that time, the Tathāgata cordially summoned Kāśyapa and offered him a co-seat, and Venerable Kāśyapa sat in the seat of the Tathāgata.[22] We should realize that Mahākāśyapa was the senior seat in the Buddha's community. To give every instance of his sustained practice throughout his lifetime would be impossible.

* * * * *

[16A:8]

第十祖波栗濕縛尊者は、一生、脇不至席なり。これ八旬老年の辨道なりといへども、當時すみやかに大法を單傳す。これ光陰をいたづらにもらさざるによりて、わづかに三箇年の功夫なりといへども、三菩提の正眼を單傳す。尊者在胎六十年なり、出胎髮白なり。誓不死臥、名脇尊者。乃至暗中手放光明、以取經法。これ生得の奇相なり。

---

21 **"saṃgha food"** (*sōjiki* 僧食): I.e., food provided by the saṃgha to its elderly and infirm members. An account of Mahākāśyapa's refusal to abandon the practice of begging can be found, e.g., in the *Ekottarāgama* (*Zengyi ahan jing* 増一阿含經, T.125.2:570b3-18). The source for Dōgen's version, told here in Japanese, is unknown.

22 **offered him a co-seat** (*hanza o yuzurimashimasu* 半座をゆづりまします): The story of the Buddha's sharing his seat with Mahākāśyapa is quite old and occurs in various sources in the Buddhist literature; see, e.g., the *Saṃyuktāgama* (*Za ehan jing* 雜阿含經, T.99.2:302a1ff).

16A. Sustained Practice, Part 1 *Gyōji* 行持 11

The Tenth Ancestor, Venerable Pārśva was one who, *throughout his life, "his side never touched the seat."*[23] Although this was his pursuit of the way as an elder of eight decades, it was at that time that he suddenly received the unique transmission of the great dharma. Due to his not frivolously wasting the years and months, he received the unique transmission of the true eye of *sambodhi* with merely three years of concentrated effort. The Venerable was sixty years in the womb; he emerged from the womb with white hair.[24] *He vowed not to recline like the dead, and thus he was called "Venerable Side."*[25] *Moreover, in the dark his hands emitted light, with which he took hold of the dharma of the sūtras.*[26] This is a wondrous sign he possessed from birth.

[16A:9]

脇尊者、生年八十垂捨家染衣。域中少年、便請之曰、愚夫朽老、一何淺智。夫出家者有二業焉、一則習定、二乃誦經。而今衰耄、無所進取。濫迹清流、徒知飽食。時脇尊者、聞諸譏議、因謝時人、而自誓曰、我若不通三藏理、不斷三界欲、不得六神通、不具八解脱、終不以脇而至於席。自爾之後、唯日不足、經行・宴坐、住立思惟。晝則研習理教、夜乃靜慮凝神。綿歷三歲、學通三藏、斷三界欲、得三明智。時人敬仰、因號脇尊者。

When Venerable Side reached nearly eighty years of age, he abandoned the home and dyed the robes.[27] *Youths in the city ridiculed him,*

---

23 **The Tenth Ancestor, Venerable Pārśva** (*daijisso Harishiba sonja* 第十祖波栗濕縛尊者): A renowned Indian scholar-monk, affiliated with the Sarvāstivāda school, active during the early second century CE. Dōgen has here reverted to the standard numbering of the ancestors, beginning with Mahākāśyapa.

"his side never touched the seat" (*kyō fushi seki* 脇不至席): A fixed expression for the *dhūta* practice of not reclining to sleep.

24 **The Venerable was sixty years in the womb** (*sonja no zaitai rokujū nen nari* 尊者の在胎六十年なり): This and the following two sentences reflect a passage in Zhanran's 湛然 (711-782) *Zhiguan fuxing zhuan hongjue* 止觀輔行傳弘決 (T.1912.46:146a26-28).

25 **"Venerable Side"** (*Kyō sonja* 脇尊者): I.e., *Pārśva*, meaning "side," or "flank."

26 **with which he took hold of the dharma of the sūtras** (*i shū kyō hō* 以取經法): Zhanran's text here (*Zhiguan fuxing zhuan hongjue* 止觀輔行傳弘決, T.1912.46:146a28) has only, "with which he took hold of the sūtras." Dōgen seems to have punctuated the passage after the initial glyph, *fa* 法 ("dharma"), of the following sentence:

手放光明以取經。法付富那奢。

His hands emitted light, with which he took hold of the sūtras. His dharma was transmitted to Puṇyayaśas.

27 **When Venerable Side reached nearly eighty years of age** (*Kyō sonja shō nen hachijū sui* 脇尊者生年八十垂): This section is taken from Xuanzang's 玄奘 *Datang xiyu ji* 大唐西域記 (T.2087.51:880b21-c2). Dōgen's version has transposed the order of the predicate in Xuanzang's text here (*nian chui bashi* 年垂八十).

abandoned the home and dyed the robes (*shake zen'e* 捨家染衣): A fixed expression for joining the Buddhist order.

12 DŌGEN'S *SHŌBŌGENZŌ* VOLUME II

saying, "Decrepit old fool, how stupid can you be?[28] Those who leave home have two tasks: first to practice meditation; second to recite the sūtras. But now you are so feeble and senile you won't make any progress. You recklessly join the clear stream, knowing only how to gorge yourself on the food."[29]

At this time, Venerable Side, upon hearing these disparaging comments, thanked these people, and then made a vow, saying, "If I do not master the principles of the three collections, do not cut off the desires of the three realms, do not attain the six spiritual powers, do not equip myself with the eight liberations, may my side never touch the seat."[30]

From then on, fearing the days were not enough, he walked, sat, stood and thought.[31] By day, he studied the teachings; by night, he reflected quietly and focused his spirit. He continued thus for three years, till his study mastered the three collections, he cut off the desires of the three realms and acquired the wisdom of the three knowledges.[32] People of the time showed their respect and admiration by calling him "Venerable Side."

[16A:10] {1:150}

しかあれば、脇尊者、處胎六十年、はじめて出胎せり。胎内に功夫なからんや。出胎よりのち、八十にならんとするに、はじめて出家學道をもとむ。託胎よりのち、一百四十年なり。まことに不群なりといへども、朽老は阿誰よりも朽老ならん。處胎にて老年あり、出胎にても老年なり。しかあれども、時人の譏嫌をかへりみず、誓願の一志不退なれば、わづかに三

---

28 **Youths in the city ridiculed him** (*jōchū shōnen ben shō shi* 域中少年便請之): Reading *shō* 誚 ("to ridicule") for *shō* 請 ("to invite").

29 **clear stream** (*seiryū* 清流): I.e., the Buddhist order.

30 **three collections** (*sanzō* 三藏): I.e., the tripiṭaka, the Buddhist canon.

three realms (*sangai* 三界): I.e., the threefold world of saṃsāra; see Supplementary Notes, s.v. "Three realms."

six spiritual powers (*roku jinzū* 六神通): I.e., the paranormal knowledges (S. *abhijñā*) accessible to advanced meditators; see Supplementary Notes, s.v. "Spiritual powers."

eight liberations (*hachi gedatsu* 八解脱): A traditional set of eight meditations leading to freedom from desire.

31 **fearing the days were not enough** (*i jitsu fusoku* 唯日不足): A fixed idiom more commonly written *i jitsu fusoku* 惟日不足.

walked, sat, stood and thought (*kinhin enza, jūryū shiyui* 經行・宴坐、住立思惟): I.e., he engaged in meditation while walking, sitting, and standing. "To stand still and think" (*jūryū shiyui* 住立思惟) is a fixed expression.

32 **wisdom of the three knowledges** (*sanmyō chi* 三明智): I.e., a standard set of three of the six spiritual powers, said to have been acquired by Buddha Śākyamuni on the night of his awakening: (1) *divya-cakṣus* (*tengen* 天眼; "the deva eye"), (2) *pūrva-nivāsānusmṛti* (*shukumyō chi* 宿命智; "recollection of former lives"), (3) *āsrava-kṣaya-jñāna* (*rojin tsū* 漏盡通; "knowledge of the elimination of the contaminants").

16A. Sustained Practice, Part 1 *Gyōji* 行持   13

歳をふるに、辨道現成するなり。たれか見賢思齊をゆるくせん、年老耄及
をうらむることなかれ。

Thus, Venerable Side emerged from the womb only after sixty years in the womb. Was he not making concentrated effort in the womb? After he emerged from the womb, only as he was turning eighty did he seek to leave home and study the way. It was one hundred forty years since his conception. Though he may have been truly beyond the crowd, he was older and more decrepit than anyone else: he was old in the womb; he was old when he emerged from the womb. Nevertheless, paying no attention to the scorn and hatred of his contemporaries, and being determined not to regress from his vow, after only three years had passed, his pursuit of the way was realized. Who could soften [the adage], "*When you meet someone good, think to equal him*"?[33] Do not regret "*reaching old age.*"[34]

[16A:11]

この生しりがたし、生か、生にあらざるか、老か、老にあらざるか。四見
すでにおなじからず、諸類の見おなじからず。ただ志氣を專修にして辨道
功夫すべきなり。辨道に生死をみるに相似せりと參學すべし、生死に辨道
するにはあらず。いまの人、あるいは五旬六旬におよび、七旬八旬におよ
ぶに、辨道をさしおかんとするは至愚なり。生來たとひいくばくの年月
と覺知すとも、これはしばらく人間の精魂の活計なり、學道の消息にあら
ず。壯齡・耄及をかへりみることなかれ、學道究辨を一志すべし。脇尊者
に齊肩なるべきなり。

This life is hard to understand: is it living or is it not living?[35] Is it old age or is it not old age? As the four views are not the same, the views of different types are not the same.[36] We should just work on pursuing the way, making a single practice of our determination. We should study that this resembles seeing life and death in our pursuit of the way; it is not pursuing the way in life and death. It is extremely stupid of people

---

33   **"When you meet someone good, think to equal him"** (*ken ken shi sei* 見賢思齊): A common saying, quoted elsewhere in the *Shōbōgenzō*, from the *Lunyu* 論語 4 (KR.1h0005.002.14b):

> 見賢思齊焉。見不賢而内自省也。
>
> When you meet someone good, think to equal him; when you meet someone not good, then look within yourself.

34   **"reaching old age"** (*nen rōmō gyū* 年老耄及): From the line in a verse by the Song-dynasty poet Louyao 楼鑰 (1137-1213): "Reaching old age and begging to go" (*nian laomao ji lü qiu qu* 年老耄及屢求去).

35   **This life is hard to understand** (*kono shō shirigatashi* この生しりがたし): This sentence could also be read, "this birth is hard to understand: is it birth or is it not birth?"

36   **four views** (*shiken* 四見): Undoubtedly, the so-called "four views of water" (*issui shiken* 一水四見): what the human sees as water, the fish sees as a dwelling, the preta sees as pus and blood, and the deva sees as jewels.

14 DŌGEN'S *SHŌBŌGENZŌ* VOLUME II

today to give up on pursuing the way when they reach their fifth decade or sixth decade or reach their seventh decade or eighth decade.[37] While we may perceive how many years there have been since our birth, this is just the life of the human spirit, not the circumstances of our studying the way. Do not consider whether you are youthful or aged; we should be solely set on studying the way and thoroughly investigating it. We should be of equal stature with Venerable Side.

[16A:12] {1:151}

塚間の一堆の塵土、あながちにしをむことなかれ、あながちにかへりみることなかれ。一志に度取せずば、たれかたれをあはれまん。無主の形骸、いたづらに偏野せんとき、眼睛をつくるがごとく正觀すべし。

Do not excessively lament the pile of dust in the cemetery; do not excessively pay it attention. If you do not set yourself solely on your deliverance, who will take pity on whom? When the masterless skeleton is randomly scattered in the fields, we should view this correctly as if seeing it with our own eyes.

* * * * *

[16A:13]

六祖は新州の樵夫なり、有識と稱しがたし。いとけなくして父を喪す、老母に養育せられて長ぜり。樵夫の業を養母の活計とす。十字の街頭にして一句の聞經よりのち、たちまちに老母をすてて大法をたづぬ。これ奇代の大器なり、拔群の辨道なり。斷臂たとひ容易なりとも、この割愛は大難なるべし、この棄恩はかろかるべからず。黄梅の會に投じて八箇月、ねぶらず、やすまず、晝夜に米をつく。夜半に衣鉢を正傳す。得法已後、なほ石臼をおひありきて、米をつくこと八年なり。出世度人説法するにも、この石臼をさしおかず、希世の行持なり。

The Sixth Ancestor was a woodcutter from Xinzhou; he could hardly be called learned.[38] While still very young, he lost his father and was raised by his mother. He made a living to support his mother by his work as a woodcutter. Upon hearing a line of a *sūtra* at a crossroad, he abruptly abandoned his old mother and set off in search of the great dharma. He was a great vessel, rare through the ages; it was an outstanding pursuit of the way. To cut off an arm is easy, but to cut off his love must have been very hard; casting aside his obligation could not have been done lightly.[39] Committing himself to the community of Huangmei, he pounded

---

37 **fifth decade or sixth decade** (*gojun rokujun* 五旬六旬): I.e., one's forties or fifties.

38 **The Sixth Ancestor** (*rokuso* 六祖): I.e., Caoxi Huineng 曹溪慧能. Xinzhou is located in present-day Guangdong province. The story here of Huineng abandoning his mother upon hearing the *Diamond Sūtra* is well known in Chan literature.

39 **To cut off an arm is easy** (*danpi tatoi yōi nari* 斷臂たとひ容易なり): Doubtless an

16A. Sustained Practice, Part 1 *Gyōji* 行持

rice day and night, without sleep, without rest, for eight months.[40] In the middle of the night, he received the direct transmission of the robe and bowl. After attaining the dharma, he continued to carry a stone mortar and pounded rice for eight years.[41] Even when he appeared in the world and preached the dharma to deliver people, he did not set aside this stone mortar — a sustained practice rare in the world.

* * * * *

[16A:14]

江西馬祖の、坐禪することは二十年なり。これ南嶽の密印を稟受するなり。傳法濟人のとき、坐禪をさしおくと道取せず。參學のはじめていたるには、かならず心印を密受せしむ。普請作務のところに、かならず先赴す。老にいたりて懈倦せず。いまの臨濟は、江西の流なり。

Mazu of Jiangxi sat in meditation for twenty years.[42] This received the secret seal of Nanyue.[43] It is not said that he set aside sitting in meditation when he was transmitting the dharma and saving people: when students first went to him, he invariably had them secretly receive the mind seal.[44] Where there was communal labor, he invariably went first; and, when he grew old, he did not rest from it. The present-day Linji [monks] belong to the Jiangxi lineage.[45]

* * * * *

---

allusion to the Second Ancestor, Huike 慧可, who is famously said to have cut off his arm and presented it to Bodhidharma as a token of the urgency of his quest for instruction; see Supplementary Notes, s.v. "Cut off an arm."

40 **the community of Huangmei** (*Ōbai no e* 黄梅の會): I.e., the followers of the Fifth Ancestor, Hongren 弘忍 (602-675), on Mount Huangmei 黄梅山, in present-day Hubei Province.

41 **pounded rice for eight years** (*kome o tsuku koto hachi nen nari* 米をつくこと八年なり): Presumably, a metaphor for Huineng's practice as a layman during the period between his designation as the Sixth Ancestor and his taking the tonsure and launching his teaching career.

42 **Mazu of Jiangxi** (*Kōzei Baso* 江西馬祖): I.e., Mazu Daoyi 馬祖道一 (709-788), disciple of Nanyue Huairang 南嶽懷讓.

43 **This received the secret seal of Nanyue** (*kore Nangaku no mitsuin o bonju suru nari* これ南嶽の密印を稟受するなり): The antecedent of "this" here is taken as Mazu's practice of sitting, though the pronoun *kore* これ might also refer to Mazu himself.

44 **he invariably had them secretly receive the mind seal** (*kanarazu shin'in o mitsuju seshimu* かならず心印を密受せしむ): Presumably, meaning that he always taught them the practice of sitting he had himself received from Nanyue.

45 **The present-day Linji [monks] belong to the Jiangxi lineage** (*ima no Rinzai wa, Kōzei no ryū nari* いまの臨濟は、江西の流なり): Linji Yixuan 臨濟義玄 (d. 866), founder of the Linji school, was a dharma descendant of Mazu in the third generation.

16 DŌGEN'S *SHŌBŌGENZŌ* VOLUME II

[16A:15]
雲巖和尚と道吾と、おなじく藥山に參學して、ともにちかひをたてて、四十年わきを席につけず、一味參究す。法を洞山の悟本大師に傳付す。洞山いはく、われ欲打成一片、坐禪辦道已二十年なり。いまその道、あまねく傳付せり。

Reverend Yunyan and Daowu studied together under Yaoshan and, making a vow that their sides would never touch the seat for forty years, investigated with a single mind.[46] Their dharma was transmitted to Great Master Wuben of Dongshan.[47] Dongshan said, "*Seeking to become one piece, I have already sat in meditation and pursued the way for twenty years.*"[48] Now, his way has been disseminated everywhere.[49]

* * * * *

[16A:16] {1:152}
雲居山弘覺大師、そのかみ三峰庵に住せしとき、天廚送食す。大師、あるとき洞山に參じて、大道を決擇して、さらに庵にかへる。天使また食を再送して師を尋見するに、三日をへて師をみることえず。天廚をまつことなし、大道を所宗とす。辦肯の志氣、おもひやるべし。

Great Master Hongjue of Mount Yunju, when long ago he was staying at the Sanfeng Hermitage, was *sent food from the kitchens of the devas.*[50] Once, the Great Master visited Dongshan, ascertained the great

---

46 **Reverend Yunyan and Daowu** (*Ungan oshō to Dōgo to* 雲巖和尚と道吾と): I.e., Yunyan Tansheng 雲巖曇晟 (782-841) and Daowu Yuanzhi 道吾円智 (769-835), fellow students of Yaoshan Weiyan 藥山惟儼 (751-834).

their sides would never touch the seat for forty years (*yonjū nen waki o seki ni tsukezu* 四十年わきを席につけず): A standard trope in the literature. Dōgen's source for the vow is unknown.

investigated with a single mind (*ichimi sankyū su* 一味參究す): The term *ichimi* 一味 (literally, "single taste") could be taken here as indicating either single-mindedness or a single intention shared by the two.

47 **Great Master Wuben of Dongshan** (*Tōzan no Gohon daishi* 洞山の悟本大師): I.e., Dongshan Liangjie 洞山良价 (807-869), successor to Yunyan Tansheng 雲巖曇晟 and founder of Dōgen's Caodong 曹洞 lineage.

48 **"become one piece"** (*tajō ippen* 打成一片): A fixed expression for the act of unifying or becoming unified. Dōgen's source for Dongshan's saying is unknown.

49 **Now, his way has been disseminated everywhere** (*ima sono dō, amaneku denpu seri* いまその道、あまねく傳付せり): This could also read, "now his words have been disseminated everywhere."

50 **Great Master Hongjue of Mount Yunju** (*Ungozan Gukaku daishi* 雲居山弘覺大師): I.e., Yunju Daoying 雲居道膺 (d. 902), disciple of Dongshan Liangjie 洞山良价. "Great Master Hongjue" 弘覺大師 is a posthumous title conferred by Emperor Zhaozong 昭宗. The Sanfeng Hermitage 三峰庵 is thought to have been on Mount Yunju 雲居山, in present-day Jiangxi Province.

16A. Sustained Practice, Part 1 *Gyōji* 行持   17

way, and then returned to the hermitage. The emissary of the devas, once again sending food, sought the Master for three days but was unable to see the Master. No longer dependent on the deva kitchens, he took the great way as his basis. We should give thought to his spirit that confirms [the way].

* * * * *

[16A:17]

百丈山大智禪師、そのかみ馬祖の侍者とありしより、入寂のゆふべにいたるまで、一日も爲衆爲人の勤仕なきヨあらず。かたじけなく一日不作、一日不食のあとをのこすといふは、百丈禪師、すでに年老臘高なり、なほ普請作務のところに、壯齡とおなじく勵力す。衆、これをいたむ、人、これをあはれむ。師やまざるなり。つひに作務のとき、作務の具をかくして、師にあたへざりしかば、師、その日一日、不食なり。衆の作務にくははらざることをうらむる意旨なり。これを百丈の、一日不作、一日不食のあと、といふ。いま大宋國に流傳せる臨濟の玄風、ならびに諸方の叢林、おほく百丈の玄風を行持するなり。

From the time when Chan Master Dazhi of Mount Baizhang served as an acolyte under Mazu, right up to the evening that he entered extinction, there was not a single day in which he did not work for the saṃgha and for people.[51] Thankfully, he left us the legacy, "*a day without working is a day without eating.*"[52] That is, Chan Master Baizhang was already an elder with seniority; still, where there was communal labor, he worked as hard as a youth. The assembly was pained by this, and people took

---

sent food from the kitchens of the devas (*tenchū sōjiki* 天廚送食): Dōgen's source for this well-known story, told here in Japanese, is not certain; it seems closest to the version given in the *Bore shin jing zhujie* 般若心經註解 (ZZ.42:79a10-13):

> 又弘覺和尚住庵、天廚送供。及再參洞山和尚後、飯菴。天神三日送食到菴、不見菴主。菴主只在菴中為何不見。皆係圓頓之法隱身之訣。所以神鬼俱不得見。

Again, when Rev. Hungjue was living at a hermitage, the kitchens of the devas sent him offerings. After he visited the Rev. Dongshan, he returned to his hermitage. The deva spirits sent food to his hermitage for three days but did not see the hermit. The hermit was within the hermitage, so why did they not see him? All who attain the perfect sudden dharma have the art of concealing the body; therefore, no spirits can see them.

51 **Chan Master Dazhi of Mount Baizhang** (*Hyakujōzan Daichi zenji* 百丈山大智禪師): I.e., Baizhang Huaihai 百丈懷海 (749-814), a disciple of Mazu. "Chan Master Great Wisdom" (*Dazhi chanshi* 大智禪師) is his title; Mount Baizhang 百丈山 is in Hongzhou 洪州, modern Jiangxi province.

52 **"a day without working is a day without eating"** (*ichinichi fusa, ichinichi fujiki* 一日不作、一日不食): Baizhang was traditionally credited with creating the first Chan monastic regulations, and this saying was widely taken as expressing the spirit of the Chan monastery. See, e.g., *Chixiu Baizhang qinggui* 勅修百丈清規, T.2025.48:1119b2. The source of Dōgen's Japanese retelling here of the saying's origin is uncertain. Here is the version given in the *Tiansheng guangdeng lu* 天聖廣燈錄 (ZZ.135:658a4-7):

18 DŌGEN'S *SHŌBŌGENZŌ* VOLUME II

pity on him; yet the Master did not stop. Finally, at work time, they hid his work tools and would not give them to the Master; so, for that entire day, the Master did not eat. By this, he showed his regret that he had not taken part in the work of the assembly. This is called the legacy of Baizhang's "*a day without working is a day without eating.*" The dark style of Linji that today has spread throughout the Land of the Great Song, as well as the monasteries in all quarters, are mostly engaging in the sustained practice of the dark style of Baizhang.[53]

* * * * *

[16A:18]

鏡清和尚、住院のとき、土地神、かつて師顔をみることえず。たよりをえざるによりてなり。

When Reverend Jingqing was abbot of a cloister, the autochthonous deity was never able to see the Master's face; for he could get no sign of him.[54]

* * * * *

[16A:19] {1:153}

三平山義忠禪師、そのかみ天廚送食す。大顛をみてのちに、天神、また師をもとむるに、みることあたはず。

Chan Master Yizhong of Mount Sanping long ago was sent food from

> 師凡作務執勞、必先於衆。衆不忍其勞、密收作具而請息之。師云。吾無德矣、爭合勞人。既徧求作具不獲、而亦不食。故有一日不作一日不食之言流播寰宇矣。
>
> The Master regularly participated in work periods and was first in the community to take on hard work. The community did not accept his working, secretly took away his tools, and asked him to stop. The Master said, "I have no virtue. Why not work with others?"
>
> Looking everywhere for his tools without finding them, he did not eat. Therefore, there is the saying that circulates everywhere, "a day without working is a day without eating."

53 **The dark style of Linji** (*Rinzai no genpū* 臨濟の玄風): A syntactically awkward sentence, in which it would appear that "the dark style of Linji" and "the monasteries in all directions" are to be taken as compound subjects of the predicate "continuously practicing."

54 **Reverend Jingqing** (*Kyōsei oshō* 鏡清和尚): I.e., Jingqing Daofu 鏡清道怤 (864-937), a disciple of Xuefeng Yicun 雪峰義存; he later resided at the Jingqing Monastery 鏡清寺 in present-day Zhejiang Province. Again, Dōgen's source for the anecdote, told in Japanese, is uncertain; again, perhaps the nearest Chinese version is found in the *Bore shin jing zhujie* 般若心經註解 (ZZ.42:79a1-2):

> 又鏡清和尚住院三年。本院土地要見師顔不能得。
>
> Again, when Reverend Jingqing was abbot of a cloister, for three years the autochthonous deity of the cloister sought to see his face but could not.

16A. Sustained Practice, Part 1 *Gyōji* 行持

the kitchens of the devas. After he met Dadian, when the devas searched for him, they could not see him.[55]

* * * * *

[16A:20]

後大潙和尚いはく、我二十年在潙山、喫潙山飯、屙潙山屙、不參潙山道。只牧得一頭水牯牛、終日露回回也。

Reverend Hou Dawei said,[56]

For twenty years, I stayed at Weishan, eating Weishan's rice and shitting Weishan's shit. I didn't study Weishan's way; I just managed to herd a single water buffalo, everywhere exposed all day long.

[16A:21]

しるべし、一頭の水牯牛は、二十年在潙山の行持より牧得せり。この師、かつて百丈の會下に參學しきたれり。しづかに二十年中の消息おもひやるべし、わするる時なかれ。たとひ參潙山道する人ありとも、不參潙山道の行持はまれなるべし。

We should realize that the water buffalo was herded by the sustained practice of "twenty years staying at Weishan." This master had once practiced in Baizhang's community. We should quietly think on the circumstances during those twenty years; do not forget them. While there are those who studied Weishan's way, a sustained practice that *"didn't study Weishan's way"* is rare.

* * * * *

[16A:22]

趙州觀音院眞際大師從諗和尚、とし六十一歳なりしに、はじめて發心求道をこころざす。瓶錫をたづさへて行脚し、遍歷諸方するに、つねにみづからいはく、七歳童兒、若勝我者、我即問伊。百歳老翁、不及我者、我即教他。

---

55 **Chan Master Yizhong of Mount Sanping** (*Sanpeizan Gichū zenji* 三平山義忠禪師): I.e., Sanping Yizhong 三平義忠 (781-872), disciple of Dadian Baotong 大顛寶通 (732-824); he later lived on Mount Sanping 三平山 in present-day Fujian Province. Dōgen's source for this anecdote has not been identified.

56 **Reverend Hou Dawei** (*Go Daii oshō* 後大潙和尚): I.e., Changqing Da'an 長慶大安 (793-883), disciple of Baizhang Huaihai 百丈懷海. Da'an was given the nickname "Later Dawei" because he succeeded Weishan Lingyou 潙山靈祐 (771-853) as abbot of the Tongqing Monastery 同慶寺 on Mount Dawei 大潙山 in present-day Hunan Province. His words here, given in Chinese, represent an abbreviated, somewhat variant version of a passage found in the *Jingde chuandeng lu* 景德傳燈錄 (T.2076.51:267c6-10); that text, which is quoted more fully in "Shōbōgenzō kajō" 正法眼藏家常, has Da'an on Weishan for thirty years. See Supplementary Notes, s.v. "Water buffalo."

20 DŌGEN'S *SHŌBŌGENZŌ* VOLUME II

Reverend Congshen, Great Master Zhenji of the Guanyin Cloister in Zhaozhou, first resolved to bring forth the mind [of bodhi] and seek the way at the age of sixty-one.[57] Taking his water flask and staff, he traveled on foot and traversed all quarters, always saying, "A *seven-year-old child who surpasses me, I'll inquire of him; a hundred-year-old elder who doesn't reach me, I'll teach him.*"[58]

[16A:23]

かくのごとくして南泉の道を學得する功夫、すなはち二十年なり。年至八十のとき、はじめて趙州城東觀音院に住して、人天を化道すること四十來年なり。いまだかつて一封の書をもて檀那につけず。僧堂おほきならず、前架なし、後架なし。あるとき牀脚おれき。一隻の燒斷の爐木を、繩をもてこれをゆいつけて、年月を經歷し修行するに、知事この牀脚をかへんと請するに、趙州ゆるさず。古佛の家風きくべし。

In this way, his concentrated effort to study the way of Nanchuan was twenty years.[59] Only when he reached the age of eighty did he take up residence at the Guanyin Cloister east of Zhaozhou City, where he guided humans and devas for forty years.[60] He never sent a single letter to his *dānapati*.[61] The saṃgha hall was not large, lacking both front shelving and back shelving.[62] Once, the leg of his platform broke off.[63] Splicing

---

57 **Reverend Congshen, Great Master Zhenji of Guanyin Cloister in Zhaozhou** (*Jōshū Kannon'in Shinsai daishi Jūshin oshō* 趙州觀音院眞際大師從諗和尚): I.e., Zhaozhou Congshen 趙州從諗 (778-897). The Guanyin Cloister in Zhaozhou was in present-day Hebei. The temple was known as Yong'an Cloister 永安院 from the Southern Song; the current name, Bailin Monastery 栢林寺, dates from the Ching.

the age of sixty-one (*toshi rokujūissai narishi* とし六十一歳なりし): Dōgen repeats this and other information on Zhaozhou here in his "Shōbōgenzō hakujushi" 正法眼藏柏樹子. The source of his claim that Zhaozhou first undertook Buddhist practice at the advanced age of sixty-one is unclear; most biographies say he became a *śrāmaṇera* as a youth.

58 **"A seven-year-old child"** (*shichisai dōji* 七歳童兒): A vow found in the *Zhaozhou lu* 趙州錄 (*Guzunsu yulu* 古尊宿語錄, ZZ.118:304b9-10).

59 **Nanquan** (*Nansen* 南泉): I.e., Zhaozhou's teacher, Nanquan Puyuan 南泉普願 (748-835).

60 **he guided humans and devas for forty years** (*ninten o kedō suru koto shijū rainen nari* 人天を化道すること四十來年なり): Some versions read *kedō* 化導 and *nenrai* 年來 here.

61 **He never sent a single letter to his *dānapati*** (*imada katsute ippū no sho o mote danna ni tsukezu* いまだかつて一封の書をもて檀那につけず): I.e., a letter to lay patrons (S. *dānapati*) seeking support for the monastery.

62 **lacking both front shelving and back shelving** (*zenka nashi, goka nashi* 前架なし、後架なし): The former term refers to shelves located in the outer section of the saṃgha hall (*sōdō* 僧堂), used for food service; the latter refers to shelves in the lavatory behind the saṃgha hall, or by extension, to the lavatory itself.

63 **the leg of his platform broke off** (*jōkyaku oreki* 牀脚をれき): I.e., the leg of his seat in the saṃgha hall. An incident recorded in the *Zhaozhou lu* 趙州錄 (ZZ.118:304b12-13), where the furniture in question is called a "cord bench" (*jōshō* 繩床), a standard term for

16A. Sustained Practice, Part 1 *Gyōji* 行持   21

a charred piece of wood to it with twine, he continued practicing on it as the months and years passed; when the stewards sought to change the platform leg, Zhaozhou would not permit it. We should listen to the house style of this old buddha.

[16A:24] {1:154}

趙州の、趙州に住することは、八旬よりのちなり、傳法よりこのかたなり。正法正傳せり。諸人これを古佛といふ。いまだ正法正傳せざらん餘人は、師よりもかろかるべし、いまだ八旬にいたらざらん餘人は、師よりも強健なるべし。壯年にして輕爾ならんわれら、なんぞ老年の崇重なるとひとしからん、はげみて辨道行持すべきなり。四十年のあひだ、世財をたくはへず、常住に米穀なし。あるいは栗子・椎子をひろうて、食物にあつ、あるいは旋轉飯食す。まことに上古龍象の家風なり、戀慕すべき操行なり。

Zhaozhou took up residence in Zhaozhou after his eighth decade, following his dharma transmission. It was the direct transmission of the true dharma. People called him an "old buddha." Others that have not received the direct transmission of the true dharma must be less significant than the Master; others that have yet to reach eighty must be more robust than the Master. How can we, who are youthful but insignificant, be equal to one who is a respected elder. We should strive to pursue the way and engage in sustained practice. For forty years, [his monastery] accumulated no worldly treasure, and its stores had no rice. Sometimes, they would collect chestnuts or beechnuts to use as food; sometimes, they would *take turns cooking*.[64] Truly, it was the house style of the dragon elephants of antiquity, conduct we should cherish.[65]

[16A:25]

あるとき、衆にしめしていはく、儞若一生不離叢林、不語十年五載、無人喚儞作啞漢、已後諸佛也不奈儞何。これ行持をしめすなり。

Once, he addressed the assembly, saying, *"If for a lifetime you don't leave the grove and don't talk for ten years or five years, no one will call you a mute; after that, even the buddhas won't know what to make of you."*[66]

This expresses sustained practice.

---

an individual monk's meditation platform.

64   **take turns cooking** (*sendenbonjiki* 旋轉飯食): An unusual term generally taken to indicate the practice of suspending the position of cook (*tenzo* 典座) and having each monk prepare his own meal.

65   **dragon elephants** (*ryūzō* 龍象): A term for superior religious practitioners. Although originally used in reference to great elephants (S. *mahānāga* or *hastināga*), it is often interpreted as "dragons and elephants."

66   **Once, he addressed the assembly** (*aru toki shu ni shimeshite* あるとき、衆にしめして): For sources of this saying and a variant version unique to Dōgen, see Supplementary Notes, s.v. "For a lifetime not leaving the grove."

[16A:26]

しるべし、十年五載の不語、おろかなるに相似せりといへども、不離叢林の功夫によりて、不語なりといへども啞漢にあらざらん。佛道かくのごとし。佛道聲をきかざらんは、不語の不啞漢なる道理あるべからず。しかあれば、行持の至妙は、不離叢林なり、不離叢林は、脱落なる全語なり。至愚のみづからは、不啞漢をしらず、不啞漢をしらせず。阿誰か遮障せざれども、しらせざるなり。不啞漢なるを、得恁麼なりときかず、得恁麼なりとしらざらんは、あはれむべき自己なり。不離叢林の行持、しづかに行持すべし。東西の風に東西することなかれ。十年五載の春風秋月、しられざれども聲色透脱の道あり。その道得、われに不知なり、われに不會なり。行持の寸陰を可惜許なりと参學すべし。不語を空然なるとあやしむことなかれ。入之一叢林なり、出之一叢林なり、鳥路一叢林なり、徧界一叢林なり。

We should realize that one who "doesn't talk for fifteen years" may look stupid, but even though one does not talk, when it is based on the concentrated effort of "*not leaving the grove*," one is not "a mute." The way of the buddhas is like this. One who does not hear the "voice of the way of the buddhas," lacks the truth that "not talking" is "not a mute."[67] Therefore, the greatest wonder of sustained practice is "*not leaving the grove*"; "*not leaving the grove*" is complete talk that is sloughed off.[68] The greatest fools do not know that they themselves are "not a mute" nor let it be known that they are "not a mute." Though no one prevents them, they do not let it be known. Those who do not hear that being "not a mute" is "getting such," who do not know it is "getting such," are selves to be pitied.[69] We should quietly engage in a sustained practice

---

the grove (*sōrin* 叢林): A common idiom for the monastery or the monastic institution.

mute (*akan* 啞漢): Used in Chan conversations for one unable to respond.

67　**"voice of the way of the buddhas"** (*butsudō shō* 佛道聲): This expression and the discussion that follows seem to reflect a verse (quoted in "Shōbōgenzō arakan" 正法眼藏阿羅漢) in the *Lotus Sūtra* (*Miaofa lianhua jing* 妙法蓮華經, T.262.9:18c20-21):

我等今者、眞是聲聞、以佛道聲、令一切聞。

Now, we
Are truly *śrāvakas*,
Who cause all to hear
The voice of the way of the buddhas.

The sūtra is playing on the term *śrāvaka* ("hearer") as "one who causes to hear" the buddhas' teaching of bodhi — the term rendered as *dō* 道 ("way") in Kumārajīva's translation here.

68　**complete talk that is sloughed off** (*datsuraku naru zengo* 脱落なる全語): Or perhaps "whole talk that is sloughing off." An unusual expression not occurring elsewhere. For the use of "slough off" (*datsuraku* 脱落), see Supplementary Notes, s.v. "Slough off."

69　**"getting such"** (*toku inmo* 得恁麼): An expression often encountered in Zen texts in casual reference to spiritual attainment — as in the well-known saying attributed to the ninth-century master Yunju Daoying 雲居道膺; see Supplementary Notes, s.v. "Such a person."

16A. Sustained Practice, Part 1 *Gyōji* 行持

of the sustained practice of "*not leaving the grove.*" Do not go east and west with the winds of east and west. Although the spring winds and autumn moons of "ten years or five years" are not noticed, they have words transcending sounds and forms.[70] Its sayings, we do not know, we do not understand. We should study that an inch of shadow of sustained practice is a sad thing.[71] Do not doubt "not talking" as merely empty. Entering is one grove; leaving is one grove; the "road of the bird" is one grove; the realms everywhere are one grove.[72]

* * * * *

[16A:27] {1:155}

大梅山は慶元府にあり。この山に護聖寺を草創す、法常禪師その本元なり。禪師は襄陽人なり。かつて馬祖の會に參じてとふ、如何是佛、と。馬祖いはく、即心是佛、と。法常、このことばをききて、言下大悟す。ちなみに大梅山の絕頂にのぼりて、人倫に不群なり。草庵に獨居、松實を食し、荷葉を衣とす。かの山に小池あり、池に荷おほし。坐禪辦道すること三十餘年なり。人事たえて見聞せず、年曆おほよそおぼえず、四山青又黄のみをみる。おもひやるにはあはれむべき風霜なり。

---

70 **they have words transcending sounds and forms** (*shōshiki tōdatsu no dō ari* 聲色透脱の道あり): An unusual expression that could also be read "there are words through which sounds and forms are liberated."

71 **an inch of shadow of sustained practice is a sad thing** (*gyōji no sun'in o kashakko nari* 行持の寸陰を可惜許なり): Presumably to be understood "[the loss of even] an inch of shadow." The term *sun'in* 寸陰 ("inch of shadow") is a literary term for "a moment of time."

72 **Entering is one grove; leaving is one grove** (*nyusshi ichi sōrin nari, shusshi ichi sōrin nari* 入之一叢林なり、出之一叢林なり): Likely reflecting a saying of Jingqing Daofu 鏡清道怤 (*Liandeng huiyao* 聯燈會要, ZZ.136:838b6-8):

師問僧、近離甚處。云三峰。師云、夏在甚處。云五峰。師云、放爾三十棒。云某甲過在甚麼處。師云、爲爾出一叢林。入一叢林。

The Master [Daofu] asked a monk, "Where did you come from?"
He said, "Three Peaks."
The Master said, "Where did you spend the summer [retreat]?"
He said, "Five Peaks."
The Master said, "I spare you the thirty blows."
He said, "Where was my mistake?"
The Master said, "Because you left one grove and entered another grove."

"road of the bird" (*chōro* 鳥路): Likely an allusion to the "path of the bird" (*chōdō* 鳥道), the first of the "three roads" (*sanro* 三路) of Dongshan Liangjie 洞山良价, cited often in Dōgen's writing; see Supplementary Notes, s.v. "Dongshan's path of the bird."

24 DŌGEN'S *SHŌBŌGENZŌ* VOLUME II

Mount Damei is in the Qingyuan Prefecture.[73] On this mountain was established the Husheng Monastery, with Chan Master Fachang as its founder.[74] The Chan Master was from Xiangyang.[75]

Once, when he was practicing in Mazu's community, he asked, "*What is a buddha?*"

Mazu said, "*This mind itself is the buddha.*"

On hearing these words, Fachang immediately had a great awakening. Thereupon, climbing to the summit of Mount Damei, he no longer mingled with humanity. He lived alone in a thatched hermitage, ate pine nuts, and wore clothes of lotus leaves. On the mountain, there was a small pond in which lotuses were plentiful. He sat in meditation pursuing the way for over thirty years. Of human affairs, he was entirely oblivious; of the passing of the years, he was wholly unaware. He saw only that "*the mountains in the four directions are green and then yellow.*"[76] When we think on it, they were winds and frosts to be pitied.[77]

[16A:28]
師の坐禪には、八寸の鐵塔一基を頂上におく。如戴寶冠なり。この塔を落地却せしめざらんと功夫すれば、ねぶらざるなり。その塔、いま本山にあり、庫下に交割す。かくのごとく辦道すること、死にいたりて懈倦なし。

When the Master sat in meditation, he placed an eight-inch iron stūpa on top of his head, as if he were wearing a jeweled crown. By the effort not to let this stūpa fall on the ground, he did not doze off. The stūpa is still at this mountain, recorded in the register of properties in the administrative office.[78] He pursued the way like this right up to his death, without ever letting up.

---

73 **Qingyuan Prefecture** (*Keigen fu* 慶元府): In the Ningbo 寧波 District of present-day Zhejiang Province.

74 **Husheng Monastery** (*Goshōji* 護聖寺): Established by Fachang 法常 circa 836.

Chan Master Fachang (*Hōjō zenji* 法常禪師): I.e., Damei Fachang 大梅法常 (752-839), a disciple of Mazu Daoyi 馬祖道一. Dōgen retells in Japanese here a version of Fachang's biography found in the *Jingde chuandeng lu* 景德傳燈錄 (T.2076.51:254c2ff).

75 **Xiangyang** (*Jōyō* 襄陽): In present-day Hubei province.

76 **"the mountains in the four directions are green and then yellow"** (*shizan sei mata ō* 四山青又黃): Quoting Facheng's own words in the conversation with the monk recounted below, section 29.

77 **winds and frosts to be pitied** (*awaremu beki fūsō* あはれむべき風霜): I.e., years spent in a pitiable state. The term *fūsō* 風霜 ("winds and frosts") refers to bitter conditions; it can also, like the similar *seisō* 星霜 ("stars and frosts"), refer to the passing of the years.

78 **recorded in the register of properties in the administrative office** (*kuka ni kōkatsu su* 庫下に交割す): A loose translation. The verb *kōkatsu su* 交割す refers to the practice of verifying the records of the public and private holdings of the monastery on the occasion of the succession of monastic officers. Dōgen's source for this information is unclear. In his

16A. Sustained Practice, Part 1 *Gyōji* 行持

[16A:29]

かくのごとくして年月を經歴するに、鹽官の會より一僧きたりて、やまに
いりて拄杖をもとむるちなみに、迷山路して、はからざるに師の庵所にい
たる。不期のなかに師をみる。すなはちとふ、和尚、この山に住してより
このかた、多少時也。師いはく、只見四山青又黄。この僧またとふ、出山
路、向什麼處去。師いはく、隨流去。この僧、あやしむこころあり。かへ
りて鹽官に舉似するに、鹽官いはく、そのかみ江西にありしとき、一僧を
曽見す。それよりのち消息をしらず。莫是此僧否。

After some years and months had passed like this, there appeared a monk
from the community of Yanguan, who, having climbed the mountain in
search of a staff, lost his way on the mountain path and by chance came
upon the Master's hermitage.[79] Upon unexpectedly seeing the Master, he
asked, "Reverend, how long have you been living on this mountain?"

The Master said, *"I see only that the mountains in the four directions
are green and then yellow."*

The monk asked again, *"Which way is the path out of the mountain?"*

The Master said, *"Follow the stream."*

The monk thought this strange. When he returned and reported it to
Yanguan, Yanguan said, "In the past, when I was in Jiangxi, I once met a
monk. Since then, I don't know what happened to him. *Couldn't he have
been this monk?"*[80]

[16A:30] {1:156}

つひに僧に令して師を請するに、出山せず。偈をつくりて答するにいは
く、摧殘枯木倚寒林、幾度逢春不變心、樵客遇之猶不顧、郢人那得苦追
尋。つひにおもむかず。これよりのちに、なほ山奥へいらんとせしちなみ
に、有頌するにいはく、一池荷葉衣無盡、數樹松華食有餘、剛被世人知住
處、更移茅舍入深居。つひに庵を山奥にうつす。

So, he sent the monk to invite the Master, but he would not leave the
mountain. He responded by composing a gāthā:

Broken dried-up tree keeping to the cold wood:
How many times has it met the spring without changing its mind?
The woodsman passes it without a backward glance;
How could a man of Ying bother to go after it?[81]

"Shōbōgenzō shisho" 正法眼藏嗣書, he reports that he stayed overnight at the Husheng
Monastery on Mount Damei; so, he may be recalling a personal experience here.

79 **Yanguan** (*Enkan* 鹽官): I.e., Yanguan Qian 鹽官齊安 (d. 842), another disciple of
Mazu Daoyi 馬祖道一.

80 **"when I was in Jiangxi"** (*Kōzei ni arishi toki* 江西にありしとき): I.e., when Yanguan was studying with Mazu.

81 **Broken dried-up tree keeping to the cold wood** (*saizan koboku i kanrin* 摧殘枯

26 DŌGEN'S *SHŌBŌGENZŌ* VOLUME II

And, in the end, he did not go. Later, when he was thinking to go further into the mountain, he composed a verse:

> *From the lotus leaves of a single pond, my clothes are inexhaustible;*
> *From the blooms of a few pines, my food is more than enough.*
> *Now that the world knows where I live,*
> *I'll move my hut to a deeper spot.*[82]

And, so, he moved his hermitage further into the mountain.

[16A:31]

あるとき、馬祖、ことさら僧をつかはしてとはしむ、和尚そのかみ馬祖を参見せしに、得何道理、便住此山なる。師いはく、馬祖われにむかひていふ、即心是佛。すなはちこの山に住す。僧いはく、近日は佛法また別なり。師いはく、作麼生別なる。僧いはく、馬祖いはく、非心非佛、とあり。師いはく、這老漢、ひとを惑亂すること、了期あるべからず。任他非心非佛、我祇管即心是佛。

Once, Mazu especially sent a monk to ask, "Reverend, formerly, when you studied with Mazu, *what truth did you get that you came to live on this mountain?*"[83]

The Master said, "Mazu told me, '*this mind itself is the buddha.*' Whereupon, I came to live on this mountain."

The monk said, "Nowadays, his buddha dharma is different."

The Master said, "How is it different?"

The monk said, "Mazu says, '*Not the mind, not the buddha.*'"

The Master said, "This old guy, there's no end to his confusing people. *Let him have his 'not the mind, not the buddha'; for me, it's just 'this mind itself is the buddha.*'"

木倚寒林): Reading *i* 倚 in the sense "to stick close to." "The cold wood" (*kanrin* 寒林) evokes the charnal ground (*shitabana* 尸多婆那; S. *śītabana*) for the disposal of corpses. The verse, cited elsewhere in the *Shōbōgenzō*, occurs at *Jingde chuandeng lu* 景德傳燈錄 (T.2076.51:254c12-13). See Supplementary Notes, s.v. "Dried-up tree."

man of Ying (*Eijin* 郢人): I.e., a maestro; in polite reference to Qian. Ying was the capital of the ancient state of Chu 楚.

82 **From the lotus leaves of a single pond, my clothes are inexhaustible** (*itchi kayō e mujin* 一池荷葉衣無盡): This verse is not found in Fachang's *Jingde chuandeng lu* 景德傳燈錄 biography but is attributed to him in the *Mingzhou Damei Fachang chanshi lu* 明州大梅法常禪師錄 (*Kanazawa bunko shiryō zensho* 金沢文庫資料全書 1:18b). However, the poem is originally the work of the eighth-century Daoist recluse Xu Xuanping 許宣平 in response to the efforts of Li Bai 李白 to visit him.

83 **Mazu especially sent a monk** (*Baso. kotosara sō o tsukawashite* 馬祖、ことさら僧をつかはして): Here, Dōgen returns to his Japanese retelling of Fachang's notice in the *Jingde chuandeng lu* 景德傳燈錄 (T.2076.51:254c14-20). As Dōgen himself notes below, this episode was well known and was recorded in several Chan sources.

16A. Sustained Practice, Part 1 *Gyōji* 行持

[16A:32] {1:157}

この道をもちて、馬祖に舉似す。馬祖いはく、梅子熟也。

He reported these words to Mazu. Mazu said, "*The plum is ripe.*"[84]

[16A:33]

この因縁は、人天みなしれるところなり。天龍は師の神足なり、俱胝は師の法孫なり。高麗の迦智は、師の法を傳持して、本國の初祖なり。いま高麗の諸師は、師の遠孫なり。

This episode is known to men and devas. Tianlong was the Master's spiritual foot; Juzhi was the Master's dharma grandson.[85] Gaji of Goryeo transmitted the Master's dharma and became the first ancestor in his land.[86] The Masters of Goryeo now are the distant descendants of the Master.

[16A:34]

生前には、一虎・一象よのつねに給侍す、あひあらそはず。師の圓寂ののち、虎・象いしをはこび、泥をはこびて師の塔をつくる。その塔、いま護聖寺に現在せり。師の行持、むかし・いまの知識とあるは、おなじくほむるところなり。劣慧のものは、ほむべしとしらず。貪名愛利のなかに佛法あらましと強爲するは、小量の愚見なり。

During his lifetime, he was attended by a tiger and an elephant, who never fought with each other. After his complete quiescence, the tiger and the elephant carried stones and carried earth to build a stūpa for the Master.[87] The stūpa still exists at the Husheng Monastery. The sustained practice of the Master is praised by all wise friends, past and present; those of inferior wisdom do not know that he is to be praised.[88] To maintain the vain hope that the buddha dharma might exist amidst craving for fame and love of profit is a small, stupid view.

---

84 **"The plum is ripe"** (*baisu juku ya* 梅子熟也): Or "Master Plum is mature"; playing on the name of Fachang's mountain, Damei 大梅 ("Great Plum").

85 **Tianlong was the Master's spiritual foot** (*Tenryū wa shi no jinsoku nari* 天龍は師の神足なり): Little is known of Fachang's disciple Tianlong 天龍 (dates unknown), teacher of Juzhi 俱胝 (dates unknown); the two masters are known primarily for their practice of teaching by holding up one finger. "Spiritual foot" here renders *jinsoku* 神足, a term for paranormal powers, used in reference to a top disciple.

86 **Gaji of Goryeo** (*Kōryō no Kaji* 高麗の迦智): Recorded as a follower of Fachang at *Jingde chuandeng lu* 景德傳燈錄 (T.2076.51:273b27). The founder of the Korean Mount Gaji 迦智山 school of Seon is usually given as Doui 道義 (d. 825), who is said to have studied with Mazu's disciples Xitang Zhizang 西堂智藏 (735-814) and Baizhang Huaihai 百丈懷海. Dōgen's source for his claim is not clear.

87 **complete quiescence** (*enjaku* 圓寂): I.e., *parinirvāṇa*.

88 **wise friends, past and present** (*mukashi ima no chishiki* むかし・いまの知識): I.e., Buddhist teachers throughout history.

28 DŌGEN'S *SHŌBŌGENZŌ* VOLUME II

* * * * *

[16A:35]

五祖の法演禪師いはく、師翁はじめて楊岐に住せしとき、老屋敗椽して、
風雨之敝、はなはだし。ときに冬暮なり。殿堂ことごとく舊損せり。その
なか、僧堂、ことにやぶれ、雪散滿牀、居不遑處なり。雪頂の耆宿、なほ
澡雪し、厖眉の尊年、皺眉のうれへあるがごとし。衆僧やすく坐禪するこ
となし。衲子、投誠して修造せんことを請せしに、師翁却之いはく、我佛
有言、時當滅劫、高岸深谷、遷變不常、安得圓滿如意、自求稱足ならん。
古往の聖人、おほく樹下露地に經行す、古來の勝躅なり、履空の玄風な
り。なんだち出家學道する、做手脚なほいまだおだやかならず、わずかに
これ四、五十歳なり。たれかいたづらなるいとまありて、豐屋をこととせ
ん。つひに不從なり。

Chan Master Fayan of Wuzu said, "When my master's father first lived
at Yangqi, the buildings were old, the rafters rotted, and the damage from
wind and rain was severe.[89] It was the end of winter. The halls were all in
disrepair. Among them, the saṃgha hall was particularly damaged, *with
snow and hail covering the platforms, so they couldn't be occupied.*"

Seniors with snowy pates still cleaned off the snow; venerable elders
with shaggy brows seemed to knit their brows in lament.[90] The monks
could not comfortably sit in meditation.

"When a patch-robed one sincerely suggested that it be repaired, my
master's father declined, saying, '*Our buddha has said that we are now
in a kalpa of decrease, with high bluffs and deep valleys changing and
impermanent.[91] How can we seek to be satisfied, with things perfectly
fulfilling our wishes?*'"

---

89 **Chan Master Fayan of Wuzu** (*Goso no Hōen zenji* 五祖の法演禪師): I.e., Wuzu
Fayan 五祖法演 (d. 1104). Dōgen here retells in Japanese a passage found in the *Chanlin
paoxun* 禪林寶訓 (T.2022.48:1018c6-11).

"When my master's father first lived at Yangqi" (*suō hajimete Yōgi ni jū seshi toki* 師
翁はじめて楊岐に住せしとき): "My master's father" renders *suō* 師翁 ("my master's
old man"; also read *shiō*), used in reference to the teacher of one's teacher. The referent here is Yangqi Fanghui 楊岐方會 (993-1046), teacher of Fayan's master, Baiyun
Shouduan 白雲守端. Yangqi 楊岐 is the name of the mountain in present-day Jiangxi
Province where Fanghui lived.

90 **Seniors with snowy pates still cleaned off the snow** (*setchō no gishuku, nao sōsetsu
shi* 雪頂の耆宿、なほ澡雪し): Dōgen here interjects this and the following sentence of
his own. The English "cleaned off the snow" tries to capture the use of the verb *sōsetsu*
澡雪 ("to clean") in a play on the "snowy pates" (*setchō* 雪頂) of the old monks.

91 **"patch-robed one"** (*nossu* 衲子): I.e., one of Fayan's monks. The term *nossu* 衲子
("patch-robed one") is synonymous with *nassō* [or *nōsō*] 衲僧 ("patch-robed monk").
Dōgen is here continuing his Japanese retelling of the *Chanlin paoxun* 禪林寶訓, at
T.2022.48:1018c7.

"Our buddha has said" (*ga butsu u gon* 我佛有言): This and the following sentence

16A. Sustained Practice, Part 1 *Gyōji* 行持   29

The sages of old often walked under a tree or in the open; this is a splendid precedent, the dark style of those who tread the sky.[92]

"'You have left home and are studying the way, but you still do not move your hands and feet gracefully.[93] It is but forty or fifty years.[94] Who has the time to waste on a fancy building?' In the end, he did not go along with it."

[16A:36] {1:158}

翌日に上堂して、衆にしめしていはく、楊岐乍住屋壁疏、滿牀盡撒雪珍珠、縮却項暗嗟嘘、翻憶古人樹下居。つひにゆるさず。しかあれども、四海五湖の雲衲霞袂、この會に掛錫するをねがふところとせり。耽道の人おほきことをよろこぶべし。この道、こころにそむべし、この語、みに銘すべし。

The following day, he held a convocation and addressed the assembly, saying,

> *When Yangqi first lived here, the walls were coming apart,*
> *The seats were all covered with scattered pearls of snow.*
> *We hunched up our shoulders, and secretly grumbled,*
> *Thinking back on those of old who lived beneath a tree.[95]*

---

are put in Chinese quoted directly from *Chanlin paoxun* 禪林寶訓 (T.2022.48:1018c8-9); some readers treat them as a quotation of "our buddha," though this seems rather unlikely.

"**kalpa of decrease**" (*genkō* 減劫): I.e., æon of decline, during which human life gradually decreases.

"**high bluffs and deep valleys**" (*kōgan shinkoku* 高岸深谷): A fixed idiom expressing great change, from the line in the *Shijing* 詩經 (Maoshi 毛詩, Shiyue zhi jiao 十月之交, KR.1c0001.019.33a):

高岸爲谷、深谷爲陵。
High bluffs become valleys; deep valleys become hills.

92 **sages of old** (*koō no shōnin* 古往の聖人): Here again, Dōgen interjects a sentence of his own. The English "walked" here translates *kinhin* 經行, a term for walking recitation or meditation.

dark style of those who tread the sky (*rikū no genpū* 履空の玄風): I.e., the practice of advanced adepts with the power of flight; the term *rikū* 履空 ("tread the sky"), which does not occur elsewhere in the *Shōbōgenzō*, is sometimes interpreted here as "walk in emptiness."

93 "**You have left home and are studying the way**'" (*nandachi shukke gakudō suru* なんだち出家學道する): Continuing Fayan's quotation, now put in Japanese, of his master's father, at *Chanlin paoxun* 禪林寶訓, T.2022.48:1018c10.

94 "**It is but forty or fifty years**'" (*wazuka ni kore shi, gojū sai nari* わずかにこれ四、五十歳なり): The antecedent of "it" (*kore* これ) is perhaps "our lives as monks."

95 **The following day** (*yokujitsu* 翌日): Continuing to retell the *Chanlin paoxun* 禪林寶訓 passage (T.2022.48:1018c11-13), through the end of the verse, which is quoted here in the Chinese.

30 DŌGEN'S *SHŌBŌGENZŌ* VOLUME II

In the end, he did not allow it.[96] Nevertheless, those robed in clouds and sleeved in mist from the four seas and five lakes sought to hang their staffs in this community.[97] It is gratifying that there were so many immersed in the way. This talk should be dyed on our minds; these words should be engraved on our bodies.

[16A:37]

演和尚、あるときしめしていはく、行無越思、思無越行。この語、おもく
すべし。日夜思之、朝夕行之。いたづらに東西南北の風にふかるるがごと
くなるべからず。いはんやこの日本國は、王臣の宮殿、なほその豊屋あら
ず、わづかにおろそかなる白屋なり。出家學道の、いかでか豊屋に幽棲す
るあらん。もし豊屋をえたる、邪命にあらざるなし、清淨なるまれなり。
もとよりあらんは論にあらず、はじめてさらに經營することなかれ。草
庵・白屋は古聖の所住なり、古聖の所愛なり。晩學したひ參學すべし、た
がゆることなかれ。

Reverend Yan once instructed, "*The practice does not exceed the thinking; the thinking does not exceed the practice.*"[98] We should take these words seriously, "*thinking on them day and night; practicing them morning and evening.*"[99] We should not be as if blown futilely by the winds of east, west, south, and north. Still less in this Land of Japan, where the palaces even of the kings and ministers lack lavish dwellings and consist merely of simple, plain dwellings.[100] How could those who

---

96 **In the end, he did not allow it** (*tsui ni yurusazu* つひにゆるさず): I.e., Fayan did not consent to have the saṃgha hall repaired. This sentence and the remainder of this section represent Dōgen's comment.

97 **robed in clouds and sleeved in mist** (*unnō kabei* 雲衲霞袂): A literary expression for the itinerant monk; akin to the more common "clouds and water" (*unsui* 雲水).

four seas and five lakes (*shikai goko* 四海五湖): I.e., the entire realm of China; a fixed expression, sometimes in reverse order. The four seas are the oceans in the four directions; the five lakes are variously listed.

hang their staffs (*kashaku* 掛錫): I.e., enroll in the monastery; see Supplementary Notes, s.v. "Staff."

98 **Reverend Yan** (*En oshō* 演和尚): Quoting again from the Fayan passage in the *Chanlin paoxun* 禪林寶訓 (T.2022.48:1018c14-15):

演祖曰、衲子守心城。奉戒律。日夜思之。朝夕行之。行無越思。思無越行。

The Ancestor Yan said, "The patch-robed who guard the citadel of the mind respect the precepts. 'Day and night, they think on them; morning and evening, they practice them. Their practice of them does not exceed their thinking on them'; their thinking on them does not exceed their practice of them."

Fayan is here adapting Zi Chan's 子産 teaching on government in the *Zuo zhuan* 左傳 (*Xiang gong er shi wu nian* 襄公二十五年, KR.c1e0001.0009.623a.).

99 **"thinking on them day and night; practicing them morning and evening"** (*nichi ya shi shi, chōseki gyō shi* 日夜思之、朝夕行之): From Fayan's use of the *Zuo zhuan*.

100 **plain dwellings** (*hakuoku* 白屋): A term for a humble cottage, sometimes derived from a dwelling thatched with kunai grass (*baimao* 白茅).

16A. Sustained Practice, Part 1 *Gyōji* 行持   31

"have left home and are studying the way" live in seclusion in lavish dwellings?[101] One does not get a lavish dwelling except from wrong livelihood; rarely is it from a pure one. If it is already there, it is not an issue, but do not construct a new one. Thatched huts and plain dwellings are the abode of the sages of old, what the sages of old loved.[102] Latter-day students should admire and study them; do not deviate from them.

[16A:38] {1:159}

黄帝・堯・舜等は、俗なりといへども草屋に居す、世界の勝躅なり。

The Yellow Emperor, Yao, and Shun, though laymen, lived in thatched dwellings, setting an excellent precedent for the world.[103]

[16A:39]

尸子曰、欲觀黄帝之行、於合宮。欲觀堯舜之行、於総章。黄帝明堂、以草蓋之、名曰合宮。舜之明堂、以草蓋之、名曰総章。

The *Shizi* says,[104]

If you wish to see the conduct of the Yellow Emperor, it is in the Hegong; if you wish to see the conduct of Yao and Shun, it is in the Zongzhang. The Mingtang of the Yellow Emperor was covered with thatch and was called the Hegong; the Mingtang of Shun was covered with thatch and was called the Zongzhang.[105]

---

101   **those who "have left home and are studying the way"** (*shukke gakudō* 出家學道): From Fayan's talk quoted in section 35, above.

102   **the abode of the sages of old, what the sages of old loved** (*koshō no shojū nari, koshō no shoai nari* 古聖の所住なり、古聖の所愛なり): Perhaps recalling Dōgen's version of lines from the poem *Caoan ge* 草菴歌, by Shitou Xiqian 石頭希遷; see above, Note 7, and Supplementary Notes, s.v. "*Reverend Shitou's Song of the Thatched Hut.*"

103   **The Yellow Emperor, Yao, and Shun** (*Kōtei Gyō Shun* 黄帝・堯・舜): I.e., the three legendary emperors of China said to have ruled in the third century BCE.

104   *Shizi* (*Shishi* 尸子): The work of the fourth-century BCE author Shi Jiao 尸佼. Much of the book was already lost by Dōgen's day; and, while this passage is quoted elsewhere in Chinese literature, it is unclear what source he used here and for the identical passage in his *Chiji shingi* 知事清規 (DZZ.6:126-128).

105   **Hegong** (*Gōkyū* 合宮); **Zongzhang** (*Sōshō* 総章); **Mingtang** (*Meidō* 明堂): The first and second are the halls in which the Yellow Emperor and the Emperor Shun respectively are said to have conducted affairs of state; the last was the hall used for formal imperial ceremony.

32   DŌGEN'S *SHŌBŌGENZŌ* VOLUME II

[16A:40]

しるべし、合宮・総章は、ともに草をふくなり。いま黄帝・堯・舜をもて、われらにならべんとするに、なほ天地の論にあらず。これなほ草蓋を明堂とせり。俗なほ草屋に居す、出家人いかでか高堂大觀を所居に擬せん、慚惶すべきなり。古人の、樹下に居し、林間にすむ、在家・出家ともに愛する所住なり。黄帝は崆峒道人廣成の弟子なり。廣成は崆峒といふ巖のなかにすむ。いま大宋國の國王・大臣、おほくこの玄風をつたふるなり。

We should know, then, that the Hegong and Zongzhang were both covered with thatch. Now, if we were to compare the Yellow Emperor, Yao, and Shun to us, it would not even be a matter of heaven and earth.[106] Yet even they used a thatched building as their Mingtang. Even laymen live in thatched dwellings; how could those who have left home propose to reside in lofty halls and stately towers? It would be shameful. The ancients stayed under trees or lived in the forest; these were abodes loved by householders and renunciants alike. The Yellow Emperor was a disciple of Guangcheng, the Daoist of Kungtong.[107] Guangcheng lived in a cave called Kongtong. Today, many kings and ministers of the Land of the Great Song follow this dark style.

[16A:41]

しかあればすなはち、塵勞中人なほかくのごとし。出家人いかでか塵勞中人よりも劣ならん、塵勞中人よりもにごれらん。向來の佛祖のなかに、天の供養をうくるおほし。しかあれども、すでに得道のとき、天眼およばず、鬼神たよりなし。そのむねあきらむべし。天衆・神道、もし佛祖の行履をふむときは、佛祖にちかづくみちあり。佛祖あまねく天衆・神道を超證するには、天衆・神道はるかに見上のたよりなく、佛祖のほとりにちかづきがたきなり。

Thus, even people in the midst of dust and toil are like this.[108] How could people who have left home be inferior to people in the midst of dust and toil, be more defiled than people in the midst of dust and toil? Among past buddhas and ancestors there were many who received offerings from the devas. However, once they gained the way, the eye of

---

106 **it would not even be a matter of heaven and earth** (*nao tenchi no ron ni arazu* なほ天地の論にあらず): I.e., the difference would be far greater than that between heaven and earth.

107 **Guangcheng, the Daoist of Kungtong** (*Kōdō dōjin Kōsei* 崆峒道人廣成): Reference to the story, found in *Zhuangzi* 莊子 11 (Zaiyou 在宥, KR.5c0126.011.8a), that the Yellow Emperor had an interview with Guang Cheng Zi 廣成子 on Mount Kongtong (though there is no mention there that the latter was living in a cave). Dōgen also refers to this story elsewhere in his writings.

108 **people in the midst of dust and toil** (*jinrōchū nin* 塵勞中人): I.e., those living in the defiled secular world. The term *jinrō* 塵勞 ("dust and toil") is a synonym for *bonnō* 煩惱 (S. *kleśa*; "defilement"). See Supplementary Notes, s.v. "Dust."

the devas did not reach them, and the spirits lacked means [to contact them].[109] We should be clear about this point. When the devas and spirits follow the conduct of the buddhas and ancestors, there is a path for them to approach the buddhas and ancestors; when the buddhas and ancestors transcend the devas and spirits everywhere, the devas and spirits have no means of looking so far up to them and cannot approach the vicinity of the buddhas and ancestors.[110]

[16A:42] {1:160}

南泉いはく、老僧、修行のちからなくして鬼神に覰見せらる。しるべし、無修の鬼神に覰見せらるるは、修行のちからなきなり。

Nanquan said, "This old monk has no strength in his practice and gets seen by spirits."[111] So, we know that being seen by the spirits that have no practice means one has no strength in his practice.

[16A:43]

太白山宏智禪師正覺和尚の會に、護伽藍神いはく、われきく、覺和尚この山に住すること十餘年なり。つねに寢堂にいたりてみんとするに不能前なり、未之識也。まことに有道の先蹤にあひあふなり。

In the community of Reverend Zhengjue, Chan Master Hongzhi of Mount Taibai, the guardian spirit of the monastery said, "I've heard that Reverend Jue has been living on this mountain for over ten years.[112] But whenever I've gone to your quarters to see you, I've been unable to proceed; so, I've yet to make your acquaintance."

Truly, we are encountering here the traces of one who has the way.

---

109 **the spirits lacked means** (*kijin tayori nashi* 鬼神たよりなし): Perhaps, recalling the examples given above, sections 16, 18, and 19, and introducing further examples below. The term *kijin* 鬼神 is regularly used for devas and other species of spiritual beings.

110 **devas and spirits** (*tenshu shindō* 天衆・神道): The term *tenshu* 天衆 refers to the "deva host"; the term *shindō* 神道 here likely means "[denizens of] the spirit realms."

transcend (*chōshō* 超證): This term, appearing several times in Dōgen's writing, is read sometimes as "rise to verification" and sometimes as "surpass verification" — neither of which would seem to work here, where the word is being used as a transitive verb.

111 **Nanquan** (*Nansen* 南泉): I.e., Nanquan Puyuan 南泉普願. His saying, paraphrased here in Japanese, occurs in an anecdote (recorded in the *Zongmen tongyao ji* 宗門統要集, ZTS.1:48a7-b1; *shinji Shōbōgenzō* 眞字正法眼藏, DZZ.5:134, case 18; etc.), in which a local spirit informs someone of Nanquan's impending arrival.

112 **Reverend Zhengjue, Chan Master Hongzhi of Mount Taibai** (*Taihakusan Wanshi zenji Shōgaku oshō* 太白山宏智禪師正覺和尚): I.e., Hongzhi Zhengjue 宏智正覺 (1091-1157); Mount Taibai is an alternative name for Mount Tiantong 天童山, in Zhejiang, site of Hongzhi's Jingdesi 景德寺. This anecdote is recorded in the *Hongzhi chanshi guanglu* 宏智禪師廣錄 (T.2001.48;121c28-29).

34 DŌGEN'S *SHŌBŌGENZŌ* VOLUME II

[16A:44]

この天童山は、もとは小院なり。覺和尚の住裏に、道士觀・尼寺・教院等
を掃除して、いまの景德寺となせり。師、遷化ののち、左朝奉大夫侍御史
王伯庠、ちなみに師の行業記を記するに、ある人いはく、かの道士觀・尼
寺・教寺をうばひて、いまの天童寺となせることを記すべし。御史いは
く、不可也、此事非僧德矣。ときの人、おほく侍御史をほむ。

This Mount Tiantong was originally a small cloister.[113] During Reverend Jue's residence, he swept away the Daoist temple, nunnery, teaching
cloister, and the like, and turned them into the present Jingde Monastery.
After the Master's transformation, the Grand Master for Court Service
of the Left, the Attendant Censor Wang Boxiang, compiled the Master's
record of deeds, on which occasion, someone said that he should record
the fact that he expropriated the Daoist temple, nunnery, teaching cloister, and the like, and turned them into the present Jingde Monastery.[114]
The Censor said, "I cannot. This is not something that would redound
to the merit of a monk." Many people at the time praised the Attendant
Censor.

[16A:45]

しるべし、かくのことくの事は、俗の能なり、僧の德にあらず。おほよそ
佛道に登入する最初より、はるかに三界の人天をこゆるなり。三界の所使
にあらず、三界の所見にあらざること、審細に咨問すべし。身・口・意お
よび依・正をきたして、功夫參究すべし。佛祖行持の功德、もとより人天
を濟度する巨益ありとも、人天さらに佛祖の行持にたすけらるると覺知せ
ざるなり。

So, we know that such affairs are the work of the laity, not the virtue of
a monk. In sum, from one's very first ascent to the way of the buddhas,
one far transcends the humans and devas of the three realms. We should
make detailed inquiries into the fact that such a one is not used by the
those of the three realms, is not seen by the those of the three realms. We
should work at and investigate this, bringing to bear our body, speech,
and mind, and our secondary and primary recompense.[115] Although of

---

113 **This Mount Tiantong** (*kono Tendōzan* この天童山): I.e., Hongzhi's monastery on
Mount Tiantong.

114 **After the Master's transformation** (*shi senge no nochi* 師遷化ののち): I.e., following Hongzhi's death.

Grand Master for Court Service of the Left, the Attendant Censor Wang Boxiang
(*sachōbu daifu jigyōshi Ō Hakushō* 左朝奉大夫侍御史王伯庠): The middle-level official
Wang Boxiang (1106-1173) compiled the "Record of Deeds" (*Xingye ji* 行業記), dated
1166, that is attached to the *Hongzhi chanshi guanglu* 宏智禪師廣錄 (T.2001.48:119b28-
121a12).

115 **secondary and primary recompense** (*eshō* 依正): I.e., the environment and the
psychophysical organism, respectively, that are the results of karma.

16A. Sustained Practice, Part 1 *Gyōji* 行持

course the merit of the sustained practice of the buddhas and ancestors has huge benefits that rescue humans and devas, the humans and devas themselves do not perceive that they are aided by the sustained practice of the buddhas and ancestors.

[16A:46] {1:161}

いま佛祖の大道を行持せんには、大隠・小隠を論ずることなく、聰明・鈍癡をいふことなかれ。ただながく名利をなげすてて、萬緣に繋縛せらるることなかれ。光陰をすごさず、頭燃をはらふべし。大悟をまつことなかれ、大悟は家常の茶飯なり。不悟をねがふことなかれ、不悟は髻中の寶珠なり。ただまさに、家郷あらんは家郷をはなれ、恩愛あらんは恩愛をはなれ、名あらんは名をのがれ、利あらば利をのがれ、田園あらんは田園をのがれ、親族あらんは親族をはなるべし。名利等なからんも、又はなるべし。すでにあるをはなる、なきをもはなるべき道理、あきらかなり。それすなはち一條の行持なり。生前に名利をなげすてて、一事を行持せん、佛壽長遠の行持なり。いまこの行持、さだめて行持に行持せらるるなり。この行持あらん身心、みづからも愛すべし、みづからもうやまふべし。

When seeking to engage in sustained practice of the great way of the buddhas and ancestors, do not discuss major hermits and minor hermits; do not speak of the wise and the stupid.[116] Just cast aside forever fame and profit, and do not be fettered by the myriad involvements. Without spending the years and months, we should brush the fire from our heads.[117] Do not wait for a great awakening; great awakening is everyday tea and rice.[118] Do not seek non-awakening; non-awakening is the precious jewel in the topknot.[119] Those with homes and hometowns should leave their homes and hometowns; those with familial affections should leave behind their familial affections; those with fame should flee their fame; those with profit should flee their profit; those with paddies and fields should flee their paddies and fields; those with kinsmen should leave their kinsmen. Those without fame, profit, and the like, should also

---

116 **major hermits and minor hermits** (*daiin shōin* 大隠・小隠): From the common trope expressed in the well-known verse by the Jin-dynasty poet Wang Kangju 王康琚:

小隠隠林藪、大隠隠朝市。

The minor hermit secludes himself in woods and marshes;
The major hermit secludes himself in court and market.

117 **brush the fire from our heads** (*zunen o harau* 頭燃をはらふ): A standard metaphor for the urgency of practice, occurring several times in the *Shōbōgenzō*.

118 **everyday tea and rice** (*kajō no sahan* 家常の茶飯): Japanese version of a fairly common expression, in both Zen texts and Dōgen's writings, for the "daily fare" of the home, or "normal practice"; see Supplementary Notes.

119 **precious jewel in the topknot** (*keichū no hōjū* 髻中の寶珠): Reference to the *Lotus Sūtra* metaphor of the sūtra as the jewel in the king's topknot that is the insignia of his sovereignty; see Supplementary Notes, s.v. "Jewel in the topknot." "Non-awakening" (*fugo* 不悟) here is often taken as indicating an inherently awakened state beyond awakening.

36 DŌGEN'S *SHŌBŌGENZŌ* VOLUME II

leave them. The principle is clear that those who have left what they already have should also leave what they do not have. This is one instance of sustained practice. Casting aside fame and wealth during this lifetime, to engage in the sustained practice of the one thing is the sustained practice of the "*length of the lifespan of the Buddha.*"[120] This present sustained practice is definitely being engaged in sustained practice by sustained practice. Bodies and minds that have this sustained practice should love themselves, should respect themselves.

* * * * *

[16A:47]

大慈寰中禪師いはく、説得一丈、不如行取一尺。説得一尺、不如行取一寸。

Chan Master Huanzhong of Daci said, "*To talk of ten feet is not like practicing one foot; to talk of one foot is not like practicing one inch.*"[121]

[16A:48]

これは、時人の行持おろそかにして、佛道の通達をわすれたるがごとくなるをいましむるににたりといへども、一丈の説は不是とにはあらず、一尺の行は一丈説よりも大功なりといふなり。なんぞただ丈尺の度量のみならん、はるかに須彌と芥子との論功もあるべきなり。須彌に全量あり、芥子に全量あり。行持の大節、これかくのごとし。いまの道得は、寰中の自爲道にあらず、寰中の自爲道なり。

Although this may resemble an admonition of those of the time who had neglected sustained practice and forgotten the penetration of the way of the buddhas, he is not saying that talking about ten feet is wrong; he is saying that the practice of one foot is of greater merit than talk of ten feet. But why is it only the gauge of ten feet and one foot? There should also be far more merit in the discussion of Sumeru and a mustard

---

120 **to engage in the sustained practice of the one thing** (*ichiji o gyōji sen* 一事を行持せん): The meaning of *ichiji* 一事 ("one thing" or "one matter") is unclear: it could mean the "one great matter" (*ichi daiji* 一大事) of buddhahood, or "this one matter" of detachment from all we have (and do not have), or simply "some one thing" that is the focus of our sustained practice.

sustained practice of the "length of the lifespan of the Buddha" (*butsuju chōon no gyōji* 佛壽長遠の行持): Presumably meaning the practice of the Buddha throughout his long lifespan. The expression *butsuju chōon* 佛壽長遠 ("length of the lifespan of the Buddha [Śākyamuni]") is borrowed from the *Lotus Sūtra* (*Miaofa lianhua jing* 妙法蓮華經, T.262.9:44b26).

121 **Chan Master Huanzhong of Daci** (*Daiji Kanchū zenji* 大慈寰中禪師): I.e., Daci Huanzhong 大慈寰中 (780-862). His saying occurs in several sources, including Dōgen's *shinji Shōbōgenzō* 眞字正法眼藏 (DZZ.5:164, case 77); see also, e.g., *Liandeng huiyao* 聯燈會要 (ZZ.136:549b12-14).

16A. Sustained Practice, Part 1 *Gyōji* 行持

seed.[122] There is a full measure in Sumeru; there is a full measure in the mustard seed.[123] The crux of sustained practice is like this. This saying is not words expressed by Huangzhong himself; it is words expressed by *huangzhong* itself.[124]

[16A:49] {1:162}

洞山悟本大師道、説取行不得底、行取説不得底。

Great Master Wuben of Dongshan said, "I talk of what can't be practiced and practice what can't be talked of."[125]

[16A:50]

これ高祖の道なり。その宗旨は、行は説に通ずるみちをあきらめ、説の行に通ずるみちあり。しかあれば、終日とくところに、終日おこなふなり。その宗旨は、行不得底を行取し、説不得底を説取するなり。

These are the words of the eminent ancestor. The essential point of this is that his practice clarifies the path to talking, and his talking has a path to practice. Therefore, in talking all day, he practices all day. The essential point is that he practices *"what can't be practiced"* and talks of *"what can't be talked of."*

---

122 **Sumeru and a mustard seed** (*Shumi to keshi* 須彌と芥子): I.e., the towering central mountain of a world system, and the tiny seed, regularly used in Buddhist literature as a metaphor for something very small. A pairing well known from the claim in the *Vimalakīrti Sūtra* (*Weimo jing* 維摩經, T.475.14:546b25-26) that the bodhisattva can put Mt. Sumeru into a mustard seed.

123 **There is a full measure in Sumeru** (*Shumi ni zenryō ari* 須彌に全量あり): Presumably meaning, "Mount Sumeru is complete in itself."

124 **This saying is not words expressed by Huangzhong himself; it is words expressed by *huangzhong* itself** (*ima no dōtoku wa, Kanchū no ji i dō ni arazu, kanchū no ji i dō nari* いまの道得は、寰中の自爲道にあらず、寰中の自爲道なり): Presumably, a play on Huangzhong's name, which has the meaning "throughout the domain" — hence "not merely a saying of Huangzhong but a saying of the whole world (or a universal saying)."

125 **Great Master Wuben of Dongshan** (*Tōzan Gohon daishi* 洞山悟本大師): I.e., Dongshan Liangjie 洞山良价. His saying here is attached as a comment on Huangzhong's saying at *Liandeng huiyao* 聯燈會要 (ZZ.136:549b14) and elsewhere, as well as at *shinji Shōbōgenzō* 眞字正法眼藏 (DZZ.5:164, case 77).

38 DŌGEN'S *SHŌBŌGENZŌ* VOLUME II

[16A:51]

雲居山弘覺大師、この道を七通八達するにいはく、説時無行路、行時無説路。

Great Master Hungjue of Mount Yunju, having thoroughly mastered these words, said, "*When he talks, he has no road of practice; when he practices, he has no road of talk.*"[126]

[16A:52]

この道得は、行・説なきにあらず。その説時は、一生不離叢林なり。その行時は、洗頭到雪峰前なり。説時無行路、行時無説路、さしおくべからず、みだらざるべし。

This saying is not that there is no practice or talk. "*When he talks*" is "*for a lifetime not leaving the grove*"; "when he practices" is "*washing his head, he presented himself to Xuefeng.*"[127] "*When he talks, he has no road of practice; when he practices, he has no road of talk*" — we should not disregard these; we should not confuse them.

* * * * *

[16A:53]

古來の佛祖いひきたれることあり、いはゆる、若人生百歳、不會諸佛機、未若生一日而能決了之。

There is something said by the buddhas and ancestors since ancient

---

126 **Great Master Hongjue of Mount Yunju** (*Ungozan Gukaku daishi* 雲居山弘覺大師): I.e., Yunju Daoying 雲居道膺, disciple of Dongshan Liangjie 洞山良价. His comment on his teacher's saying here is attached to Huangzhong's saying at *Liandeng huiyao* 聯燈會要 (ZZ.136:549b14) and elsewhere.

thoroughly mastered (*shittsū hattatsu* 七通八達): A free translation of an expression, more literally rendered by something like "seven penetrations and eight masteries," that plays with the term *tsūdatsu* 通達 ("to penetrate"; "to master"); appears often in Dōgen's writing.

"When he talks, he has no road of practice; when he practices, he has no road of talk" (*setsu ji mu gyōro, gyō ji mu setsuro* 説時無行路、行時無説路): It is also possible to read this, "When he talks, it is his road of no practice; when he practices, it is his road of no talking," in a play on Dongshan's famous "three roads" (*sanro* 三路). See Supplementary Notes, s.v. "Dongshan's three roads."

127 **"for a lifetime not leaving the grove"** (*isshō furi sōrin* 一生不離叢林): From the saying of Zhaozhou Congshen 趙州從諗 quoted above, section 25.

"washing his head, he presented himself to Xuefeng" (*sentō tō Seppō zen* 洗頭到雪峰前): I.e., Xuefeng Yicun 雪峰義存 (822-908). From a story, recorded in Dōgen's *shinji Shōbōgenzō* 眞字正法眼藏 (DZZ.5:218, case 183), Dahui's 大慧 *Zhengfayanzang* 正法眼藏 (ZZ.118:7b12-17), and elsewhere. Xuefeng challenges a hermit who had let his hair grow long to say something or have his head shaved. The hermit just washes his head (in preparation for the shaving) and comes to Xuefeng. Dōgen cites both this and the preceding saying of Zhaozhou in his "Shōbōgenzō dōtoku" 正法眼藏道得.

16A. Sustained Practice, Part 1 *Gyōji* 行持

times: "*Should a person live a hundred years without understanding the crux of the buddhas, it would still not be like living one day having definitively comprehended it.*"[128]

[16A:54]

これは一佛二佛のいふところにあらず、諸佛の道取しきたれるところ、諸佛の行取しきたれるところなり。百千萬劫の回生回死のなかに、行持ある一日は、髻中の明珠なり、同生同死の古鏡なり、よろこぶべき一日なり、行持力みづからよろこばるるなり。行持のちからいまだいたらず、佛祖の骨髓うけざるがごときは、佛祖の身心をおしまず、佛祖の面目をよろこばざるなり。佛祖の面目骨髓、これ不去なり、如去なり、如來なり、不來なりといへども、かならず一日の行持に稟受するなり。

This is not something said by one or two buddhas; it is something that all the buddhas have been saying, something all the buddhas have been practicing. Within the repeated births and repeated deaths of a hundred thousand myriad kalpas, one day in which there is sustained practice is the bright jewel in the topknot, is the old mirror that is born together and dies together [with us]; it is a day in which to rejoice; it is the power of sustained practice itself able to rejoice.[129] Those who have not reached the power of sustained practice and have not received the bones and marrow of the buddhas and ancestors do not hold dear the body and mind of the buddhas and ancestors, do not rejoice in the face of the buddhas and ancestors. The face and the bones and marrow of the buddhas and ancestors, though they may be not gone, thus gone, thus come, not come, are invariably received in the sustained practice of one day.[130]

---

128 **something said by the buddhas and ancestors** (*busso iikitareru koto* 佛祖いひきたれること): A saying attributed to the Buddha by a boy claiming to be a hundred years old. The boy became the eighteenth ancestor of Zen in India, Gayaśata. The story appears in several Chan sources; see, e.g., *Jingde chuandeng lu* 景德傳燈錄 (T.2076.51:212b15-17).

"the crux of the buddhas" (*shobutsu ki* 諸佛機): Usually understood as the key point made by (or about) the buddhas.

129 **bright jewel in the topknot** (*keichū no myōju* 髻中の明珠): See above, section 46.

old mirror that is born together and dies together (*dōshō dōshi no kokyō* 同生同死の古鏡): Likely recalling the story of Gayaśata that was the source for the quotation in the preceding section: as recounted in "Shōbōgenzō kokyō" 正法眼藏古鏡, when the boy was born, there was a round mirror "born together" with him.

power of sustained practice itself able to rejoice (*gyōjiriki mizukara yorokobaruru nari* 行持力みづからよろこばるるなり) Taking the predicate as a potential form.

130 **not gone, thus gone, thus come, not come** (*fuko nari, nyoko nari, nyorai nari. furai nari* 不去なり、如去なり、如來なり、不來なり): No doubt reflecting the common play in Mahāyāna literature with the term *tathāgata* ("thus come" or "thus gone") as an epithet of the buddhas: when seen as empty of real referent, a "tathāgata" neither comes nor goes.

40 DŌGEN'S *SHŌBŌGENZŌ* VOLUME II

[16A:55] {1:163}

しかあれば、一日はおもかるべきなり。いたづらに百歳いけらんは、うらむべき日月なり、かなしむべき形骸なり。たとひ百歳の日月は、聲色の奴婢と馳走すとも、そのなか一日の行持を行取せば、一生の百歳を行取するのみにあらず、百歳の他生をも度取すべきなり。この一日の身命は、たふとぶべき身命なり、たふとぶべき形骸なり。かるがゆえに、いけらんこと一日ならんは、諸佛の機を會せば、この一日を曠劫多生にもすぐれたりとするなり。このゆえに、いまだ決了せざらんときは、一日をいたづらにつかふことなかれ。この一日は、をしむべき重寶なり。尺璧の價直に擬すべからず、驪珠にかふることなかれ。古賢、をしむこと、身命よりもすぎたり。

Therefore, one day must be valued. For those who live in vain for a hundred years, it is years and months to be regretted, it is a body to be pitied. Even if we have run about as slaves to sights and sounds for the years and months of a hundred years, if within that we have practiced sustained practice for one day, it is not only practicing a hundred years of a whole life but is delivering that life of a hundred years.[131] The life of this one day is a life to be valued, a body to be valued. For that reason, those with but one day to live, if they have "understood the crux of the buddhas," take this one day as superior to the many lives of vast kalpas. Therefore, when you have not yet "definitively comprehended" it, do not waste one day. This one day is a weighty treasure to be held dear. It should not be compared to the value of a one-foot jewel; do not exchange it for the black dragon's pearl.[132] The worthies of old held it dearer than their lives.

[16A:56]

しづかにおもふべし、驪珠はもとめつべし、尺璧はうることもあらん、一生百歳のうちの一日は、ひとたびうしなはん、ふたたびうることなからん。いづれの善巧方便ありてか、すぎにし一日をふたたびかへしえたる。紀事の書にしるさざるところなり。もしいたづらにすごさざるは、日月を皮袋に包含して、もらさざるなり。しかあるを、古聖・先賢は、日月ををしみ、光陰ををしむこと、眼睛よりもをしむ、國土よりもをしむ。そのい

---

131 **it is not only practicing a hundred years of a whole life but is delivering that life of a hundred years** (*isshō no hyakusai o gyōshu suru nomi ni arazu, hyakusai no tashō o mo doshu subekei nari* 一生の百歳を行取するのみにあらず、百歳の他生をも度取すべきなり): I.e., the efficacy of the practice extends not only to this lifetime but to that lifetime (or lifetimes) to come.

132 **one-foot jewel** (*sekiheki* 尺璧): I.e., a jewel one "foot" in diameter; from the old Chinese saying, "The sage does not value a one-foot jewel but gives weight to an inch of shadow (*sun'in* 寸陰) [i.e., a moment of time]." (See *Huainanzi* 淮南子, Yuandao xun 原道訓, KR.3j0010.001-12a.)

black dragon's pearl (*riju* 驪珠): Reference to the precious pearl held under the chin of the black dragon; a symbol of a most precious treasure, best known from the *Zhuangzi* 莊子 (Lie Yukou 列御寇, KR.5c0126.032.9a.).

16A. Sustained Practice. Part 1 *Gyōji* 行持

たづらに蹉過するといふは、名利の浮世に濁亂しゆくなり。いたづらに蹉過せずといふは、道にありながら、道のためにするなり。

We should quietly think that, while we might find the black dragon's pearl, and we could get the one-foot jewel, once we lose one day in the hundred years of life, there is no getting it back again. With what skillful device can we retrieve one day that has passed? It is something not recorded in the history books. Not spending time in vain is wrapping up the years and months in this bag of skin and not allowing it to leak out.[133] Thus, the sages of old and prior worthies held dear the days and months, held dear the years and months, more than they held dear their eyes, more than they held dear their land. To spend time in vain means to become confused in the floating world of fame and profit; not to spend time in vain means to act for the sake of the way while being on the way.

[16A:57] {1:164}

すでに決了することをえたらん、又一日をいたづらにせざるべし。ひとへに道のために行取し、道のために説取すべし。このゆえにしりぬ、古來の佛祖、いたづらに一日の功夫をつひやさざる儀、よのつねに觀想すべし。遲遲華日も、明窓に坐しておもふべ⌐、蕭蕭雨夜も、白屋に坐してわするることなかれ。光陰なにとしてかわが功夫をぬすむ。一日をぬすむのみにあらず、多劫の功德をぬすむ。光陰とわれと、なんの怨家ぞ。うらむべし、わが不修のしかあらしむるなるべし。われ、われとしたしからず、われ、われをうらむるなり。佛祖も恩愛なきにあらず、しかあれどもなげすてきたる。佛祖も諸緣なきにあらず、しかあれどもなげすてきたる。たとひをしむとも、自他の因緣、をしまるべきにあらざるがゆえに、われもし恩愛をなげすてずば、恩愛かへりてわれをなげすつべき云爲あるなり。恩愛をあはれむべくは、恩愛をあはれむべし。恩愛をあはれむといふは、恩愛をなげすつるなり。

Those who have already attained the "definitive comprehension" should not again spend one day in vain. We should solely practice for the sake of the way and speak for the sake of the way. Therefore, we know that we should constantly reflect on the behavior of the past buddhas and ancestors, who did not idly waste the effort of one day. On a leisurely day of spring flowers, as we sit by a bright window, we should think on it; on a dismal night of autumn rains, as you sit in a simple hut, do not forget it. Why do the years and months rob us of our efforts? They rob us not only of one day; they rob us of the merit of many kalpas. The years and months and I — what enemies are we? Sadly, my failure to practice must have made it so. Not being close to myself, I resent myself. The buddhas and ancestors are also not without familial affections, but they have cast them aside; the buddhas and ancestors are not without worldly involvements, but they have cast them aside. Though we may hold dear

---

133 **bag of skin** (*hitai* 皮袋): I.e., the human body; see Supplementary Notes.

42   DŌGEN'S *SHŌBŌGENZŌ* VOLUME II

familial affections, they are the causes and conditions of self and other, not to be held dear; hence, if we do not cast them aside, it can turn out that they instead cast us aside. Those who may cherish familial affections should cherish familial affections; to cherish familial affections is to cast aside familial affections.

* * * * *

[16A:58]

南嶽大慧禪師懷讓和尚、そのかみ曹溪に參じて、執侍すること十五秋なり。しかうして傳道授業すること、一器水瀉一器なることをえたり。古先の行履、もとも慕古すべし。十五秋の風霜、われをわづらはすおほかるべし。しかあれども、純一に究辨す。これ晚進の龜鏡なり。寒爐に炭なく、ひとり虛堂にふせり、涼夜に燭なく、ひとり明窓に坐する。たとひ一知半解なくとも、無爲の絕學なり。これ行持なるべし。

Reverend Huairang, Chan Master Dahui of Nanyue, in the past consulted Caoxi, attending him for fifteen autumns.[134] Thus, he attained the transmission of the way and bestowal of the work, the pouring of the water from one vessel to another vessel.[135] We should admire the ancients most of all in the conduct of our old forebears. The wind and frost of fifteen autumns must have caused him much suffering; yet he purely pursued a thorough investigation. This is a tortoise shell mirror for latecomers.[136] With no charcoal in the cold winter stove, he slept alone in the empty hall; with no candle in the cool summer night, he sat alone at the bright window. Even without a single knowledge and a half understanding, he was "finished learning with nothing to do."[137] This must be sustained practice.

---

134   **Reverend Huairang, Chan Master Dahui of Nanyue** (*Nangaku Daie zenji Ejō oshō* 南嶽大慧禪師懷讓和尚): I.e., Nanyue Huairang 南嶽懷讓.

Caoxi (*Sōkei* 曹溪): I.e., the Sixth Ancestor, Huineng of Caoxi 曹溪慧能.

135   **transmission of the way and bestowal of the work** (*dendō jugō* 傳道授業): A phrase, appearing elsewhere in the *Shōbōgenzō*, that is the result of splitting two familiar compound terms: "transmit and bestow" (*denju* 傳授) and "the work of the way" (*dōgō* 道業).

136   **tortoise shell mirror for latecomers** (*banshin no kikyō* 晚進の龜鏡): I.e., a model for later practitioners. The reference is to the ancient Chinese practice of augury by the use of tortoise shells. A "latecomer" is one who has come to Zen practice late, either in his or her own life or recently in the history of the tradition. An expression occurring elsewhere in the *Shōbōgenzō*.

137   **a single knowledge and a half understanding** (*itchi hange* 一知半解): A set phrase for little or shallow knowledge.

"finished learning with nothing to do" (*mui no zetsugaku* 無爲の絕學): I.e., has completed the study of Buddhism. From the opening line of the *Zhengdao ge* 證道歌, attributed to Yongjia Xuanjue 永嘉玄覺 (or Zenjue 眞覺, d. 713) (T.2014.48:395c9):

絕學無爲閑道人。

A person versed in the way, finished learning, with nothing to do.

16A. Sustained Practice, Part 1 *Gyōji* 行持 43

[16A:59] {1:165}

おほよそ、ひそかに貪名愛利をなげすてきたりぬれば、日日に行持の積功のみなり。このむねわするることなかれ。説似一物即不中は、八箇年の行持なり。古今のまれなりとするところ、賢・不肖ともにこひねがふ行持なり。

More generally, when we have privately cast aside greed for fame and love of profit, our sustained practice simply accumulates merit day after day. Do not forget this point. "To say that it's like any thing doesn't hit it" is eight years of sustained practice.[138] It is something recognized as rare in past and present, a sustained practice sought by the wise and otherwise alike.

* * * * *

[16A:60]

香嚴の智閑禪師は、大潙に耕道せしとき、一句を道得せんとするに數番、つひに道不得なり。これをかなしみて、書籍を火にやきて、行粥飯僧となりて、年月を經歴しき。のちに武當山にいりて、大證の舊跡をたづねて、結草爲庵し、放下幽棲す。一日、わづかに道路を併淨するに、礫のほとばしりて、竹にあたりて聲をなすによりて、忽然として悟道す。のちに香嚴寺に住して、一盂一衲を平生に不換なり。奇巖清泉をしめて、一生偃息の幽棲とせり。行跡おほく本山にのこれり。平生に山をいでざりけるといふ。

Chan Master Zhixian of Xiangyan, when cultivating the way under Dawei, tried several times to say a single phrase but, in the end, could not say anything.[139] Saddened by this, he burnt his books and spent the years and months as a monk serving meals. Later, entering Mount Wudang and visiting Dazheng's old site, he bundled grass and made a her-

---

138 **"To say that it's like any thing doesn't hit it" is eight years of sustained practice** (*setsuji ichimotsu soku fuchū wa hakko nen no gyōji nari* 説似一物即不中は八箇年の行持なり): Allusion to Huairang's response, given (in Dōgen's version) after eight years, to Huineng's question, "What thing is it that comes like this?" From the anecdote, appearing regularly throughout Dōgen's writings, recorded in his *shinji Shōbōgenzō* 眞字正法眼藏 (DZZ.5:178, case 101); see Supplementary Notes, s.v. "What thing is it that comes like this?"

139 **Chan Master Zhixian of Xiangyan** (*Kyōgen no Chikan zenji* 香嚴の智閑禪師): I.e., Xiangyan Zhixian 香嚴智閑 (d. 898). Dōgen here recalls in Japanese a famous story he recounts in his "Shōbōgenzō keisei sanshoku" 正法眼藏溪聲山色; the original can be found in several sources: see, e.g., *Liandeng huiyao* 聯燈會要, ZZ.136:565b12-566a9; *Jingde chuandeng lu* 景德傳燈錄, T.2076.51:283c27-284a18; *shinji Shōbōgenzō* 眞字正法眼藏, DZZ.5:134, case 17.

cultivating the way under Dawei (*Daii ni kōdō seshi* 大潙に耕道せし): I.e., Weishan Lingyou 潙山靈祐. "Cultivating (or tilling) the way" (*kōdō* 耕道) is a venerable mixed metaphor for spiritual training not occurring elsewhere in the *Shōbōgenzō*.

44 DŌGEN'S *SHŌBŌGENZŌ* VOLUME II

mitage, abandoning all and dwelling in obscurity.[140] One day, while he was sweeping off the path a bit, a piece of tile flew up and struck a bamboo; at the sound, he suddenly awakened to the way. Later, he resided at Xiangyan Monastery, never exchanging his single bowl and single robe his whole life. He occupied the strange crags and pure springs, where he spent his life tranquilly dwelling in obscurity. Many traces of his deeds remain at this mountain. It is said that he never left the mountain his whole life.

* * * * *

[16A:61]
臨濟院の慧照大師は、黃檗の嫡嗣なり。黃檗の會にありて三年なり。純一に辨道するに、睦州陳尊宿の教訓によりて、佛法の大意を黃檗にとふこと三番するに、かさねて六十棒を喫す。なほ励志たゆむことなし。大愚にいたりて大悟することも、すなはち黃檗・睦州兩尊宿の教訓なり。祖席の英雄は、臨濟・德山といふ。しかあれども、德山いかにしてか臨濟におよばん。まことに臨濟のごときは、群に群せざるなり。そのときの群は、近代の拔群よりも拔群なり。行業純一にして行持拔群せりといふ。幾枚幾般の行持なりとおもひ擬せんとするに、あたるべからざるものなり。

Great Master Huizhao of Linji Cloister was the legitimate heir of Huangbo.[141] He was in Huangbo's community for three years. While he was purely pursuing the way, when, following the instructions of Venerable Chen of Muzhou, he asked Huangbo three times the great meaning of the buddha dharma, he received a total of sixty blows.[142] Yet his determination was unflagging. His going to Dayu and having a great awakening was also at the instruction of the two Venerables, Huangbo and Muzhou.[143] It is said that the heroes of the ancestral seat were Linji and Deshan; but how could Deshan match Linji?[144] Truly one like Linji

---

140 **entering Mount Wudang and visiting Dazheng's old site** (*Butōzan ni irite, Daishō no kyūseki o tazunete* 武當山にいりて、大證の舊跡をたづねて): I.e., the mountain range in present-day Hubei where Nanyang Huizhong 南陽慧忠 (d.775) once lived.

141 **Great Master Huizhao of Linji Cloister** (*Rinzai in no Eshō daishi* 臨濟院の慧照大師): I.e., Linji Yixuan 臨濟義玄, disciple of Huangbo Xiyun 黃檗希運 (dates unknown). Dōgen here recounts an abbreviated Japanese version of the famous story of Linji's study under Huangbo, which appears in several sources (see, e.g., *Tiansheng guangdeng lu* 天聖廣燈錄, ZZ.135:683b3-684a18; *shinji Shōbōgenzō* 眞字正法眼藏, DZZ.5:138-142, case 27) and is repeated in "Shōbōgenzō bukkyō" 正法眼藏佛經.

142 **Venerable Chen of Muzhou** (*Bokushū Chin sonshuku* 睦州陳尊宿): In some versions of the story, the head monk (*shuso* 首座) who prompted Linji to pose a question to Huangbo is identified as Muzhou Daozong 睦州道蹤 (or Daoming 道明, whose family name was Chen 陳; dates unknown).

143 **Dayu** (*Daigu* 大愚): I.e., Gaoan Dayu 高安大愚 (dates unknown), to whom Linji was sent after he left Huangbo.

144 **heroes of the ancestral seat** (*soseki no eiyū* 祖席の英雄): I.e., great figures in the

16A. Sustained Practice, Part 1 *Gyōji* 行持

45

is not to be grouped with the crowd; and the crowd of his time was more outstanding than the outstanding of recent times. It is said that his behavior was pure and his sustained practice was outstanding. We cannot imagine how many kinds of sustained practice it was.

[16A:62] {1:166}

師在黃檗、與黃檗栽松杉次、黃檗問師曰、深山裏栽許多樹作麼。師曰、一與山門爲境致、二與後人作標榜。乃將鍬拍地兩下。黃檗拈起拄杖曰、雖然如是、汝已喫我三十棒了也。師作嘘嘘聲。黃檗曰、吾宗到汝大興於世。

When the Master was at Huangbo, he was planting pine and fir with Huangbo, when Huangbo asked the Master, "Why are we planting so many trees deep in the mountains?"[145]

The Master said, "First, for the monastery, for the sake of its grounds; second, for later people, to serve as a marker."

Then, he struck the ground two times with his hoe. Huangbo raised his staff and said, "Maybe so, but you've already tasted my thirty blows."

The Master went, "Whew, whew."[146]

Huangbo said, "Having reached you, our lineage will flourish greatly in the world."

[16A:63]

しかあればすなはち、得道ののちも杉松などをうゑけるに、てづからみづから鍬柄をたづさへけるとしるべし。吾宗到汝大興於世、これによるべきものならん。栽松道者の古蹟、まさに單傳直指なるべし。黃檗も臨濟とともに栽樹するなり。黃檗のむかしは、捨衆して、大安精舍の勞侶に混迹して、殿堂を掃灑する行持あり。佛殿を掃灑し、法堂を掃灑す。心を掃灑すると行持をまたず、ひかりを掃灑すると行持をまたず。裴相國と相見せし、この時節なり。

Thus, we know that, even after gaining the way, he himself took hold of the hoe to plant cedars and pines. "*Having reached you, our lineage will flourish greatly in the world*" must have been [said] because of this. The ancient traces of the Pine-planting Practitioner must have been uniquely

---

Zen lineage; an expression that, while seemingly not common in Chan literature, occurs several times in Dōgen's writing.

Deshan (*Tokusan* 德山): I.e., Deshan Xuanjian 德山宣鑑 (780-865). Deshan and Linji are similarly linked elsewhere in the *Shōbōgenzō*, where Dōgen is dismissive of both.

145 **When the Master was at Huangbo** (*shi zai Ōbaku* 師在黃檗): Or "when the Master [i.e., Linji] was with Huangbo" — "Huangbo" being the name of the mountain (in present-day Fujian) from which Huangbo Xiyun got his name. This conversation, quoted here in Chinese, appears in the *Linji lu* 臨濟錄 (T.1985.47:505a5-9) and several other Chan texts.

146 **The Master went, "Whew, whew"** (*shi sa kyokyo shō* 師作嘘嘘聲): An audible exhalation, usually understood here as dismissive.

46 DŌGEN'S *SHŌBŌGENZŌ* VOLUME II

transmitted and directly indicated.[147] Huangbo also planted trees with Linji. In his past, Huangbo had abandoned the assembly and, hiding his traces among the laborers at the Da'an Vihāra, engaged in the sustained practice of washing down the halls.[148] He washed down the buddha hall; he washed down the dharma hall. He did not wait for a sustained practice that would wash down the mind; he did not wait for a sustained practice that would wash down the radiance.[149] It was at this time that he met Minister of State Pei.[150]

* * * * *

[16A:64] {1:167}

唐宣宗皇帝は、憲宗皇帝第二の子なり。少而より敏黠なり。よのつねに結跏趺坐を愛す。宮にありてつねに坐禪す。穆宗は宣宗の兄なり。穆宗在位のとき、早朝罷に、宣宗すなはち戯而して、龍床にのぼりて揖群臣の勢をなす。大臣これをみて、心風なりとす。すなはち穆宗に奏す。穆宗みて、宣宗を撫而していはく、我弟乃吾宗之英冑也。ときに宣宗、とし、はじめて十三なり。

Emperor Xuanzong of the Tang was the second son of Emperor Xianzong.[151] He was quick witted from childhood. He was always fond of cross-legged sitting and regularly practiced seated meditation in the palace. Muzong was Xuanzong's elder brother. When Muzong was on the throne, following the morning court, Xuanzong playfully climbed into the dragon

---

147　**Pine-planting Practitioner** (*Saishō Dōsha* 栽松道者): Reference no doubt to Huangmei Hongren 黄梅弘忍, the Fifth Ancestor, who is said to have been a "practitioner who planted pines" in his previous life. Dōgen tells the story in his "Shōbōgenzō busshō" 正法眼藏佛性. "Uniquely transmitted and directly indicated" (*tanden jikishi* 單傳直指) is a fixed phrase occurring often in Chan literature in reference to the handing down of the tradition from generation to generation.

148　**In his past, Huangbo had abandoned the assembly** (*Ōbaku no mukashi wa, shashu shite* 黄檗のむかしは、捨衆して): Reference to an incident recorded at *Jingde chuandeng lu* 景德傳燈錄 (T.2076.51:293a29-b1); *shinji Shōbōgenzō* 眞字正法眼藏 (DZZ.5:130, case 9).

Da'an Vihāra (*Daian Shōja* 大安精舎): Monastery in present-day Jiangxi province.

149　**wash down the radiance** (*hikari o sōsai suru* ひかりを掃灑する): Likely a reference to the "light" of the inherent buddha mind.

150　**Minister of State Pei** (*Hai shōkoku* 裴相國): I.e., Pei Xiu 裴休 (797-870), a lay student of Huangbo and Gueifeng Zongmi 圭峰宗密; he compiled a record of Huangbo's teachings under the title *Chuanxin fayao* 傳心法要 (T.2012A). His meeting with Huangbo at Da'an is recorded at *Jingde chuandeng lu* 景德傳燈錄, T.2076.51:293a29ff.

151　**Emperor Xuanzong** (*Sensō kōtei* 宣宗皇帝): Li Chen 李忱 (810-859), reigned 846-859. His father, Emperor Xianzong 憲宗 (r. 805-820), had twenty sons, of whom Li Chen was the thirteenth and the second to become emperor, after his elder brother Li Heng (Emperor Muzong 穆宗, r. 821-824). Dōgen's account of Xuanzong, from here through the following three sections, tells in Japanese a passage also found in the *Biyan lu* 碧巖錄 (T.2003.48:152b18-c10).

16A. Sustained Practice, Part 1 *Gyōji* 行持 47

seat and made as if to greet the assembled ministers.[152] A great minister, seeing this, thought he was deranged and reported it to Wuzong. On seeing him, Wuzong patted Xuanzong and said, "*My younger brother is an excellent descendant of our line.*" At the time, Xuanzong was but thirteen.

[16A:65]

穆宗は、長慶四年晏駕あり。穆宗に三子あり。一は敬宗、二は文宗、三は武宗なり。敬宗、父位をつぎて三年に崩ず。文宗繼位するに、一年といふに、内臣謀而これを易す。武宗即位するに、宣宗いまだ即位せずして、をひのくににあり。武宗つねに宣宗をこゝに癡叔といふ。武宗は會昌の天子なり、佛法を癈せし人なり。武宗あるとき宣宗をめして、昔日ちちのくらゐにのぼりしことを罰して、一頓打殺して、後華園のなかにおきて、不淨を潅するに復生す。

Muzong departed this life in the fourth year of the Changqing era.[153] Muzong had three sons: the first was Jingzong; the second was Wenzong; the third was Wuzong. Jingzong met his demise three years after succeeding to his father's throne.[154] Wenzong inherited the throne, but within one year, the inner court conspired to replace him. When Wuzong came to the throne, Xuanzong, who had yet to come to the throne, was living in the territory of his nephew. Wuzong always called Xuanzong "my idiot uncle." Wuzong was son of heaven during the Huichang; he was the person who suppressed the buddha dharma.[155] Once, Wuzong summoned Xuanzong and, angry that he had long ago climbed into his father's throne, had him struck dead and put out in the rear garden; but when he was pissed on, he revived.

---

152 **dragon seat** (*ryūshō* 龍床): The imperial throne.

153 **departed this life in the fourth year of the Changqing era** (*Chōkei yonen anga ari* 長慶四年晏駕あり): I.e., died in 824. 'Departed this life" is a loose translation for the term *anga* 晏駕 ("late carriage") used in euphemistic reference to the passing of an emperor.

154 **Jingzong met his demise three years after succeeding to his father's throne** (*Keisō, fui o tsugite sannen ni hōzu* 敬宗、父位をつぎて三年に崩ず): Dōgen's Japanese here and in the following sentence departs both from historical fact and from the corresponding passage in the vulgate *Biyan lu* 碧巌録 (T.2003.48:152b24-25):

> 敬宗繼父位、二年内臣謀易之。文宗繼位、一十四年。
>
> Jingzong succeeded to his father's throne, but after two years the inner court conspired to replace him. Wenzong succeeded to the throne for fourteen years.

The Emperor Jingzong 敬宗 reigned 824-827, at which latter date he was assassinated by conspirators in the court. His brother Wenzong 文宗 reigned 827-840 and, though his reign was also marked by continued court intrigue, managed to die in bed after picking his brother Wuzong as his successor. Wuzong 武宗 reigned 840-846.

155 **Huichang** (*Kaishō* 會昌): I.e., the Huichang era (841-846), during which the Tang government undertook a persecution of the Buddhist saṃgha. This sentence does not occur in the *Biyan lu* 碧巌録 passage.

DŌGEN'S *SHŌBŌGENZŌ* VOLUME II

[16A:66]

つひに父王の邦をはなれて、ひそかに香嚴禪師の會に參じて、剃頭して沙彌となりぬ。しかあれど、いまだ不具戒なり。志閑禪師をともとして遊方するに、廬山にいたる。ちなみに志閑みづから瀑布を題していはく、穿崖透石不辞勞、遠地方知出處高。この兩句をもて沙彌を釣他して、これいかなる人ぞと、みんとするなり。沙彌、これを續していはく、溪澗豈能留得住、終歸大海作波濤。この兩句をみて、沙彌はこれつねの人にあらず、としりぬ。

Later, he left the land of his father, the sovereign, and, secretly joining the community of Chan Master Xiangyan, shaved his head and became a *śrāmaṇera*, though he remained without the full precepts.[156] He went wandering with Chan Master Zhixian as companion. When they came to Mount Lu, Zhixian composed a verse entitled "Waterfall":[157]

> *It bores through the cliff and penetrates the rocks, without refusing its labors;*
> *Yet even from afar, we know how high the place from which it springs.*

With these two lines, he sought to hook the *śrāmaṇera*, in order to see what sort of person he was. The *śrāmaṇera* continued, saying,

> *How can the cataract be brought to a halt?*
> *In the end, it returns to the sea to form waves.*

Seeing these two lines, he knew that the *śrāmaṇera* was no ordinary person.

[16A:67] {1:168}

のちに杭州鹽官齊安國師の會にいたりて、書記に充するに、黃檗禪師、ときに鹽官の首座に充す。ゆえに黃檗と連單なり。黃檗、ときに佛殿にいたりて禮佛するに、書記いたりてとふ、不著佛求、不著法求、不著僧求、長老用禮何爲。かくのごとく問著するに、黃檗便掌して沙彌書記にむかひて道す、不著佛求、不著法求、不著僧求、常禮如是事。かくのごとく道しをはりて、又掌すること一掌す。書記いはく、太麤生なり。黃檗いはく、遮裏是什麼所在、更說什麼麤細。また書記を掌すること一掌す。書記ちなみに休去す。

Later, he went to the community of the National Teacher Qi'an of Yanguan in Hangzhou, where he was appointed secretary.[158] At the time,

---

156 **Chan Master Xiangyan** (*Kyōgen zenji* 香嚴禪師): I.e., Xiangyan Zhixian 香嚴智閑 (d. 898); see above, section 60.

157 **Mount Lu** (*Rozan* 廬山): Mountain in present-day Jiangxi Province famous for its Buddhist sites.

158 **National Teacher Qi'an of Yanguan in Hangzhou** (*Kōshū Enkan Seian kokushi* 杭州鹽官齊安國師): I.e., Yanguan Qi'an 鹽官齊安 (d. 842), a disciple of Mazu Daoyi 馬祖道一. Yanguan is a district near Hangzhou in present-day Zhejiang.

16A. Sustained Practice, Part 1 *Gyōji* 行持　　　49

Chan Master Huangbo was serving as the head seat of Yanguan.[159] Hence, he was an adjacent seat to Huangbo.[160] Once, when Huangbo had gone to the buddha hall and was bowing to the buddha, the secretary went to him and asked, "'*Not to seek it in the buddha; not to seek it in the dharma; not to seek it in the saṃgha.*'[161] *What is the Elder doing by bowing?*"

Questioned thus, Huangbo immediately slapped him and said to the *śrāmaṇera* secretary, "'*Not to seek it in the buddha; not to seek it in the dharma; not to seek it in the saṃgha.*' *I always bow in this way.*"

After saying this, he slapped him once again. The secretary said, "How rough!"

Huangbo said, "*Where are we here that we're talking of rough or fine?*" He slapped the secretary once again, and the secretary desisted.

[16A:68]
武宗ののち、書記つひに還俗して即位す。武宗の廢佛法を廢して、宣宗すなはち佛法を中興す。宣宗は即位在位のあひだ、つねに坐禪をこのむ。未即位のとき、父王のくにをはなれて、遠地の溪澗に遊方せしとき、純一に辨道す。即位ののち、晝夜に坐禪すといふ。まことに、父王すでに崩御す、兄帝また晏駕す、をひのために打殺せらる。あはれむべき窮子なるがごとし。しかあれども、勵志うつらず辨道功夫す。奇代の勝躅なり、天眞の行持なるべし。

After Wuzong, the secretary at last returned to lay life and assumed the throne.[162] Abandoning Wuzong's persecution of the buddha dharma, Xuanzong revived the buddha dharma. Throughout his time on the throne, Xuanzong always enjoyed sitting in meditation. Before he assumed the throne, when he left the land of his father, the sovereign, to wander to the cataracts of distant places, he had purely pursued the way; after he assumed the throne, it is said he practiced seated meditation day and night. His father, the sovereign, had met his demise, his elder brother had passed away, and he had been beaten to death by his nephew. Truly, he was like

---

159　**head seat** (*shuso* 首座): The leader of the saṃgha hall assembly.

160　**Hence, he was an adjacent seat to Huangbo** (*yue ni Ōbaku to rentan nari* ゆえに黄檗と連單なり): A sentence not found in the *Biyan lu* 碧巌録 account. "Adjacent seat" (*rentan* 連單) refers to someone with whom one shares the meditation platform in the monks' hall.

161　**"Not to seek it in the buddha; not to seek it in the dharma; not to seek it in the saṃgha"** (*fujaku butsu gu, fujaku hō gu, fujaku sō gu* 不著佛求、不著法求、不著僧求): From the *Vimalakīrti Sūtra* (*Weimo jing* 維摩經, T.475.14:546a11-12). The object of "seek" in the sūtra passage is "the dharma."

162　**After Wuzong** (*Busō no nochi* 武宗ののち): Dōgen here departs from the version in the *Biyan lu* to give his own conclusion to this section on Xuanzong.

50 DŌGEN'S *SHŌBŌGENZŌ* VOLUME II

the pitiful "impoverished son."[163] Yet his determination never budged as he worked at pursuing the way. His was an excellent precedent, rare through the ages; it must have been a case of inherent sustained practice.

* * * * *

[16A:69] {1:169}

雪峰眞覺大師義存和尚、かつて發心よりこのかた、掛錫の叢林、および行程の接待、みちはるかなりといへども、ところをきらはず、日夜の坐禪おこたることなし。雪峰草創の露堂堂にいたるまで、おこたらずして坐禪と同死す。咨參のそのかみは、九上洞山、三到投子する、奇世の辦道なり。行持の清嚴をすすむるには、いまの人、おほく雪峰高行といふ。雪峰の昏昧は、諸人とひとしといへども、雪峰の剞利は、諸人のおよぶところにあらず。これ行持のしかあるなり。いまの道人、かならず雪峰の澡雪をまなぶべし。しづかに雪峰の、諸方に參學せし筋力をかへりみれば、まことに宿有靈骨の功德なるべし。

Reverend Yicun, Great Master Zhenjue of Mount Xuefeng, after he brought forth the mind [of bodhi], never neglected seated meditation day or night, indifferent to the place, whether it be a "grove" where he hung his staff or lodging along the way on distant paths.[164] Until the founding of Xuefeng was exposed and imposing, he died together with seated meditation, without ever neglecting it.[165] In his former inquiries, his "*nine times climbing Mount Dong; three times going to Touzi*" was a pursuit of the way rare in the world.[166] In promoting purity and rigor in sustained practice, many people today cite the lofty conduct of Xuefeng. Xuefeng's ignorance may have been the same as anyone else, but his intelligence was beyond the reach of anyone else. His sustained practice was like this. People today should learn from Xuefeng's cleaning off the snow.[167] When we quietly reflect on the physical strength with which

---

163 **"impoverished son"** (*gūji* 窮子): In the *Lotus Sūtra*; see above, section 2.

164 **Reverend Yicun, Great Master Zhenjue of Mount Xuefeng** (*Seppō Shinkaku daishi Gison oshō* 雪峰眞覺大師義存和尚): I.e., Xuefeng Yicun 雪峰義存.

165 **Until the founding of Xuefeng was exposed and imposing** (*Seppō sōsō no rodōdō ni itaru made* 雪峰草創の露堂堂にいたるまで): An odd phrase, presumably meaning something like, "from the establishment of his monastery on Mount Xuefeng till it [or he] became widely known." The term *rodōdō* 露堂堂 ("exposed and imposing") is an expression commonly used in reference to a person's majestic bearing or manner.

166 **"nine times climbing Mount Dong; three times going to Touzi"** (*ku jō Tōzan, san tō Tōsu* 九上洞山、三到投子): I.e., nine visits to Dongshan Liangjie 洞山良价 and three visits to Touzi Datong 投子大同 (819-914). A fixed expression found often in accounts of Xuefeng; see, e.g., *Liandeng huiyao* 聯燈會要, ZZ.136:781b1.

167 **Xuefeng's cleaning off the snow** (*Seppō no sōsetsu* 雪峰の澡雪): An attempt to render Dōgen's play with the glyph for "snow" (*setsu* 雪) in Xuefeng's name and the term "to clean"; see above, Note 90.

16A. Sustained Practice, Part 1 *Gyōji* 行持   51

Xuefeng studied [with masters] in all quarters, truly it must have been the virtue of his sacred bones from a previous existence.[168]

[16A:70]

いま、有道の宗匠の會をのぞむに、眞實、請參せんとするとき、そのたよ
り、もとも難辨なり。ただ二十、三十箇の皮袋にあらず、百千人の面面な
り。おのおの實歸をもとむ。授手の日くれなんとす、打春の夜あけなんと
す。あるひは師の普説するときは、わが耳目なくして、いたづらに見聞を
へだつ。耳目そなはるときは、師また道取おはりぬ。耆宿尊年の老古錐、
すでに拊掌笑呵呵のとき、新戒晩進のおのれとしては、むしろのすゑを接
するたより、なほまれなるがごとし。堂奥にいるといらざると、師決をき
くときかざるとあり。光陰は矢よりもすみやかなり、露命は身よりももろ
し。師はあれども、われ參不得なるうらみあり、參ぜんとするに、師不得
なるかなしみあり。かくのごとくの事、まのあたり見聞せしなり。

Now, in seeking the community of a teacher who has the way, when we truly seek instruction, it is most difficult to get the opportunity. It is not simply twenty or thirty skin bags; it is a hundred or a thousand people, each seeking "the true refuge." The days of offering a hand grow dark; the nights of pounding the mortar grow bright.[169] Sometimes, when the master is giving a public sermon, we have no eyes or ears and vainly keep our distance from seeing and hearing it; then, by the time we get back our eyes and ears, the master has finished speaking. When the venerable old awls, the seniors of venerable years, are already *clapping their hands and laughing "ha ha,"* it seems rare for those of us, as latecomers newly ordained, even to get a place at the edge of the mat.[170] There are those who enter the interior of the hall and those who do not enter; there are those who hear the master's definitive teachings and those who do not hear them.[171] The years and months are swifter than an arrow; the life of the dewdrop, more fragile than the body. There is the bitterness of having a master with whom one cannot study; there is the sadness of wanting to study but having no master. I have directly witnessed such things.

---

168 **sacred bones from a previous existence** (*shukuu reikotsu* 宿有靈骨): Presumably, meaning "an extraordinary body produced by past karma"; a fixed expression not occurring elsewhere in the *Shōbōgenzō*. The term "sacred bones" (*reikotsu* 靈骨) is used in reference to the body of a Daoist immortal as well as the relics of a Buddhist saint.

169 **The days of offering a hand grow dark; the nights of pounding the mortar grow bright** (*jushu no hi kurenan to su, tashō no yo akenan to su* 授手の日くれなんとす、打春の夜あけなんとす): I.e., the time during which the master can teach and the student can train is limited. "Pounding the mortar" (*tashō* 打春) alludes to the practice of the Sixth Ancestor, Huineng; see above, section 16.

170 **clapping their hands and laughing "ha ha"** (*fushō shō kaka* 拊掌笑呵呵): A fixed expression for rejoicing in one's understanding; more often written *bushō* 撫掌.

171 **the master's definitive teachings** (*shiketsu* 師決): I.e., the master's final word on something; akin to *shinketsu* 眞訣 ("true arcanum").

[16A:71] {1:170}

大善知識、かならず人をしる徳あれども、耕道功夫のとき、あくまで親近する良縁まれなるものなり。雪峰のむかし、洞山にのぼれりけんにも、投子にのぼれりけんにも、さだめてこの事煩をしのびけん。この行持の法操、あはれむべし、參學せざらんは、かなしむべし。

Although great wise friends always have the virtue of recognizing a person, when they are working at cultivating the way, opportunities to get as close as possible to them are rare. In the past, when Xuefeng climbed Dongshan and climbed Touzi, he surely endured this difficulty. We should cherish this fidelity to the dharma; we should pity those who do not study it.

正法眼藏行持第十六上
Treasury of the True Dharma Eye
Sustained Practice
Number 16, Part One

[Ryūmonji MS:]

于時天文丁未麥秋仲旬。喆肏賢衲寫焉
Copied, middle of wheat harvest [fourth month], junior fire year of the sheep, Tenbun [April 1547]. The monk Tessō Ken[172]

[Tōmonji MS:]

仁治癸卯正月十八日書寫了
同三月八日校點了。懷奘
Copied eighteenth day, first month of the junior water year of the rabbit, Ninji [8 February 1243].
Proofed eighth day, third month of the same [year] [29 March 1243].
Ejō

于時永正七年庚午五月日、於阿陽路勝浦縣桂林寺得月亭上、
住山小比丘用兼七十三歲謹以書寫焉
Respectfully copied in the Tokugatsu Pavilion, Keirin Monastery, Katsuura District, Ayōji; fifth month, senior metal year of the horse, the seventh year of Eishō [June-July 1510], by the abbot, a humble bhikṣu, Yōken, in his seventy third year[173]

---

172 **Tessō Ken** 喆肏賢: I.e., Tessō Hōken 喆肏芳賢 (d. 1551), copyist of the Ryūmonji 龍門寺 MS, which lacks a colophon by Dōgen for Part 1 of this chapter.

173 **Yōken** 用兼: I.e., Kinkō Yōken 金岡用兼 (1437–1513?).

Treasury of the True Dharma Eye

Number 16B

Sustained Practice
Part 2

Gyōji

行持

Sustained Practice

Gyōji

Part 2

INTRODUCTION

As mentioned above, in the introduction to the translation of "Gyōji" Part 1, this chapter is treated as number 17 in the sixty-chapter *Shōbōgenzō*, where it bears the end title "Busso gyōji" 佛祖行持 ("Sustained Practice of the Buddhas and Ancestors") and a colophon stating that it was composed in the spring of 1242, at Kōshōji. In the seventy-five-chapter compilation, as well as the ninety-chapter vulgate edition, it represents Part 2 of Chapter 16.

While somewhat longer than Part 1, this text deals with only half as many exemplars of sustained practice and, unlike Part 1, limits its coverage to monks of the Chinese Chan tradition. By far the longest section, fully one-third of the whole, is devoted to praise of the first Chan ancestor, Bodhidharma, with which the work opens. It closes with another lengthy section, on Dōgen's own Chinese master, Tiantong Rujing 天童如淨. Throughout, the text is laced with fervent admonitions to undertake the sustained practice it describes.

正法眼藏第十六
Treasury of the True Dharma Eye
Number 16

行持 下
Sustained Practice
Part 2

[16B:1] {1:171}

眞丹初祖の西來東土は、般若多羅尊者の教勅なり。航海三載の霜華、その
風雪いたましきのみならんや、雲煙いくかさなりの嶮浪なりとかせん。不
知のくににいらんとす、身命をおしまん凡類、おもひよるべからず。これ
ひとへに傳法救迷情の大慈よりなれる行持なるべし。傳法の自己なるがゆ
えにしかあり、傳法の遍界なるがゆえにしかあり、盡十方界は眞實道なる
がゆえにしかあり、盡十方界自己なるがゆえにしかあり、盡十方界盡十方
界なるがゆえにしかあり。いづれの主緣か王宮にあらざらん、いづれの王
宮か道場をさへん。このゆえに、かくのごとく西來せり。救迷情の自己な
るがゆえに、驚疑なく、怖畏せず。救迷情の遍界なるゆえに、驚疑せず、
怖畏なし。ながく父王の國土を辭して、大舟をよそふて、南海をへて廣州
にとづく。使船の人おほく、巾瓶の曽あまたありといへども、史者、失錄
せり。著岸よりこのかた、しれる人なし。すなはち梁代の普通八年丁未歳
九月二十一日なり。廣州の刺史蕭昂といふもの、主禮をかざりて迎接した
てまつる。ちなみに、表を修して武帝にきこゆる、蕭昂が勤恪なり。武帝
すなはち奏を覽して欣悦して、使に詔をもたせて迎請したてまつる。すな
はちそのとし十月一日なり。

The First Ancestor in Cīnasthāna came from the west to the Land of
the East at the instruction of Venerable Prajñātāra.[1] During the frost and
flowers of the three years of his sea voyage, not only did he suffer the
bitter winds and snow, but through the clouds and mist how many towering waves must have surged?[2]

---

1 **First Ancestor in Cīnasthāna** (*Shintan shoso* 眞丹初祖): I.e., Bodhidharma. "Cīnasthāna" is a Sanskrit name for China, here transliterated by the Chinese *zhendan* 眞丹.

Venerable Prajñātāra (*Hannyatara sonja* 般若多羅尊者): I.e., Bodhidharma's master,
the Twenty-seventh Ancestor in the traditional lineage of Zen transmission in India.

2 **frost and flowers of the three years of his sea voyage** (*kōkai sansai no sōka* 航海
三載の霜華): I.e., the cycle of seasons of "autumn frosts and spring flowers" during his
three years at sea. The tradition that Bodhidharma was at sea for "three cycles of cold
and heat" (*san shū kansho* 三周寒暑) can be seen in his notice in the *Jingde chuandeng
lu* 景德傳燈錄 (T.2076.51:219a13).

winds and snow (*fūsetsu* 風雪): Or "wind-driven snow"; used as a metaphor for difficult

56   DŌGEN'S *SHŌBŌGENZŌ* VOLUME II

He was about to enter an unknown land, something ordinary types who value their lives could not imagine. This was surely his sustained practice derived solely from his great compassion "*to transmit the dharma and save deluded sentient beings.*"[3] This is so because transmitting the dharma is his self; it is so because transmitting the dharma is the realms everywhere; it is so because all the worlds in the ten directions are the true way; it is so because all the words in the ten directions are the self; it is true because all the worlds in the ten directions are all the worlds in the ten directions.[4] What conditions of birth are not a royal palace?[5] What royal palace is precluded from being a practice place?

Therefore, he came from the west like this. Because saving deluded sentient beings was his self, he was not bewildered, not fearful; because saving deluded sentient beings was the realms everywhere, he was not bewildered, not fearful. Leaving forever the land of his father, the king, he readied a great ship, crossed the Southern Sea, and arrived in Guangzhou. Although there were many aboard the ambassadorial vessel, and numerous towel and flask monks, historians failed to record them.[6] Ever since

---

circumstances or painful experience (though seemingly incongruous in an account of a sea voyage from south India to south China).

clouds and mist (*un'en* 雲煙): Used in reference to the sea or the experience of being at sea.

3   **"to transmit the dharma and save deluded sentient beings"** (*denbō gu meijō* 傳法救迷情): From Bodhidharma's transmission verse (e.g., at *Jingde chuandeng lu* 景德傳燈錄, T.2076.51:219c17-18):

> 吾本來茲土、傳法救迷情、一華開五葉、結果自然成。
>
> I originally came to this land
> To transmit the dharma and save deluded sentient beings.
> A single blossom opens five petals;
> The fruit forms, ripening naturally of itself.

See Supplementary Notes, s.v. "A single flower opens five petals."

4   **all the worlds in the ten directions are the true way** (*jin jippō kai wa shinjitsu dō naru* 盡十方界は眞實道なる): An unusual phrase, likely playing on a saying of Xuansha Shibei 玄沙師備 (835-908) cited elsewhere in the *Shōbōgenzō*: "All the worlds in the ten directions are this true human body" (*jin jippō kai ze ko shinjitsu nintai* 盡十方界是箇眞實人體). See Supplementary Notes, s.v. "True human body."

all the worlds in the ten directions are the self (*jin jippō kai jiko naru* 盡十方界自己なる): Variation on the words, quoted elsewhere in the *Shōbōgenzō*, of Changsha Jingcen 長沙景岑 (dates unknown); see Supplementary Notes, s.v. "All the worlds in the ten directions are the single eye of the *śramaṇa*."

5   **What conditions of birth are not a royal palace** (*izure no shōen ka ōgū ni arazaran* いづれの生緣か王宮にあらざらん): I.e., which of us is not born in a palace? Doubtless an allusion to the tradition, mentioned below, that Bodhidharma (like Prince Siddhārtha) was born into a royal family.

6 **towel and flask monks** (*kinbyō no sō* 巾瓶の僧): Monks in attendance on Bodhidharma; from the use of "towel and flask" (*kinbyō* 巾瓶) in reference to a teacher's close attendants.

16B. Sustained Practice, Part 2 *Gyōji* 行持   57

the party landed, no one has known [of them].[7] It was the twenty-first day of the ninth month of the junior fire year of the sheep, the eighth year of Putong in the Liang dynasty.[8] The prefect of Guangzhou, one Xiao Ang, received him with ceremony; that he also composed a memorial informing the Emperor Wu was [a mark of] Xiao Ang's diligence.[9] Emperor Wu straightaway read the memorial and, overjoyed, dispatched a messenger with a decree of invitation. It was on the first day of the tenth month of that year.[10]

[16B:2] {1:172}

初祖、金陵にいたりて梁武と相見するに、梁武とふ、朕即位已來、造寺・寫經・度僧、不可勝紀、有何功德。師曰、竝無功德。帝曰、　　何以無功德。師曰、此但人天小果、有漏之因。如影隨形、雖有非實。帝曰、如何是眞功德。師曰、淨智妙圓、體自空寂。如是功德、不以世求。帝又問、如何是聖諦第一義諦。師曰、廓然無聖。帝曰、對朕者誰。師曰、不識。帝不領悟。師知機不契。

> When the First Ancestor arrived in Jinling and had an audience with Liang Wu, Liang Wu inquired, "*Since ascending the throne, I have had monasteries built, sūtras copied, and monks ordained beyond enumeration. What merit is there in this?*"[11]
>
> *The Master said, "No merit at all."*
>
> *The Emperor said, "Why is there no merit?"*

---

7   **no one has known [of them]** (*shireru hito nashi* しれる人なし): The object of the verb is unexpressed; the translation asssumes it is those whom the historians failed to record. It is often taken as "Bodhidharma"; but this seems odd, given that Dōgen immediately hereafter reports the tradition that Bodhidharma received an official reception.

8   **the twenty-first day of the ninth month of the junior fire year of the sheep, the eighth year of Putong in the Liang dynasty** (*Ryōdai no Futsū hachinen chōmi sai kugatsu nijūichinichi* 梁代の普通八年丁未歲九月二十一日): I.e., October 31, 527, in the Gregorian calendar. From here to the end of this section, Dōgen is retelling in Japanese the Chinese text at *Jingde chuandeng lu* 景德傳燈錄, T.2076.51:219a14-16. There is, of course, no contemporaneous evidence for this account.

9   **Xiao Ang** (*Shōgō* 蕭昂): Styled Ziming 子明 (483-535); his biography is found at *Liangshu* 梁書, KR.2a0018.024.5a.

Emperor Wu (*Butei* 武帝): 484-549; the founding emperor of the Liang dynasty and enthusiastic patron of Buddhism.

10   **It was on the first day of the tenth month of that year** (*sunawachi sono toshi jūgatsu ichijitsu nari* すなはちそのとし十月一日なり): Dōgen seems to have broken off the Chinese in mid-sentence here: the *Jingde chuandeng lu* 景德傳燈錄, T.2076.51:219a16 reads:

十月一日至金陵。

On the first day of the tenth month, they arrived in Jinling.

11   **When the First Ancestor arrived in Jinling** (*shoso Kinryō ni itarite* 初祖金陵にいたりて): Dōgen here quotes in Chinese the famous encounter between Bodhidharma and the Liang Emperor Wu 武, as recorded at *Jingde chuandeng lu* 景德傳燈錄 (T.2076.51:219a22-28). Jinling 金陵 was the Liang capital.

58 DŌGEN'S *SHŌBŌGENZŌ* VOLUME II

The Master said, "These are merely the minor effects of humans and devas, contaminated causes.[12] *They're like the shadow that follows the body: they may exist but they're not real."*

The Emperor said, "So what is true merit?"

The Master said, "Pure wisdom, wondrous and perfect; the body, naturally empty and quiescent. Merit such as this is not to be sought in the mundane world."

The Emperor asked further, "What is the prime truth of the sacred truths?"

The Master said, "Completely open with nothing sacred."

The Emperor said, "Who is it that faces me?"

The Master said, "I don't know."

The Emperor did not comprehend. The Master knew that his abilities were no match.[13]

[16B:3]

ゆえにこの十月十九日、ひそかに江北にゆく。そのとし十一月二十三日、洛陽にいたりぬ。嵩山少林寺に寓止して、面壁而坐、終日黙然なり。しかあれども、魏主も不肖にしてしらず、はぢつべき理もしらず。

Therefore, on the nineteenth day of the tenth month, he secretly traveled north of the river; and, on the twenty-third day of the eleventh month of that year, he arrived in Luoyang.[14] Lodging at Shaolin Monastery at Mount Song, *he sat facing a wall, silent all day long.*[15] However, the ruler of the Wei was also incompetent and neither knew of this nor recognized that he should be ashamed of the fact.[16]

12　**contaminated causes** (*uro shi in* 有漏之因): I.e., karma contaminated by the mental "defilements" (*bonnō* 煩惱; S. *kleśa*).

13　**The Master knew that his abilities were no match** (*shi chi ki fukei* 師知機不契): I.e., Bodhidharma realized that the emperor was not spiritually qualified for his teachings.

14　**on the nineteenth day of the tenth month** (*kono jūgatsu jūkunichi* この十月十九日): Dōgen here shifts back to Japanese translation of the text at *Jingde chuandeng lu* 景德傳燈錄 (T.2076.51:219a28-b4). "North of the river" (*kōhoku* 江北) refers to the territory north of the Yangzi — at the time, governed by the Northern Wei dynasty, with its later capital at Luoyang.

15　**Shaolin Monastery at Mount Song** (*Sūzan Shōrinji* 嵩山少林寺): The monastery, long associated with Bodhidharma, on the Shaoshi Peak 少室峰 of Songshan 嵩山, in present-day Henan.

16　**ruler of the Wei** (*Gishū* 魏主): I.e., the Emperor Xiaoming 孝明 (r. 515-528), who was only seventeen in 527 (and would be poisoned by his mother the following year). This sentence is Dōgen's interpolation, not found in the Chinese text.

16B. Sustained Practice, Part 2 *Gyōji* 行持

[16B:4] {1:173}

師は南天竺の刹利種なり、大國の皇子なり。大國の王宮、その法ひさしく慣熟せり。小國の風俗は、大國の帝者に爲見のはぢつべきあれども、初祖、うごかしむるこころあらず。くにをすてず、人をすてず。ときに菩提流支の訕謗を救せず、にくまず。光統律師が邪心をうらむるにたらず、きくにおよばず。かくのごとくの功德おほしといへども、東地の人物、ただ尋常の三藏および經論師のごとくにおもふは、至愚なり、小人なるゆえなり。あるいはおもふ、禪宗とて一途の法門を開演するが、自餘の論師等の所云も、初祖の正法も、おなじかるべき、とおもふ。これは佛法を濫穢せしむる小畜なり。

The Master was of the kṣatriya class of South Sindhu, the prince of a great country.[17] Over the years, he had become thoroughly familiar with the rites of the royal palace of a great country. Although the customs of a small country might well appear shameful to royalty of a great country, the First Ancestor was unshaken: he did not forsake the country; he did not forsake its people. At the time, he did not defend himself against nor did he hate the slander of Bodhiruci; he did not bother to resent the wrong thoughts of the Vinaya Master Guangtong nor even listen to him.[18] The fact that, despite his many such merits, the people of the Land of the East thought of him as merely like an ordinary tripiṭaka master or teacher of sūtras and treatises represents the ultimate stupidity, a consequence of their being small-minded people. Some thought that what is called the Zen school promulgated a dharma gate of one path, but what was said by other treatise teachers and their ilk was the same as the true dharma of the First Ancestor. These were little creatures who contaminate the buddha dharma.

[16B:5]

初祖は、釋迦牟尼佛より二十八世の嫡嗣なり。父王の大國をはなれて、東地の衆生を救濟する、たれの、かたをひとしくするかあらん。もし祖師西來せずば、東地の衆生、いかにしてか佛正法を見聞せん。いたづらに名相の沙石にわづらふのみならん。いまわれらがごときの邊地遠方の披毛戴角までも、あくまで正法をきくことをえたり。いまは田夫・農父・野老・村童までも見聞する、しかしながら祖師航海の行持にすくはるるなり。西天

17　**The Master was of the kṣatriya class of South Sindhu** (*shi wa nan Tenjiku no setsuri shu nari* 師は南天竺の刹利種なり): I.e., Bodhidharma was of the ruling class in south India. Chinese geography recognized a division of the Indian subcontinent into the "fivefold Sindhu" (*go Tenjiku* 五天竺), based on the four cardinal directions and the center.

18　**Bodhiruci** (*Bodairushi* 菩提流支); **Vinaya Master Guangtong** (*Kōzu risshi* 光統律師): Allusion to the tradition (found, for example, at *Jingde chuandeng lu* 景德傳燈錄, T.2076.51:220a23-27) that these two monks poisoned Bodhidharma out of jealousy. The former figure is the prolific north Indian translator who was active in Luoyang in the first decades of the sixth century; the latter is the vinaya scholar Huiguang 慧光 (468-537), who worked on some of Bodhiruci's translations.

と中華と、土風、はるかに勝劣せり、方俗、はるかに邪正あり。大忍力の大慈にあらずよりは、傳持法藏の大聖、むかふべき處在にあらず。住すべき道場なし、知人の人まれなり。しばらく嵩山に掛錫すること九年なり。人、これを壁觀婆羅門といふ。史者、これを習禪の列に編集すれども、しかにはあらず。佛佛嫡嫡相傳する正法眼藏、ひとり祖師のみなり。

The First Ancestor was the legitimate heir in the twenty-eighth generation from Buddha Śākyamuni. In his leaving the great country of his father, the king, and saving living beings of the Land of the East, who could stand shoulder to shoulder with him? Had the Ancestral Master's coming from the west not taken place, how would the living beings of the Land of the East have experienced the true dharma of the Buddha?[19] They would only have fretted in vain over the sand and pebbles of names and appearances.[20] Now, even [creatures] like us, clad in fur and crowned by horns in remote border lands, have been able fully to hear the true dharma.[21] That now even field hands and farmers, rural elders and village youths, hear it means they have all been saved by the sustained practice of the Ancestral Master's crossing the sea. Between Sindh in the West and China, there is a great difference in the value of their indigenous cultures and the correctness of their local customs.[22] Were he not one with the great compassion capable of great tolerance, it would not have been an appropriate destination for the great sage who transmitted and maintained the treasury of the dharma. Practice places where he could live were nonexistent, and people who could know the person were rare.[23]

Hanging his staff for a while at Mount Song, he spent nine years there.[24]

---

19 **Ancestral Master's coming from the west** (*soshi seirai* 祖師西來): A fixed expression for Bodhidharma's mission to China; see Supplementary Notes, s.v. "Intention of the Ancestral Master's coming from the west."

20 **sand and pebbles of names and appearances** (*myōsō no shaseki* 名相の沙石): Likely meaning something like, "the odds and ends of doctrinal distinctions."

21 **clad in fur and crowned by horns** (*himō taikaku* 披毛戴角): A fixed expression for "beasts."

22 **Between Sindh in the West and China** (*Saiten to Chūka to* 西天と中華と): "China" here renders *Chūka* 中華 ("Central Flower"), the traditional term for China as a cultural center. Dōgen seems here to favor Indian civilization over that of China; elsewhere (in the "Shōbōgenzō tashin tsū" 正法眼藏他心通) he seems to be dismissive of the local customs of the Buddha's homeland (and below he will favor China over Japan).

23 **know the person** (*chinin* 知人): I.e., recognize the spiritual status of an individual.

24 **Hanging his staff for a while at Mount Song** (*shibaraku Sūzan ni kashaku suru* しばらく嵩山に掛錫する): Dōgen here returns to the narrative of Bodhidharma's career from section 3 above. "To hang one's staff" (*kashaku* 掛錫) refers to a monk's registration or residence at a monastery.

16B. Sustained Practice, Part 2 *Gyōji* 行持

People called him "the wall-contemplating brahman."[25] Although an historian recorded him among the practitioners of dhyāna, this was not accurate.[26] The treasury of the true dharma eye transmitted by buddha after buddha and successor after successor was [transmitted by] the Ancestral Master alone.

[16B:6] {1:174}

石門林間錄云、菩提達磨、初自梁之魏。經行於嵩山之下、倚杖於少林。面壁燕坐而已、非習禪也。久之人莫測其故、因以達磨爲習禪。夫禪那諸行之一耳、何足以盡聖人。而當時之人以之、爲史者、又從而傳於習禪之列、使與枯木死灰之徒爲伍。雖然聖人非止於禪那、而亦不違禪那。如易于陰陽、而亦不違乎陰陽。梁武初見達磨之時、即問、如何是聖諦第一義。答曰、廓然無聖。進曰、對朕者誰。又曰、不識。使達磨不通方言、則何於是時使能爾耶。

In Shimen's Grove Record, it is said,[27]

When Bodhidharma first went from Liang to Wei, he proceeded to the foot of Mount Song, where he rested his staff at Shaolin. There he just sat facing a wall. It was not the practice of dhyāna, but after a while others, unable to fathom what he was doing, made Bodhidharma a practioner of dhyāna. Now, dhyāna is but one among various practices; how could it suffice to exhaust [the practice of] the sage? Nevertheless, people of the time took it in this way; and those who wrote histories followed this and recorded him among practitioners of dhyāna, thus making him a confederate of the partisans of dried-up trees and dead ashes.[28] Although the sage does not stop at dhyāna, he does not

---

25 **"the wall-contemplating brahman"** (*hekigan baramon* 壁觀婆羅門): A characterization found in several Chan texts; here, probably reflecting *Jingde chuandeng lu* 景德傳燈錄, T.2076.51:219b4-5.

26 **an historian recorded him among the practitioners of dhyāna** (*shisha, kore o shūzen no retsu ni henshū su* 史者、これを習禪の列に編集す): Likely a reference to Daoxuan 道宣 (596-667), whose *Xu gaoseng zhuan* 續高僧傳 (T.260.50:551b27ff) includes Bodhidharma's biographical notice in the section of the work devoted to eminent monks who were "practitioners of dhyāna" (*shūzen* 習禪). Dōgen here reflects the text of the *Linjian lu* 林間錄 that he will quote at length in the following section. See Supplementary Notes, s.v. "Practitioner of dhyāna."

27 **Shimen's *Grove Record*** (*Sekimon Rinkan roku* 石門林間錄): "Shimen" 石門 is a sobriquet for the author Juefan Huihong 覺範慧洪 (1071-1128). Dōgen runs together here two passages from Huihong's *Linjian lu* 林間錄 that are not related in the original: the first (found at ZZ.148:590b7-12; also cited in "Shōbōgenzō butsudō" 正法眼藏佛道 and *Eihei kōroku* 永平廣錄) is concerned to distinguish the Chan tradition of Bodhidharma from the use of *chan* 禪 as a transliteration of Sanskrit *dhyāna*; the second (at 594a15-17) is offered as evidence that, upon his arrival in China, Bodhidharma was already fluent in the spoken language of the Liang dynasty.

28 **dried-up trees and dead ashes** (*kuboku shikai* 枯木死灰): Or "dead wood and cold ashes"; a common expression in Chan texts, often used in a pejorative sense, for the mind in trance; see Supplementary Notes, s.v. "Dried-up tree."

62 DŌGEN'S *SHŌBŌGENZŌ* VOLUME II

oppose dhyāna. It is like change, which [emerges] from yin and yang and yet does not oppose yin and yang. . . .[29]

When Liang Wu first met Dharma, he asked, "What is the first principle of the sacred truths?"

He answered, "Completely open with nothing sacred."

He continued, "Who is it that faces me?"

He spoke again, "I don't know."

Had Dharma not been fluent in the local language, how could this have taken place at the time?

[16B:7]

しかあればすなはち、梁より魏へゆくことあきらけし。嵩山に經行して、少林に倚杖す。面壁燕坐すといへども、習禪にはあらざるなり。一卷の經書を將來せざれども、正法傳來の正主なり。しかあるを、史者あきらめず、習禪の篇につらぬるは、至愚なり、かなしむべし。

Thus, it is clear that he went from the Liang to the Wei. Proceeding to Mount Song, he rested his staff at Shaolin. Though he may have sat facing a wall, this was not the practice of dhyāna. Though he did not bring a single scripture, he was a true master who transmitted the true dharma. That the historian nevertheless did not understand and listed him in the section on "dhyāna practitioners" was the height of stupidity and quite deplorable.

[16B:8] {1:175}

かくのごとくして嵩山に經行するに、犬あり、堯をほゆ。あはれむべし、至愚なり。たれのこころあらんか、この慈恩をかろくせん。たれのこころあらんか、この恩を報ぜざらん。世恩なほわすれず、おもくする人おほし、これを人といふ。祖師の大恩は、父母にもすぐるべし、祖師の慈愛は、親子にもたくらべざれ。われらが卑賤、おもひやれば驚怖しつべし。中土をみず、中華にむまれず、聖をしらず、賢をみず、天上にのぼれる人いまだなし、人心ひとへにおろかなり。開闢よりこのかた、化俗の人なし、國をすますときをきかず。いはゆるは、いかなるか清、いかなるか濁、としらざるによる。二柄・三才の本末にくらきによりて、かくのごとくなり。いはんや五才盛衰をしらんや。この愚は、眼前の聲色にくらきによりてなり。くらきことは、經書をしらざるによりてなり、經書に師なきによりてなり。その師なしといふは、この經書、いく十卷といふことをしらず、この經、いく百偈・いく千言としらず、ただ文の説相をのみよむ、いく千偈・いく萬言といふことをしらざるなり。すでに古經をしり、古書をよむがごときは、すなはち慕古の意旨あるなり。慕古のこころあれば、古經きたり現前するなり。漢高祖および魏太祖、これら天象の偈をあきらめ、地形の言をつたへし帝者なり。かくのごときの經典あきらむるとき、いささか三才あきらめきたるなり。いまだかくのごとくの聖君の化にあわざる百姓のともがらは、いかなるを事君とならひ、いかなるを事親となら

---

29 **like change, which [emerges] from yin and yang** (*nyo i u onyō* 如易于陰陽): Supplying the predicate *shutsu* 出 ("emerge") that is missing in Dōgen's text.

16B. Sustained Practice, Part 2 *Gyōji* 行持

ふとしらざれば、君子としてもあはれむべきものなり、親族としてもあは
れむべきなり。臣となれるも、子となれるも、尺璧もいたづらにすぎぬ、
寸陰もいたづらにすぎぬるなり。かくのごとくなる家門にむまれて、國土
のおもき職、なほさづくる人なし、たろき官位なほをしむ。にごれるとき
なほしかあり、すめらんときは見聞もまれならん。かくのごときの邊地、
かくのごときの卑賤の身命をもちながら、あくまで如來の正法をきかんみ
ちに、いかでかこの卑賤の身命をおしむこころあらん。おしんでのちに、
なにもののためにかすてんとする。おもくかしこからん、なほ法のために
おしむべからず、いはんや卑賤の身命をや。たとひ卑賤なりといふとも、
爲道・爲法のところにおしまずすつることあらば、上天よりも貴なるべ
し、輪王よりも貴なるべし。おほよそ、天神地祇・三界衆生よりも貴なる
べし。

In this way, when he proceeded to Mount Song, there were dogs that
barked at Yao.[30] How pathetic, the height of stupidity. How could anyone with a heart take lightly his compassion? How could anyone with a
heart not repay his kindness? There are many people who do not forget
even mundane kindness and take it seriously; they are called humans.
The great kindness of the Ancestral Master is surely superior to that of
one's father and mother; do not compare the compassionate love of the
Ancestral Master with that of a parent for a child. When we reflect on our
lowly status, we must surely be startled and fearful. We have not seen the
Central Land; we were not born in China.[31] We do not know of the sages;
we do not see the worthies. There are none who have ascended to the
heavens. The people's minds are entirely foolish. Since its foundation,
there has been no one to educate the common people, and we do not hear
of a time when the land was purified. This is because we do not know
what is pure and what is polluted. We are like this because we are in the
dark about the roots and branches of the two levers and the three powers;
how much less do we know the waxing and waning of the five powers.[32]

---

30 **there were dogs that barked at Yao** (*inu ari, Gyō o hoyu* 犬あり、堯をほゆ):
From the saying, "Zhi's dog barked at Yao" (*Zhi gou fei Yao* 蹠狗吠堯; i.e., the thief's
dog barks at the sage emperor), used in reference to the jealousy of the lowly toward
their betters; here, presumably, allusion to the jealousy of Bodhiruci and Guangtong
toward Bodhidharma.

31 **We have not seen the Central Land** (*chūdo o mizu* 中土をみず): Usually understood as a reference, like the following *Chūka* 中華 ("Central Flower"), to China as a
center of culture; but one could also take it as referring to India or as meaning simply
"a central land." The unspoken grammatical subject here is, of course, "we people of
Japan."

32 **two levers** (*nihei* 二柄); **three powers** (*sansai* 三才); **five powers** (*gosai* 五才):
Categories of traditional Chinese historiography. The first most likely refers to the two
"levers" of authority: rewards and punishments (or civil and military, though some take
it as indicating yin and yang, or heaven and earth); the second refers to the trinity of
heaven, earth, and human; the third refers to the five elements: metal, wood, water, fire,
and earth.

64 DŌGEN'S *SHŌBŌGENZŌ* VOLUME II

This stupidity is due to our being in the dark about the sights and sounds right before our eyes. Our being in the dark is due to our lack of knowledge of the scriptures, is due to our lack of teachers of the scriptures. Our lack of a teacher means that without knowing how many tens of scrolls these scriptures are, without knowing how many hundreds of gāthās, how many thousands of words, these sūtras are, we simply read the explanations of the texts, without realizing how many thousands of gāthās, how many myriads of words, there are. Those who know the ancient sūtras and read the ancient texts have the intention to emulate the ancients. When we have the intention to emulate the ancients, the ancient sūtras will come and appear before us.

The Eminent Ancestor of the Han and the Grand Ancestor of the Wei were emperors who understood the gāthās of celestial phenomena and transmitted the words of terrestrial shapes.[33] When they understood such scriptures, they had some understanding of the three powers. Commoners who have never enjoyed the teachings of such sagely lords, since they do not know what it means to learn how to serve one's lord or to learn how to serve one's parents, are pitiful for their lords and are pitiful for their families. Whether they are subjects or children, they pass in vain the one-foot jewel, they pass in vain the one-inch shadow.[34] No one born into such families surrenders an important state office; even minor official ranks are begrudged. Even in times of corruption, this is the case; in times of tranquility, it is rarely seen.[35]

In such a peripheral land, while having such a lowly life, on the way where we fully hear the true dharma of the Tathāgata, how could we begrudge this lowly life? Once we begrudge it, for what would we cast it aside later? Were we important and wise, for the sake of the dharma we still should not begrudge [our lives]; how much less, then, our lowly lives. Even though [our lives] may be lowly, if, without begrudging them, we cast them aside for the sake of the way and the sake of the

---

33 **The Eminent Ancestor of the Han and the Grand Ancestor of the Wei** (*Kan kōso oyobi Gi taiso* 漢高祖および魏太祖): I.e., Liu Bang 劉邦 (256 [or 247]–195 BCE), founder of the Han dynasty; and Cao Cao 曹操 (155-220), founder of the Wei dynasty (220-265).

gāthās of celestial phenomena (*tenshō no ge* 天象の偈); **words of terrestrial shapes** (*chigyō no gon* 地形の言): I.e., the texts of heaven and earth.

34 **one-foot jewel** (*sekiheki* 尺璧); **one-inch shadow** (*sun'in* 寸陰): From the old Chinese saying, "The sage does not value a one-foot jewel but gives weight to an inch of shadow (*sun'in* 寸陰, i.e., a moment of time)." (See *Huainanzi* 淮南子, Yuandao xun 原道訓, KR.3j0010.001-12a.)

35 **Even in times of corruption, this is the case** (*nigoreru toki nao shika ari* にごれるときなほしかあり): The point is presumably that, even when the official posts are worth little, they are not surrendered.

16B. Sustained Practice, Part 2 *Gyōji* 行持

dharma, we are more noble than the highest devas, more noble than the wheel-turning monarch. We are, in sum, more noble than the heavenly gods and earthly deities, and living beings of the three realms.

[16B:9]

しかあるに、初祖は南天竺國香至王の第三皇子なり。すでに天竺國の帝胤なり、皇子なり。高貴のうやまふべき、東地邊國には、かしづきたてまつるべき儀もいまだしらざるなり。香なし、華なし。坐褥おろそかなり、殿台つたなし。いはんやわがくには、遠方の絶岸なり、いかでか大國の皇をうやまふ儀をしらん。たとひならふとも、迂曲してわきまふべからざるなり。諸侯と帝者と、その儀ことなるべし、その禮も輕重あれども、わきまへしらず。自己の貴賤をしらざれば、自己を保任せず、自己を保任せざれば、自己の貴賤、もともあきらむべきなり。

The First Ancestor, however, was the third prince of King Xiangzhi of a country of South Sindhu.[36] He was of imperial descent in the Land of Sindhu, a royal prince. He was deserving of the respect due a nobleman; but, in a peripheral land of the eastern regions, the proper forms for waiting upon him were unknown. There was no incense; there were no flowers; the sitting mats were simple; the buildings poor. Worse still is our land of distant cliffs: how could we know the forms of respect for the ruler of a great country? Even were we to learn them, they are so involved that we could not distinguish among them. The forms for the nobility and for the emperor would be different, and the rites would be more or less formal; but we would not know how to distinguish among them. When we do not know our own status, we will not maintain ourselves; when we do not maintain ourselves, we should first and foremost clarify our own status.

[16B:10] {1:177}

初祖は、釋尊第二十八世の付法なり。道にありてよりこのかた、いよいよおもし。かくのごとくなる大聖至尊、なほ師勅によりて、身命をおしまざるは、傳法のためなり、救生のためなり。眞丹國には、いまだ初祖西來よりさきに、嫡嫡單傳の佛子をみず、嫡嫡面授の祖面を面授せず、見佛いまだしかりき。のちにも、初祖の遠孫のほか、さらに西來せざるなり。曇華の一現はやすかるべし、年月をまちて算數しつべし、初祖の西來は、ふたたびあるべからざるなり。しかあるに、祖師の遠孫と稱するともがらも、楚國の至愚にゑふて、玉石いまだわきまへず、經師論師も齊肩すべきとおもへり、少聞薄解によりてしかあるなり。宿殖般若の正種なきやからは、祖道の遠孫とならず、いたづらに名相の邪路に跰蹰するもの、あはれむべし。

---

36 **third prince of King Xiangzhi of a country of South Sindhu** (*nan Tenjiku koku Kōshi ō no daisan ōji* 南天竺國香至三の第三皇子): A common claim in Chan texts (see, e.g., *Jingde chuandeng lu* 景德傳燈錄, T.2076.51:217a9-10), though the king's name is not attested elsewhere. The translation of *nan Tenjiku koku* 南天竺國 as "a country of South Sindhu" assumes that Dōgen was not imagining a country called South India.

66　　　　　　　　DŌGEN'S *SHŌBŌGENZŌ* VOLUME II

The First Ancestor was the twenty-eighth generation heir to the dharma of Śākya, the Honored One. Since entering the way, he had gradually gained in stature. That such a great sage and most honored one, at the command of his teacher, did not begrudge his life was in order to transmit the dharma, in order to save living beings. In Cīnasthāna, before the First Ancestor came from the west, no one had seen a child of the Buddha with the unique transmission from successor to successor; no one had made a face-to-face conferral of the face of an ancestor with the face-to-face conferral from successor to successor; and no one had seen a buddha. Thereafter as well, no one came from the west except distant descendants of the First Ancestor.[37] The appearance of the *udumbara* flower is a simple matter: one just keeps count while waiting for the years and months to pass; but the First Ancestor's coming from the west will not happen again.[38] Nevertheless, intoxicated like the great fool of the state of Chu, unable to distinguish between jade and stone, even some who call themselves distant descendants think that sūtra masters and treatise masters are of equal stature [with the First Ancestor].[39] They do so because they are short on learning and shallow in understanding. Those who lack the true seeds of prajñā grown in former lives do not become distant descendants on the way of the ancestors; how pitiful are those who wander the false roads of names and appearances.

[16B:11]
梁の普通よりのち、なほ西天にゆくものあり、それ、なにのためぞ。至愚のはなはだしきなり。惡業のひくによりて、他國に跉跰するなり。歩歩に謗法の邪路におもむく、歩歩に親父の家郷を逃逝す。なんだち、西天にいたりてなんの所得かある、ただ山水に辛苦するのみなり。西天の東來する宗旨を學せず、佛法の東漸をあきらめざるによりて、いたづらに西天に迷路するなり。佛法をもとむる名稱ありといへども、佛法をもとむる道念なきによりて、西天にしても正師にあはず、いたづらに論師經師にのみあへり。そのゆえは、正師は西天にも現在せれども、正法をもとむる正心なきによりて、正法、なんだちが手にいらざるなり。西天にいたりて正師をみたるといふ、たれかその人、いまだきこえざるなり。もし正師にあはば、いくそばくの名稱をも自稱せん。なきによりて自稱いまだあらず。

37　**no one came from the west except distant descendants of the First Ancestor** (*shoso no onson no hoka, sara ni seirai sezaru nari* 初祖の遠孫のほか、さらに西來せざるなり): It is unlikely that Dōgen thought all the monks arriving in China from the west after Bodhidharma were somehow his descendants; more likely he means here that, after Bodhidharma brought it to China, the lineage of ancestors ended in the west and was, therefore, never reintroduced.

38　*udumbara* **flower** (*donge* 曇華): Blossom of a legendary tree said to bloom only once every three thousand years.

39　**the great fool of the state of Chu** (*Sokoku no shigu* 楚國の至愚): Exemplar of a person who cannot judge authenticity; from the well-known tale of the fool of the ancient kingdom of Song 宋 who mistook a stone from Yan 燕 for a gem.

16B. Sustained Practice, Part 2 *Gyōji* 行持

Even after the Putong era of the Liang there were those who went to Sindh in the West. But for what? It was the height of extreme stupidity. Pulled along by their bad karma, they wandered in other lands; step by step, they followed the wrong road that disparages the dharma; step by step they fled the homeland of their fathers.[40] What do you gain by going to Sindh in the West?[41] Just the hardships and pain of the mountains and waters. Because you failed to study the essential point that Sindh in the West had come to the east and had not clearly understood the spread of the buddha dharma to the east, you lost your way in Sindh in the West. You may have reputations for seeking the buddha dharma, but because you lacked the commitment to the way that seeks the buddha dharma, even in Sindh in the West you did not meet any true masters but met only treatise masters and sūtra masters to no avail.[42] The reason is that, though there were true masters in Sindh in the West, because you lacked the true mind that seeks the true dharma, the true dharma did not fall into your hands. Who are the people said to have gone to Sindh in the West and met true masters? We have yet to hear of any. Had they met true masters, they would themselves have pronounced some number of names. Because there were not any, they have not pronounced any.

[16B:12] {1:178}

また眞丹國にも、祖師西來よりのち、經論に倚解して、正法をとぶらはざる僧侶おほし。これ經論を披閲すといへども、經論の旨趣にくらし。これ黑業は今日の業力のみにあらず、宿生の惡業力なり。今生つひに如來の眞訣をきかず、如來の正法をみず、如來の面授にてらされず、如來の佛心を使用せず、諸佛の家風をきかざる、かなしむべき一生ならん。隋・唐・宋の諸代、かくのごときのたぐひおほし。ただ宿殖般若の種子ある人は、不期に入門せるも、あるは算砂の業を解脱して祖師の遠孫となれりしは、ともに利根の機なり、上上の機なり。正人の正種なり。愚蒙のやから、ひさしく經論の草庵に止宿するのみなり。しかあるに、かくのごとくの嶮難あるさかひを、辭せず、いとはず、初祖西來する玄風、いまなほあふぐところに、われらが臭皮袋をおしむで、つひになにゝかせん。

---

40 **they wandered in other lands** (*takoku ni reihei suru* 他國に跉跰する): Dōgen is no doubt recalling here the famous parable in the *Lotus Sūtra* (*Miaofa lianhua jing* 妙法蓮華經, T.262.9:16b7-19a12), of the son who runs away from his wealthy father's land and wanders for years in abject poverty.

41 **What do you gain by going to Sindh in the West?** (*nandachi, Saiten ni itarite nan no shotoku ka aru* なんだち、西天にいたりてなんの所得かある): Dōgen here addresses the pilgrims to India directly.

42 **met only treatise masters and sūtra masters to no avail** (*itazura ni ronshi kyōshi ni nomi aeri* いたづらに論師經師にのみあへり): Dōgen likely has in mind here such famous Tang pilgrims to India as Xuanzang 玄奘 (602–664) and Yijing 義淨 (635–713), both of whom studied at the great Buddhist university at Nālanda.

68 DŌGEN'S *SHŌBŌGENZŌ* VOLUME II

Again, in the Land of Cīnasthāna as well, following the Ancestral Master's coming from the west, there have been many clerics who relied on the sūtras and treatises for their interpretations and thus failed to inquire into the true dharma. While they may open and peruse the sūtras and treatises, they are in the dark about the point of the sūtras and treatises. This black karma represents not only the force of their present karma but bad karma of their previous lifetimes. In their present lifetimes, they do not hear the true arcanum of the tathāgatas, do not meet with the true dharma of the tathāgatas, are not illumined by the personal transmission of the tathāgatas, do not use the body and mind of the tathāgatas, and do not hear of the house styles of the buddhas; it is a lifetime to be pitied. There have been many such types during the Sui, Tang, and Song dynasties.[43] But among people with the seeds of prajña grown in former lives, even those who entered the gate without expectation, those that were liberated from the karma of counting sand and became distant descendants of the Ancestral Master were all followers with sharp faculties, followers of the highest grade, with the true seeds of the true person.[44] The stupid types just remain for long dwelling in the thatched huts of the sūtras and treatises. Still, he did not reject or hate such a difficult place; and now, when the dark style of the First Ancestor's coming from the west is still something we look up to, what is the point in the end of begrudging our stinking bags of skin?[45]

[16B:13]
香嚴禪師いはく、百計千方只爲身、不知身是塚中塵、莫言白髮無言語、此是黃泉傳語人。

Chan Master Xiangyan said,[46]

A hundred stratagems and a thousand devices, all for the sake of this body,
Without realizing this body is but dust in the grave.
Don't say the white-haired have nothing to say:
They're messengers from the Yellow Springs.[47]

---

43 **during the Sui, Tang, and Song dynasties** (*Zui Tō Sō no shodai* 隋・唐・宋の諸代): I.e., in the period from the time of Bodhidharma in the sixth century till Dōgen's day in the thirteenth century.

44 **counting sand** (*sansha* 算砂): A common pejorative for the study of the details of doctrine; see Supplementary Notes.

45 **he did not reject or hate such a difficult place** (*kaku no gotoku no kennan aru sakai o, jisezu, itowazu* かくのごとくの嶮難あるさかひを、辭せず、いとはず): Presumably, the unexpressed grammatical subject is "Bodhidharma."

46 **Chan Master Xiangyan** (*Kyōgen zenji* 香嚴禪師): Presumably, Xiangyan Zhixian 香嚴智閑 (d. 898), though the source of this quotation is unknown.

47 **Yellow Springs** (*kōsen* 黃泉): A pre-Buddhist Chinese term for the netherworld inhabited by the spirits of the dead.

16B. Sustained Practice, Part 2 *Gyōji* 行持

[16B:14] {1:179}

しかあればすなはち、おしむにたとひ百計千方をもてすといふとも、つひにはこれ塚中一堆の塵と化するものなり。いはんやいたづらに小國の王民につかはれて、東西に馳走するあひだ、千辛萬苦いくばくの身心をかくるしむる。義によりては身命をかろくす、殉死の禮、わすれざるがごとし。恩につかはるる前途、ただ暗頭の雲霧なり。小臣につかはれ、民間に身命をすつるもの、むかしよりおほし。おしむべき人身なり、道器となりぬべきゆえに。いま正法にあふ、百千恒沙の身命をすてても、正法を參學すべし。いたづらなる小人と、廣大深遠の佛法と、いづれのためにか身命をすつべき。賢・不肖ともに進退にわづらふべからざるものなり。しづかにおもふべし、正法、よに流布せざらんときは、身命を正法のために拋捨せんことをねがふとも、あふべからず。正法にあふ今日のわれらを、ねがふべし、正法にあふて、身命をすてざるわれらを、慚愧せん。はづべくは、この道理をはづべきなり。しかあれば、祖師の大恩を報謝せんことは、一日の行持なり。自己の身命をかへりみることなかれ。禽獣よりもおろかなる恩愛、をしむですててざることなかれ。たとひ愛惜すとも、長年のともなるべからず。あくたのごとくなる家門、たのみてとどまることなかれ。たとひとどまるとも、つひの幽棲にあらず。むかし佛祖のかしこかりしに、みな七寶・千子をなげすて、玉殿・朱楼をすみやかにすつ。涕唾のごとくみる、糞土のごとくみる。これらみた、古來の佛祖の、古來の佛祖を報謝しきたれる知恩・報恩の儀なり。病雀、なほ恩をわすれず、三府の璟、よく報謝あり。窮龜、なほ恩をわすれず、餘不の印、よく報謝あり。かなしむべし、人面ながら畜類よりも愚劣ならんことは。

Thus, while we may use "a hundred stratagems and a thousand devices" to preserve ourselves, in the end, we become a heap of dust in the grave. Worse yet, while futilely chasing east and west in service to the king and people of a small country, in how many bodies and minds are we afflicted by the thousand hardships and myriad sufferings?[48] We take our lives lightly for the sake of righteousness, and the ritual of following [one's lord] into death seems still not to have been forgotten. The way ahead for those subject to obligations is dark clouds and mists. Since ancient times, there have been many who, subject to petty officials, have thrown away their lives among the people. They were human bodies that should have been preserved; for they could have become vessels of the way. Now, we have encountered the true dharma; we should study the true dharma, even if we must throw away lives numerous as the sands of hundreds of thousands of Ganges. Worthless petty people, or the buddha dharma, "broad, great, deep, and far-reaching" — for the sake of which

---

48 **the thousand hardships and myriad sufferings** (*senshin banku* 千辛萬苦): A fixed idiom for extreme hardships, here no doubt used to balance Xiangyan's "a hundred stratagems and a thousand devices."

70 DŌGEN'S *SHŌBŌGENZŌ* VOLUME II

should we throw away our lives?[49] Neither the wise nor the otherwise should trouble themselves over advancing or retreating.[50]

We should think about this quietly. When the true dharma has not spread in the world, though we may wish to cast aside our bodies for the sake of the true dharma, we will not encounter it. We should wish it for ourselves now that we have encountered the true dharma; we will be ashamed of ourselves for having encountered the true dharma but not throwing away our lives. If we should be ashamed [of anything], we should be ashamed of this truth. Hence, repaying the great blessings of the Ancestral Master is a single day's sustained practice. Do not be concerned about your own life. Do not value and fail to abandon your feelings of love, more stupid than those of the birds and beasts. Though you feel love for them, they will not accompany you for long years. Do not remain dependent on the family, which is like garbage; though you remain with it, it is not in the end a dark dwelling.[51] In the old days, the buddhas and ancestors were wise: they all cast aside the seven treasures and a thousand children and immediately abandoned their jeweled palaces and vermilion towers.[52] They saw them as snot and spittle; they saw them as dung and dirt.[53] These are all deeds acknowledging blessings and repaying blessings through which the buddhas and ancestors of the past have expressed their gratitude to the buddhas and ancestors of the past. Even the sick sparrow did not forget its blessings and expressed its gratitude with the rings of the three offices; even the distressed tortoise did not forget its blessings and expressed its gratitude with the seal of Yubu.[54] How sad to have human faces and yet be more stupid than beasts.

---

49 **"broad, great, deep, and far-reaching"** (*kō dai jin on* 廣大深遠): A fixed expression, used most often in reference to the knowledge of a tathāgata.

50 **trouble themselves over advancing or retreating** (*shintai ni wazurau* 進退にわづらふ): Presumably, meaning "have any doubts about pursuing the way or backsliding."

51 **dark dwelling** (*yūsei* 幽棲): A poetic term for a peaceful place of refuge.

52 **the seven treasures and a thousand children** (*shippō senshi* 七寶・千子): I.e., their most prized possessions; a fixed expression from the royal possessions of the *cakravartin* ruler.

53 **dung and dirt** (*fundo* 糞土): Or simply "filth," "muck."

54 **the sick sparrow** (*byōjaku* 病雀): Allusion to the story, found in the Tang anthology *Mengqiu* 蒙求 (Yang Bao huang qui 楊寶黃雀, KR.3k0010.001.121a-b), of Yang Bao 楊寶 of the Later Han dynasty, who as a boy saved a baby sparrow; he was subsequently visited by an emissary of the Queen Mother of the West, who gave him four rings symbolizing the four generations of his descendants who would hold the three highest government offices.

the distressed tortoise (*kyūki* 窮龜): Allusion to the story, also found in the *Mengqiu* 蒙求 (Kong Yu fang gui 孔愉放龜, KR.3k0010.002.68a-b), of Kong Yu 孔愉 of the Jin dynasty, governor of Yubu 餘不, who once released a tortoise from captivity; as the tor-

16B. Sustained Practice, Part 2 *Gyōji* 行持

[16B:15] {1:180}

いまの見佛聞法は、佛祖面面の行持よりきたれる慈恩なり。佛祖もし單傳せずば、いかにしてか今日にいたらん。一句の恩、なほ報謝すべし、一法の恩、なほ報謝すべし。いはんや正法眼藏無上大法の大恩、これを報謝せざらんや。一日に無量恆河沙の身命、すてんことねがふべし。法のためにすてんかばねは、世世のわれら、かへりて禮拜供養すべし。諸天龍神、ともに恭敬尊重し、守護讚嘆するところなり。道理それ必然なるがゆえに。

Our seeing the buddha and hearing the dharma now is the compassionate kindness come to us from the sustained practice of each buddha and ancestor. If the buddhas and ancestors had not uniquely transmitted it, how could it have reached us today?[55] For the kindness even of a single line, we should express our thanks; for the kindness even of a single dharma, we should express our thanks. How much more, then, the great kindness of the unsurpassed great dharma of the treasury of the true dharma eye — how could we not express our thanks for it? We should seek to cast aside in a single day lives equal to the incalculable sands of the Ganges. We will return in lifetime after lifetime to pay obeisance and make offerings to the corpse we cast aside for the sake of the dharma. It will be revered and venerated protected and celebrated by devas, dragons, and gods; for, according to principle, this is inevitable.

[16B:16]

西天竺國には、髑髏をうり髑髏をたふ婆羅門の法、ひさしく風聞せり。これ聞法の人の髑髏形骸の、功德おほきことを尊重するなり。いま、道のために身命をすてざれば、聞法の功德いたらず。身命をかへりみず聞法するがごときは、その聞法成熟するなり。この髑髏は、尊重すべきなり。いまわれら、道のためにすてざらん髑髏は、他日にさらされて野外にすてらるとも、たれかこれを禮拜せん、たれかこれを賣買せむ。今日の精魂、かへりてうらむべし。鬼の先骨をうつゐりき、天の先骨を禮せしあり。いたづらに塵土に化するときをおもひやえば、いまの愛惜なし、のちのあはれみあり。もよほさるるところは、みゃ人のなみだのごとくなるべし。いたづらに塵土に化して、人にいとはれん髑髏をもて、よくさいわいに佛正法を行持すべし。このゆえに、寒苦をおづることなかれ、寒苦、いまだ人をやぶらず、寒苦、いまだ道をやぶらず。ただ不修をおづべし、不修、それ人をやぶり、道をやぶる。暑熱をおづることなかれ、暑熱、いまだ人をやぶらず、暑熱、いまだ道をやぶらず。不修、よく人をやぶり、道をやぶる。麦をうけ蕨をとるは、道俗の勝躅なり。血をもとめ、乳をもとめて、鬼畜にならわざるべし。ただまさに行持なる一日は、諸佛の行履なり。

---

toise swam away it turned its head to the left to look back at him. Thereafter, when the tortoise depicted on the governor's seal was cast, the head seemed to be turned to the left.

55 If the buddhas and ancestors had not uniquely transmitted it (*busso moshi tanden sezuba* 佛祖もし單傳せずば): The grammatical object is unexpressed; presumably, "the buddha dharma."

72 DŌGEN'S *SHŌBŌGENZŌ* VOLUME II

It has long been heard that, in the Land of Sindhu in the West, there was a practice among brahmans of selling skulls and buying skulls.[56] This reflects the value placed on the wealth of merit associated with the skull and skeleton of someone who has heard the dharma. If now we do not cast aside our life for the sake of the way, we gain no merit from hearing the dharma. Hearing the dharma matures in those who hear the dharma without regard for their lives; and this skull should be valued. The skull that we do not now cast aside for the sake of the way — though it will one day be cast aside in a field, bleached by the sun, who will pay obeisance to it? Who will buy or sell it? We will resent our present spirit.[57] There was the demon that beat its former bones; there was the deva that paid obeisance to its former bones.[58]

When we think about the time we are meaninglessly turned to dust, our feelings of love now are gone, and we feel pity for ourselves then. What we feel is rather like the tears of an onlooker. With the skull that will futilely turn to dust and be despised, happily we can and should engage in the sustained practice of the true dharma of the buddha. Therefore, do not fear the pangs of cold: the pangs of cold have yet to break a person; the pangs of cold have yet to break the way. Just fear not practicing: not practicing breaks the person, breaks the way. Do not fear the heat: the heat has yet to break a person; the heat has yet to break the way. Not practicing breaks the person, breaks the way. Accepting the barley and gathering the bracken are splendid examples, Buddhist and secular.[59]

---

56 **selling skulls and buying skulls** (*dokuro o uri dokuro o kau* 髑髏をうり髑髏を かふ): Likely a reference to the story of the brahman in Pāṭaliputra who sold skulls, the value of which depended on the degree to which the original owner of the skull had heard and understood the dharma (as determined by the depth to which one could pass a probe through the ear cavity). See *Fayuan zhulin* 法苑珠林 (T.2122.53:412b4-17); *Zhiguan fuxing zhuan hongjue* 止觀輔行傳弘決 (T.1912.46:147b2-15).

57 **We will resent our present spirit** (*konnichi no seikon* 今日の精魂): Presumably meaning that, in a future life, when we see the skull we have today discarded in a field, we will resent the spirit that now inhabits that skull for not taking better care of its future.

58 **the demon that beat its former bones** (*ki no senkotsu o utsu* 鬼の先骨をうつ); **the deva that paid obeisance to its former bones** (*ten no senkotsu o rai seshi* 天の先 骨を禮せし): Reference to stories in which a demon punishes the remains of its former self for creating the bad karma resulting in its present state; and a deva thanks the remains of its former self for the good karma that led to its being reborn in heaven. The two stories appear together at *Tianzun shuo Ayuwang piyu jing* 天尊説阿育王譬喩經 (T.2044.50:171c10-22).

59 **Accepting the barley and gathering the bracken** (*mugi o uke warabi o toru* 麦を うけ蕨をとる): Allusion to two stories of ascetic practice. In the first, the Buddha and his monks spend a summer retreat deprived of alms, eating only the feed of horses (see, e.g., *Zhong benqi jing* 中本起經, T.196.4:162c15–163a21). In the second, non-Buddhist story (found at *Shiji* 史記, Liezhuan 列傳, Bo Yi liezhuan 伯夷列傳, KR.2a0001.500.2a-

16B. Sustained Practice, Part 2 *Gyōji* 行持 73

We should not imitate the ghost and the beast in seeking blood and seeking milk.[60] Truly, a single day of sustained practice is the conduct of the buddhas.

* * * * *

[16B:17] {1:181}

眞丹第二祖、大祖正宗普覺大師は、神鬼ともに嚮慕す、道俗おなじく尊重せし高德の祖なり、曠達の士なり。尹洛に久居して、群書を博覽す。くにのまれなりとするところ、人のあひがたきなり。法高德重のゆえに、神物倐見して、祖にかたりていふ、將欲受果、何滯此耶。大道匪遠、汝其南矣。

The Second Ancestor in Cīnasthāna, Great Master Pujue, Great Ancestor Zhengzong, was an ancestor of high virtue and a "gentleman of broad thinking," admired by both gods and demons, revered alike by cleric and laity.[61] "Dwelling for long between the Yi and Luo, he read broadly in a multitude of books."[62] Considered rare in the land, he was the sort of person hard to meet. Because of the loftiness of his dharma and weightiness of his virtue, a spiritual being suddenly appeared and addressed the Ancestor, saying, "*If you wish to reap the fruit, why linger here? The great way is not far. Go south.*"[63]

4a), two brothers, from a sense of shame, go into self-imposed exile in the mountains and starve to death living only on ferns.

60 **seeking blood and seeking milk** (*chi o motome, chichi o motomete* 血をもとめ、乳をもとめて): From the tradition that the hungry ghost (*gaki* 餓鬼; S. *preta*) drinks blood.

61 **The Second Ancestor in Cīnasthāna, Great Master Pujue, Great Ancestor Zhengzong** (*Shintan daini so taiso Shōshū Fukaku daishi* 眞丹第二祖大祖正宗普覺大師): I.e., Huike 慧可 (487–593). Dōgen's account here draws on material on Huike in the *Jingde chuandeng lu* 景德傳燈錄, beginning in the notice on Bodhidharma (T.2076.51:219b5ff).

"gentleman of broad thinking" (*kōtatsu no shi* 曠達の士): Here and below, Dōgen borrows from the description of Huike in the *Jingde chuandeng lu* 景德傳燈錄 (T.2076.51:219b5-6):

時有僧神光者、曠達之士也。久居伊洛、博覽群書善談玄理。

At the time [when Bodhidharma was sitting before the wall at Songshan], there was a monk, Shenguang [i.e., Huike], a gentleman of broad thinking. Dwelling for long between the Yi and Luo, he read broadly in a multitude of books and discussed skillfully the dark principles.

62 **"Dwelling for long between the Yi and Luo"** (*I Raku ni kugo shite* 伊洛に久居して): I.e., in the capital region of Luoyang, where flow the Yi and Luo Rivers. In Dōgen's day (though not yet in 1004, when the *Jingde chuandeng lu* 景德傳燈錄 was written), "Yi Luo 伊洛" was the name of the school of Confucian learning associated with the Cheng 程 brothers.

63 **a spiritual being suddenly appeared** (*shinmotsu shukugen shite* 神物倐見して):

74 DŌGEN'S *SHŌBŌGENZŌ* VOLUME II

[16B:18]

あくる日、にわかに頭痛すること刺がごとし。其師、洛陽龍門香山寳靜禪
師、これを治せんとする。ときに、空中有聲曰、此乃換骨、非常痛也。祖
遂以見神事白于師。師視其頂骨、即如五峰秀出矣。乃曰、汝相、吉祥、當
有所證。神汝南者、斯則少林寺達磨大士、必汝之師也。

The next day, he suddenly felt a pain in his head as if he had been
stabbed.[64] When his master, Chan Master Baojing of Xiangshan at Longmen in Luoyang, tried to cure him,[65]

*There was a voice in midair saying, "This is exchanging the bones;
it is not ordinary pain."[66] The Ancestor then told his master about his
encounter with the deity. When the Master examined his cranium, it
was as if five peaks protruded from it. He said, "Your physiognomy
is auspicious; you will have a realization. The deity [having you] go
south means the Great One Dharma of Shaolin Monastery is to be your
master."*

[16B:19] {1:182}

この教をききて、祖、すなはち少室峰に参ず。神はみづからの久遠修道の
守道神なり。このとき窮臘寒天なり、十二月初九夜といふ。天大雨雪なら
ずとも、深山高峰の冬夜は、おもひやるに人物の窓前に立地すべきにあら
ず、竹節なほ破す、おそれつべき時候なり。しかあるに、大雪匝地、埋山
没峰なり。破雪して道をもとむ、いくばくの嶮難なりとかせん。つひに祖
室にとづくといへども、入室ゆるされず、顧眄せざるがごとし。この夜、
ねぶらず、坐せず、やすむことなし。堅立不動にしてあくるをまつに、夜
雪、なさけなきがごとし。ややつもりて腰をうづむあひだ、おつるなみだ
滴滴こほる。なみだをみるになみだをかさぬ、身をかへりみて身をかへ
りみる。自惟すらく、昔人求道、敲骨取髄、刺血齊飢。布髪淹泥、投崖飼
虎。古尚若此、我又何人。かくのごとくおもふに、志氣いよいよ励志あ
り。いまいふ古尚若此、我又何人を、晩進もわすれざるべきなり。しばら
くこれをわするるとき、永劫の沈溺あるなり。かくのごとく自惟して、法
をもとめ道をもとむる志氣のみかさなる。澡雪の操を操とせざるにより

Again borrowing from the *Jingde chuandeng lu* 景德傳燈錄 (T.2076.51:220c5-6):

於寂默中、倐見一神人。謂曰、將欲受果、何滯此耶。大道匪遙。汝其南矣。

In the still silence [of Huike's meditation], there suddenly appeared a spiritual person, who addressed him, saying, "If you wish to reap the fruit, why linger here? The
great way is not distant. Go south."

64 **The next day** (*akuru hi* あくる日): Dōgen continues retelling the account in the
Jingde chuandeng lu 景德傳燈錄 (T.2076.51:220c7-11), shifting to direct quotation of
the Chinese after the second sentence here.

65 **Chan Master Baojing of Xiangshan at Longmen in Luoyang** (*Rakuyō Ryūmon
Kōzan Hōjō zenji* 洛陽龍門香山寳靜禪師): Said to have been the teacher under whom
Huike took the tonsure (*Jingde chuandeng lu* 景德傳燈錄, T.2076.51:220c3). Xiangshan
香山 is a range (and later a monastery) by the Longmen mountains near Luoyang.

66 **exchanging the bones** (*kankotsu* 換骨): The mystical process by which the Daoist
wizard is transformed into an immortal.

16B. Sustained Practice, Part 2 *Gyōji* 行持

て、しかありけるなるべし。遅明のよるの消息、はからんとするに肝胆も
くだけぬるがごとし。ただ身毛の寒白せらるるのみなり。

Hearing this instruction, the Ancestor went immediately to Shaoshi Peak. The deity was his own guardian deity from his long practice of the way. The time was the end of the year, and the weather was cold; it is said to have been the night of the ninth day of the twelfth month.[67] Even had there been no great snowstorm, on a winter night on a high peak deep in the mountains, we can well imagine that no one should be standing outside a window; it was a frightful time of year, [cold enough] to break even the bamboo joint.[68] Yet, a great snow covered the ground, burying the mountain and submerging the peak. Breaking through the snow in search of the way — what an ordeal it must have been. Finally, he reached the Ancestor's quarters, but he was not permitted to enter the room; it was as if he never glanced back at him.[69]

That night, he never rested, neither sleeping nor sitting. As he stood erect without moving, waiting for the dawn, the night's snow fell as if without mercy. While it gradually piled up, burying him to the waist, the tears he shed froze drop by drop. Seeing his tears, he redoubled his tears; reflecting on himself, he reflected on himself. He thought to himself, "*When the ancients sought the way, they pummeled their bones to extract the marrow, drew their blood to save the starving, spread their hair to cover the mud, flung themselves from precipices to feed a tiger.*[70]

67　**it is said to have been the night of the ninth day of the twelfth month** (*jūni gatsu shokyū ya to iu* 十二月初九夜といふ): From the *Jingde chuandeng lu* 景德傳燈錄 (T.2076.51:219b11).

68　**Even had there been no great snowstorm** (*ten dai usetsu narazu tomo* 天大雨雪ならずとも): Reference to the report (at *Jingde chuandeng lu* 景德傳燈錄, T.2076.51:219b12) that, on the night of the ninth, there was a great snowfall.

break even the bamboo joint (*chikusetsu nao ha su* 竹節なほ破す): Perhaps reflecting the use of the bamboo as symbol of constancy and commitment.

69　**it was as if he never glanced back at him** (*komen sezaru ga gotoshi* 顧眄せざるがごとし): I.e., Bodhidharma ignored Huike. Recalling the account in the *Jingde chuandeng lu* 景德傳燈錄 (T.2076.51:219b):

師常端坐面牆、莫聞誨勵。

The Master [Bodhidharma] just continued sitting facing the wall and did not offer any encouragement.

70　**He thought to himself** (*jiyui suraku* 自惟すらく): Here, Dōgen switches to direct quotation of the Chinese version of Huike's thoughts (at *Jingde chuandeng lu* 景德傳燈錄, T.2076.51:219b9-11).

"pummeled their bones to extract the marrow" (*kō kotsu shu zui* 敲骨取髓): Likely a reference to the story of Bodhisattva Sadāprarudita, who, in order to buy a gift for his teacher, sold his body to a brahman seeking body parts for a ritual (see, e.g., *Da bore boluomiduo jing* 大般若波羅蜜多經, T.220.6:1063a23-24).

76 DŌGEN'S *SHŌBŌGENZŌ* VOLUME II

When the ancients were like this, what kind of person am I?"

Thinking thus, he became all the more resolved. His saying here, *"When the ancients were like this, what kind of person am I?"* should not be forgotten by latecomers as well.[71] When we forget it even briefly, we are sunk for everlasting kalpas. As he thought to himself in this way, his determination to seek the dharma and seek the way was redoubled. He must have been like this because he did not regard his commitment to wash the snow as a commitment.[72] To imagine his state during that night awaiting the late dawn is enough to rend one's guts; it fairly makes one's hair stand on end.[73]

"drew their blood to save the starving" (*rakketsu sai ki* 剌血齊飢): Reference to the story of Buddha Śākyamuni as a benevolent king in a previous life, who gave his blood to feed a starving plague deity (see *Xianyu jing* 賢愚經, T.202.4:360b8ff).

"spread their hair to cover the mud" (*fu hatsu en dei* 布髮淹泥): More often written *en dei* 掩泥. Reference to the story of Buddha Śākyamuni in a previous life as Bodhisattva Mānava, who invited Buddha Dīpaṃkara to cross a muddy patch stepping on his hair (see, e.g., *Dazhidu lun* 大智度論, T.1509.25:87a15-16).

"flung themselves from precipices to feed a tiger" (*tō gai shi ko* 投崖飼虎): Reference to the story of Buddha Śākyamuni in a previous life as a prince who jumped into a pit to feed his body to a starving mother tiger (see, e.g., *Jin guangming zuishengwang jing* 金光明最勝王經, T.665.16:451b1ff).

71 **latecomers** (*banshin* 晚進): I.e., those of us who have come later to Buddhist practice.

72 **he did not regard his commitment to wash the snow as a commitment** (*sōsetsu no sō o sō to sezaru* 澡雪の操を操とせざる): Perhaps meaning something like, "he did not make much of his own self control." The translation attempts to retain Dōgen's play (seen also in "Shōbōgenzō gyōji" 正法眼藏行持, part 1) with the compound term *sōsetsu* 澡雪 ("to clean"), the second element of which (*setsu* 雪) can also mean "snow" and the first element of which (*sō* 澡) is cognate with *sō* 操 ("constancy," "integrity"; translated here "commitment").

73 **his state during that night awaiting the late dawn** (*chimei no yoru no shōsoku* 遲明のよるの消息): Recalling the description in the *Jingde chuandeng lu* 景德傳燈錄 (T.2076.51:219b12):

遲明積雪過膝。

By dawn, the snow had accumulated above his knees.

enough to rend one's guts (*kantan mo kudakenuru ga gotoshi* 肝胆もくだけぬるがごとし): The expression *kantan o kudaku* 肝胆を碎く normally means "to do something fully, with all one's might"; here, perhaps, used in the sense *kantan o samukarashimu* 肝胆を寒からしむ ("to send a chill through one's guts").

makes one's hair stand on end (*shinmō no kanpaku seraruru* 身毛の寒怕せらるる): I.e., the hair of one's body (not that of the monk's bald pate).

16B. Sustained Practice, Part 2 *Gyōji* 行持　　77

[16B:20] {1:183}

初祖あはれみて、昧旦にとふ、汝久立雪中、當求何事。かくのごとくきくに、二祖、悲涙ますますおとしていはく、惟願和尚、慈悲開甘露門、廣度群品。かくのごとくまうすに、初祖曰、諸佛無上妙道、曠劫精勤、難行能行、非忍而忍。豈以小德小智・輕心慢心、欲冀眞乘、徒勞勤苦。このとき、二祖ききていよいよ誨励す。ひそかに利刀をとりて、みづから左臂を斷て、置于師前するに、初祖ちなみに、二祖これ法器なりとしりぬ。乃曰、諸佛最初求道、爲法忘形。汝今斷臂吾前、求亦可在。

As dawn was breaking, taking pity on him, the First Ancestor asked, *"You've been standing in the snow for a long time. What is it you seek?"*[74]

Hearing this, the Second Ancestor shed even more tears of grief and said, *"I only beg that, in his compassion, the Reverend open the ambrosia gate through which beings are delivered everywhere."*

When he had said this, *the First Ancestor said, "The unsurpassed wondrous way of the buddhas takes vast kalpas of spiritual fortitude, practicing what is difficult to practice, enduring the unendurable. For one of little virtue and little wisdom, of frivolous mind and vain mind, to aspire to the true vehicle would be labor in vain."*

Upon hearing this, the Second Ancestor was further encouraged. Secretly taking a sharp knife, he cut off his own left arm and placed it before the Master. Seeing this, the First Ancestor knew that the Second Ancestor was a vessel of the dharma. So, he said, *"When the buddhas first seek the way, they forget their bodies for the sake of the dharma. Now you have cut off your arm before me, your quest too is possible."*[75]

[16B:21]

これより堂奥にいる。執侍八年、勤勞千萬、まことにこれ人天の大依怙なるなり、人天の大導師なるなり。かくのごときの勤勞は、西天にもきかず、東地はじめてあり。破顔は古をきく、得髓は祖に學す。

Thereafter, he entered the interior of the hall.[76] *His attendance was eight years; his exertions, a thousand myriad.* Truly he was a great recourse for humans and devas, a great guide for humans and devas. Ex-

---

74　**taking pity on him** (*aware mite* あはれみて): This section retells in Japanese the account in the *Jingde chuandeng lu* 景德傳燈錄 (T.2076.51:219b12-20), with the speeches left in Chinese.

75　**"your quest too is possible"** (*kyū eki ka zai* 求亦可在): The *Jingde chuandeng lu* 景德傳燈錄 passage (T.2076.51:219b19-20) concludes here:

師遂因與易名曰慧可。

The Master [Bodhidharma] thereupon changed [the Second Ancestor's] name [from Shenguang 神光] to Huike 慧可 ["Capable of Wisdom"].

76　**he entered the interior of the hall** (*dōō ni iru* 堂奥にいる): I.e., was accepted as Bodhidharma's close disciple.

78 DŌGEN'S *SHŌBŌGENZŌ* VOLUME II

ertions such as his, unheard of even in Sindh in the West, first occurred in the Land of the East. Breaking into a smile is heard of from ancient times; getting the marrow is studied in this ancestor.[77]

[16B:22] {1:184}

しづかに觀想すらくは、初祖いく千萬の西來ありとも、二祖もし行持せずば、今日の飽學措大あるべからず。今日、われら正法を見聞するたぐひとなれり、祖の恩、かならず報謝すべし。その報謝は、餘外の法はあたるべからず、身命も不足なるべし、國城もおもきにあらず。國城は他人にもうばはる、親子にもゆづる。身命は無常にもまかす、主君にもまかす、邪道にもまかす。しかあれば、これを擧して報謝に擬するに、不道なるべし。ただまさに日日の行持、その報謝の正道なるべし。いはゆるの道理は、日日の生命を等閑にせず、わたくしにつひやさざらんと行持するなり。そのゆえはいかん。この生命は、前來の行持の餘慶なり、行持の大恩なり、いそぎ報謝すべし。かなしむべし、はづべし、佛祖行持の功德分より生成せる形骸を、いたづらなる妻子のつぶねとなし、妻子のもてあそびにまかせて、破落をおしまざらんことは。邪狂にして身命を名利の羅利にまかす、名利は一頭の大賊なり。名利をおもくせば、名利をあはれむべし。名利をあはれむといふは、佛祖となりぬべき身命を、名利にまかせてやぶらしめざるなり。妻子・親族あはれまんことも、またかくのごとくすべし。名利は夢幻空華と學することなかれ、衆生のごとく學すべし。名利をあはれまず、罪報をつもらしむることなかれ。參學の正眼、あまねく諸法をみんこと、かくのごとくなるべし。

What we should quietly contemplate is that, no matter how many thousand myriad times the First Ancestor were to come from the west, had the Second Ancestor not engaged in sustained practice, there would be no one today who was learned and skilled.[78] Today, we have become those who experience the true dharma; we should certainly express our gratitude for the blessings of the Ancestor. To express our gratitude, other means are no good: our life is insufficient; a country or a city is not important. Countries and cities are seized by outsiders or passed down from parent to child; our lives are at the mercy of impermanence, at the mercy of our lord, at the mercy of false ways. Thus, to think to express our gratitude with these would be the wrong way. Just sustained practice day after day is the true way to express that gratitude.

The principle of this is to engage in sustained practice, without neglect-

---

77   **Breaking into a smile** (*hagan* 破顏); **getting the marrow** (*tokuzui* 得髓): The first expression refers to the first transmission of the "treasury of the true dharma eye" (*shōbōgenzō* 正法眼藏) from Śākyamuni to Mahākāśyapa at an assembly on Vulture Peak; see Supplementary Notes, s.v. "Break into a smile." The second expression refers to the story of the first transmission in China, when Huike expressed his understanding of Bodhidharma's teaching by bowing in silence, and Bodhidharma said, "You've gotten my marrow." See Supplementary Notes, s.v. "Skin, flesh, bones, and marrow."

78   **learned and skilled** (*hogaku sodai* 飽學措大): I.e., trained and capable in the buddha dharma; literally "replete with learning and [capable of] handling great matters."

16B. Sustained Practice, Part 2 *Gyōji* 行持

ing the life of each day, without squandering it on private matters. What is the reason? This life is a blessing from our prior sustained practice, a great blessing of our sustained practice, for which we should quickly express our gratitude. How sad, how shameful, that this body, born from the merit of the sustained practice of the buddhas and ancestors, should be made the worthless slave of wives and children, allowed to become the plaything of wives and children, without any regret for its deterioration. Misguided and mad, we give our lives over to the *rākṣasa* of fame and profit; fame and profit are one great thief.[79] If we take fame and profit seriously, we should care for fame and profit. To care for fame and profit means not to let the life that will become a buddha and ancestor be given over to and ruined by fame and profit. Caring for one's wife and children and one's family should be regarded in the same way. Do not study fame and profit as dreams, illusions, and sky flowers; we should study them as living beings do.[80] Do not pile up recompense for evil by failing to care for fame and profit. Seeing all the dharmas with the true eye of study should be like this.

[16B:23]

世人のなさけある、金銀珍玩の蒙恵、なほ報謝す、好語好聲のよしみ、こころあるはみな報謝のなさけをはげむ。如來無上の正法を見聞する大恩、たれの人面かわするるときあらん。これをわすれざらん、一生の珍寶なり。この行持を不退轉ならん形骸・髑髏は、生時死時、おなじく七寶塔におさめ、一切人天皆應供養の功德なり。かくのごとく大恩ありとしりなば、かならず草露の命をいたづらに零落せしめず、如山の德をねんごろに報ずべし、これすなはち行持なり。この行持の功は、祖佛として行持するわれありしなり。おほよそ初祖・二祖、かつて精藍を草創せず、薙草の繁務なし。および三祖・四祖もまたかくのごとし。五祖・六祖、寺院を自草せず、青原・南嶽もまたかくのごとし。

Even a worldly person with any feelings expresses gratitude for the gift of gold, silver, or precious objects; for the friendliness of pleasant words and pleasant voice, anyone with a heart strives to [demonstrate] the feelings of expressing gratitude. The great beneficence of experiencing the unsurpassed true dharma of the Tathāgata — will there ever come a time when anyone with a human face could forget it? Not to forget this is a lifelong treasure. The body or skull of one who does not regress from this sustained practice has such merit, whether in life or in death, that it [should be] placed in a stūpa of the seven treasures, where

---

79 *rākṣasa* **of fame and profit** (*myōri no rasetsu* 名利の羅刹): The *rākṣasa* is a class of flesh-eating demon.

80 **sky flowers** (*kūge* 空華): Spots appearing to the diseased eye; a standard metaphor in Buddhist texts for what is mere appearance without objective reality; see Supplementary Notes, s.v. "Clouded eyes and sky flowers."

DŌGEN'S *SHŌBŌGENZŌ* VOLUME II

"all humans and devas should make offerings to it."[81] Having recognized that we have such great blessings, without letting our lives of dew on the grass simply fall into ruin, we should earnestly repay the mountain-like virtue.[82] This is precisely sustained practice. The merit of this sustained practice exists in us who are engaged in sustained practice as ancestors and buddhas. In sum, the First Ancestor and the Second Ancestor did not found monastic complexes and had no onerous task of clearing the grass.[83] And the Third Ancestor and the Fourth Ancestor were also like this. The Fifth Ancestor and Sixth Ancestor did not themselves build monasteries; and Qingyuan and Nanyue were also like this.[84]

* * * * *

[16B:24] {1:185}

石頭大師は、草庵を大石にむすびて、石上に坐禪す。晝夜にねぶらず、坐せざるときなし。衆務を齷齪せずといへども、十二時の坐禪、かならずつとめきたれり。いま青原の一派の、天下に流通すること、人天を利潤せしむることは、石頭大力の行持堅固のしかあらしむるなり。いまの雲門・法眼のあきらむるところある、みな石頭大師の法孫なり。

Great Master Shitou built a thatched hut atop a large rock and sat in meditation on the rock.[85] He did not sleep day or night; there was no time he was not sitting. Although he was not remiss in other tasks, he

---

81 **"all humans and devas should make offerings to it"** (*issai ninten kai ō kuyō* 一切人天皆應供養): From the *Lotus Sūtra* (*Miaofa lianhua jing* 妙法蓮華經, T.262.9:46a1-2), where the reference is to a stūpa that should be erected and worshiped wherever anyone who "accepts and keeps, reads and recites this sūtra" has sat, stood, or walked.

82 **the mountain-like virtue** (*nyosen no toku* 如山の德): Presumably, the [Second Ancestor's] great virtue of bestowing blessings on us.

83 **onerous task of clearing the grass** (*chisō no hanmu* 薙草の繁務): Presumably, in a reference to preparing the site of monastic buildings.

84 **the Third Ancestor and the Fourth Ancestor** (*Sanso Shiso* 三祖四祖); **The Fifth Ancestor and Sixth Ancestor** (*Goso Rokuso* 五祖六祖); **Qingyuan and Nanyue** (*Seigen Nangaku* 青原南嶽): I.e., Sengcan 僧璨 (d. 606) and Dayi Daoxin 大醫道信 (580-651); Daman Hongren 大滿弘忍 (602-675) and Caoxi Huineng 曹溪慧能; and the Sixth Ancestor's two major disciples, Qingyuan Xingsi 青原行思 (d. 740) and Nanyue Huairang 南嶽懷讓 (677-744). Dōgen is here listing the generations from the Second Ancestor to Shitou 石頭, the subject of the following section.

85 **Great Master Shitou** (*Sekitō daishi* 石頭大師): I.e., Shitou Xiqian 石頭希遷 (700-791), disciple of Qingyuan Xingsi 青原行思. Shitou's sobriquet "Reverend Stone Head" (Shitou heshang 石頭和尚) was said to derive from the boulder on which he is supposed to have built a thatched hut. (See, e.g., *Jingde chuandeng lu* 景德傳燈錄, T.2076.51:309b10-12.)

16B. Sustained Practice, Part 2 *Gyōji* 行持   81

was always practicing seated meditation throughout the twelve times.[86] That the Qingyuan lineage has now spread everywhere under heaven and brings benefits to humans and devas was made possible by the resoluteness of the sustained practice of Shitou's great effort. Those who have clarified something in the present Yunmen and Fayan are all the dharma descendants of Great Master Shitou.[87]

* * * * *

[16B:25]

第三十一祖大医禪師は、十四歳のそのかみ、三祖大師をみしより、服勞九載なり。すでに佛祖の祖風を嗣續するより、攝心無寐にして脇不至席なること僅六十年なり。化、怨親にかうぶらしめ、德、人天にあまねし。眞丹の四祖なり。

The Thirty-first Ancestor, Chan Master Dayi, after meeting the Great Master, the Third Ancestor, at the age of fourteen, labored under him for nine years.[88] After inheriting the ancestral style of the buddhas and ancestors, he concentrated his mind without sleep, his side not touching the seat for nearly sixty years.[89] His proselytizing was received by friend

---

86   **twelve times** (*jūni ji* 十二時): I.e., the twenty-four hours of the day, traditionally reckoned in twelve two-hour periods.

87   **Yunmen and Fayan** (*Unmon Hōgen* 雲門・法眼): I.e., Chan "houses" founded by Yunmen Wenyen 雲門文偃 (864-949) and Fayan Wenyi 法眼文益 (885-958), both of whom belonged to a lineage stemming from Shitou.

88   **Thirty-first Ancestor, Chan Master Dayi** (*daisanjūisso Daii zenji* 第三十一祖大医禪師): I.e., the fourth Chinese ancestor, Daoxin 道信.

Great Master, the Third Ancestor (*sanso daishi* 三祖大師): I.e., Sengcan 僧璨. Daoxin's nine years of labor (*fukurō kyūsai* 服勞九載) under the Third Ancestor reflects a passage in Sengcan's biography in the *Jingde chuandeng lu* 景德傳燈錄 (T.2076.51:221c18-21):

有沙彌道信、年始十四。來禮師曰、願和尚慈悲乞與解脱法門。師曰、誰縛汝。曰無人縛。師曰、何更求解脱乎。信於言下大悟。服勞九載。

There was a śrāmaṇera Daoxin, barely fourteen years of age. He came and paid his respects to the Master, saying, "I beg the Reverend in his compassion to give me the dharma gate to liberation."
The Master said, "Who has bound you?"
He said, "No one has bound me."
The Master said, "Then why are you seeking liberation?"
Under these words, Shin had a great awakening. He labored [under Sengcan] for nine years.

89   **After inheriting the ancestral style of the buddhas and ancestors** (*sude ni busso no sofū o shizoku suru yori* すでに佛祖の祖風を嗣續するより): This sentence is a Japanese translation of a passage in Daoxin's biography in the *Jingde chuandeng lu* 景德傳燈錄 (T.2076.51:222b3-5), though Dōgen has parsed the passage in an odd manner:

幼慕空宗諸解脱門、宛如宿習既嗣祖風。攝心無寐脇不至席者、僅六十年。

From a young age, he admired the doors to liberation of the emptiness teaching,

82 DŌGEN'S *SHŌBŌGENZŌ* VOLUME II

and foe alike; his virtue extended to humans and devas everywhere. He was the Fourth Ancestor in Cīnasthāna.

[16B:26]

貞觀癸卯歲、太宗嚮師道味、欲瞻風彩、詔赴京。師上表遜謝、前後三返、竟以疾辭。第四度、命使曰、如果不赴、即取首來。使至山諭旨。師乃引頸就刃、神色儼然。使異之、廻以狀聞。帝彌加歎慕。就賜珍繒、以遂其志。

In the junior water year of the rabbit in Zhenguan, Taizong, attracted to the flavor of the Master's way and wishing to behold his demeanor, summoned him to the capital.[90] Thrice submitting his apologies, [the Master] declined on grounds of ill health. The fourth time, [the Emperor] instructed his emissary, saying, "If it turns out he will not come, then bring back his head." When the emissary arrived at the mountain and advised him of his orders, the Master stretched his neck against the sword, his expression composed. The emissary thought it extraordinary and, when he returned, informed [the Emperor] in his report. The Emperor came to admire him even more. He presented him with rare silks, and [the Master] prevailed in his determination.

[16B:27] {1:186}

しかあればすなはち、四祖禪師は、身命を身命とせず、王臣に親近せざらんと行持せる行持、これ千載の一遇なり。太宗は有義の國主なり、相見のものうかるべきにあらざれども、かくのごとく先達の行持はありけると參學すべきなり。人主としては、身命をしまず、引頸就刃して身命ををしまざる人物をも、なほ歎慕するなり。これいたづらなるにあらず、光陰をををしみ、行持を專一にするなり。上表三返、奇代の例なり。いま澆季には、もとめて帝者にまみえんとねがふあり。

Thus, the Chan Master, the Fourth Ancestor, did not take his life as his life; his sustained practice that engaged in the sustained practice of not approaching kings and ministers is something encountered once in a thousand years. Taizong was a righteous ruler, and [the Ancestor] need not have been reluctant to meet him; yet we should study that our predecessors nevertheless had such sustained practice. As a ruler, [the Emperor] still admired an individual who, not begrudging his life, would "*stretch his neck against the sword*" without begrudging his life. This

---

almost as if he had studied in a previous life and had already inherited the ancestral style. He concentrated his mind without sleeping, his side not touching the seat for nearly sixty years.

his side not touching the seat (*kyō fushi seki* 脇不至席): A fixed expression for the ascetic practice of not reclining to sleep.

90 **In the junior water year of the rabbit in Zhenguan** (*Jōkan kibo sai* 貞觀癸卯歲): I.e., 643 CE, the seventeenth year of the Zhenguan era of the Tang Emperor Taizong 太宗 (r. 626-649). This section is a direct quotation from the Chinese at *Jingde chuandeng lu* 景德傳燈錄, T.2076.51:222b23-28.

16B. Sustained Practice, Part 2 *Gyōji* 行持

was no frivolous act: he begrudged the years and months and was solely devoted to sustained practice.[91] His three submissions to the throne are an example rare through the ages. In this late season of shallowness, there are those who eagerly seek an audience with the emperor.[92]

[16B:28]

高宗永徽辛亥歲閏九月四日、忽垂誠門人曰、一切諸法、悉皆解脱、汝等各自護念、流化未來。言訖安坐而逝、壽七十有二、塔于本山。明年四月八日、塔戸無故自開、儀相如生。爾後門人不敢復閉。

> On the fourth day of the intercalary ninth month of the junior metal year of the pig in Yonghui in the reign of Gaozong, [the Fourth Ancestor] suddenly admonished his followers, saying, "All dharmas without exception are liberated. Each of you should bear this in mind and pass it on to the future."[93] After saying this, he sat peacefully and departed. He was seventy-two. They located his stūpa at this mountain.[94] On the eighth day of the fourth month of the following year, the door of the stūpa opened by itself for no reason.[95] He appeared as if alive. Thereafter, his followers dared not close it up again.

[16B:29] {1:187}

しるべし、一切諸法、悉皆解脱なり。諸法の空なるにあらず、諸法の諸法ならざるにあらず、悉皆解脱なる諸法なり。いま四祖には、未入塔時の行持あり、既在塔時の行持あるなり。生者かならず滅あり、と見聞するは小見なり、滅者は無思覺、と知見せるは小聞なり。學道には、これらの小聞・小見をならふことなかれ。生者の滅なきもあるべし、滅者の有思覺なるもあるべきなり。

We should recognize that "*all dharmas without exception are liberated.*" It is not that the dharmas are empty; it is not that the dharmas are not the dharmas: they are dharmas that are "*without exception liberated.*"

---

91 **years and months** (*kōin* 光陰): I.e., the passing time. Literally, "light and shade," in reference to the sun and moon; variously understood as "years and months," "days and months," and "days and nights."

92 **late season of shallowness** (*gyōki* 澆季): A standard Chinese expression for a later, degenerate age.

93 **fourth day of the intercalary ninth month of the junior metal year of the pig in Yonghui in the reign of Gaozong** (*Kōsō Eiki shingai sai jun kugatsu shinichi* 高宗永徽辛亥歲閏九月四日): October 23, 651, the second year of the Yonghui era of the Tang Emperor Gaozong 高宗 (r. 649-683). This section is a direct quotation from the passage at *Jingde chuandeng lu* 景德傳燈録, T.2076.51:22b28-33.

94 **this mountain** (*honzan* 本山): I.e., Dongshan 東山 at Mount Huangmei 黄梅 in present-day Hubei.

95 **eighth day of the fourth month of the following year** (*myōnen shigatsu hachinichi* 明年四月八日): May 21, 652; in East Asia, the eighth of the fourth lunar month is the traditional date of the birthday of Buddha Śākyamuni.

The Fourth Ancestor had a sustained practice when he had yet to enter his stūpa, and he had a sustained practice after he was in the stūpa. To perceive that the living invariably die is a small view; to know that the dead are without awareness is a small perception. In studying the way, do not learn small perceptions and small views. There should be the living that do not die; there should be the dead that have awareness.

* * * * *

[16B:30]

福州玄沙宗一大師、法名師備、福州閩縣人也。姓謝氏、幼年より垂釣をこのむ。小艇を南臺江にうかめて、もろもろの漁者になれきたる。唐の咸通のはじめ、年甫三十なり。たちまちに出塵をねがふ。すなはち釣舟をすてて、芙蓉山靈訓禪師に投じて落髮す。豫章開元寺道玄律師に具足戒をうく。

Great Master Zongyi, Xuansha of Fuzhou, whose dharma name was Shibei, was from the Min Prefecture of Fuzhou.[96] His surname was Xie. As a youth he enjoyed fishing; he sailed a little boat on the Nantai River and became familiar with the fishermen.[97] At the beginning of the Gantong era of the Tang, when he was thirty years of age, he suddenly sought to leave the dusty world.[98] Immediately abandoning his fishing boat, he committed himself to Chan Master Linxun of Mount Furong and took the tonsure.[99] He received the full precepts from Vinaya Master Daoxuan of the Kaiyuan Monastery in Yuzhang.[100]

[16B:31]

布衲芒履、食纔接氣、常終日宴坐。衆皆異之。與雪峰義存、本法門昆仲、而親近若師資。雪峰以其苦行、呼爲頭陀。一日雪峰問曰、阿那箇是備頭陀。師對曰、終不敢誑於人。異日雪峰召曰、備頭陀何不徧參去。師曰、達磨不來東土、二祖不往西天。雪峰然之。

---

96 **Great Master Zongyi, Xuansha of Fuzhou** (*Fukushū Gensha Sōitsu daishi* 福州玄沙宗一大師): I.e., Xuansha Shibei 玄沙師備. This section represents a Japanese translation of the opening lines of Xuansha's biography in the *Jingde chuandeng lu* 景德傳燈錄 (T.2076.51:343c27-344a2).

97 **Nantai River** (*Nantai kō* 南臺江): The Minjiang 閩江, in present-day Fujian.

98 **Gantong era of the Tang** (*Tō no Kantsū* 唐の咸通): Spanning the years 860-874. The year in question would have been 865.

99 **Chan Master Linxun of Mount Furong** (*Fuyōzan Reikun zenji* 芙蓉山靈訓禪師): I.e., Furong Linxun 芙蓉靈訓 (dates unknown), disciple of Guizong Zhichang 歸宗智常 (dates unknown).

100 **Vinaya Master Daoxuan of the Kaiyuan Monastery in Yuzhang** (*Yoshō Kaigenji Dōgen risshi* 豫章開元寺道玄律師): Otherwise unknown monk. Yuzhang is present-day Jiangxi; the Kaiyuan Monastery was one of a series of similarly named institutions established by the Emperor Xuanzong 玄宗 in the twenty-sixth year of Kaiyuan (738).

16B. Sustained Practice, Part 2 *Gyōji* 行持

85

With a patched robe of plant fiber and shoes made of grass, with food barely enough to sustain life, he always sat calmly all day.[101] *The assembly all thought him eccentric. He and Xuefeng Yicun were originally brothers in that dharma gate, and their close relationship was like that of teacher and disciple.*[102] *Xuefeng called him "Dhūta" because of his arduous practice.*[103]

One day, Xuefeng asked him, "What is Bei Dhūta?"

The Master replied, "I would never deceive anyone."

Another day, Xuefeng addressed him, saying, "Bei Dhūta, why don't you go off on an extensive study?"[104]

The Master said, "Dharma didn't come to the Land of the East; the Second Ancestor didn't go to Sindh in the West."

Xuefeng approved this.

[16B:32] {1:188}

つひに象骨にのぼるにおよむで、すなはち師と同力締構するに、玄徒臻萃せり。師の入室咨決するに、晨昏にかはることなし。諸方の玄學のなかに、所未決あるは、かならず師にしたがひて請益するに、雪峰和尚いはく、備頭陀にとふべし。師、まさに仁にあたりて不讓にして、これをつとむ。拔群の行持にあらずよりは、慇懃の行履あるべからず。終日宴坐の行持、まれなる行持なり。いたづらに聲色に馳騁することはおほしといへども、終日の宴坐は、つとむる人まれなるなり。いま晚學としては、のこりの光陰のすくなきことをおそりて、終日宴坐、これをつとむべきなり。

When eventually [Xuefeng] climbed Xianggu and collaborated with the Master to build [a monastery], followers of the dark learning congregated there.[105] Whether morning or evening, the Master would enter the room to seek a resolution.[106] Those among the [followers of] the dark

---

101 **With a patched robe of plant fiber and shoes made of grass** (*funō bōri* 布衲芒履): This section is direct quotation from the *Jingde chuandeng lu* 景德傳燈錄 (T.2076.51:344a2-7). "Plant fiber" here translates the Chinese *bu* 布 (Japanese *fu*), which can refer to any cloth made from plants (ramie, hemp, linen, cotton, etc.,) — as opposed to silk or wool.

102 **Xuefeng Yicun** (*Seppō Gison* 雪峰義存): 822-908. Xuefeng would become Xuansha's teacher.

103 **"Dhūta"** (*zuda* 頭陀): A Sanskrit term for "austerities."

104 **"extensive study"** (*henzan* 徧參): More often written 遍參; the practice of traveling widely to study with various masters.

105 **Xianggu** (*Zōkotsu* 象骨): I.e., Mount Xuefeng 雪峰山, in present-day Fujian province. The first five sentences of this section (through the saying of Confucius) represent Dōgen's Japanese rendering (with some omission) of the passage at *Jingde chuandeng lu* 景德傳燈錄, T.2076.51:344a8-12.

106 **enter the room to seek a resolution** (*nisshitsu shiketsu* 入室咨決): I.e., visit Xuefeng's quarters to receive instruction.

86 DŌGEN'S *SHŌBŌGENZŌ* VOLUME II

learning from all quarters who had unresolved issues would always accompany the Master and request instruction. Reverend Xuefeng would tell them, "Ask Bei Dhūta." The Master, not deferring when it comes to humaneness, would work [to answer them].[107] Were it not for his extraordinary sustained practice, there could not be such conduct. The sustained practice of "sitting calmly all day" is a rare instance of sustained practice. While there are many cases of meaninglessly chasing after sights and sounds, rare are those who work at sitting calmly all day. Now, as late students, fearing that the years and months remaining are few, we should work at sitting calmly all day.

* * * * *

[16B:33]

長慶の慧稜和尚は、雪峰下の尊宿なり。雪峰と玄沙とに往來して、參學することは僅二十九年なり。その年月に、蒲團二十枚を坐破す。いまの人の坐禪を愛するあるは、長慶をあげて慕古の勝躅とす。したふはおほし、およぶすくなし。

Reverend Huileng of Changqing was a venerable under Xuefeng.[108] Moving back and forth between Xuefeng and Xuansha, he studied for almost twenty-nine years.[109] Over those years, he sat through twenty reed cushions.[110] People today who have a love of seated meditation take Changqing as a splendid example for those who admire the ancients. There are many who admire him, few who equal him.

[16B:34]

しかあるに、三十年の功夫むなしからず、あるとき凉簾を卷起せしちなみに、忽然として大悟す。三十來年、かつて郷土にかへらず、親族にむかはず、上下肩と談笑せず、専一に功夫す。師の行持は三十年なり。疑滞を疑滞とせること三十年、さしおかざる利機といふべし、大根といふべし。励志の堅固なる、傳聞するは或從經卷なり。ねがふべきをねがひ、はづべき

---

107 **not deferring when it comes to humaneness** (*nin ni atarite fujō ni shite* 仁にあたりて不讓にして): From the saying of Confucius (*Lunyu* 論語 15; KR.1h0005.008.9a):

當仁不讓於師。

When it comes to humaneness, do not defer to the teacher.

108 **Reverend Huileng of Changqing** (*Chōkei no Eryō oshō* 長慶の慧稜和尚): I.e., Changqing Huileng 長慶慧稜 (854-932), dharma heir of Xuefeng. His biography can be found at *Jingde chuandeng lu* 景德傳燈錄, T.2076.51:347b16ff.

109 **he studied for almost twenty-nine years** (*sangaku suru koto kin nijūku nen nari* 參學すること僅二十九年なり): Likely reflecting the *Jingde chuandeng lu* 景德傳燈錄 (T.2076.51:34712).

110 **he sat through twenty reed cushions** (*futon nijū mai o zaha su* 蒲團二十枚を坐破す): I.e., wore out twenty meditation cushions; a trope often associated with Changqing (though some sources give the number as a mere seven).

16B. Sustained Practice Part 2 *Gyōji* 行持

をはぢとせん、長慶に相逢すべきなり。實を論ずれば、ただ道心なく、操行つたなきによりて、いたづらに名利には繋縛せらるるなり。

Thus, his thirty years of concentrated effort were not in vain: once, while rolling up a bamboo blind, he suddenly had a great awakening.[111] For thirty years, he never returned to his birthplace; he did not meet with his relatives; he did not chat with those [who sat] shoulder to shoulder with him: he worked away single-mindedly.[112] The Master's sustained practice lasted thirty years. Thirty years of taking his doubts as his doubts — we can call him one of sharp faculties who would not let up; we can call him one of great abilities. To hear of the firmness of his dedication is *whether from a sūtra scroll*.[113] To desire what should be desired and be ashamed of what is shameful is to meet Chanqing. To tell the truth, it is because we lack the mind of the way and our conduct is poor that we are meaninglessly in bondage to fame and profit.

* * * * *

[16B:35] {1:189}

大潙山大圓禪師は、百丈の授記より、直に潙山の峭絶にゆきて、鳥獸爲伍して、結草修練す。風雪を辭勞することなし、橡栗充食せり。堂宇なし、常住なし。しかあれども、行持の見成すること、四十來年なり。のちには海内の名藍として、龍象蹴踏するものなり。梵刹の現成を願ぜんにも、人情をめぐらすことなかれ、佛法の行持を堅固にすべきなり。修練ありて堂閣なきは、古佛の道場なり、露地・樹下の風、とほくきこゆるなり。この處在、ながく結界となる。まさに一人の行持あれば、諸佛の道場につたはるべきなり。末世の愚人、いたづらに堂閣の結構につかるることなかれ、佛祖いまだ堂閣をねがはず。自己の眼目いまだあきらめず、いたづらに殿堂・精藍を結構する、まったく諸佛に佛宇を供養せんとにはあらず、おのれが名利の窟宅とせんがためなり。潙山のそのかみの行持、しづかにおもひやるべきなり。おもひやるといふは、わがいま潙山にすめらんがごとくおもふべし。深夜のあめの聲、こけをうがつのみならんや、巖石を穿却するちからもあるべし。冬天のゆきの夜は、禽獸もまれなるべし、いはんや人煙の、われをしるあらんや。命をかろくし法をおもくする行持にあらずば、しかあるべからざる活計なり。薙草すみやかならず、土木いとなま

---

111   **once, while rolling up a bamboo blind, he suddenly had a great awakening** (*aru toki ryōren o kanki seshi chinami ni, kotsunen toshite daigo su* あるとき凉簾を卷起せしちなみに、忽然として大悟す): Dōgen records the story of Changqing's awakening in his *shinji Shōbōgenzō* 眞字正法眼藏 (DZZ.5:206-208, case 156), probably based on the version in Dahui Zonggao's 大慧宗杲 *Zengfayanzang* 正法眼藏 (ZZ.118:93a12-b3) — though this latter text gives Changqing's quest as lasting twenty (not thirty) years.

112   **those [who sat] shoulder to shoulder with him** (*jōge ken* 上下肩): I.e., those on either side of his seat in the meditation hall.

113   **whether from a sūtra scroll** (*waku jū kyōkan* 或從經卷): I.e., "[to hear of Huileng's commitment is] like reading scripture." From the fixed expression, occurring often in Dōgen's writing, "whether from a wise friend, whether from a sūtra scroll" (*waku jū chishiki waku jū kyōkan* 或從知識或從經卷); see Supplementary Notes.

ず。ただ行持修練し、辦道功夫あるのみなり。あはれむべし、正法傳持の嫡祖、いくばくか山中の嶮岨にわづらふ。溈山をつたへきくには、池あり、水あり、こほりかさなり、きりかさなるらん。人物の、堪忍すべき幽棲にあらざれども、佛道と玄奥と、化成することあらたなり。かくのごとく行持しきたれりし道得を見聞す。身をやすくしてきくべきにあらざれども、行持の勤勞すべき報謝をしらざれば、たやすくきくといへども、こころあらん晩學、いかでかそのかみの溈山を、目前のいまのごとくおもひやりてあはれまざらん。この溈山の行持の道力化功によりて、風輪うごかず、世界やぶれず、天衆の宮殿おだやかなり、人間の國土も保持せるなり。溈山の遠孫にあらざれども、溈山は祖宗なるべし。のちに仰山きたり侍奉す。仰山、もとは百丈先師のところにして、問十答百の鷙子なりといへども、溈山に參侍して、さらに看牛三年の功夫となる。近來は斷絶し、見聞することなき行持なり。三年の看牛、よく道得を人にもとめざらしむ。

Chan Master Dayuan of Mount Dawei, after receiving Baizhang's prediction, went directly to the steep heights of Mount Wei, where he made friends with the birds and beasts, fashioned a thatched hut, and undertook training.[114] He was undaunted by the snowstorms; chestnuts sufficed for his food. There were no monastic halls; there was no monastic property. Nevertheless, the realization of his sustained practice there lasted forty years. Later on, as a monastery famed within the seas, it was a place where "the dragon elephants tread."[115] Even if one should wish to realize a *brahma-kṣetra*, do not be caught up in human feelings: we should remain firm in our sustained practice of the buddha dharma.[116] A place where there is training with no hall is the practice place of the old buddhas: the style [of practicing] in the open or under a tree is known from the distant past. These places become permanent restricted realms.[117] If there is the sustained practice of a single person, [the place] will be passed down as the practice place of the buddhas.

---

114   **Chan Master Dayuan of Mount Dawei** (*Daiisan Daien zenji* 大溈山大圓禪師): I.e., Weishan Lingyou (771-853; also sometimes read Guishan Lingyou). Mount Wei 溈山 is in present-day Hunan. The opening lines of this section retell in Japanese a description found in Weishan's biography in the *Jingde chuandeng lu* 景德傳燈錄 (T.2076.51:264c13-15).

Baizhang's prediction (*Hyakujō no juki* 百丈の授記): I.e., the validation of Lingyou's spiritual status by his teacher, Baizhang Huaihai 百丈懷海 (749-814; according to some sources, 720-814).

115   **monastery famous within the seas** (*kaidai no meiran* 海内の名藍): I.e., a monastery famous throughout the land; *kaidai* 海内 ("within the seas") refers to the seas in the four directions (*shikai* 四海), or "everywhere."

"the dragon elephants tread" (*ryūzō shūtō* 龍象蹴踏): A fixed expression for the congregation of powerful practitioners; from a line in the *Vimalakīrti Sūtra* (*Weimo jing* 維摩經, T.475.14:547a26) likening the bodhisattva to a great elephant.

116   **brahma-kṣetra** (*bonsetsu* 梵刹): I.e., a monastic establishment; the transliteration of a Sanskrit term for a "pure field," or sacred space.

117   **restricted realms** (*kekkai* 結界): Sacred precincts, ritually marked off.

16B. Sustained Practice, Part 2 *Gyōji* 行持

89

Fools of the final age, do not wear yourselves out in the vain construction of monastic halls. The buddhas and ancestors have never wished for halls. Those who vainly construct halls and monasteries when their own eye is not yet clear are by no means offering Buddhist buildings to the buddhas; they are doing it to make a den for their own fame and profit. We should calmly think on the sustained practice of Weishan in his day. To "think on" means we should think of ourselves now as if living on Mount Wei. The sound of the rain in the dead of night has a force that not only penetrates the moss but pierces the very boulders; on a snowy night under a winter sky, even the birds and beasts would be rare; how much less would there be the smoke of humans aware of us.[118] It is a way of life of a sort impossible without the sustained practice that takes life lightly and gives weight to the dharma. He did not hurry to clear the grass; he did not engage in construction; he just trained himself in sustained practice, in concentrated effort to pursue the way. How sad that a legitimate ancestor who had transmitted and maintained the true dharma should have suffered so many hardships in the rugged mountain. They say that Mount Wei has ponds and streams; the ice must be thick, the mist thick. Although it was not a secluded life that human beings could bear, the fusing of the way of the buddhas and the dark interior is obvious.[119] We hear the sayings about how he practiced continuously in this way. We should not hear them in a relaxed posture; but even if we hear them casually, not recognizing the thanks we should strive to express for his sustained practice, when we think on the Weishan of that time as if he were here before our eyes, how could any late student with a heart not feel for him? Owing to the power of the way and the merit of conversion arising from this sustained practice of Weishan, the disk of wind does not move, the world does not crumble, the palaces of the devas are calm, and the countries of humans are maintained.[120]

118 **smoke of humans** (*jin'en* 人煙): A poetic reference to the smoke of home fires as a sign of human habitation.

119 **fusing of the way of the buddhas and the dark interior is obvious** (*butsudō to gen'ō to, kejō suru koto arata nari* 佛道と玄奥と、化成することあらたなり): I.e., it is clearly a combination of Buddhist practice and deep understanding. A tentative interpretation of a phrase variously understood; the translation takes the term *arata* in the sense "immediately apparent"; others take it here in the sense "new" (hence, "there is something new created from the combination of the way of the buddhas and the dark interior").

120 **power of the way and the merit of conversion** (*dōriki kekō* 道力化功): An unusual combination, probably meaning something like Weishan's "spiritual strength and teaching effectiveness."

disk of wind (*fūrin* 風輪): Or "wind wheel" (S. *vāyu-maṇḍala*) of Buddhist cosmology, according to which the earth rests on disks of (in ascending order) space, wind, water, and metal.

90   DŌGEN'S *SHŌBŌGENZŌ* VOLUME II

Even if we are not the distant descendants of Weishan, Weishan is our ancestor.[121]

Later, Yangshan arrived and served him.[122] Although, originally, at his former master Baizhang's place, Yangshan was said to have been a Śāriputra, with "a hundred answers for ten questions," attending Weishan, he worked further for "three years tending the ox."[123] This is a sustained practice that has gone extinct in recent times and is no longer known.

121　**Even if we are not the distant descendants of Weishan** (*Isan no onson ni arazaredomo* 潙山の遠孫にあらざれども): I.e., even for those of us who are not in the lineage of the Weiyang 潙仰 house of Chan descended from Weishan.

122　**Yangshan** (*Kyōzan* 仰山): I.e., Weishan's successor Yangshan Huiji 仰山慧寂 (807-883), who together with Weishan, was later considered the founder of the Weiyang school of Chan.

123　**at his former master Baizhang's place** (*Hyakujō senshi no tokoro ni shite* 百丈先師のところにして): I.e., the monastery of Baizhang Huaihai 百丈懷海. Dōgen is drawing here on a conversation he records in his *shinji Shōbōgenzō* 眞字正法眼藏 (DZZ.5:190, case 118), which begins with Weishan saying to Yangshan,

承聞子在百丈先師處、問一答十問十答百。

I hear that when you were at our former master Baizhang's place, you had ten answers for one question and a hundred answers for ten questions.

The conversation is found in the *Liandeng huiyao* 聯燈會要 (ZZ.136:559a4-10) and elsewhere. Note that, if our date of 814 for Baizhang's death is correct, Yangshan would have been only seven years old at the time. Yangshan's biographies (e.g., at *Jingde chuandeng lu* 景德傳燈錄, T.2076.51:282a29-b1) have him entering the order at the age of seventeen.

A well-known story about Weishan's other famous disciple Xiangyan Zhixian 香嚴智閑 (e.g., at Dahui's 大慧 *Zhengfayanzang* 正法眼藏, ZZ.118:72a5-9) also begins with the line:

山問、我聞汝在百丈先師處、問一答十問十答百。

[Wei]shan questioned him. "I hear that, when you were with our former master Baizhang, you gave ten answers for one question, a hundred answers for ten questions."

a Śāriputra, with "a hundred answers for ten questions" (*mon jū tō hyaku no Shūshi* 問十答百の鷲子): Though it does not occur elsewhere in the *Shōbōgenzō*, the expression, "a hundred answers for ten questions" is a common phrase in Chan literature for a smart student. Śāriputra was the disciple of Buddha Śākyamuni recognized for his mastery of doctrine. Although in the story of Weishan's interview with Yangshan, the latter is not compared to Śāriputra, in another story recorded by Dōgen (see, e.g., *shinji Shōbōgenzō* 眞字正法眼藏, DZZ.5:158, case 61), Weishan likens his two disciples, Yangshan and Xiangyan, to Śāriputra and Maudgalyāyana respectively.

"three years tending the ox" (*kan gyū sannen* 看牛三年): Typically understood as a metaphor for spiritual training. Taken here from the line (*shinji Shōbōgenzō* 眞字正法眼藏, DZZ.5:190, case 118):

便發心看牛三年

Then, bringing forth the mind [of bodhi], he tended the ox for three years.

For more on this metaphor, see Supplementary Notes, s.v. "Water buffalo."

16B. Sustained Practice. Part 2 *Gyōji* 行持

91

Tending the ox for three years left him no longer seeking sayings from others.[124]

* * * * *

[16B:36] {1:190}

芙蓉山の楷祖、もはら行持見成の本源なり。國主より定照禪師號ならびに紫袍をたまふに、祖うけず、修表具辭す。國主とがめあれども、師つひに不受なり。米湯の法味、つたはれり。芙蓉山に庵せしに、道俗の川湊するもの、僅數百人なり。日食粥一杯なるゆえに、おほく引去す。師はちかひて赴齋せず。あるとき、衆にしめすにいはく、

Ancestor Kai of Mount Furong was a source of the realization of single-minded sustained practice.[125] When the ruler conferred on him the title Chan Master Dingzhao together with a purple robe, the Ancestor would not accept them and composed a memorial stating his refusal.[126] Although the ruler reprimanded him, the Master still did not accept. The dharma taste of his rice broth has been passed down. When he made his hermitage at Mount Furong, the clerics and laymen who flowed to the place were nearly several hundred in number.[127] But, since they only got a daily fare of one bowl of gruel, many of them withdrew. The Master made a vow not to go for meal offerings.[128] Once, in addressing the assembly, he said,[129]

---

124 **left him no longer seeking sayings from others** (*yoku dōtoku o hito ni moto-mezarashimu* よく道得を人にもとめざらしむ): Reflecting the final lines of the story (*shinji Shōbōgenzō* 眞字正法眼藏, DZZ.5:190, case 118):

一日師入山見、在樹下坐禪。師以杖点點背一下。仰廻首。師云、寂子道得也未。仰曰、雖道不得、且不就人別借口。師云、寂子會也。

One day, upon entering the mountain, the Master [Weishan] saw him [Yangshan] sitting in meditation under a tree. The Master tapped him once on the shoulder with his staff. Yangshan turned his head. The Master said, "Can you say it yet?" Yangshan said, "I can't say it, but at least I don't borrow someone else's words." The Master said, "You've understood it."

125 **Ancestor Kai of Mount Furong** (*Fuyōzan no Kai so* 芙蓉山の楷祖): I.e., Furong Daokai 芙蓉道楷 (1043-1118). This section is based on a passage found at *Jiatai pudeng lu* 嘉泰普燈錄, ZZ.137:82a5-b5.

126 **the ruler** (*kokushu* 國主): The Song Emperor Huizong 徽宗 (r. 1100-1125). Daokai 道楷 was briefly exiled for his defiance of Huizong. An account of the incident can be found at *Jiatai pudeng lu* 嘉泰普燈錄, ZZ.137:82a5ff.

127 **When he made his hermitage at Mount Furong** (*Fuyōzan ni an seshi ni* 芙蓉山に庵せしに): This and the following sentence represent a Japanese translation of the text at *Jiatai pudeng lu* 嘉泰普燈錄, ZZ.137:82b4-5. Daokai's temple was on Lake Furong 芙蓉湖, in his home district of Shandong.

128 **go for meal offerings** (*fusai* 赴齋): I.e., attend the noon meal offered at the home of a lay person.

129 **Once, in addressing the assembly, he said** (*aru toki, shu ni shimesu ni iwaku* あると

DŌGEN'S *SHŌBŌGENZŌ* VOLUME II

[16B:37] {1:191}

夫出家者、爲厭塵勞求脱生死、休心息念、斷絕攀緣、故名出家。豈可以等
閑利養、埋没平生。直須兩頭撤開、中間放下、遇聲遇色、如石上栽華、見
利見名、似眼中著屑。況從無始以來、不是不曾經歷、又不是不知次第、不
過翻頭作尾。止於如此、何須苦苦貪恋。如今不歇、更待何時。所以先聖教
人只要盡却今時。能盡今時、更有何事。若得心中無事、佛祖猶是冤家。一
切世事、自然冷淡、方始那邊相應。

> To go forth from the household means to hate the afflictions and seek
> liberation from birth and death, to rest the mind, stop thoughts, and cut
> off mental objects; therefore, it's called going forth from the house-
> hold. How can we bury our daily lives in frivolous benefits? We should
> straightaway let go of duality and cast aside the middle; when we en-
> counter sounds and encounter sights, they're like flowers planted on a
> rock; when we see profit and see fame, they're like dirt in the eye. After
> all, it's not as if, from the beginningless past, we've never experienced
> this and don't know how it goes; it's nothing more than switching the
> head for the tail.[130] Since this is all it is, why must we so fervently per-
> sist in our craving and longing? If we don't stop it now, what are we
> waiting for? Therefore, the prior sages always had people exhaust the
> present moment; when we exhaust the present moment, what else is
> there?[131] When we've got a mind without concerns, even the buddhas
> and ancestors will be our enemies.[132] Only once we're naturally cool to
> all the concerns of this world, will we accord with over there.[133]

[16B:38]

儞不見、隱山至死不肯見人、趙州至死不肯告人、區担拾橡栗爲食、大梅以
荷葉爲衣、紙衣道者只披紙、玄太上座只著布。石霜置枯木堂與衆坐卧、只
要死了儞心。投子使人辦米、同煮共餐、要得省取儞事。且從上諸聖、有如
此榜樣。若無長處、如何甘得。諸仁者、若也於斯體究、的不虧人。若也不
肯承當、向後深恐費力。

き、衆にしめすにいはく): The following six sections (through 42) represent direct quotation in Chinese from the text found at *Jiatai pudeng lu* 嘉泰普燈錄, ZZ.137:346a5-347a7.

130 **we've never experienced this** (*fuzō kyōryaku* 不曾經歷): The antecedent of "this"
(unexpressed in the original) here is likely the practice of detachment from the objects
of our desires.

switching the head for the tail (*han zu sa bi* 翻頭作尾): An idiomatic expression for
what we might call "getting priorities straight."

131 **exhaust the present moment** (*jinkyaku konji* 盡却今時): A fixed expression found
elsewhere in Chan literature, meaning something like "focus entirely on each moment."

132 **mind without concerns** (*shinchū buji* 心中無事): A common expression for a state
of mind in which there is no felt need to do anything; akin to *kyōkin buji* 胸襟無事
("breast without concerns").

133 **over there** (*nahen* 那邊): A colloquial expression, regularly used in Chan texts in
casual reference to what lies beyond "here" (*shahen* 這邊).

16B. Sustained Practice, Part 2 *Gyōji* 行持 93

Have you not seen that, until his death, Yinshan was unwilling to meet anyone;[134] that, until his death, Zhaozhou was unwilling to tell anyone;[135] that Biandan gathered chestnuts for his food;[136] that Damei used lotus leaves for his clothes;[137] that Practitioner Zhiyi wore only paper;[138] that Senior Seat Xuantai wore only plant fiber?[139] Shixiang's establishing a dried-up tree hall, where he sat and slept with the assembly, was just so you could kill off your mind;[140] Touzi's having people prepare the rice that they cooked and ate together was to enable you to reduce your affairs.[141] Now, the previous sages had models like these; if they didn't have their value, why would they have been willing to do them? Gentlemen, if you personally investigate them, truly you'll be one who lacks nothing; if you're unwilling to accede to them, I deeply fear that henceforth you'll be wasting your efforts.

---

134 **Yinshan** (*Inzan* 隠山): The sobriquet (meaning "hidden in the mountains") of Tanzhou Longshan 潭州龍山 (dates unknown), a follower of Mazu Daoyi 馬祖道一 (709-788), said never to have left his mountain abode.

135 **Zhaozhou** (*Jōshū* 趙州): I.e., Zhaozhou Congshen 趙州從諗 (778-897).

136 **Biandan** (*Hentan* 區担): I.e., Biandan Xiaoliao 區担曉了 (dates unknown), a disciple of the Sixth Ancestor.

137 **Damei** (*Daibai* 大梅): I.e., Damei Fachang 大梅法常 (752-839), a disciple of Mazu Daoyi 馬祖道一. Dōgen discusses him in "Shōbōgenzō gyōji" 正法眼藏行持, part 1.

138 **Practitioner Zhiyi** (*Shie dōsha* 紙衣道者): "Practitioner Paper Robe," the sobriquet of Zhuozhou Kefu 涿州克符 (dates unknown), a follower of Linji Yixuan 臨濟義玄 (d. 866).

139 **Senior Seat Xuantai** (*Gentai jōza* 玄太上座): I.e., Nanyue Xuantai 南嶽玄太 (also written 玄泰, dates unknown), disciple of Shixiang Qingzhu 石霜慶諸, sometimes known as "Plant Fiber Patched Robed Tai" (*Tai funō* 泰布衲). "Senior seat" (*jōza* 上座) is an honorific for a senior monk, used variously for an abbot, a head monk, an elder, a monk of over twenty years standing, etc.

140 **Shixiang** (*Sekisō* 石霜): I.e., Xuantai's master, Shishuang Qingzhu 石霜慶諸 (807-888).

dried-up tree hall (*koboku dō* 枯木堂): I.e., a meditation hall. "Dried-up tree" (or "dead wood") is a common term for meditation, as in the expression "dried-up trees and dead ashes" (*koboku shikai* 枯木死灰); see Supplementary Notes, s.v. "Dried-up tree."

141 **Touzi** (*Tōsu* 投子): I.e., Touzi Datong 投子大同 (819-914).

94 DŌGEN'S *SHŌBŌGENZŌ* VOLUME II

[16B:39]

山僧行業無取、忝主山門。豈可坐費常住、頓忘先聖附囑。今者輒欲略傚古
人爲住持體例。與諸人儀定、更不下山、不赴齋、不發化主。唯將本院莊課
一歳所得、均作三百六十分、日取一分用之、更不隨人添減。可以備飯則作
飯、作飯不足則作粥、作粥不足則作米湯。新到相見茶湯而已、更不煎點。
唯置一茶堂、自去取用。務要省緣、專一辦道。

*This mountain monk, though his practice is not noteworthy, is honored
to serve as head of this monastery. How could I simply sit by while
the monastic property is wasted, suddenly forgetting what prior sages
have entrusted to us. So now, first of all, I want to learn a bit from
the precedents for abbots left by the ancients. Having consulted with
everyone, henceforth, we will not descend the mountain, will not go
for meal offerings, and will not dispatch proselytizing masters.[142] We
shall divide the annual yield of this cloister's fields into three hundred
sixty equal parts and use one part each day, regardless of the increase
or decrease of the residents. If there is enough rice, we'll make rice; if
there's not enough to make rice, we'll make gruel; if there's not enough
to make gruel, we'll make rice water. In greeting new arrivals, we shall
simply offer tea, without providing refreshments. We shall provide a
single tea room, which individuals may use. We should strive to reduce
involvements and single-mindedly pursue the way.*

[16B:40] {1:192}

又況活計具足、風景不疏。華解笑、鳥解啼。木馬長鳴、石牛善走。天外之
青山寡色、耳畔之鳴泉無聲。嶺上猿啼、露湿中霄之月。林間鶴唳、風回清
曉之松。春風起時、枯木龍吟、秋葉凋而寒林華散。玉堦鋪苔蘚之紋、人面
帯煙霞之色。音塵寂爾、消息宛然。一味蕭條、無可趣向。

Moreover,
There's plenty to live on,
The landscape hardly wanting.
The flowers can smile;
The birds can sing.
The wood horse whinnies long;
The stone ox gallops well.
Beyond the heavens, the hues of the blue mountains pale;
Beside our ears, the voice of the singing spring is still.
On the peak, a monkey chatters;
The dew moistens the moon in the firmament.[143]
In the wood, a crane cries;

---

142 **proselytizing masters** (*keshu* 化主): A term used for monks soliciting donations
in the lay community.

143 **The dew moistens the moon in the firmament** (*ro shitsu chūshō shi getsu* 露湿中
霄之月): I.e., the moon is reflected in the dew.

16B. Sustained Practice, Part 2 *Gyōji* 行持 95

The wind circles the pines at daybreak.
When the spring breeze arises, the dragons sing amidst the dried-up trees;[144]
The autumn leaves wither; their blossoms scatter in the cold wood.
The jeweled stairs are patterned with moss;
The faces of the people, wrapped in hazy hues.
The noise is stilled; the situation, just the same.[145]
A single solitude, with nowhere to go.

[16B:41]

山僧今日、向諸人面前説家門。已是不著便、豈可更去陞堂入室、拈槌竪
拂、東喝西棒、張眉努目、如癇病發相似。不唯屈沈上座、況亦辜負先聖。

Today, this mountain monk is talking to you about our house.[146] *Since this doesn't involve expedients, how can we go on to ascend to the hall and enter the room, take up the mallet and hold up the whisk, shout to the east and beat to the west, arch our brows and bulge our eyes like someone having convulsions?*[147] *It would not only be condescending to you senior seats but would also let down the prior sages.*

[16B:42]

儞不見、達磨西來、到少室山下、面壁九年。二祖至於立雪斷臂、可謂、受
艱辛。然而達磨不曽措了一詞、二祖不曽問著一句。還喚達磨作不爲人得
麼、喚二祖做不求師得麼。山僧每至説著古聖做處、便覺無地容身、慚愧後
人軟弱。又況百味珍羞、遞相供養。道我四事具足、方可發心、只恐做手脚
不迭、便是隔生隔世去也。時光似箭、深爲可惜。雖然如是、更在他人從長
相度。山僧也強教儞不得。諸仁者、還見古人偈麼。山田脱粟飯、野菜淡黄
虀、喫則從君喫、不喫任東西。伏惟同道、各自努力。珍重。

Have you not seen that Dharma came from the west, went to the foot of Mount Shaoshi, and faced the wall for nine years? For the Second Ancestor to stand in the snow and cut off his arm, we have to say was

---

144   **the dragons sing amidst the dried-up trees** (*koboku ryūgin* 枯木龍吟): A set phrase evoking the sound of the wind in bare branches; often used in Chan to suggest action within repose, or the power of life within the lifeless; see Supplementary Notes, s.v. "Dried-up tree."

145   **The noise is stilled; the situation, just the same** (*onjin jakuji, shōsoku enzen* 音塵寂爾、消息宛然): Both "the noise" (*onjin* 音塵) and "the situation" (*shōsoku* 消息) can refer especially to "news" or "communication" from the outside world.

146   **our house** (*kamon* 家門): I.e., the tradition of Zen teachings.

147   **Since this doesn't involve expedients** (*i ze fuchakuben* 已是不著便): The exact sense is subject to varied interpretation; perhaps meaning that this is enough. The translation takes *ben* 便 here as equivalent to *hōben* 方便 ("expedient means"; S. *upāya*), the pedagogic devices of the Buddhist teacher.

ascend to the hall and enter the room (*shindō nisshitsu* 陞堂入室): I.e., the rituals of the abbot's public lecture in the dharma hall (*jōdō* 上堂) and the student's private interview in the master's quarters. The remaining actions in this sentence are all common in descriptions of the teaching techniques of the Chan masters.

DŌGEN'S *SHŌBŌGENZŌ* VOLUME II

suffering pain; yet Dharma never expressed a single word, and the Second Ancestor never asked for a single line. Can we then say that Dharma didn't act for the sake of others? Or say the Second Ancestor didn't seek out a teacher? Whenever this mountain monk talks about what the sages of old did, I feel there's no place for me here and feel ashamed of our weakness as a people of a later generation. Worse still, we offer each other delicacies of the hundred flavors. We say that only once we're provided with the four things, can we bring forth the mind [of bodhi].[148] But I'm afraid that this trick won't work and will go on from lifetime to lifetime and generation to generation.[149] Time is like an arrow; we should deeply regret [its passing]. While this is so, there will be others who consider this at greater length; as for this mountain monk, I can't force the teachings on you.[150] Have you gentlemen seen the gāthā by an ancient?[151]

> Unpolished rice from the mountain fields,
> Pale yellow pickle of wild vegetables:
> If they'll eat this, they can help themselves;
> If not, they can go where they like.

I sincerely hope that my fellow wayfarers will each strive hard. Please take care of yourselves.

---

148   **the four things** (*shiji* 四事): Although there are several lists of the "four things," here, likely the four requisites of the monk: food, clothing, bedding, and medicine.

149   **this trick won't work** (*soshukyaku futetsu* 做手脚不迭): The expression *soshukyaku* ("make with the hands and feet") is often read here as meaning "behavior"; the translation takes it in the idiomatic sense "scam," "fraud," etc.

150   **there will be others who consider this at greater length** (*kō zai tanin jūchō sōdo* 更在他人從長相度): A tentative translation of a phrase variously interpreted. Many take the term *sōdo* 相度 (rendered here "to consider") as "to deliver" (or "to be delivered"), and the term *jūchō* 從長 ("at length") in the sense "according to strength" (i.e., "skillfully"); hence, e.g., "others may deliver [you] (or be delivered) in accord with their strengths." (The punctuation in Kawamura's text after *jū* 從 must be a typo; and the reading that takes the following *sansō* 山僧 "mountain monk" as the object of *sōdo* 相度 seems unlikely.

151   **gāthā by an ancient** (*kojin ge* 古人偈): Reflecting the words of Niutou Wei 牛頭微 (dates unknown), dharma heir of Touzi Datong 投子大同, in a conversation found in the *Jingde chuandeng lu* 景德傳燈錄 (T.2076.51:324c13-16):

僧問、如何是和尚家風。師曰、山畬粟米飯、野菜澹黃虀。僧曰、忽遇上客來又作麽生。師曰、喫即從君喫、不喫任東西。

A monk asked, "What is the Reverend's house style?"
The Master said, "Unpolished rice from the mountain fields, yellowed pickle of wild vegetables."
The monk said, "What do you do when honored guests suddenly arrive?"
The Master said, "If they'll eat it, they can help themselves; if not, they can go where they like."

16B. Sustained Practice, Part 2 *Gyōji* 行持 97

[16B:43] {1:194}

これすなはち祖宗單傳の骨髓なり。高祖の行持おほしといへども、しばら
くこの一枚を擧するなり。いまわれらが晩學なる、芙蓉山に修練せし行
持、したひ參學すべし、それすなはち祇園の正儀なり。

This is the bones and marrow uniquely transmitted by the ancestors.
While there are many instances of the sustained practice of the Eminent Ancestor, here I have offered just this one. Now, we who are later
students should admire and study the sustained practice undertaken on
Mount Furong.[152] It is the proper deportment of the Jeta Grove.[153]

* * * * *

[16B:44] {1:195}

洪州江西開元寺大寂禪師、諱道一、漢州十方縣人なり。南嶽に參侍するこ
と十餘載なり。あるとき、郷里にかへらんとして、半路にいたる。半路よ
りかへりて焼香・禮拜するに、南嶽。ちなみに偈をつくりて馬祖にたまふ
にいはく、勸君莫歸郷、歸郷道不行。竝舍老婆子、説汝舊時名。

Chan Master Daji, of the Kaiyuan Monastery in Jiangxi in Hongzhou,
named Daoyi, was from the Shifang District of Hanzhou.[154] He attended
Nanyue for more than ten years. Once, on his way back to his home village, he had reached halfway when he turned back.[155] When he burned

---

152 **the sustained practice undertaken on Mount Furong** (*Fuyōzan ni shuren seshi
gyōji* 芙蓉山に修練せし行持): Some versions of the text here read "the sustained practice
undertaken by the Eminent Ancestor Furong on Mount Furong" (*Fuyō kōso no Fuyōsan ni
shuren seshi gyōgi* 芙蓉高祖の芙蓉山に修練せし行儀).

153 **It is the proper deportment of the Jeta Grove** (*sore sunawachi Gion no shōgi
nari* それすなはち祇園の正儀なり): I.e., the orthodox practice of Buddha Śākyamuni
at the famous Jetavana Monastery, where the Buddha is said to have spent twenty-five
rainy season retreats. The antecedent of "it" (*sore* それ) here is ambiguous: it may be the
"continuous practice on Mount Furong," the "admiration and study of later students,"
or Daokai's sermon as a whole, which is preserved as a separate text entitled *Proper
Deportment of Jeta Grove* (*Qiyuan chengyi* 祇園正儀, ZZ.111:169a1-170a15).

154 **Chan Master Daji, of the Kaiyuan Monastery in Jiangxi in Hongzhou** (*Kōshū
Kōzei Kaigenji Daijaku zenji* 洪州江西開元寺大寂禪師): I.e., Mazu Daoyi 馬祖道一
(709–788), famed disciple of Nanyue Huairang 南岳懷讓.

Hanzhou (*Kanshū* 漢州): In present-day Sichuan; "Shifang" 十方 is also written 什邡.

155 **Once, on his way back to his home village** (*aru toki, kyōri ni kaeran toshite* ある
とき、郷里にかへらんとして): Dōgen's source for this anecdote is unknown. A simi-
lar story appears in the *Wujia zhengzong zan* 五家正宗贊 (ZZ.135:907b15-17), in which
Mazu does return to his home, is treated with contempt by the village women, and himself
composes a slightly different version of the poem that Dōgen attributes here to Nanyue:

勸君莫還郷。還郷道不成。溪邊老婆子。喚我舊時名。

I recommend that you not return home;
If you do, the way won't be attained.

incense and paid obeisance, Nanyue composed a gāthā and presented it to Mazu:

I recommend that you not return home;
If you return home, the way won't be practiced.
The old women next door
Will call you by your old name.

[16B:45]

この法語をたまふに、馬祖、うやまひたまはりて、ちかひていはく、われ生生にも漢州にむかはざらん、と誓願して、漢州にむかひて一歩をあゆまず。江西に一住して、十方を往来せしむ。わづかに即心是佛を道得するほかに、さらに一語の爲人なし。しかありといへども、南嶽の嫡嗣なり、人天の命脈なり。

When presented with these dharma words, Mazu accepted them respectfully and vowed, "In any life, I shall never go toward Hanzhou." Having made this vow, he never took a single step toward Hanzhou. Settling permanently in Jiangxi, he let the monks of the ten directions come to him there. Apart from saying "*this mind itself is the buddha,*" he had not a single word of benefit for others.[156] Nevertheless, he was the legitimate heir of Nanyue and a vital artery for humans and devas.

[16B:46]

いかなるかこれ莫歸郷。莫歸郷とはいかにあるべきぞ。東西南北の歸去來、ただこれ自己の倒起なり。まことに歸郷道不行なり。道不行なる歸郷なりとや行持する、歸郷にあらざるとや行持する。歸郷なにによりてか道不行なる。不行にさへらるとやせん、自己にさへらるとやせん。並舍老婆子は、説汝舊時名なりとはいはざるなり。並舍老婆子、説汝舊時名なり、といふ道得なり。南嶽いかにしてかこの道得ある、江西いかにしてかこの法語をうる。その道理は、われ向南行するときは、大地おなじく向南行するなり。餘方もまたしかあるべし。須彌・大海を量として、しかあらずと疑殆し、日月・星辰に格量して、猶滞するは、少見なり。

What is his "not returning home"?[157] What would it mean for him "not to return home"? Returning to and from north, south, east, and west is just [Mazu] himself falling down and getting up. Truly this is, "*if you re-*

    The local old women
    Call me by my old name.

156 **"this mind itself is the buddha"** (*soku shin ze butsu* 即心是佛): Or "this very mind is the buddha." Cited in Dōgen's *shinji Shōbōgenzō* 眞字正法眼藏 (DZZ.5:266, case 278) and many other Zen sources; see Supplementary Notes.

157 **What is his "not returning home"?** (*ikanaru ka kore maku kikyō* いかなるかこれ莫歸郷): The translation here and below assumes that, though not explicit, Dōgen is talking throughout about Mazu.

16B. Sustained Practice, Part 2 *Gyōji* 行持 99

turn home, the way won't be practiced."[158] Does he engage in a sustained practice such that "the way won't be practiced" is his "returning home," or does he engage in a sustained practice such that it is his "not returning home"? Why is "returning home" "the way won't be practiced"? Is it obstructed by "won't be practiced"?[159] Is it obstructed by [Mazu] himself? "The old women next door" is not saying they are "calling you by your old name": it is the saying, "Old Women Next Door" is "calling you by your old name."[160] Why did Nanyue have this saying? Why did Jiangxi get these dharma words? The principle here is, when I head south, the whole earth also heads south. The other directions must be the same. It is a small view that doubts this is so, taking Sumeru and the great oceans as the measure, or hesitates over this, taking the sun, moon, and stars as the scale.[161]

* * * * *

[16B:47] {1:196}

第三十二祖大満禪師は、黄梅人なり。俗姓は周氏なり、母の姓を稱なり。師は無父而生なり。たとへば、李老君のごとし。七歳傳法よりのち、七十有四にいたるまで、佛祖正法眼藏、よくこれを住持し、ひそかに衣法を慧能行者に附属する、不群の行持なり。衣法を神秀にしらせず、慧能に附属するゆえに、正法の壽命不斷なるなり。

The Thirty-second Ancestor, Chan Master Daman, was from Huangmei.[162] His secular surname was Zhou, which was his mother's family name. The Master was born without a father, like Lord Li Lao.[163] Following his transmission of the dharma at age seven until the age of seventy-four, he upheld the treasury of the true dharma eye of the buddhas

---

158 **Truly this is, "if you return home, the way won't be practiced"** (*makoto ni kikyō dō fugyō nari* まことに歸郷道不行なり): While Dōgen is quoting Nanyue's poem here, the sentence could also be read, "Truly, the way that returns home is not practiced."

159 **Is it obstructed by "won't be practiced"?** (*fugyō ni saeraru to ya sen* 不行にさへらるとやせん): The passive construction *ni saeraru* ("is obstructed by") here is probably best taken in the sense "is identified with," "is defined by," a usage common throughout Dōgen's writing.

160 **it is the saying, "Old Women Next Door" is "calling you by your old name"** (*heisha rōba su, setsu nyo kyūji myō nari, to iu dōtoku nari* 迸舍老婆子、説汝舊時名なり、といふ道得なり): I.e., "your old name is 'Old Women Next Door.'"

161 **taking Sumeru and the great oceans as the measure** (*Shumi daikai o ryō toshite* 須彌大海を量として): I.e. on the basis of the Buddhist world system, in which Mount Sumeru stands at the center surrounded by a series of oceans.

162 **Chan Master Daman** (*Daiman zenji* 大満禪師): I.e., the Fifth Ancestor, Huangmei Hongren 黄梅弘忍, thirty-second in descent from Buddha Śākyamuni.

163 **Lord Li Lao** (*Li Lao kun* 李老君): I.e., Laozi 老師, who is traditionally said to have been conceived when his mother saw a shooting star and to have remained in the womb for sixty-two (or, in some accounts, more) years.

100 DŌGEN'S *SHŌBŌGENZŌ* VOLUME II

and ancestors and secretly entrusted the robe and dharma to the postulant Huineng — an outstanding example of sustained practice.[164] Because, without informing Shenxiu of the robe and dharma, he entrusted them to Huineng, the lifespan of the true dharma was not cut off.[165]

* * * * *

[16B:48]

先師天童和尚は、越上人事なり。十九歳にして、教學をすてて參學するに、七旬におよむでなほ不退なり。嘉定の皇帝より紫衣・師號をたまはるといへども、つひにうけず、修表辭謝す。十方の雲衲、ともに崇重す、遠近の有識、ともに隨喜するなり。皇帝、大悦して御茶をたまふ。しれるものは奇代の事と讚歡す。まことにこれ眞實の行持なり。そのゆえは、愛名は犯禁よりもあし、犯禁は一時の非なり、愛名は一生の累なり。おろかにしてすてざることなかれ、くらくしてうくることなかれ。うけざるは行持なり、すつるは行持なり。六代の祖師、おのおの師號あるは、みな滅後の勅諡なり、在世の愛名にあらず。

My former master, Reverend Tiantong, was from Yue.[166] At the age of nineteen, he abandoned doctrinal learning and undertook [Chan] study, from which he never regressed even into his seventh decade.[167] Although he was granted the purple robe and the title of master by the Jiading Emperor, in the end he did not accept and submitted a memorial formally declining them.[168] Those robed in clouds in the ten directions all respected him for this; those of learning near and far all rejoiced.[169] The Emperor was delighted and presented him with his own tea. Those who knew of it praised it as a rare event. Truly, this was authentic sustained practice. The reason is that loving fame is even worse than violating the prohibitions: violating the prohibitions is a one-time error; loving fame

---

164 **transmission of the dharma at age seven** (*shichisai denbō* 七歳傳法): Dōgen recounts Hongren's meeting with the Fourth Ancestor in "Shōbōgenzō busshō" 正法眼藏佛性.

the postulant Huineng (*Enō anja* 慧能行者): I.e., The Sixth Ancestor, Huineng 慧能, who was a lay postulant in Hongren's monastery at the time he was bequeathed Bodhidharma's robe.

165 **Shenxiu** (*Jinshū* 神秀): The head seat of Hongren's monastery, who, according to legend, sought to succeed the Fifth Ancestor, but whose lineage died out.

166 **My former master, Reverend Tiantong** (*senshi Tendō oshō* 先師天童和尚): I.e., Tiantong Rujing 天童如淨 (1162-1227). Yue 越 refers to the eastern area of present-day Zhejiang province.

167 **his seventh decade** (*shichijun* 七旬): I.e., "his sixties."

168 **Jiading Emperor** (*Katei no kōtei* 嘉定の皇帝): I.e., the Emperor Ningzong 寧宗 (r. 1194-1224), who used Jiading 嘉定 as an era name through much of his reign.

169 **robed in clouds** (*unnō* 雲衲): A literary term for monks.

16B. Sustained Practice, Part 2 *Gyōji* 行持

is lifelong trouble.[170] Do not stupidly fail to abandon it; do not ignorantly accept it. Not accepting it is sustained practice; abandoning it is sustained practice. That the six generations of ancestral masters each had the title of master was in every case due to posthumous names granted by the emperor following their deaths, not due to their love of fame while they were in the world.[171]

[16B:49]

しかあれば、すみやかに生死の愛名をすてて、佛祖の行持をねがふべし。貪愛して禽獣にひとしきことなかれ。おもからざる吾我をむさぼり愛するは、禽獣もそのおもひあり、畜生もそのこころあり。名利をすつることは、人天もまれなりとするところ、佛祖、いまだすてざるはなし。あるがいはく、衆生利益のために貪名愛利す、といふ。おほきなる邪説なり、附佛法の外道なり、謗正法の魔儻なり。なんぢがいふがごとくならば、不貪名利の佛祖は利生なきか。わらふべし、わらふべし。又、不貪の利生あり、いかん。又そこばくの利生あることを學せず、利生にあらざるを利生と稱する、魔類なるべし。なんぢに利益せられん衆生は、堕獄の種類なるべし。一生のくらきことをかなしむべし、愚蒙を利生に稱することなかれ。しかあれば、師號を恩賜すとも上表辞謝する、古來の勝蹰なり、晩學の參究なるべし。まのあたり先師をみる、これ人にあふなり。

Hence, we should quickly abandon our love of fame in [the realm of] birth and death, and seek the sustained practice of the buddhas and ancestors. Do not be the same as the birds and beasts, craving and loving. To crave and love one's own insignificant self — the birds and beasts have such thoughts; the animals have such feelings. To abandon fame and profit, something considered rare even among humans and devas — among the buddhas and ancestors, there are none who have not abandoned them. There are those who say, "It is for the benefit of living beings that we crave fame and love profit." This is a major heresy; it is an other path attached to the buddha dharma; it is the minions of Māra who slander the true dharma.[172] If it is as you say, do the buddhas and ancestors, who do not crave fame and profit, have no benefit for living

---

170 **lifelong trouble** (*isshō no rui* 一生の累): Or, perhaps, "the accumulation of a lifetime."

171 **six generations of ancestral masters** (*rokudai no soshi* 六代の祖師): I.e., the first six ancestors in China, from Bodhidharma through Huineng 慧能.

172 **other path attached to the buddha dharma** (*fu buppō no gedō* 附佛法の外道): I.e., a non-Buddhist teaching within Buddhism, a term appearing several times in the *Shōbōgenzō*; traditionally used especially in critical reference to the Vātsīputrīya, a school of early Buddhism said to have held to the reality of the self and to have followed a more lenient set of precepts. (See *Mohe zhiguan* 摩訶止觀, T.1911.46:132b2-3, b22-c-5.)

minions of Māra (*matō* 魔黨): Also written 魔儻. Followers of Māra, the Evil One (S. *pāpīyān*), lord of the sixth heaven of the realm of desire (S. *kāma-loka*), who seeks to obstruct Buddhist awakening; a common pejorative in Dōgen's writings.

102   DŌGEN'S *SHŌBŌGENZŌ* VOLUME II

beings? Laughable! Laughable! Again, there is benefiting living beings in non-craving — what about that?[173] Again, those who do not study how many kinds of benefiting human beings there are and claim that what is not benefiting living beings is benefiting living beings — these must be Māra types. The living beings who benefit from you must be types who will fall into hell. It is pitiful that you spend your whole life in the dark. Do not call your stupid ignorance "benefiting living beings." Thus, though granted the title of master, to submit a memorial formally declining it is a splendid precedent from the past, and something to be thoroughly investigated by later students. To have seen my former master with my own eyes — this was to meet a person.

[16B:50] {1:197}

先師は、十九歳より、離郷尋師、辦道功夫すること、六十五載にいたりて、なほ不退不轉なり。帝者に親近せず、帝者にみえず、丞相と親厚ならず、官員と親厚ならず。紫衣・師號を表辭するのみにあらず、一生、まだらなる袈裟を搭せず、よのつねに上堂・入室、みなくろき袈裟・褊子をもちいる。

My former master never regressed from his concentrated effort in pursuit of the way, from the age of nineteen, when he left his hometown to seek a master, till he reached the age of sixty-five. He did not approach the emperor; he was not seen by the emperor; he was not close to the prime minister; he was not close to officials. Not only did he decline a purple robe and the title of master, throughout his life he never donned a patterned *kāṣāya* but, in both ascending to the hall and entering the room, he always used a black *kāṣāya* and robe.[174]

[16B:51]

褊子を教訓するにいはく、參禪學道は、第一有道心、これ學道のはじめなり。いま二百來年、祖師道すたれたり、かなしむべし。いはんや一句を道得せる皮袋すくなし。某甲、そのかみ徑山に掛錫するに、光佛照、そのときの粥飯頭なりき。上堂していはく、佛法禪道、かならずしも他人の言句をもとむべからず、ただ各自理會。かくのごとくいひて、僧堂裏都不管なりき。雲來兄弟也都不管なり、祇管與官客相見追尋するのみなり。佛照、ことに佛法の機關をしらず、ひとへに貪名愛利のみなり。佛法、もし各自理會ならば、いかでか尋師訪道の老古錐あらん。眞箇是光佛照、不曽參禪也。いま諸方長老無道心なる、ただ光佛照箇兒子也。佛法那得他手裏有、

---

173 **there is benefiting living beings in non-craving** (*futon no rishō ari* 不貪の利生あり): Or, perhaps, "non-craving has benefits for living beings."

174 **ascending to the hall and entering the room** (*jōdō nisshitsu* 上堂・入室): See above, section 41. The term *jōdō* 上堂, translated rather literally here, refers to the abbot's formal teaching in the dharma hall to the assembled community; rendered below as "convocation."

kāṣāya and robe (*kesa tossu* 袈裟・褊子): I.e., the outer vestment and habit, or *jikitotsu* 直裰.

16B. Sustained Practice, Part 2 *Gyōji* 行持 103

可惜可惜。かくのごとくいふに、佛照兒孫、おほくきくものあれど、うらみず。

In instructing the patch-robed, he said,[175]

In practicing meditation and studying the way, the first thing is to have the mind of the way: this is the beginning of learning the way. How sad that now for the last two hundred years the way of the ancestral masters has been abandoned. Not to mention that there are few skin bags who have said a single line.[176] In the past, when I hung my staff at Mount Jing, Guang Fozhao was head of meals at the time.[177] In his convocations, he would say, "In the way of Chan in the buddha dharma, we should not seek it in the words of others; it is each of us understanding for ourselves." Saying this, *he took no interest at all in the monks' hall, no interest at all in the brothers arriving in clouds*; he just *chased after interviews with official visitors*.[178] Fozhao especially knew nothing about the workings of the buddha dharma and only craved fame and loved profit. If the buddha dharma were "each of us understanding for ourselves," how could there be venerable old awls who sought out teachers and inquired about the way?[179] *Truly this Guang Fozhao never practiced Chan*. The elders in all quarters now who lack the mind of the way are just the children of Guang Fozhao.[180] *How could the buddha dharma rest in their hands? Deplorable! Deplorable!*

When he said this, though there were many descendants of Fozhao listening to him, they did not resent it.

---

175 **In instructing the patch-robed** (*nossu o kyōkun suru ni* 衲子を教訓するに): I.e., "in teaching his monks." What follows here is mostly in Japanese; the source is unknown.

176 **skin bags who have said a single line** (*ikku o dōtoku seru hitai* 一句を道得せる皮袋): I.e., monks with anything significant to say. "Skin bag" (*hitai* 皮袋) is a common term in Chan literature for "person" or "human being," especially used in reference to monks. For the meaning of the metaphor and other examples of its usage, see Supplementary Notes, s.v. "Bag of skin."

177 **when I hung my staff at Mount Jing** (*Kinzan ni kashaku suru ni* 徑山に掛錫するに): I.e., when Rujing was in residence at Wanshou Monastery 萬壽寺 at Mount Jing, in Zhejiang.

Guang Fozhao (*Kō Busshō* 光佛照): I.e., Zhuoan Deguang 拙菴德光 (1121-1203), disciple of Dahui Zonggao 大慧宗杲; he received the title Chan Master Fozhao 佛照禪師 from the Song Emperor Xiaozong 孝宗 (r. 1189-1194). "Head of meals" (*shukuhantō* 粥飯頭) refers to an abbot.

178 **Brothers arriving in clouds** (*unrai kyōdai* 雲來兄弟): I.e., the many monks that came to the monastery.

179 **venerable old awls** (*rō kosui* 老古錐): A common term for Chan masters.

180 **elders in all quarters** (*shohō chōrō* 諸方長老): I.e., abbots of monasteries throughout the land.

104 DŌGEN'S *SHŌBŌGENZŌ* VOLUME II

[16B:52] {1:198}

又いはく、參禪者身心脱落也、不用燒香・禮拜・念佛・修懺・看經、祇管坐始得。

   Again, he said, "*Studying Chan is body and mind sloughed off.*[181] *There is no need to burn incense, make bows, recollect the buddha, practice repentance, or read the sūtras. You'll only get it when you just sit.*"

[16B:53]

まことに、いま大宋國の諸方に、參禪に名字をかけ、祖宗の遠孫と稱する皮袋、ただ一、二百のみにあらず、稻麻竹葦なりとも、打坐を打坐に勸誘するともがら、たえて風聞せざるなり。ただ四海五湖のあひだ、先師天童のみなり。諸方もおなじく天童をほむ、天童、諸方をほめず。又すべて天童をしらざる大刹の主もあり。これは中華にむまれたりといへども、禽獸の流類ならん。參ずべきを參ぜず、いたづらに光陰を蹉過するがゆえに。あはれむべし、天童をしらざるやからは、胡説乱道をかまびすしくするを、佛祖の家風と錯認せり。

   Truly, in all quarters of the Land of the Great Song now, the skin bags who identify themselves as studying Chan and call themselves the distant descendants of the ancestors are not just one or two hundred but like rice, hemp, bamboo, and reeds; yet, of any who encourage sitting as sitting, we hear nothing.[182] Within the four seas and five lakes, it is only my former master, Tiantong.[183] Those in all quarters praised Tiantong; Tiantong did not praise those in all quarters. Again, there are heads of great monasteries who know nothing of Tiantong. Though born in China, they are akin to birds and beasts; for they pass the years and months in vain, not studying what should be studied. How pitiful that fellows who do not know of Tiantong mistake the noise of reckless talk and wild words for the house style of the buddhas and ancestors.

[16B:54] {1:199}

先師、よのつねに普説す、われ十九歳よりこのかた、あまねく諸方の叢林をふるに、爲人師なし。十九載よりこのかた、一日一夜も不礙蒲團の日夜あらず。某甲、未住院よりこのかた、郷人とものがたりせず、光陰、をし

---

181 **"Studying Chan is body and mind sloughed off"** (*sanzen sha shinjin datsuraku ya* 參禪者身心脱落也): A saying slightly variant versions of which Dōgen attributes to Rujing in several places; see Supplementary Notes, s.v. "Body and mind sloughed off."

182 **rice, hemp, bamboo, and reeds** (*tō ma chiku i* 稻麻竹葦): I.e., dense and profuse; a simile from Kumārajīva's translation of the *Lotus Sūtra* (*Miaofa lianhua jing* 妙法蓮華經, T.262.9:6a13); see Supplementary Notes.

encourage sitting as sitting (*taza o taza ni kanyū suru* 打坐を打坐に勸誘する): Or, perhaps, "encourage sitting for sitting."

183 **the four seas and five lakes** (*shikai goko* 四海五湖): I.e., all of China; a fixed expression, sometimes in reverse order. The four seas are the oceans in the four directions; the five lakes are variously listed.

16B. Sustained Practice, Part 2 *Gyōji* 行持

きによりてなり。掛錫の處在にあり、庵裏・寮舍、すべていりてみること
なし。いはんや游山翫水に功夫をつひやさんや。雲堂公界の坐禪のほか、
あるいは閣上、あるいは屛處をもとめて、獨子ゆきて、穩便のところに坐
禪す。つねに袖裏に蒲團をたづさへて、あるいは巖下にも坐禪す。つねに
おもひき、金剛座を坐破せんと。これ、もとむる所期なり。臀肉の爛壞す
るときどきもありき。このとき、いよいよ坐禪をこのむ。某甲今年六十五
載、老骨頭懶、不會坐禪なれども、十方兄弟をあはれむによりて、住持山
門、曉諭方來、爲衆傳道なり。諸方長老、那裏有什麼佛法なるゆえに。

In his public sermons, my former master regularly said,

Ever since the age of nineteen, I have passed through the groves in all
quarters without finding masters who benefit people.[184] Ever since the
age of nineteen, day and night, there has been no day or night I have
not pressed down the rush cushion.[185] Even since before I was abbot
of a cloister, I have not chatted with the local people; for the years and
months are precious. Wherever I hung my staff, I never visited the
hermitages or monks' dormitories, much less spent time and effort in
rambling in the mountains and sporting by the waters.[186] Besides the
seated meditation in the common area of the cloud hall, I sought out
upper floors or secluded places, where I went alone to practice seated
meditation in peace and quiet.[187] Always carrying a rush cushion in my
sleeve, I sometimes sat in meditation beneath a cliff. I always thought
to wear down the vajra seat; this is what I wanted.[188] There were times
when my buttocks festered; at such times, I enjoyed seated meditation
even more. *This year, I am sixty-five; my bones are old, my head is
slow, and I cannot do seated meditation.* Still, from concern for the
brothers in the ten directions, *I assumed the abbotship of the monastery, to instruct the new arrivals and transmit the way for the sake of
the assembly; for what buddha dharma is there in the places of the
elders in all quarters?*

---

184   **groves in all quarters** (*shohō no sōrin* 諸方の叢林): I.e. the monasteries throughout China.

185   **I have not pressed down the rush cushion** (*fuge futon* 不礙蒲團): I.e., "I have
not occupied my meditation cushion." The rendering "press down" (or "cover") for *ge*
礙 ("to obstruct") here is uncertain; its use with *futon* 蒲團 is unusual but also occurs in
Dōgen's *Bendō hō* 辦道法 (DZZ.6:30).

186   **rambling in the mountains and sporting by the waters** (*yusan gansui* 游山翫水):
A fixed expression for amusing oneself on outings in the countryside.

187   **cloud hall** (*undō* 雲堂): I.e., the saṃgha hall (*sōdō* 僧堂).

188   **to wear down the vajra seat** (*kongō za o zaha sen* 金剛座を坐破せん): To "sit till
one breaks" (*zaha* 坐破) one's meditation seat; the "vajra seat" (*kongō za* 金剛座) refers
to the seat where Buddha Śākyamuni attained awakening under the bodhi tree.

106   DŌGEN'S *SHŌBŌGENZŌ* VOLUME II

[16B:55]
かくのごとく上堂し、かくのごとく普説するなり。又、諸方の雲水の人事
の産をうけず。

This is how he held convocations; this is how he gave public sermons. Furthermore, he did not accept the personal gifts of the monks from all quarters.[189]

[16B:56]
趙提擧は、嘉定聖主の胤孫なり。知明州軍州事、管内勸農使なり。先師を
請して、州府につきて陞座せしむるに、銀子壱萬鋌を布施す。

Minister Zhao was a descendant of the sage ruler of Jiading.[190] He was supervisor of the commandery and prefecture of Mingzhou and commissioner for the promotion of agriculture within the jurisdiction.[191] He invited my former master to the prefectural headquarters, had him mount the seat, and presented him with ten thousand ingots of silver.[192]

[16B:57]
先師、陞座了に、提擧にむかふて謝していはく、某甲依例出山陞座、開演
正法眼藏涅槃妙心、謹以薦福先公冥府。但是銀子、不敢拜領。僧家不要這
般物子、千萬賜恩、依舊拜還。

After my former master had finished his "mounting the seat" sermon, he addressed the Minister and declined, saying, "*Following custom, I have left the mountain and mounted the seat to propound the treasury of the true dharma eye, the wondrous mind of nirvāṇa.[193] I respectfully dedicate the merit to your late father in the court of darkness.[194] However, this silver, I dare not accept. A monk has no use for such things. Appreciating your thousand myriad kindnesses, I respectfully return this as it was.*"

---

189   **personal gifts of the monks from all quarters** (*shohō no unsui no jinji no san* 諸方の雲水の人事の産): I.e., presents for the abbot brought by newly arrived itinerant monks (*unsui* 雲水).

190   **Minister Zhao** (*Chō teiko* 趙提擧): Otherwise unknown. "The sage ruler of Jiading" (*Katei seishu* 嘉定聖主) refers to the Emperor Ningzong 寧宗; the Jiading era of his reign covered the years 1208-1224).

191   **Mingzhou** (*Meishū* 明州): Corresponding to present-day Zhejiang.

192   **mount the seat** (*shinzo* 陞座): I.e., give a formal instruction from the seat on the altar of a dharma hall.

193   **he addressed the Minister and declined, saying** (*teiko ni mukaute sha shite iwaku* 提擧にむかふて謝していはく): The following conversation between Zhao and Rujing is given almost entirely in Chinese, as if copied from the source Dōgen will identify in section 62, below.

194   **"court of darkness"** (*meifu* 冥府): I.e., the realm of the dead.

16B. Sustained Practice, Part 2 *Gyōji* 行持   107

[16B:58] {1:200}

提擧いはく、和尚、下官忝以皇帝陛下親族、到處且貴、寶貝見多。今以先
父冥福之日、欲資冥府、和尚如何不納。今日多幸、大慈大悲、卒留少襯。
先師曰、提擧臺命且巖、不敢遜謝。只有道理、某甲陞座説法、提擧聡聽得
否。提擧曰、下官只聽歡喜。

The Minister said, *"Your Reverence, this humble official, I am ashamed
to say, as a relative of his imperial majesty, is respected wherever he
goes and has wealth obviously great. Now, on a day for my late father's blessings in the dark realm, I wish to provide for him in the
court of darkness.*[195] *Why will your reverence not accept? Today, I am
exceedingly fortunate. In your great pity and great compassion, please
just keep my meager donation."*[196]

*My former master said, "The minister's order is strict, and I dare not
refuse. Still, I do have a justification. When I mounted the seat and
preached the dharma, could the minister clearly hear me or not?"*

The Minister said, "This humble official heard you with joy."

[16B:59]

先師いはく、提擧聡明、照鑑山語、不勝皇恐。更望臺臨、鈞候萬福。山僧
陞座時、説得甚麼法、試道看。若道得、拜領銀子壹萬鋌。若道不得、便府
使收銀子。提擧起向先師云、即辰伏惟、和尚法候、動止萬福。

*My former master said, "I am truly in awe that the minister is so intelligent
he has thoroughly understood this mountain monk's words. And I hope
that the esteemed condition of he who has so honored us with his exalted
presence may enjoy myriad blessings. When this mountain monk mounted the seat, what was the dharma he preached? Try to say it. If you can say
it, I shall respectfully accept the ten thousand ingots of silver; if you cannot say it, then have the prefectural representatives take back the silver."*

*The Minister rose and said to my former master, "With all respect,
today the dharma condition and deportment of your reverence were
manifoldly blessed."*

[16B:60] {1:201}

先師いはく、這箇是擧來底、那箇是聽得底。提擧擬議。

My former master said, *"This is what I presented. What was it that you heard?"*

The Minister hesitated.

---

195 **"I wish to provide for him in the court of darkness"** (*yoku shi meifu* 欲資冥府):
Zhao's argument is based on the common belief that the merit derived from making a
donation to the Buddhist clergy can be dedicated to the welfare of one's ancestors in the
other world; hence, it is an act of compassion for Rujing to accept the donation.

196 **"my meager donation"** (*shōshin* 少襯): The glyph *shin* 襯 here is a substitute for
shin 嚫, from *tasshin* 達嚫, the transliteration of the Sanskrit *dakṣiṇā* ("donation").

108 DŌGEN'S *SHŌBŌGENZŌ* VOLUME II

[16B:61]

先師いはく、先公冥福圓成、襯施は且待先公臺判。

My former master said, *"The blessings for your late father in the dark realm are complete. The matter of the donation, let us leave to the honored judgment of your late father."*

[16B:62]

かくのごとくいひて、すなはち請暇するに、提擧いはく、未恨不領、且喜見師。かくのごとくいひて先師をおくる。浙東・浙西の道俗、おほく讃歎す。このこと、平侍者が日録にあり。

When, having said this, he excused himself, the Minister said, *"I do not regret that I have not understood, but in any case, I am delighted to have met the Master."*

So saying, he saw off my former master. Both east of the Zhe and west of the Zhe, many clerics and laypersons praised this.[197] It is in the daily log of the Acolyte Ping.[198]

[16B:63]

平侍者いはく、這老和尚、不可得人、那裏容易得見。

The Acolyte Ping said, *"This old reverend is the sort of person you don't find. Where could you easily meet him?"*

[16B:64]

たれか諸方にうけざる人あらん、壱萬鋌の銀子。ふるき人のいはく、金銀珠玉、これをみんこと糞土のごとくみるべし。たとひ金銀のごとくみるとも、不受ならんは衲子の風なり。先師にこの事あり、餘人にこのことなし。先師つねにいはく、三百年よりこのかた、わがごとくなる知識いまだいでず、諸人、審細に辨道功夫すべし。

Ten thousand ingots of silver — is there anyone anywhere who would not accept it? An ancient has said, "Gold and silver, pearls and gems — we should see them as dung and dirt."[199] Even if we see them as gold and silver, not to accept them is the custom of the patch-robed. My former master kept this; others do not. My former master always said, "For the last three hundred years, there has not appeared a wise friend like me. You should all carefully make concentrated effort to pursue the way."

---

197 **east of the Zhe and west of the Zhe** (*Settō Sessei* 浙東・浙西): I.e., throughout present-day Zhejiang.

198 **Acolyte Ping** (*Hei jisha* 平侍者): Likely a reference to Rujing's attendant Guangping 廣平, whose name appears in Dōgen's *Busso shōden bosatsu kai sahō* 佛祖正傳菩薩戒作法 (DZZ.6:188).

199 **An ancient** (*furuki hito* ふるき人): It is not clear whether Dōgen had a specific source in mind for this saying, given here in Japanese.

16B. Sustained Practice, Part 2 *Gyōji* 行持

[16B:65]

先師の會に、西蜀の綿州人にて、道昇とてありしは、道家流なり。徒黨五
人、ともにちかうていはく、われら一生に佛祖の大道を辦取すべし、さら
に郷土にかへるべからず。先師、ことに隨喜して經行・道業、ともに衆僧
と一如ならしむ。その排列のときは、比丘尼のしもに排立す、奇代の勝躅
なり。又、福州の僧、その名善如、ちかひていはく、善如、平生さらに一
歩をみなみにむかひてうつすべからず、もはら佛祖の大道を參ずべし。先
師の會に、かくのごとくのたぐひあまたあり、まのあたりみしところな
り。餘師のところになしといへども、大宋國の僧宗の行持なり。われらに
この心操なし、かなしむべし。佛法にあふときなほしかあり、佛法にあは
ざらんときの身心、はぢてもあまりあり。

In the assembly of my former master, there was a native of Mianzhou
in Western Shu named Daosheng, who was a follower of Daoism.[200] A
group of five of them took a vow together, saying, "We will pursue the
great way of the buddhas and ancestors for our entire lives and will never again return to our home lands." My former master was especially
delighted and, in circumambulations and other practices, let them join
in with the monks.[201] When they were lined up, they stood below the
bhikṣuṇīs, a splendid example, rare through the ages.[202] Again, a monk
from Fuzhou, whose name was Shanru, made a vow, saying, "For the
rest of his life, Shanru will never again take a single step toward the
south, but will single-mindedly practice the great way of the buddhas
and ancestors."[203] There were many such people in the assembly of my
former master; something I myself witnessed. Though there may not
have been any at other masters' places, this is the sustained practice that
is the essence of the saṃgha in the Land of the Great Song.[204] We lack
this integrity. How sad. Even when we meet the buddha dharma, we
are like this; when we have not met the buddha dharma, our bodies and
minds are beyond shame.

---

200 **a native of Mianzhou in Western Shu named Daosheng** (*Seishoku no Menshūjin
nite Dōshō* 西蜀の綿州人にて道昇): Otherwise unknown. "Western Shu" (*Seishoku* 西
蜀) refers to the area of present-day Sichuan, the ancient kingdom of Shu.

201 **circumambulations and other practices** (*kinhin dōgō* 經行道業): The term *dōgō*
道業 ("work of the way") can have the general sense of Buddhist practices but here likely refers to the formal observances ordinarily reserved for monks.

202 **they stood below the *bhikṣuṇīs*** (*bikuni no shimo ni hairyū su* 比丘尼のしもに排
立す): I.e., they were treated as laymen, a status lower than nuns.

203 **a monk from Fuzhou, whose name was Shanru** (*Fukushū no sō sono na Zennyo*
福州の僧その名善如): Otherwise unknown. Fuzhou 福州 is the city in present-day Fujian, south of Zhejiang.

204 **the sustained practice that is the essence of the saṃgha** (*sōshū no gyōji* 僧宗の
行持): I.e., such practices reflect what is fundamental to the monastic calling.

110 DŌGEN'S *SHŌBŌGENZŌ* VOLUME II

[16B:66] {1:202}

しづかにおもふべし、一生いくばくにあらず、佛祖の語句、たとひ三三兩
兩なりとも道得せんは、佛祖を道得せるならん。ゆえはいかん。佛祖は身
心如一なるがゆえに、一句兩句、みな佛祖のあたたかなる身心なり。かの
身心きたりてわが身心を道得す。正當道取時、これ道得きたりてわが身心
を道取するなり。此生道取累生身なるべし。かるがゆえに、ほとけとな
り、祖となるに、佛をこえ、祖をこゆるなり。三三兩兩の行持の句、それ
かくのごとし。いたづらなる聲色の名利に馳騁することなかれ、馳騁せざ
れば、佛祖單傳の行持なるべし。すすむらくは、大隱小隱、一箇半箇なり
とも、萬事萬緣をなげすてて、行持を佛祖に行持すべし。

We should think quietly: a lifetime is not long; to speak the words of
the buddhas and ancestors, even if only in twos and threes, is to have
spoken the buddhas and ancestors.[205] Why? Since the body and mind
of the buddhas and ancestors are one, one line or two lines are all the
warm body and mind of the buddhas and ancestors.[206] That body and
mind comes and speaks our body and mind. When it is speaking, it is the
speaking coming and speaking our body and mind.[207] It is, *in this life, we
speak the bodies of accumulated lives.*[208] Therefore, in becoming a buddha or becoming an ancestor, we surpass the buddhas and surpass the ancestors. The words in twos and threes on sustained practice are like this.

---

205 **is to have spoken the buddhas and ancestors** (*busso o dōtoku seru naran* 佛祖を
道得せるならん): Perhaps meaning "is to have expressed the truth of the buddhas and
ancestors," though it might also be interpreted "is to have given voice to the buddhas
and ancestors" or "is to have invoked the buddhas and ancestors." "In twos and threes"
here translates *sansan ryōryō* 三三兩兩 ("three and three, two and two"), an idiomatic
Chinese expression for "a few."

206 **Since the body and mind of the buddhas and ancestors are one** (*busso wa shinjin
nyoitsu naru ga yue ni* 佛祖は身心如一なるがゆえに): Perhaps meaning that the body
and the mind of any given buddha or ancestor are somehow identical or unified, though
it might also be read that the bodies and minds of all the buddhas and ancestors are the
same. It is difficult to see how either interpretation would yield Dōgen's conclusion here,
which would seem to require some reading like, "since the body and mind of the buddhas
and ancestors are one [with their words]."

207 **When it is speaking** (*shōtō dōshu ji* 正當道取時): Taking the unexpressed agent
("it") to be the "body and mind" of the buddhas and ancestors that "comes and speaks
our body and mind."

208 **in this life, we speak the bodies of accumulated lives** (*shi shō dōshu ruishō
shin* 此生道取累生身): Variation on a line in a verse, quoted in the "Shōbōgenzō keisei sanshoku" 正法眼藏溪聲山色, by Longya Judon 龍牙居遁 (835-923), disciple of
Dongshan Liangjie 洞山良价 (807-869) (*Chanmen zhuzushi jisong* 禪門諸祖師偈頌,
ZZ.116:923b12-13):

昔生未了今須了、此生度取累生身、古佛未悟同今者、悟了今人即古人。

What in past lives we have not finished, now we should finish.
In this life, we can deliver the bodies of accumulated lives.
When the old buddhas were not yet awakened, they were the same as those now.
Once awakened, people now are the people of old.

Do not chase after the meaningless fame and profit of sights and sounds; when we do not chase after them, it is the sustained practice uniquely transmitted by the buddhas and ancestors. Whether we are a major hermit or a minor hermit,[209] whether one or a half, I urge that, casting aside the myriad affairs and myriad involvements, we should engage in the sustained practice of the sustained practice as buddhas and ancestors.[210]

正法眼藏佛祖行持下第十六
Treasury of the True Dharma Eye
Sustained Practice of the Buddhas and Ancestors, Part 2
Number 16

[Ryūmonji MS:]
仁治三年壬寅四月五日、書于觀音導利興聖寶林寺
Written at Kannon Dōri Kōshō Hōrin Monastery; fifth day, fourth month of the senior water year of the tiger, the third year of Ninji [6 May 1242][211]

[Tōunji MS:]
正法眼藏佛祖行持第十七、下終
Treasury of the True Dharma Eye
Sustained Practice of the Buddhas and Ancestors
Number 17, Part 2, end

同四年癸卯正月十八日書寫、同三月八日校點了。懷奘
Copied eighteenth day, first month of the junior water year of the rabbit, Ninji [8 February 1243].
Proofed eighth day, third month of the same [year] [29 March 1243].
Ejō

---

209 **a major hermit or a minor hermit** (*daiin shōin* 大隱小隱): From the common trope expressed in the well-known verse by the Jin-dynasty poet Wang Kangju 王康琚:

小隱隱林藪、大隱隱朝市。
The minor hermit secludes himself in woods and marshes;
The major hermit secludes himself in court and market.

210 **we should engage in the sustained practice of the sustained practice as buddhas and ancestors** (*gyōji o busso ni gyōji su beshi* 行持を佛祖に行持すべし): Taking the particle *ni* に in the sense *ni shite* にして; it might also be read as the locative *ni okite* におきて ("in," "among").

211 The Tōunji 洞雲寺 MS shares an identical colophon.

112 DŌGEN'S *SHŌBŌGENZŌ* VOLUME II

于峕永正七年庚午六月日、於阿陽路勝浦縣桂林寺得月亭上。住山小比丘用
兼七十三歳謹以書寫焉

*Respectfully copied in the Tokugatsu Pavilion, at Keirin Monastery,
Katsuura District, Ayōji; twentieth day, sixth month, senior metal year
of the horse, the seventh year of Eishō [25 July 1510].
By the abbot, a humble bhikṣu, Yōken, in his seventy-third year*[212]

---

212 **Yōken** 用兼: I.e., Kinkō Yōken 金岡用兼 (1437–1513?).

TREASURY OF THE TRUE DHARMA EYE

NUMBER 17

Such
Inmo
恁麼

Such

Inmo

INTRODUCTION

This work was composed at Kōshōji in the spring of 1242, a period to which many *Shōbōgenzō* chapters are dated. It represents number 17 in the seventy-five-chapter compilation and number 29 in both the sixty-chapter compilation and the ninety-five-chapter Honzan edition.

The title theme of "Inmo" is the Chinese word "*renme*" 恁麼, a colloquial term, dating from the late Tang, used adverbially in the sense "like this," "in this way," "thus," etc.; and as an adjective for "this kind of," "such," etc. Hence, it is a word that can give informal expression to the Buddhist term *nyoze* 如是 ("such," "suchness;" "thus," "thusness"; S. *tathā*, *yathā*, etc.), used in reference to what is just what it is, what is beyond further predication.

Dōgen opens his essay with one of the best-known examples of Zen use of this term, the saying by the ninth-century figure Yunju Daoying 雲居道膺, "If you wish to get such a thing, you should be such a person. Since you are such a person, why worry about such a thing?" Though the saying seems to question our aspiration to get such a thing, in his comments, Dōgen emphasizes that it is precisely because we want to get such a thing that we are such a person. He then offers examples of what it means to want such a thing and be such a person, and concludes with one of his favorite lines from Chan literature, the Sixth Ancestor's question, "What sort of thing is it that comes like this?"

正法眼藏第十七
Treasury of the True Dharma Eye Number 17

恁麼

Such

[17:1] {1:203}

雲居山弘覺大師は、洞山の嫡嗣なり。釋迦牟尼佛より第三十九世の法孫なり。洞山宗の嫡祖なり。一日、示衆云、欲得恁麼事、須是恁麼人。既是恁麼人、何愁恁麼事。

Great Master Hongjue of Mount Yunju was the legitimate heir of Dongshan.[1] He was a dharma descendant in the thirty-ninth generation from Buddha Śākyamuni; he was a legitimate ancestor in the lineage of Dongshan. *One day, he addressed the assembly, saying,*

> *If you want to get such a thing,*
> *You should be such a person;*
> *Since you are such a person,*
> *Why worry about such a thing?*

[17:2]

いはゆるは、恁麼事をえんとおもふは、すべからくこれ恁麼人なるべし。すでにこれ恁麼人なり、なんぞ恁麼事をうれへん。この宗旨は、直趣無上菩提、しばらくこれを恁麼といふ。この無上菩提のていたらくは、すなはち盡十方界も無上菩提の少許なり、さらに菩提の、盡界よりもあまるべし。われらも、かの盡十方界の中にあらゆる調度なり。なににによりてか恁麼あるとする。いはゆる、身心ともに盡界にあらはれて、われにあらざるゆえに、しかありとしるなり。

---

1 **such** (*inmo* 恁麼): A colloquial expression, dating from the late Tang, used adverbially in the sense "like this," "in this way," "thus," etc.; and (as here) as an adjective for "this kind of," "such," etc. Appears regularly in Zen literature and throughout Dōgen's writing. In order to maintain semantic consistency, the translation will render it with the word "such" (or "suchness") throughout this essay, even when this results in rather awkward English.

   Great Master Hongjue of Mount Yunju (*Ungozan Kōkaku daishi* 雲居山弘覺大師): I.e., Yunju Daoying 雲居道膺 (d. 902), a follower of Dongshan Liangjie 洞山良价 (807-869); Great Master Hongjue is a posthumous title. His famous words quoted here can be found at *Jingde chuandeng lu* 景德傳燈錄, T.2076.51:335c19-20.

116 DŌGEN'S *SHŌBŌGENZŌ* VOLUME II

What this says is that, if you wish to get "such a thing," you should be "such a person."[2] Since you are "such a person," why worry about "such a thing"? The essential point of this is that, for now, *proceeding directly to unsurpassed bodhi* is called "such."[3] The state of this unsurpassed bodhi is such that even all the worlds in the ten directions are but a bit of unsurpassed bodhi: bodhi must exceed all the worlds. We too are all the implements in all those worlds in the ten directions. How do we know it is "such"?[4] We know it is so because our bodies and minds both appear in all the worlds without being ourselves.[5]

[17:3] {1:204}

身すでにわたくしにあらず、いのちは光陰にうつされてしばらくもとどめがたし。紅顔いづくへかさりにし、たづねんとするに蹤跡なし。つらつら觀ずるところに、往事のふたたびあふべからざるおほし。赤心もとどまらず、片片として往來す。たとひまことありといふとも、吾我のほとりにとどこほるものにあらず。恁麼なるに、無端に發心するものあり。この心おこるより、向來もてあそぶところをなげすてて、所未聞をきかんとねがひ、所未證を證せんともとむる、ひとへにわたくしの所爲にあらず。しるべし、恁麼人なるゆえに、しかあるなり。なにをもてか恁麼人にてありとしる。すなはち恁麼事をえんとおもふによりて、恁麼人なりとしるなり。すでに恁麼人の面目あり、いまの恁麼事をうれふべからず。うれふるも、これ恁麼事なるがゆえに、うれへにあらざるなり。又、恁麼事の、恁麼あるにもおどろくべからず。たとひおどろきあやしまるる恁麼ありとも、さらにこれ恁麼なり。おどろくべからずといふ恁麼あるなり。これただ佛量にて量すべからず、心量にて量すべからず、法界量にて量すべからず、盡界量にて量すべからず。ただまさに既是恁麼人、何愁恁麼事なるべし。このゆえに、聲色の恁麼は、恁麼なるべし、身心の恁麼は、恁麼なるべし、諸佛の恁麼は、恁麼なるべきなり。たとへば、因地倒者のときを恁麼なりと恁麼會なるに、必因地起の恁麼のとき、因地倒をあやしまざるなり。

My body is not I: my life is carried along by the years and months, hard to stop even for a moment.[6] Where have those rosy cheeks gone?[7]

---

2 **What this says** (*iwayuru wa* いはゆるは): This and the following sentence merely provide Dōgen's translation of Daoying's Chinese saying into Japanese.

3 **proceeding directly to unsurpassed bodhi** (*jikishu mujō bodai* 直趣無上菩提): A fixed phrase, best known from a line in a verse by Li Zunxu 李遵勖 (988-1038); see Supplementary Notes, s.v. "Man of iron."

4 **How do we know it is "such"?** (*nani ni yorite ka inmo aru to shiru* なにによりてか恁麼あるとしる): I.e., "how do we know this is so?" Dōgen is here playing with the term *inmo*.

5 **without being ourselves** (*ware ni arazaru* われにあらざる): I.e., we are the mere "implements" of suchness because we lack a separate self.

6 **the years and months** (*kōin* 光陰): Literally, "light and shade," in reference to the sun and moon; variously understood as "years and months," "days and months," and "days and nights."

7 **Where have those rosy cheeks gone?** (*kōgan izuku e ka sarinishi* 紅顔いづくへかさりにし): Literally the "red face" (*kōgan* 紅顔) associated with youth.

17. Such *Inmo* 恁麼   117

When we search for them, there are no traces of them. Where we look carefully, there are many things in the past that we will never meet again. The bare mind also does not stand still but comes and goes in pieces; though there may be truth in it, it is not something that lingers in the vicinity of the self.[8]

"Such" being the case, there are those who, for no apparent reason, bring forth the mind [of bodhi].[9] Once this mind arises, casting aside what we have previously enjoyed, we aspire to hear what we have not yet heard and seek to verify what we have not yet verified. This is not entirely of our own doing. We should realize that this is so because we are "such a person." How do we know that we are "such a person"? It is because we wish to get "such a thing" that we know we are "such a person."

Since we already have the face of "such a person," we should not worry about this "such a thing." Because worrying too is "such a thing," it is not worry. Moreover, we should not be surprised that "such a thing" is "such."[10] Although there is the "suchness" of being surprised and in doubt, this again is "such." There is a "suchness" about which we should not be surprised. This should not be measured by the measure of the buddha; it should not be measured by the measure of the mind; it should not be measured by the measure of the dharma realm; it should not be measured by the measure of all the worlds. It should just be, "*since you are such a person, why worry about such a thing?*" Therefore, the "suchness" of sound and form should be "such"; the "suchness" of body and mind should be "such"; the "suchness" of the buddhas should be "such." For example, when there is "such" an understanding that the time when "one falls because of the ground" is "such," at the time of the "suchness" of "*one always gets up because of the ground,*" we do not have doubts about "falling because of the ground."[11]

---

8 **bare mind** (*sekishin* 赤心): A standard term for the true, sincere, or dedicated mind. The following "in pieces" (*henpen* 片片) derives from the common expression in Zen texts, "the bare mind in pieces" (*sekishin henpen* 赤心片片); see Supplementary Notes, s.v. "Bare mind in pieces."

though there may be truth in it (*tatoi makoto ari to iutomo* たとひまことありといふ とも): Generally taken to mean that, "while the bare mind may be true," it is not ours.

9 **bring forth the mind** (*hosshin* 發心) I.e., arouse the aspiration for buddhahood (S. *cittotpāda*); see Supplementary Notes.

10 **we should not be surprised that "such a thing" is "such"** (*inmo ji no, inmo aru ni mo odoroku bekarazu* 恁麼事の、恁麼あるにもおどろくべからず): Dōgen begins here a series of plays with the term *inmo*. The translation seeks to retain the single equivalent "such" (or "suchness") throughout, even when the resulting English is awkward at best.

11 **when there is "such" an understanding that the time when "one falls because**

118 DŌGEN'S *SHŌBŌGENZŌ* VOLUME II

[17:4] {1:205}

古昔よりいひきたり、西天よりいひきたり、天上よりいひきたれる道あり。いはゆる、若因地倒、還因地起、離地求起、終無其理。

There is a saying that has come down to us from ancient times, come down to us from Sindh in the West, come down to us from the heavens above:

If one falls down because of the ground,
One gets up because of the ground.
If one seeks to get up apart from the ground,
It will never be possible.[12]

[17:5]

いはゆる道は、地によりてたふるるものは、かならず地によりておく、地によらずしておきんことをもとむるは、さらにうべからず、となり。しかあるを擧拈して、大悟をうるはしとし、身心をもぬくる道とせり。このゆえに、もし、いかなるか諸佛成道の道理なる、と問著するにも、地にたふるるものの、地によりておくるがごとし、といふ。これを參究して、向來をも透脱すべし、末上をも透脱すべし、正當恁麼時をも透脱すべし。大悟・不悟、却迷・失迷、被悟礙・被迷礙、ともにこれ地にたふるるものの、地によりておくる道理なり。これ天上・天下の道得なり、西天・東地の道得なり。古往・今來の道得なり、古佛・新佛の道得なり。この道得、さらに道未盡あらず、道虧闕あらざるなり。

These words mean that someone who falls down because of the ground will necessarily get up because of the ground; to seek to get up without relying on the ground is impossible.[13] What is like this has been taken up and seen as the starting point for getting the great awakening, has been seen as the way that escapes body and mind.[14] Therefore, when asked what is the principle through which the buddhas attain the way, it is said that it is like someone falling to the ground who gets up by the ground.

---

of the ground" is "such" (*in ji tōsha no toki o inmo nari to inmo e naru ni, hitsu in ji ki no inmo no toki* 因地倒者のときを恁麼なりと恁麼會なるに、必因地起の恁麼のとき): The translation struggles to retain the convoluted syntax of the original. Apart from the word play, the point of this sentence would seem to be that we are not surprised that the same ground that trips us up also supports us, a reference to the adage introduced in the following section.

12 **There is a saying** (*dō ari* 道あり): From a verse said to have been given by the deva Brahmā to convert Māra, the Evil One (see, e.g., *Jingde chuandeng lu* 景德傳燈錄, T.2076.51:207b16-17); hence, Dōgen's claim that the saying originates in the heavens.

13 **These words** (*iwayuru dō* いはゆる道): This sentence simply translates the Chinese quotation into Japanese.

14 **What is like this has been taken up** (*shikaaru o konen shite* しかあるを擧拈して): I.e., what is meant by these words has been taken up as a topic for comment, presumably, by past interpreters of this saying.

17. Such *Inmo* 恁麼 119

Investigating this, we should transcend the past, should transcend the future, should transcend precisely "such" a time.[15]

Great awakening and not awakening; reverting to delusion and losing delusion; obstructed by awakening and obstructed by delusion — these are all the principle that one who falls to the ground gets up by the ground.[16] This is a saying of the heavens above and beneath the heavens, a saying of Sindh in the West and the Land of the East; it is a saying going back to the past and coming down to the present, a saying of old buddhas and new buddhas.[17] This saying lacks anything not exhaustively said, anything not sufficiently said.

[17:6]

しかあれども、恁麼會のみにして、さらに不恁麼會なきは、このことばを參究せざるがごとし。たとひ古佛の道得は恁麼つたはれりといふとも、さらに古佛として古佛の道を聞著せんとき、向上の聞著あるべし。いまだ西天に道取せず、天上に道取せずといへども、さらに道著の道理あるなり。いはゆる、地によりてたふるるもの、もし地によりておきんことをもとむるには、無量劫をふるに、さらにおくべからず。まさにひとつの活路より、おくることをうるなり。いはゆる、地によりてたふるるものは、かならず空によりておき、空によりてたふるるものは、かならず地によりておくるなり。もし恁麼あらざらんは、つひにおくることあるべからず。諸佛諸祖みなかくのごとくありしなり。

Nevertheless, "such" an understanding, without a further understanding that is not "such," is like not investigating these words. Even though

---

15 **should transcend the future** (*matsujō o mo tōdatsu su beshi* 末上をも透脱すべし): Here as elsewhere in his writings, Dōgen seems to be taking the expression *matsujō* 末上 as "last," rather than its usual sense of "first."

precisely "such" a time (*shōtō inmo ji* 正當恁麼時): I.e., the present. The translation tries to preserve the use of *inmo* in this common expression in Dōgen's writing, often translated "this very moment."

16 **reverting to delusion and losing delusion** (*kyakumei shitsumei* 却迷・失迷): "To revert to delusion" (*kyakumei* 却迷; also written 郤迷) is typically understood as the "return" of the awakened practitioner to the world of everyday experience.

obstructed by awakening and obstructed by delusion (*hi go ge hi mei ge* 被悟礙・被迷礙): Dōgen regularly (perhaps as here) uses terms for "obstruction" (*ge* 礙, *keige* 罣礙, *gaige* 罣礙, etc.) in the sense "to delimit," "to define."

17 **This is a saying of the heavens above and beneath the heavens, a saying of Sindh in the West and the Land of the East** (*kore tenjō tenka no dōtoku nari, Saiten Tōchi no dōtoku nari* これ天上・天下の道得なり、西天・東地の道得なり): Dōgen plays here with "heaven and earth" (*tenchi* 天地), from the "ground," or "earth" (*chi* 地) of the verse. "Heavens above" (*tenjō* 天上) refers to the deva realms; "beneath the heavens" (*tenka* 天下) is a common expression for "the whole world," "the whole realm [of China]." The translation "Sindh in the West and the Land of the East" (*Saiten Tōchi* 西天東地), in reference to India and China respectively, masks the more literal sense "Western Heavens and Eastern Earth."

120 DŌGEN'S *SHŌBŌGENZŌ* VOLUME II

the saying of the old buddha has had "such" a transmission, when we go on to hear the words of the old buddha as an old buddha, we should have a higher hearing. Though it may never have been said in Sindh in the West, never said in the heavens above, there is a further truth to be spoken. It is that one who falls down because of the ground, should they seek to get up by relying on the ground, will never get up though they spend innumerable kalpas. In fact, there is one way out by which one can get up: it is that one who falls down because of the ground always gets up because of the sky; one who falls down because of the sky always gets up because of the ground.[18] If "such" is not the case, one will never get up. The buddhas and the ancestors have all been like this.

[17:7] {1:206}

もし人ありて恁麼とはん、空と地と、あひさること いくばくぞ。恁麼問著せんに、かれにむかひて恁麼いふべし、空と地と、あひさること十萬八千里なり。若因地倒、必因空起、離空求起、終無其理。若因空倒、必因地起、離地求起、終無其理。もしいまだかくのごとく道取せざらんは、佛道の地・空の量、いまだしらざるなり、いまだみざるなり。

Suppose someone were to ask "such" a question: "How far apart are the sky and the ground?" Being asked "such" a question, we should give "such" an answer: "The sky and the ground are one hundred eight thousand miles apart."[19]

If one falls down because of the ground,
One always gets up because of the sky.
If one seeks to get up apart from the sky,
It will never be possible.
If one falls down because of the sky,
One always gets up because of the ground.
If one seeks to get up apart from the ground,
It will never be possible.

If we have not yet said it like this, we do not yet know, do not yet see, the measure of the ground and sky of the way of the buddhas.

---

18 **one way out** (*hitotsu no katsuro* ひとつの活路): Though sometimes interpreted as "vital path," the term *katsuro* 活路 typically refers, as no doubt here, to an "escape route" from a dangerous situation.

the sky (*kū* 空): The term "*kū*" 空 is also used to render Sanskrit "*śūnyatā*" and is taken by some here as "emptiness." For the sake of consistency, the translation continues to use "ground" for *chi* 地, though here and in the subsequent discussion of "sky" one might prefer "the earth."

19 **"one hundred eight thousand miles"** (*jū man hassen ri* 十萬八千里): An idiomatic expression indicating a great distance. The value of the Chinese "mile" (*li* 里) varies throughout history, generally around one-third of the English mile. From this point to the end of his answer, Dōgen switches to Chinese.

17. Such *Inmo* 恁麼   121

* * * * *

[17:8]

第十七代の祖師、僧伽難提尊者、ちなみに伽耶舎多、これ法嗣なり。ある
とき、殿にかけてある鈴鐸の、風にふかれてなるをききて、伽耶舎多にと
ふ、風のなるとやせん、鈴のなるとやせん。伽耶舎多まふさく、風の鳴に
あらず、鈴の鳴にあらず、我心の鳴なり。僧伽難提尊者いはく、心はまた
なにぞや。伽耶舎多まふさく、ともに寂静なるがゆえに。僧伽難提尊者い
はく、善哉善哉、わが道を次ぐべきこと、子にあらずよりはたれぞや。つ
ひに正法眼藏を傳付す。

The seventeenth ancestral master was Venerable Saṃghanandi; Gayaśata was his dharma heir.[20] Once, upon hearing the ringing of a bell hanging in a hall when blown by the wind, he asked Gayaśata, "Is it the ringing of the wind, or is it the ringing of the bell?"

Gayaśata said, "It's neither the ringing of the wind nor the ringing of the bell: it's the ringing of one's mind."

Venerable Saṃghanandi said, "And what is mind?"

Gayaśata said, "Because both are quiescent."

Venerable Saṃghanandi said, "Excellent! Excellent! Who but the young master could succeed to my way?"

And eventually, he transmitted to him the treasury of the true dharma eye.

[17:9] {1:207}

これは、風の鳴にあらざるところに、我心鳴を學す。鈴のなるにあらざる
とき、我心鳴を學す。我心鳴はたとひ恁麼なりといへども、倶寂静なり。

This means we study "the ringing of one's mind" where there is no "ringing of the wind"; we study "the ringing of one's mind" when there is no "ringing of the bell." Though "the ringing of one's mind" may be "such," "both are quiescent."

---

20 **Venerable Saṃghanandi** (*Sōgyananadai sonja* 僧伽難提尊者); **Gayaśata** (*Kayasha-ta* 伽耶舎多): (The reconstruction of the Chinese *Qieyesheduo* 伽耶舎多 as Gayaśata is uncertain.) Usually listed as the seventeenth and eighteenth ancestors respectively in the Indian lineage leading from Mahākāśyapa to Bodhidharma (though some sources differ). Their conversation, recounted in Japanese here, can be found at *Jingde chuandeng lu* 景德傳燈錄, T.2076.51:212b20-24.

122   DŌGEN'S *SHŌBŌGENZŌ* VOLUME II

[17:10]

西天より東地につたはれ、古代より今日にいたるまで、この因縁を學道の
標準とせるに、あやまるたぐひおほし。伽耶舍多の道取する、風のなるに
あらず、鈴のなるにあらず、心のなるなり、といふは、能聞の恁麼時の正
當に念起あり、この念起を心といふ。この心念、もしなくば、いかでか鳴
響を緣ぜん。この念によりて聞を成ずるによりて、聞の根本といひぬべき
によりて、心のなる、といふなり。これは邪解なり、正師のちからをえざ
るによりてかくのごとし。たとへば、依主・隣近の論師の釋のごとし。か
くのごとくなるは、佛道の玄學にあらず。

In its transmission from Sindh in the West to the Land of the East, from
ancient times down to the present day, when this episode has been taken
as a standard for studying the way, there have been many who were mistaken. [They hold that] the words of Gayaśata, "it is neither the ringing
of the wind nor the ringing of the bell: it is the ringing of one's mind,"
mean that in the hearer precisely at "such a time" there is the arising of a
thought, and this arising of a thought is called "mind." If this thought did
not exist, how could it take the sound of the ringing as an object? Since
the achieving of hearing depends on this thought, it may be called the
root of hearing; therefore, he says the mind rings. This is an erroneous
understanding. They are like this because they have not had the help of
a true master. It is, for example, like the treatise masters' interpretations
of dependent and proximate.[21] What is like this is not the dark learning
of the way of the buddhas.[22]

[17:11]

しかあるを、佛道の嫡嗣に學しきたれるには、無上菩提正法眼藏、これを
寂靜といひ、無爲といひ、三昧といひ、陀羅尼といふ。道理は、一法わづ
かに寂靜なれば、萬法ともに寂靜なり、風吹寂靜なれば鈴鳴寂靜なり、こ
のゆえに倶寂靜といふなり。心鳴は、風鳴にあらず、心鳴は、鈴鳴にあら
ず、心鳴は心鳴にあらず、と道取するなり。親切の恁麼なるを究辦せんよ
りは、さらにただいふべし、風鳴なり、鈴鳴なり、吹鳴なり、鳴鳴なり、
ともいふべし。何愁恁麼事のゆえに、恁麼あるにあらず、何關恁麼事なる
によりて、恁麼なるなり。

---

21 **the treatise masters' interpretations of dependent and proximate** (*eshu ringon
no ronji no shaku* 依主・隣近の論師の釋): "Dependent" and "proximate" here translate
eshu 依主 and *ringon* 隣近, respectively, technical terms in the analysis of compounds
in Sanskrit grammar. The former renders Sanskrit *tat-puruṣa* (in which the first term
qualifies the second); the latter, *avyayībhāva* (in Sanskrit, an indeclinable compound;
in Chinese, a compound in which one term carries a sense specific to the compound).
"Treatise master" (*ronji* 論師) refers to Buddhist scholastics; a common pejorative in
Dōgen's writings.

22 **dark learning of the way of the buddhas** (*butsudō no gengaku* 佛道の玄學): I.e.,
study of the profundities of Buddhism. "Dark learning" (*gengaku* 玄學) is a standard
term, used for both Daoism and Buddhism.

17. Such *Inmo* 恁麼　　　123

However, for one who has studied under a legitimate successor on the way of the buddhas, the unsurpassed bodhi, the treasury of the true dharma eye — this is called "quiescence," is called "unconditioned," is called "samādhi," is called "*dhāraṇī*."[23] The principle is that, when even one dharma is quiescent, the myriad dharmas are all quiescent; when the blowing of the wind is quiescent, the ringing of the bell is quiescent. Therefore, he says, "both are quiescent." It says that the ringing of the mind is not the ringing of the wind; the ringing of the mind is not the ringing of the bell; the ringing of the mind is not the ringing of the mind. Once we thoroughly investigate what is intimately "such," we should go on just to say, "it is the ringing of the wind; it is the ringing of the bell; it is the ringing of the blowing, it is the ringing of the ringing." It is not "such" because of "*why worry about such a thing?*"; it is "such" because of "*why be involved with such a thing?*"[24]

* * * * *

[17:12]

第三十三祖大鑑禪師、未剃髮のとき、廣州法性寺に宿するに、二僧あり て相論するに、一僧いはく、幡の動ずるなり。一僧いはく、風の動ずる なり。かくのごとく相論往來して休歇せざるに、六祖いはく、風動にあら ず、旛動にあらず、仁者心動なり。二僧ききて、すみやかに信受す。

At the time that the Thirty-third Ancestor, Chan Master Dajian, was not yet tonsured, while he was staying at the Faxing Monastery in Guangzhou, there were two monks arguing.[25] One monk said, "It's the flag that's moving"; the other monk said, "It's the wind that's moving."

In this way, as they argued back and forth without stopping, the Sixth Ancestor said, "It's not the wind moving; it's not the flag moving; it's your minds moving."

The two monks, on hearing this, immediately accepted it.

23　**this is called "quiescence," is called "unconditioned"** (*jakujō to ii, mui to ii* 寂 靜といひ、無爲といひ): Dōgen is redefining the term "quiescence" (*jakujō* 寂靜) from Gayaśata's answer; both this term and the following "unconditioned" (*mui* 無爲) are synonyms for nirvāṇa.

24　**it is "such" because of "why be involved with such a thing"** (*ka kan inmo ji naru ni yorite, inmo naru nari* 何關恁麼事なるによりて、恁麼なるなり): Dōgen has here merely substituted the verb *kan* 關 ("to be related, connected, concerned," etc.) for *shū* 愁 ("to worry") in Hongjue's saying. The significance of the substitution is subject to varied interpretation.

25　**the Thirty-third Ancestor, Chan Master Dajian** (*dai sanjūsan so Daikan zenji* 第 三十三祖大鑑禪師): I.e., the famous Sixth Ancestor, Huineng 慧能, thirty-third in the Zen lineage from Mahākāśyapa. Dajian is an honorary title. This story can be found at *Jingde chuandeng lu* 景德傳燈錄, T.2076.51:235c3-6, and elsewhere, as well as in Dō-gen's *shinji Shōbōgenzō* 眞字正法眼藏 (DZZ.5:202, case 146).

124 DŌGEN'S *SHŌBŌGENZŌ* VOLUME II

[17:13] {1:208}

この二僧は、西天よりきたれりけるなり。しかあればすなはち、この道著は、風も旛も動も、ともに心にてある、と六祖は道取するなり。まさにいま六祖の道をきくといへども、六祖の道をしらず、いはんや六祖の道得を道取することをえんや。爲甚麼恁麼道。いはゆる仁者心動の道をききて、すなはち仁者心動といはんとしては、仁者心動、と道取するは、六祖をみず、六祖をしらず、六祖の法孫にあらざるなり。いま六祖の兒孫として、六祖の道を道取し、六祖の身體髮膚をえて道取するには、恁麼いふべきなり。いはゆる仁者心動はさもあらばあれ、さらに仁者動といふべし。爲甚麼恁麼道。いはゆる動者動なるがゆえに、仁者仁者なるによりてなり。　既是恁麼人なるがゆえに、恁麼道なり。

These two monks had come from Sindh in the West. Thus, with these words, the Sixth Ancestor said that the wind, the flag, and the movement are all the mind. Although they may have heard the words of the Sixth Ancestor, they did not understand the words of the Sixth Ancestor, let alone were they able to say what the Sixth Ancestor said. *Why do we say "such"?*[26] Because, hearing the words, "it's your minds moving," to try to express "it's your minds moving" by saying "it's your minds moving" is not to see the Sixth Ancestor, not to know the Sixth Ancestor, not to be a dharma descendant of the Sixth Ancestor. Now, as the descendants of the Sixth Ancestor, to speak the words of the Sixth Ancestor, to speak having got the body, hair, and skin of the Sixth Ancestor, we should say "such": "Let 'it's your minds moving' be as it may, we should go on to say, 'it's you moving.'"[27] *Why do we say "such"?* Because "moving" moves, because "you" are you.[28] It is because "*since you are such a person*" that we say "such."

[17:14]

六祖のむかしは、新州の樵夫なり。山をもきはめ、水をもきはむ。たとひ青松の下に功夫して根源を截斷せりとも、なにとしてか明窓のうちに從容して、照心の古教ありとしらん、澡雪たれにかならふ。いちにありて經をきく、これみづからまちしところにあらず、他のすすむるにあらず。いとけなくして父を喪し、長じては母をやしなふ。しらず、このころもにかかれりける一顆珠の、乾坤を照破することを。たちまちに發明せしより、老母をすてて知識をたづぬ、人のまれなる儀なり。恩愛のたれかかろから

26　**Why do we say "such"?** (*i jinmo inmo dō* 爲甚麼恁麼道): Or, more colloquially, "why do we say so?" Here and below, the awkward translation of this sentence in Chinese seeks to preserve a consistent rendering of *inmo*.

27　**we should say "such"** (*inmo iu beki nari* 恁麼いふべきなり): Or, more colloquially, "we should say it like this." Again, the translation retains "such" for *inmo*.

28　**Because "moving" moves, because "you" are you** (*iwayuru dōsha dō naru ga yue ni, ninsha ninsha naru ni yorite nari* いはゆる動者動なるがゆえに、仁者仁者なるによりてなり): Or perhaps "because the mover moves." The term *ninsha* 仁者, translated here "you," is more literally the polite second person address "one who is benevolent"; Dōgen borrows the element *sha* 者 ("one who is" or "that which is") for his phrase *dōsha dō* 動者動.

17. Such *Inmo* 恁麼 125

ん、法をおもくして恩をかろくするによりて、棄恩せしなり。これすなは
ち有智若聞、即能信解の道理なり。

In the past, the Sixth Ancestor had been a wood-cutter in Xinzhou,
who was thoroughly familiar with the mountains, thoroughly familiar
with the waters.[29] Although, working away beneath the green pines he
had cut the root,[30] how could he have known of the old teaching that
illumines the mind as one sits at ease by the bright window?[31] Under
whom had he learned to cleanse himself?[32] In the marketplace, he heard
the sūtra, not something he had expected nor had been urged upon him
by another.[33] He had lost his father while still very young and, growing
up, had cared for his mother. Little did he realize that the jewel attached
to his clothing would illuminate heaven and earth.[34] Immediately after
having understood, he abandoned his old mother and went in search of
a wise friend — behavior rare in a person.[35] Who could treat the debt
of gratitude and love so lightly?[36] It is because he gave weight to the

---

29   **Xinzhou** (*Shinshū* 新州): A province in Tang times located in the present-day
Xinxing District 新興縣 of Guangzhou.

30 **he had cut the root** (*kongen o setsudan seri* 根源を截斷せり): Perhaps, recalling
a line from the famous poem *Zhengdao ge* 證道歌, attributed to the early Chan figure
Yongjia Xuanjue 永嘉玄覺 (d. 723) (T.2014.48:395c21-22):

直截根源佛所印。摘葉尋枝我不能。

Directly cutting off the root source — this is sealed by the Buddha;
Plucking at the leaves and searching the branches — this I can't do.

31 **the old teaching that illumines the mind as one sits at ease at the bright window**
(*meisō no uchi ni, shōyō shite shōshin no kokyō* 明窓のうちに、從容して照心の古教):
I.e., the Buddhist teachings studied by monks. "Bright window" (*meisō* 明窓) refers to
monastic windows providing light for reading scriptures; see Supplementary Notes.

32 **cleanse himself** (*sōsetsu* 澡雪): A Chinese compound expression meaning "to wash
and wipe clean," though elsewhere Dōgen seems to play on the second element, *setsu* 雪,
to suggest a reading "wash away the snow."

33 **In the marketplace, he heard the sūtra** (*ichi ni arite kyō o kiku* いちにありて經を
きく): Traditionally said to have been the *Diamond Sūtra*.

34 **the jewel attached to his clothing** (*koromo ni kakarerikeru ikka ju* ころもにかかれ
りける一顆珠): Allusion to the famous parable in the *Lotus Sūtra*, in which a poor man
is unaware that he has a jewel sewn into the lining of his garment; see Supplementary
Notes, s.v. "Jewel in the robe." The jewel is often taken as a metaphor for the buddha
nature present in all beings.

illuminate heaven and earth (*kenkon o shōha suru* 乾坤を照破する): Japanese rendering of the Chinese expression *zhaopo qiankun* 照破乾坤 found in several Zen texts.

35 **wise friend** (*chishiki* 知識): I.e., a Buddhist teacher.

36 **Who could treat the debt of gratitude and love so lightly?** (*on'ai no tare ka karo-
karan* 恩愛のたれかかろからん): I.e., the debt of gratitude a son owes to his mother.
Huineng's abandonment of his elderly mother in his quest for the dharma is praised as
well in "Shōbōgenzō gyōji" 正法眼藏行持, part 1.

126 DŌGEN'S *SHŌBŌGENZŌ* VOLUME II

dharma and took gratitude lightly that he cast aside his debt of gratitude. This is the truth of "*if those having wisdom hear it, they will believe and understand it.*"[37]

[17:15] {1:209}

いはゆる智は、人に學せず、みづからおこすにあらず。智よく智につたはれ、智すなはち智をたづぬるなり。五百の蝙蝠は、智おのづから身をつくる、さらに身なし、心なし。十千の游魚は、智したしく身にてあるゆえに、縁にあらず、因にあらずといへども、聞法すれば即解するなり。きたるにあらず、入にあらず。たとへば東君の春にあふがごとし。智は有念にあらず、智は無念にあらず、智は有心にあらず、智は無心にあらず。いはんや大小にかかはらんや、いはんや迷悟の論ならんや。いふところは、佛法はいかにあることともしらず、さきより聞取するにあらざれば、したふにあらず、ねがふにあらざれども、聞法するに、恩をかろくし身をわするるは、有智の身心、すでに自己にあらざるがゆえに、しかあらしむるなり。これを即能信解といふ。しらず、いくめぐりの生死にか、この智をもちながら、いたづらなる塵勞にめぐる。なほし石の玉をつつめるが、玉も石につつまれりともしらず、石も玉をつつめりともしらざるがごとし。人、これをしる、人、これをとる。これすなはち玉の期せざるところ、石のまたざるところ、石の知見によらず、玉の思量にあらざるなり。すなはち人と智とあひしらざれども、道かならず智にきかるるがごとし。

This "wisdom" is not learned from someone; it is not generated by oneself: wisdom transmits to wisdom; wisdom seeks out wisdom. [In the case of] the five hundred bats, wisdom itself created their bodies; they had no other body, no other mind.[38] [In the case of] the ten thousand swimming fish, it was because of the wisdom intimately present in their bodies — not conditions, not causes — that, when they heard the dharma, they immediately understood it.[39] It is not that it has come; it is not that it enters: it is like the Lord of the East meeting the spring.[40] Wisdom is not having thought; wisdom is not lacking thought; wisdom is not

---

37 **"if those having wisdom hear it, they will believe and understand it"** (*uchi nyaku mon, soku nō shinge* 有智若聞、即能信解): Quoting the *Lotus Sūtra* (*Miaofa lianhua jing* 妙法蓮華經, T.262.9:19c12-13).

38 **five hundred bats** (*gohyaku no henpuku* 五百の蝙蝠): Allusion to the story, recorded in Xuanzang's *Datang xiyuji* 大唐西域記 (T.2087.51:882a11-21), of five hundred bats in a tree that had caught fire, who were so taken with the recitation of the Buddhist *abhidharma* teachings that they remained in the tree and perished in the flames. They were subsequently reborn as humans, joined the Buddhist order, and became the five hundred arhats who compiled the great Sarvāstivāda treatise known as the *Mahāvibhāṣa*.

39 **the ten thousand swimming fish** (*jūsen no yūgyo* 十千の游魚): Allusion to a *jātaka* tale recorded in the *Jing guangming jing* 金光明經 (T.663.16:352b15ff), in which ten thousand fish swimming in a pond received the teaching of the twelvefold chain of causes and conditions and were subsequently reborn in the Heaven of the Thirty-three Devas. Dōgen's reference here to "causes" (*in* 因) and "conditions" (*en* 緣) could either be to the teaching of the twelvefold chain or to the karmic fruit of hearing the teaching.

40 **the Lord of the East** (*Tōkun* 東君): I.e., the god of the sun, or of spring.

17. Such *Inmo* 恁麼 — 127

having mind; wisdom is not lacking mind.[41] Still less does it have to do with great and small; still less is it a question of delusion and awakening.

What this is saying is that, not knowing what the buddha dharma is, since he had not heard of it, he did not yearn for it, did not desire it; yet upon hearing the dharma, that he took gratitude lightly and forgot about himself occurred as it did because the body and mind possessed of wisdom were not his own.[42] This is called *they will believe and understand it.*" There is no knowing through how many rounds of birth and death, even while possessed of this wisdom, we have turned round in meaningless afflictions.[43] It is just like a stone containing a gem: the gem does not know it is contained in the stone, nor does the stone know that it contains the gem.[44] A person knows of it; the person takes it. This is something the gem did not expect, something the stone did not anticipate; it does not depend on the stone's knowledge, nor is it the thinking of the gem. That is, although the person and wisdom do not know each other, it seems the words are heard by wisdom.

[17:16] {1:210}

無智疑怪、即爲永失といふ道あり。智かならずしも有にあらず、智かならずしも無にあらざれども、一時の春松なる有あり、秋菊なる無あり。この無智のとき、三菩提みな疑怪となる、盡諸法みな疑怪なり。このとき、永失即爲なり。所聞すべき道、所證なるべき法、しかしながら疑怪なり。われにあらず、徧界かくるるところなし。たれにあらず、萬里一條鐵なり。たとひ恁麼して抽枝なりとも、十方佛土中、唯有一乘法なり。たとひ恁麼して葉落すとも、是法住法位、世間相常住なり。既是恁麼事なるにより て、有智と無智と、日面と月面となり。

There is the saying, "*Those lacking wisdom will doubt and suspect it, and thereby lose it forever.*"[45] Wisdom is not necessarily "having";

---

41   **having thought** (*unen* 有念); **lacking thought** (*munen* 無念); **having mind** (*ushin* 有心); **lacking mind** (*mushin* 無心): Probably to be taken here as two states much valued in early Chan texts — "no thought" (*munen* 無念) and "no mind" (*mushin* 無心) — as well as their opposites.

42   **What this is saying** (*iu tokoro wa* いふところは): Presumably, Dōgen is returning here to the story of the Sixth Ancestor.

43   **turned round in meaningless afflictions** (*itazura naru jinrō ni meguru* いたづらなる塵勞にめぐる): I.e., been reborn in vain in afflicted states. The term *jinrō* 塵勞 (literally, "dust and toil") is regularly used for *kleśa* (*bonnō* 煩惱; "defilements"). See Supplementary Notes, s.v. "Dust."

44   **a stone containing a gem** (*naoshi ishi no tama o tsutsumeru* なほし石の玉をつつめる): Variation on a common Buddhist metaphor of gold hidden in ore.

45   **There is the saying** (*dō ari* 道あり): The second half of the passage from the *Lotus Sūtra* quoted above, section 14. The original (*Miaofa lianhua jing* 妙法蓮華經, T.262.9:19c10c13), reads "those lacking wisdom will have doubts and regrets" (*muchi gige* 無智疑悔).

128 DŌGEN'S *SHŌBŌGENZŌ* VOLUME II

wisdom is not necessarily "lacking." Nevertheless, there is the having that is one moment of the pine in spring; there is the lacking that is [one moment of] the chrysanthemum in autumn.[46] At the moment of this "lacking wisdom," *saṃbodhi* becomes "doubt and suspicion"; all dharmas are "doubt and suspicion." At this moment, to "*lose it forever*" "*is it.*"[47] The words one should hear, the dharmas one should verify, are all of them "doubt and suspicion." They are not I: in the realms everywhere, there is nothing hidden; they are not other: they are "*one strip of iron for ten thousand miles.*"[48] Although "such" is the budding of branches, "*in the buddha lands of the ten directions, there is only the dharma of the one vehicle*"; although "such" is the leaves falling, "*the dharmas abide in their dharma positions; the marks of the world constantly abide.*"[49] Due to its being "*since it is such a thing*," it is "having wisdom" and "lacking wisdom," the face of the sun and the face of the moon.[50]

---

46 **there is the having that is one moment of the pine in spring; there is the lacking that is [one moment of] the chrysanthemum in autumn** (*ichiji no shunshō naru u ari, shūkiku naru mu ari* 一時の春松なる有あり、秋菊なる無あり): Or "there is the being . . . there is the non-being . . . ." Dōgen is playing in this section with the verbs *u* 有 ("to exist," "to have") and *mu* 無 ("not to exist," "to lack") in the sūtra's expressions "those having wisdom" (*uchi* 有智) and "those lacking wisdom" (*muchi* 無智), respectively.

47 **At this moment, to "lose it forever" "is it"** (*kono toki, yō shitsu soku i nari* このとき、永失即爲なり): A tentative translation of a sentence in which Dōgen has reversed the order of the sūtra's phrase *soku i yō shitsu* 即爲永失 ("thereby lose it forever"). Perhaps to be understood that "losing it forever" is itself the "doubt and suspicion" of "lacking wisdom."

48 **in the realms everywhere, there is nothing hidden** (*henkai kakururu tokoro nashi* 徧界かくるるところなし); **"one strip of iron for ten thousand miles"** (*banri ichijō tetsu* 萬里一條鐵): Two set phrases appearing often in Zen literature. The former is a variation in Japanese on the saying "in the realms everywhere, it has never been hidden" (*henkai fu zō zō* 徧界不曾藏), suggesting the ubiquity of the ultimate truth (or the buddha dharma); the latter is an idiom expressing the ultimate unity of the myriad phenomena. See Supplementary Notes, s.v. "In the realms everywhere, it has never been hidden," "One strip of iron for ten thousand miles."

49 **Although "such" is the budding of branches** (*tatoi inmo shite chūshi nari tomo* たとひ恁麼して抽枝なりとも); **although "such" is the leaves falling** (*tatoi inmo shite yōraku su tomo* たとひ恁麼して葉落すとも): Or, more naturally, "although the branches sprout in this way," "although the leaves fall in this way." Another evocation of the spring and autumn seasons seen above in the "spring pine" and "autumn chrysanthemum."

"in the buddha lands of the ten directions, there is only the dharma of the one vehicle" (*jippō butsudo chū yui u ichijō hō* 十方佛土中唯有一乘法); **"the dharmas abide in their dharma positions; the marks of the world constantly abide"** (*ze hō jū hōi, seken sō jō jū* 是法住法位、世間相常住): Quoting two passages from the *Lotus Sūtra*; see Supplementary Notes, s.v. "Dharmas abide in their dharma positions."

50 **the face of the sun and the face of the moon** (*nichimen to gachimen to* 日面と月面と): Terms that may be taken either as referring to the sun and moon, or as allusion to

17. Such *Irmo* 恁麼   129

[17:17]

恁麼人なるがゆえに、六祖も發明せり。つひにすなはち黄梅山に參じて、
大満禪師を拜するに、行堂に投下せしむ。晝夜に米を碓こと、僅に八箇月
をふるほどに、あるとき、夜ふかく更たけて、大満みづからひそかに碓坊
にいりて、六祖にとふ、米白也未と。六祖いはく、白也未有篩在と。大
満、つえして臼をうつこと三下するに、六祖、箕にいれる米をみたび簸
る。このときを、師資の道あひかなふといふ。みづからもしらず、他も不
會なりといへども、傳法・傳衣、まさしく恁麼の正當時節なり。

Because he was "such a person," the Sixth Ancestor had an understanding. Subsequently, he visited Mount Huangmei and paid his respects to
Chan Master Daman, who had him lodged in the postulants' hall.[51] After
he had pounded rice day and night for some eight months, at one point,
deep in the night, Daman himself secretly entered the pounding room
and asked the Sixth Ancestor, "*Is the rice whitened yet?*"

The Sixth Ancestor said, "*It's whitened but not yet sifted.*"

Daman struck the mortar with his staff three times, and the Sixth Ancestor sifted the rice in the winnow three times.[52] It is said that, at this
time, the ways of master and disciple came together. Though they themselves did not know it, and it was not understood by others, the transmission of the dharma and transmission of the robe, was precisely at "such"
a moment.

* * * * *

[17:18]

南嶽山無際大師、ちなみに藥山とふ、三乘十二分教、某甲粗知、嘗聞南方
直指人心、見性成佛、實未明了。伏望和尚、慈悲指示。

Sun Face and Moon Face, two buddhas given in the *Foming jing* 佛名經; see Supplementary Notes, s.v. "Sun face, moon face."

51　**Mount Huangmei** (*Ōbaisan* 黄梅山): The mountain in Qizhou 蘄州, present-day
Hubei, that was the site of the communities of the Fourth and Fifth Ancestors.

Chan Master Daiman (*Daiman zenji* 大満禪師): I.e., the Fifth Ancestor, Daman
Hongren 大滿弘忍 (602-675).

had him lodged in the postulants' hall (*andō ni tōge seshimu* 行堂に投下せしむ): As
a layman, Huineng was housed with the lay members of the monastery. The verb *tōge* 投
下 should probably be taken in the sense *tōshuku* 投宿 ("to lodge").

52　**the Sixth Ancestor sifted the rice in the winnow three times** (*Rokuso, mi ni ireru
kome o mitabi hiru* 六祖、箕にいれる米をみたび簸る): Most versions of this story do
not have Huineng winnowing the rice three times but, rather, entering the Fifth Ancestor's
room at the third watch of the night and there receiving the transmission of Bodhidharma's robe. (See, e.g., *Tiansheng guangdeng lu* 天聖廣燈錄, ZZ.135:645a9-11.) Dōgen
repeats his version several times in the *Eihei kōroku* 永平廣錄.

130   DŌGEN'S *SHŌBŌGENZŌ* VOLUME II

Great Master Wuji of Mount Nanyue was once asked by Yaoshan, *"The three vehicles and twelvefold teachings, I roughly know.*[53] *I once heard that in the south [they say], 'pointing directly at the person's mind, seeing the nature and attaining buddhahood' — this I haven't really understood yet.*[54] *I humbly hope your reverence will compassionately instruct me about it."*

[17:19] {1:211}

これ藥山の問なり。藥山は本爲講者なり、三乘十二分教は、通利せりけるなり。しかあるは、佛法さらに昧然なきがごとし。むかしは別宗いまだおこらず、ただ三乘十二分教をあきらむるを、教學の家風とせり。いま、人おほく鈍致にして、各各の宗旨をたてて佛法を度量する、佛道の法度にあらず。

This is Yaoshan's question. Yaoshan was originally a lecturer, well versed in the three vehicles and twelvefold teachings. So it seemed there was nothing in the buddha dharma about which he was in the dark. In the old days, before the rise of separate lineages, it was the style of learning simply to clarify the three vehicles and twelvefold teachings. Nowadays, many people, obtuse in the extreme, set up their own individual tenets to gauge the buddha dharma — this is not the norm on the way of the buddhas.

[17:20]

大師いはく、恁麼也不得、不恁麼也不得、恁麼不恁麼總不得。汝作麼生。

The Great Master said, *"Such can't be got; not such can't be got; both such and not such can't be got.*[55] *What will you do?"*

---

53   **Great Master Wuji of Mount Nanyue** (*Nangakusan Musai daishi* 南嶽山無際大師): I.e., Shitou Xiqian 石頭希遷 (700-790), disciple of Qingyuan Xingsi 青原行思 and teacher to Yaoshan Weiyan 藥山惟儼 (751-834). "Great Master Wuji" (*Wuji dashi* 無際大師) is a posthumous title. This incident is found at *Liandeng huiyao* 聯燈會要, ZZ.136:738b1-4.

"three vehicles and twelvefold teachings" (*sanjō jūnibun kyō* 三乘十二分教): I.e., the Buddhism of the Buddhist canon. The "three vehicles" (*sanjō* 三乘) refers to the teachings for the *śrāvaka*, *pratyeka-buddha*, and bodhisattva; the "twelvefold teachings" (*jūnibun kyō* 十二分教) is synonymous with the "twelvefold division of the canon" (*jūnibu kyō* 十二部經), a traditional division of the canonical texts by genre. Dōgen treats the topic in "Shōbōgenzō bukkyō" 正法眼藏佛教. See Supplementary Notes, s.v. "Three vehicles and twelvefold teachings."

54   **"in the south"** (*nanpō* 南方): A reference to the "sudden teachings" attributed to the Southern school of the Sixth Ancestor, Huineng 慧能.

"'pointing directly at the person's mind, seeing the nature and attaining buddhahood'" (*jikishi ninshin, kenshō jōbutsu* 直指人心、見性成佛): A famous dictum of Zen, traditionally attributed to Bodhidharma; see Supplementary Notes, s.v. "Pointing directly at the person's mind, seeing the nature and attaining buddhahood."

55   **"Such can't be got; not such can't be got; both such and not such can't be got"** (*inmo ya futoku, fuinmo ya futoku, inmo fuinmo sō futoku* 恁麼也不得、不恁麼也不得、

17. Such *Inmo* 恁麼

[17:21]

これすなはち、大師の、藥山のためにする道なり。まことにそれ恁麼・不恁麼総不得なるゆえに、恁麼不得なり、不恁麼不得なり。恁麼は恁麼をいふなり。有限の道用にあらず、無限の道用にあらず。恁麼は不得に參學すべし、不得は恁麼に問取すべし。這箇の恁麼および不得、　ひとへに佛量のみにかかはるにあらざるなり。會不得なり、悟不得なり。

These are the words that the Great Master spoke for Yaoshan. Truly, it is because "*both such and not such can't be got*" that "*such can't be got*," and "*not such can't be got*." "Such" is how he expresses "such."[56] He is not saying it is limited; he is not saying it is unlimited.[57] We should study "such" in "can't be got"; we should question "can't be got" in "such." This "such" and "can't be got" do not have to do only with the measure of the buddha: understanding "can't be got"; awakening "can't be got."[58]

⁕ ⁕ ⁕ ⁕ ⁕

[17:22]

曹溪山大鑑禪師、ちなみに南嶽大慧禪師にしめすにいはく、是什麼物恁麼來 。

Chan Master Dajian of Mount Caoxi once addressed Chan Master Dahui of Nanyue saying, "*What thing is it that comes such?*"[59]

恁麼不恁麼総不得): Or, more naturally, "You can't be like this; you can't not be like this; you can't be either like this or not like this." For the full context in which Shitou Xiqian 石頭希遷 (700-790) spoke these words to Yaoshan Weiyan 藥山惟儼 (751-834), see Supplementary Notes, s.v. "Slough off."

56 **"Such" is how he expresses "such"** (*inmo wa inmo o iu nari* 恁麼は恁麼をいふなり): Probably meaning, "this is the way that he [i.e., Wuji] talks about *inmo*."

57 **He is not saying it is limited; he is not saying it is unlimited** (*ugen no dōyū ni arazu, mugen no dōyū ni arazu* 有限の道用にあらず、無限の道用にあらず): The term *dōyū* 道用 (also read *dōyō*), translated here as "saying," occurs most often in the sense of a Buddhist religious implement; here, however, it is often interpreted to mean "function of words," or what we might call "usage." The antecedent of "it" here is unclear; perhaps best taken as Wuji's statement that "such can't be got and not such can't be got."

58   **measure of the buddha** (*butsuryō* 佛量): A term that appears several times in Dōgen's writings, sometimes interpreted in the sense "the thinking of a buddha" (*butsu no shiryō* 佛の思量); see Supplementary Notes, s.v. "Measure of the buddha."

59 **Chan Master Dajian of Mount Caoxi** (*Sōkeizan Daikan zenji* 曹溪山大鑑禪師): I.e., the Sixth Ancestor, Huineng 慧能. Mount Caoxi is in present-day Guangdong province, the location of Huineng's Baolin Monastery 寶林寺. "Chan Master Dahui of Nanyue" refers to Huineng's follower Nanyue Huairang 南嶽懷讓 (677-744). Huineng's question here occurs in a famous dialogue included in the *shinji Shōbōgenzō* 眞字正法眼藏 (DZZ.5:178, case 101) and much quoted by Dōgen; see Supplementary Notes, s.v. "What thing is it that comes like this?"

132 DŌGEN'S *SHŌBŌGENZŌ* VOLUME II

[17:23]

この道は、恁麼はこれ不疑なり、不會なるがゆえに、是什麼物なるがゆえに、萬物まことにかならず什麼物なると參究すべし、一物まことにかならず什麼物なると參究すべし。什麼物は疑著にはあらざる、恁麼來なり。

These words mean that, because "such" is not to be doubted, is not to be understood, because it is "what thing," truly we should always investigate the myriad things as being "what thing," truly we should always investigate a single thing as "what thing." That "what thing" is not to be doubted is "comes such."

正法眼藏恁麼第十七
Treasury of the True Dharma Eye
Such
Number 17

[Ryūmonji MS:]

爾時仁治三年壬寅三月二十六日、在于觀音導利興聖寶林寺示衆

Presented to the assembly at Kannon Dōri Kōshō Hōrin Monastery; twenty-sixth day, third month of the senior water year of the tiger, the third year of Ninji [27 April 1242][60]

[Tōunji MS:]

寬元元年癸卯四月十四日、書寫之侍者寮。懷奘

Copied this at the acolyte's quarters; fourteenth day, fourth month of the junior water year of the rabbit, the first year of Kangen [14 May 1243]. Ejō

于嘗永正七年庚午六月廿四日、於阿陽勝浦縣桂林寺丈室中。
用兼七十三歲、謹寫之

In the abbot's quarters of Keirin Monastery, Katsuura District, Ayō; twenty-fourth day, sixth month, senior metal year of the horse, the seventh year of Eishō [29 July 1510]. Yōken, in his seventy-third year, respectfully copied this[61]

---

60 The Tōunji 洞雲寺 MS shares an identical colophon.

61 **Yōken** 用兼: I.e., Kinkō Yōken 金岡用兼 (1437–1513?).

TREASURY OF THE TRUE DHARMA EYE

NUMBER 18

Avalokiteśvara

Kannon

觀音

Avalokiteśvara

Kannon

INTRODUCTION

This chapter is dated in the spring of 1242, soon after the start of the summer retreat. Although the location is not given in the colophon, we can assume that Dōgen was at Kōshōji, his monastery in Uji, where, in the week before he composed this text, he had produced the "Kaiin zanmai" 海印三昧 and "Juki" 授記 chapters of the *Shōbōgenzō*. Our work here appears as number 18 in both the seventy-five- and sixty-chapter compilations and as number 33 in the Honzan edition.

The "Kannon" chapter is devoted entirely to Dōgen's comments on a single conversation, between two Tang-dynasty monks, Yunyan Tansheng 雲巌曇晟 and Daowu Yuanzhi 道吾圓智, who were fellow disciples of Yaoshan Weiyan 藥山惟儼. The topic of the conversation is the eponymous Bodhisattva Avalokiteśvara, known in Japan as Kannon 觀音. Avalokiteśvara, perhaps the single most popular figure in the Mahāyāna pantheon, is represented in many forms; the form under discussion here is that known as the Thousand-armed Avalokiteśvara (*Senju Kannon* 千手觀音), whose great compassionate activity is expressed through a thousand arms, each with an eye in the palm of its hand. The question raised by Yunyan is how the bodhisattva uses these many hands and eyes; the answer proposed by Daowu is that it is like someone groping for a pillow in the dark.

In his commentary, Dōgen analyzes every sentence of the conversation, often finding surprising meanings in the two masters' statements and proposing playful reworkings of the Chinese text. In this, the "Kannon" chapter is often representative of characteristic features of Dōgen's notoriously challenging approach to reading and interpreting the Chinese kōan literature.

The chapter ends with an unusual postscript (or appendix), in which Dōgen points out that, while he has focused here on the best discussion of Avalokiteśvara, there are several other references to the bodhisattva in the Chan corpus, some examples of which he simply notes with little comment.

正法眼藏第十八

Treasury of the True Dharma Eye
Number 18

觀音

Avalokiteśvara

[18:1] {1:213}

雲巖無住大師、問道吾山修一大師、大悲菩薩、用許多手眼作麼。道吾曰、
如人夜間背手摸枕子。雲巖曰、我會也、我會也。道吾曰、汝作麼生會。雲
巖曰、遍身是手眼。道吾曰、道也太煞道、祇道得八九成。雲巖曰、某甲祇
如此、師兄作麼生。道吾曰、通身是手眼。

Great Master Wuzhu of Yunyan asked Great Master Xiuyi of Mount
*Daowu, "How does the Bodhisattva of Great Compassion use so many
hands and eyes?"*[1]

*Daowu said, "Like a person groping behind for their pillow in the
night."*

Yunyan said, "I understand. I understand."

Daowu said, "How do you understand it?"

Yunyan said, "His body everywhere is hands and eyes."

*Daowu said, "You talk big talk, but it's just eight or nine tenths of a
saying."*[2]

---

1 **Great Master Wuzhu of Yunyan** (*Ungan Mujū daishi* 雲巖無住大師); **Great Master Xiuyi of Mount Daowu** (*Dōgozan Shuitsu daishi* 道吾山修一大師): The former is
Yunyan Tansheng 雲巖曇晟 (782-841), disciple of Yaoshan Weiyan 藥山惟儼 (751-834),
in the lineage of Qingyuan Xingsi 青原行思; the latter is Daowu Yuanzhi 道吾圓智 (769-
835), who studied together with Yunyan under Yaoshan. A slightly variant version of
their conversation is recorded in Dōgen's *shinji Shōbōgenzō* 眞字正法眼藏 (DZZ.5:182,
case 105). The dialogue appears in several Chan sources; see, e.g., *Zongmen tongyao ji*
宗門統要集, ZTS.1:149d-150a.

Bodhisattva of Great Compassion (*daihi bosatsu* 大悲菩薩): I.e., Bodhisattva
Avalokiteśvara.

so many hands and eyes (*kota shugen* 許多手眼): Reference to the form of Avalokiteśvara known as "Kannon of a Thousand Arms and a Thousand Eyes" (*senju sengen kannon* 千手千眼觀音), represented in iconography as having an eye in the palm of each of
his thousand hands. The question, "how does [he] use" (*yō . . . so ma* 用 . . . 作麼) may
be taken both as "in what way does he use" and "to what end does he use."

2 **"You talk big talk"** (*dō ya taisatsu dō* 道也太煞道): Loose translation for the Chinese idiom *taisha dao* 太煞道 ("extreme speech"; also written 太殺道).

136 DŌGEN'S *SHŌBŌGENZŌ* VOLUME II

Yunyan said, "I'm just like this. How about my elder brother?"

Daowu said, "His body throughout is hands and eyes."[3]

[18:2]

道得觀音は、前後の聞聲、ままにおほしといへども、雲巖・道吾にしかず。觀音を參學せんとおぼえば、　雲巖・道吾のいまの道也を參究すべし。いま道取する大悲菩薩といふは、觀世音菩薩なり、觀自在菩薩ともいふ。諸佛の父母とも參學す、諸佛よりも未得道なりと學することなかれ。過去正法明如來なり。

Although one hears many voices, both before and after them, speaking of Kannon, they are not like those of Yunyan and Daoyu.[4] If we would study Kannon, we should study this talk of Yunyan and Daowu.[5] The "Bodhisattva of Great Compassion" they are speaking of here is Bodhisattva Kanzeon, also called Bodhisattva Kanjizai.[6] We study him also as the parent of the buddhas; do not study that, compared to the buddhas, he has not yet gained the way.[7] He is the past Tathāgata Shōbō Myō.[8]

---

eight or nine tenths of a saying (*dōtoku hakku jō* 道得八九成): I.e., "not bad"; see Supplementary Notes, s.v. "Eight or nine tenths complete."

3　**"body everywhere"** (*henshin* 遍身); **"body throughout"** (*tsūshin* 通身): The two terms are roughly synonymous, meaning "everywhere throughout the body," "the entire body," etc. The latter term can also have a more general sense of "completeness," "totality," etc.; hence, "he is completely hands and eyes." The former term is also written 徧身.

4　**speaking of Kannon** (*dōtoku Kannon* 道得觀音): I.e., talking about Bodhisattva Avalokiteśvara. Dōgen uses the most common form of the bodhisattva's name, rendered here and below in the Japanese reading.

5　**this talk** (*ima no dōya* いまの道也): In the odd form *dōya* 道也, Dōgen seems to be playing with the Chinese of Daowu's remark translated above as "You talk big talk" (*dōya taisatsu dō* 道也太煞道), where the element *ya* 也 is functioning merely as a grammatical particle marking the topic.

6　**Bodhisattva Kanzeon** (*Kanzeon bosatsu* 觀世音菩薩): "Bodhisattva Observer of the Sounds of the World"; the Chinese rendering of the name "Avolokiteśvara" favored by the translator Kumārajīva.

Bodhisattva Kanjizai (*Kanjizai bosatsu* 觀自在菩薩): "Bodhisattva Observing Lord"; the rendering of the name adopted by the Chinese translator Xuanzang.

7　**parent of the buddhas** (*shobutsu no bumo* 諸佛の父母): A role reflecting the treatment of Avalokiteśvara in some esoteric traditions.

compared to the buddhas, he has not yet gained the way (*shobutsu yori mo mitokudō* 諸佛よりも未得道): I.e., is still on the bodhisattva path leading to buddhahood.

8　**the past Tathāgata Shōbō Myō** (*kako Shōbōmyō nyorai* 過去正法明如來): "Tathāgata Knowledge of the True Dharma"; the name given to Avalokiteśvara in texts that treat him as having attained buddhahood in the distant past. See, e.g., *Qian shou qian yan guanshiyin pusa dayuanman wuai dabeixin tuoluoni jing* 千手千眼觀世音菩薩廣大圓滿無礙大悲心陀羅尼經 (T.1060.20:110a11-12):

善男子此觀世音菩薩。不可思議威神之力。已於過去無量劫中。已作佛竟號正法明如來。

18. Avalokiteśvara *Kannon* 觀音　　137

[18:3] {1:214}

しかあるに、雲巖道の大悲菩薩用許多手眼作麼の道を舉拈して、參究すべきなり。觀音を保任せしむる家門あり、觀音を未夢見なる家門あり。雲巖に觀音あり、道吾と同參せり。ただ一、兩の觀音のみにあらず、百、千の觀音、おなじく雲巖に同參す。觀音を眞箇に觀音ならしむるは、ただ雲巖會のみなり。所以はいかん。雲巖道の觀音と、餘佛道の觀音と、道得・道不得なり。餘佛道の觀音は、ただ十二面なり、雲巖しかあらず。餘佛道の觀音は、わづかに千手眼なり、雲巖しかあらず。餘佛道の觀音は、しばらく八萬四千手眼なり、雲巖しかあらず。なにをもてかしかありとしる。

Thus, we should take up and study Yunyan's words, "*How does the Bodhisattva of Great Compassion use so many hands and eyes?*" There are houses that maintain Kannon; there are houses that have never dreamt of Kannon.[9] There is a Kannon in Yunyan; he studied together with Daowu.[10] Not merely one or two Kannons but a hundred, a thousand, Kannons similarly studied together with Yunyan. Kannon is truly made Kannon only in the community of Yunyan. Why is this? The Kannon Yunyan speaks of and the Kannon other buddhas speak of are saying it and not saying it.[11] The Kannon other buddhas speak of is twelve faces; Yunyan is not like this.[12] The Kannon other buddhas speak of is just a thousand hands and eyes; Yunyan is not like this. The Kannon other buddhas speak of is temporarily eighty-four thousand hands and eyes; Yunyan is not like this.[13] How do we know this?

[The World-Honored One said,] "Good men, this Bodhisattva Observer of the Sounds of the World has inconceivable majestic powers. In innumerable kalpas past, he already became a buddha named Tāthāgata Knowledge of the True Dharma."

9　**houses that maintain Kannon** (*Kannon o hōnin seshimuru kamon* 觀音を保任せしむる家門): Presumably, Buddhist traditions in which Kannon plays a significant role.

10　**There is a Kannon in Yunyan; he studied together with Daowu** (*Ungan ni Kannon ari, Dōgo to dōsan seri* 雲巖に觀音あり、道吾と同參せり): The first clause here suggests that "Yunyan" 雲巖 refers to the location of that name (in Youxian 攸縣, present-day Hunan); the second clause suggests it refers to the person, Tansheng 曇晟.

11　**saying it and not saying it** (*dōtoku dōfutoku* 道得道不得): I.e., Yunyan is able truly to express what should be said of Kannon, whereas "other buddhas" are not; the affirmative and negative forms of the Chinese idiomatic *daode* 道得, "to say"; especially "to be able to say" something significant.

12　**twelve faces** (*jūni men* 十二面): An unusual number of faces for Avalokiteśvara; presumably, the eleven-headed version, in whose iconography the eleven heads sometimes emerge from a central head.

13　**temporarily eighty-four thousand hands and eyes** (*shibaraku hachiman shisen shugen* しばらく八萬四千手眼): A figure (S. *caturasīti-sahasra*) regularly used in Buddhist literature to designate a great number; here, perhaps, meant to suggest the common trope that a buddha has eighty-four thousand teachings to counteract the eight-four thousand afflictions. The force of the adverb *shibaraku* しばらく, translated here "temporarily," is unclear: it may indicate that Kannon sometimes manifests eighty-four thousand

138 DŌGEN'S *SHŌBŌGENZŌ* VOLUME II

[18:4]

いはゆる雲巌道の大悲菩薩用許多手眼は、許多の道、ただ八萬四千手眼の
みにあらず、いはんや十二および三十二、三の數般のみならんや。許多
は、いくそばくといふなり。如許多の道なり、種般かぎらず。種般すでに
かぎらずば、無邊際量にもかぎるべからざるなり。用許多のかず、その宗
旨かくのごとく參學すべし。すでに無量無邊の邊量を超越せるなり。いま
雲巌道の許多手眼の道を拈來するに、道吾、さらに道不著といはず、宗旨
あるべし。

The words "so many" in Yunyan's saying, "*How does the Bodhisattva of Great Compassion use so many hands and eyes?*" are not merely eighty-four thousand hands and eyes, let alone varieties numbering twelve, or thirty-two or three.[14] *Xuduo* ["so many"] means "how many?"[15] It is saying, "so many," without limiting the varieties. Since the varieties are not limited, it must not be limited even to a limitless amount. Regarding the number in "use so many," we should study its meaning in this way. It has transcended the limit of the incalculable and limitless. There is an essential point in the fact that, in taking up Yunyan's "so many hands and eyes" here, Daoyu does not say that his words do not say it.[16]

[18:5] {1:215}

雲巌・道吾は、かつて薬山に同參・齊肩より、すでに四十年の同行とし
て、古今の因縁を商量するに、不是處は剗却し、是處は證明す。恁麼しき
たれるに、今日は許多手眼と道取するに、雲巌道取し、道吾證明する。し
るべし、兩位の古佛、おなじく同道取せる許多手眼なり。許多手眼は、あ
きらかに雲巌・道吾同參なり。いまは用作麼を道吾に問取するなり。この
問取を、經師・論師ならびに十聖・三賢等の問取にひとしめざるべし。こ
の問取は、道取を擧來せり、手眼を擧來せり。いま用許多手眼作麼と道取
するに、この功業をちからとして成佛する古佛・新佛あるべし。使許多手
眼作麼とも道取しつべし。作什麼とも道取し、動什麼とも道取し、道什麼
とも道取ありぬべし。

---

hands and eyes; or it may suggest simply that Kannon is occasionally spoken of as having this number of hands and eyes.

14 **varieties numbering twelve, or thirty-two or three** (*jūni oyobi sanjū ni, san no su-han* 十二および三十二、三の數般): Dōgen here seems to be referring, not to the number of hands and eyes of Kannon, but to the twelve faces represented in some iconography and to the thirty-two or thirty-three manifestations of Kannon given in some sources.

15 ***Xuduo* means "how many?"** (*kota wa ikusobaku to iu nari* 許多はいくそばくといふなり): Dōgen is here merely providing a Japanese equivalent, "how many" (*ikusobaku* いくそばく) for the Chinese expression *xuduo* 許多.

16 **his words do not say it** (*dō fujaku* 道不著): I.e., Yunyan's words are insufficient. A loose translation of the Chinese idiomatic *dao buzhao* 道不著, a form not appearing else-where in Dōgen's writings; roughly synonymous with the much more common *dao bude* 道不得, translated as "not saying it," in section 3 above. The antecedent of the pronoun is, of course, Yunyan.

18. Avalokiteśvara *Kannon* 觀音   139

Yunyan and Daowu once studied together and were equals under Yaoshan. Thereafter, as fellow travelers for forty years, discussing episodes past and present, they "leveled what was wrong and confirmed what was right."[17] In this way, today, in saying "*how many hands and eyes*," Yunyan says it, and Daowu confirms it. We should know that, for both old buddhas, it is the "*how many hands and eyes*" that they say together. "*How many hands and eyes*" is clearly Yunyan and Daowu studying together.

Now, he asks Daowu, "*How does he use them?*" We should not equate this question with the questions of the sūtra masters and treatise masters, the ten sages and three worthies, and the like.[18] This question has brought up a saying, has brought up "hands and eyes." In saying, "*how does he use so many hands and eyes*," there should be old buddhas and new buddhas who attain buddhahood through the strength of this meritorious deed.[19] We may also say, "*how does he employ so many hands and eyes?*"[20] We may also say, "What does he do with them?" We may also say, "How does he move them?" There should also be a saying, "How does he speak of them?"

---

17   **fellow travelers** (*dōgyō* 同行): Or "fellow practitioners."

"leveled what was wrong and confirmed what was right" (*fuzesho wa senkyaku shi, zesho wa shōmyō su* 不是處は剗却し、是處は證明す): Reflecting a remark to Xuefeng Yicun 雪峰義存 (822-908) by Yantou Quanhuo 巖頭全奯 (828–887) (*Lengdeng huiyao* 聯燈會要, ZZ.136:782b17-18):

> 是處與儞證明、不是處與儞剗却。
>
> Where you're right, I confirm it for you; where you're wrong, I shave it off for you.

18   **sūtra masters and treatise masters** (*kyōji ronji* 經師論師): I.e., specialists in the interpretation of the sūtras and treatises; scholastics. A pejorative term commonly found in Dōgen's works.

ten sages and three worthies (*jisshō sanken* 十聖・三賢): I.e., those on the ten advanced stages (*ji* 地; S. *bhūmi*) of the bodhisattva path and the three preliminary stages preceding these.

19   **old buddhas and new buddhas who attain buddhahood through the strength of this meritorious deed** (*kono kugō o chikara toshite jōbutsu suru kobutsu shinbutsu* この功業をちからとして成佛する古佛・新佛): I.e., buddhas, both ancient and modern, who achieve buddhahood through Yunyan's question; see Supplementary Notes, s.v. "Old buddha."

20   **"how does he employ so many hands and eyes?"** (*shi kota shugen somo* 使許多手眼作麼): Dōgen here begins a series of plays with the Chinese question, in which he substitutes other possible verbs for *yō* 用 ("to use"). The second instance here, if translated in parallel with the others, would read "how does he do them?" (*so jūmo* 作什麼); in ordinary parlance, it would be taken as the Chinese idiomatic "what's it for?" "what good is it?" etc.

[18:6]

道吾いはく、如人夜間背手摸枕子。いはゆる宗旨は、たとへば、人の夜間に手をうしろにして、枕子を摸索するがごとし。摸索するといふは、さぐりもとむるなり。夜間はくらき道得なり、なほ日裏看山と道取せんがごとし。用手眼は、如人夜間背手摸枕子なり。これをもて用手眼を學すべし。夜間を日裏よりおもひやると、夜間にして夜間なるときと、撿點すべし、すべて晝夜にあらざらんときと撿點すべきなり。人の摸枕子せん、たとひこの儀すなはち觀音の用手眼のごとくなる、會取せざれども、かれがごとくなる道理、のがれ・のがるべきにあらず。

Daowu says, "*Like a person groping behind them for their pillow in the night.*" The meaning of this is, for example, like a person in the night reaching behind them and groping for their pillow.[21] *Mosuo* ["groping"] means "to search for." "In the night" is a saying about the dark, like saying, "*seeing the mountain in the daylight.*"[22] "Using hands and eyes" is "*like a person groping behind them for their pillow in the night.*" With this, we should study "*using hands and eyes.*" We should examine it as considering "the night" from the daylight and as the time when "the night" is "the night" itself.[23] We should examine it as the time when there is neither day nor night. "A person's groping for a pillow" — though we do not understand that this behavior is like Kannon's using his hands and eyes, we cannot avoid the truth that it is [in fact] like that.

[18:7]

いまいふ如人の人は、ひとへに譬喩の言なるべきか。又この人は平常の人にして、平常の人なるべからざるか。もし佛道の平常人なりと學して譬喩のみにあらずば、摸枕子に學すべきところあり。枕子も、咨問すべき何形段あり。夜間も、人天晝夜の夜間のみなるべからず。しるべし、道取するは、取得枕子にあらず、牽挽枕子にあらず、推出枕子にあらず。夜間背手摸枕子、と道取する道吾の道底を撿點せんとするに、眼の夜間をうる、見るべし、すごさざれ。手の、まくらをさぐる、いまだ劑限を著手せず。背手の機要なるべくは、背眼すべき機要のあるか。夜間をあきらむべし。手眼世界なるべきか、人手眼のあるか、ひとり手眼のみ飛霹靂するか、頭正尾正なる手眼の一條・兩條なるか。もしかくのごとくの道理を撿點すれば、用許多手眼はたとひありとも、たれかこれ大悲菩薩、ただ手眼菩薩のみきこゆるがごとし。恁麼いはば、手眼菩薩、用許多大悲菩薩作麼、と問取しつべし。

---

21 **The meaning of this** (*iwayuru shūshi* いはゆる宗旨): Dōgen is here and in the next sentence simply providing the Japanese meaning of the Chinese sentence.

22 **a saying about the dark** (*kuraki dōtoku* くらき道得): Literally, "a dark saying"; a somewhat odd locution, perhaps to be understood as "a saying that it is dark."

"seeing the mountain in the daylight" (*nichiri kanzan* 日裏看山): Perhaps meaning "as clear as seeing a mountain in broad daylight." Likely reflecting the words of Yunmen Wenyen 雲門文偃 (864-949); see Supplementary Notes.

23 **considering "the night" from the daylight** (*yakan o nichiri yori omoiyaru* 夜間を日裏よりおもひやる): I.e., "the night" as seen from, or perhaps in contrast to, the daylight — as opposed to the following night as it is in itself.

18. Avalokiteśvara *Kannon* 觀音   141

The "person" in this "like a person" — should it be solely a metaphorical term? Again, should this "person" be an ordinary person, or should it not be an ordinary person? If we study them as the ordinary person on the way of the buddhas and not as a metaphor, there is something to be studied in their "groping for thrir pillow." And the pillow as well, what shape it has should be questioned. "The night" as well must not be the night of the day and night of humans and devas. We should know that the saying is not that they get their pillow, not that they draw in their pillow, not that they "push away their pillow."[24] When one would investigate Daoyu's saying that says "*groping behind them for their pillow in the night*," we should see that the eye must get "the night"; do not overlook this. The hand's searching for the pillow has not set its hand on its limit.[25] If the "hand behind" them is essential, is it essential to do an "eye behind" them?[26] We should clarify "the night." Is it a world of hands and eyes? Are there human hands there? Or do the hands and eyes by themselves dart like a thunderbolt? Is it one or two instances of hands and eyes true from head to tail? When we examine its principles like this, although there may be "*using so many hands and eyes*," who is the Bodhisattva of Great Compassion? It sounds as if there is just Bodhisattva Hands and Eyes. If we put it like this, we should ask, "*How does Bodhisattva Hands and Eyes use so many Bodhisattvas of Great Compassion?*"

---

24 **"push away their pillow"** (*suishutsu chinsu* 推出枕子): Likely recalling a story about Yangshan Huiji 仰山慧寂 (803-887) (*Lengdeng huiyao* 聯燈會要, ZZ.136:565a3-4):

> 僧問、法身還會説法也。師云、我説不得、別有一人説得。云、説得底人在甚麼處。師推出枕子。
>
> A monk asked, "Can the dharma body really preach the dharma?"
> The Master [Yangshan] said, "I say it can't, but there's someone else who says it can."
> [The monk] said, "Where is the ore who says it can?"
> The Master pushed away his pillow.

25 **The hand's searching for the pillow has not set its hand on its limit** (*te no, makura o saguru, imada saigen o chakushu sezu* 手の、まくらをさぐる、いまだ劑限を著手せず): I.e., the searching for the pillow has no limit. The translation tries to capture the play with "hand" in the verb *chakushu* 著手 ("set its hand"), which would ordinarily suggest "to undertake," "to embark on."

26 **If the "hand behind" him is essential, is it essential to do an "eye behind" him?** (*haishu no kiyō naru beku wa, haigen su beki kiyō no aru ka* 背手の機要なるべくは、背眼すべき機要のあるか): Dōgen has here formed a strange noun, *haishu* 背手 ("hand behind"), from Daowu's Chinese and then created a stranger new verb, *haigen su* 背眼 す ("to eye behind").

142   DŌGEN'S *SHŌBŌGENZŌ* VOLUME II

[18:8] {1:216}
しるべし、手眼はたとひあひ罣礙せずとも、用作麼は恁麼用なり、用恁麼
なり。恁麼道得するがごときは、徧手眼は不曾藏なりとも、徧手眼と道得
する期をまつべからず。不曾藏の那手眼ありとも、這手眼ありとも、自己
にはあらず、山海にはあらず、日面・月面にあらず、即心是佛にあらざる
なり。

We should know that, while the hands and eyes do not obstruct each
other, "*how does he use*" is such use, is using such.[27] In such a saying,
while "*hands and eyes everywhere*" "have never been hidden," they do
not await our saying they are "hands and eyes everywhere."[28] While
there are those hands and eyes and these hands and eyes that "have never been hidden," they are not the self; they are not the mountains and
oceans; they are not the sun face and moon face; they are not "*this mind
itself is the buddha.*"[29]

[18:9]
雲巖道の我會也、我會也は、道吾の道を我會するといふにあらず。用恁麼
の手眼を道取に道得ならしむるには、我會也、我會也なり。無端用這裏な
るべし、無端須入今日なるべし。

Yunyan's saying, "*I understand, I understand*," is not saying, "I understand Daowu's words." To make a statement that can speak of the

---

27   **obstruct each other** (*shugen wa tatoi ai keige sezu tomo* 手眼はたとひあひ罣礙
せずとも): Here, and in the following two sentences, the logic of the argument suggests
that we might take the concessive form "X *tomo*" ("while X") in the sense, "given X."
Dōgen often uses the verb *keige su* 罣礙す ("to obstruct," "to hinder") in the sense "to
define," "to identify."

"how does he use" is such use, is using such (*yō somo wa inmo yō nari, yō inmo nari* 用
作麼は恁麼用なり、用恁麼なり): "Such" translates the colloquial Chinese expression
renmo 恁麼 ("in this way," "like this," etc.), typically understood here as invoking the
Buddhist use of "suchness," or "thusness" (*nyoze* 如是; S. *tathatā*) to indicate what is
beyond predication — a practice very common in Dōgen's writing.

28   **while "hands and eyes everywhere" "have never been hidden"** (*hen shugen wa fu
zō zō nari tomo* 徧手眼は不曾藏なりとも): Dōgen is here playing with the expression,
"in the realms everywhere, it has never been hidden" (*henkai fu zō zō* 徧界不曾藏), a
popular saying attributed to Chan Master Shishuang Qingzhu 石霜慶諸 (807-888); see
Supplementary Notes, s.v. "In the realms everywhere, it has never been hidden."

29   **sun face and moon face** (*nichimen gachimen* 日面・月面): The terms may be taken
either as referring to the sun and moon or as allusion to Sun-faced and Moon-faced, two
buddhas given in the *Foming jing* 佛名經, or to a famous saying by Mazu Daoyi 馬祖道
一 (709-788); see Supplementary Notes, s.v. "Sun face, moon face."

"this mind itself is the buddha" (*soku shin ze butsu* 即心是佛): Or "this very mind is
the buddha." A very common phrase in Zen literature, cited in Dōgen's *shinji Shōbōgenzō* 眞字正法眼藏 (DZZ.5:266, case 278) and many other Zen sources; see Supplementary Notes.

18. Avalokiteśvara *Kannon* 觀音　　143

hands and eyes that use such, it is, "*I understand, I understand.*" It must
be *unexpectedly using here; it must be unexpectedly taking on today.*[30]

[18:10] {1:217}

道吾道の儞作麼生會は、いはゆる我會也、たとひ我會也なるを罣礙するに
あらざれども、道吾に儞作麼生會の道取あり。すでにこれ我會儞會なり、
眼會手會なからんや。現成の會なるか、未現成の會なるか。我會也の會を
我なりとすとも、儞作麼生會に儞あることを功夫ならしむべし。

Daowu's saying, "*How do you understand it?*" is "I understand"; while
it does not obstruct "I understand," Daowu has the saying, "*How do you
understand it?*"[31] Since it is "I understand" and "you understand," could
it not be "eyes understand" and "hands understand"? Is it a manifest understanding? Or is it an unmanifest understanding?[32] Though we take the
understanding of "I understand" as "I," the existence of "you" in "*how
do you understand it?*" should be made the object of our concentrated
effort.[33]

30　**It must be unexpectedly using here; it must be unexpectedly taking on today**
(*mutan yō shari naru beshi, mutan shunyū konnichi naru beshi* 無端用這裏なるべし、
無端須入今日なるべし): Presumably, meaning that Yunyan's "I understand, I understand"
unexpectedly expresses the "use" of "hands and eyes" "here" and "today." "Unexpectedly"
translates *mutan* 無端, a term suggesting "for no reason," "without grounds," "out of nowhere"; some interpretations take it as "without limit" and treat this sentence as describing
Kannon's unlimited use of his hand and eyes. "Taking on today" (*shunyū konnichi* 須入
今日) is an unusual phrase, found also in the "Shōbōgenzō raihai tokuzui" 正法眼藏禮拜
得髓. While the predicate *shunyū* 須入 is regularly read here as the deontic verb "should
enter," the translation takes it in the sense "to employ," "to make use of."

31　**"How do you understand it?" is "I understand"** (*ni somosan e wa, iwayuru
ga e ya* 儞作麼生會は、いはゆる我會也): I.e., Daowu's question is his way of saying
what Yunyan expressed by "I understand!" A tentative translation of a passage open to
interpretation. The English here follows the common practice of reading *ga e ya* 我會
也 ("I understand it") as a predicate nominative, and taking *ni somosan e* 儞作麼生會
("How do you understand it?") as the subject of the following "does not obstruct." An
alternative reading would treat *ni somosan e* 儞作麼生會 as the sentence topic and take
ga e ya 我會也 as the subject — yielding, "Regarding Daoyu's saying, 'How do you understand it?': although 'I understand' does not obstruct its being 'I understand,' Daowu
has the saying, 'How do you understand it?'" Such a reading would take the point to be
that Yunyan's saying "I understand" is, as Dōgen has argued above, not to be restricted
to his understanding of Daowu's saying (taking *keigi su* 罣礙す ["obstruct"] in the sense
"to define").

32　**manifest understanding** (*genjō no e* 現成の會); **unmanifest understanding** (*mi
genjō no e* 未現成の會): Perhaps in the sense, "apparent in the words of the dialogue."

33　**the existence of "you" in "how do you understand it?"** (*ni somosan e ni ni aru
koto* 儞作麼生會に儞あること): Presumably, meaning that, while we are familiar with
the "I" in "I understand it," we need to study the "you" in "how do you understand it."

144 DŌGEN'S *SHŌBŌGENZŌ* VOLUME II

[18:11]

雲巖道の遍身是手眼の出現せるは、夜間背手摸枕子を講誦するに、遍身こ
れ手眼なり、と道取せると參學する觀音のみおほし。この觀音たとひ觀音
なりとも、未道得なる觀音なり。雪巖の遍身是手眼といふは、手眼是身遍
といふにあらず。遍はたとひ遍界なりとも、身手眼の正當恁麼は、遍の所
遍なるべからず。身手眼にたとひ遍の功德ありとも、攙奪行市の手眼にあ
らざるべし。手眼の功德は、是と認ずる見取・行取・説取あらざるべし。
手眼すでに許多といふ、千にあまり、萬にあまり、八萬四千にあまり、無
量無邊にあまる。ただ遍身是手眼の、かくのごとくあるのみにあらず、度
生説法も、かくのごとくなるべし、國土放光も、かくのごとくなるべし。
かるがゆえに、雲巖道は遍身是手眼なるべし、手眼を遍身ならしむるには
あらず、と參學すべし。遍身是手眼を使用すといふとも、動容進止せしむ
といふとも、動著することなかれ。

On the appearance here of Yunyan's saying, "h*is body everywhere is
hands and eyes*": when reciting "*groping behind them for their pillow in
the night*," there are many Kannons who study that it says "*his body everywhere*" *is* "*hands and eyes.*"[34] While these Kannons may be Kannons,
they are Kannons who have not yet said it. Yunyan's "his body everywhere is hands and eyes" is not saying "hands and eyes" are everywhere
in his body.[35] While "everywhere" may be "the realms everywhere," the
body hands and eyes just as such are not where "everywhere" is.[36] While
the body hands and eyes may have the virtue of being "everywhere,"
they are not hands and eyes that *dominate the market*.[37] There should
be no view, practice, or teaching that recognizes the virtue of hands and
eyes as "is."[38] The hands and eyes are said to be "so many"; they exceed

---

34 **there are many Kannons who study that it says "his body everywhere" is "hands
and eyes"** (*henshin kore shugen nari, to dōshu seru to sangaku suru Kannon nomi ooshi*
遍身これ手眼なり、と道取せると參學する觀音のみおほし): Dōgen has here simply
put the Chinese sentence, "the body everywhere is hands and eyes," into its Japanese
reading. Note that he uses "Kannon" here for those who study Kannon.

35 **"hands and eyes" are everywhere in his body** (*shugen ze shinpen* 手眼是身遍):
A tentative translation, based on what seems to be the logic of this passage. The term
shinpen 身遍 could as well be interpreted as "his body [present] everywhere."

36 **the body hands and eyes just as such are not where "everywhere" is** (*shin shugen
no shōtō inmo wa, hen no shohen naru bekarazu* 身手眼の正當恁麼は、遍の所遍なる
べからず): The translation struggles here to retain the consistent use of "everywhere" for
hen 遍. If we substitute a term like "pervasion" here, this sentence might read, "While
pervasion may pervade the realms, the body hands and eyes just as such are not pervaded
by pervasion." "The body hands and eyes" translates the ambiguous *shin shugen* 身手眼,
taken here as "the hands and eyes that are the body"; it might also be rendered simply as
"the body, the hands and eyes."

37 **dominate the market** (*zandatsu kōshi* 攙奪行市): An idiomatic expression, found in
Chan texts, for arbitrary or arrogant behavior; see Supplementary Notes. Here, perhaps,
used in the sense, fully capturing the significance of "everywhere."

38 **recognizes the virtue of hands and eyes as "is"** (*shugen no kudoku wa, ze to ninzu-*

18. Avalokiteśvara *Kannon* 觀音 145

a thousand, exceed ten thousand, exceed eighty-four thousand, exceed the incalculable and limitless. It is not only "*his body everywhere is hands and eyes*" that is like this: his *delivering beings and preaching the dharma* are also like this; his *land and radiance* are also like this.[39] Because of that, Yuyan's saying is "*his body everywhere is hands and eyes*"; we should study that he does not make "hands and eyes" "his body everywhere." Whether he employs and uses "*his body everywhere is hands and eyes*," whether he makes it move or rest, proceed or stop, do not move![40]

[18:12]
道吾道取す、道也太瞁道、祇道得八九成。いはくの宗旨は、道得は太瞁道なり。太瞁道といふは、いひあて、いひあらはす、のこれる未道得なし、といふなり。いますでに未道得の、つひに道不得なるべきのこりあらざるを道取するときは、祇道得八九成なり。

Daowu said, "You *talk big talk, but it's just eight or nine tenths of a saying.*" The essential point here is that a "saying" is "big talk." *Taisha dao* means "to say spot on," "to express," "to say with nothing left unsaid."[41] When one finally says what was hitherto unsaid, with nothing remaining that has not been said, this is "*just eight or nine tenths of a saying.*"

[18:13] {1:218}
いふ意旨の參學は、たとひ十成なりとも、道未盡なる力量にてあらば、參究にあらず。道得は八九成なりとも、道取すべきを、八九成に道取すると、十成に道取すると、なるべし。當恁麼の時節に、百千萬の道得に道取すべきを、力量の妙なるがゆえに、些子の力量を擧して、わづかに八九成に道得するなり。たとへば、盡十方界を百千萬力に拈來するあらんも、拈來せざるにはすぐるべし。しかあるを、一力に拈來せんは、よのつねの力量なるべからず。いま八九成のこころ、かくのごとし。しかあるを、佛祖の祇道得八九成の道をききては、道得十成なるべきに、道得いたらずして

---

ru 手眼の功德は、是と認ずる): "Is" here translates the copula *ze* in the phrase *henshin ze shugen* 遍身是手眼 ("his body everywhere is hands and eyes"). The same word could be translated as "this" or as "right."

39 **delivering beings and preaching the dharma** (*dosho seppo* 度生説法); **his land and radiance** (*kokudo hoko* 國土放光): I.e., the salvific activities of the bodhisattva. "Land" (*kokudo* 國土) refers to the bodhisattva's acquiring a buddha field (S. *kṣetra*) over which to preside — here, likely Avalokiteśvara's Potalaka (*Fudaraku* 補陀落); "radiance" (*hoko* 放光) refers to the nimbus (*komyo* 光明) surrounding his body — often used as a metaphor for the spreading of his wisdom.

40 **do not move!** (*dojaku suru koto nakare* 動著することなかれ): A common expression of Zen masters that can mean, "do not make a move," "do not move [the thing under discussion]," or "do not be moved" [by the thing under discussion].

41 ***Taisha do*** (*taisatsu do* 太瞁道): Dogen is here simply giving a Japanese definition of the Chinese idiom.

146 DŌGEN'S *SHŌBŌGENZŌ* VOLUME II

八九成といふと會取す。佛法、もしかくのごとくならば、今日にいたるべからず。いはゆるの八九成は、百千といはんがごとし、許多といはんがごとし、參學すべきなり。すでに八九と道取す、はかりしりぬ、八九にかぎるべからずといふなり。佛祖の道話、かくのごとく參學するなり。

The study of what this means is that, even if it is ten tenths, it is not an investigation if it lacks the power to say it exhaustively. A saying may be eight or nine tenths, but it should be one that says what should be said, whether eight or nine tenths or ten tenths. At precisely such a juncture — where he should say it with a hundred, a thousand, ten thousand sayings — because his power is so wondrous, he shows a bit of this power and says it just eight or nine tenths. For example, though we take up all the worlds in the ten directions with a hundredfold, a thousandfold, a myriadfold power, it surpasses not taking them up; but to take them up with a single power, is no ordinary power. "Eight or nine tenths" here is like this. But, hearing the words of the buddha and ancestor, "*just eight or nine tenths of a saying*," [people] understand it to be saying that, where his saying should be ten tenths, his saying is just eight or nine tenths.[42] If the buddha dharma were like this, it would not have reached us today.[43] We should study "eight or nine tenths" as like saying "a hundred thousand," like saying "so many." Since he says, "eight or nine tenths," we know that it must not be limited to eight or nine tenths. This is how we should study the talk of the buddha and ancestor.

[18:14]

雲巖道の、某甲祇如是、師兄作麼生は、道吾のいふ道得八九成の道を道取せしむるがゆえに、祇如是と道取するなり。これ不留朕迹なりといへども、すなはち臂長衫袖短なり。わが適來の道を道未盡ながらさしおくを、某甲祇如是といふにはあらず。

On Yunyan's saying, "*I'm just like this. How about my elder brother?*": he says, "just like this," to have him say what Daowu calls "eight or nine tenths of a saying."[44] While we may say *it leaves no signs or traces*,

---

42 **buddha and ancestor** (*busso* 佛祖): Here and in the final sentence of this section, most likely an epithet for Daowu, though it could also be read in the generic sense, "buddhas and ancestors."

43 **If the buddha dharma were like this, it would not have reached us today** (*buppō, moshi kaku no gotoku naraba, konnichi ni itaru bekarazu* 佛法、もしかくのごとくならば、今日にいたるべからず): Japanese version of a common lament of Chinese Chan masters, variously phrased. Similar expressions occur frequently throughout the *Shōbōgenzō*; this one seems akin to the phrasing of a remark by the monk Baoen Xuanze 報恩玄則 that Dōgen cites at *shinji Shōbōgenzō* 眞字正法眼藏, DZZ.5:192, case 122:

佛法若如是不到今日。

If the buddha dharma were like this, it would never have reached today.

44 **to have him say what Daowu calls "eight or nine tenths of a saying"** (*Dōgo no iu dōtoku hakku jō no dō o dōshu seshimuru* 道吾のいふ道得八九成の道を道取せしむる):

18. Avalokiteśvara *Kannon* 觀音   147

it is *a long arm and a short sleeve*.[45] He is not saying, "I'm just like this," in the sense, "while my previous words have not fully expressed it, I'll leave at that."

[18:15]

道吾いはく、通身是手眼。いはゆる道は、手眼たがひに手眼として通身なりといふにあらず、手眼の通身を、通身是手眼といふなり。

Daowu said, "*His body throughout is hands and eyes*." These words do not say that the hands and eyes, as hands and as eyes, are "throughout the body"; he is calling the body throughout of hands and eyes "*his body throughout is hands and eyes*."[46]

[18:16]

しかあれば、身はこれ手眼なり、といふにはあらず。用許多手眼は、用手・用眼の許多なるには、手眼かならず通身是手眼なるなり。用許多身心作麼と問取せんには、通身是作麼なる道得もあるべし。いはんや雲巌の遍と道吾の通と、道得盡、道未盡にはあらざるなり。雲巌の遍と道吾の通と、比量の論にあらずといへども、おのおの許多手眼は、恁麼の道取あるべし。

Therefore, it is not that he is saying that the body is hands and eyes. When "*using so many hands and eyes*" is the "so many" of "using hands" and of "using eyes," it is necessarily "*the body throughout is hands and eyes*." When we ask, "*how does he use so many bodies and minds*," there must also be the saying, "*the body throughout is 'how'?*"[47] Still less is it the case that Yunyan's "everywhere" and Daowu's "throughout" are saying it exhaustively and not saying it exhaustively.[48] Although Yunyan's "everywhere" and Daowu's "throughout" are not an issue of comparison, each of their "*so many hands and eyes*" can have such sayings.

I.e., to cause Daowu to offer his own saying; assuming that the agent of the causative is Daowu. See Supplementary Notes, s.v. "Eight or nine tenths complete."

45 **it leaves no signs or traces** (*furyū chinshaku* 不留朕迹): Also written 不留朕跡. A fixed expression of appreciation often encountered in Zen texts.

a long arm and a short sleeve (*hi chō sanshū tan* 臂長衫袖短): A Zen idiom generally taken to indicate that the meaning surpasses the words, or one's true intentions are exposed.

46 **body throughout of hands and eyes** (*shugen no tsūshin* 手眼の通身): I.e., the body throughout that is itself hands and eyes.

47 **"body throughout is 'how'"** (*tsūshin ze somo* 通身是作麼): Substituting the "how" of "how does he use" for the "hands and eyes" of "the body throughout is hands and eyes," a play that seems to suggest that the hands and eyes are how he uses them.

48 **saying it exhaustively and not saying it exhaustively** (*dōtoku jin, dō mijin* 道得盡、道未盡): I.e., one has fully expressed it and the other has not.

148 DŌGEN'S *SHŌBŌGENZŌ* VOLUME II

[18:17]

しかあれば、釋迦老子の道取する觀音は、わづかに千手眼なり、十二面なり。三十三身、八萬四千あり。雲巖・道吾の觀音、許多手眼なり。しかあれども、多少の道にはあらず。雲巖・道吾の許多手眼の觀音を參學するとき、一切諸佛は觀音の三昧を成八九成するなり。

Thus, the Avalokiteśvara spoken of by Old Master Śākya is just a thousand hands and eyes, just twelve faces.[49] He has thirty-three bodies, or eighty-four thousand. The Avalokiteśvara of Yunyan and Daowu is "so many hands and eyes." But this is not talk of quantity. When they study Yunyan and Daowu's Avalokiteśvara of "so many hands and eyes," all the buddhas realize "eight or nine tenths" of the samādhi of Avalokiteśvara.

正法眼藏觀音第十八

Treasury of the True Dharma Eye

Kannon

Number 18

[Ryūmonji MS:]

爾時仁治三年壬寅四月二十六日示

Presented on the twenty-sixth day, fourth month of the senior water year of the tiger, the third year of Ninji [27 May 1242]

[18:18]

いま佛法西來よりこのかた、佛祖おほく觀音を道取すといへども、雲巖・道吾におよはざるゆゑに、ひとりこの觀音を道取す。永嘉の眞覺大師に、不見一法名如來、方得名爲觀自在の道あり。如來と觀音と、即現此身なりといへども、他身にはあらざる證明なり。

Ever since the buddha dharma came from the west, many buddhas and ancestors have spoken of Avalokiteśvara; but, since they do not approach Yunyan and Daowu, we have spoken [here] solely of this Avalokiteśvara. Great Master Zhenjue of Yongjia has the words, "*Not seeing a single dharma is called the Thus Come One; again, it can be called The Lord Who Observes.*"[50] Though we say that the Tathāgata and

---

49 **Old Master Śākya** (*Shaka rōshi* 釋迦老子): I.e., Buddha Śākyamuni, in the sūtras; a common expression of familiarity used in Zen literature.

50 **Great Master Zhenjue of Yongjia** (*Yōka no Shinkaku daishi* 永嘉の眞覺大師): I.e., Yongjia Xuanjue 永嘉玄覺 (d. 723), a disciple of the Sixth Ancestor, Huineng 慧能. His saying here occurs in the *Zhengdao ge* 證道歌, the famous poem attributed to him (T.2014.48:396c11-12). "The Lord Who Observes" translates (*Kanjizai* 觀自在), Xuanzang's rendering of the name Avalokiteśvara.

18. Avalokiteśvara *Kannon* 觀音　　149

Avalokiteśvara *"then manifest this body,"* this is verification that they are not different bodies.[51]

[18:19]

麻谷・臨濟に、正手眼の相見あり。許多の一一なり。雲門に、見色明心、聞聲悟道の觀音あり。いづれの聲色か見聞の觀世音菩薩にあらざらん。百丈に入理の門あり。楞嚴會に圓通觀音あり。法華會に普門示現觀音あり。みな與佛同參なり、與山河大地同參なりといへども、なほこれ許多手眼の一二なるべし。

There is the encounter of the true hands and eyes of Magu and Linji: they are each one of "so many."[52] Yunmen has an Avalokiteśvara of *"seeing forms and clarifying the mind; hearing sounds and understanding the way"*: what sounds and forms are not Bodhisattva Observer of the Sounds of the World who sees and hears?[53] Baizhang has the "gateway

---

51　**the Tathāgata and Avalokiteśvara "then manifest this body"** (*Nyorai to Kannon to soku gen shi shin* 如來と觀音と即現此身): Likely reflecting the passage on Kannon in the *Lotus Sūtra* explaining the thirty-three manifestations of the bodhisattva: in each case, he appears in whatever body is appropriate to the deliverance of his audience. See Supplementary Notes, s.v. "Manifesting a body to preach the dharma."

52　**Magu and Linji** (*Mayoku Rinzai* 麻谷・臨濟): I.e., Magu Baoche 麻谷寶徹 (dates unknown) and Linji Yixuan 臨濟義玄 (d. 866). Their encounter on the true hands and eyes of Kannon appears in the *Linji lu* 臨濟錄 (T.1985.47:496c5-9):

> 時麻谷出問、大悲千手眼、那箇是正眼。師云、大悲千手眼、那箇是正眼。速道速道。麻谷拽師下座。麻谷却坐。師近前云、不審。麻谷擬議。師亦拽麻谷下座。師却坐。麻谷便出去。師便下座。
>
> At that time, Magu came forward and asked, "Among the thousand hands and eyes of Great Compassion, which is the true eye?"
> The Master [Linji] said, "Among the thousand hands and eyes of Great Compassion, which is the true eye? Speak! Speak!"
> Magu pulled the Master down from his seat and took the seat himself.
> The Master approached and said, "I don't understand."
> As Magu thought to answer, the Master pulled him down from the seat and took the seat himself. Magu withdrew, and the Master then came down from the seat.

they are each one of "so many" (*kota no ichiichi nari* 許多の一一なり): A tentative translation of a sentence subject to varied interpretation. Some would take the duplicated *ichiichi* ("each one") here as referring to each of the two actors in the story; others suggest that the story is "one" with "so many"; still others, that the story is but one of "so many."

53　**Yunmen** (*Unmon* 雲門): I.e., Yunmen Wenyen 雲門文偃. His saying on Kannon can be found in Dōgen's *shinji Shōbōgenzō* 眞字正法眼藏 (DZZ.5:258, case 257); see also the *Yunmen yulu* 雲門語錄 (T.1988.47:554a13-15):

> 擧古云、聞聲悟道見色明心。師云、作麼生是聞聲悟道見色明心。乃云、觀世音菩薩將錢來買餬餅。放下手云、元來秖是饅頭。
>
> Taking up an old saying, [Yunmen] said, "Hearing sounds and understanding the way; seeing forms and clarifying the mind." The Master [Yunmen] said, "What is this 'hearing sounds and understanding the way; seeing forms and clarifying the mind'?" Then he said, "Bodhisattva Observer of the Sounds of the World comes

150 DŌGEN'S *SHŌBŌGENZŌ* VOLUME II

for entering principle."[54] In the *Śūraṃgama* assembly, there is the Kannon of Perfect Penetration; in the *Lotus* assembly there is the Kannon of Universal Manifestation.[55] While these are all studying together with the buddha, studying together with the mountains, rivers, and the whole earth, they are still one or two of "so many hands and eyes."

[Tōunji MS:]

爾時仁治三年壬寅四月二十六日示

Presented on the twenty-sixth day, fourth month of the senior water year of the tiger, the third year of Ninji [27 May 1242][56]

仁治壬寅仲夏十日書寫之。懷奘

Copied this on the tenth day of mid-summer, senior water year of the tiger, Ninji [9 June 1242]. Ejō

---

with cash to buy rice cakes." He put down his hand and said, "Basically, they're just dumplings."

54 **Baizhang** 百丈: I.e., Baizhang Huaihai 百丈懷海 (749-814). His saying on Kannon occurs in a story in the *Jingde chuandeng lu* 景德傳燈錄 (T.2076.51:250a4-8):

因普請钁地次、忽有一僧聞飯鼓鳴舉起钁頭大笑便歸。師云、俊哉此是觀音入理之門。師歸院乃喚其僧問、適來見什麼道理便恁麼。對云、適來只聞鼓聲動歸喫飯去來。師乃笑。

Once, when all were hoeing the fields, a certain monk, upon hearing the sound of the meal drum, picked up his hoe, gave a great laugh, and returned.
The Master [Baizhang] said, "Excellent! This is Guanyin's gateway for entering principle."
When the Master returned to the cloister, he called that monk and asked him, "What principle did you see just then that you were like that?"
He replied, "When I heard the sound of the drum just then, I just took off and came back to eat."
The Master laughed.

55 *Śūraṃgama* **assembly** (*Ryōgon e* 楞嚴會): Likely a reference to the assembly at which the Buddha was supposed to have preached the *Śūraṃgama-sūtra*, the sixth chapter of which contains discussion of the perfect penetration (*entsū* 圓通) of Bodhisattva Avalokiteśvara. (*Shoulengyan jing* 首楞嚴經, T.945.9:128b11ff.)

Lotus **assembly** (*Hokke e* 法華會): Reference either to the assembly at which the *Saddharma-puṇḍarīka-sūtra* was originally preached, or to convocations dedicated to the sūtra, which contains the popular chapter on Kannon, entitled "Universal Gateway" (*Fumon* 普門), in which the bodhisattva manifests himself in whatever form is appropriate for his intended audience.

56 This colophon in the Tōunji 洞雲寺 MS is followed by a postscript identical to that of the Ryūmonji 龍門寺 MS given above.

TREASURY OF THE TRUE DHARMA EYE

NUMBER 19

The Old Mirror
Kokyō

古鏡

The Old Mirror

Kokyō

INTRODUCTION

This essay was composed at Kōshōji in late autumn of 1241. It occurs as number 19 in both the seventy-five and sixty-chapter *Shōbōgenzō* compilations and as number 20 in the vulgate edition.

In common parlance, "old mirror" refers to the ancient bronze mirrors of China, often thought of as somehow magical for their reflective power. More importantly for our essay is the Buddhist use of the mirror as a metaphor for consciousness, especially for the type or feature of consciousness that perfectly reflects its object — the "mirror wisdom," often said to be inherent in all consciousness and fully realized in the awakened mind.

Dōgen's essay takes up a series of passages on this mirror appearing in Zen literature — from the strange case of the Indian Zen ancestor Gayaśata, who was from birth always accompanied by a mirror, through the famous poem by the Sixth Ancestor, Huineng 慧能, on polishing the mirror of the mind, and the odd discussion between the ninth-century masters Xuefeng Yicun 雪峰義存 and Xuansha Shibei 玄沙師備 about what happens when two mirrors reflect each other, to the story, much cited in the *Shōbōgenzō*, of Nanyue Huairang's 南嶽懷讓 likening Mazu Daoyi's 馬祖道一 meditating in order to become a buddha to someone's trying to make a mirror by polishing a clay tile. Not surprisingly, given his emphasis on practice, Dōgen ends his essay by encouraging us to take up our own tile and make ourselves a mirror.

正法眼藏第十九

Treasury of the True Dharma Eye
Number 19

古鏡

The Old Mirror

[19:1] {1:221}

諸佛諸祖の受持し單傳するは、古鏡なり。同見同面なり、同像同鑄なり、
同參同證す。胡來胡現、十萬八千、漢來漢現、一念萬年なり。古來古現
し、今來今現し、佛來佛現し、祖來祖現するなり。

What the buddhas and the ancestors receive and keep and uniquely transmit is the old mirror. They are the same view, the same face;
they are the same image, the same casting; they study together, and
verify together.[1] It is, *when a foreigner comes, a foreigner appears —
one hundred eight thousand; when a Han comes, a Han appears — ten
thousand years in one moment of thought.*[2] It is, when the past comes,
the past appears; when the present comes, the present appears; when a
buddha comes, a buddha appears; when an ancestor comes, an ancestor
appears.

* * * * *

[19:2]

第十八祖伽耶舍多尊者は、西域の摩提國の人なり。姓は鬱頭藍、父名天
蓋、母名方聖。母氏かつて夢見にいはく、ひとりの大神、おほきなるかが
みを持してむかへりと。ちなみに懷胎す。七日ありて師をむめり。師、は
じめて生ぜるに、肌體、みがける瑠璃のごとし。いまだかつて洗浴せざる

---

1 **the same image, the same casting** (*dōzō dōchū* 同像同鑄): The term "image" here
may refer either to an image, or reflection, in a mirror or to an image, or icon, such as a
painting or statue of a buddha or an ancestor. Both senses are at play in this essay. The
term "casting" may refer to the making either of an image or of a metal (typically bronze)
mirror. It is not clear what terms are being identified by the adjectives "same" (*dō* 同) in
this sentence; it could be the "the buddhas" and "the ancestors" but is more likely "the
buddhas and the ancestors" and "the old mirror."

2 **when a foreigner comes, a foreigner appears** (*ko rai ko gen* 胡來胡現); **when a Han
comes, a Han appears** (*kan rai kan gen* 漢來漢現) : Dōgen is here introducing a saying
of Xuefeng Yicun 雪峰義存 (822-908) that he will discuss below, section 19.

ten thousand years in one moment of thought (*ichinen bannen* 一念萬年): A common
expression in Zen literature for eternity in each moment.

に、自然に香潔なり。いとけなくより閑靜をこのむ、言語、よのつねの童子にことなり。

The Eighteenth Ancestor, Venerable Gayaśata, was a person of the Land of Magadha in the Western Regions.[3] His family name was Yutoulan; his father's name was Tiange; his mother's name was Fangsheng.[4] His mother once reported a dream in which a great deity came to her holding a large mirror. She then became pregnant, and, after seven days, the Master was born. When the Master was first born, his skin was like burnished *vaiḍūrya*, and before he was bathed, he was naturally fragrant and clean.[5] From an early age, he loved the quiet, and his words were different from those of ordinary boys.

[19:3]

むまれしより、一の淨明の圓鑑、おのづから同生せり。圓鑑とは圓鏡なり。奇代の事なり。同生せり、といふは、圓鑑も母氏の胎よりむめるにはあらず。師は胎生す、師の出胎する同時に、圓鑑きたりて、天眞として師のほとりに現前して、ひごろの調度のごとくありしなり。この圓鑑、その儀、よのつねにあらず。童子むかひきたるには、圓鑑を兩手にささげきたるがごとし。しかあれども、童面かくれず。童子さりゆくには、圓鑑をおうてさりゆくがごとし。しかあれども、童身かくれず。童子睡眠するときは、圓鑑そのうへにおほふ、たとへば華蓋のごとし。童子端坐のときは、圓鑑その面前にあり。おほよそ動容進止にあひしたがふなり。しかのみにあらず、古來今の佛事、ことごとくこの圓鑑にむかひてみることをう。また天上・人間の衆事諸法、みな圓鑑にうかみてくもれるところなし。たとへば、經書にむかひて照古照今をうるよりも、この圓鑑よりみるはあきらかなり。

When he was born, a clear, bright, round mirror was born together with him. The term *enkan* means "round mirror."[6] It was a rare event.

---

3 **The Eighteenth Ancestor, Venerable Gayaśata** (*daijūhachi so Kayashata sonja* 第十八祖伽耶舍多尊者): Dōgen is here retelling in Japanese a biography of the ancestor that can be found in the *Jingde chuandeng lu* 景德傳燈錄 (T.2076.51:212c). The Sanskrit name is unattested and the reconstruction tentative.

the Land of Magadha (*Madai koku* 摩提國): Kingdom of north India corresponding roughly to modern Bihar.

the Western Regions (*saiiki* 西域): A term broadly used for regions west of China, including, as in this case, India.

4 **Yutoulan** (*Uzzuran* 鬱頭藍); **Tiange** (*Tengai* 天蓋); **Fangsheng** (*Hōshō* 方聖): Chinese names for which, given that Gayaśata is unknown from Sanskrit sources, there are likely no Indic originals.

5 *vaiḍūrya* (*ruri* 瑠璃): Also written *ruri* 琉璃; a Sanskrit term used for beryl, crystal, and other minerals; one of the seven precious substances.

6 **The term *enkan* means "round mirror"** (*enkan to wa enkyō nari* 圓鑑とは圓鏡なり): Dōgen is here simply offering a synonym for the graph *kan* 鑑, used in the preceding sentence. The tradition that Gayaśata was born with a mirror, as well as the following

19. The Old Mirror *Kokyō* 古鏡 155

To say that it was born together with him does not mean that the round mirror was born from his mother's womb; the Master was born, and, at the same time that he emerged from the womb, the round mirror came and spontaneously appeared in the vicinity of the Master, just like an ordinary implement. The behavior of this round mirror was not ordinary: when the child approached, he seemed to be holding up the round mirror with both hands, but the boy's face was not hidden [by it]; when he departed, he seemed to be carrying the round mirror on his back, but the boy's body was not hidden. When the boy slept, the round mirror covered him, like a flowered canopy; when the boy sat up, the round mirror was in front of him. It followed him when he moved or was still, when he advanced or stopped. Morever, all Buddhist affairs from the past to the present could be seen in this round mirror. Again, the affairs and phenomena in the heavens and among humans all floated without any blurring on this round mirror. What was seen, for example, with this mirror was clearer than the illumination of the past and illumination of the present one could get from consulting books.

[19:4] {1:222}

しかあるに、童子すでに出家・受戒するとき、圓鑑、これより現前せず。このゆえに近里・遠方、おなじく奇妙なりと讃歎す。まことにこの裟婆世界に比類すくなしといふとも、さらに他那裏に親族のかくのごとくなる種胤あらんことを莫怪なるべし、遠慮すべし。まさにしるべし、若樹・若石に化せる經卷あり、若田・若里に流布する知識あり、かれも圓鑑なるべし、いまの黄紙朱軸は圓鑑なり。

However, once the boy had left home and received the precepts, the round mirror no longer appeared. Hence, those in nearby villages and distant quarters alike praised this as rare and marvelous. Truly there are few comparable examples in this Sahā world, but we should not be suspicious of, should be circumspect about, the fact that, elsewhere over there, there may be families that have such progeny.[7] We should realize that, "*whether on trees or on rocks*," there are sūtra scrolls that convert [beings]; "*whether in fields or in villages*," there are wise friends that

---

account of its presence throughout his life as a householder, does not occur in his biography in the *Jingde chuandeng lu* 景德傳燈錄. A source here has not been identified.

7 **elsewhere over there** (*ta nari ni* 他那裏に): Presumably, in worlds other than our Sahā world.

156 DŌGEN'S *SHŌBŌGENZŌ* VOLUME II

spread [the dharma].[8] They are also the round mirror. This yellow paper and vermilion spindle are the round mirror.[9]

[19:5]

あるとき、出遊するに、僧伽難提尊者にあうて、直にすすみて難提尊者の前にいたる。尊者とふ、汝が手中なるは、まさに何の所表かある。有何所表、を問著にあらずとききて参學すべし。

Once, as he was traveling, upon meeting Venerable Saṃghānandi, he went right up in front of Saṃghānandi.[10] The Venerable asked, "What is shown in what you have in your hands?"

We should study this, hearing it not as a question about "*what is shown.*"[11]

[19:6] {1:223}

師いはく、諸佛大圓鑑、内外無瑕翳、兩人同得見、心眼皆相似。

---

8   **"whether on trees or on rocks," there are sūtra scrolls that convert [beings]** (*nyaku ju nyaku seki ni keseru kyōkan ari* 若樹若石に化せる經卷あり); **"whether in fields or in villages," there are wise friends that spread [the dharma]** (*nyaku den nyaku ri ni rufu suru chishiki ari* 若田若里に流布する知識あり): The former phrase is associated with the tale, in the *Nirvāṇa Sūtra*, of the "boy of the Himalayas" who vowed to write the teachings of the Buddha on trees and rocks; see Supplementary Notes, s.v. "Whether on trees or on rocks." The latter phrase is associated with the account, in the *Lotus Sūtra*, of followers of the Buddha preaching the dharma in fields and villages; see Supplementary Notes, s.v. "Whether in fields or in villages." The juxtaposition of "sūtra scrolls" (*kyōkan* 經卷) and "wise friends" (*chishiki* 知識; i.e., teachers) here likely reflects the fixed expression, "whether from a wise friend, whether from a sūtra scroll" (for which, see Supplementary Notes); the phrase, occurring several times in Dōgen's writing, appears below, in section 8.

9   **yellow paper and vermilion spindle** (*ōshi shujiku* 黄紙朱軸): I.e., the paper and spindle of a roll of text; here, doubtless a scriptural text. Some manuscript witnesses follow this sentence with the line, "Who could think that the Master alone was extraordinary?" (*tare ka shi o hitoe ni kii nari to omowan* たれか師をひとへに希夷なりとおもはん). The "Master" here no doubt refers to Gayaśata.

10   **Once, as he was traveling** (*aru toki, shutsuyū suru ni* あるとき、出遊するに): Dōgen here retells in Japanese part of a conversation that appears in the biographical notice of the Seventeenth Ancestor, Saṃghānandi (*Sengjianandi* 僧伽難提), at *Jingde chuandeng lu* 景德傳燈錄, T.2076.51:212b17-19. In the original, Saṃghānandi encounters Gayaśata as a boy dwelling on a mountain peak covered by purple clouds. After their conversation, Saṅghānandi inducts him into the Buddhist order and gives him the name Gayaśata.

11   **hearing it not as a question about "what is shown"** (*u ka shohyō, o monjaku ni arazu to kikite* 有何所表、を問著にあらずとききて): Usually interpreted to mean that we should not take Saṅghānandi's words as a question. "What is shown" translates the four-word interrogative phrase of the Chinese source, *yu he suo biao* 有何所表, which, if read as a declarative, could only yield something strange like, "Being is the expression of what."

19. The Old Mirror *Kokyō* 古鏡   157

The Master said,

> *The great round mirror of the buddhas,*
> *Without flaw or blur inside or out.*
> *Both people can see the same;*
> *Mind and eye, all alike.*[12]

[19:7]

しかあれば、諸佛大圓鑑、なにとしてか師と同生せる。師の生來は大圓
鑑の明なり。諸佛は、この圓鑑に同參同見なり、諸佛は、大圓鑑の鑄像
なり。大圓鑑は、智にあらず、理にあらず、性にあらず、相にあらず。十
聖・三賢等の法のなかにも大圓鏡の名あれども、いまの諸佛大圓鑑にあら
ず。諸佛かならずしも智にあらざるがゆえに、諸佛に智慧あり、智慧を諸
佛とせるにあらず。

Such being the case, how could the great round mirror of the buddhas
be born together with the Master? The birth of the Master is the bright-
ness of the great round mirror. The buddhas study together and see together by this round mirror. The buddhas are the cast image of the great
round mirror. The great round mirror is not wisdom, is not principle, is
not the nature, is not the form. The term "great round mirror" may occur
in the dharma of the ten sages and three worthies, but it is not this great
round mirror of the buddhas.[13] Since the buddhas are not necessarily [the
same as] wisdom, the buddhas have wisdom; we do not identify wisdom
as the buddhas.[14]

---

12 **The Master said** (*shi iwaku* 師いはく): Dōgen here quotes Gayaśata's verse in Chinese. Exactly who is indicated in the phrase, "both people can see the same" (*ryōnin dō
tokuken* 兩人同得見) is unclear; it could refer to both the person holding and the person
looking at the mirror or to both the person looking at and the person appearing in the mirror.

Mind and eye, all alike (*shingen kai sōji* 心眼皆相似): One might well prefer to read
this "the mind's eye, all alike"; the translation here seeks to accommodate Dōgen's discussion of the phrase below, sections 9-10.

13 **ten sages and three worthies** (*jisshō sanken* 十聖三賢): I.e., the traditional path of
the bodhisattva: the ten stages, or "grounds" (*chi* 地; S. *bhūmi*), of the "sage," or "noble"
(*shō* 聖; S. *ārya*) — i.e., those on the advanced levels of the path — and the three types of
"worthy" (*ken* 賢; S. *bhadra*) — i.e., those on the levels just preceding the ārya.

14 **we do not identify wisdom as the buddhas** (*chie o shobutsu to seru ni arazu* 智
慧を諸佛とせるにあらず): I.e., Buddhas may have wisdom, but they cannot be defined
simply by their wisdom. The point here seems to be that, while the mirror is commonly
used in Buddhist literature as a metaphor for wisdom, the mirror under discussion here
is not limited to this virtue of the buddhas. The English of the two final sentences of
this paragraph follows the most common punctuation of the text. It is also possible (and
seems to make somewhat better sense) to read the Japanese here as follows:

> The term "great round mirror" may occur in the dharma of the "ten sages and three
> worthies," but it is not this great round mirror of the buddhas, since the buddhas are
> not necessarily [the same as] wisdom. The buddhas have wisdom; we do not identify
> wisdom as the buddhas.

158 DŌGEN'S *SHŌBŌGENZŌ* VOLUME II

[19:8]

参學しるべし、智を説著するは、いまだ佛道の究竟説にあらざるなり。すでに諸佛大圓鑑、たとひわれと同生せりと見聞すといふとも、さらに道理あり。いはゆるこの大圓鑑、この生に接すべからず、他生に接すべからず。玉鏡にあらず、銅鏡にあらず、肉鏡にあらず、髓鏡にあらず。圓鑑の言偈なるか、童子の説偈なるか。童子この四句の偈をとくことも、かつて人に學習せるにあらず、かつて或從經卷にあらず、かつて或從知識にあらず、圓鑑をささげてかくのごとくとくなり。師の幼稚のときより、かがみにむかふの常儀とせるのみなり。生知の辯慧あるがごとし。大圓鑑の、童子と同生せるか、童子の、大圓鑑と同生せるか、まさに前後生もあるべし。大圓鑑は、すなはち諸佛の功德なり。

Students should realize that to talk of wisdom is not the ultimate talk of the way of the buddhas. Although we experience that the great round mirror of the buddhas has been born together with us, there is a further principle: that we do not contact this great round mirror in this birth, we do not contact it in that birth.[15] It is not a jeweled mirror; it is not a bronze mirror; it is not a flesh mirror; it is not a marrow mirror.[16] Is this a gāthā said by the round mirror? Is this a gāthā spoken by the boy? The boy's speaking this four-line gāthā is not something ever learned from another, not *whether from a sūtra scroll*, not *whether from a wise friend*; he spoke this way from holding up the round mirror.[17] From his childhood, the Master made it his usual practice to face the mirror. It is as if he had the discriminating wisdom of knowledge at birth.[18] Was the great round mirror born together with the boy? Was the boy born together with the great round mirror? There should also be births before or after.[19] The great round mirror is the virtue of the buddhas.

---

15 **we experience** (*kenmon su* 見聞す): Or, perhaps, "we learn." A common compound verb (literally, "see and hear") that can mean "to perceive" or "to experience," "to learn of," "to have knowledge (or information) about," etc.

this birth (*kono shō* この生); **that birth** (*tashō* 他生): Or "this life," "that life." The translation tries to retain the repetition here of the term *shō* in the preceding "born together."

16 **flesh mirror** (*nikukyō* 肉鏡); **marrow mirror** (*zuikyō* 髓鏡): Dōgen is here alluding to the phrase "skin, flesh, bones, and marrow" (*hi niku kotsu zui* 皮肉骨髓), regularly appearing in his writings to indicate the essence or entirety of the Zen transmission; see Supplementary Notes, s.v. "Skin, flesh, bones, and marrow."

17 **whether from a sūtra scroll** (*waku jū kyōkan* 或從經卷); **whether from a wise friend** (*waku jū chishiki* 或從知識): See above, Note 8.

18 **knowledge at birth** (*shōchi* 生知): I.e., innate knowledge, a term that could be applied to the inherent wisdom suggested by the story of Gayaśata's birth with the mirror. See Supplementary Notes, s.v. "Knowledge at birth."

19 **births before or after** (*zengo shō* 前後生): I.e., boy and mirror born at different times.

19. The Old Mirror *Kokyō* 古鏡 159

[19:9]

このかがみ、内外にくもりなし、といふは、外にまつ内にあらず、内にく
もれる外にあらず。面背あることなし、両箇おなじく得見あり、心と眼と
あひにたり。相似といふは、人の人にあふなり。たとひ内の形像も、心・
眼あり、同得見あり。たとひ外の形像も、心眼あり、同得見あり。いま現
前せる依報・正報、ともに内に相似なり、外に相似なり。われにあらず、
たれにあらず、これは両人の相見なり、両人の相似なり。かれもわれとい
ふ、われもかれとなる。

To say that this mirror is without blurring "inside and out" is not [refer-
ring to] an inside that depends on an outside or an outside blurred by an
inside. It does not have front or back; "both can see the same; mind and
eye are alike."[20] To say they are "alike" means a person meets a person.
The image on the inside has mind and eye, and "both can see"; the image
on the outside has mind and eye, and "both can see." This secondary recompense and primary recompense before us are alike on the inside and
alike on the outside.[21] They are not I; they are not another. This is "both
people" seeing each other, "both people" alike. The other is also called
"I"; I am also the other.

[19:10] {1:224}

心と眼と皆相似、といふは、心は心に相似なり、眼は眼に相似なり。相似
は心・眼なり。たとへば、心眼各相似といはんがごとし。いかならんかこ
れ心の心に相似せる、いはゆる三祖・六祖なり。いかならんかこれ眼の眼
に相似なる、いはゆる道眼被眼礙なり。

To say that the mind and eye are "all alike" means the mind is like the
mind, means the eye is like the eye, means "alike" is "mind and eye." It
is as if we were to say that mind and eye each are like each. What is the
mind like the mind? It is the Third Ancestor and the Sixth Ancestor.[22]

---

20 **"both can see the same; mind and eye are alike"** (*ryōko onajiku tokuken ari, shin
to gan to ainitari* 両箇おなじく得見あり、心と眼とあひにたり*): Putting the last two
lines of Gayaśata's verse into Japanese, though Dōgen has altered the numerical classifier from the poem's "both people" (*ryōnin* 両人) to what would more commonly indicate
"both things" (*ryōko* 両箇). Hence, his version might suggest that both "front and back"
can see, though his subsequent comments seem to refer to the person and image.

21 **secondary recompense and primary recompense** (*ehō shōhō* 依報正報): Standard
Buddhist terms for the two aspects of karmic consequences: the environment, or circumstances, into which one is born; and the makeup of the person — hence, the self and its
world. See Supplementary Notes.

22 **the Third Ancestor and the Sixth Ancestor** (*sanso rokuso* 三祖・六祖): It is not
obvious why Dōgen picks out these two ancestors here. Most commentators suggest that
it is simply because both have the glyph for "mirror" (*jian* 鑑) in their names: respectively, Jianzhi ("Mirror Wisdom") Sengcan 鑑智僧璨 and Dajian ("Great Mirror") Huineng
大鑑慧能.

160 DŌGEN'S *SHŌBŌGENZŌ* VOLUME II

What is the eye like the eye? It is "*the eye of the way is obstructed by the eye.*"[23]

[19:11]
いま師の道得する宗旨、かくのごとし。これはじめて僧伽難提尊者に奉覲する本由なり。この宗旨を擧拈して、大圓鑑の佛面・祖面を參學すべし、古鏡の眷屬なり。

Such is the essential point of this saying of the Master. This is the original account of how he first had audience with Venerable Saṅghānandi. Taking up this essential point, we should study the buddha faces and ancestor faces of the great round mirror.[24] They are the attendants of the old mirror.

* * * * *

[19:12]
第三十三祖大鑑禪師、かつて黄梅山の法席に功夫せしとき、壁書して祖師に呈する偈にいはく、菩提本無樹、明鏡亦非臺、本來無一物、何處有塵埃。

Once, when the Thirty-third Ancestor, Chan Master Dajian, was working away at the dharma seat of Mount Huangmei, he said in a gāthā written on a wall and presented to the Ancestral Master,[25]

> *Bodhi originally has no tree,*
> *The bright mirror, no stand.*
> *From the beginning, not one thing;*
> *Where is there any dust?*[26]

---

23 **"the eye of the way is obstructed by the eye"** (*dōgen hi gen ge* 道眼被眼礙): After the words of Fayan Wenyi 法眼文益 (885-958), quoted in Dōgen's *shinji Shōbōgenzō* 眞字正法眼藏 (DZZ.5:186, case 111); see Supplementary Notes, s.v. "Obstructed by the eye."

24 **buddha faces and ancestor faces** (*butsumen somen* 佛面・祖面): Dōgen is here beginning to play with the numerical classifier *men* 面, used to count flat objects like mirrors, which has the primary senses, "face," "surface." He will continue to exploit this term in his subsequent commentary. See Supplementary Notes, s.v. "Buddha faces, ancestor faces."

25 **the Thirty-third Ancestor, Chan Master Dajian** (*dai sanjūsan so Daikan zenji* 第三十三祖大鑑禪師): I.e., the Sixth Ancestor, Huineng 慧能.

Mount Huangmei (*Ōbaisan* 黄梅山): The mountain in present-day Hunan that was the site of the communities of the Fourth and Fifth Ancestors. According to his legend, as a layman, Huineng was put to work at the Fifth Ancestor's monastery.

the Ancestral Master (*soshi* 祖師): I.e., the Fifth Ancestor, Hongren 弘忍 (602-675). According to the famous legend, Hongren held a contest to determine his successor. The head monk Shenxiu 神秀 (d. 706) wrote a poem on a monastery wall to which Huineng's poem was a response.

26 **Bodhi originally has no tree** (*bodai hon mu ju* 菩提本無樹): Huineng's famous

19. The Old Mirror *Kokyō* 古鏡 161

[19:13]

しかあれば、この道取を學取すべし。大鑑高祖、よの人、これを古佛とい
ふ。圜悟禪師いはく、稽首曹溪眞古佛。しかあればしるべし、大鑑高祖の
明鏡をしめす、本來無一物、何處有塵埃、なり。明鏡非臺、これ命脈あ
り、功夫すべし。明明はみな明鏡なり、かるがゆえに、明頭來明頭打とい
ふ。いづれのところ、にあらざれば、いづれのところ、なし。いはんや、
かがみにあらざる一塵の、盡十方界にのこれらんや。かがみにあらざる一
塵、かがみにのこらんや。しるべし、盡界は塵刹にあらざるなり、ゆえに
古鏡面なり。

Thus, we should study these words. People in the world called the Eminent Ancestor Dajian an "old buddha." The Chan Master Yuanwu said,
"*I make prostrations to Caoxi, a true old buddha.*"[27] Thus, we should
realize that the Eminent Ancestor Dajian shows the bright mirror: it
is, "*From the beginning, not one thing; where is there any dust?*" "*The
bright mirror, no stand*": this has the vital artery. We should work away
at it. All that is "perfectly clear" is the bright mirror.[28] Hence, it is said,
"*when the bright comes, the bright does it.*"[29] Since it is not anywhere,
there is no "where."[30] How much less does there remain throughout all
the worlds in the ten directions one mote of "dust" that is not the mirror;
how much less does there remain on the mirror one mote of "dust" that
is not the mirror. We should realize that all the worlds are not *kṣetra* like
dust motes.[31] Hence, they are the face of the old mirror.

---

verse appears in several slightly variant versions. Dōgen's version here follows that re-
corded at *Tiansheng guangdeng lu* 天聖廣燈錄, ZZ.135:645a6-7. The verse to which
Huineng is responding also has several slight variants; see Supplementary Notes, s.v.
"Bright mirror."

27 **The Chan Master Yuanwu** (*Engo zenji* 圜悟禪師): I.e., Yuanwu Keqin 圜悟克
勤 (1063-1135). His words can be found at *Yuanwu Foguo chanshi yulu* 圜悟佛果禪師
語錄 (T.1997.47:807b8). "Caoxi" 曹溪 is the place, in present-day Guangdong, where
Huineng is said to have resided.

28 **"perfectly clear"** (*meimei* 明明): The translation loses the repetition of *mei* 明, the
term being otherwise translated here as "bright." Possibly an allusion to the words of
Layman Pang (*Hō koji* 龐居士; 740?-808), cited elsewhere in Dōgen's writing; see Supplementary Notes, s.v. "Perfectly clear, the tips of the hundred grasses."

29 **"when the bright comes, the bright does it"** (*meitō rai meitō ta* 明頭來明頭打):
A tentative rendering of a vexed saying attributed to the Chan monk Puhua 普化 (dates
unknown), quoted in Dōgen's *shinji Shōbōgenzō* 眞字正法眼藏 (DZZ.5:136-138, case
22); see Supplementary Notes.

30 **there is no "where"** (*izure no tokoro, nashi* いづれのところ、なし): From the final
line of Huineng's verse: "Where is there any dust?"

31 **all the worlds are not *kṣetra* like dust motes** (*jinkai wa jinsetsu ni arazaru* 盡界
は塵刹にあらざる): The translation tries to retain Dōgen's punning on the term *jinsetsu*
塵刹, which refers to "lands as numerous as motes of dust." See Supplementary Notes,
s.v. "Dust."

162　　DŌGEN'S *SHŌBŌGENZŌ* VOLUME II

* * * * *

[19:14] {1:225}

南嶽大慧禪師の會に、ある僧とふ、如鏡鑄像、光歸何處。師云、大德、未出家時相貌、向甚麼處去。僧曰、成後爲甚麼不鑑照。師云、雖不鑑照、瞞他一點也不得。

> In the community of Chan Master Dahui of Nanyue, a monk asked, "*If a mirror were cast as an image, where would its light return?*"[32]
>
> *The Master said, "Most Virtuous One, your appearance before you left home — where has it gone?"*
>
> *The monk said, "After it's finished, why doesn't it reflect?"*
>
> *The Master said, "Even though it doesn't reflect, it can't deceive anyone even one jot."* [33]

[19:15]

いまこの萬像は、なにものとあきらめざるに、たづぬれば鏡を鑄成せる證明、すなはち師の道にあり。鏡は金にもあらず、玉にもあらず、明にあらず、像にあらずといへども、たちまち鑄像なる、まことに鏡の究辨なり。

While it is not clear what the ten thousand images are, when we seek them, the proof that they are cast from a mirror is in the words of the Master.[34] The mirror is not metal; it is not jewel; it is not bright; it is not an image. Yet that it is immediately a cast image is truly the ultimate discernment of the mirror.

[19:16]

光歸何處は、如鏡鑄像の如鏡鑄像なる道取なり。たとへば、像歸像處なり、鑄能鑄鏡なり。

"*Where would its light return?*" is a saying in which "*a mirror cast as an image*" is "*a mirror cast as an image.*" For example, *the image returns where the image is; the casting casts a mirror.*[35]

32　**Chan Master Dahui of Nanyue** (*Nangaku Daie zenji* 南嶽大慧禪師): I.e., Nanyue Huairang 南嶽懷讓 (677-744), disciple of the Sixth Ancestor, Huineng 慧能. This story appears in many Zen collections; see, e.g., *Zongmen tongyao ji* 宗門統要集 (ZTS.1:46c10-d2); *shinji Shōbōgenzō* 眞字正法眼藏 (DZZ.5:188-190, case 116).

"**If a mirror were cast as an image**" (*nyo kyō chū zō* 如鏡鑄像): I.e., if a bronze mirror were recast as an icon.

33　"**Even though it doesn't reflect, it can't deceive anyone even one jot**" (*man ta itten ya futoku* 瞞他一點也不得): Usually interpreted to mean that the recast image is not a reflection that one might mistake for the real thing.

34　**the ten thousand images** (*banzō* 萬像): A common term usually denoting "the myriad things" that appear in the world. Dōgen seems here to be shifting the sense of "image" from the icon to phenomena.

35　**the image returns where the image is** (*zō ki zō sho* 像歸像處); **the casting casts a**

19. The Old Mirror *Kokyō* 古鏡　　163

[19:17]

大德未出家時相貌、向甚麼處去、といふは、鏡をささげて照面するなり。
このとき、いづれの面面かすなはち自己面ならん。

His saying, "*Most Virtuous One, your appearance before you left home — where has it gone?*" holds up the mirror and reflects the face. At this time, which of the faces is his own face?[36]

[19:18]

師いはく、雖不鑑照、瞞他一點也不得、といふは、鑑照不得なり、瞞他不
得なり。海枯不到露底を參學すべし、莫打破、莫動著なり。しかありとい
へども、さらに參學すべし、拈像鑄鏡の道理あり。當恁麼時は、百千萬の
鑑照にて、瞞瞞點點なり。

"The Master said, '*Even though it doesn't reflect, it can't deceive anyone even one jot.*'" This says, "*the mirror can't reflect*"; it says, "*it can't deceive anyone.*"[37] We should learn that "*though the ocean dries up, it does not reveal the bottom.*"[38] It is, "*Don't spoil it; don't move!*"[39] Nevertheless, we should study it further. There is a principle of taking up an image to cast a mirror. This very time is deception after deception, jot after jot, in a hundred, thousand, myriad reflections.

* * * * *

---

mirror (*shu nō shu kyō* 鑄能鑄鏡): Usually interpreted to mean that the image is just the image, the casting is just the casting.

36 **which of the faces is his own face?** (*izure no menmen ka sunawachi jiko men naran* いづれの面面かすなはち自己面ならん): The referent of "own" (*jiko* 自己) here is unclear; the question could as well be put, "which of the faces is our own face?" or "which of the faces is the face of the self?"

37 **"the mirror can't reflect"** (*kanshō futoku* 鑑照不得); **"it can't deceive anyone"** (*man ta futoku* 瞞他不得): Presumably this means that there is a perspective from which the mirror is not merely a reflector that might "deceive" someone by its images.

38 **"though the ocean dries up, it does not reveal the bottom"** (*kai ko futō rotei* 海枯不到露底): Variation on a saying, drawn from a verse by the poet Du Xunhe 杜荀鶴 (846-907), that occurs often in Zen literature (see, e.g., *Zongjing lu* 宗鏡錄, T.2016.48:564b12):

海枯終見底、人死不知心。

When the ocean dries up, we finally see the bottom;
When a person dies, we do not know his mind.

39 **"Don't spoil it; don't move!"** (*maku taha, maku dōjaku* 莫打破、莫動著): Colloquial expressions sometimes used in Zen texts to warn students away from erroneous words or deeds.

164 DŌGEN'S *SHŌBŌGENZŌ* VOLUME II

[19:19] {1:226}

雪峰眞覺大師、あるとき衆にしめすにいはく、要會此事、我這裏如一面古鏡相似。胡來胡現、漢來漢現。時玄沙出問、忽遇明鏡來時如何。師云、胡漢俱隱。玄沙曰、某甲即不然。峰云、儞作麼生。玄沙曰、請和尚問。峰云、忽遇明鏡來時如何。玄沙曰、百雜碎。

> Great Master Zhenjue of Xuefeng once addressed the assembly, saying, *"If you wish to understand this matter, I'm here like one old mirror: a foreigner comes, a foreigner appears; a Han comes, a Han appears."*[40]

> At that time, Xuansha came forth and asked, *"How about when all of a sudden a bright mirror comes?"*[41]

> The Master said, *"Foreigner and Han would both disappear."*

> Xuansha replied, *"I'm not like this."*

> Feng said, *"How about you?"*

> Xuansha replied, *"Ask me, Reverend."*

> Feng said, *"How about when all of a sudden a bright mirror comes?"*

> Xuansha replied, *"A hundred fragments."*

[19:20]

しばらく雪峰道の、此事、といふは、是什麼事と參學すべし。しばらく雪峰の古鏡をならひみるべし。如一面古鏡、の道は、一面とは、邊際ながく斷じて、内外さらにあらざるなり、一珠走盤の自己なり。いま胡來胡現は、壱隻の赤鬚なり。漢來漢現は、この漢は、混沌よりこのかた、盤古よりのち、三才・五才の現成せるといひきたれるに、いま雪峰の道には、古鏡の功德の、漢現せり。いまの漢は漢にあらざるがゆえに、すなはち漢現なり。いま雪峰道の胡漢俱隱、さらにいふべし、鏡也自隱なるべし。玄沙道の百雜碎は、道也須是恁麼道なりとも、比來責儞還吾碎片來、如何還我明鏡來なり。

We should study for awhile Xuefeng's saying, "this matter," as *"what matter is this?"*[42] We should try learning for awhile about Xuefeng's old mirror. In the words, *"like one old mirror,"* the [numerical classifier] "one face" means limits long severed, without any inside and outside;

40　**Great Master Zhenjue of Xuefeng** (*Seppō Shinkaku daishi* 雪峰眞覺大師): Posthumous title of Xuefeng Yicun 雪峰義存. A version of this exchange can be found at *Liandeng huiyao* 聯燈會要, ZZ.136:784a7-10.

"one old mirror" (*ichimen kokyō* 一面古鏡): See Supplementary Notes, s.v. "Old mirror." The translation loses the numerical counter, *ichimen* (literally "one face"), with which Dōgen will play in his comment.

41　**Xuansha** (*Gensha* 玄沙): I.e., Xuefeng's disciple Xuansha Shibei 玄沙師備 (835-908).

42　**"what matter is this?"** (*ze jūmo* [or *shimo*] *ji* 是什麼事): The sentence could be understood simply as, "We should study 'what this matter is' that Xuefeng calls 'this matter'"; but it also lends itself to a reading, "We should study 'this matter' as 'what matter'" (i.e., an ineffable ultimate matter).

19. The Old Mirror *Kokyō* 古鏡   165

it means the self of a pearl rolling on a tray.[43] This "a foreigner comes, a foreigner appears" is one red beard.[44] On [the saying,] "*a Han comes, a Han appears,*" it has been said of this Han that, since the chaos, following Pangu, the three powers or five powers appeared [as Han]; but now, in Xuefeng's saying, the virtues of the old mirror have "appeared as Han."[45] Because this Han is not a Han, "a Han appears." Where Xuefeng says, "*Foreigner and Han would both disappear,*" we should say further, "*the mirror will itself disappear.*" On Xuefeng's saying, "A hundred fragments," while *what he says should be said like this, I've been asking you to return the fragments; why have you returned the bright mirror?*[46]

* * * * *

[19:21] {1:227}

黄帝のとき、十二面の鏡あり。家訓にいはく、天授なり。また廣成子の崆峒山にして與授せりけるともいふ。その十二面のもちいる儀は、十二時に時時に一面をもちいる、又十二月に毎月毎面にもちいる、十二年に年年面面にもちいる。いはく、鏡は廣成子の經典なり。黄帝に傳授するに、十二時等は鏡なり。これより照古照今するなり。十二時、もし鏡にあらずよりは、いかでか照古あらん。十二時、もし鏡にあらずは、いかでか照今あ

---

43 **"one face"** (*ichi men* 一面): Dōgen is here playing with the numerical counter for mirror in Xuefeng's "like one old mirror."

a pearl rolling on a tray (*isshu sōban* 一珠走盤): An idiom expressing unhampered movement.

44 **one red beard** (*isseki no shakushu* 壱隻の赤鬚): The term "red beard" is regularly used for a foreigner from the west. The significance of the numerical classifier *seki* 隻 here is ambiguous; it is used to count some types of animals, as well as to indicate one of a pair. In any case, the implication seems to be that there is one foreigner who both "comes" and "appears."

45 **the chaos** (*konton* 混沌); **Pangu** (*Banko* 盤古): References to the formation of the world according to Chinese cosmological accounts. The mythical figure Pangu is said to have been born from the primordial chaos and, in dying, created the heaven and earth.

three powers or five powers (*sansai gosai* 三才・五才): Chinese cosmological categories: the former refers to the triad, heaven, earth, and human; the latter, to the five phases (*wu xing* 五行): wood, fire, earth, metal, and water.

the virtues of the old mirror have "appeared as Han" (*kokyō no kudoku no, kangen seri* 古鏡の功徳の、漢現せり): Or, perhaps, "'a Han appears' as the virtues of the old mirror." The original has the awkward play, "The virtues of the old mirror have 'Han-appeared.'"

46 **what he says should be said like this** (*dō ya shu ze inmo dō* 道也須是恁麼道): I.e., Xuefeng has said it right. Here and in the following sentence, Dōgen shifts to Chinese, replicating a classical style of Chan comment.

return the fragments (*gen go saihen rai* 還吾碎片來); **returned the bright mirror** (*gen ga myōkyō rai* 還我明鏡來): The Chinese imperative construction here, *huan wu . . . lai* 還吾 . . . 來, and the closely similar *huan wo . . . lai* 還我 . . . 來 ("give me back . . ."), is a fairly common challenge in Chan texts, appearing several times in the *Shōbōgenzō*.

166 DŌGEN'S *SHŌBŌGENZŌ* VOLUME II

らん。いはゆる十二時は、十二面なり、十二面は、十二鏡なり、古今は十
二時の所使なり、この道理を指示するなり。これ俗の道取なりといへど
も、漢現の十二時中なり。

At the time of the Yellow Emperor, there were twelve mirrors.[47] It is said in house instructions that they are the bestowal of heaven; again, it is also said that Guang Chengzi bestowed them at Mount Kongtong.[48] The rites for using these twelve mirrors were to use one for each of the twelve times, or to use one every month of the twelve months, or to use mirror after mirror in year after year over the twelve years.[49] This is to say that the mirrors were the scripture of Guang Chengzi. When he bestowed them on the Yellow Emperor, the twelve times and the rest were mirrors; thereafter, they reflected the past and reflected the present.[50] If the twelve times were not a mirror, how could they reflect the past? If the twelve times were not a mirror, how could they reflect the present? This means the twelve times are twelve faces; the twelve faces are twelve mirrors.[51] Past and present are what the twelve times use; it is pointing out the reason for this.[52] Though this is a secular saying, the "Han appearing" is within the twelve times.

---

47 **Yellow Emperor** (*Kōtei* 黄帝): Legendary early Chinese ruler and cultural hero, traditionally dated in the third millennium BCE. Twelve great mirrors are mentioned in the *Shiwu jiyuan* 事物紀原 (KR.3k0014.008.18b), where it is said that the emperor cast the mirrors and used one of them each month. Beginning here, Dōgen embarks on an excursus, to discuss mirrors in China and Japan; he will return to his commentary on the conversation between Xuefeng and Xuansha in section 26, below.

48 **house instructions** (*kakun* 家訓): I.e., records of traditions and admonitions passed down within a family, though the referent here is unknown.

Guang Chengzi (*Kō Seishi* 廣成子); **Mount Kongtong** (*Kōtōzan* 崆峒山): Reference to a legend that the Yellow Emperor visited the sage Guang Chengzi on Kongtong. The story is found in *Zhuangzi* 莊子 11 (Zaiyou 在宥, KR.5c0126.011.8a), but no mention is made there of the twelve mirrors.

49 **the twelve times** (*jūni ji* 十二時); **the twelve years** (*jūni nen* 十二年): The twelve times are the periods, of two hours each, into which the day was divided in traditional China; the twelve years represent one cycle through the traditional Chinese astrological signs.

50 **the twelve times and the rest** (*jūni ji tō* 十二時等): Presumably, "the twelve times, the twelve months, and the twelve years. Dōgen is here beginning his comment on the tradition of the twelve mirrors as themselves times.

thereafter, they reflected the past and reflected the present (*kore yori shō ko shō kon suru nari* これより照古照今するなり): Perhaps, in the sense that history (*kokon* 古今; "past and present") was illumined through the marking off of the divisions of time.

51 **the twelve times are twelve faces; the twelve faces are twelve mirrors** (*jūni ji wa, jūni men nari, jūni men wa, jūni kyō nari* 十二時は、十二面なり、十二面は、十二鏡な り): The translation attempts to preserve something of Dōgen's play here again with the numerical classifier for mirrors, *men* 面 ("face," or "surface").

52 **it is pointing out the reason for this** (*kono dōri o shiji suru nari* この道理を指示す るなり): The subject here is unexpressed; most likely, "this story of the twelve mirrors of the Yellow Emperor."

19. The Old Mirror *Kokyō* 古鏡   167

[19:22]

軒轅黄帝膝行進崆峒、問道乎廣成子。于時廣成子曰、鏡是陰陽本、治身長久。自有三鏡云天、云地、云人。此鏡、無視無聽。抱神以靜、形將自正。必靜必清、無勞汝形、無搖汝精、乃可以長生。

> The Yellow Emperor Xuan Yuan approached Kongtong on his knees and questioned Guang Chengzi.[53]

> At that time, Guang Chengzi said, "The mirror is the root of yin and yang. Governing the body and prolonging the span come from three mirrors: heaven, earth, and human. These mirrors are without seeing and without hearing. They embrace the spirit and make it calm; the body will naturally be correct. Always calm, always pure, your body is without troubles, your spirit without agitation. And thus, you will extend your life."

[19:23] {1:228}

むかしはこの三鏡をもちて、天下を治し、大道を治す。この大道にあきらかなるを、天地の主とするなり。俗のいはく、太宗は人をかがみとせり、安危理亂、これによりて照悉する、といふ。三鏡のひとつをもちいるなり。人を鏡とするときては、博覽ならん人に古今を問取せば、聖賢の用舍をしりぬべし、たとへば魏徵をえしがごとく、房玄齡をえしがごとし、とおもふ。これをかくのごとく會取するは、太宗の、人を鏡とする、と道取する道理にはあらざるなり。人を鏡とす、といふは、鏡を鏡とするなり、自己を鏡とするなり、五行を鏡とするなり、五常を鏡とするなり。人物の去來をみるに、來無迹、去無方を人鏡の道理といふ。賢・不肖の萬般なる、天象に相似なり。まことに經緯なるべし。人面鏡面・日面月面なり。五嶽の精、および四瀆の精、よをへて四海をすます、これ鏡の慣習なり。人物をあきらめて經緯をはかるを、太宗の道といふなり。博覽人をいふにあらざるなり。

In ancient times, they used these three mirrors to govern the realm and govern the great way. The one who is clear about the great way is considered the lord of heaven and earth. The secular [sources] say that Taizong made the human his mirror; from this, he fully reflected security and danger, order and disorder.[54] He used one of the three mirrors. One

---

53   **The Yellow Emperor Xuan Yuan** (*Ken'en kōtei* 軒轅黄帝): Dōgen seems here to be quoting from a Chinese text, but his source is unclear. Most commentators cite the *Zhuangzi* 莊子 story noted above, Note 48. This text does begin with the Yellow Emperor approaching Kongtong on his knees, as well as the passage beginning, "Without seeing and without hearing"; however, the conversation here is not about the three mirrors but about the supreme way (*zhidao* 至道).

54   **Taizong** (*Taisō* 太宗): Second Tang emperor, reigned 627-650. His use of people as one of his three mirrors occurs in the account of his rule, the *Zhenguan zhengyao* 貞觀政要 (Renxian 任賢, KR.2e0006.002.8b):

夫以銅為鏡、可以正衣冠。以古為鏡、可以知興替。以人為鏡、可以明得失。

With bronze as the mirror, one can adjust one's attire; with the past as the mirror,

168   DŌGEN'S *SHŌBŌGENZŌ* VOLUME II

thinks, upon hearing that he made the human his mirror, that because he questioned people of broad learning about past and present, he knew how to employ the sage and the worthy — as, for example, he got Wei Zheng and got Fang Xuanling.[55] To understand it in this way is not the meaning of the saying that Taizong made the human his mirror. To make the human a mirror is to make a mirror a mirror; it is to make oneself a mirror; it is to make the five phases a mirror; it is to make the five constants a mirror.[56] In watching the going and coming of beings, that they come without traces and go without direction is called the meaning of the human mirror. The wise and the otherwise are of ten thousand types, resembling heavenly bodies, truly like the warp and woof.[57] It is the human face, the mirror face, the sun face, the moon face.[58] The essence of the five peaks and the essence of the four channels, passing through the world, purify the four seas.[59] This is the familiar practice of this mirror.

---

one can know prosperity and decline; with a person as the mirror, one can clarify gain and loss.

55   **Wei Zheng** (*Gi Chō* 魏徵): 580-643. Famous Chinese statesman; served as Grand Councilor (*zaixiang* 宰相) and trusted advisor under Taizong, who lamented after Wei Zheng's death that he had lost one of his mirrors. Wei was the lead author of the *Suishu* 隋書, the official history of the Sui dynasty.

Fang Xuanling (*Bō Genrei* 房玄齡): 579-648. Along with Du Ruhui 杜如晦 (585-630), often held up as an exemplary minister; served Li Shimin 李世民 during the campaign to establish the Tang dynasty and rose to Grand Councilor (*zaixiang* 宰相) after Li took the throne as Emperor Taizong 太宗. Fang was the lead author of the *Jinshu* 晉書, the official history of the Jin dynasty.

56   **five phases** (*gogyō* 五行); **five constants** (*gojō* 五常): The "five phases" (*gogyō* 五行) are equivalent to the five "powers" (*gosai* 五才; see above, Note 45). Which of the lists of "five constants" (*gojō* 五常; C. *wuchang*) Dōgen had in mind here is not obvious. It is usually thought to be the five virtues of traditional Chinese ethical thought: benevolence (*ren* 仁), righteousness (*yi* 義), propriety (*li* 禮), wisdom (*zhi* 智), and sincerity (*xin* 信); but he might as well have been thinking of the five social relationships (*gorin* 五倫; C. *wulun*): ruler and subject (*jun chen* 君臣), father and son (*fu zi* 父子), brother and brother (*xiong di* 兄弟), husband and wife (*fu qi* 夫妻), and friend and friend (*peng you* 朋友).

57   **the warp and woof** (*keii* 經緯): I.e., the very structure of the world.

58   **It is the human face, the mirror face, the sun face, the moon face** (*ninmen kyōmen nichimen gachimen* 人面鏡面 · 日面月面): Dōgen is again exploiting the term *men*. In addition to referring to the sun and moon, the terms "Sun Face" and "Moon Face" appear in Buddhist literature as the names of buddhas; see Supplementary Notes, s.v. "Sun face, moon face." Presumably the subject here is still the "human mirror."

59   **five peaks** (*gogaku* 五嶽): Sacred mountains located at the four cardinal directions and the center of China; the list varies with the source, the most common being Taishan 泰山 (east), Hengshan 衡山 (south), Huashan 華山 (west), Hengshan 恆山 (north), and Songshan 嵩山 (center).

four channels (*shitoku* 四瀆): Four great rivers of China: the Huang 黃, Chang 長 (i.e., Yangze), Huai 淮, and Ji 濟.

19. The Old Mirror *Kokyō* 古鏡　　169

To measure the warp and woof by clarifying beings is called the way of Taizong; we are not talking about people of broad learning.[60]

[19:24]

日本國自神代有三鏡、璽之與劔、而共傳來至今。一枚在伊勢太神宮、一枚在紀伊國日前社、一枚在内裏内侍所。

The Land of Japan, from the age of the gods, has had three mirrors.[61] They have been transmitted down to the present, together with the seal and the sword. One is at the Grand Shrine at Ise; one is at the Hinokuma Shrine in the Land of Kii; one is within the imperial court.

[19:25] {1:229}

しかあればすなはち、國家みな鏡を傳持すること、あきらかなり。鏡をえたるは、國をえたるなり。人つたふらくは、この三枚の鏡は、神位とおなじく傳來せり、天神より傳來せりと相傳す。しかあれば、百練の銅も、陰陽の化成なり、今來今現、古來古現ならん。これ古今を照臨するは、古鏡なるべし。

Thus, it is clear that countries all transmit and keep mirrors. To get a mirror is to get a country. In what is reported by the people, it is handed down that these three mirrors have all been transmitted like the divine seat, transmitted from the gods.[62] Therefore, the bronze refined a hundred times is also fashioned by yin and yang.[63] This might be [put], "*the present comes, the present appears; the past comes, the past appears.*"[64] It would mean the reflection of past and present is the old mirror.

---

four seas (*shikai* 四海): A term used for all the water surrounding China.

60　**we are not talking about people of broad learning** (*hakurannin o iu ni arazaru nari* 博覽人をいふにあらざるなり): I.e., we are not talking about Taizong's using learned people as mirrors.

61　**The Land of Japan** (*Nihon koku* 日本國): Dōgen here again shifts to Chinese, as if quoting a text; the source, if any, is unidentified. The Japanese imperial regalia includes (along with a sword and jewel) the so-called *yata no kagami* 八咫鏡 ("eight-foot mirror"), said today to be housed at the Grand Shrine at Ise; but whether it corresponds to any of the three mirrors Dōgen mentions is uncertain.

62　**the divine seat** (*shin'i* 神位): Usually the altar, tablet, or image in which a divine being is thought to reside; here, likely applied to the imperial throne.

63　**bronze refined a hundred times** (*hyakuren no dō* 百練の銅): I.e., even though the mirror is the result of the human activity of refining the bronze, it is ultimately the product of the cosmic forces of yin and yang.

64　**This might be [put]** (*naran* ならん): An attempt to suggest Dōgen's use here of the dubative form of the copula *nari*; the subject is unexpressed. Perhaps the implication is something like, "the above might be expressed by the statement . . ." The translation is based on the assumption that, in these last two sentences, Dōgen is summarizing his excursus into mirror legends and bringing the reader back to his interpretation of the conversation between Xuefeng and Xuansha on the "old mirror."

DŌGEN'S *SHŌBŌGENZŌ* VOLUME II

* * * * *

[19:26]

雪峰の宗旨は、新羅來新羅現、日本來日本現ともいふべし、天來天現、人
來人現ともいふべし。現來をかくのごとくの參學すといふとも、この現、
いまわれら本末をしれるにあらず、ただ現を相見するのみなり。かならず
しも來現を、それ知なり、それ會なり、と學すべきにあらざるなり。いま
いふ宗旨は、胡來は胡現なり、といふか。胡來は一條の胡來にて、胡現は
一條の胡現なるべし、現のための來にあらず。古鏡たとひ古鏡なりとも、
この參學あるべきなり。

Xuefeng's essential point can also be put, "*a [person of] Silla comes, a
[person of] Silla appears; a [person of] Japan comes, a [person of] Japan
appears.*"[65] It can also be put, "*a deva comes, a deva appears; a human
comes, a human appears.*" While we study "appearing" and "coming"
in this way, we do not know the root and branches of this "appearing."[66]
We just see the "appearing." We should not learn that "coming and appearing" is what we know or what we understand. Is the point of what
is said here that the "foreigner coming" is the "foreigner appearing"?
The foreigner coming is the single instance of a foreigner coming; the
foreigner appearing must be the single instance of a foreigner appearing:
it is not coming in order to appear.[67] The old mirror is the old mirror, but
there should be this sort of study.

[19:27]

玄沙いでてとふ、たちまちに明鏡來にあはんに、いかん。この道取、たづ
ねあきらむべし。いまいふ明の道得は、幾許なるべきぞ。いはくの道は、
その來はかならずしも胡・漢にはあらざるを、これは明鏡なり、さらに
胡・漢と現成すべからず、と道取するなり。明鏡來はたとひ明鏡來なり
とも、二枚なるべからざるなり。たとひ二枚にあらずといふとも、古鏡は
これ古鏡なり、明鏡はこれ明鏡なり。古鏡あり明鏡ある證驗、すなはち雪
峰と玄沙と道取せり。これを佛道の性相とすべし。これ、玄沙の明鏡來の
道話の、七通八達なるとしるべし、八面玲瓏なること、しるべし。逢人に
は即出なるべし、出即には接渠なるべし。しかあれば、明鏡の明と、古鏡
の古と、同なりとやせん、異なりとやせん。明鏡に、古の道理ありやなし
や、古鏡に、明の道理ありやなしや。古鏡といふ言によりて、明なるべ
し、と學することなかれ。宗旨は、吾亦如是あり、汝亦如是あり。西天諸
祖亦如是の道理、はやく練磨すべし。祖師の道得に、古鏡は磨あり、と道
取す。明鏡もしかあるべきか、いかん。まさにひろく諸佛諸祖の道にわた
る參學あるべし。

---

65 **"a [person of] Silla comes"** (*Shinra rai* 新羅來); **"a [person of] Japan comes"**
(*Nihon rai* 日本來): I.e., a native of the ancient kingdom of Silla on the Korean peninsula
and a native of Japan.

66 **root and branches** (*honmatsu* 本末): A common expression for "the nature and
characteristics" or "source and outcome" of something.

67 **it is not coming in order to appear** (*gen no tame no rai ni arazu* 現のための來に
あらず): I.e., the "coming" is just coming; the "appearing" just appearing.

19. The Old Mirror *Kokyō* 古鏡   171

Xuansha came forth and asked, "How about when all of a sudden a bright mirror comes?"

We should pursue and clarify this saying. What is the extent of the word "bright" mentioned here? These words are saying that the "bright mirror" is the fact that the "coming" is not necessarily [that of] the foreigner or the Han, and that it should not appear as the foreigner or the Han. A bright mirror coming may be a bright mirror coming, but they are not two things.[68] They may not be two, but the old mirror is the old mirror, the bright mirror is the bright mirror. The proof that there is an old mirror and there is a bright mirror is in what Xuefeng and Xuansha said. We should take this as the nature and marks of the words of the buddha. We should understand that Xuansha's remark on the bright mirror coming is seven passes and eight arrivals; we should understand that it is eight sides crystal clear.[69] It should be, in "meeting a person," "I immediately come forth"; it should be, in "coming forth immediately," I engage [the person].[70] This being the case, should we take the "bright" of the "bright mirror" and the "old" of the "old mirror" as the same or as different? Is there a principle of "old" in the "bright mirror" or not? Is there a principle of "bright" in the "old mirror" or not? Do not learn from the words "old mirror" that it must be "bright." The essential point lies in "*I'm also like this,*" in "*you're also like this.*" We should quickly polish the principle that "*the ancestors of Sindh in the West are also like this.*"[71] In the words of the Ancestral Master, it says that there is polish-

---

68   **they are not two things** (*nimai naru bekarazaru nari* 二枚なるべからざるなり): While the antecedent of the pronoun here is unclear, the sentence that follows suggests it should be "the old mirror" and "the bright mirror."

69   **seven passes and eight arrivals** (*shittsū hattatsu* 七通八達): A common expression in Dōgen's writings and earlier Chan texts for "thorough understanding," "complete mastery."

eight sides crystal clear (*hachimen reirō* 八面玲瓏): A common term for perfect clarity; the image is of the sound of a crystal (*reirō*) throughout the eight points of the compass.

70   **"immediately come forth"** (*sokushutsu* 即出); **"coming forth immediately"** (*shutsusoku* 出即): The translation here struggles to preserve Dōgen's play with the words of Sansheng 三聖 and Xinghua 興化, quoted in case 92 of the *shinji Shōbōgenzō* 眞字正法眼藏 (DZZ.5:172) and alluded to elsewhere in the *Shōbōgenzō*:

> 三聖院慧然禪師〈嗣臨濟〉道、我逢人即出、出即不爲人。興化道、我逢人即不出、出即便爲人。
>
> Chan Master Huiran of the Sansheng Cloister (succeeded Linji) said, "When I meet a person, I come forth; but, when I come forth, I don't benefit the person."
> Xinghua said, "When I meet a person, I don't come forth; but, when I do come forth, I benefit the person.

Dōgen treats the Chinese adverbial glyph *ji* 即 ("then," "as soon as"; also "is namely") as if it were part of two compound verbs, *jichu* 即出 and *chuji* 出即.

71   **"I'm also like this"** (*go yaku nyo ze* 吾亦如是); **"you're also like this"** (*nyo yaku*

172 DŌGEN'S *SHŌBŌGENZŌ* VOLUME II

ing of the "old mirror."[72] Is this true as well of the "bright mirror"? How about it? More broadly, there should be [such] study across the words of the buddhas and the ancestors.

[19:28] {1:230}

雪峰道の胡漢俱隱は、胡も漢も、明鏡時は俱隱なり、となり。この俱隱の道理、いかにいふぞ。胡・漢すでに來現すること、古鏡を相罣礙せざるに、なにとしてかいま俱隱なる。古鏡は、たとひ胡來胡現、漢來漢現なりとも、明鏡來は、おのづから明鏡來なるがゆえに、古鏡現の胡・漢は、俱隱なるなり。しかあれば、雪峰道にも古鏡一面あり、明鏡一面あるなり。正當明鏡來のとき、古鏡現の胡漢を罣礙すべからざる道理、あきらめ決定すべし。いま道取する古鏡の胡來胡現、漢來漢現は、古鏡上に來現すといはず、古鏡裏に來現すといはず、古鏡外に來現すといはず、古鏡と同參來現すといはず、この道を聽取すべし。胡漢來現の時節は、古鏡の、胡・漢を現來せしむるなり。胡漢俱隱ならん時節も、鏡は存取すべきと道得せるは、現にくらく、來におろそかなり。錯亂といふにおよばざるものなり。

Xuefeng's saying, "*Foreigner and Han would both disappear*," means that, at the time of the "bright mirror," the foreigner and the Han would both disappear.[73] How do we express the principle of this "both disappear"? Since the coming and appearing of the foreigner and Han do not obstruct the "old mirror," why do they both disappear? The "old mirror" may be "*a foreigner comes, a foreigner appears; a Han comes, a Han appears*," but because the "bright mirror comes" is itself "the bright mirror comes," the foreigner and the Han that appear in the "old mirror" both disappear. Therefore, in Xuefeng's words, there is the one "old mirror," there is the one "bright mirror." We should clarify and be certain of the principle that, precisely at the time that the "bright mirror comes," it does not obstruct the foreigner and Han that appear in the "old mirror." This saying, "a foreigner comes, a foreigner appears; a Han comes, a Han appears," of the "old mirror," is not saying that they come and appear on the "old mirror," not saying that they come and appear within the "old mirror," not saying that they come and appear outside the "old

---

nyo ze 汝亦如是); **"the ancestors of Sindh in the West are also like this"** (*Saiten shoso yaku nyo ze* 西天諸祖亦如是): Words of the Sixth Ancestor, Huineng, in response to his disciple Nanyue Huairang's 南嶽懷讓 claim that he is undefiled by Buddhist practice and verification; a conversation, recorded in the *shinji Shōbōgenzō* 眞字正法眼藏 (DZZ.5:178, case 101) and much cited by Dōgen; see Supplementary Notes, s.v. "You're also like this, I'm also like this."

72 **In the words of the Ancestral Master, it says that there is polishing of the "old mirror"** (*soshi no dōtoku ni, kokyō wa ma ari, to dōshu su* 祖師の道得に、古鏡は磨あり、と道取す): No doubt a reference to the words of Chan Master Guotai Hungou 國泰弘瑫 in the story Dōgen will quote below, section 48.

73 **at the time of the "bright mirror," the foreigner and the Han would both disappear** (*ko mo kan mo, meikyō ji wa guin nari* 胡も漢も、明鏡時は俱隱なり): Dōgen seems here simply to be explaining the Chinese passage in Japanese.

19. The Old Mirror *Kokyō* 古鏡　　173

mirror"; it is not saying that they come and appear together with the "old mirror." We should hear these words. On the occasion that the foreigner and the Han come and appear, the "old mirror" causes the foreigner and the Han to appear and come. On the occasion as well when foreigner and Han may both disappear, to say that the mirror remains is ignorant of appearing and oblivious to coming; to say it is confused is hardly the word for it.

[19:29] {1:231}

ときに玄沙いはく、某甲はすなはちしかあらず。雪峰いはく、なんぢ作麼生。玄沙いはく、請すらくは和尚とふべし。

> At that time, Xuansha said, "I'm not like this."[74]
> Xuefeng said, "How about you?"
> Xuansha replied, "Ask me, Reverend."

[19:30]

いま玄沙のいふ請和尚問のことば、いたづらに蹉過すべからず。いはゆる和尚問の來なる、和尚問の請なる、父子の投機にあらずは、爲甚如此なり。すでに請和尚問ならん時節は、恁麼人さだめて問處を若會すべし。すでに問處の霹靂するには、無廻避處なり。

> We should not idly pass over Xuansha's words, "*Ask me, Reverend.*" The coming of the Reverend's asking and the requesting of the Reverend's asking, were they not father and child in perfect fit, would be, *why is it like this?*[75] At the moment of "*Ask me, Reverend,*" such a person surely understood what is asked.[76] Since what is asked thunders, there is no place to escape.

74　**At that time, Xuansha said** (*toki ni Gensha iwaku* ときに玄沙いはく): Dōgen here provides Japanese translation of his Chinese text.

75　**father and child in perfect fit** (*fushi no tōki* 父子の投機): I.e., master and disciple in accord. The term *tōki* is a colloquial expression meaning "harmonious" or, as we might say, "to see eye to eye."

why is it like this? (*i jin nyo shi* 爲甚如此): Dōgen here slips into Chinese. I.e., How could they talk like this if Xuefeng's question and Xuangsha's request were not an instance of a perfect fit.

76　**such a person surely understood what is asked** (*inmo nin sadamete monsho o nyakue su beshi* 恁麼人さだめて問處を若會すべし): "Such a person" (*inmo nin* 恁麼人) can be used in reference to an awakened person, as in the Chan saying, "if you want such a thing, you must be such a person": here, likely indicating "a person in perfect fit with his teacher" — i.e., Xuansha. See Supplementary Notes, s.v. "Such a person."

174 DŌGEN'S *SHŌBŌGENZŌ* VOLUME II

[19:31]

雪峰いはく、忽遇明鏡來時如何。この問處は、父子ともに參究する一條の古鏡なり。

Xuefeng said, "How *about when all of a sudden a bright mirror comes?*"

What is asked here is an instance of the old mirror in which father and child investigate together.

[19:32]

玄沙いはく、百雜碎。この道取は、百千萬に雜碎するとなり。いはゆる忽遇明鏡來時は、百雜碎なり。百雜碎を參得せんは、明鏡なるべし、明鏡を道得ならしむるに、百雜碎なるべきがゆえに。雜碎のかかれるところ、明鏡なり。さきに未雜碎なるときあり、のちにさらに不雜碎ならん時節を管見することなかれ。ただ百雜碎なり、百雜碎の對面は孤峻の一なり。しかあるに、いまいふ百雜碎は、古鏡を道取するか、明鏡を道取するか。更請一轉語なるべし。また古鏡を道取するにあらず、明鏡を道取するにあらず。古鏡・明鏡はたとひ間來得なりといへども、玄沙の道取を擬議するとき、沙礫牆壁のみ現前せる舌端となりて、百雜碎なりぬべきか。碎來の形段作麼生。萬古碧潭空界月。

Xuansha said, "A hundred fragments."

This saying means to be fragmented into a hundred, thousand, myriad pieces. When "*all of a sudden a bright mirror comes*" is "a hundred fragments." That which studies "a hundred fragments" is the bright mirror; for, when one is made to speak of the "bright mirror," it is "a hundred fragments." Where the fragments hang is the "bright mirror."[77] Do not take the narrow view that there is previously a time that is not yet "fragments," or there is subsequently again a time of not "fragments." It is just "a hundred fragments." Facing a hundred fragments is one that is solitary and steep.[78] So, is the "hundred fragments" mentioned here speaking of the "old mirror," or is it speaking of the "bright mirror"? We should ask for a turning word.[79] Again, it is not speaking of the "old mirror"; it is not speaking of the "bright mirror." We have been asking about the "old mirror" and the "bright mirror," but when we consider

---

77 **Where the fragments hang is the "bright mirror"** (*zassui no kakareru tokoro, myōkyō nari* 雜碎のかかれるところ、明鏡なり): This passage could also be parsed differently: "That which studies 'the fragments' is the bright mirror. When one is made to speak of the bright mirror, it is 'a hundred fragments'; for where the fragments hang is the 'bright mirror.'"

78 **one that is solitary and steep** (*koshun no itsu* 孤峻の一): "One" (*itsu* 一) here is usually interpreted as referring to the unity of the mirror; "solitary and steep" suggests an unapproachable, insurmountable state.

79 **turning word** (*itten go* 一轉語): A phrase, often encountered in Zen dialogues, for a statement that expresses what is at stake in the conversation.

19. The Old Mirror *Kokyō* 古鏡   175

Xuansha's saying, was it only the sand, pebbles, fences, and walls appearing before us that become the tip of the tongue and are "a hundred fragments"?[80] *What about their shape* when they've been fragmented? *"Blue depths ten thousand ages old, the moon in an empty realm."*[81]

* * * * *

[19:33] {1:232}

雪峰眞覺大師と三聖院慧然禪師と行次に、ひとむれの獼猴をみる。ちなみに雪峰いはく、この獼猴、おのおの一面の古鏡を背せり。

> Once, when Great Master Shenjue of Xuefeng and Chan Master Huiran of Sansheng Cloister were traveling, they saw a group of monkeys.[82]
>
> Xuefeng said, "Each of these monkeys is bearing an old mirror on its back."

[19:34]

この語、よくよく參學すべし、獼猴といふは、さる、なり、いかならんか雪峰のみる獼猴。かくのごとく問取して、さらに功夫すべし、經劫をかへりみることなかれ。おのおの一面の古鏡を背せり、とは、古鏡たとひ諸佛祖面なりとも、古鏡は向上にも古鏡なり。獼猴おのおの面面に背せり、といふは、面面に大面・小面あらず、一面古鏡なり。背す、といふは、たとへば、繪像の佛のうらをおしつくるを、背す、とはいふなり。獼猴の背を背するに、古鏡にて背するなり。使得什麼糊來。こころみにいはば、さるのうらは古鏡にて背すべし、古鏡のうらは獼猴にて背するか。古鏡のうらを古鏡にて背す、さるのうらをさるにて背す。各背一面、のことば、虛設なるべからず、道得是の道得なり。しかあれば、獼猴か、古鏡か。畢竟作麼生道。われらすでに獼猴か、獼猴にあらざるか、たれにか問取せん。自己の獼猴にある、自知にあらず、他知にあらず。自己の自己にある、摸索およばず。

---

80   **sand, pebbles, fences, and walls** (*sha ryaku shō heki* 沙礫牆壁): I.e., the myriad things of the world around us. Compare Supplementary Notes, s.v. "Fences, walls, tiles, and pebbles."

become the tip of the tongue (*zettan to nari* 舌端となり): I.e., get put into words.

81   **"Blue depths ten thousand ages old, the moon in an empty realm"** (*banko hekitan kūkai getsu* 萬古碧潭空界月): Quoting the *Shi xuantan* 十玄談, by Tong'an Changcha 同安常察 (dates unknown) (*Jingde chuandeng lu* 景德傳燈錄, T.2076.51:455c7).

82   **Great Master Shenjue of Xuefeng** (*Seppō Shinkaku daishi* 雪峰眞覺大師): I.e., Xuefeng Yicun 雪峰義存; see above, Note 40.

Chan Master Huiran of Sansheng Cloister (*Sanshōin E'nen zenji* 三聖院慧然禪師): A Tang monk (dates unknown), who studied with Linji and other masters. Sansheng Cloister 三聖院 was in present-day Hebei. Slightly variant versions of this story appear in several Chan sources, none of which seems exactly to match Dōgen's account here. For the version recorded in Dōgen's *shinji Shōbōgenzō* 眞字正法眼藏, see Supplementary Notes, s.v. "Old mirror."

176 DŌGEN'S *SHŌBŌGENZŌ* VOLUME II

We should study these words well. [The term] *mikō* means "monkey."[83] How about these monkeys Xuefeng saw? We should ask like this and go on to work on it. Do not look around at the passing kalpas.[84] "Each is bearing on its back an old mirror" means that, while the old mirror is the face of the buddhas and ancestors, the old mirror is the old mirror beyond as well.[85] To say that each of the monkeys bears on its back its own mirror does not mean that among the mirrors there are large ones and small ones: they are one old mirror. To say they "bear on their backs" is, for example, to say of a painted buddha image that it "bears on its back" what is attached behind it. When the monkeys bear their backs, they bear them as the old mirror.[86] *What kind of paste have they used?*[87]

If we try to say this, the backs of the monkeys are the old mirrors that they bear on their backs. Are the backs of the old mirrors the monkeys that they bear on their backs? The backs of the old mirrors are borne on the backs of the old mirrors; the backs of the monkeys are borne on the backs of the monkeys. The words "each bears one" are not an empty contrivance; they are a saying that says it right.[88] Therefore, is it old mirrors? Is it monkeys? In the end, what can we say? Are we monkeys or not monkeys? Whom can we ask? That we are monkeys is not something we know, not something others know. That we are ourselves, our gropings do not reach.

[19:35]

三聖いはく、歴劫無名なり、なにのゆえにかあらはして古鏡とせん。これは、三聖の、古鏡を證明せる一面・一枚なり。歴劫といふは、一心・一念未萌以前なり、劫裏の不出頭なり。無名といふは、歴劫の日面月面、古鏡面なり、明鏡面なり。無名、眞箇に無名ならんには、歴劫いまだ歴劫にあらず。歴劫すでに歴劫にあらずば、三聖の道得、これ道得にあらざるべし。しかあれども、一念未萌以前といふは、今日なり、今日を蹉過せしめ

83　*mikō* means "monkey" (*mikō to iu wa, saru, nari* 獼猴といふは、さる、なり): Dōgen is here simply defining the Chinese word *mihou* 獼猴 for his Japanese audience.

84　**Do not look around at the passing kalpas** (*kyōkō o kaerimiru koto nakare* 經劫をかへりみることなかれ): I.e., don't waste time.

85　**the old mirror is the old mirror beyond as well** (*kokyō wa kōjō ni mo kokyō nari* 古鏡は向上にも古鏡なり): Dōgen is playing here with the physical features of "face" and "back." The mirrors borne on the backs of the monkeys are "beyond" the "faces" of the buddhas and ancestors.

86　**When the monkeys bear their backs** (*miko no hai o hai suru ni* 獼猴の背を背するに): Dōgen is here exploiting the term *hai* 背 in its two meanings of "back" and "to bear on the back."

87　**What kind of paste have they used?** (*shi toku jūmo* [or *shimo*] *ko rai* 使得什麼糊來): Dōgen here shifts to Chinese, as if quoting a saying, though the source is unknown.

88　**not an empty contrivance** (*kosetsu* 虛設): I.e., not a statement empty of significance.

19. The Old Mirror *Kokyō* 古鏡   177

ず練磨すべきなり。まことに歴劫無名、この名、たかくきこゆ。なにをあらはしてか古鏡とする、龍頭蛇尾。

Sansheng said, "It has been *nameless across the kalpas*. Why do you express it as 'an old mirror'?"

This is one face, one piece, with which Sansheng has demonstrated the old mirror. "Across the kalpas" means *before one mind or one thought has yet to sprout*; it means without putting oneself forward for a kalpa.[89] "Nameless" means the sun face, moon face, old mirror face across the kalpas; it means the bright mirror face. When "nameless" is truly "nameless," "across the kalpas" is not yet "across the kalpas." Since "across the kalpas" is not "across the kalpas," Sansheng's saying must not be a saying. Nevertheless, "before one thought has yet to sprout" means today. We should polish it so as not to let today pass us by. Truly, "nameless across the kalpas" is a name of high repute. What is it you express as "an old mirror"? The head of a dragon with the tail of a snake.[90]

[19:36] {1:233}

このとき、三聖にむかひて雲峰いふべし、古鏡古鏡、と。雪峰、恁麼いはず。さらに、瑕生也、といふは、きずいできぬる、となり。いかでか古鏡に瑕生也ならんとおぼゆれども、古鏡の瑕生也は、歴劫無名とらいふをきずとせるなるべし。古鏡の瑕生は、全古鏡なり。三聖いまだ古鏡の瑕生也の窟をいでさりけるゆゑに、道來せる參究は、一任に古鏡瑕なり。しかあれば、古鏡にも瑕生なり、瑕生なるも古鏡なりと參學する、これ古鏡を參學するなり。

At this time, Xuefeng should address Sansheng and say, "The old mirror. The old mirror." Xuefeng does not say it. He goes on to say, "a flaw's developed," meaning a scratch has appeared.[91] We may think, how could it be that "a flaw's developed" on the old mirror? But [to say that] "a flaw's developed" on the old mirror is taking the scratch as say-

---

89   **before one mind or one thought has yet to sprout** (*isshin ichinen mibō izen* 一心一念未萌以前): The expression "before X has yet to sprout" (*mibō izen* 未萌以前) is a common one in Zen for the state preceding the appearance of X. Perhaps best known in a phrase that Dōgen also uses, "before any portent has yet to sprout" (*chinchō mibō izen* 朕兆未萌已前).

without putting oneself forward for a kalpa (*kōri no fushuttō* 劫裏の不出頭): Literally, "putting forth the head," *shutō* is a colloquial idiom for making an appearance or for making one's way in the world.

90   **The head of a dragon with the tail of a snake** (*ryūtō dabi* 龍頭蛇尾): An idiom usually used pejoratively to indicate something that seems impressive at the outset but fails to deliver. Often used in Zen texts to describe a person who pretends to be awakened but is actually deluded. Here, seemingly, a criticism of Sansheng's saying.

91   **meaning a scratch has appeared** (*kizu idekinuru, to nari* きずいできぬる、となり): Dōgen is simply explaining the Chinese phrase *xia sheng ye* 瑕生也 in the original text.

178 DŌGEN'S *SHŌBŌGENZŌ* VOLUME II

ing "nameless across the kalpas." "A flaw's developed" on the old mirror is the whole old mirror. Because Sansheng has not yet emerged from the cave of "a flaw's developed" on the old mirror, the investigation he speaks of is entirely given over to a flaw on the old mirror.[92] Thus, we study that a flaw develops even on the old mirror, that a flaw develops is the old mirror. This is the study of the old mirror.

[19:37]

三聖いはく、有什麼死急、話頭也不識。いはくの宗旨は、なにとしてか死急なる。いはゆるの死急は、今日か、明日か、自己か、他門か、盡十方界か、大唐國裏か、審細に功夫參學すべきなり。話頭也不識は、話といふは、道來せる話あり、未道得の話あり、すでに道了也の話あり。いまは話頭なる道理現成するなり。たとへば、話頭も大地有情同時成道しきたれるか、さらに再全の錦にはあらざるなり。かるがゆえに不識なり。對朕者不識なり、對面不相識なり。話頭はなきにあらず、祇是不識なり。不識は、條條の赤心なり、さらにまた明明の不見なり。

> Sansheng said, *"What's your predicament? I don't even know what you're talking about."*[93]

The meaning of what he says is, "What is your predicament?"[94] We should make concentrated effort on and study of this "predicament" in detail. Is it today? Is it tomorrow? Is it ourselves? Is it another?[95] Is it all the worlds in the ten directions? Is it in the Land of the Great Tang?

In regard to the "talking" of *"I don't even know what you're talking about,"* there is talking that is said; there is talking that has not been said; there is talking that was already said. Here, the meaning that is "what you're talking about" appears. For example, has "what you're talking about" *"attained the way together with the whole earth and sentient*

---

92 **is entirely given over to a flaw on the old mirror** (*ichinin ni kokyō ka nari* 一任に古鏡瑕なり): I.e., only talks about the flaw. The phrase might also indicate that Sansheng's remark is itself a flaw on the old mirror.

93 **"What's your predicament? I don't even know what you're talking about"** (*u jūma shikyū, watō ya fushiki* 有什麼死急、話頭也不識): The grammatical subject is unexpressed; so the phrase could be read, "You don't even know what you're talking about." Dōgen here seems to be following the text at *Jingde chuandeng lu* 景德傳燈錄 (T.2076.51:328b2); other versions (including Dōgen's own *shinji Shōbōgenzō* 眞字正法眼藏) read:

一千五百人善知識話頭也不識。

Fifteen hundred wise friends wouldn't even know what you're talking about.

94 **The meaning of what he says** (*iwaku no shūshi* いはくの宗旨): Dōgen merely puts Sansheng's question into Japanese.

95 **Is it another?** (*tamon* 他門): A term usually referring to another house, tradition, or teaching; here, probably just "someone else." The only occurrence in the *Shōbōgenzō*.

19. The Old Mirror *Kokyō* 古鏡   179

beings"?[96] It is not refinished brocade.[97] Therefore, he "doesn't know." It is *"the one before us doesn't know"*; it is *"face-to-face, they don't know each other."*[98] It is not that there is nothing he is "talking about"; it is *just that he "doesn't know."* "Not knowing" is "the bare mind in each instance"; furthermore, it is not seeing what is perfectly clear.[99]

[19:38] {1:234}

雪峰いはく、老僧罪過。いはゆるは、あしくいひにける、といふにも、かくいふこともあれども、しかはこころうまじ。老僧、といふことは、屋裏の主人翁なり。いはゆる餘事を參學せず、ひとへに老僧を參學するなり。千變萬化あれども、神頭鬼面あれども、參學は唯老僧一著なり。佛來祖來、一念萬年あれども、參學は、唯老僧一著なり。罪過は、住持事繁なり。おもへばそれ、雪峰は德山の一角なり、三聖は臨濟の神足なり。兩位の尊宿、おなじく系譜いやしからず、青原の遠孫なり、南嶽の遠派なり。古鏡を住持しきたれる、それかくのごとし。晩進の龜鏡なるべし。

Xuefeng said, *"This old monk made a mistake."*[100]

---

96 **"attained the way together with the whole earth and sentient beings"** (*daichi ujō dōji jōdō* 大地有情同時成道): A reference to the Buddha's awakening under the bodhi tree. The expression, which appears in several of Dōgen's texts, is from a line that he will quote in his "Shōbōgenzō hotsu bodai shin" 正法眼藏發菩提心 chapter (DZZ.2:164; also quoted in *Eihei kōroku* 永平廣錄 (DZZ.3:28, no. 37):

> 釋迦牟尼佛言、明星出現時、我與大地有情、同時成道。
>
> Buddha Śākyamuni said, "When the dawn star appeared, I, together with the whole earth and sentient beings, simultaneously attained the way."

Although the passage appears in Chan texts from this period (see, e.g, *Jianzhong Jingguo xudeng lu* 建中靖國續燈錄, ZZ.136:36b17-18), it has not been located in any extant sūtra. The translation here follows the usual reading of *daichi ujō* 大地有情 as a compound subject; the phrase could also be read, "sentient beings of the whole earth."

97 **refinished brocade** (*saizen no nishiki* 再全の錦): An idiom suggesting something akin to English "icing on the cake": i.e., something that provides an additional value; from the tradition of the brocades of Szechuan, which are said to have become more lustrous with washing.

98 **"the one before us doesn't know"** (*tai chin sha fushiki* 對朕者不識): "Us" (*chin* 朕) here refers to the Emperor Wu 武 of Liang. An allusion to the story of Bodhidarma's encounter with him. When asked by the Emperor who he was, Bodhidharma replied, "I don't know" (*Jingde chuandeng lu* 景德傳燈錄, T.2076.51:219a27-28).

"face-to-face, they don't know each other" (*taimen fusōshiki* 對面不相識): A fairly common idiom in Zen texts, perhaps best known from a saying of the early figure Yang Danian 楊大年 (dates unknown) (e.g., at *Chanlin sengbao juan* 禪林僧寶傳, ZZ.137:522b2-3).

99 **"bare mind in each instance"** (*jōjō no sekishin* 條條の赤心): A "bare (or 'red') mind" (*chixin* 赤心) is a common Chinese idiom for a sincere, or straightforward, mind (or heart). Compare Supplementary Notes, s.v. "Bare mind in pieces."

100 **"This old monk made a mistake"** (*rōsō zaika* 老僧罪過): Again, seeming to reflect the *Jingde chuandeng lu* 景德傳燈錄 (T.2076.51:328b3).

180 DŌGEN'S *SHŌBŌGENZŌ* VOLUME II

This is saying, "I said it wrong"; while such may be said, it may not be understood like this. Saying "this old monk" means the old man who is master within the house: that is, one who does not study other things and solely studies "this old monk."[101] He may have a *thousand changes and a myriad transformations*, he may have spirit heads and demon faces; but his study is just the *one move of "this old monk."*[102] *Buddhas may come and ancestors may come, for ten thousand years in one moment of thought*; but his study is just the one move of "this old monk."[103] His "mistake" is "the abbot's business is complicated."[104] If we think about it, Xuefeng is a single horn of Deshan; Sansheng is the spirit foot of Linji.[105] The genealogy of these two venerables is not humble: they are distant descendants of Qingyuan, a distant branch of Nanyue.[106] They have maintained the old mirror like this. They should be a tortoise mirror for latecomers.[107]

---

101   **the old man who is master within the house** (*okuri no shujin ō* 屋裏の主人翁): Typically interpreted as the true person inside the body.

102   **a thousand changes and a myriad transformations** (*senpen banka* 千變萬化): A fixed phrase found throughout Chinese Buddhist texts and appearing elsewhere in the *Shōbōgenzō*.

spirit heads and demon faces (*jinzu kimen* 神頭鬼面): I.e., "weird things"; a fixed phrase used in self-deprecating reference to monks.

one move (*itchaku* 一著): From a move in a board game, often used in Zen texts for a "move" in a dialogue.

103   **ten thousand years in one moment of thought** (*ichinen bannen* 一念萬年): A common expression in Zen literature for eternity in each moment.

104   **"the abbot's business is complicated"** (*jūji ji han* 住持事繁): Quoting Xuefeng's "excuse" for his "mistake." The final exchange between Sansheng and Xuefeng in this story exactly matches another of their well-known conversations (see, e.g., *Dahui yulu* 大慧語錄, T.1998A.47:823c3-5; *shinji Shōbōgenzō* 眞字正法眼藏, DZZ.5:152, case 52):

> 三聖問雪峰、透網金鱗以何爲食。峯云、待汝出網來向汝道。三聖云、一千五百
> 人善知識話頭也不識。峯云、老僧住持事繁。
>
> Sansheng asked Xuefeng, "The golden-scaled one that slips the net — what does it eat?"
> Feng said, "Wait till you're out of the net, and I'll tell you."
> The Master [Sansheng] said, "Fifteen hundred wise friends wouldn't even know what you're talking about."
> Feng said, "This old monk's abbot's business is complicated."

105   **a single horn of Deshan** (*Tokusan no ikkaku* 德山の一角); **the spirit foot of Linji** (*Rinzai no jinsoku* 臨濟の神足): Both "single horn" and "spirit foot" are used to indicate top disciples.

106   **distant descendants of Qingyuan** (*Seigen no onson* 青原の遠孫); **a distant branch of Nanyue** (*Nangaku no onpa* 南嶽の遠派): I.e., Xuefeng belongs to the lineage descended from Qingyuan Xingsi 青原行思 (d. 740); Sansheng, to the lineage of Nanyue Huairang 南嶽懷讓.

107   **a tortoise mirror for latecomers** (*banshin no kikyō* 晚進の龜鏡): Reference to the ancient Chinese practice of augury by the use of tortoise shells. A "latecomer" (*banshin* 晚進) here refers to latter-day students of the tradition.

19. The Old Mirror *Kokyō* 古鏡   181

* * * * *

[19:39]

雪峰示衆云、世界闊一丈、古鏡闊一丈。世界闊一尺、古鏡闊一尺。時玄沙
指火爐云、且道、火爐闊多少。雪峰云、似古鏡闊。玄沙云、老和尚、脚跟
未點地在。

*Xuefeng addressed the assembly saying, "If the breadth of the world
is ten feet, the breadth of the old mirror is ten feet; if the breadth of the
world is one foot, the breadth of the old mirror is one foot."*[108]

*At that point, Xuansha pointed at the brazier and said, "Tell me, what's
the breadth of the brazier?"*[109]

Xuefeng said, "It's like the breadth of the old mirror."

Xuansha said, "The old Reverend's heels haven't touched the earth."[110]

[19:40]

一丈、これを世界といふ、世界は、これ一丈なり。一尺、これを世界と
す、世界、これ一尺なり。而今の一丈をいふ、而今の一尺をいふ、さら
にことなる尺丈にはあらざるなり。この因縁を參學するに、世界のひろさ
は、よのつねにおもはくは、無量無邊の三千世界、および無盡法界といふ
も、ただ小量の自己にして、しばらく隣里の彼方をさすがごとし。この世
界を拈じて、一丈とするなり。このゆえに雪峰いはく、古鏡闊一丈、世界
闊一丈。この一丈を學せんには、世界闊の一端を見取すべし。

He says ten feet is the world; the world is ten feet. He takes one foot as
the world; the world is one foot. He is speaking of the present ten feet;
he is speaking of the present one foot; there are no other ten feet or one
foot. When we study this episode, we think that the breadth of the world
is the incalculable, limitless three-thousandfold world, or the inexhaust-
able dharma realms; but this is like being the small self just pointing
out what is outside the village.[111] Taking up this world, he takes it as ten
feet. Hence, Xuefeng says, *"the breadth of the old mirror is ten feet; the*

---

108 **Xuefeng addressed the assembly** (*Seppō jishu* 雪峰示衆): An episode recorded
in various texts; see, e.g., *Liandeng huiyao* 聯燈會要, ZZ.136:819a18-b2; *shinji Shōbōgenzō* 眞字正法眼藏, DZZ.5:184, case 109.

ten feet (*ichijō* 一丈); **one foot** (*isshaku* 一尺): The Chinese unit *zhang* 丈 varied somewhat with time and place; the *chi* 尺 was one tenth of a *zhang*.

109 **brazier** (*karo* 火爐): Probably a charcoal hibachi or stove used for heating.

110 **"The old Reverend's heels haven't touched the earth"** (*rō oshō, kyakukon miten
chi zai* 老和尚、脚跟未點地在): The term "heels," rather like "nose," is often used in
Zen talk as a synecdoche for the person.

111 **three-thousandfold world** (*sanzen sekai* 三千世界): A standard Buddhist reference to the cosmos, also given as "worlds of three thousand, great thousand" (*sanzen
daisen sekai* 三千大千世界; S. *tri-sāhasra mahā-sāhasra loka-dhātu*). One billion
worlds. (Some versions of the text give *sanzen daisen sekai* 三千大千世界 here.)

180

breadth of the world is one foot." In studying this "ten feet," we should see one edge of the breadth of the world.

[19:41] {1:235}

又古鏡の道を聞取するにも、一枚の薄氷の見をなす、しかにはあらず。一丈の闊は、世界の闊一丈に同参なりとも、形興かならずしも世界の無端に齊肩なりや、同参なりやと功夫すべし。古鏡さらに一顆珠のごとくにあらず。明昧を見解することなかれ、方圓を見取することなかれ。盡十方界、たとひ一顆明珠なりとも、古鏡にひとしかるべきにあらず。しかあれば、古鏡は胡・漢の來現にかかはれず、縱横の玲瓏に條條なり。多にあらず、大にあらず。闊はその量を擧するなり、廣をいはんとにはあらず。闊といふは、よのつねの二寸・三寸といひ、七箇・八箇とかぞふるがごとし。佛道の算數には、大悟・不悟と算數するに、二兩・三兩をあきらめ、佛佛祖祖と算數するに、五枚・十枚を見成す。一丈は古鏡闊なり、古鏡闊は一枚なり。

Again, on hearing the words "old mirror," we take the view that it is one sheet of thin ice. This is not the case. Its ten-foot breadth practices together with the ten-foot breadth of the world, but we should work on [the questions,] is its shape of equal stature to, does it practice together with, the limitlessness of the world? The old mirror is not like "one bright pearl."[112] Do not understand it as bright or dark; do not see it as square or round. Even if all the worlds in the ten directions are "one bright pearl," they are not equal to the old mirror. Hence, the old mirror, regardless of the coming and appearing of the foreigner and the Han, is each instance in the crystal clarity of vertical and horizontal. It is not many; it is not big. "Breadth" holds up its measure; it does not mean its width. To say "breadth" is like saying the ordinary two inches or three inches, or counting seven things or eight things.[113] In calculations on the way of the buddhas, when we calculate great awakening or not awakening, we clarify two taels or three taels; when we calculate by buddha after buddha and ancestor after ancestor, we present five sheets or ten sheets.[114] Ten feet is the breadth of the old mirror; the breadth of the old mirror is one sheet.

---

112 **"one bright pearl"** (*ikka myōju* 一顆明珠): Some versions of the text give *ikka ju* 一顆珠 here. From a conversation, featuring Xuansha, about the saying, "all the worlds in the ten directions are one bright pearl," recorded in Dōgen's *shinji Shōbōgenzō* 眞字正法眼藏 (DZZ.5:132, case 15) and discussed in "Shōbōgenzō ikka myōju" 正法眼藏一顆明珠. See Supplementary Notes, s.v. "One bright pearl."

113 **two inches or three inches** (*nisun sansun* 二寸三寸): The Chinese unit *cun* 寸 is one tenth of a *chi* 尺; approximately an inch.

114 **two taels or three taels** (*niryō sanryō* 二兩三兩): The Chinese *liang* 兩 is a unit of weight, sometimes translated "ounce," that varied with time and place; also, a coin of that weight.

five sheets or ten sheets (*gomai jūmai* 五枚十枚): An awkward attempt to preserve Dōgen's play with numerical classifiers. Here, he uses the counter *mai* 枚, normally

19. The Old Mirror *Kokyō* 古鏡　　183

[19:42]

玄沙のいふ火爐闊多少。かくれざる道得なり、千古・萬古にこれを參學すべし。いま火爐をみる、たれ人となりてかこれをみる。火爐をみるに、七尺にあらず、八尺にあらず。これは動執の時節話にあらず、新條特地の現成なり。たとへば是什麼物恁麼來なり。闊多少の言きたりぬれば、向來の多少は、多少にあらざるべし。當處解脱の道理、うたがはざりぬべし。火爐の、諸相・諸量にあらざる宗旨は、玄沙の道をきくべし。現前の一團子、いたづらに落地せしむることなかれ、打破すべし、これ功夫なり。

Xuansha's saying, "*what's the breadth of the brazier?*" is a saying that is not hidden.[115] We should study it for a thousand ages, ten thousand ages. [On] seeing the brazier, who is it we become when we see it? When we see the brazier, it is not seven feet, it is not eight feet.[116] This is not talk about the moment of moving and grasping; it is the realization of a new instance and a special place.[117] It is, for example, "*what thing is it that comes like this?*"[118] When "what's the breadth?" has been said, what has been the size in the past will not be the size. We should no longer doubt the principle of liberation in this very place. The essential point that the brazier is not forms or measures, we should hear [in] Xuansheng's words. Do not idly let the dumpling right before you fall on the ground.[119] We should break it. This is our concentrated effort.

---

indicating flat things (like mirrors), for buddhas and ancestors.

115　**a saying that is not hidden** (*kakurezaru dōtoku* かくれざる道得): I.e., a statement the meaning of which is obvious.

116　**it is not seven feet, it is not eight feet** (*shichi shaku ni arazu, hachi shaku ni arazu* 七尺にあらず、八尺にあらず): Perhaps reflecting a conversation between Chan Masters Xuansha Shibei 玄沙師備 (835-908) and Xuefeng Yicun 雪峰義存 (822-908) on which Dōgen comments in "Shōbōgenzō juki" 正法眼藏授記; see Supplementary Notes, s.v. "Seven feet or eight feet."

117　**realization of a new instance and a special place** (*shinjō tokuchi no genjō* 新條特地の現成): Generally taken to mean that the brazier talked about here is not the familiar thing of our ordinary world of "moving and grasping."

118　**"what thing is it that comes like this?"** (*ze jūmo butsu inmo rai* 是什麼物恁麼來): The question put to Nanyue Huairang 南嶽懷讓 by the Sixth Ancestor in the conversation quoted above, Note 71.

119　**Do not idly let the dumpling right before you fall on the ground** (*genzen no ichi dansu, itazura ni rakuchi seshimuru koto nakare* 現前の一團子、いたづらに落地せしむることなかれ): Some take the term *ichi dansu* 一團子 here to refer to a "single lump," rather than a "dumpling." In either case, the reference would seem to be to the "brazier" in Xuangsheng's words.

184 DŌGEN'S *SHŌBŌGENZŌ* VOLUME II

[19:43] {1:236}

雪峰いはく、如古鏡闊。この道取、しづかに照顧すべし。火爐闊一丈とい
ふべきにあらざれば、かくのごとく道取するなり。一丈といはんは道得是
にて、如古鏡闊は道不是なるにあらず、如古鏡闊の行履をかがみるべし。
おほく人のおもはくは、火爐闊一丈といはざるを道不是とおもへり。闊の
獨立をも功夫すべし、古鏡の一片をも鑑照すべし、如如の行李をも蹉過せ
しめざるべし。動容揚古路、不堕悄然機なるべし。

Xuefeng said, "*It's like the breadth of the old mirror.*" We should quietly reflect on these words. Since he ought not say the breadth of the
brazier is ten feet, he says this. It is not that saying "ten feet" says it
right, while saying "*like the breadth of the old mirror*" says it wrong. We
should consider the conduct of "*like the breadth of the old mirror.*"[120]
Many people have thought that not to say, "*the breadth of the brazier is
ten feet,*" is to say it wrong. We should work on the independent positing
of "breadth"; we should reflect on the one piece of "the old mirror"; we
should not let pass the conduct of "like."[121] This is "*action and rest promote the old path; I won't be sinking into worry.*"[122]

[19:44]

玄沙いはく、老漢脚跟未點地在。いはくのこころは、老漢といひ、老和尚
といへども、かならず雪峰にあらず、雪峰は老漢なるべきがゆえに。脚跟
といふはいづれのところぞ、と問取すべきなり、脚跟といふはなにをいふ
ぞ、と參究すべし。參究すべし、といふは、　脚跟とは、正法眼藏をいふ
か、虚空をいふか、盡地をいふか、命脈をいふか。幾箇ある物ぞ、一箇あ
るか、半箇あるか、百千萬箇あるか、怎麼勤學すべきなり。

Xuansha said, "*The old Han's heels haven't touched the earth.*"[123] The
point here is that, though we call him "the old Han" or we call him "the
old Reverend," this is not necessarily Xuefeng; for Xuefeng is an "old

---

120　**the conduct of "like the breadth of the old mirror"** (*nyo kokyō katsu no anri* 如
古鏡闊の行履): I.e., what Xuefeng is doing when he says, "like the breadth of the old
mirror."

121　**the independent positing of "breadth"** (*katsu no dokuryū* 闊の獨立); **the one
piece of "the old mirror"** (*kokyō no ippen* 古鏡の一片); **the conduct of "like"** (*nyonyo
no anri* 如如の行李): Dōgen is here encouraging us to take apart Xuefeng's sentence and
consider each of its individual words in turn.

122　**"action and rest promote the old path; I won't be sinking into worry"** (*dōyō
yō koro, fuda shōnen ki* 動容揚古路、不堕悄然機): Lines from a verse celebrating his
awakening by Xiangyan Zhixian 香嚴智閑 (d. 898); quoted in "Shōbōgenzō keisei sanshoku" 正法眼藏溪聲山色. (See *Jingde chuandeng lu* 景德傳燈錄, T.2076.51:284a16;
shinji Shōbōgenzō 眞字正法眼藏, DZZ.5:134, case 17.)

123　**"The old Han's heels haven't touched the earth"** (*rōkan kyakukon miten chi zai*
老漢脚跟未點地在): Dōgen here replaces Xuansha's "old Reverend" with "old Han"
(presumably to invoke Xuefeng's earlier comment about the Han coming and appearing); hence, his following comment.

19. The Old Mirror *Kokyō* 古鏡

185

Han." About "heels," we should ask, "where are they?" We should investigate, "What are heels?" "We should investigate" means, is it the treasury of the true dharma eye? Is it empty space? Is it all the earth? Is it the vital artery? How many are there? Is there one? Is there a half? Are there a hundred, thousand, myriad? We should diligently study like this.

[19:45]

未點地在は、地といふは、是什麼物なるぞ。いまの大地といふ地は、一類の所見に準じて、しばらく地といふ。さらに諸類、あるひは不思議解脱法門とみるあり、諸佛諸行道とみる一類あり。しかあれば、脚跟の點ずべき地は、なにものをか地とせる。地は實有なるか、實無なるか。又おほよそ地といふものは、大道のなかに寸許もなかるべきか。問來問去すべし、道他道己すべし。脚跟は點地也是なる、不點地也是なる。作麼生なればか、未點地在と道取する。大地無寸土の時節は、點地也未、未點地也未なるべし。しかあれば、老漢脚跟未點地在は、老漢の消息なり、脚跟の造次なり。

"*Haven't touched the earth.*" What is it that he calls "the earth"? The earth of the present whole earth, he calls "the earth," for the time being, in accordance with the view of one type. There are types that see it as the dharma gate of inconceivable liberation. There is a type that sees it as the way practiced by the buddhas. Therefore, in regard to the earth that heels should touch, what is it that we take as earth? Does earth really exist? Really not exist? Again, more generally, we should keep asking again and again, we should keep saying to others and ourselves, is there not, on the great way, even an inch or so of what we call earth? For "heels," is touching the earth right, or is not touching the earth right? Why is it that he says, "haven't touched the earth"? At the time when "*there isn't an inch of ground on the whole earth,*" "*touched the earth*" is "*haven't*" and "*haven't touched the earth*" is "*haven't.*"[124] Therefore, "*the old Han's heels haven't touched the earth*" is the circumstances of "the old Han," the quickness of his "heels."

* * * * *

---

124 **"there isn't an inch of ground on the whole earth"** (*daichi mu sun do* 大地無寸土): An expression occurring several times in the *Shōbōgenzō*, common in Chan texts; see, e.g., *Jingde chuandeng lu* 景德傳燈錄, T.2076.51:464a26:

若人識得心、大地無寸土。

If a person knows the mind, there isn't an inch of ground on the whole earth.

"touched the earth" is "haven't" and "haven't touched the earth" is "haven't" (*ten chi ya mi, miten chi ya mi* 點地也未、未點地也未): Or "'touched the earth' is 'not yet'; 'not yet touched the earth' is 'not yet.'" The translation struggles to preserve Dōgen's odd Chinese syntax.

186 DŌGEN'S *SHŌBŌGENZŌ* VOLUME II

[19:46] {1:237}

婺州金華山國泰院弘瑫禪師、ちなみに僧とふ、古鏡未磨時如何。師云、古
鏡。僧曰、磨後如何。師云、古鏡。

Chan Master Hungtou of Guotai Cloister on Mount Jinhua in Wuzhou
was once asked by a monk, *"Before the old mirror is polished, what's
it like?"*[125]
The Master said, "The old mirror."
The monk said, "After it's polished, what's it like?"
The Master said, "The old mirror."

[19:47]

しるべし、いまいふ古鏡は、磨時あり、未磨時あり、磨後あれども、一面
に古鏡なり。しかあれば、磨時は、古鏡の全古鏡を磨するなり。古鏡にあ
らざる水銀等を和して磨するにあらず。磨自・自磨にあらざれども、磨古
鏡あり。未磨時は、古鏡くらきにあらず、くろしと道取すれども、くらき
にあらざるべし、活古鏡なり。おほよそ鏡を磨して鏡となす、甎を磨して
鏡となす、　甎を磨して甎となす、鏡を磨して甎となす。磨してなさざる
あり、なることあれども磨することえざるあり。おなじく佛祖の家業な
り。

We should realize that this old mirror has a time of polishing, a time
before polishing, a time after polishing; yet it is a single old mirror.
Therefore, at the time of polishing, it is the old mirror polishing the
whole old mirror. It is not polishing by mixing in something other than
the mirror like mercury; it is not polishing itself or self polishing.[126] Yet
there is "polishing the old mirror." In the time before it is polished, the
old mirror is not dim; we may say it is dark, but it is not dim: it is the
living old mirror. Generally speaking, we polish a mirror to make a mirror; we polish a tile to make a mirror; we polish a tile to make a tile;
we polish a mirror to make a tile.[127] There is polishing without making;
there is making without being able to polish. They are both the family
occupation of the buddhas and ancestors.[128]

---

125 **Chan Master Hungtou of Guotai Cloister on Mount Jinhua in Wuzhou** (*Mushū
Kinkasan Kokutaiin Kōtō zenji* 婺州金華山國泰院弘瑫禪師): Guotai Hungou 國泰弘瑫
(dates unknown), disciple of Xuansha Shibei 玄沙師備. This dialogue appears at *Jingde
chuandeng lu* 景德傳燈錄, T.2076.51:373a14-15; *shinji Shōbōgenzō*, DZZ.5:190, case
117.

126 **polishing itself or self polishing** (*ma ji ji ma* 磨自・自磨): Or, as this phrase is
often understood, "polishing the self or the self polishing."

127 **we polish a tile to make a mirror** (*sen o mashite kyō to nasu* 甎を磨して鏡とな
す): Dōgen is here introducing the material from the story of Huairang 懷讓 and Mazu
馬祖 that he will discuss in the next section.

128 **the family occupation of the buddhas and ancestors** (*busso no kagō* [or *kagyō*]
佛祖の家業): I.e., the spiritual practice in the "house" of the buddhas and ancestors.

19. The Old Mirror *Kokyō* 古鏡　　187

* * * * *

[19:48]

江西馬祖、むかし南嶽に參學せしに、南嶽かつて心印を馬祖に密受せし
む、磨甎のはじめのはじめなり。馬祖、傳法院に住して、よのつねに坐
禪すること、わづかに十餘歳なり。雨夜の草菴、おもひやるべし、封雪の
寒牀に、おこたるといはず。南嶽、あるとき馬祖の菴にいたるに、馬祖侍
立す。南嶽とふ、儞近日作什麼。馬祖いはく、近日道一祇管打坐するのみ
なり。南嶽いはく、坐禪なにごとをか圖する。馬祖いはく、坐禪は作佛を
圖す。南嶽すなはち一片の甎をもちて、馬祖の菴のほとりの石にあてて磨
す。馬祖これをみてすなはちとふ、和尚作什麼。南嶽いはく、磨甎。馬祖
いはく、磨甎用作什麼。南嶽いはく、磨作鏡。馬祖いはく、磨甎豈得成鏡
耶、南嶽いはく、坐禪豈得作佛耶。

In the past, when Xiangxi Mazu was studying with Nanyue, Nanyue
had Mazu secretly receive the mind seal.[129] It was the beginning of the
beginning of "polishing a tile."[130] For over ten years, Mazu, residing at
Chuanfa Cloister, always did seated mediation. We should try to think of
his grass hermitage on a rainy night It is not said he neglected his cold
couch sealed in by snow.[131]

One time, when Nanyue went to Mazu's hermitage, Mazu stood to
attend him. Nanyue asked, "*What are you doing these days?*"[132]

Mazu said, "*These days, Daoyi just sits.*"[133]

Nanyue said, "What are you figuring to do, sitting in meditation?"

Mazu said, "I'm sitting in meditation figuring to make a buddha."

Nanyue thereupon took up a tile and polished it on a stone by Mazu's
hermitage. Upon seeing this, Mazu asked, "*Reverend, what are you
doing?*"

129　**Xiangxi Mazu** (*Kōzei Baso* 江西馬祖). **Nanyue** (*Nangaku* 南嶽): I.e., the famous
Tang-dynasty master Mazu Daoyi 馬祖道一 (709-788) and his master, Nanyue Huairang
南嶽懷讓 (see above, Note 32).

130　**the beginning of the beginning of "polishing a tile"** (*masen no hajime no hajime*
磨甎のはじめのはじめ): I.e., Huairang's granting of the mind seal was the initial instance of the "polishing a tile" that will be discussed here.

131　**his cold couch sealed in by snow** (*hōsetsu no kanjō* 封雪の寒牀): The "couch"
here no doubt refers to the seat, or dais, on which monks practice meditation.

132　**One time** (*aru toki* あるとき): A vernacular retelling of a famous story found at
Jingde chuandeng lu 景德傳燈錄 (T.2076.51:240c18-28), as well as at Dōgen's *shinji
Shōbōgenzō* 眞字正法眼藏 (DZZ.5:128-130, case 8). Reference to it appears frequently
in the *Shōbōgenzō*. See Supplementary Notes, s.v. "Nanyue polishes a tile." After the
first sentence here, Dōgen adds his own interpolation; he returns to the Chinese sources
beginning with Nanyue's question, "What are you figuring to do, sitting in meditation."

133　**"Daoyi just sits"** (*Dōitsu shikan taza suru nomi* 道一祇管打坐するのみ): Though
not found in any extant source for this story, Dōgen introduces here one of his favorite
and most famous terms for Zen practice; see Supplementary Notes, s.v. "Just sit."

188 DŌGEN'S *SHŌBŌGENZŌ* VOLUME II

Nanyue said, "*I'm polishing a tile.*"

Mazu said, "*What's the use of polishing a tile?*"

Nanyue said, "*I'm polishing it to make a mirror.*"

Mazu said, "*How can you produce a mirror by polishing a tile?*"

Nanyue said, "*How can you make a buddha by sitting in meditation?*"

[19:49] {1:238}

この一段の大事、むかしより數百歳のあひだ、人おほくおもふらくは、南嶽ひとへに馬祖を勸勵せしむる、と。いまだかならずしもしかあらず。大聖の行履、はるかに凡境を出離せるのみなり。大聖もし磨甎の法なくば、いかでか爲人の方便あらん。爲人のちからは、佛祖の骨髓なり。たとひ搆得すとも、なほこれ家具なり。家具調度にあらざれば、佛家につたはれざるなり。いはんやすでに馬祖を接することすみやかなり。はかりしりぬ、佛祖正傳の功德、これ直指なることを。まことにしりぬ、磨甎の、鏡となるとき、馬祖作佛す。馬祖作佛するとき、馬祖すみやかに馬祖となる。馬祖の、馬祖となるとき、坐禪すみやかに坐禪となる。かるがゆゑに、甎を磨して鏡となすこと、古佛の骨髓に住持せられきたる。

From the past for several hundred years, many people have thought that the great matter of this passage was simply Nanyue's exhorting Mazu. This is not necessarily the case. The conduct of the great sages simply escapes the realm of the commoner. If the great sages had no dharma of polishing a tile, how could they have expedient means to help people? The power to help people is the bones and marrow of the buddhas and ancestors. Though they construct it, it is their domestic furnishings. If it is not their domestic furnishings and implements, it is not passed down in the house of the buddhas.[134] How much more, then, does this immediately engage Mazu.[135] [From this] we know that the virtues directly transmitted by the buddhas and ancestors are direct pointing.[136] Truly we know that when polishing a tile becomes a mirror, Mazu makes a buddha; when Mazu makes a buddha, Mazu quickly becomes Mazu. When Mazu becomes Mazu, seated meditation quickly becomes seated

---

134 **domestic furnishings and implements** (*kagu chōdo* 家具調度): Dōgen is here playing with the metaphor of the Zen tradition as the "house of the buddhas" (*bukke* 佛家).

135 **How much more, then, does this immediately engage Mazu** (*iwanya sude ni Baso o sessuru koto sumiyaka nari* いはんやすでに馬祖を接することすみやかなり): The exact implication of this sentence is unclear; from the context, presumably it means something like, "how much more does Nanyue use his skill in helping others directly to instruct Mazu."

136 **direct pointing** (*jikishi* 直指): As in the famous line, sometimes attributed to Bodhidharma, "pointing directly at the person's mind" (*jikishi ninshin* 直指人心); see Supplementary Notes, s.v. "Pointing directly at the person's mind, seeing the nature and attaining buddhahood."

19. The Old Mirror *Kokyō* 古鏡   189

meditation. Therefore, polishing a tile to make a mirror has been maintained in the bones and marrow of the old buddhas.

[19:50]

しかあれば、甎のなれる古鏡あり。この鏡を磨しきたるとき、從來も未染汚なるなり。甎の、ちりあるにはあらず、ただ甎なるを磨甎するなり。このところに、作鏡の功德の現成する、すなはち佛祖の功夫なり。磨甎もし作鏡せずば、磨鏡も作鏡すべからざるなり。たれか、はかることあらん、この作に作佛あり、作鏡あることを。又疑著すらくは、古鏡を磨するとき、あやまりて甎と磨しなすことのあるべきか。磨時の消息は、餘時のはかるところにあらず。しかあれども、南嶽の道、まさに道得を道得すべきがゆえに、畢竟じてすなはちこれ磨甎作鏡なるべし。いまの人も、いまの甎を拈じ磨してこころみるべし、さだめて鏡とならん。甎、もし鏡とならずば、人、ほとけになるべからず。甎、泥團なりとかろしめば、人も泥團なりとかろからん。人、もし心あらば、甎も心あるべきなり。たれかしらん、甎來甎現の鏡子あることを。又たれかしらん、鏡來鏡現の鏡子あることを。

Therefore, there are old mirrors made from a tile. When we have been polishing this mirror, even up till now it is not stained. It is not the case that the tile has dirt. We just polish a tile that is a tile. From this, the virtue of making a mirror is realized. This is the concentrated effort of the buddhas and ancestors. If polishing a tile did not make a mirror, polishing a mirror would not make a mirror. Who could think that, in this "making," there is making a buddha or making a mirror? Again, what I doubt is, when we are polishing the old mirror, could we mistakenly polish it as a tile? The circumstances at the time of polishing are not something that can be judged by other times. Nevertheless, because Nanyue's words must say a saying, ultimately they should be "*polishing a tile to make mirror.*" Present people should try taking up present tiles and polishing them. They will surely become mirrors. If tiles do not become mirrors, people do not become buddhas. If we disdain tiles as clods of mud, we will disdain people as clods of mud. If people have minds, tiles should also have minds. Who knows that there are mirrors of "*a tile comes, a tile appears*"? Who knows that there are mirrors where "*a mirror comes, a mirror appears*"?

正法眼藏古鏡第十九
Treasury of the True Dharma Eye
The Old Mirror
Number 19

190 DŌGEN'S *SHŌBŌGENZŌ* VOLUME II

[Ryūmonji MS:]

仁治二年辛丑九月九日、觀音導利興聖寶林寺示衆

*Presented to the assembly at Kannon Dōri Kōshō Hōrin Monastery;
ninth day, ninth month of the junior metal year of the ox, the second
year of Ninji [15 November 1241]*[137]

[Tōunji MS:]

同四年癸卯正月十三日、書寫于栴檀林裡

*Copied at the Sendan Grove; thirteenth day, first month, junior water
year of the rabbit, the fourth year of the same [era] [3 February 1510]*

于時永正七年庚午五月吉日於桂林室中、用兼書之

*Copied in the abbot's quarters of Keirin; auspicious [first] day,
fifth month, senior metal year of the horse, the seventh year of Eishō
[7 June 1510], by Yōken*[138]

---

137 The Tōunji 洞雲寺 MS shares an identical colophon.
138 **Yōken** 用兼: I.e., Kinkō Yōken 金岡用兼 (1437–1513?).

TREASURY OF THE TRUE DHARMA EYE

NUMBER 20

Sometimes
Uji
有時

Sometimes

Uji

INTRODUCTION

This relatively short essay is one of the most celebrated, most closely studied chapters of the *Shōbōgenzō*. It is dated in the autumn of 1240, when Dōgen was living at Kōshōji, his monastery just south of the capital of Heiankyō (modern Kyoto). It occurs as number 20 in both the seventy-five- and sixty-chapter compilations of the *Shōbōgenzō* and as number 11 in the Honzan edition.

The essay famously plays with two senses of its title. The Sino-Japanese expression *uji* 有時 (Chinese *youshi*; Japanese *aru toki*) is normally used as an adverb meaning "at times," "sometimes," "at one time," and so on. Dōgen cites examples of such use at the outset of his essay and again in quotations from Chan masters Mazu Daoyi 馬祖道一 and Shexian Guixing 葉縣歸省 later in the piece. For his part, however, Dōgen also sees in this familiar adverb two terms of considerable metaphysical weight: *u* 有, "to exist," regularly used as a noun for "being" in the abstract and for individual "beings"; and *ji* 時, "time," used both in the abstract and in reference to specific "times" — moments, hours, periods, seasons, occasions, and so on. Seeing the expression in this way, he can re-imagine it as a dvandva, a compound in which "being" and "time" coalesce. (Hence, the common practice of translating the expression as "being-time.") Thus, he begins his comments with the statement, "[The expression] 'sometimes' means times are themselves beings; all beings are times." He then proceeds in the essay to an exploration of some of the implications of this novel reading.

正法眼藏第二十

Treasury of the True Dharma Eye
Number 20

有時

Sometimes

[20:1] {1:240}

古佛言、有時高高峰頂立、有時深深海底行、有時三頭八臂、有時丈六八尺、有時拄杖拂子、有時露柱燈籠、有時張三李四、有時大地虛空。

The old buddhas say,[1]

> Sometimes, standing atop the highest peak; sometimes, walking the floor of the deepest ocean. Sometimes, three heads and eight arms; sometimes, sixteen feet and eight feet.[2] Sometimes, a staff and a whisk; sometimes, pillars and lanterns.[3] Sometimes, Zhang's third

---

1   **old buddhas** (*kobutsu* 古佛): There is no known source for these lines given here in Chinese, and the translation therefore reads the term *kobutsu* ("old buddha") here as a reference to the various Chan masters in whose sayings one can find such expressions. (See Supplementary Notes, s.v. "Old buddha.") The passage is often treated as if a quotation from Yaoshan Weiyan 藥山惟儼 (751–834), to whom is attributed a variant version of the first two lines, at *Jingde chuandeng lu* 景德傳燈錄, T.2076.51:440c13:

須向高高峰頂立、深深海底行。

You should stand atop the highest peak, walk the floor of the deepest ocean.

2   **three heads and eight arms** (*sanzu happi* 三頭八臂): A fixed expression, used in reference to certain wrathful forms of Buddhist divinities. Its use here may reflect the words of Yuanwu Keqin 圜悟克勤 (1063–1135). See Supplementary Notes, s.v. "Three heads and eight arms."

sixteen feet and eight feet (*jōroku hasshaku* 丈六八尺): Reference to the body of a buddha, reckoned as sixteen *zhang* 丈 when standing, eight *chi* 尺 when seated. (The Chinese measurement *zhang* 丈 [J. *jō*], while varying somewhat according to time and place, equals roughly 10 feet; the *chi* 尺 [J. *shaku*] is one-tenth of a *zhang*.) This body is sometimes said to be the "small" body, in which a buddha manifests himself, in contrast to his "great" body, which fills all of space.

3   **a staff and a whisk** (*shujō hossu* 拄杖拂子): Two items appearing regularly in the records of Zen masters. The staff (*shujō* 拄杖) is a walking stick, often carried by the master when he "ascends to the hall" (*jōdō* 上堂; i.e., holds a formal convocation); the whisk (*hossu* 拂子) is a ceremonial fly whisk, often held by the master during lectures and other rituals. See Supplementary Notes, s.v. "Staff," "Whisk."

194 DŌGEN'S *SHŌBŌGENZŌ* VOLUME II

and Li's fourth; sometimes, the whole earth and empty space.[4]

[20:2]
いはゆる有時は、時すでにこれ有なり、有はみな時なり。丈六金身、これ時なり、時なるがゆえに時の莊嚴光明あり、いまの十二時に習學すべし。三頭八臂、これ時なり、時なるがゆえに、いまの十二時に一如なるべし。十二時の長遠・短促、いまだ度量せずといへども、これを十二時といふ。去來の方跡あきらかなるによりて、人、これを疑著せず、疑著せざれども、しれるにあらず。衆生もとより、しらざる毎物毎事を疑著すること一定せざるがゆえに、疑著する前程、かならずしもいまの疑著に符合することなし。ただ疑著しばらく時なるのみなり。

"Sometimes" means times are themselves beings; all beings are times.[5] The sixteen-foot golden body is a time; because it is a time, it has the adornments and radiance of time.[6] We should study it in the present twelve times.[7] The "three heads and eight arms" are a time; because they are a time, they are one with the present twelve times. Although we have not gauged how long or short the twelve times are, we call them the "twelve times."[8] Since the traces of their coming and going are clear, people do not doubt them; though they do not doubt them, they have not understood them. Since, naturally, living beings' doubtings of the things and events they do not understand are not fixed, the future of their

---

pillars and lanterns (*rochū tōrō* 露柱燈籠): Two terms appearing often in Zen texts and in Dōgen's writings, used especially as symbols of the objective, insentient world; see Supplementary Notes, s.v. "Pillars and lanterns."

4 **Zhang's third and Li's fourth** (*Chōsan Rishi* 張三李四): From the Chinese idiom *Zhang san Li si* 張三李四 ("Zhang's third son, Li's fourth son"), used (as we might use "Tom, Dick, and Harry") to indicate any ordinary person.

5 **times are themselves beings; all beings are times** (*ji sude ni kore u nari, u wa mina ji nari* 時すでにこれ有なり、有はみな時なり): Or, as sometimes read, "time is itself being; all being is time." Dōgen here takes apart the compound term *uji* 有時 ("sometimes") into its component elements, *u* 有 ("there are"; "being") and *ji* 時 ("time").

6 **sixteen-foot golden body** (*jōroku konjin* 丈六金身): I.e., a buddha body; equivalent to "sixteen feet and eight feet" (*jōroku hasshaku* 丈六八尺) in section 1, above. The choice of this expression here may reflect a well-known Zen trope, invoked elsewhere in the *Shōbō-genzō*, that equates a single blade of grass with the sixteen-foot body of the buddha; see Supplementary Notes, s.v. "One blade of grass."

adornments and radiance (*shōgon kōmyō* 莊嚴光明): Standard attributes describing the body of a buddha.

7 **present twelve times** (*ima no jūni ji* いまの十二時): I.e., the twenty-four hours of the day, which was traditionally divided into twelve two-hour periods.

8 **Although we have not gauged how long or short the twelve times are** (*jūni ji no chōon tansoku, imada takuryō sezu to iedomo* 十二時の長遠・短促、いまだ度量せずといへども): Presumably, an ironic suggestion that we might somehow use time to measure time.

20. Sometimes *Uji* 有時　　195

doubtings will not necessarily match their present doubts. It is just that the doubting is a time for a while.[9]

[20:3] {1:241}

われを排列しをきて盡界とせり、この盡界の頭頭物物を、時時なりと覷見すべし。物物の相礙せざるは、時時の相礙せざるがごとし。このゆえに、同時發心あり、同心發時なり。および修行・成道もかくのごとし。われを排列してわれこれをみるなり。自己の時なる道理、それかくのごとし。

We have lined ourselves up and make it all the worlds; we should see the individual things of all these worlds as times.[10] That the things do not obstruct each other is like the times not obstructing each other. Therefore, there is bringing forth the mind [of bodhi] at the same time; it is bringing forth the time at the same mind.[11] And practicing and attaining the way are also like this. Lining ourselves up, we see this. The reasoning that the self is time is like this.

[20:4]

恁麼の道理なるゆえに、盡地に萬象・百草あり、一草・一象おのおの盡地にあることを參學すべし。かくのごとくの往來は、修行の發足なり。到恁麼の田地のとき、すなはち一草・一象なり、會象・不會象なり、會草・不會草なり。正當恁麼時のみなるがゆえに、有時みな盡時なり、有草・有象ともに時なり。時時の時に盡有・盡界あるなり。しばらく、いまの時にもれたる盡有・盡界ありや、なしや、と觀想すべし。

Since it is such reasoning, we should study that there are on all the earth the myriad forms, the hundred grasses; and that a single blade of grass, a single form is all the earth. Coming and going like this is the

---

9　**doubting is a time for a while** (*gijaku shibaraku ji naru* 疑著しばらく時なる): Often read "doubt is temporarily time." The translation takes the phrase to mean that, in the ongoing, shifting course of our doubts, each act of doubting time is itself a brief time.

10　**all the worlds** (*jinkai* 盡界): Typically taken as an abbreviation for "all the worlds in the ten directions" (*jin jippō kai* 盡十方界) — i.e., the entire universe.

we should see the individual things of all these worlds as times (*kono jinkai no zuzu motsumotsu o, jiji nari to shoken su beshi* この盡界の頭頭物物を、時時なりと覷見すべし): The translation loses the rhetorical device of repetition of the nouns here — a pattern that might be rendered, "We should see each and every thing after thing as time after time."

11　**bringing forth the mind [of bodhi] at the same time** (*dōji hosshin* 同時發心): "Bringing forth the mind" (or "producing the thought") translates *hosshin* 發心 (S. *cittotpāda*), the standard term for the bodhisattva's aspiration for buddhahood. See Supplementary Notes, s.v. "Bring forth the mind," "Practice and verification."

it is bringing forth the time at the same mind (*dōshin hotsuji nari* 同心發時なり): Dōgen's play on the preceding expression. Some texts read *ari* ("there is") here for *nari* ("it is"). This phrase could also be read, "it is the same mind bringing forth the time."

196 DŌGEN'S *SHŌBŌGENZŌ* VOLUME II

start of practice.[12] When one reaches such a field, it is one blade of grass, one phenomenon; it is understanding the form, not understanding the form, understanding the grass, not understanding the grass.[13] Since they are only at just such times, all "sometimes" are all the times, and both some grass and some forms are times.[14] In the time of time after time, there are all the beings, all the worlds. We should reflect for a while whether there are or are not all the beings or all the worlds that are left out of this present time.

[20:5]
しかあるを、佛法をならはざる凡夫の時節に、あらゆる見解は、有時のことばをきくにおもはく、あるときは三頭八臂となれりき、あるときは丈六八尺となれりき、たとへば、河をすぎ、山をすぎしがごとくなり、と。いまは、その山河たとひあるらめども、われすぎきたりて、いまは玉殿朱楼に處せり、山河とわれと、天と地となり、とおもふ。

Nevertheless, when we are common people who have yet to learn the buddha dharma, we all take the view upon hearing the word *uji* that, at some time, they became "three heads and eight arms"; at some time, they became "sixteen feet and eight feet," as if having crossed a river or crossed a mountain.[15] We think that, while that mountain and river may exist, I have crossed them, and now reside in jade palaces and vermilion towers; the mountain and river and I are like heaven and earth.[16]

---

12   **Coming and going like this** (*kaku no gotoku no ōrai* かくのごとくの往來): The exact sense is unclear; perhaps something like, "studying back and forth like this between the two ways of thinking about phenomena and grasses."

13   **When one reaches such a field** (*tō inmo no denchi no toki* 到恁麼の田地のとき): Japanese rendering of the common Chinese phrase *dao renme tiandi* 到恁麼田地, meaning "to reach this point," "to arrive at such a stage."

14   **all "sometimes" are all the times, and both some grass and some forms are times** (*uji mina jinji nari, usō uzō tomo ni ji nari* 有時みな盡時なり、有草・有象ともに時なり): Here, Dōgen is playing with the graph *u* 有 ("being"; the "some" of "sometimes"), attaching it to "grass" and "forms." Outside of such play, the terms *usō* 有草 and *uzō* 有象 could probably be read simply "any grass," "any form."

15   **at some time, they became "three heads and eight arms"; at some time, they became "sixteen feet and eight feet"** (*aru toki wa sanzu happi to nareriki, aru toki wa jōroku hasshaku to nareriki* あるときは三頭八臂となれりき、あるときは丈六八尺となれりき): Using the term *uji* 有時 here in its Japanese reading, *aru toki* あるとき. The grammatical subjects of the verbs "became" here are unstated. It is possible to take them as "all the beings" (*jin'u* 盡有) of the previous sentence, but it is perhaps easier to read the sentence as saying simply, "At some time, the three heads and eight arms and the sixteen feet and eight feet became what they now are."

16   **jade palaces and vermilion towers** (*gyokuden shurō* 玉殿朱楼): A phrase best known from the *Caoan ge* 草庵歌, by Shitou Xiqian 石頭希遷 (700-790) (*Jingde chuandeng lu* 景德傳燈錄, T.2076.51:461c15-16):

青松下明窓内。玉殿朱樓未爲對。

20. Sometimes *Uji* 有時

[20:6]

しかあれども、道理この一條のみにあらず。いはゆる、山をのぼり、河を
わたりし時に、われありき、われに時あるべし。われすでにあり、時、さ
るべからず。時、もし去來の相にあらずば、上山の時は有時の而今なり。
時、もし去來の相を保任せば、われに有時の而今ある、これ有時なり。か
の上山・度河の時、この玉殿朱楼の時を呑却せざらんや、吐却せざらん
や。三頭八臂は、きのふの時なり、丈六八尺は、けふの時なり。しかあれ
ども、その昨今の道理、ただこれ山のなかに直入して、千峰萬峰をみわた
す時節なり、すぎぬるにあらず。三頭八臂も、すなはちわが有時にて一經
す、彼方にあるににたれども而今なり。丈六八尺も、すなはちわが有時に
て一經す、彼處にあるににたれども而今なり。

However, this is not the only line of reasoning. At the time I climbed
the mountain or crossed the river, I existed, and the time should exist
with me. Since I exist, the time should not pass away. If time does not
have the character of coming and going, the time of climbing the mountain is the present of "sometimes"; if time does maintain the character
of coming and going, the present of "sometimes" exists with me. This is
"sometimes." Does not the time of climbing the mountain and crossing
the river swallow up and vomit out the time of the jade palaces and vermilion towers? The "three heads and eight arms" are yesterday's time;
the "sixteen feet and eight feet" are today's time. Nevertheless, the principle of yesterday and today is that they are just the time when I enter
directly into the mountains and gaze out at the thousand peaks, the ten
thousand peaks; they do not pass away. The "three heads and eight arms"
pass as my "sometimes"; they seem to be over there, but they are now.
The "sixteen feet and eight feet" pass as my "sometimes"; they seem to
be elsewhere, but they are now.

[20:7] {1:241}

しかあれば、松も時なり、竹も時なり。時は飛去するとのみ解會すべから
ず、飛去は時の能とのみは學すべからず。時、もし飛去に一任せば、間隙
ありぬべし。有時の道を經聞せざるは、すぎぬるとのみ學するによりてな
り。要をとりていはば、盡界にあらゆる盡有は、つらなりながら時時な
り、有時なるによりて吾有時なり。

By the bright window, beneath green pines:
Jade palaces and vermilion towers can't compare.

For the full context, see Supplementary Notes, s.v. *"Reverend Shitou's Song of the
Thatched Hut."* The "bright window" (*meisō* 明窓) is a reference to the windows providing light in sūtra reading halls (*kankindō* 看經堂) and other facilities where monks
studied scriptures.

like heaven and earth (*ten to chi to nari* 天と地となり): I.e., are as distant as heaven
from earth.

198　　DŌGEN'S *SHŌBŌGENZŌ* VOLUME II

Thus, the pine is time; the bamboo is time.[17] Do not understand time simply as flying away; do not study only that flying away is the function of time. If time resigned itself entirely to flying away, there would be gaps.[18] That one has not heard the word "sometimes" is due to one's studying only that it has passed.[19] In essence, in all the worlds, all the beings, while connected, are time after time; because they are "sometimes," they are my "sometimes."[20]

[20:8]

有時に經歷の功德あり、いはゆる、今日より明日へ經歷す、今日より昨日に經歷す、昨日より今日に經歷す、今日より今日に經歷す、明日より明日に經歷す、經歷は、それ時の功德なるがゆえに。古今の時、かさなれるにあらず、ならびつもれるにあらざれども、青原も時なり、黄檗も時なり、江西も石頭も時なり。自他すでに時なるがゆえに、修證は諸時なり、入泥入水、おなじく時なり。いまの凡夫の見、および見の因縁、これ凡夫のみるところなりといへども、凡夫の法にあらず、法、しばらく凡夫を因縁せるのみなり。この時・この有は、法にあらずと學するがゆえに、丈六金身はわれにあらずと認ずるなり。われを丈六金身にあらずとのがれんとする、またすなはち有時の片片なり、未證據者の看看なり。

"Sometimes" has the virtue of passage: it passes from today to tomorrow; it passes from today to yesterday; it passes from yesterday to today; it passes from today to today; it passes from tomorrow to tomorrow — for passage is a virtue of time.[21] Although the times of past and present do not pile up or accumulate in a row, Qingyuan is a time, Huangbo is a

---

17　**the pine is time; the bamboo is time** (*matsu mo toki nari, take mo toki nari* 松も時なり、竹も時なり): One could as well read this, "the pines are times; the bamboos are times." Both trees are common symbols of longevity.

18　**there would be gaps** (*kenkyaku arinu beshi* 間隙ありぬべし): Generally taken to mean that, were there no continuity in time, each time would be separated from what precedes and follows it; perhaps, reflecting a traditional Buddhist argument to the effect that, if time is strictly defined as a series of indivisible instants, there could be no relation between any two such instants.

19　**That one has not heard the word "sometimes"** (*uji no dō o kyōmon sezaru wa* 有時の道を經聞せざるは): Presumably, meaning, "that one has not heard the meaning of the word as explained here." We may note in passing Dōgen's use here of the verb *kyōmon* 經聞 ("undergo the hearing"?), a *hapax legomenon* in his corpus that takes advantage of the glyph *kyō* 經 from *kyōryaku* 經歷 ("passage").

20　**because they are "sometimes," they are my "sometimes"** (*uji naru ni yorite go uji nari* 有時なるによりて吾有時なり): The translation masks what is likely the point here: "because these times are the times of beings, they are times of my being."

21　**for passage is a virtue of time** (*kyōryaku wa, sore ji no kudoku naru ga yue ni* 經歷は、それ時の功德なるがゆえに): The translation here follows the punctuation at Kawamura 1:242.15. It is also possible to end the sentence after "tomorrow to tomorrow" and read this phrase as introducing the following sentence: "Because passage is a virtue of time, past and present times do not pile up . . . ."

20. Sometimes *Uji* 有時　　199

time, Jiangxi is a time, Shitou is a time.[22] Since self and other are times, practice and verification are times; entering the mud and entering the water are similarly times.[23]

The views of the common people here and the conditions of those views, though they may be what the common people see, are not the dharma of the common people: it is merely that the dharma has temporarily conditioned the common people.[24] Because we learn that this time, this being, is not the dharma, we consider the sixteen-foot golden body as not myself. Trying to escape myself as not the sixteen-foot golden body is also bits and pieces of "sometimes." It is "looking, looking" by "those who haven't verified it."[25]

[20:9] {1:243}

いま世界に排列せるむま・ひつじをあらしむるも、住法位の恁麼なる昇降・上下なり。ねずみも時なり、とらも時なり。生も時なり、佛も時なり。この時、三頭八臂にて盡界を證し、丈六金身にて盡界を證す。それ盡界をもて盡界を界盡するを、究盡するとはいふなり。丈六金身をもて丈六金身するを、發心・修行・菩提・涅槃と現成する、すなはち有なり、時なり。盡時を盡有と究盡するのみ、さらに剩法なし、剩法これ剩法なるがゆえに。たとひ半究盡の有時も、半有時の究盡なり。たとひ蹉過すとみゆる形段も、有なり。さらにかれにまかすれば、蹉過の現成する前後ながら、

22　Although the times of past and present do not pile up or accumulate in a row (*kokon no toki, kasanareru ni arazu, narabitsumoreru ni arazaredomo* 古今の時、かさなれるにあらず、ならびつもれるにあらざれども): The point here would seem to be that, while it does not make sense to speak of two times occurring at the same time in history, we can nevertheless speak of the past Chan masters as "times," even when some of them are contemporaries.

Qingyuan (*Seigen* 青原): I.e., Chan Master Qingyuan Xingsi 青原行思 (d. 740); **Huangbo** (*Ōbaku* 黃檗): Huangbo Xiyun 黃檗希運 (dates unknown); **Jiangxi** (*Kōzei* 江西; also read *Kōsai*): Mazu Daoyi 馬祖道一 (709-738); **Shitou** (*Sekitō* 石頭): Shitou Xiqian 石頭希遷.

23　entering the mud and entering the water (*nyūdei nyūsui* 入泥入水; also read *nyūdei nissui*): A common idiom referring to the Zen master's "getting his hands dirty," as we might say, in the teaching of his students; synonymous with *dadei taisui* 拖泥帶水 ("dragged through the mud and drenched with water"). See Supplementary Notes, s.v. "Dragged through the mud and drenched with water." Teaching for the "other" is here contrasted with "practice and verification" for the "self."

24　it is merely that the dharma has temporarily conditioned the common people (*hō, shibaraku bonbu o innen seru nomi nari* 法、しばらく凡夫を因縁せるのみなり): This passage might be paraphrased, "What the ordinary person sees is not the ordinary person's real situation (dharma); it is merely how that situation appears to the person. It is because we do not recognize this time and our being as our real situation that we think the buddha is something other."

25　It is "looking, looking" by "those who haven't verified it" (*mishōkosha no kankan nari* 未證據者の看看なり): After words, common in Zen teachings, often attributed to Linji Yixuan 臨濟義玄 (d. 866). See Supplementary Notes, s.v. "True person of no rank."

200　　　DŌGEN'S *SHŌBŌGENZŌ* VOLUME II

有時の住位なり。住法位の活鱍鱍地なる、これ有時なり。無と動著すべからず、有と強爲すべからず。

What brings about the horse and the sheep presently lined up in the world is also the ascent and descent, the rise and fall, that is the suchness of "abiding in their dharma positions."[26] The rat is a time; the tiger is a time.[27] Living beings are times; the buddhas are times. At this time, they verify all the worlds as "three heads and eight arms," they verify all the worlds as the sixteen-foot golden body.[28] Using all the worlds, to exhaust the worlds of all the worlds is called exhaustively investigating.[29] Using the sixteen-foot golden body, to manifest being the sixteen-foot golden body as bringing forth the mind, practice, bodhi, and nirvāṇa — this is being; this is time.[30] One only exhaustively investigates all the times as all the beings: there are no extra dharmas; for an extra dharma is an extra dharma.[31] Even the "sometimes" of a half exhaustive investigation is the exhaustive investigation of a half "sometimes." Even shapes seen

---

26　**the horse and the sheep** (*muma hitsuji* うま・ひつじ): I.e., the hours of the horse (*go* 午; 11:00 a.m.-1:00 p.m.) and the sheep (*bi* 未; 1:00-3:00 p.m.).

the suchness of "abiding in their dharma positions" (*jū hōi no inmo* 住法位の恁麼): Perhaps meaning something like, "the way things really are in each moment." The expression "to abide in their dharma positions" (*jū hōi* 住法位) can express the view that each thing occurs in its own proper moment, without extending into the subsequent moment; it reflects a traditional reading of a phrase in Kumārajīva's translation of the *Lotus Sūtra*. See Supplementary Notes, s.v. "Dharmas abide in their dharma positions."

27　**The rat** (*nezumi* ねずみ); **the tiger** (*tora* とら): The hour of the rat (*shi* 子; 11:00 p.m.-1:00 a.m.); the hour of the tiger (*in* 寅; 3:00-5:00 a.m.).

28　**At this time** (*kono ji* この時): The phrase could also be read as the grammatical subject of the sentence: "This time verifies . . . ."

29　**Using all the worlds, to exhaust the worlds of all the worlds is called exhaustively investigating** (*jinkai o mote jinkai o kaijin suru o, gūjin suru to wa iu nari* 盡界をもて盡界を界盡するを、究盡するとはいふなり): The translation, strain as it may, fails to capture Dōgen's play with the term *jin* 盡, variously rendered here "all," "to exhaust," and "exhaustively." "To exhaust the worlds" (or perhaps "to world exhaustively") represents the neologism *kaijin su* 界盡す, the transposition of *jinkai* 盡界 ("all the worlds") used as a transitive verb.

30　**to manifest being the sixteen-foot golden body as bringing forth the mind, practice, bodhi, and nirvāṇa** (*jōroku konjin suru o, hosshin shugyō bodai nehan to genjō suru* 丈六金身するを、發心・修行・菩提・涅槃と現成する): Perhaps, meaning something like, "to express buddhahood as the four basic stages of becoming a buddha." "Being (or, perhaps, 'doing') the sixteen-foot golden body" attempts to render the novel verbal form "to sixteen-foot golden body" (*jōroku konjin suru* 丈六金身する).

31　**for an extra dharma is an extra dharma** (*jōhō kore jōhō naru ga yue ni* 剩法これ剩法なるがゆえに): Presumably, meaning something like, "because whatever is not included in the investigation of times as beings is nevertheless still included in 'sometimes.'" The translation here follows Kawamura's punctuation at DZZ.1:243.10. The phrase could also be (and is probably more often) read with the following sentence:

20. Sometimes *Uji* 有時 201

as mistakes are beings. If, moreover, we leave it to them, what precedes and follows the appearance of the mistake is itself "sometimes" abiding in its state.[32] The brisk liveliness of abiding in its dharma position is "sometimes."[33] We should not move to take it as nothing; we should not insist on taking it as being.

[20:10]

時は一向にすぐるとのみ計功して、未到と解會せず。解會は時なりといへ
ども、他にひかるる緣なし。去來と認じて、住位の有時と見徹せる皮袋な
し。いはんや透關の時あらんや。たとひ住位を認ずとも、たれか既得恁麼
の保任を道得せん。たとひ恁麼と道得せることひさしきを、いまだ面目現
前を摸捺せざるなし。凡夫の有時なるに一任すれば、菩提・涅槃もわづか
に去來の相のみなる有時なり。

Calculating times solely as passing away, we do not understand them as not yet arrived. Although our understandings are times, they are not occasioned by them.[34] There is no skin bag who, recognizing them as coming and going, has discerned them as the "sometimes" of "abiding in their state."[35] How much less have they had a time of passing through the barrier?[36] Even if they recognize "abiding in their state," who can say something that maintains their "having got such"?[37] Even if they have long said

---

"Because an extra dharma is an extra dharma, even the 'sometimes' of a half entire investigation is the entire investigation of a half 'sometimes.'"

32 If, moreover, we leave it to them (*sara ni kare ni makasureba* さらにかれにまかすれば): Perhaps meaning something like, "if we go on to take [these mistaken forms] as dharmas."

"sometimes" abiding in its state (*uji no jūi* 有時の住位): I.e., instances of "sometimes" in their proper moments.

33 brisk liveliness (*kappatsupatchi* 活鱍鱍地): A loose translation of a Chinese idiom expressing the quick, powerful movements of a fish; see Supplementary Notes, s.v. "Brisk and lively."

34 they are not occasioned by them (*ta ni hikaruru en nashi* 他にひかるる緣なし): Literally, "they lack a condition [or object] drawn from that"; perhaps meaning, "those understandings have no real basis in the times."

35 skin bag (*hitai* 皮袋): A common term for the body, especially of humans; for the meaning of the metaphor and other examples of its usage, see Supplementary Notes, s.v. "Bag of skin."

36 a time of passing through the barrier (*tōkan no ji* 透關の時): To "pass the barrier" is a common Zen expression for understanding, as in the phrase, "the eye that passes through the barrier" (*tōkan gen* 透關眼). The phrase here is ambiguous: it could mean "a time when [the skin bags] pass the barrier" or "a time that is passing the barrier."

37 can say something that maintains their "having got such" (*ki toku inmo no hōnin o dōtoku sen* 既得恁麼の保任を道得せん): I.e. "can truly express what they have recognized." The phrase "having got such" (*ki toku inmo* 既得恁麼) suggests the famous saying attributed to Yunju Daoying 雲居道膺 (d. 902); see Supplementary Notes, s.v. "Such a person."

202 DŌGEN'S *SHŌBŌGENZŌ* VOLUME II

it is such, they cannot but grope for it in front of their faces.[38] If we leave them to the "sometimes" of common people, even bodhi and nirvāṇa are merely the "sometimes" only of the attributes of coming and going.

[20:11] {1:244}

おほよそ、籠籠とどまらず有時現成なり。いま右界に現成し、左方に現成する天王天衆、いまもわが盡力する有時なり。その餘外にある水陸の衆有時、これわがいま盡力して現成するなり。冥陽に有時なる諸類・諸頭、みなわが盡力現成なり、盡力經歴なり。わがいま盡力經歴にあらざれば、一法・一物も現成することなし、經歴することなし、と參學すべし。

In sum, they are the appearance of "sometimes" unimpeded by nets and cages.[39] The deva kings and deva hosts, now appearing in realms to the right and appearing in quarters to the left, are the "sometimes" of our even now using all our strength.[40] The "sometimes" of those elsewhere, in the water and on land, appear as we now use all our strength. The types and individuals that are the "sometimes" in the dark and in the light are all the appearance of our using all our strength, are the passage of our using all our strength. We should learn that, if they were not the passage of our using all our strength, there would not appear, there would not pass, even a single dharma, a single thing.

[20:12]

經歴といふは、風雨の東西するがごとく學しきたるべからず、盡界は不動轉なるにあらず、不進退なるにあらず、經歴なり。經歴は、たとへば春のごとし、春に許多般の様子あり、これを經歴といふ。外物なきに經歴すると參學すべし。たとへば、春の經歴はかならず春を經歴するなり。經歴は春にあらざれども、春の經歴なるがゆえに、經歴いま春の時に成道せり。審細に參來・參去すべし。經歴をいふに、境は外頭にして、能經歴の法は、東にむきて百千世界をゆきすぎて、百千萬劫をふる、とおもふは、佛道の參學、これのみを専一にせざるなり。

---

38 **they cannot but grope for it in front of their faces** (*imada menmoku genzen o mōsaku sezaru nashi* いまだ面目現前を摸撈せざるなし): Or "There are as yet none who fail to grope in front of their faces"; i.e., they are still seeking to experience it directly for themselves.

39 **In sum, they are the appearance of "sometimes" unimpeded by nets and cages** (*ōyoso, rarō todomarazu uji genjō nari* おほよそ、籠籠とどまらず有時現成なり): The grammatical subject of the copula *nari* なり is unstated; the translation "they are" takes it to be the "times" of the preceding section.

nets and cages (*rarō* 籠籠): I.e., for trapping fish and keeping birds and animals; regularly used in Zen texts for the limiting categories of our understanding. See Supplementary Notes, s.v. "Nets and cages."

40 **using all our strength** (*waga jinriki suru* わが盡力する): The translation strains to retain the parallel in the term *jinriki* 盡力 ("to exhaust one's strength," "to make every effort") with the uses of *jin* 盡 above, in *jinkai* ("all the worlds"), *jinchi* 盡地 ("all the earth"), *jinji* 盡時 ("all the times"), and *jin'u* 盡有 ("all the beings").

20. Sometimes *Uji* 有時   203

We should not have been learning that the meaning of "passage" is like the wind and rain moving east to west. All the worlds are not immoveable; they are not not advancing and retreating: they are passing. Passage is like the spring: spring takes many forms; this is its "passage." We should study that it passes without any external thing.[41] For example, the passage of spring always passes spring. The passage is not the spring; but, since it is the passage of spring, passage has attained the way at this time of spring.[42] We should study this, coming and going, in detail. To think that, in saying "passage," we mean that, while the object is external, the dharma accomplishing the passage proceeds to the east a hundred thousand worlds, over a hundred thousand myriad kalpas — this is not devoting oneself single-mindedly solely to the study of the way of the buddhas.[43]

* * * * *

[20:13]

薬山弘道大師、ちなみに無際大師の指示によりて、江西大寂禪師に參問す、三乘十二分教、某甲、ほぼその宗旨をあきらむ、如何是祖師西來意。かくのごとくとふに、大寂禪師いはく、有時教伊揚眉瞬目、有時不教伊揚眉瞬目、有時教伊揚眉瞬目者是、有時教伊揚眉瞬目者不是。薬山、ききて大悟し、大寂にまふす、某甲かつて石頭にありし、蚊子の鐵牛にのぼれるがごとし。

Great Master Hongdao of Yaoshan, on the advice of Great Master Wuji, once questioned Chan Master Jiangxi Daji, "I've largely clarified the essential point of the three vehicles and the twelvefold teachings, but *what is the intention of the Ancestral Master's coming from the west?*"[44]

---

41 **it passes without any external thing** (*gaimotsu naki ni kyōryaku suru* 外物なきに経歴する): I.e., there is nothing else that it passes.

42 **passage has attained the way at this time of spring** (*kyōryaku ima haru no toki ni jōdō seri* 経歴いま春の時に成道せり): The predicate here is a standard term for the attainment of bodhi, perhaps in the sense, "has been fully realized."

43 **while the object is external, the dharma accomplishing the passage** (*kyō wa getō ni shite, nō kyōryaku no hō wa* 境は外頭にして、能経歴の法は): Dōgen here introduces terms commonly used to distinguish the object of perception (*kyō* 境) from the perceiver (*nō* 能); here perhaps indicating merely a fixed, external field across which something passes.

44 **Great Master Hongdao of Yaoshan** (*Yakusan Gudō daishi* 薬山弘道大師): Posthumous title of Yaoshan Weiyan 薬山惟儼. "Great Master Wuji" (*Musai daishi* 無際大師): Honorific title of Yaoshan's teacher, Shitou Xiqian 石頭希遷. "Chan Master Jiangxi Daji" (*Kōzei Daijaku zenji* 江西大寂禪師): I.e., Mazu Daoyi 馬祖道一. There is no known source for this version of Yaoshan's exchange with Mazu, told here in a mixture of Chinese and Japanese. In his *shinji Shōbōgenzō* 眞字正法眼藏 (DZZ.5:204, case 150), Dōgen quotes only Mazu's famous answer, without Yaoshan's question. A variant of the conversation occurs at *Liandeng huiyao* 聯燈會要, ZZ.136:738b1-10; see also *Zongmen*

204 DŌGEN'S *SHŌBŌGENZŌ* VOLUME II

Questioned like this, Chan Master Daji said, "*Sometimes, I have him raise his eyebrows and blink his eyes; sometimes, I don't have him raise his eyebrows and blink his eyes.*[45] *Sometimes, having him raise his eyebrows and blink his eyes is it; sometimes, having him raise his eyebrows and blink his eyes is not it.*"[46]

Hearing this, Yaoshan had a great awakening and said to Daji, "When I was with Shitou, it was like a mosquito on an iron bull."

[20:14] {1:245}

大寂の道取するところ、餘者とおなじからず。眉目は山海なるべし、山海は眉目なるゆえに。その教伊揚は山をみるべし、その教伊瞬は海を宗すべし。是は伊に慣習せり、伊は教に誘引せらる。不是は不教伊にあらず、不教伊は不是にあらず、これらともに有時なり。山も時なり、海も時なり。時にあらざれば山海あるべからず、山海の而今に時あらずとすべからず。時もし壊すれば、山海も壊す、時もし不壊なれば、山海も不壊なり。この道理に明星出現す、如來出現す、眼睛出現す、拈華出現す。これ時なり、時にあらざれば不恁麼なり。

What Daji says is not the same as others. The "eyebrows" and "eyes" must be the mountains and oceans; for mountains and oceans are eye-

---

tongyao ji 宗門統要集, ZTS.1:141a8-b7. For the full story as it appears at *Wudeng huiyuan* 五燈會元, ZZ.138:163a9-b10, see Supplementary Notes, s.v. "Slough off."

three vehicles and the twelvefold teachings (*sanjō jūnibun kyō* 三乘十二分教): A fairly standard expression for the teachings of the Buddhist canon: the teachings of the three vehicles (*śrāvaka*, *pratyeka-buddha*, and bodhisattva), and the twelvefold division of the canon according to genre. See Supplementary Notes, s.v. "Three vehicles and twelvefold teachings."

intention of the Ancestral Master's coming from the west (*soshi seirai i* 祖師西來意): A popular fixed phrase in Zen literature, often the subject of lectures and discussions; the title theme of Dōgen's "Shōbōgenzō soshi seirai i" 正法眼藏祖師西來意. The "Ancestral Master" here is, of course, the first ancestor of Chan in China, Bodhidharma, said to have come from India in the sixth century. See Supplementary Notes, s.v. "Intention of the Ancestral Master's coming from the west."

45 **"Sometimes, I have him raise his eyebrows and blink his eyes"** (*uji kyō i yōbi shunmoku* 有時教伊揚眉瞬目): The expression "raise the eyebrows and blink the eyes" (*yōbi shunmoku* 揚眉瞬目) is a set phrase used in Zen texts to represent the ordinary actions through which Buddhism is expressed; see Supplementary Notes, s.v. "Raise the eyebrows and blink the eyes." The antecedent of "him" (*i* 伊) here is unclear. One might posit "the Ancestral Master" of Yaoshan's question, or Mazu speaking of himself in the third person. Or the reference may be to Shitou Xiqian 石頭希遷 (700-790), whose words Mazu is responding to in the version of the story that appears in *Wudeng huiyuan* 五燈會元, ZZ.138:163a9-b10; see Supplementary Notes, s.v. "Slough off." It is sometimes suggested that the expression alludes to Buddha Śākyamuni's "blinking" as he famously held up the flower on Vulture Peak; see Supplementary Notes, s.v. "Holding up a flower and blinking the eyes." However, that version of the story of the first transmission of Chan, found in Dōgen's writings, was not widespread China.

46 **"it"** (*ze* 是); **"not it"** (*fuze* 不是): Or, "right," "not right."

20. Sometimes *Uji* 有時   205

brows and eyes.[47] "Having him raise" them is to see the mountains; "having him blink" them is to merge with the oceans.[48] "It" is familiar to "him"; "him" is enticed by "having."[49] "Not it" is not "I don't have him"; "I don't have him" is not "not it": they are both "sometimes."[50]

The mountains are times; the oceans are times. If they were not times, there would be no mountains and oceans; we should not take it that there are no times in the present of the mountains and oceans. If the times are destroyed, the mountains and oceans are destroyed; if the times are not destroyed, the mountains and oceans are not destroyed. By this principle, the dawn star appears; the Tathāgata appears; his eye appears; the flower he held up appears.[51] They are times; if they were not times, they would not be such as this.

* * * * *

[20:15]

葉縣の歸省禪師は、臨濟の法孫なり、首山の嫡嗣なり。あるとき、大衆にしめしていはく、有時意到句不到、有時句到意不到、有時意句兩倶到、有時意句倶不到。

---

47 **for mountains and oceans are eyebrows and eyes** (*sangai wa bimoku naru yue ni* 山海は眉目なるゆえに): Following Kawamura's punctuation at DZZ.1:245:4-5; this phrase could instead be read with the following sentence: "Because mountains and oceans are eyebrows and eyes, 'having him raise' them is to see the mountains; 'having him blink' them is to merge with oceans." The expression "mountains and oceans" (*sangai*; also read *sengai* 山海) can serve as a synecdoche for "the world around us," but it is also regularly used for the great distance (across which the Ancestral Master passed) separating India from East Asia.

48 **merge with the oceans** (*umi o shū su beshi* 海を宗すべし): Taking the unusual verbal form *shū su* 宗す in the sense *chōsō* 朝宗, used to describe the convergence of rivers in the sea.

49 **"It" is familiar to "him"; "him" is enticed by "having"** (*ze wa i ni kanjū seri, i wa kyō ni yūin seraru* 是は伊に慣習せり、伊は教に誘引せらる): With this novel play with the terms of the quotation, Dōgen seems to be identifying both what is "it" and the person ("him") with his practiced acts. "Having" here translates the glyph *kyō* 教 ("teaching"), used as the causative marker in Mazu's "having him raise his eyebrows and blink his eyes."

50 **"Not it" is not "I don't have him"** (*fize wa fukyō i ni arazu* 不是は不教伊にあらず): Presumably, meaning that we should not equate the sentence, "Sometimes, having him raise his eyebrows and blink his eyes is not it," with the sentence, "Sometimes, I don't have him raise his eyebrows and blink his eyes."

51 **the dawn star appears** (*myōjō shutsugen su* 明星出現す): Reference to the tradition that Siddhārtha attained awakening upon the appearance of the planet Venus.

the flower he held up appears (*nenge shutsugen su* 拈華出現す): Reference to the flower held up by the Buddha on the occasion of his transmission of the treasury of the true dharma eye to Mahākāśyapa on Vulture Peak; see Supplementary Notes, s.v. "Hold up a flower."

206 DŌGEN'S *SHŌBŌGENZŌ* VOLUME II

Chan Master Guixing of Shexian was a descendant of Linji, the direct heir of Shoushan. On one occasion, addressing the great assembly, he said,[52]

Sometimes, the intention reaches it, and the words don't reach it. Sometimes, the words reach it, and the intention doesn't reach it. Sometimes, both the intention and the words reach it. Sometimes, neither the intention nor the words reach it.

[20:16]

意・句ともに有時なり、到・不到ともに有時なり。到時未了なりといへども不到時來なり。意は驢なり、句は馬なり。馬を句とし、驢を意とせり。到それ來にあらず、不到これ未にあらず、有時かくのごとくなり。到は到に罣礙せられて不到に罣礙せられず、不到は不到に罣礙せられて、到に罣礙せられず。意は意をさへ、意をみる。句は句をさへ、句をみる。礙は礙をさへ、礙をみる。礙は礙を礙するなり、これ時なり。礙は他法に使得せらるといへども、他法を礙する礙いまだあらざるなり。我逢人なり、人逢人なり、我逢我なり、出逢出なり。これらもし時をえざるには、恁麼ならざるなり。又、意は現成公案の時なり、句は向上關棙の時なり、到は脱體の時なり、不到は即此離此の時なり。かくのごとく辦肯すべし、有時すべし。

"The intention" and "the words" are both "sometimes." "Reaching it" and "not reaching it" are both "sometimes." Although *the time of "reaching it" is not yet done, the time of "not reaching it" arrives.*[53] "The intention" is the donkey; "the words" are the horse: he has taken the horse as "the words" and taken the donkey as "the intention."[54] "Reaching it" is not "coming"; "not reaching it" is not "not yet" — "sometimes" is like

---

52   **Chan Master Guixing of Shexian** (*Sekken no Kisei zenji* 葉縣の歸省禪師); **Shoushan** (*Shuzan* 首山):

I.e., Shexian Guixing 葉縣歸省 (dates unknown) and Shoushan Shengnian 首山省念 (926-993). This saying, told here in a mixture of Chinese and Japanese, appears at *Liandeng huiyao* 聯燈會要, ZZ.136:622b13-15.

53   **Although the time of "reaching it" is not yet done, the time of "not reaching it" arrives** (*tō ji miryō nari to iedomo futō ji rai nari* 到時未了なりといへども不到時來なり): Perhaps meaning that when the intention or the words have not yet "reached it," this is itself the distinct time of "not reaching it." Dōgen is playing with the donkey and horse saying he alludes to in his next sentence here.

54   **"The intention" is the donkey; "the words" are the horse** (*i wa ro nari, ku wa ba nari* 意は驢なり、句は馬なり): Allusion to a saying first attributed to Lingyun Zhiqin 靈雲志勤 (dates unknown) (*Jingde chuandeng lu* 景德傳燈錄, T.2076.51:285b12-13):

僧問、如何是佛法大意。師曰、驢事未去馬事到來。

A monk asked, "What is the great meaning of the buddha dharma?"

The Master said, "Before the donkey business is gone, the horse business arrives." The saying is generally taken to mean something like, "It's just one damned thing after another."

20. Sometimes *Uji* 有時   207

this.[55] "Reaching it" is obstructed by "reaching it," not obstructed by "not reaching it."[56] "Not reaching it" is obstructed by "not reaching it," not obstructed by "reaching it." "The intention" blocks "the intention" and sees "the intention"; "the words" block "the words" and see "the words." The obstruction blocks the obstruction and sees the obstruction; the obstruction obstructs the obstruction — these are times. Although we say obstruction is made use of by another dharma, there is no obstruction that obstructs another dharma.[57] It is "I meet a person"; it is the person meets the person; it is I meet myself; it is "coming forth" meets "coming forth."[58] Where these do not get a time, they are not like this. Again, "the intention" is the time of the realized kōan; "the words" are the time of the higher pivot.[59] "Reaching it" is the time of the body stripped; "not reaching it" is the time of identical with this, apart from this.[60] In this

---

55 **"Reaching it" is not "coming"; "not reaching it" is not "not yet"** (*tō sore rai ni arazu, futō kore mi ni arazu* 到それ來にあらず、不到これ未にあらず): Presumably, meaning that the sense of "reach" in Guixing's saying is not the same as that of "arrive" in Lingyun's saying, nor "not reach" in the former the same as "not yet" in the latter.

56 **"Reaching it" is obstructed by "reaching it," not obstructed by "not reaching it"** (*tō wa tō ni keige serarete futō ni keige serarezu* 到は到に罣礙せられて不到に罣礙せられず): Probably meaning that "reaching it" is just "reaching it," not the opposite of "not reaching it." Reflecting a recurrent use in Dōgen's writings of the passive *keige seraru* 罣礙せらる ("to be obstructed or impeded") in the sense "to be identified or defined."

57 **Although we say obstruction is made use of by another dharma, there is no obstruction that obstructs another dharma** (*ge wa tahō ni shitoku seraru to iedomo, tahō o ge suru ge imada arazaru nari* 礙は他法に使得せらるといへども、他法を礙する礙いまだあらざるなり): Perhaps best interpreted to mean that, while in one sense things are contingent on other things, each thing retains its identity — a reiteration of the preceding claim that "reaching it" is obstructed by itself.

58 **"I meet a person"** (*ga hō nin* 我逢人): Dōgen seems to have in mind here the words of Sansheng 三聖 and Xinghua 興化, quoted in case 92 of the *shinji Shōbōgenzō* 眞字正法眼藏 (DZZ.5:172) and alluded to elsewhere in the *Shōbōgenzō*:

> 三聖院慧然禪師〈嗣臨濟〉道、我逢人即出、出即不爲人。興化道、我逢人即不出、出即便爲人。

> Chan Master Huiran of the Sansheng Cloister (succeeded Linji) said, "When I meet a person, I come forth; but, when I come forth, I don't benefit the person."

> Xinghua said, "When I meet a person, I don't come forth; but, when I do come forth, I benefit the person."

59 **realized kōan** (*genjō kōan* 現成公案): Or "settled case"; also written 見成公案. A Dōgen favorite, the title theme of one of the most celebrated chapters of his *Shōbōgenzō*; see Supplementary Notes.

higher pivot (*kōjō kanrei* 向上關捩): The term *kanreisu* 關捩子 (also written 關振子) refers to the pivots at the top and bottom of a door frame, on which the door turns; hence, the pivotal point of something.

60 **body stripped** (*dattai* 脱體): A term indicating a state of liberation; in Zen texts, it often carries the sense "to reveal all," or, as we might say, "to say it like it is" —

208　　DŌGEN'S *SHŌBŌGENZŌ* VOLUME II

way, we should confirm them, we should be "sometimes."[61]

[20:17] {1:246}

向來の尊宿、ともに恁麼いふとも、さらに道取すべきところなからんや。いふべし、意句半到也有時、意句半不到也有時。かくのごとくの參究あるべきなり。

Previous venerables have all spoken like this, but is there nothing fur-ther to be said? We should say, *"the intention and the words half reach-ing it is 'sometimes'; the intention and the words half not reaching it is 'sometimes.'"* There should be an investigation like this.

[20:18]

教伊揚眉瞬目也半有時、教伊揚眉瞬目也錯有時、　　不教伊揚眉瞬目也錯錯有時。

Making him raise his eyebrows and blink his eyes is a half "some-times"; making him raise his eyebrows and blink his eyes is a wrong "sometimes"; not making him raise his eyebrows and blink his eyes is a wrong, wrong "sometimes."[62]

---

hence, "the very thing itself," "the 'naked' thing." See Supplementary Notes, s.v. "Body stripped."

identical with this, apart from this (*soku shi ri shi* 即此離此): Perhaps reflecting a question posed by Baizhang Huaihai 百丈懷海 (749-814) to his teacher, Mazu Daoyi 馬祖道一 (e.g., at *Baizhang Huaihai chanshi yulu* 百丈懷海禪師語錄, *Sijia yulu* 四家語錄, ZZ.119:6a3-7):

祖目視繩床角拂子。師曰、即此用離此用。祖曰、汝向後開兩片皮、將何爲人。師取拂子豎起。祖曰、即此用離此用。師挂拂子於舊處。

Mazu was looking at a whisk on the corner of his bench. The Master [Baizhang] said, "Is it identical with its use or apart from its use?"
Mazu said, "In the future, when you open those two pieces of skin, what will you have for people?"
The Master took the whisk and stood it up.
Mazu said, "Is it identical with its use or apart from its use?"
The Master placed the whisk back where it had been.

61　**we should be "sometimes"** (*uji su beshi* 有時すべし): The translation seeks to pre-serve Dōgen's novel use of *uji* here as an imperative verb.

62　**wrong, wrong "sometimes"** (*shaku shaku uji* 錯錯有時): "Wrong! Wrong!" (or "Mistake! Mistake!") is a common retort of Chan masters, sometimes used in ironic praise. This entire passage is put in Chinese, of which some texts give a variant version that creates a novel *catuṣkoṭi*:

教伊揚眉瞬目也半有時、教伊揚眉瞬目也錯有時、不教伊揚眉瞬目也半有時、不教伊揚眉瞬目也錯有時。

Making him raise his eyebrows and blink his eyes is a half "sometimes"; making him raise his eyebrows and blink his eyes is a wrong "sometimes"; not making him raise his eyebrows and blink his eyes is a half "sometimes"; not making him raise his eyebrows and blink his eyes is a wrong "sometimes."

20. Sometimes *Uji* 有時

[20:19]

恁麼のごとく參來・參去、參到・參不到する、有時の時なり。

In this way, *studying coming, studying going, studying "reaching it," and studying "not reaching it"* are the times of "sometimes."

正法眼藏有時第二十

Treasury of the True Dharma Eye
Sometimes
Number 20

[Ryūmonji MS:]

仁治元年庚子開冬日、書于興聖寶林寺

Written at Kōshō Hōrin Monastery; first day of winter, senior metal year of the rat, the first year of Ninji [17 October 1240][63]

[Tōunji MS:]

寛元癸卯夏安居、書寫之。懷奘

Copied this during the summer retreat, junior water year of the rabbit, Kangen [16 April-15 July 1243]. Ejō

于当永正七年庚午年四月日、於桂林精舍丈室書寫焉。用兼拜

Copied in the abbot's quarters of Keirin [Monastery]; on a day in the fourth month, the senior metal year of the horse, the seventh year of Eishō [May-June 1510]. Yōken[64]

For the meaning of "raise the eyebrows and blink the eyes," see Supplementary Notes.

63   The Tōunji 洞雲寺 MS shares an identical colophon.

first day of winter (*kaitōbi* 開冬日): I.e., the first day of the tenth lunar month.

64   **Yōken** 用兼: I.e., Kinkō Yōken 金岡用兼 (1437-1513?).

Treasury of the True Dharma Eye

Number 21

Prediction
Juki

授記

Prediction

Juki

INTRODUCTION

This work was composed at Kōshōji in May of 1242, during a one-week period in which are dated the "Kaiin zanmai" 海印三味, "Juki" 授記, and "Kannon" 觀音 chapters. "Juki" represents number 21 in the seventy-five- and sixty-chapter compilations of the *Shōbōgenzō* and number 32 in the Honzan edition.

The title theme of the text derives from the Buddhist tradition that bodhisattvas are supposed to study under many buddhas, from one of whom they will receive a prediction, or confirmation (*vyākaraṇa*), of future buddhahood. Insofar as Dōgen wishes to treat the ancestral masters of Zen as equivalent to the buddhas, the question naturally arises how he understands this tradition of prediction. His answer, given in the opening sections here, is that, rightly understood, prediction goes far beyond the standard understanding: it is conferred on all beings; indeed, it is the truth of all things, of "the mountains, rivers, and the whole earth, of Mount Sumeru and the vast oceans."

In the second half of the essay, Dōgen cites a series of passages from his favorite scripture, the *Lotus Sūtra*, in which Buddha Śākyamuni confers predictions on all beings, human and nonhuman, in his audience and, indeed, on all beings who ever hear and rejoice in even so much as a single line of the sūtra. The text ends with a passage from the *Vimalakīrti Sūtra*, in which Vimalakīrti tells Bodhisattva Maitreya, predicted to be the next buddha, that at the ultimate stage there is no such thing as a prediction. Dōgen takes Vimalakīrti to task here, as he does elsewhere, saying he does not realize that the ultimate stage is precisely prediction.

正法眼藏第二十一
Treasury of the True Dharma Eye
Number 21

授記
Prediction

[21:1] {1:247}

佛祖單傳の大道は、授記なり。佛祖の參學なきものは、夢也未見なり。その授記の時節は、いまだ菩提心をおこさざるものにも授記す、無佛性に授記す、有佛性に授記す、有身に授記し、無身に授記す、諸佛に授記す。諸佛は、諸佛の授記を保任するなり。得授記ののちに作佛す、と參學すべからず、作佛ののちに得授記す、と參學すべからず。授記時に作佛あり、授記時に修行あり。このゆえに、諸佛に授記あり、佛向上に授記あり。自己に授記す、身心に授記す。授記に飽學措大なるとき、佛道に飽學措大なり。身前に授記あり、身後に授記あり。自己にしらるる授記あり、自己にしられざる授記あり。他をしてしらしむる授記あり、他をしてしらしめざる授記あり。

The great way uniquely transmitted by the buddhas and ancestors is prediction.[1] Those lacking study with the buddhas and ancestors *have never seen it even in their dreams*. At the time of the prediction, it is conferred even on those who have not yet aroused the thought of bodhi; it is conferred on those without buddha nature, conferred on those with buddha nature, conferred on those with a body, conferred on those without a body, conferred on the buddhas.[2] The buddhas maintain the prediction

---

1 **prediction** (*juki* 授記): The conferral of a prediction (S. *vyākaraṇa*) of future spiritual status, paradigmatically by a buddha regarding a bodhisattva's eventual buddhahood. In much Buddhist literature, such a prediction is considered a necessary event in the bodhisattva career.

2 **the thought of bodhi** (*bodai shin* 菩提心): S. *bodhi-citta*, the bodhisattva's aspiration to attain the supreme perfect awakening of a buddha; see Supplementary Notes, s.v. "Bring forth the mind." While the prediction of future buddhahood typically occurs after the bodhisattva has aroused the aspiration for buddhahood, Buddhist texts are not necessarily consistent on this point; see, e.g., the *Śūraṅgama-samādhi-sūtra* (*Shoulengyan sanmei jing* 首楞嚴三昧經, T.642.15:638c14), where prediction before the arousal of bodhi-citta is listed as the first of four types of prediction: before the arousal of the aspiration, just after the arousal, in secret, and upon achieving patience in regard to the non-arising of dharmas (*mushō hō nin* 無生法忍; S. *anutpattika-dharma-kṣānti*).

those without buddha nature (*mu busshō* 無佛性): While this could be taken as a reference to the *icchantika* (*issendai* 一闡提), a being without the potential to become a buddha, the more likely sense here is the Zen use of this term to express a higher understanding of

214 DŌGEN'S *SHŌBŌGENZŌ* VOLUME II

of the buddhas. We should not study that one becomes a buddha after getting the prediction; we should not study that one gets the prediction after becoming a buddha: at the time of the prediction, there is becoming a buddha; at the time of the prediction, there is practice. Therefore, there are predictions for the buddhas, and there are predictions beyond the buddha. Predictions are conferred on the self; predictions are conferred on the body and mind. When one is learned and skilled in prediction, one is learned and skilled in the way of the buddhas.[3] There are predictions before the body; there are predictions after the body.[4] There are predictions known to the self; there are predictions unknown to the self.[5] There are predictions made known to the other; there are predictions not made known to the other.

[21:2]
まさにしるべし、授記は自己を現成せり、授記これ現成の自己なり。この ゆえに、佛佛祖祖嫡嫡相承せるは、これただ授記のみなり、さらに一法と しても授記にあらざるなし。いかにいはんや、山河大地・須彌巨海あらん や、さらに一箇半箇の張三李四なきなり。かくのごとく參究する授記は、 道得一句なり、聞得一句なり、不會一句なり、會取一句なり、行取なり、 説取なり。退歩を教令せしめ、進歩を教令せしむ。いま得坐披衣、これ古 來の得授記にあらざれば、現成せざるなり。合掌頂戴なるがゆえに、現成 は授記なり。

We should realize that prediction manifests the self, that prediction is the self manifested. Therefore, what is inherited by successor after successor of buddha after buddha and ancestor after ancestor is nothing but prediction. There is not even a single dharma that is not prediction. Much less are there the mountains, rivers, and the whole earth, Sumeru and the vast oceans.[6] And further, there is not one or a half of Zhang's

---

buddha nature, as in sayings such as, "all living beings have no buddha nature" (*issai shujō mu busshō* 一切衆生無佛性) — seen, e.g., in a saying of Yanguang Qian 鹽官齋安 (d. 842) (see *shinji Shōbōgenzō* 眞字正法眼藏, DZZ.5:188, case 115), quoted in "Shōbōgenzō busshō" 正法眼藏佛性.

3 **learned and skilled** (*hōgaku sodai* 飽學措大): An idiom literally meaning "replete with learning and [capable of] handling great matters."

4 **before the body** (*shinzen* 身前); **after the body** (*shingo* 身後): Can mean before and after death, or previous and future lives; the former expression is sometimes taken in a metaphysical sense, to refer to what precedes existence in this body. Appears several times in the *Shōbōgenzō*, more often in the form *shinsen shingo* 身先身後.

5 **predictions known to the self** (*jiko ni shiraruru juki* 自己にしらるる授記): This and the following three types of prediction would seem to anticipate the eight types of prediction introduced in section 3, below.

6 **the mountains, rivers, and the whole earth, Sumeru and the vast oceans** (*senga daichi Shumi kokai* 山河大地・須彌巨海): I.e., the natural world. "The mountains, rivers, and the whole earth" (*senga daichi* 山河大地) is a fixed expression common in Zen

21. Prediction *Juki* 授記 215

third and Li's fourth.[7] The prediction we study like this is saying one line; it is hearing one line; it is not understanding one line; it is understanding one line; it is practicing it; it is talking about it.[8] It instructs us to step back and instructs us to step forward.[9] That now we can take our seat and don the robe — this would not occur were they not the ancient prediction; it is because we join our palms and place it on our heads that their occurrence is the prediction.[10]

[21:3] {1:248}
佛言、それ授記に多般あれども、しばらく要略するに八種あり。いはゆる、

The Buddha said that, although there are many kinds of predictions, to summarize them briefly here, there are eight types — to wit:[11]

---

texts and in Dōgen's writings. "Sumeru" (*shumi* 須彌) refers to the mountain, surrounded by a series of oceans, at the center of a Buddhist world system.

7 **Zhang's third and Li's fourth** (*Chō san Ri shi* 張三李四): I.e., everyone. From the Chinese idiom *Zhang san Li si* 張三李四 ("Zhang's third son, Li's fourth son"), used (as we might use "Tom, Dick, and Harry") to indicate anyone at all.

8 **saying one line** (*dōtoku ikku* 道得一句): A common expression in Zen texts for saying something significant.

it is practicing it; it is talking about it (*gyōshu nari, sesshu nari* 行取なり、説取なり): Perhaps reflecting a passage recorded in the *shinji Shōbōgenzō* 眞字正法眼藏 (DZZ.5:164, case 77):

杭州大慈山性空大師〈嗣百丈、諱寰中〉示衆云、説得一丈、不如行取一尺、説得一尺、不如行取一寸。洞山曰、説取行不得底、行取説不得底。

Great Master Xinggong of Mount Daci in Hangzhou (named Huangzhong) addressed the assembly saying, "To talk about ten feet is not like practicing one foot; to talk about one foot is not like practicing one inch."
Dongshan said, "He talks about what can't be practiced; he practices what can't be talked about."

9 **step back** (*taiho* 退步); **step forward** (*shinpo* 進步): "Stepping forward and stepping back" (*shinpo taiho* 進步退步) is an expression occurring regularly in Dōgen's writings; it can refer simply to all the ordinary movements of the agent, or more specifically, to motion forward and back; see Supplementary Notes, s.v. "Stepping forward and stepping back." Here, possibly, instructions for a ritual practice.

10 **we can take our seat and don the robe** (*tokuza hie* 得坐披衣); **we join our palms and place it on our heads** (*gasshō chōdai* 合掌頂戴): Two common expressions in Zen texts. The former typically refers to becoming established as a teacher (though, here, we might want to read it more literally); the latter recalls the monks' ritual at morning meditation of placing the *kāṣāya* on their heads and chanting its praises.

11 **The Buddha said** (*butsu gon* 佛言): What follows here is a teaching of the *Pusa yingluo jing* 菩薩瓔珞經 (T.656.16:81b12-c12), as summarized in the *Fahua wenju* 法華文句 (T.1718.34:97b3-5), attributed to the Tiantai figure Zhiyi 智顗 (538–597). The vulgate Honzan edition of this chapter, as well as the Kenkon'in 乾坤院 (1488) and Shōbōji 正法寺 (1512) manuscripts of the seventy-five-chapter *Shōbōgenzō* compilation, include interlinear comments (*warichū* 割注) quoting Zhiyi's explanation of each type of prediction. These comments, thought to have been added to the text in the early fifteenth

216   DŌGEN'S *SHŌBŌGENZŌ* VOLUME II

[21:4]

一者自己知他不知。二者衆人盡知自己不知。三者自己・衆人倶知。四者自己・衆人倶不知。五者近覺遠不覺。六者遠覺、近不知覺。七者倶覺。八者倶不覺。

First, the individual knows, but others do not know.[12] *Second, other people all know, but the individual does not know.*[13] *Third, both the individual and other people know.*[14] *Fourth, neither the individual nor other people know.*[15] *Fifth, those nearby are aware of it, but those distant are not.*[16] *Sixth, those distant are aware of it, but those nearby are not aware of it.*[17]

---

century, do not appear in Kawamura's edition but are collected at DZZ.1:500b-c; they are translated in Notes 12-19, below.

12 **First** (*issha* 一者): This and the following seven notes record Zhiyi's explanations of the eight types, as provided in the Honzan version of our text:

己知他不知者、發心自誓未廣及人、未得四無所畏、未得善權故。

The individual knows, but others do not know: because one has brought forth the mind [of bodhi] and made the vow, but has not extended it to others; one has not yet attained the four types of fearlessness, and one has not yet attained skillful expedience.

13 **Second** (*nisha* 二者):

衆人盡知、己不知者、發心廣大得無畏善權故。

Other people all know, but the individual does not know: because one's bringing forth the mind has extended broadly; one has attained the four types of fearlessness and expedience.

14 **Third** (*sansha* 三者):

皆知者、位在七地、無畏善權、得空觀故。

Everyone knows: because one's rank is the seventh *bhūmi* [of the bodhisattva path]; one has fearlessness and skillful expedience, and has attained insight into emptiness.

15 **Fourth** (*shisha* 四者):

皆不知者、未入七地、未得無著行。

No one knows: one has not yet entered the seventh stage and has not yet attained detached action.

16 **Fifth** (*gosha* 五者):

遠者不覺者、彌勒是也。根具足、不如來無著行故。

Those at a distance are not aware of it: Maitreya is this type; because one possesses the faculties but not the detached action of a tathāgata.

17 **Sixth** (*rokusha* 六者):

近者不覺者、此人未能演賢聖之行、師子膺是也。

Those nearby are not aware of it: this type cannot yet display the actions of the worthy or sage; Shiziying is this type.

21. Prediction *Juki* 授記　　　217

Seventh, both are aware of it.[18] *Eighth, neither is aware of it.*[19]

[21:5]

かくのごとく授記あり。しかあれば、いまこの臭皮袋の精魂に識度せられ
ざるには授記あるべからず、と活計することなかれ、未悟の人面にたやす
く授記すべからず、といふことなかれ。よのつねにおもふには、修行功満
じて作佛決定するとき授記すべし、と學しきたるといへども、佛道はしか
にはあらず。或從知識して一句をきき、或從經卷して一句をきくことある
は、すなはち得授記なり。これ諸佛の本行なるがゆえに、百草の善根なる
がゆえに。もし授記を道取するには、得記人みな究竟人なるべし。しるべ
し、一塵なほ無上なり、一塵なほ向上なり。授記なんぞ一塵ならざらん、
授記なんぞ一法ならざらん、授記なんぞ萬法ならざらん、授記なんぞ修
證ならざらん、授記なんぞ佛祖ならざらん、授記なんぞ功夫辨道ならざら
ん、授記なんぞ大悟・大迷ならざらん。授記はこれ吾宗到汝、大興于世な
り、授記はこれ汝亦如是、吾亦如是なり、授記これ標榜なり、授記これ何
必なり、授記これ破顔微笑なり、授記これ生死去來なり、授記これ盡十方
界なり、授記これ徧界不曾藏なり。

There are such predictions. This being so, do not live by [the notion
that] there ought not be a prediction when it is not discerned by the spirit
of this stinking skin bag; do not say one ought not readily confer a prediction on the face of a person who is not yet awakened.[20] Although, in
the common understanding, we learn that predictions are conferred when
the merits of practice are fulfilled and becoming a buddha is assured, in
the way of the buddhas, this is not the case. The fact that, *whether from
a wise friend,* one hears a single line, *whether from a sūtra scroll,* one
hears a single line — this is receiving a prediction.[21] For it is the original

---

18　**Seventh** (*shichisha* 七者):

近遠倶覺者、根具足、不無著之行、柔順菩薩是也。

Both those nearby and those distant are aware of it: one possesses the faculties but
lacks detached action; Bodhisattva Roushun is this type.

19　**Eighth** (*hassha* 八者):

近遠倶不覺者、未得善權、不能悉知如灾藏、等行菩薩是也。

Neither those nearby nor those distant are aware of it: one has not yet attained skillful
expedients, and cannot know fully the tathāgata-garbha; Bodhisattva Dengxing is
this type.

20　**do not live by [the notion that]** (*to kakkei suru koto nakare* と活計することなか
れ): The term *kakkei* 活計 ("livelihood," "to make a living," etc.) occurs regularly in
Dōgen's writing, sometimes (as perhaps here) in a pejorative sense of being "occupied
with," "given over to," etc.

the face of a person who is not yet awakened (*migo no ninmen* 未悟の人面): The odd
term *ninmen* 人面 ("human face") could well be taken simply as "person."

21　**whether from a wise friend** (*waku jū chishiki* 或從知識); **whether from a sūtra
scroll** (*waku jū kyōkan* 或從經卷): I.e., whether from a teacher or from a text. Fixed expressions occurring together several times in the *Shōbōgenzō*; see Supplementary Notes,
s.v. "Whether from a wise friend, whether from a sūtra scroll."

218   DŌGEN'S *SHŌBŌGENZŌ* VOLUME II

practice of the buddhas; for it is the good roots of the hundred grasses.[22] When we speak of prediction, the people who receive the prediction should all be perfected people.[23]

We should realize that even a single dust mote is unsurpassed; even a single dust mote is beyond. How could prediction not be a single dust mote? How could prediction not be a single dharma? How could prediction not be myriad dharmas? How could prediction not be practice and verification? How could prediction not be the buddhas and ancestors? How could prediction not be concentrated effort and pursuit of the way? How could prediction not be great awakening and great delusion? Prediction is, "*When my lineage has reached you, it will flourish greatly in the world.*"[24] Prediction is "*You're also like this, I'm also like this.*"[25]

---

22 **the original practice of the buddhas** (*shobutsu no hongyō* 諸佛の本行): While the term *hongyō* 本行 could be understood as "fundamental practice," it probably reflects a passage in the *Lotus Sūtra* (*Miaofa lianhua jing* 妙法蓮華經, T.262.9:42c22-23) cited in several places in the *Shōbōgenzō*:

諸善男子、我本行菩薩道所成壽命、今猶未盡、復倍上數。

Good sons, the lifespan attained by my original practice of the bodhisattva path is even now still not exhausted; it is twice the above number.

the good roots of the hundred grasses (*hyakusō no zenkon* 百草の善根): A play with vegetative metaphors: "good roots" (*zenkon* 善根; S. *kuśala-mūla*) refers to what we might call one's moral character or spiritual propensities; "the hundred grasses" (*hyakusō* 百草) is used in reference to "all phenomena."

23 **perfected people** (*kukyō nin* 究竟人): Probably to be taken as those who have attained the ultimate stage (S. *niṣṭhā*) of buddhahood. Does not occur elsewhere in the *Shōbōgenzō*.

24 **"When my lineage has reached you, it will flourish greatly in the world"** (*goshū tō nyo, daikō o se* 吾宗到汝、大興于世): A remark of Huangbo Xiyuan 黃蘗 希運 (dates unknown) to his student Linji Yixuan 臨濟義玄 (d. 866); *Linji lu* 臨濟錄, T.1985.47:505a5-9:

師栽松次。黃蘗問。深山裏栽許多作什麼。師云。一與山門作境致。二與後人作 標榜。道了將钁頭打地三下。黃蘗云。雖然如是。子已喫吾三十棒了也。師又以 钁頭打地三下。作嘘嘘聲。黃蘗云。吾宗到汝大興於世。

When the Master [Linji] was planting pines, Huangbo asked, "Why plant so many in the deep mountains?"

The Master said, "First, to form a border for the mountain gate; second, to make a signpost for later people." After speaking, he struck the ground three times with his shovel.

Huangbo said, "Maybe so, but you've already tasted my thirty blows!"

The Master again struck the ground three times with his shovel and made a hissing sound.

Huangbo said, "When my lineage has reached you, it will flourish greatly in the world."

25 **"You're also like this, I'm also like this"** (*nyo yaku nyo ze, go yaku nyo ze* 汝亦 如是、吾亦如是): A remark of the Sixth Ancestor, Caoxi Huineng 曹溪慧能 (638–713) to his student Nanyue Huairang 南嶽懷讓 (677–744) in a conversation recorded in the

21. Prediction *Juki* 授記　　219

Prediction is "a signpost"; prediction is "why must that be?"[26] Prediction is *breaking into a smile*.[27] Prediction is birth and death, coming and going. Prediction is all the worlds in the ten directions. Prediction is *in the realms everywhere, it has never been hidden*."[28]

* * * * *

[21:6] {1:249}

玄沙院宗一大師、侍雪峰行次、雪峰指面前地云、這一片田地、好造箇無縫塔。玄沙曰、高多少。雪峰乃上下顧視。玄沙云、人天福報即不無、和尚靈山授記、未夢見在。雪峰云、儞作麼生。玄沙曰、七尺八尺。

> *Great Master Zongyi of Xuansha Cloister was walking in attendance on Xuefeng.*[29] *Xuefeng pointed at the ground in front of them and said, "This piece of land would be a good place to build a seamless stūpa."*[30]
>
> *Xuansha said, "How tall would it be?"*
>
> *Xuefeng looked up and down.*
>
> *Xuansha said, "It's not that you lack the blessings of humans and devas, but the prediction on Vulture Peak, the Reverend hasn't seen even in his dreams."*
>
> *Xuefeng said, "What do you make of it?"*
>
> *The Master said, "Seven feet or eight feet."*

[21:7]

いま玄沙のいふ和尚靈山授記、未夢見在は、雪峰に靈山の授記なし、とい

---

shinji Shōbōgenzō 眞字正法眼藏 (DZZ.5:178, case 101) and much cited by Dōgen; see Supplementary Notes, s.v. "You're also like this, I'm also like this."

26 **"a signpost"** (*hyōbō* 標榜): Likely reflecting the remark by Linji 臨濟 in the conversation alluded to just above.

"why must that be?" (*ka hitsu* 何必): An expression often used rhetorically in the sense "not necessarily," somewhat akin to our usage of the dubious, "oh really?"

27 **breaking into a smile** (*hagan mishō* 破顏微笑): Reference to the famous story of the first transmission of the "treasury of the true dharma eye" (*shōbōgenzō* 正法眼藏) from Śākyamuni to Mahākāśyapa at an assembly on Vulture Peak. Dōgen records one version in his *shinji Shōbōgenzō* 眞字正法眼藏 (DZZ.5:258, case 253); see Supplementary Notes, s.v. "Break into a smile."

28 **"in the realms everywhere, it has never been hidden"** (*henkai fuzō zō* 徧界不曾藏): A popular saying attributed to Chan Master Shishuang Qingzhu 石霜慶諸 (807-888); see Supplementary Notes, s.v. "In the realms everywhere, it has never been hidden."

29 **Great Master Zongyi of Xuansha Cloister** (*Genshain Sōitsu daishi* 玄沙院宗一大師): I.e., Xuansha Shibei 玄沙師備 (835-908), disciple of Xuefeng Yicun 雪峰義存 (822-908). For their conversation, included in the *shinji Shōbōgenzō* 眞字正法眼藏 (DZZ.5:185, case 60), see Supplementary Notes, s.v. "Seven feet or eight feet."

30 **"seamless stūpa"** (*muhō tō* 無縫塔): I.e., a stone memorial for a monk.

220 DŌGEN'S *SHŌBŌGENZŌ* VOLUME II

ふにあらず、雪峰に靈山の授記あり、といふにあらず、和尚靈山授記、未
夢見在といふなり。

Xuansha's saying here, "*The prediction on Vulture Peak, the Reverend hasn't seen even in his dreams,*" does not say that Xuefeng lacks the prediction on Vulture Peak; it does not say that Xuefeng has the prediction on Vulture Peak: it says, "*The prediction on Vulture Peak, the Reverend hasn't seen even in his dreams.*"

[21:8] {1:250}

靈山の授記は、高著眼なり。吾有正法眼藏涅槃妙心、附囑摩訶迦葉なり。
しるべし、青原の、石頭に授記せしときの同參は、摩訶迦葉も青原の授記
をうく、青原も釋迦の授記をさづくるがゆえに、佛佛祖祖の面面に、正法
眼藏附囑有在なることあきらかなり。ここをもて、曹溪すでに青原に授記
す、青原すでに六祖の授記をうくるとき、授記に保任せる青原なり。この
とき、六祖・諸祖の參學、正直に青原の授記によりて行取しきたれるな
り。これを明明百草頭、明明佛祖意といふ。

"The prediction on Vulture Peak" is a higher point of view.[31] It is "*I have the treasury of the true dharma eye, the wondrous mind of nirvāṇa, which I bequeath to Mahākāśyapa.*"[32] We should realize that, as a fellow student at the time that Qingyuan conferred his prediction on Shitou, Mahākāśyapa also received Qingyuan's prediction, and Qingyuan also conferred the prediction of Śākyamuni; hence, it is clear that, in face after face of buddha after buddha and ancestor after ancestor, *the bequest of the treasury of the true dharma eye is retained.*[33] According to this,

31 **a higher point of view** (*kō chaku gan* 高著眼): An idiom meaning either "to lift one's gaze" or "to take a higher perspective."

32 **"I have the treasury of the true dharma eye, the wondrous mind of nirvāṇa, which I bequeath to Mahākāśyapa"** (*go u shōbōgenzō nehan myōshin, fuzoku Makakashō* 吾有正法眼藏涅槃妙心、附囑摩訶迦葉): One version of the famous line spoken by Buddha Śākyamuni on Vulture Peak in announcing the first transmission of the dharma (see above, Note 27).

33 **Qingyuan** (Seigen 青原); **Shitou** (Sekitō 石頭): I.e., Qingyuan Xingsi 青原行思 (d. 740), the disciple of the Sixth Ancestor, Caoxi Huineng 曹溪慧能, and his dharma heir Shitou Xiqian 石頭希遷 (700–790).

the bequest of the treasury of the true dharma eye is retained (*shōbōgenzō fuzoku uzai* 正法眼藏附囑有在): An expression in Chinese syntax; the use here of *fuzoku uzai* 附囑有在 (literally, something like "the bequest is still present") seems to associate the transmission of the *Shōbōgenzō* with a passage in Kumārajīva's translation of the *Lotus Sūtra* on the entrustment of the text to later generations (*Miaofa lianhua jing* 妙法蓮華經, T.262.9:33c14-15):

佛欲以此妙法華經付囑有在。

The Buddha wishes to bequeath this *Sūtra of the Blossom of the Wondrous Dharma* that it remain present.

The same usage is found, e.g., at *Xuansha Shibei chanshi yulu* 玄沙師備禪師語錄; ZZ.126:431a5.

21. Prediction *Juki* 授記

once Caoxi had conferred his prediction on Qingyuan, and Qingyuan had received the prediction of the Sixth Ancestor, he was Qingyuan maintained by the prediction. At this point, the study of the Sixth Ancestor and the other ancestors had been directly practiced based on the prediction of Qingyuan. This is called, "*perfectly clear, the tips of the hundred grasses; perfectly clear, the intention of the buddhas and ancestors.*"[34]

[21:9]

しかあればすなはち、佛祖いづれか百草にあらざらん、百草なんぞ吾・汝にあらざらん。至愚にしておもふことなかれ、みづからに具足する法は、みづからかならずしるべしと、みるべしと。恁麼にあらざるなり。自己の知する法、かならずしも自己の有にあらず。自己の有、かならずしも自己のみるところならず、自己のしるところならず。しかあれば、いまの知見思量分にあたはざれば自己にあるべからず、と疑著することなかれ。いはんや靈山の授記といふは、釋迦牟尼佛の授記なり。この授記は、釋迦牟尼佛の、釋迦牟尼佛に授記しきたれるなり。授記の未合なるには、授記せざる道理なるべし。その宗旨は、すでに授記あるに授記するに罣礙なし、授記なきに授記するに剩法せざる道理なり。虧闕なく、剩法にあらざる、これ諸佛祖の、諸佛祖に授記しきたれる道理なり。

This being so, which buddha or ancestor is not "the hundred grasses"; how could "the hundred grasses" not be you and I? Do not stupidly think that the dharmas with which you are endowed you must necessarily know, must necessarily see. This is not so. The dharmas that one knows are not necessarily one's own; and what is one's own is not necessarily something seen by one, not necessarily known by one. Therefore, do not have doubts that, if it does not accord with what we know and think, it must not be ours.

Needless to say, "the prediction on Vulture Peak" was the prediction of Śākyamuni: this prediction is Śākyamuni having conferred a prediction on Śākyamuni. This must be the principle that prediction is not conferred where there is not accord with the prediction. The essential point of this is the principle that there is no obstacle to conferring a prediction where there is already a prediction, and nothing extra in conferring a prediction where there is no prediction. Neither deficient nor extra — this is the principle by which the buddhas and ancestors have conferred predictions on the buddhas and ancestors.

---

34 **"perfectly clear, the tips of the hundred grasses; perfectly clear, the intention of the buddhas and ancestors"** (*meimei hyakusō tō, meimei busso i* 明明百草頭、明明佛祖意): Variant of a fixed expression best known in Zen literature from its use by Layman Pang Yun 龐蘊居士 (740?-808), in a passage recorded in Dōgen's *shinji Shōbōgenzō* 眞字正法眼藏 (DZZ.5:168, case 88); see Supplementary Notes, s.v. "Perfectly clear, the tips of the hundred grasses."

222　DŌGEN'S *SHŌBŌGENZŌ* VOLUME II

[21:10] {1:251}

このゆえに古佛いはく、古今擧拂示東西、大意幽微肯易參、此理若無師教授、欲將何見語玄談。

> Therefore, an old buddha has said,[35]
>
> *In past and present, they raise the whisk, instructing east and west.*
> *Their grand intent, obscure and subtle; how could it easily be approached?*
> *Without a teacher to teach and confer this truth,*
> *With what view would you discuss the dark talk?[36]*

[21:11]

いまの玄沙の宗旨を參究するに、無縫塔の高多少を量するに、高多少の道得あるべし。さらに五百由旬にあらず、八萬由旬にあらず。これによりて、上下を顧視するをきらふにあらず。ただこれ人天の福報は即不無なりとも、無縫塔高を顧視するは、釋迦牟尼佛の授記にはあらざるのみなり。釋迦牟尼佛の授記をうるは、七尺・八尺の道得あるなり。眞箇の釋迦牟尼佛の授記を點撿することは、七尺・八尺の道得をもて撿點すべきなり。しかあればすなはち、七尺・八尺の道得を是・不是せんことはしばらくおく、授記はさだめて雪峰の授記あるべし、玄沙の授記あるべきなり。いはんや授記を擧して無縫塔高の多少を道得すべきなり。授記にあらざらんを擧して佛法を道得するは、道得にはあらざるべきなり。

In investigating Xuansha's essential point here, when he measures "how tall" the seamless stūpa is, he should say "how tall" it is. It is not, moreover, five hundred yojana; it is not eighty thousand yojana.[37] Hence, he does not disapprove of looking up and down; it is just that, while it may "not lack" the blessings of human and devas, looking at the height of the seamless stūpa is not the prediction of Buddha Śākyamuni. What gets the prediction of Buddha Śākyamuni is the saying, "seven feet or eight feet." Really to examine the prediction of Buddha Śākyamuni we should examine it with the saying "seven feet or eight feet." This being the case, setting aside for now the question of whether the saying "seven feet or eight feet" is right or not, as predictions, there is definitely a

---

35　**an old buddha** (*kobutsu* 古佛): Slightly variant version of the opening and closing lines from the poem "Gujin dayi" 古今大意, attributed to Yunding Defu 雲頂德敷 (dates unknown), a dharma heir of Wuguo Zhiyuan 護國智遠 (dates unknown) and a fourth generation descendant of Dongshan Liangjie 洞山良价 (807–869). The poem appears in the *Jingde chuandeng lu* 景德傳燈錄 (T.2076.51:456b7-11) and elsewhere.

36　**dark talk** (*gendan* 玄談): Or "profound talk"; an expression for Buddhist discourse, common enough in Buddhist writing but not in the *Shōbōgenzō*.

37　**five hundred yojana** (*gohyaku yujun* 五百由旬): A yojana (*yujun* 由旬) is a measure of distance, varying greatly depending on the source, but often said to range from seven to nine miles. "Five hundred yojana" is the height given for the famous jeweled stūpa of Buddha Prabhūtaratna in the *Lotus Sūtra* (*Miaofa lianhua jing* 妙法蓮華經, T.262.9:32b17).

21. Prediction *Juki* 授記 223

prediction of Xuefeng and a prediction of Xuansha. Obviously, taking up prediction, they should say how tall the seamless stūpa is. To speak of the buddha dharma by taking up what is not prediction is not to say anything.

[21:12]

自己の、眞箇に自己なるを會取し、聞取し、道取すれば、さだめて授記の現成する公案あるなり。授記の當陽に、授記と同參する功夫きたるなり。授記を究竟せんために、如許多の佛祖は現成正覺しきたれり。授記の功夫するちから、諸佛を推出するなり。このゆえに、唯以一大事因緣故出現といふなり。その宗旨は、向上には非自己かならず非自己の授記をうるなり。このゆえに、諸佛は諸佛の授記をうるなり。

When one understands, hears, and says that one's self is really oneself, there is definitely the kōan that realizes prediction. In the immediacy of prediction, there emerges the concentrated effort that studies together.[38] It is in order to fulfill prediction that so many buddhas and ancestors have appeared and attained right awakening. The power of the concentrated effort of prediction pushes out the buddhas. Therefore, it is said that [the buddhas] *"appear for the reason of one great matter alone."*[39] The essential point of this is that, at a higher level, the non-self always receives prediction from the non-self. Therefore, the buddhas receive the prediction of the buddhas.

[21:13] {1:252}

おほよそ授記は、一手を擧して授記し、両手を擧して授記し、千手眼を擧して授記し、授記せらる。あるいは優曇華を擧して授記す、あるいは金襴衣を拈じて授記する、ともにこれ強爲にあらず、授記の云爲なり。内よりうる授記あるべし、外よりうる授記あるべし。内外を參究せん道理は、授記に參學すべし。授記の學道は、萬旦一條鐵なり。授記の兀坐は、一念萬年なり。

In sum, regarding predictions, predictions are conferred by raising one hand, predictions are conferred by raising both hands, predictions are

---

38 **In the immediacy of prediction** (*juki no tōyō ni* 授記の當陽に): The term *tōyō* 當陽, translated loosely here as "immediacy," while unusual in Dōgen's writing, occurs often in Zen literature, in the sense "direct," "straightforward," "head on," etc. In ordinary Chinese, the term usually refers to the accession of the emperor, whose location in court "faces the sun" in the south.

39 **"appear for the reason of one great matter alone"** (*yui i ichidaiji innen ko shutsugen* 唯以一大事因緣故出現): A passage, in Chinese, quoting famous words of Śākyamuni in the *Lotus Sūtra* (*Miaofa lianhua jing* 妙法蓮華經, T.262.9:7a21-22), where the "one great matter" is the mission to lead all beings to buddhahood. See Supplementary Notes, s.v. "Buddhas, the world-honored ones, appear in the world for the reason of one great matter alone."

224 DŌGEN'S *SHŌBŌGENZŌ* VOLUME II

conferred and received by raising a thousand hands and eyes.[40] Conferring predictions by raising the *udumbara* flower, or conferring predictions by taking up the robe of gold brocade — none of these is a forced act: they are the words and deeds of prediction.[41] There are predictions received from inside; there are predictions received from outside. The principle of investigating "inside" and "outside," we should study in prediction. The study of the way of prediction is *one strip of iron for ten thousand miles*; the fixed sitting of prediction is *ten thousand years in one moment of thought*.[42]

---

40 **raising one hand** (*isshu o koshite* 一手を擧して); **raising both hands** (*ryōshu o koshite* 兩手を擧して): The verb "to raise" (*kosu* 擧す) often suggests "to hold up for examination," "to take up for consideration"; here, it may reflect the opening line of the verse in section 10, above: "In past and present, they raise the whisk, instructing east and west." It is not clear whether Dōgen has particular historical examples of hand-raising in mind here, but commentators sometimes offer the case of Yaoshan Weiyan 藥山惟儼 (751-834) responding to a question on the way from the official Li Ao (771-841) by pointing to the heavens and pointing to a water jug (see, e.g., *Hongzhi chanshi guanglu* 宏智禪師廣錄, T.2001.48:5b17-19); and the case of Baizhang Weizheng 百丈惟政 (757–842) explaining the great meaning by spreading out his hands (*Jingde chuandeng lu* 景德傳燈錄, T.2076.51:268c1-3).

a thousand hands and eyes (*sen shugen* 千手眼): Likely an allusion to the conversation between Yunyan Tansheng 雲巖曇晟 (782–841) and Guannan Daowu 關南道吾 (dates unknown) over how Bodhisattva Avalokiteśvara (described as having a thousand hands, each with an eye in the palm) uses so many hands and eyes (see, e.g., *Biyan lu* 碧巖錄, T.2003.48:213c19-26); the case is discussed at length in "Shōbōgenzō Kannon" 正法眼藏觀音.

41 ***udumbara* flower** (*udonge* 優曇華): The *udumbara* is a plant said to blossom only very rarely; hence a symbol of what is rare and precious. The reference here is undoubtedly to the famous story of Buddha Śākyamuni's teaching the dharma on Vulture Peak by holding up a flower (see above, Note 20); though there seems to be no explicit precedent for this in Chinese sources, Dōgen elsewhere identifies the flower as the *udumbara* (see, *Eihei kōroku* 永平廣錄, DZZ.4:12, no. 428).

robe of gold brocade (*kinran'e* 金襴衣): Though not quite an example of prediction, the reference here would seem to be to the legend that Buddha Śākyamuni bestowed a gold brocade robe on Mahākāśyapa, to be handed on to the next buddha, Maitreya (see, e.g., *Jingde chuandeng lu* 景德傳燈錄, T.2076.51:205c3-5).

none of these is a forced act: they are the words and deeds of prediction (*tomo ni kore gōi ni arazu, juki no un'i nari* ともにこれ強爲にあらず、授記の云爲なり): An unusual usage, seen elsewhere in Dōgen's writing, that contrasts *gōi* 強爲 (translated here "forced act") and *un'i* 云爲 ("words and deeds"); the former suggests intentional, premeditated action, while the latter seems to be used for behavior that comes naturally — hence, here, the natural activity of prediction.

42 **one strip of iron for ten thousand miles** (*banri ichijō tetsu* 萬里一條鐵): A common Zen idiom for the ultimate unity of the myriad phenomena; see Supplementary Notes, s.v. "One strip of iron."

ten thousand years in one moment of thought (*ichinen bannen* 一念萬年): A common expression in Zen literature for eternity in each moment.

21. Prediction *Juki* 授記   225

* * * * *

[21:14]

古佛いはく、相繼得成佛、轉次而授記。

An old buddha has said,[43]

In succession, they attained buddhahood,
And, in turn, next conferred predictions.

[21:15]

いはくの成佛は、かならず相繼するなり、相繼する少許を成佛するなり。
これを授記の轉次するなり。轉次は轉得轉なり、轉次は次得次なり。たと
へば造次なり、造次は施爲なり。その施爲は、局量の造身にあらず、局量
の造境にあらず、度量の造作にあらず、造心にあらざるなり。まさに造
境・不造境、ともに轉次の道理に一任して究辨すべし。造作・不造作、
ともに轉次の道理に一任して究辨すべし。いま諸佛諸祖の現成するは、施
爲に轉次せらるるなり。五佛六祖の西來する、施爲に轉次せらるるなり。
いはんや運水般柴は、轉次しきたるなり。即心是佛の現生する、轉次な
り。即心是佛の滅度する、一滅度・二滅度をめづらしくするにあらず、如
許多の滅度を滅度すべし、如許多の弍道を成道すべし、如許多の相好を相
好すべし。これすなはち相繼得成佛なり、相繼得滅度等なり、相繼得授記
なり、相繼得轉次なり。轉次は本來にあらず、ただ七通八達なり。いま佛
面・祖面の面面に相見し、面面に相逢するは相繼なり。佛授記・祖授記の
轉次する、廻避のところ間隙にあらず。

"Attaining buddhahood" is always to be "in succession." A few "in succession" "attain buddhahood."[44] This, prediction does "in turn, next."[45]
"In turn, next" is "in turn" attaining "turning"; "in turn, next" is "next"
attaining "next."[46] For example, it is a "hasty act," and a "hasty act" is

---

43 **An old buddha** (*kobutsu* 古佛): I.e., Buddha Śākyamuni in the *Lotus Sūtra*, speaking of the ancient Buddha Dīpaṅkara and his seven brothers (*Miaofa lianhua jing* 妙法
蓮華經, T.262.9:5b1).

44 **A few "in succession" "attain buddhahood"** (*sōzoku suru shōko o jōbutsu suru
nari* 相繼する少許を成佛するなり): Reacing *shōko o jōbutsu suru* 少許を成佛する as
"to make a buddha of a few." Perhaps meaning that, within the ongoing succession, there
are a few cases (e.g., Dīpaṅkara and his brothers?) in which buddhahood occurs. This
section represents an extended exploration, difficult to capture in translation, of the two
adverbial expressions in the quotation from the *Lotus Sūtra*: *sōkei* 相繼 ("in succession,"
which, as here, Dōgen also uses as the verb *sōkei su* 相繼す, "to succeed [one another]"),
and *tenji* 轉次 (translated, somewhat awkwardly, as "in turn, next," which Dōgen will
also treat as the verb *tenji su* 轉次す, "to do [or be] in turn").

45 **This, prediction does "in turn, next"** (*kore o juki no tenji suru nari* これを授記の
轉次するなり): Presumably, meaning something like, "this buddhahood is what prediction does repeatedly."

46 **"in turn" attaining "turning"** (*ten toku ten* 轉得轉); **"next" attaining "next"**
(*ji toku ji* 次得次): Dōgen here breaks apart the expression *tenji* 轉次 ("in turn, next")
into the primary meanings of its two component glyphs: "to turn" and "next." Perhaps
the meaning is that, while the succession of predictions follows one after another, each

226 DŌGEN'S *SHŌBŌGENZŌ* VOLUME II

an "activity."[47] That activity is not the constricted, constructed body, not the constricted, constructed object, not a gauged, constructed action or constructed mind.[48] Both construction of the body and non-construction of the body, we should thoroughly investigate by relying entirely on the principle of "in turn, next"; both constructed action and non-constructed action, we should thoroughly investigate by relying entirely on the principle of "in turn, next."

The present advent of the buddhas and the ancestors is done "in turn next" by the activity; the coming from the west of five buddhas or six ancestors is done "in turn, next" by the activity.[49] Needless to say, then, *"bearing water and hauling firewood"* is done "in turn, next."[50] The ad-

---

successive instance is complete in itself. The verb *toku* 得 ("attain") probably indicates identity: "turning" is just "turning"; "next" is just "next."

47 **it is a "hasty act"** (*zōji nari* 造次なり): I.e., the glyph *ji* 次 ("next") in *tenji* 轉次 ("in turn, next") is the *ji* 次 in *zōji* 造次, a term meaning "hasty," "briefly," "instantly," something done quickly or casually.

a "hasty act" is an "activity" (*zōji wa sei nari* 造次は施爲なり): I.e., the term *zōji* 造次 implies "doing," "performing," or "implementing" (*sei* 施爲) something.

48 **the constricted, constructed body** (*kyokuryō no zōshin* 局量の造身): Dōgen begins here a series using the element *zō* 造 of *zōji* 造次 ("hasty act") in its primary sense "to construct"; the resulting terms can be read either as adjective-noun compounds ("constructed body," etc.) or verb-object compounds ("constructing the body").

49 **the coming from the west of five buddhas or six ancestors** (*gobutsu rokuso no seirai suru* 五佛六祖の西來する): Dōgen turns here to an investigation of "in turn, next" (*tenji* 轉次) through a series of references to buddhahood. The first in the series seems to refer to the coming of the buddhas from India to China. Supplementary Notes, s.v. "Coming from the west." The apparent combination here of "five buddhas" (*gobutsu* 五佛), a teaching normally associated with esoteric Buddhism, with the "six ancestors" (*rokuso* 六祖) central to Zen tradition seems quite unlikely; probably, the phrase *gobutsu rokuso* should be taken as "five or six buddhas and ancestors" (*goroku busso* 五六佛祖). Still, which (if any) historical figures Dōgen might have had in mind here is unclear; and some MS witnesses replace the phrase with the more familiar *soshi* 祖師 ("Ancestral Master") — i.e., the First Ancestor, Bodhidharma; see Supplementary Notes, s.v. "Intention of the Ancestral Master's coming from the west."

50 **"bearing water and hauling firewood"** (*unsui hansai* 運水般柴; also written as 運水搬柴): I.e., the everyday actions of the buddhas and ancestors. Words made famous in a line attributed to the Layman Pang 龐居士 (see, e.g., *Jingde chuandeng lu* 景德傳燈錄, T.2076.51:263b12):

神通並妙用。運水及搬柴

The spiritual powers and the wondrous functions:
Bearing water and hauling firewood.

The expression "spiritual powers and wondrous functions" alludes to the paranormal attributes of a buddha; the saying also recalls a famous story in the *Lotus Sūtra* of the prior career of Buddha Śākyamuni, in which he "drew water and gathered firewood" (*kyūsui shūshin* 汲水拾薪) for his teacher, the future Devadatta (*Miaofa lianhua jing* 妙法蓮華經, T.262.9:34c6).

21. Prediction *Juki* 授記   227

vent of "*this mind itself is the buddha*" is "in turn, next." The extinction of "this mind itself is the buddha" is not something we should take as occurring rarely, in one extinction or two extinctions: it should render extinct so many extinctions; it should attain the way of so many attainments of the way; it should mark and sign so many marks and signs.[51] This is "*in succession, they attained buddhahood*"; it is *in succession, they attained extinction*; it is *in succession, they attained prediction*; it is in succession, they attained "in turn, next." "In turn, next" is not inherent: it is only seven penetrations and eight masteries.[52] Buddha faces and ancestor faces each seeing each other, each meeting each other — this is "in succession." In the being "in turn, next" of buddha predictions and ancestor predictions, there is no interval into which to escape.

[21:16] {1:253}

古佛いはく、我今從佛聞授記莊嚴亭、及轉次受決、身心遍歡喜。

Old buddhas have said,[53]

> *Now that we hear from the Buddha*
> *Of the splendid matter of prediction,*
> *And receive assurance of our turn next,*
> *Our bodies and minds everywhere rejoice.*

---

51   **The advent of "this mind itself is the buddha"** (*soku shin ze butsu no genshō suru* 即心是佛の現生する); **The extinction of "this mind itself is the buddha"** (*soku shin ze butsu no metsudo suru* 即心是佛の滅度する): I.e., the appearance in the world and the entrance into nirvāṇa of a buddha that is this mind itself. Reference to a famous saying attributed to Mazu Daoyi 馬祖道一 (709-788), cited in Dōgen's *shinji Shōbōgenzō* 眞字正法眼藏 (DZZ.5:266, case 278) and many other Zen sources; see Supplementary Notes, s.v. "This mind itself is the buddha."

render extinct so many extinctions (*nyokota no metsudo o metsudo su* 如許多の滅度を滅度す); **attain the way of so many attainments of the way** (*nyokota no jōdō o jōdō su* 如許多の成道を成道す); **mark and sign so many marks and signs** (*nyokota no sōgō o sōgō su* 如許多の相好を相好す): Probably meaning that the buddha that is "this mind itself" should experience many nirvāṇas, many awakenings, and many physical marks and signs of its buddhahood. In each of these phrases, Dōgen treats the feature of the buddha as a transitive verb having itself as object. "Marks and signs" translates *sōgō* 相好, a reference to the thirty-two primary marks and eighty auspicious signs on the physical body of a buddha — a term highly improbable as a verb.

52   **seven penetrations and eight masteries** (*shittsū hattatsu* 七通八達): I.e., complete mastery. A fixed expression, not infrequent in Dōgen's writing, that plays with the term *tsūdatsu* 通達 ("to penetrate," "to understand fully").

53   **Old buddhas** (*kobutsu* 古佛): A quotation from the *Lotus Sūtra* (*Miaofa lianhua jing* 妙法蓮華經, T.262.9:29b20-21). The speakers here are not in fact "old buddhas" but Ājñātakauṇḍinya and other disciples of Buddha Śākyamuni celebrating in verse their having received predictions of their future buddhahood. See Supplementary Notes, s.v. "Old buddha."

228 DŌGEN'S *SHŌBŌGENZŌ* VOLUME II

[21:17]

いふところは、授記莊嚴事、かならず我今從佛聞なり。我今從佛聞の及轉
次受決するといふは、身心遍歡喜なり。及轉次は我今なるべし、過・現・
當の自他にかかはるべからず。從佛聞なるべし、從他聞にあらず、迷悟に
あらず、衆生にあらず、草木國土にあらず、從佛聞なるべし。授記莊嚴事
なり、及轉次受決なり。轉次の道理、しばらくも一隅にとどまりぬること
なし、身心遍歡喜しもてゆくなり。歡喜なる及轉次受決、かならず身と同
參して遍參し、心と同參して遍參す。さらに又、身はかならず心に遍ず、
心はかならず身に遍ずるゆえに、身心遍といふ。すなはちこれ遍界遍方、
遍身遍心なり。これすなはち特地一條の歡喜なり。その歡喜、あらはに
瘖痖を歡喜せしめ、迷悟を歡喜せしむるに、おのおのと親切なりといへど
も、おのおのと不染汚なり。かるがゆえに、轉次而受決なる、授記莊嚴事
なり。

What this says is that "*the splendid matter of prediction*" is always
"*now that we hear from the Buddha.*" To say that "*now that we hear from
the Buddha*" represents "*and receive assurance of our turn next*" means
"*our bodies and minds everywhere rejoice.*"[54] "*And our turn next*" is "we
now"; it has nothing to do with self or other of past, present, or future.
It is "hearing from the Buddha"; it is not hearing from another; it is not
delusion or awakening; it is not living beings; it is not the grasses, trees,
and lands: it is "hearing from the Buddha."[55] It is "*the splendid matter of
prediction*"; it is "*and receive assurance of our turn next.*" The principle
of "*our turn next*" does not pause even briefly at one corner but proceeds
to "*our bodies and minds everywhere rejoice.*" The "*and receive assurance of our turn next*" that is "rejoicing" is always study everywhere
studying together with the body, study everywhere studying together
with the mind.[56] Going further, because the body is always everywhere

---

54 **To say that "now what we hear from the Buddha" represents "and receive
assurance of our turn next" means "our bodies and minds everywhere rejoice"** (*ga
kon jū butsu mon no kyū tenji juketsu suru to iu wa, shinjin hen kanki nari* 我今從佛聞
の及轉次受決するといふは、身心遍歡喜なり): The awkward translation struggles to
make sense of Dōgen's play with the Chinese phrases of the sūtra, in which the first line
has become the grammatical subject of a verb created from the next line. A rephrasing
of this odd sentence might yield something like, "what we now hear from the Buddha
is the assurance that we shall follow in turn — this is the joy that pervades our bodies
and minds."

55 **grasses, trees, and lands** (*sōmoku kokudo* 草木國土): A common expression for the
natural world, as in the saying, "grasses, trees, and lands all attain buddhahood" (*sōmoku
kokudo shikkai jōbutsu* 草木國土悉皆成佛); here, paired with the preceding "living beings" (*shujō* 衆生).

56 **The "and receive assurance of our turn next" that is "rejoicing" is always study
everywhere studying together with the body, study everywhere studying together
with the mind** (*kanki naru kyū tenji juketsu, kanarazu shin to dōsan shite henzan shi,
shin to dōsan shite henzan su* 歡喜なる及轉次受決、かならず身と同參して遍參し、
心と同參して遍參す): Dōgen here uses the Chinese of the entire third line of his quo-

21. Prediction *Juki* 授記   229

in the mind, and the mind is always everywhere in the body, it is called "our bodies and minds everywhere." This is the realms everywhere, the directions everywhere, the body everywhere, the mind everywhere.[57] This is a single, special joy. When that joy clearly makes waking and sleeping joyful, makes delusion and awakening joyful, while it may be intimate with each of them, it is not defiled by any of them. Therefore, it is *"in turn" "receiving assurance"*; it is *"the splendid matter of prediction."*

* * * * *

[21:18]

釋迦牟尼佛、因藥王菩薩、告八萬大士、藥王、汝見是大衆中、無量諸天・龍王・夜叉・乾闥婆・阿修羅・迦棲羅・緊那羅・摩睺羅伽、人與非人、及比丘・比丘尼・優婆塞・優婆夷、求聲聞者、求辟支佛者、求佛道者、如是等類、咸於佛前、聞妙法華經一偈一句、乃至一念隨喜者、我皆與授記。當得阿耨多羅三藐三菩提。

Buddha Śākyamuni addressed the eighty thousand great beings, beginning with Bodhisattva Medicine King,[58]

Medicine King, you see in this great assembly incalculable devas, dragon kings, yakṣas, gandharvas, asuras, garuḍas, kiṃnaras, mahoragas, humans and nonhumans, as well as bhikṣus, bhikṣuṇīs, upāsakas, and upāsikās, those who seek to become śrāvakas, those who seek to become pratyeka-buddhas, and those who seek the way of the buddhas.[59] *Upon all such types in the presence of the buddha who hear*

---

tation, "and receive assurance of our turn next," as the grammatical subject modified by "rejoicing." He then treats the "everywhere" (*hen* 遍) of "bodies and minds everywhere," by associating it with "study everywhere" (*henzan* 遍參, or "extensive consultation"), a term for the monk's practice of traveling about to study with various teachers. The meaning would seem be that the mental and physical joy of receiving assurance of buddhahood is the study of Buddhism with body and mind.

57 **the realms everywhere, the directions everywhere, the body everywhere, the mind everywhere** (*henkai henhō, henshin henshin* 遍界遍方、遍身遍心): Playing with the word *hen* 遍 (also written 徧), found in such familiar expressions as "the realms everywhere" (*henkai* 遍界, as in the saying "in the realms everywhere, it has never been hidden" [*henkai fu zō zō* 遍界不曾藏]) and "his body everywhere" (*henshin* 遍身, as in "the body everywhere is hands and eyes" [*henshin ze shugen* 遍身是手眼]). See Supplementary Notes, s.v. "In the realms everywhere, it has never been hidden," "His body everywhere is hands and eyes."

58 **Buddha Śākyamuni** (*Shakamuni butsu* 釋迦牟尼佛): A passage from the *Lotus Sūtra* (*Miaofa lianhua jing* 妙法蓮華經, T.262.9:30b29–c7).

59 **devas, dragon kings, *yakṣas*, gandharvas, *asuras*, garuḍas, *kiṃnaras*, mahoragas** (*shoten ryūō yasha kendabba ashura karura kinnara magoraga* 諸天・龍王・夜叉・乾闥婆・阿修羅・迦棲羅・緊那羅・摩睺羅伽): A standard list of the eight kinds of beings (*hachibu ju* 八部聚) often in attendance at the preaching of the Mahāyāna sūtras.

230 DŌGEN'S *SHŌBŌGENZŌ* VOLUME II

a single *gāthā* or a single line of the *Sūtra of the Wondrous Dharma
Blossom* and rejoice for even a single thought, I confer a prediction on
all that they will attain *anuttara-samyak-saṃbodhi*."

[21:19] {1:254}

しかあればすなはち、いまの無量なる衆會、あるいは天王・龍王・四部・
八部、所求・所解ことなりといへども、たれか妙法にあらざらん一句一偈
をきかしめん。いかならんなんぢが乃至一念も、他法を隨喜せしめん。如
是等類といふは、これ法華類なり。咸於佛前といふは、咸於佛中なり。人
與非人の、萬像に錯認するありとも、百草に下種せるありとも、如是等類
なるべし。如是等類は、我皆與授記なり。我皆與授記の頭正尾正なる、す
なはち當得阿耨多羅三藐三菩提なり。

Thus, in the "incalculable" "assembly," while what is sought and what
is understood by "the devas, dragon kings," the four groups, and eight
groups may differ, which would hear "a single line or a single *gāthā*" of
what is not "the wondrous dharma?"[60] Which of you would "rejoice" in
another dharma for "even a single thought?" "Such types" means types
of "dharma blossom"; "all in the presence of the buddha" means "all
within the buddha." "Humans and nonhumans," whether they mistakenly discern the myriad forms, or whether they have planted seeds in the
hundred grasses, are "such types."[61] "Such types" are "*I confer a prediction on all*." That "*I confer a prediction on all*" is true from head to tail is
"they will attain *anuttara-samyak-saṃbodhi*."

"Devas" (*ten* 天): heavenly beings, inhabiting the upper reaches of Mount Sumeru and
the celestial realms; "dragon kings" (*ryūō* 龍王; S. *nāga, nāga-rāja*): great serpents living in the clouds or bodies of water and associated with rain; "*yakśas*" (*yasha* 夜叉):
flesh-eating flying demons; "*gandharvas*" (*kendabba* 乾闥婆): spirit musicians who subsist on scents; "*asuras*" (*ashura* 阿修羅): demigods, or titans, who war with the gods;
"*garuḍas*" (*karura* 迦樓羅): mythical birds that feed on *nāgas*; "*kiṃnaras*" (*kinnara* 緊
那羅): heavenly musicians, sometimes described as part god, part human, part animal;
"*mahoragas*" (*magoraga* 摩睺羅伽): giant python-like snakes.

bhikṣus, bhikṣunīs, upāsakas, and *upāsikās (biku bikuni ubasoku ubai* 比丘比丘尼・優
婆塞・優婆夷): Monks, nuns, lay men and lay women.

srāvakas (shōmon 聲聞); *pratyeka-buddhas (byakushibutsu* 辟支佛); **the way of the
buddhas** (*butsudō* 佛道): I.e., the traditional three vehicles of Buddhism, *śrāvaka,
pratyeka-buddha,* and bodhisattva, only the last of which would ordinarily receive a
prediction of the unsurpassed, perfect awakening of buddhahood offered here.

60　**four groups, and eight groups** (*shibu hachi bu* 四部・八部): I.e., the monks, nuns, lay
men, and lay women; and the eight classes of non-human beings mentioned in the sūtra passage.

61　**whether they mistakenly discern the myriad forms, or whether they have planted seeds in the hundred grasses** (*banzō ni sakunin suru ari tomo, hyakusō ni geshu
seru ari tomo* 萬像に錯認するありとも、百草に下種せるありとも): The exact sense
is uncertain; possibly suggesting, "whether [the distinctions among] the types of beings
are based on the nature of their perception or of their karmic causes."

21. Prediction *Juki* 授記　　　231

[21:20]

釋迦牟尼佛告藥王、又如來滅度之後、若有人聞妙法華經、乃至一偈一句、
一念隨喜者、我亦與授阿耨多羅三藐三菩提記。

Buddha Śākyamuni addressed Medicine King,[62]

*Moreover, if, after the extinction of the Tathāgata, there are people
who hear even a single gāthā or a single line of the Sūtra of the Wondrous Dharma Blossom and rejoice for a single thought, I also confer
a prediction on them that they will attain anuttara-samyak-saṃbodhi."*

[21:21] {1:255}

いまいふ如來滅度之後は、いづれの時節到來なるべきぞ。四十九年なる
か、八十年中なるか。しばらく八十年中なるべし。若有人聞妙法華經、乃
至一偈一句、一念隨喜といふは、有智の所聞なるか、無智の所聞なるか、
あやまりてきくか、あやまらずしてきくか。爲他道せば、若有人の所聞な
るべし、さらに有智・無智等の諸類なりとすることなかれ。いふべし、
聞法華經はたとひ甚深無量なるいく佛智慧なりとも、きくにはかならず一
句なり、きくにかならず一偈なり、きくにかならず一念隨喜なり。このと
き、我亦與授阿耨多羅三藐三菩提記なるべし。亦與授記あり、皆與授記あ
り。蹉過の張三に一任せしむることなかれ、審細の功夫に同參すべし。句
偈隨喜を若有人聞なるべし、皮肉骨髓を頭上安頭するにいとまあらず。見
授阿耨多羅三藐三菩提記は、我願既滿なり、如許皮袋なるべし。衆望亦足
なり、如許若有人聞ならん。拈松枝の授記あり、拈優曇華の授記あり、拈
瞬目の授記あり、拈破顔の授記あり、靴鞋を轉授せし蹤跡あり。そこばく
の是法非思量分別之所能解なるべし。我身是也の授記あり、汝身是也の授
記あり。この道理、よく過去・現在・未來を授記するなり。授記中の過
去・現在・未來なるがゆえに、自授記に現成し、他授記に現成するなり。

This "after the extinction of the Tathāgata" — at what point does it arrive? Is it forty-nine years? Is it in eighty years?[63] For now, let us say it
should be in eighty years. *"If there are people who hear even a single
gāthā or a single line of the Sūtra of the Wondrous Dharma Blossom and
rejoice for a single thought"* — is this heard by "those having wisdom,"
or is it heard by "those lacking wisdom"?[64] Do they hear it mistaken-

---

62　**Buddha Śākyamuni** (*Shakamuni butsu* 釋迦牟尼佛): Quoting the passage in the
Lotus Sūtra immediately following that cited in section 18, above (*Miaofa lianhua jing*
妙法蓮華經, T.262.9:30c7-9).

63　**Is it forty-nine years? Is it in eighty years?** (*shijūkyū nen naru ka, hachijū nenchū
naru ka* 四十九年なるか、八十年中なるか): I.e., is Śākyamuni's nirvāṇa to be mea-
sured as the end of his teaching career (in some accounts figured as forty-nine years) or
at the end of his human life (at age eighty).

64　**"those having wisdom"** (*uchi* 有智); **"those lacking wisdom"** (*muchi* 無智):
Doubtless alluding to the lines in the *Lotus Sūtra* (*Miaofa lianhua jing* 妙法蓮華經,
T.262.9:19c12-13):

有智若聞、則能信解。無智疑悔、則爲永失。

If those having wisdom hear it,

232 DŌGEN'S *SHŌBŌGENZŌ* VOLUME II

ly, or hear it unmistakenly? *Speaking for others*, it should be what is heard by "if there are people"; do not further take them as types such as "those having wisdom" or "those lacking wisdom."[65] We should say that, in hearing the *Sūtra of the Dharma Blossom*, though it may be the wisdom of however many buddhas, "profound and incalculable," the hearing is always "a single line"; the hearing is always "a single gāthā"; the hearing is always "rejoicing for a single thought."[66] This time should be "*I also confer a prediction of anuttara-samyak-saṃbodhi.*" There is "*I also confer a prediction*"; there is "*on all I confer a prediction.*"[67] Do not leave them to the oblivious Zhang's third; working at them in detail, we should study together with them.[68] They should be, "*if there are people, they hear*" the "line," the "gāthā," and the "rejoicing"; there is no spare time for the *putting a head on top of your head* of the skin, flesh, bones, and marrow.[69] "*To have conferred on us a prediction of anuttara-*

They will believe and understand it;
Those lacking wisdom will have doubts and regrets,
And, therefore, lose it forever.

65 **Speaking for others** (*i ta dō seba* 爲他道せば): Dōgen here uses the Chinese phrase describing the Zen master answering his own question.

66 **the wisdom of however many buddhas, "profound and incalculable"** (*jinjin muryō naru iku butsu chie* 甚深無量なるいく佛智慧): Recalling the opening line of the "Upāya-kauśalya" (*Fangbian* 方便) chapter of the *Lotus Sūtra* (*Miaofa lianhua jing* 妙法蓮華經, T.262.9:5b25-26):

爾時世尊從三昧安詳而起、告舍利弗、諸佛智慧甚深無量。

At that time the World-Honored One arose serenely from his samādhi and addressed Śāriputra. "The wisdom of the buddhas is profound and incalculable."

67 **There is "I also confer a prediction"; there is "on all I confer a prediction"** (*yaku yo juki ari, kai yo juki ari* 亦與授記あり、皆與授記あり): I.e., there are two versions of the prediction in the two passages of the *Lotus Sūtra* quoted above in sections 21 and 18, respectively.

68 **the oblivious Zhang's third** (*shaka no Chō san* 蹉過の張三): I.e., the ordinary person who misses the import of the text. For "Zhang's third" (*Chō san* 張三), see above, Note 7.

69 **They should be, "if there are people, they hear" the "line," the "gāthā," and the "rejoicing"** (*ku ge zuiki o nyaku u nin mon naru beshi* 句偈隨喜を若有人聞なるべし): Perhaps meaning that the predictions are simply the hearing and rejoicing of the people.

there is no spare time for the putting a head on top of your head of the skin, flesh, bones, and marrow (*hi niku kotsu zui o zujō an zu suru ni itoma arazu* 皮肉骨髓を頭上安頭するにいとまあらず): Perhaps meaning that we should not waste time looking for a prediction beyond the "skin, flesh, bones, and marrow" of the hearing and rejoicing themselves. The expression "skin, flesh, bones, and marrow" (*hi niku kotsu zui* 皮肉骨髓) is commonly used by Dōgen to indicate the essence or truth or entirety of something or someone, as handed down in the ancestral tradition of Zen; see Supplementary Notes, s.v. "Skin, flesh, bones, and marrow." "Putting a head on top of your head" (*zujō an zu* [also read *tōjō an tō*] 頭上安頭) is a common expression in Zen texts for the mistake of adding

21. Prediction *Juki* 授記   233

samyak-saṃbodhi" is "*to have our aspirations fulfilled*" and should be a number of skin bags; it is "our wishes would also be satisfied" and would be a number of "if there are people who hear."[70]

There are predictions that take up a pine branch; there are predictions that take up an *udumbara* blossom; there are predictions that take up blinking the eyes; there are predictions that take up breaking into a smile; and there are the traces of passing on shoes.[71] They are so many cases of "*this dharma is not something that can be understood by thinking or discrimination*."[72] There are predictions of "I myself am this"; there are

something superfluous, of saying something unnecessary, or imagining or seeking something one already has; see Supplementary Notes, s.v. "Putting a head on top of your head."

70 **"To have conferred on us a prediction of *anuttara-samyak-saṃbodhi*"** (*kenju anokutara sanmyaku sanbodai* 見授阿耨多羅三藐三菩提記); **"to have our aspirations fulfilled"** (*ga gan ki man* 我願既滿); **"our wishes would also be satisfied"** (*shumō yaku soku* 衆望亦足): Quoting the words of Ānanda and Rāhula soliciting predictions in the *Lotus Sūtra* (*Miaofa lianhua jing* 妙法蓮華經, T.262.9:29b28-c1):

若佛見授阿耨多羅三藐三菩提記者、我願既滿、衆望亦足。

Were the Buddha to confer on us a prediction of *anuttara samyak saṃbodhi*, our aspirations would be fulfilled, and our wishes would also be satisfied.

a number of skin bags (*nyoko hitai* 如許皮袋); **a number of "if there are people who hear"** (*nyoko nyaku u nin mon* 如許若有人聞): Likely meaning that the preceding clauses refer to everyone, not only to the speakers, Ānanda and Rāhula. See Supplementary Notes, s.v. "Bag of skin."

71 **predictions that take up a pine branch** (*nen shōshi no juki* 拈松枝の授記): In his "Shōbōgenzō shisho" 正法眼藏嗣書, Dōgen also refers to "inheriting a pine branch" (*shōshi o sōshi shi* 松枝を相嗣し); neither there nor here is the reference certain. It may be that he is thinking simply of the use of pine boughs in dharma transmission ceremonies. Some suggest that he may have in mind the story, told in "Shōbōgenzō busshō" 正法眼藏佛性, of the Fifth Ancestor, Hongren 弘忍 (602-675), who received promise of dharma transmission in a previous life, when he was a "pine-planting practitioner" (*sai shō dōsha* 栽松道者); others propose the conversation, told in "Shōbōgenzō gyōji" 正法眼藏行持 (and alluded to above, in section 5) of Huangbo 黄檗 acknowledging Linji 臨濟 as his successor while the latter was planting pines at the monastery.

predictions that take up an *udumbara* blossom (*nen udonge no juki* 拈優曇華の授記); **blinking the eyes** (*shunmoku* 瞬目); **breaking into a smile** (*hagan* 破顔): References to the story of the first transmission of Zen on Vulture Peak (see above, Note 27).

traces of passing on shoes (*shōai o tenju seshi shōseki* 靸鞋を轉授せし蹤跡): Thought to be an allusion to the case in which, before he died, Dayang Jingxuan 太陽警玄 (942–1027) entrusted his portrait (*shinzō* 眞像), robe (*jikitotsu* 直裰), shoes (*hiri* 皮履), and verse (*ge* 偈) to Fushan Fayuan 浮山法遠 (991–1067), who turned them over to Touzi Yiqing 投子義青 (1032–1083) with the request that the latter become the deceased Jingxuan's heir.

72 **"this dharma is not something that can be understood by thinking or discrimination"** (*ze hō hi shiryō funbetsu shi shonōge* 是法非思量分別之所能解): From a famous line in the *Lotus Sūtra* (*Miaofa lianhua jing* 妙法蓮華經, T.262.9:7a18-20):

我以無數方便種種因緣譬喻言辭演說諸法。是法非思量分別之所能解。

234 DŌGEN'S *SHŌBŌGENZŌ* VOLUME II

predictions of "you yourself are this."[73] This principle confers predictions on past, present, and future. Because they are the past, present, and future within prediction, they are realized in predictions of the self, they are realized in predictions of the other.

* * * * *

[21:22] {1:256}
維摩詰謂彌勒言、彌勒、世尊授仁者記、一生當得阿耨多羅三藐三菩提、
爲用何生得受記乎。過去耶、未來耶、現在耶。若過去生、過去生已滅。
若未來生、未來生未至。若現在生、現在生無住。如佛所説、比丘、汝今即
時、亦生・亦老・亦滅。若以無生得受記者、無生即是正位。於正位中、亦
無受記、亦無得阿耨多羅三藐三菩提。云何彌勒受一生記乎。爲從如生得受
記耶、爲從如滅得受記耶。若以如生得受記者、如無有生。若以如滅得受記
者、如無有滅。一切衆生皆如也、一切法亦如也。衆聖賢亦如也。至於彌勒
亦如也。若彌勒得受記者、一切衆生亦應受記。所以者何。夫如者、不二不
異。若彌勒得阿耨多羅三藐三菩提者、一切衆生皆亦應得。所以者何。一切
衆生即菩提相。

Vimalakīrti addressed Maitreya saying,[74]

Maitreya, the World-Honored One has conferred on you a prediction that, in one birth, you will attain anuttara-samyak-saṃbodhi. For what birth did you receive this prediction? For the past? For the future? For the present? If for a past birth, past births have already passed away; if for a future birth, future births have not yet arrived; if for a present birth, the present birth is without abiding. As has been said by the Buddha, "Bhikṣu, at this very moment, you are being born, aging, and ceasing." If it was by the unborn that you received the prediction, the unborn is the true stage.[75] At the true stage, there is no prediction, nor is there attaining anuttara-samyak-saṃbodhi. How, then did Maitreya receive a prediction of one birth? Did you receive the prediction from such a birth? Did

---

I use innumerable techniques, and various stories, parables, and figures of speech to expound the dharmas. This dharma is not something that can be understood by thinking or discrimination.

73 **"I myself am this"** (*gashin ze ya* 我身是也); **"you yourself are this"** (*nyoshin ze ya* 汝身是也): Phrases from the *Lotus Sūtra*, in which Bodhisattva Mañjuśrī explains to the Bodhisatta Maitreya that, in the distant past, Mañjuśrī himself was a bodhisattva named Varaprabha and Maitreya was a bodhisattva named Yaśaskāma. (See *Miaofa lianhua jing* 妙法蓮華經, T.262.9:4b15-16.)

74 **Vimalakīrti** (*Yuimakitsu* 維摩詰): Quoting the *Vimalakīrti Sūtra* (*Weima jing* T.475.14:542b1–17).

75 **the unborn is the true stage** (*mushō soku ze shōi* 無生即是正位): I.e., the ultimate reality in which no dharma arises is the final state of bodhi. "The true stage" (*shōi* 正位) is understood here as referring to buddhahood, the ultimate stage of the spiritual path.

21. Prediction *Juki* 授記 235

you receive the prediction from such a cessation?[76] *If you received the prediction by such a birth, in suchness there is no birth; if you received the prediction by such a cessation, in suchness there is no cessation. All living beings are such; all dharmas are also such. The sages and worthies are also such. And Maitreya is also such. If Maitreya received a prediction, then all living beings should also receive a prediction. Why? Because in suchness there is no duality, no differentiation. If Maitreya attains anuttara-samyak-sambodhi, all living beings should also attain it. Why? Because all living beings are marked by bodhi.*

[21:23] {1:257}

維摩詰の道取するところ、如來これを不是といはず。しかあるに、彌勒の得受記、すでに決定せり。かるがゆえに、一切衆生の得受記、おなじく決定すべし。衆生の受決あらずば、彌勒の受記あるべからず。すでに一切衆生、即菩提相なり。菩提の、菩提の授記をうるなり。受記は今日の命なり。しかあれば、一切衆生は彌勒と同發心するゆえに、同受記なり、同成道なるべし。ただし維摩道の、於正位中、亦無受記は、正位即授記をしらざるがごとし、正位即菩提といはざるがごとし。また過去生已滅、未來生未至、現在生無住とらいふ。過去かならずしも已滅にあらず、未來かならずしも未至にあらず、現在かならずしも無住にあらず。無住・未至・已滅等を過・未・現と學すといふとも、未至のすなはち過・現・未なる道理、かならず道取すべし。

What Vimalakīrti says, the Tathāgata does not say is incorrect. Given this, Maitreya's having "received a prediction" is certain. Therefore, "all living beings" having received a prediction is similarly certain. Were living beings not to receive assurance, Maitreya would not receive the prediction. Since "*All living beings are marked by bodhi,*" it is bodhi receiving the prediction of bodhi. "Receiving prediction" is today's life. This being the case, "all living beings," because they bring forth the mind [of bodhi] together with Maitreya, must receive prediction together with him and attain the way together with him. But in Vimalakīrti's saying, "*At the true stage, there is no prediction,*" it seems he does not know that *the true stage is precisely prediction*; it seems he does not say that the true stage is precisely bodhi. Again, he says, "*Past births have already passed away, future births have not yet arrived, the present birth is without abiding.*" But the past is not necessarily "already passed away"; the future is not necessarily "not yet arrived"; the present is not necessarily "without abiding." While he may say that we regard "without abiding," "not yet arrived," and "already passed away" as past, future, present, he should certainly speak of the principle that "not yet arrived" is itself past, present, and future.

---

76 **such a birth** (*nyo shō* 如生); **such a cessation** (*nyo metsu* 如滅): I.e., the arising and ceasing of "suchness" (or, that is "such").

236 DŌGEN'S *SHŌBŌGENZŌ* VOLUME II

[21:24]

しかあれば、生滅ともに得記する道理あるべし、生滅ともに得菩提の道理あるなり。一切衆生の、授記をうるとき、彌勒も受記をうるなり。しばらくなんぢ維摩にとふ、彌勒は衆生と同なりや異なりや、試道看。すでに、若彌勒得記せば、一切衆生も得記せん、といふ。彌勒は衆生にあらず、といはば、衆生は衆生にあらず、彌勒も彌勒にあらざるべし、いかん。正当恁麼時、また維摩にあらざるべし。維摩にあらずば、この道得用不著ならん。

Thus, there should be a principle that both birth and cessation get predictions, a principle that both birth and cessation get bodhi. When "all living beings" receive a prediction, Maitreya also receives a prediction. Now, let us just ask you, Vimalakīrti, "Are Maitreya and living beings the same or different?" Try to say something. You say that, if Maitreya got a prediction, all living beings also got a prediction. If you say Maitreya is not living beings, then living beings will not be living beings, and Maitreya will not be Maitreya. What about this? At this very moment, you will not be Vimalakīrti; and, if you are not Vimalakīrti, *what you say here is useless.*

[21:25] {1:258}

しかあればいふべし、授記の、一切衆生をあらしむるとき、一切衆生および彌勒はあるなり。授記、よく一切をあらしむべし。

Thus, we should say, when prediction causes "all living beings" to appear, there are all living beings and Maitreya. Prediction should cause all of them to appear.

正法眼藏授記第二十一

Treasury of the True Dharma Eye
Prediction
Number 21

[Ryūmonji MS:]

仁治三年壬寅夏四月二十五日、記于觀音導利興聖寶林寺

Recorded at Kannon Dōri Kōshō Hōrin Monastery; twenty-fifth day, fourth month, summer of the senior water year of the tiger, the third year of Ninji [25 May 1242][77]

[Tōunji MS:]

寛元二年甲辰正月廿日書寫之、在于越州吉峰寺侍者寮

Copied this at the acolyte's quarters, Kippō Monastery, Esshū; twentieth day, first month of the senior wood year of the dragon, the second year of Kangen [29 February 1244]

---

77 The Tōunji 洞雲寺 MS shares an identical colophon.

TREASURY OF THE TRUE DHARMA EYE

NUMBER 22

Full Function
Zenki

全機

Full Function

Zenki

INTRODUCTION

This essay, number 22 in the seventy-five-chapter *Shōbōgenzō*, is number 23 in the sixty-chapter compilation and number 41 in the Honzan edition. According to its colophon, it was delivered at the residence of Dōgen's warrior patron, Hatano Yoshishige 波多野義重, located in Rokuharamitsuji 六波羅蜜寺, a quarter of Heiankyō that housed the offices of the new military government in the imperial capital. "Zenki" is dated in the winter of 1243; in the following spring, Dōgen would deliver another text, the "Kobutsushin" 古佛心, at this location, and in the summer, he would abandon his mission in the capital area to take up residence in his patron's domain in Echizen.

This brief essay, one of the shortest pieces in the *Shōbōgenzō*, reflects a verse by the famed Song-dynasty master Yuanwu Keqin 圓悟克勤. Commenting on the Tang figure Daowu Yuanzhi's 道吾圓智 refusal to say whether a corpse was alive or dead, Yuanwu said, "Alive, the manifestation of the full function; dead, the manifestation of the full function." In his own comments, Dōgen explores this "complete working," or fundamental activity, that encompasses both life and death.

正法眼藏第二十二

Treasury of the True Dharma Eye
Number 22

全機

Full Function

[22:1] {1:259}

諸佛の大道、その究盡するところ、透脱なり、現成なり。その透脱といふ
は、あるひは生も生を透脱し、死も死を透脱するなり。このゆえに、出
生死あり、入生死あり、ともに究盡の大道なり。　捨生死あり、度生死あ
り、とも究盡の大道なり。現成これ生なり、生これ現成なり。その現成の
とき、生の全現成にあらずといふことなし、死の全現成にあらずといふこ
となし。

The great way of the buddhas, where it is exhaustively investigated,
is transcendence, is realization. This "transcendence" means life transcends life, and death transcends death.[1] Therefore, there is leaving life
and death, and there is entering life and death; and both are the great
way exhaustively investigated. There is abandoning life and death; there
is delivering life and death; and both are the great way exhaustively
investigated.[2] Realization is life; life is realization.[3] At the time of their
realization, there is nothing that is not the full realization of life; there is
nothing that is not the full realization of death.

---

1   **life transcends life, and death transcends death** (*shō mo shō o tōdatsu shi, shi
mo shi o tōdatsu suru* 生も生を透脱し、死も死を透脱する): This could also be read
"life liberates life; death liberates death." Here and below, the word *shō* 生, translated as
"life," could also be rendered by "birth." The word is used in reference to the "arising"
of phenomena, to the "birth" or the "lifetime" of a sentient being, to the state of "living," or being "alive," etc. Although, often in what follows, one would ordinarily prefer
the English "birth," for the sake of semantic consistency, the translation will use "life"
throughout, in order to reflect the sense of the word as "alive," in contrast to "dead," in
the saying of Yuanwu Koqin 圜悟克勤 that is the focus of this essay.

2   **delivering life and death** (*do shōji* 度生死): An unusual expression that could be
understood either as "deliverance from life and death" or "deliverance of life and death."

3   **Realization is life; life is realization** (*genjō kore shō nari, shō kore genjō nari*
現成これ生なり、生これ現成なり): "Realization" here translates *genjō* 現成, Dōgen's
much-loved term for "manifestation," "appearance," "occurrence," etc. — as in *genjō
kōan* 現成公案 ("realized kōan").

240 DŌGEN'S *SHŌBŌGENZŌ* VOLUME II

[22:2]
この機關、よく生ならしめ、よく死ならしむ。この機關の現成する正當恁
麼時、かならずしも大にあらず、かならずしも小にあらず、遍界にあら
ず、局量にあらず、長遠にあらず、短促にあらず。いまの生は、この機關
にあり、この機關は、いまの生にあり。

This function makes life what it is, makes death what it is.[4] At the very
moment that this function occurs, it is not necessarily great, is not necessarily small; it is not the realms everywhere, is not restricted; it is not
long-lasting, is not brief. The present life is in this function; this function
is in the present life.

[22:3]
生は來にあらず、生は去にあらず、生は現にあらず、生は成にあらざるな
り。しかあれども、生は全機現なり、死は全機現なり。しるべし、自己に
無量の法あるなかに、生あり、死あるなり。

Life is not coming; life is not going; life is not manifestation; life is
not realization.[5] Nevertheless, it is "alive, the manifestation of the full
function; dead, the manifestation of the full function."[6] We should recognize that among the incalculable dharmas in the self, there is life and
there is death.

[22:4] {1:260}
しづかに思量すべし、いまこの生、および生と同生せるところの衆法は、
生にともなりとやせん、生にともならずとやせん。一時・一法として、生
にともならざることなし。一事・一心としても、生にともならざるなし。

We should quietly consider this present life and the multiple phenomena that are born together with life: do they accompany life, or do they not

---

4　**This function** (*kono kikan* この機關): The antecedent of the pronoun "this" (*kono*
この) is not clear; perhaps the "realization" of life and death. The translation takes *kikan*
機關 ("function," "workings," "mechanism," "device," etc.) to be equivalent to the *ki* 機
of *zenki* 全機 ("full function"); see Supplementary Notes, s.v. "Manifestation of the full
function."

5　**Life is not coming; life is not going** (*shō wa rai ni arazu, shō wa ko ni arazu* 生は
來にあらず、生は去にあらず): Reflecting the common phrase, occurring often in the
Shōbōgenzō, "birth (or life) and death, coming and going" (*shōji korai* 生死去來), used
in reference to life after life in saṃsāra.

life is not manifestation; life is not realization (*shō wa gen ni arazu, shō wa jō ni
arazaru* 生は現にあらず、生は成にあらざる): Dōgen has here split into its two ele-
ments the compound term *genjō* 現成, translated above as "realization" and "realized."

6　**"alive, the manifestation of the full function; dead, the manifestation of the
full function"** (*shō wa zenki gen nari, shi wa zenki gen nari* 生は全機現なり、死は全
機現なり): Dōgen here anticipates in Japanese the Chinese saying he will quote below,
section 6.

22. Full Function *Zenki* 全機 241

accompany life?[7] A single moment, a single dharma — there is nothing that does not accompany life; a single event, a single thought — there is nothing that does not accompany life.

[22:5]
生といふは、たとへば、人の、ふねにのれるときのごとし。このふねは、われ、帆をつかひ、われ、かぢをとれり、われ、さほをさすといへども、ふね、われをのせて、ふねのほかにわれなし。われ、ふねにのりて、このふねをもふねならしむ。この正當恁麼時を功夫參學すべし。この正當恁麼時は、舟の世界にあらざることなし。天も水も岸も、みな舟の時節となれり、さらに舟にあらざる時節とおなじからず。このゆえに、生はわが生ぜしむるなり、われをば生のわれならしむるなり。舟にのれるには、身心依正、ともに舟の機關なり。盡大地・盡虚空、ともに舟の機關なり。生なるわれ、われなる生、それかくのごとし。

"Life" is like that time when a person is riding in a boat. On this boat, although I may use a sail, I may take the rudder, or I may do the poling, the boat carries me, and I do not exist apart from the boat. I make this boat a boat by riding on it. We should make concentrated effort and study this very moment. At this very moment, there is nothing that is not the world of the boat. The heavens, the water, the sky — all have become the time of the boat, not the same as the time that is not the boat. Therefore, life gives life to me; life makes me into me. When I am riding in the boat, my body and mind, my secondary and primary recompense, are all the function of the boat.[8] All the whole earth, all empty space, are all the function of the boat. The I that is alive, the life that is I, are like this.

* * * * *

7   **do they accompany life, or do they not accompany life?** (*shō ni tomo nari to ya sen, shō ni tomo narazu to ya sen* 生にともなりとやせん、生にともならずとやせん): A rhetorical question, presumably meaning "do the multiple phenomena occur together with life (or birth) or not?"

8   **secondary and primary recompense** (*eshō* 依正): A standard Buddhist term for the results of past karma reflected respectively in the circumstances into which one is born and the mental and physical makeup of the person; see Supplementary Notes, s.v. "Secondary and primary recompense."

242　DŌGEN'S *SHŌBŌGENZŌ* VOLUME II

[22:6]

圜悟禪師克勤和尚云、生也全機現、死也全機現。

　*Reverend Keqin, Chan Master Yuanwu, said, "Alive, the manifesta-
tion of the full function; dead, the manifestation of the full function."*[9]

[22:7]

この道取、あきらめ參究すべし。參究すといふは、生也全機現の道理、は
じめ・おはりにかかはれず、盡大地・盡虚空なりといへども、生也全機現
をあひ罣礙せざるのみにあらず、死也全機現をも罣礙せざるなり。死也
全機現のとき、盡大地・盡虚空なりといへども、死也全機現をあひ罣礙
せざるのみにあらず、生也全機現をも罣礙せざるなり。このゆえに、生は
死を罣礙せず、死は生を罣礙せざるなり。盡大地・盡虚空、ともに生にも
あり、死にもあり。しかあれども、一枚の盡大地、一枚の盡虚空を、生に
も全機し、死にも全機するにはあらざるなり。一にあらざれども異にあら
ず、異にあらざれとも即にあらず、即にあらざれども多にあらず。このゆ
えに、生にも全機現の衆法あり、死にも全機現の衆法あり、生にあらず死
にあらざるにも全機現あり。全機現に生あり、死あり。このゆえに、生死
の全機は、壯士の臂を屈伸するがごとくにもあるべし、如人夜間背手摸枕
子にてもあるべし。これに許多の神通光明ありて現成するなり。正當現成
のときは、現成に全機せらるるによりて、現成よりさきに現成あらざりつ
ると見解するなり。しかあれども、この現成よりさきは、さきの全機現な
り。さきの全機現ありといへども、いまの全機現を罣礙せざるなり。この
ゆえに、しかのごとく見解、きほひ現成するなり。

　We should investigate and clarify these words. To "investigate" it
means that the principle of "*alive, the manifestation of the full function*,"
while it may, regardless of its beginning or end, be all the whole earth and
all empty space, this not only does not obstruct "*alive, the manifestation
of the full function*," it also does not obstruct "*dead, the manifestation
of the full function*." And, when it is "*dead, the manifestation of the full
function*," while it may be all the whole earth and all empty space, this
not only does not obstruct "*dead, the manifestation of the full function*,"
it also does not obstruct "*alive, the manifestation of the full function*."
Therefore, life does not obstruct death; death does not obstruct life. All
the whole earth and all empty space are both in life and in death.

9　**Reverend Keqin, Chan Master Yuanwu** (*Engo zenji Kokugon oshō* 圜悟禪師
克勤和尚): I.e., Yuanwu Keqin 圜悟克勤 (1063–1135). Yuanwu 圜悟 is a posthumous
title granted by the Emperor Gaozong 高宗. Also known as Foguo Keqin 佛果克勤,
after the posthumous title granted by the Emperor Huizong 徽宗. This quotation derives
from a verse comment that Yuanwu attached to an exchange involving Daowu Yuanzhi
道悟圓智 (769–835) and the latter's dharma heir Jianyuan Zhongxing 漸源仲興 (dates
unknown); for the exchange and Yuanwu's verse, see Supplementary Notes, s.v. "Manifestation of the full function."

Nevertheless, it is not that a single "all the whole earth" or a single "all empty space" fully functions in life and fully functions in death.[10] They are not one, yet they are not different; they are not different, yet they are not identical; they are not identical, yet they are not many. Therefore, there are the multiple phenomena of the manifestation of the full function in life; there are the multiple phenomena of the manifestation of the full function in death; there is the manifestation of the full function in what is neither life nor death. There is life and there is death in the manifestation of the full function.

Therefore, the full function of life and death must be like a strong youth bending and flexing his arm, must be *like a person groping behind for a pillow in the night.*[11] It is realized with so many spiritual powers and radiances.[12] When it is realized, since it is being fully functioned by the realization, we assume that prior to the realization there was no realization.[13] However, prior to this realization, there is a prior manifestation of the full function. And, though there may be a prior manifestation of the full function, it does not obstruct the present manifestation of the full function. It is for this reason that such assumptions are realized in profusion.

---

10 **it is not that a single "all the whole earth" or a single "all empty space" fully functions in life and fully functions in death** (*ichimai no jin daichi, ichimai no jin kokū o, shō ni mo zenki shi, shi ni mo zenki suru ni wa arazaru nari* 一枚の盡大地、一枚の盡虚空を、生にも全機し、死にも全機するにはあらざるなり): Perhaps meaning "it is not the case that there is a single 'thing' (all the whole earth or all empty space) that is manifest as life and death."

11 **like a strong youth bending and flexing his arm** (*sōshi no hiji o kusshin suru ga gotoku* 壯士の臂を屈伸するがごとく); **"like a person groping behind for a pillow in the night"** (*nyo nin yakan hai shu mo chinsu* 如人夜間背手摸枕子): The former phrase derives from a simile in the *Guan wuliangshou jing* 觀無量壽經 (T.365.12:345c4-5) for the speed with which one could be born after death into the Pure Land of Amitābha. The latter phrase is from the saying attributed to Daowu Yuanzhi 道吾円智 (769-835) in answer to the question of how the thousand-armed Bodhisattva Avalokiteśvara uses so many hands — a case that Dōgen records in his *shinji Shōbōgenzō* 眞字正法眼藏 (DZZ.5:182, case 105) and discusses at length in his "Shōbōgenzō Kannon" 正法眼藏觀音.

12 **so many spiritual powers and radiances** (*kota no jinzū kōmyō* 許多の神通光明): Two properties with which buddhas are endowed: the paranormal powers of a accomplished yogi and the nimbus that surrounds his body; see Supplementary Notes, s.v. "Spiritual powers. Presumably, the unexpressed grammatical subject here and in the next sentence is still "the full function."

13 **since it is being fully functioned by the realization** (*genjō ni zenki seraruru ni yorite* 現成に全機せらるるによりて): An awkward attempt to render Dōgen's creation of a passive verb from the term "full function." The point here would seem to be that each event in each moment, even if new, is an expression of the full function.

244 DŌGEN'S *SHŌBŌGENZŌ* VOLUME II

正法眼藏全機第二十二

Treasury of the True Dharma Eye
Full Function
Number 22

[Ryūmonji MS:]

爾時仁治三年壬寅十二月十七日、在雍州六波羅蜜寺側雲州刺史幕下示衆

Presented to the assembly at the residence of the governor of Unshū, by Rokuharamitsuji, in Yōshū; seventeenth day, twelfth month of the senior water year of the tiger, the third year of Ninji [9 January 1243][14]

[Tōunji MS:]

同四年癸卯正月十九日、書寫之。懷奘

Copied this the nineteenth day, first month of the junior water year of the rabbit, the fourth year of the same [era] [9 February 1243]. Ejō

---

14 The Tōunji 洞雲寺 MS shares an identical colophon.

governor of Unshū (*Unshū shishi* 雲州刺史): Dōgen's patron, Hatano Yoshishige 波多野義重, former governor of Izumo 出雲 (Unshū 雲州). Rokuharamitsuji 六波羅蜜寺 is a quarter in the capital city of Heiankyō that housed the offices of the military government.

TREASURY OF THE TRUE DHARMA EYE

NUMBER 23

The Moon
Tsuki

都機

The Moon

Tsuki

INTRODUCTION

This short chapter was composed at Kōshōji, in the first days of 1243. Number 23 in the seventy-five-chapter *Shōbōgenzō*, it represents number 22 in the sixty-chapter compilation and number 42 in the ninety-five-chapter Honzan edition.

The title theme of the chapter, the moon (*tsuki* 都機, written using *hentaigana* 変体仮名 syllabary glyphs not found elsewhere in the *Shōbōgenzō*), is a common and multivalent symbol in Buddhist literature. Most famously, perhaps, it is the reality pointed at by the teachings taken as "a finger pointing at the moon." It is the transcendental truth reflected in the immanent "moon in the water." It is the round and perfect light behind the passing clouds of ignorance; it is the waxing and waning night glow in contrast to the constant sun of the day.

Dōgen takes up here several passages in the Buddhist literature, both in the sūtras and the sayings of the Zen masters, that invoke these and other images of the moon. The moon is the mind, he says, and everything takes place in the moonlight.

正法眼藏第二十三
Treasury of the True Dharma Eye
Number 23

都機
The Moon

[23:1] {1:262}

諸月の圓成すること、前三三のみにあらず、後三三のみにあらず。圓成の
諸月なる、前三三のみにあらず、後三三のみにあらず。このゆえに、

That moons become full is not only "*three three in front*," not only "*three three in back*"; that the fullness is the moons is not only "*three three in front*," not only "*three three in back*."[1] Therefore,

[23:2]

釋迦牟尼佛言、佛眞法身、猶若虛空．應物現形、如水中月。

Buddha Śākyamuni said, "The true dharma body of a buddha is just like empty space. It manifests its shape in response to beings, like the moon in the water."[2]

[23:3]

いはゆる如水中月の如如は、水月なるべし、水如・月如・如中・中如なる
べし。相似を如と道取するにあらず、如は是なり。佛眞法身は、虛空の猶
若なり、この虛空は、猶若の佛眞法身なり。佛眞法身なるがゆえに、盡地

---

1 **The Moon** (*tsuki* 都機): The title uses the orthography of *manyōgana* 万葉仮名, in which the Japanese word *tsuki* is written with Chinese glyphs used for their sound value. When read for their semantic value, the graphs could be understood as "all functions," "the whole works," etc., akin to *zenki* 全機 ("full function").

  That moons become full (*shogetsu no enjō suru koto* 諸月の圓成すること); **that the fullness is the moons** (*enjō no shogetsu naru* 圓成の諸月なる): The term *enjō* 圓成 ("round and complete"), translated "full" here, is a standard Buddhist technical term for "perfection"; the plurality of moons suggests the trope of the multiple reflections of the moon in water — hence, the sense of individual phenomena reaching perfection, and of perfection expressed as individual phenomena.

"three three in front" (*zen sansan* 前三三); **"three three in back"** (*go sansan* 後三三): Or, perhaps, "three and three of the former"; "three and three of the latter." From a well-known kōan, appearing in several Zen collections and recorded in Dōgen's *shinji Shōbōgenzō* 眞字正法眼藏 (DZZ.5:194-195, case 127); see Supplementary Notes.

2 **Buddha Śākyamuni** (*Shakamuni butsu* 釋迦牟尼佛): From the *Jin guangming jing* 金光明經, T.663.16:344b3-4.

248　DŌGEN'S *SHŌBŌGENZŌ* VOLUME II

盡界、盡法盡現、みづから虚空なり。現成せる百草萬像猶若なる、しかし
ながら佛眞法身なり、如水中月なり。月のときはかならず夜にあらず、夜
かならずしも暗にあらず。ひとへに人間の小量にかかはることなかれ。日
月なきところにも晝夜あるべし、日月は晝夜のためにあらず、日月ともに
如如なるがゆえに、一月兩月にあらず、千月萬月にあらず。月の自己、た
とひ一月兩月の見解を保任すといふとも、これは月の見解なり、かならず
しも佛道の道取にあらず、佛道の知見にあらず。しかあれば、昨夜たとひ
月ありといふとも、今夜の月は昨月にあらず、今夜の月は初・中・後とも
に今夜の月なりと參究すべし。月は月に相嗣するがゆえに、　月ありとい
へども、新舊にあらず。

The "suchnesses" of "*like the moon in the water*" must be "*the water*" and "*the moon*"; they must be "*the water*" is "*such*," "*the moon*" is
"*such*," the "*suchness*" is "*in*," the "*in*" is "*such*."[3] It is not that he calls a
resemblance "like": "like" is "is."[4] "The true dharma body of a buddha"
is the "*just like*" of "empty space"; this "empty space" is "the true dharma body of a buddha" that is "*just like*."[5] Because it is "the true dharma
body of a buddha," *all the earth, all the realms, all dharmas, all the manifestations* are themselves "empty space."[6] That the manifest hundred
grasses and myriad images are "just like" is precisely "the true dharma
body of a buddha," is "*like the moon in the water*."[7]

The time of the moon is not necessarily the night; the night is not
necessarily dark. Do not be simply caught up in the small dimensions of
humans. There must be places without sun or moon where there is day
and night. The sun and moon do not exist for day and night. Since both
sun and moon are "suchnesses," they are not one moon or two moons,
not a thousand moons or ten thousand moons. Even though the moon
itself might maintain the view of one moon or two moons, this is the

---

3　**The "suchnesses" of "like the moon in the water"** (*iwayuru nyo sui chū getsu no
nyonyo* いはゆる如水中月の如如): The translation obscures Dōgen's play here with the
term *nyo* 如, rendered "like" in the phrase "like the moon in the water," but also used
in Buddhist writing for "such" (*tathā*) or "suchness" (*tathatā*). Hence, each term in the
phrase (including the locative "in" [*chū* 中]) is an instance of the "suchnesses" in the
phrase.

4　**"like" is "is"** (*nyo wa ze nari* 如は是なり): I.e., the term *nyo* 如 ("like," "such") here
should not be taken in the sense, "A is like B," but in the sense, "A is B."

5　**the "just like" of "empty space"** (*kokū no yū'nyaku* 虚空の猶若): Continued play
with the terms in the sūtra passage. Here, Dōgen creates a noun from the predicate "to
be just like" (*yū'nyaku* 猶若) and uses it, in a manner akin to his treatment of *nyo* 如, to
express the true identity of "empty space."

6　**all the manifestations** (*jingen* 盡現): An unusual expression probably derived here
from the phrase "it manifests its shape" (*gengyō* 現形) in the sūtra passage.

7　**the manifest hundred grasses and myriad images** (*genjō seru hyakusō banzō* 見
成せる百草萬像): I.e., all the phenomena occurring in the world. Some witnesses read
banzō 萬象 ("myriad forms"). See Supplementary Notes, s.v. "Myriad forms."

23. The Moon *Tsuki* 都機   249

moon's view: it is not necessarily what is said on the way of the buddhas, not necessarily what is known on the way of the buddhas. This being so, though there may have been a moon last night, tonight's moon is not last night's moon. We should investigate the fact that tonight's moon, whether early, middle, or late, is tonight's moon. Because the moon succeeds the moon, while there may be a moon, it is not new or old.

* * * * *

[23:4] {1:263}

盤山寶積禪師云、心月孤圓、光吞萬象。光非照境、境亦非存。光境俱亡、復是何物。

Chan Master Baoji of Mount Pan said,[8]

> The mind moon, alone and full,
> Its light swallows the myriad forms.
> It's not that the light illumines the object,
> Nor that the object remains.
> Light and object, both gone;
> Now, what is it?

[23:5]

いまいふところは、佛祖・佛子、かならず心月あり、月を心とせるがゆえに。月にあらざれば心にあらず、心にあらざる月なし。孤圓といふは、虧欠せざるなり。兩三にあらざるを萬象といふ。萬象これ月光にして萬象にあらず、このゆえに光吞萬象なり。萬象おのづから月光を吞盡せるがゆえに、光の、光を吞却するを、光吞萬象といふなり。たとへば、月吞月なるべし、光吞月なるべし。ここをもて、光非照境、境亦非存と道取するなり。得恁麼なるゆえに、應以佛身得度者のとき、即現佛身而爲説法なり。應以普現色身得度者のとき、即現普現色身而爲説法なり。これ月中の轉法輪にあらずといふことなし。たとひ陰精・陽精の光象するところ、火珠・水珠の所成なりとも、即現成なり。この心すなはち月なり、この月おのづから心なり。佛祖・佛子の、心を究理・究事すること、かくのごとし。

What he is saying here is that buddhas and ancestors, and disciples of the buddhas, always have the mind moon, for they take the moon as their mind. If it is not the moon, it is not the mind; and there is no moon that is not the mind. "Alone and full" means lacking nothing. What is not two or three is called "the myriad forms." "The myriad forms" are moonlight, not myriad forms; therefore, "its light swallows the myriad forms." Since "the myriad forms" have themselves swallowed up the

---

8   **Chan Master Baoji of Mount Pan** (*Banzan Hōshaku zenji* 盤山寶積禪師): Dates unknown; a follower of Mazu Daoyi 馬祖道一 (709-788), who taught on Panshan 盤山 in Youzhou 幽州, in present-day Hobei province. His words, much quoted in Zen literature, can be found at *Jingde chuandeng lu* 景德傳燈録, T.2076.51:253b15-17.

250 DŌGEN'S *SHŌBŌGENZŌ* VOLUME II

moonlight, he calls the light swallowing the light "the light swallows the myriad forms." For example, it could be "the moon swallows the moon"; it could be "the light swallows the moon." With this, he says, *"It's not that the light illumines the object, nor that the object remains."* Because it is like this, when it is *"those who ought to attain deliverance by a buddha body," "then he manifests a buddha body and preaches the dharma to them."*[9] When it is *those who ought to attain deliverance by a universally manifest form body, then he manifests a universally manifest form body and preaches the dharma to them.* There is no case where this is not turning the dharma wheel in the moon. Even if the lighting of forms by the spirit of yin and the spirit of yang is created by the fire pearl and water pearl, it is the realization of "then he manifests."[10] This mind is precisely the moon; this moon is itself the mind. Such is the way that the buddhas and ancestors, and the disciples of the buddha, investigate the principle and investigate the fact of the mind.

* * * * *

---

9   **"those who ought to attain deliverance by a buddha body"** (*ō i busshin tokudo sha* 應以佛身得度者): From a famous passage in the *Lotus Sūtra* (*Miaofa lianhua jing* 妙法蓮華經, T.262.9:57a23-24) describing the thirty-three manifestations of Bodhisattva Avalokiteśvara, according to the needs of his audience.

> 佛告無盡意菩薩、善男子、若有國土衆生應以佛身得度者、觀世音菩薩即現佛身而爲説法。

> The Buddha addressed Bodhisattva Akṣayamati, "Good man, if there are in the land living beings who ought to attain deliverance by a buddha body, Bodhisattva Avalokiteśvara manifests a buddha body and preaches the dharma to them."

The following sentence here on the "universally manifest form body" (*fugen shikishin* 普現色身), modeled on but not in fact taken from the sūtra, refers to the general phenomenon of buddhas and bodhisattvas appearing in human form to guide sentient beings.

10   **the spirit of yin and the spirit of yang** (*insei yōsei* 陰精・陽精): I.e., the moon and sun respectively.

the fire pearl and water pearl (*kaju suiju* 火珠・水珠): Likely metaphors for the sun and moon respectively; see, e.g., *Dazhidu lun* 大智度論 (T.1509.25:113c3-4), where fire is associated with the "sun pearl" (*rizhu* 日珠), and water, with the "moon pearl" (*yuezhu* 月珠).

it is the realization of "then he manifests" (*soku genjō* 即現成): I.e., it is an instance of Avalokiteśvara's manifestations, as described in the *Lotus Sūtra*. This interpretation takes the element *gen* 現 to be functioning simultaneously for the sūtra's *soku gen* 即現 ("then he manifests") and *genjō* 現成 ("realization"). Some witnesses read here *soku gen genjō* 即現現成.

23. The Moon *Tsuki* 都機

251

[23:6] {1:264}

古佛いはく、一心一切法、一切法一心。

An old buddha said, *"One mind, all dharmas; all dharmas, one mind."*[11]

[23:7]

しかあれば、心は一切法なり、一切法は心なり。心は月なるがゆえに、月は月なるべし。心なる一切法、これことごとく月なるがゆえに、遍界は遍月なり、通身ことごとく通月なり。たとひ直須萬年の前後三三、いづれか月にあらざらん。いまの身心依正なる日面佛・月面佛、おなじく月中なるべし。生死去來ともに月にあり、盡十方界は、月中の上下・左右なるべし。いまの日用、すなはち月中の明明百草頭なり、月中の明明祖師心なり。

Thus, the mind is all dharmas, and all dharmas are the mind. Since the mind is the moon, the moon must be the moon. Since all the dharmas that are the mind are, every one of them, the moon, the realms everywhere are the moon everywhere, and bodies throughout are, every one of them, the moon throughout.[12] Even the "three three before and after" of *"it would surely take ten thousand years"* — which of them is not the moon?[13] The Sun-faced Buddha and Moon-faced Buddha that are the present body and mind, the secondary and primary recompense, must similarly be within the moon.[14] Birth and death, coming and going are all

---

11 **An old buddha** (*kobutsu* 古佛): The source of this saying is uncertain. While there does not appear to be an exact equivalent in the extant Chinese materials, a similar phrase occurs in Zhiyi's 智顗 *Mohe zhiguan* 摩訶止觀 (T.1911.46:54a15-16):

心是一切法。一切法是心。
The mind is all dharmas; all dharmas are the mind.

A variant version is used in Yanshou's 延壽 *Zongjing lu* 宗鏡錄 (T.2016.48:437a17):

一切法是心。心是一切法。
All dharmas are the mind; the mind is all dharmas.

12 **bodies throughout** (*tsūshin* 通身): Recalling the saying of Daowu Yuanzhi 道吾圓智 (769-835) regarding the thousand-armed, thousand-eyed Bodhisattva Avalokiteśvara (*senju sengen Kannon* 千手千眼觀音) that "his body throughout is hands and eyes." See Supplementary Notes.

13 **"three three before and after" of "it would surely take ten thousand years"** (*jikishu bannen no zengo sansan* 直須萬年の前後三三): Presumably, meaning something like, "all that happens over all the years." For the expression "three three before and after" (*zengo sansan* 前後三三), see above, Note 1. The expression *jikishu bannen* 直須萬年 ("it will surely take ten thousand years") is a fixed phrase, cited elsewhere in the *Shōbōgenzō*, perhaps best known from a saying, attributed to Shishuang Chingzhu 石霜慶諸 (807-888); see *shinji Shōbōgenzō* 眞字正法眼藏 (DZZ.5:166, case 85); and Supplementary Notes, s.v. "It would surely take ten thousand years."

14 **Sun-faced Buddha and Moon-faced Buddha** (*Nichimen butsu Gachimen butsu* 日面佛・月面佛): Two buddhas given in the *Foming jing* 佛名經, best known in Zen from a kōan involving Mazu Daoyi 馬祖道一 (709-788); see Supplementary Notes, s.v. "Sun face, moon face."

in the moon; all the worlds in the ten directions must be the up and down, left and right within the moon. The present daily activities are precisely "*perfectly clear, the tips of the hundred grasses*" within the moon, "*perfectly clear, the mind of the Ancestral Master*" within the moon.[15]

* * * * *

[23:8]
舒州投子山慈濟大師、因僧問、月未圓時如何。師云、呑却三箇四箇。僧曰、圓後如何。師云、吐却七箇八箇。

> *Great Master Ciji of Mount Touzi in Shuzhou was once asked by a monk, "What about when the moon is not yet full?"*[16]
>
> *The Master said, "Swallowing three or four."*
>
> *The monk said, "What about after it's full?"*
>
> *The Master said, "Vomiting seven or eight."*

[23:9]
いま參究するところは、未圓なり、圓後なり、ともにそれ月の造次なり。月に三箇・四箇あるなかに、未圓の一枚あり。月に七箇・八箇あるなかに、圓後の一枚あり。呑却は三箇・四箇なり。このとき、月未圓時の見成なり。吐却は七箇・八箇なり。このとき、圓後の見成なり。月の、月を呑却するに、三箇・四箇なり。呑却に月ありて現成す、月は呑却の見成なり。月の、月を吐却するに、七箇・八箇あり。吐却に月ありて現成す、月は吐却の見成なり。このゆえに、呑却盡なり、吐却盡なり。盡地盡天吐却なり、蓋天蓋地呑却なり。呑自呑他すべし、吐自吐他すべし。

What is investigated here is "not yet full" and "after it's full," both of which are the hasty acts of the moon. Among the "three or four" of the moon, there is the single "not yet full"; among the "seven or eight" of the moon, there is the single "after it's full." The "swallowing" is the "three or four"; this time is the appearance of "when the moon is

---

secondary and primary recompense (*eshō* 依正): I.e., the circumstances and psychophysical makeup of the individual, respectively; see Supplementary Notes, s.v. "Secondary and primary recompense."

15 **"perfectly clear, the tips of the hundred grasses"** (*meimei hyaku sōtō* 明明百草頭); **"perfectly clear the mind of the Ancestral Master"** (*meimei soshi shin* 明明祖師心): Variant of a phrase best known from a saying of the Layman Pang Yun 龐蘊居士 (740?-808) included in the *shinji Shōbōgenzō* 眞字正法眼藏 (DZZ.5:168, case 88); see Supplementary Notes, s.v. "Perfectly clear, the tips of the hundred grasses."

16 **Great Master Ciji of Mount Touzi in Shuzhou** (*Joshū Tōsuzan Jisai daishi* 舒州投子山慈濟大師): I.e., Touzi Datong 投子大同 (819-914), a disciple of Cuiwei Wuxue 翠微無學, in the lineage of Qingyuan Xingsi 青原行思. "Great Master Ciji" 慈濟大師 is a posthumous title. Shuzhou 舒州 is in the vicinity of present-day Anqing 安慶 in Anhui. This conversation can be found in the *Liandeng huiyao* 聯燈會要, ZZ.136:776b15-16, and elsewhere, including *shinji Shōbōgenzō* 眞字正法眼藏 (DZZ.5:132, case 13).

23. The Moon *Tsuki* 都機   253

not yet full." The "vomiting" is the "seven or eight"; this time is the appearance of "after it's full." When the moon swallows the moon, it is the "three or four." In the swallowing, the moon exists and appears; the moon is the appearance of the swallowing. When the moon vomits the moon, there are the "seven or eight." In the vomiting, the moon exists and appears; the moon is the appearance of the vomiting. Therefore, it swallows entirely; it vomits entirely. *All the earth and all the heaven are vomited; the whole of heaven and the whole of earth are swallowed.* It must be swallowing self and swallowing other; it must be vomiting self and vomiting other.

* * * * *

[23:10] {1:265}

釋迦牟尼佛、告金剛藏菩薩言、譬如動目能揺湛水、又如定眼猶廻轉火。雲駛月運、舟行岸移 、亦復如是。

Buddha Śākyamuni addressed Bodhisattva Vajragarbha, saying,[17]

For example, it is like the case of the moving eye that can stir still water, or again like the stationary eye that yet spins fire. As the clouds race past, the moon moves; as the boat proceeds, the shore shifts: these are also like this.

[23:11]

いま佛演説の雲駛月運、舟行岸移、あきらめ參究すべし。倉卒に學すべからず、凡情に順すべからず。しかあるに、この佛説を佛説のごとく見聞するものまれなり。もしよく佛説のごとく學習するといふは、圓覺かならずしも身心にあらず、菩提涅槃にあらで、菩提涅槃かならずしも圓覺にあらず、身心にあらざるなり。

We should clarify and investigate [the words] "*as the clouds race past, the moon moves; as the boat proceeds, the shore shifts*" that the Buddha expounds here. We should not study in haste; we should not follow common sentiment. Yet those who perceive this preaching of the Buddha as it is preached by the Buddha are rare. If we study it as it is preached by the Buddha, perfect awakening is not necessarily body and mind, not necessarily bodhi and nirvāṇa; and bodhi and nirvāṇa are not necessarily perfect awakening, not necessarily body and mind.

---

17   **Buddha Śākyamuni** (*Shakamuni butsu* 釋迦牟尼佛): From the *Da fangguang yuanjue xiuduoluo liaoyi jing* 大方廣圓覺修多羅了義經 (T.842.17:915c4-6), giving examples of optical illusions. "Spinning fire" (*kaitenka* 廻轉火) likely refers to the phenomenon, commonly noted in Buddhist texts, of the apparent circle of light created by a swiftly spun fire brand.

254 DŌGEN'S *SHŌBŌGENZŌ* VOLUME II

[23:12]

いま如來道の雲駛月運、舟行岸移は、雲駛のとき、月運なり、舟行のとき、岸移なり。いふ宗旨は、雲と月と、同時同道して同歩同運すること、始終にあらず、前後にあらず。舟と岸と、同時同道して同歩同運すること、起止にあらず、流轉にあらず。たとひ人の行を學すとも、人の行は起止にあらず、起止の行は人にあらざるなり。起止を擧揚して人の行に比量することなかれ。雲の駛も月の運も、舟の行も岸の移も、みなかくのごとし。おろかに少量の見に局量することなかれ。雲の駛は東西南北をとはず、月の運は晝夜・古今に休息なき宗旨、わすれざるべし。舟の行および岸の移、ともに三世にかかはれず、よく三世を使用するものなり。このゆえに、直至如今飽不飢なり。しかあるを、愚人おもはくは、くものはしるによりて、うごかざる月をうごくとみる、舟のゆくによりて、うつらざる岸をうつるとみゆる、と見解せり。もし愚人のいふがごとくならんは、いかでか如來の道ならん。佛法の宗旨、いまだ人天の少量にあらず。ただ不可量なりといへども、隨機の修行あるのみなり。たれか舟岸を再三撈摝せざらん、たれか雲月を急著眼看せざらん。

The words of the Tathāgata, "*As the clouds race past, the moon moves; as the boat proceeds, the shore shifts,*" mean that, when "the clouds race past," it is "the moon moves"; when "the boat proceeds," it is "the shore shifts." The essential point is that, the walking together and moving together, at the same time on the same path, of the "the clouds" and "the moon" are not [qualified by] beginning and end, before and after; the walking together and moving together, at the same time on the same path, of "the boat" and "the shore" are not [qualified by] starting and stopping, drifting and turning. Even in studying the movements of a person, the person's movements are not starting and stopping, and the starting and stopping of the movements are not the person. Do not hold up starting and stopping as comparable to a person's movement. The "racing" of "the clouds," the "moving" of "the moon," the "proceeding" of "the boat," the "shifting" of "the shore," are all like this. Do not foolishly restrict yourself to petty views.

We should not forget the essential point that the "racing" of "the clouds" is not about north, south, east, or west, and the "movement" of "the moon" is ceaseless day and night, past and present. The "proceeding" of "the boat" and the "shifting" of "the shore" have nothing to do with the three times; they make use of the three times. Therefore, right up till now, I've been full and not hungry.[18] Yet stupid people take the view that, due to the clouds racing past, the moon that does not move appears to move, and due to the boat proceeding, the shore that does not shift appears to shift. If it were as the stupid people say, how could it be

---

18 **right up till now, I've been full and not hungry** (*jikishi nyokon hō fuki* 直至如今飽不飢): A fixed expression common in Chan texts; also written 直至如今飽不饑. Generally understood to mean that one is complete from the beginning.

23. The Moon *Tsuki* 都機   255

the words of the Tathāgata? The essential point of the buddha dharma is not [captured by] the petty calculations of humans and devas. It may be incalculable, but it exists solely in the practice appropriate to each capacity.[19] Who would not "*scoop up two or three times*" "the boat" and "the shore"?[20] Who would not "*look!*" at "the clouds" and "the moon"?[21]

[23:13]

しるべし、如來道は雲を什麼法に譬せず、月を什麼法に譬せず、舟を什麼法に譬せず、岸を什麼法に譬せざる道理、しづかに功夫參究すべきなり。月の一歩は如來の圓覺なり、如來の圓覺は月の運爲なり。動止にあらず、進退にあらず。すでに月運は譬論にあらざれば、孤圓の性相なり。

We should realize that we should quietly make concentrated effort at the investigation of the principle that the words of the Tathāgata do not liken "the clouds" to any dharma, do not liken "the moon" to any dharma, do not liken "the boat" to any dharma, do not liken "the shore" to any dharma.[22] A single pace of the moon is the perfect awakening of the Tathāgata; the perfect awakening of the Tathāgata is the movement of the moon. It is not motion or rest; it is not advancing or retreating. Since "the moon moves" is not a metaphor, it is the nature and marks of "alone and full."[23]

[23:14]

しるべし、月の運度はたとひ駛なりとも、初・中・後にあらざるなり。このゆえに、第一月、第二月あるなり。第一、第二、おなじくこれ月なり。正好修行、　　　これ月なり、正好供養、これ月なり、拂袖便行、これ月なり。圓尖は去來の輪轉にあらざるなり。去來輪轉を使用し、使用せず、放行し、把定し、逞風流するがゆえに、かくのごとくの諸月なるなり。

We should realize that the passage of "the moon," even if it is "racing," is not beginning, middle, and end. Therefore, there are the first moon and the second moon.[24] First or second, they are both "the moon." "Just

---

19   **the practice appropriate to each capacity** (*zuiki no shugyō* 隨機の修行): I.e., the spiritual aptitude of each individual.

20   **"scoop up two or three times"** (*saisan rōroku* 再三撈摝): Reflecting a verse found in the *Shi xuantan* 十玄談, by Tong'an Changcha 同安常察 (dates unknown); see Supplementary Notes.

21   **"look!"** (*kyū chakugan kan* 急著眼看): A fixed colloquial imperative common in Zen texts.

22   **do not liken "the clouds" to any dharma** (*kumo o jūmo hō ni hi sezu* 雲を什麼法に譬せず): I.e., are not using "clouds," etc., as a metaphor for something.

23   **the nature and marks of "alone and full"** (*koen no shōsō* 孤圓の性相): Recalling Baoji's line (above, section 4), "the mind moon, alone and full." The term *shōsō* 性相 is a standard Buddhist expression for the essential nature and phenomenal characteristics of something.

24   **the first moon and the second moon** (*daiichi getsu daini getsu* 第一月第二月): A

256
DŌGEN'S *SHŌBŌGENZŌ* VOLUME II

right for practice" — this is "the moon"; "just right for offerings" — this is "the moon"; "shaking out his sleeves and leaving" — this is "the moon."[25] Its fullness and pointedness are not a matter of the cycle of its waxing and waning. They make use of the cycle of waxing and waning, or they do not make use of it, because they "let it go, hold it fast, and are full of style," they are the various moons like this.[26]

正法眼藏都機第二十三
Treasury of the True Dharma Eye
The Moon
Number 23

"second moon" is a common example of an optical illusion in Buddhist texts. Perhaps best known in Chan sources from a conversation between Yunyan Tansheng 雲巖曇晟 (782-841) and fellow student Daowu Yuanzhi 道吾圓智 that is recorded in Dōgen's *shinji Shōbōgenzō* 眞字正法眼藏 (DZZ.5:166, case 83):

> 潭州雲巖山曇晟禪師〈嗣藥山〉一日掃地次、道吾曰、太區區生。師云、有不區區者。吾曰、恁麼則有第二月也。師豎起掃箒云、這箇是第幾月。吾休去。

Chan Master Tansheng of Mount Yunyan in Tanzhou (succeeded Yaoshan), was sweeping one day, when Daowu said, "How attentive!"
The Master said, "There's one who's not attentive."
Wu said, "If so, there's a second moon."
The Master stood up his broom and said, "What number moon is this?"
Wu desisted.

25 **"Just right for practice"** (*shōkō shugyō* 正好修行); **"just right for offerings"** (*shōkō kuyō* 正好供養); **"shaking out his sleeves and leaving"** (*hosshū ben kō* 拂袖便行): From an account of four monks discussing the moon, found in various sources, including, e.g., *Dahui Pujue chanshi yulu* 大慧普覺禪師語錄 (T.1998A.47:826b16-8):

> 馬祖與西堂南泉百丈、中秋翫月次、祖指月云、正當恁麼時如何。西堂云、正好修行。百丈云、正好供養。南泉拂袖便行。祖云、經入藏禪歸海、唯有普願獨超物外。

Mazu, together with Xitang, Nanchuan, and Baizhang, was enjoying the mid-autumn moon, when Zu pointed at the moon and said, "Right now, how about it?"
Xitang said, "Just right for practice."
Baizhang said, "Just right for offerings."
Nanchuan shook out his sleeves and left.
Zu said, "The sūtras are entered in the canon; Chan returns to the ocean; but there's only Puyuan [i.e., Nanchuan] who rises alone beyond things."

26 **"let it go, hold it fast, and are full of style"** (*hōgyō shi, hajō shi, tei fūryū suru* 放行し、把定し、逞風流する): Also read *ei fūryū* 逞風流; taking 逞 as 盈. Slightly variant Japanese rendering of a line by Tiantong Rujing 天童如淨 (1162-1227) (*Rujing chanshi yulu* 如淨禪師語錄, T.2002A.48:122c18):

> 放行把住逞風流。

Letting go and holding on, full of style.

23. The Moon *Tsuki* 都機

[Ryūmonji MS:]

仁治癸卯端月六日、書于觀音導利興聖寶林寺。沙門

Written at Kannon Dōri Kōshō Hōrin Monastery; sixth day, head month of the junior water year of the rabbit, in Ninji [27 January 1243]. The Śramaṇa[27]

[Tōunji MS:]

寛元癸卯解制前日、書寫之。懷奘

Copied on the day preceding the unbinding of the rule, the junior water year of the rabbit, in Kangen [1 August 1243]. Ejo

---

27 The Tōunji 洞雲寺 MS shares an almost identical colophon.

TREASURY OF THE TRUE DHARMA EYE
NUMBER 24

Painted Cakes
Gabyō
畫餅

Painted Cakes

Gabyō

INTRODUCTION

This essay was composed at Kōshōji, in late autumn of 1242. It represents number 24 in both the seventy-five and sixty-chapter compilations of the *Shōbōgenzō* and number 40 in the Honzan edition.

"Gabyō" concerns the famous saying, best known from the story of the ninth-century figure Xiangyan Zhixian 香嚴智閑, that "a painted cake doesn't satisfy hunger." In this story, which Dōgen had two years earlier recounted in his "Keisei sanshoku" 溪聲山色, Xiangyan is challenged by his teacher, Weishan Lingyou 潙山靈祐, to say something "from the time before your father and mother were born." Unable to find anything in his books, he uttered his famous saying in despair.

The painted cake is thus a traditional symbol of representations of reality, including the Buddhist representations in Xiangyan's books, as opposed to the real thing that is held to be the proper concern of Zen. But Dōgen has a different view. The teachings of Buddhism are the real thing. The representation of the cake is the real thing. The real things around us — the cakes, the humans, the mountains, the buddhas — are, all of them, painted. Therefore, Dōgen concludes at the end of his essay, only a painted cake can satisfy our hunger; for our hunger is also painted, our satisfaction is also painted.

正法眼藏第二十四

Treasury of the True Dharma Eye
Number 24

畫餅

Painted Cakes

[24:1] {1:268}

諸佛これ證なるゆえに、諸物これ證なり。しかあれども、一性にあらず、一心にあらず。一性にあらず・一心にあらざれども、證のとき、證證さまたけず現成するなり。現成のとき、現現あひ接することなく現成すべし。これ、祖宗の端的なり。一・異の測度を擧して、參學の力量とすることなかれ。

Since the buddhas are verification, things are verification.[1] Nevertheless, they are not one nature, they are not one mind. Although they are not one nature and are not one mind, at the time of verification, the verifications appear without obstructing one another; at the time of appearance, the appearances will appear without engaging one another. This is an obvious truth of the ancestors. Do not hold up reckonings of oneness and difference as the power of study.

[24:2]

このゆえにいはく、一法繊通萬法通。いふところの一法通は、一法の從來せる面目を奪却するにあらず、一法を相對せしむるにあらず、一法を無對ならしむるにあらず。無對ならしむるは、これ相礙なり。通をして通の礙なからしむるに、一通これ萬通、これなり。一通は一法なり、一法通、これ萬法通なり。

Therefore, it is said, "*A single dharma barely penetrated and the myriad dharmas are penetrated.*"[2] It is not that the "single dharma penetrated" spoken of here snatches away the previous face of the "single

---

1 **Since the buddhas are verification, things are verification** (*shobutsu kore shō naru yue ni, shomotsu kore shō nari* 諸佛これ證なるゆえに、諸物これ證なり): The word for "things" (*shomotsu* 諸物) can also be read *shobutsu*, a homophone for "the buddhas" (*shobutsu* 諸佛).

2 **"A single dharma barely penetrated and the myriad dharmas are penetrated"** (*ippō san tsū banpō tsū* 一法繊通萬法通: A sentence in Chinese that appears to be a quotation but for which no source has been identified. The phrase "a single dharma barely penetrated" (*ippō san tsū* 一法繊通) is found in:

a) A saying of the twelfth-century figure Nantang Yuanjing 南堂元靜 (dates unknown) (see, e.g., *Xu chuandeng lu* 續傳燈錄, T.2077.51:678c8):

262 DŌGEN'S *SHŌBŌGENZŌ* VOLUME II

dharma"; it is not that the "single dharma" is opposed; it is not that the "single dharma" is unopposed.[3] To make it unopposed would be a mutual obstruction.[4] When the obstacle of penetration is eliminated from the "penetration," a single penetration is myriad penetrations.[5] A single penetration is "a single dharma"; "a single dharma penetrated" is "the myriad dharmas penetrated."

* * * * *

[24:3]

古佛言、畫餅不充飢。

An old buddha has said, "A painted cake doesn't satisfy hunger."[6]

[24:4] {1:269}

この道を參學する雲衲霞袂、この十方よりきたれる菩薩・聲聞の名位をひ
とつにせず、かの十方よりきたれる神頭鬼面の皮肉、あつく、うすし。
これ古佛・今佛の學道なりといへども、樹下草菴の活計なり。このゆえ
に、家業を正傳するに、あるひはいはく、經論の學業は眞智を熏修せしめ
ざるゆえにしかのごとくいふ、といひ、あるひは、三乘・一乘の教學さら

一法纔通、法法周。

A single dharma barely penetrated, every dharma throughout.

b) The tenth-century *Zongjing lu* 宗鏡錄 (T.2016.48:589a3):

一法纔通、萬像盡歸心地。

A single dharma barely penetrated, and the myriad dharmas all return to the mind ground.

3 **snatches away the previous face of the "single dharma"** (*ippō no jūrai seru menmoku o dakkyaku suru* 一法の從來せる面目を奪却する): Perhaps meaning something like, "denies the identity of the dharma in question."

the "single dharma" is opposed (*ippō o sōtai seshimuru* 一法を相對せしむる); **the "single dharma" is unopposed** (*ippō o mutai narashimuru* 一法を無對ならしむる): Exactly to what the "single dharma" is (or is not) opposed is not clear; perhaps, to other dharmas (though it might also be taken as the "penetration").

4 **mutual obstruction** (*sōge* 相礙): Presumably, meaning that the "single dharma" and other dharmas would obstruct each other (though, again, one might imagine an obstruction between the "dharma" and its "penetration").

5 **obstacle of penetration** (*tsū no ge* 通の礙): Or "obstacles to penetration."

a single penetration is myriad penetrations (*ittsū kore bantsū kore nari* 一通これ萬通これなり): Some would read this "it is just one penetration and myriad penetrations."

6 **An old buddha** (*kobutsu* 古佛): I.e., Xiangyan Zhixian 香嚴智閑 (d. 898), after searching in vain in texts for something with which to answer his teacher's demand that he say something "from the time before your father and mother were born" (*bumo mishō* 父母未生). The story that is the context of this saying is included in Dōgen's *shinji Shōbōgenzō* 眞字正法眼藏 (DZZ.5:134, case 17) and discussed in the "Shōbōgenzō keisei sanshoku" 正法眼藏谿聲山色; see Supplementary Notes, s.v. "A painted cake can't satisfy hunger."

24. Painted Cakes *Gabyō* 畫餅　　263

に三菩提のみちにあらずといはむとして恁麼いふなり、と見解せり。おほ
よそ、假立なる法は眞に用不著なるをいはんとして恁麼の道取ありと見解
する、おほきにあやまるなり。祖宗の功業を正傳せず、佛祖の道取にくら
し。この一言をあきらめざらん、たれか餘佛の道取を參究せりと聽許せ
む。

Those robed in clouds and sleeved in mist who study these words, the bodhisattvas and *śrāvakas* coming from the ten directions, are not of one name or rank; the skin and flesh of the spirit heads and demon faces arriving from the ten directions are thick and are thin.[7] While they may be studying the way of the old buddhas and present buddhas, they make their living under trees and in thatched huts. Therefore, in directly transmitting the family enterprise, some say that this is said because the work of studying the sūtras and treatises does not inculcate true wisdom; some hold the view that such words are to say that instruction in the three vehicles and the one vehicle is not the path to *saṃbodhi*.[8] In general, those who hold the view that such words are to say that provisionally established dharmas are actually worthless are greatly mistaken.[9] They do not directly transmit the work of the ancestors; they are in the dark about the words of the buddhas and ancestors. If they are not clear about this one statement, who would acknowledge that they have investigated the sayings of other buddhas?

7　**robed in clouds and sleeved in mist** (*unnō kabei* 雲衲霞袂): A literary expression for the monk, imagined as wandering the landscape; akin to the more common "clouds and water" (*unsui* 雲水).

the skin and flesh of the spirit heads and demon faces arriving from the ten directions are thick and are thin (*kano jippō yori kitareru jinzu kimen no hiniku, atsuku, usushi* かの十方よりきたれる神頭鬼面の皮肉、あつく、うすし): I.e., the many different monks everywhere who have studied this saying. "Spirit heads and demon faces" (*jinzu kimen* 神頭鬼面; i.e., "weird things") is used in self-deprecating reference to monks.

8　**family enterprise** (*kagō* 家業): I.e., Buddhism.

instruction in the three vehicles and the one vehicle (*sanjō ichijō no kyōgaku* 三乗・一乗の教學): I.e., doctrinal learning in the vehicles of *śrāvaka*, *pratyeka-buddha*, and bodhisattva, and the one, buddha vehicle; see Supplementary Notes, s.v. "Three vehicles."

9　**provisionally established dharmas** (*keryū naru hō* 假立なる法): I.e., the teachings of Buddhism based on conventional categories.

[24:5]

畫餅不能充飢と道取するは、たとへば、諸惡莫作、衆善奉行と道取するがごとし、是什麼物恁麼來と道取するがごとし、吾常於是切といふがごとし。しばらくかくのごとく參學すべし。

To say, "*a painted cake can't satisfy hunger*" is like saying, for example, "*Do no evil, practice the good*"; like saying, "*What thing is it that comes like this?*"; like saying, "*I'm always close to this.*"[10] We should study it like this for a while.

---

10 **"a painted cake can't satisfy hunger"** (*gabyō funō jūki* 畫餅不能充飢): This version of the saying, with the auxiliary verb "can" (*nō* 能) does not seem to occur in the Chinese sources.

"Do no evil, practice the good" (*shoaku maku sa shuzen bugyō* 諸惡莫作衆善奉行): From the famous "Verse of the Common Precepts of the Seven Buddhas," found throughout the Buddhist canon (see, e.g., *Da banniepan jing* 大般涅槃經 T.374.12:451c11-12):

諸惡莫作、諸善奉行、自淨其意、是諸佛教。

To do not evil,
Practice the good,
And purify one's mind:
This is the teaching of the buddhas.

"What thing is it that comes like this?" (*ze jūmo butsu inmo rai* 是什麼物恁麼來): A question famously put by the Sixth Ancestor, Huineng 慧能, upon greeting Nanyue Huairang 南嶽懷讓 (677-744), from a dialogue recorded in the *shinji Shōbōgenzō* 眞字正法眼藏 (DZZ.5:178, case 101) and often cited by Dōgen; see Supplementary Notes.

"I'm always close to this" (*go jō o ze setsu* 吾常於是切): Variant of the phrase *go jō o shi setsu* 吾常於此切 that occurs in the "Jinzu" 神通 and "Henzan" 遍參 chapters of the *Shōbōgenzō*. The sense of the glyph *setsu* 切 here is subject to interpretation: the translation takes it as *sekkin* 切近 ("to be familiar with," "to be intimate with"), but it could also be, and has been, understood as *shinsetsu* 深切 ("to be ardent," "to care deeply," etc.). From a remark attributed to Dongshan Liangjie 洞山良价 (807-869), in answer to a question about the three bodies of a buddha. The *Dongshan yulu* 洞山語錄 (T.1986A.47:510b24-25) gives the question as:

問、三身之中、阿那身不墮衆數。

[A monk] asked, "Among the three bodies [of the buddha], which body doesn't fall among the numbered?"

Dōgen's *shinji Shōbōgenzō* 眞字正法眼藏 (DZZ.5:152, case 55) has a variant version:

洞山因僧問、三身中那身説法。師曰、吾常於此切。僧後問曹山、洞山道吾常於此切、意旨云何。山云、要頭斫將去。僧又問雪峰。峯以拄杖劈口打曰、我也曾到洞山來。

Dongshan was asked by a monk, "Among the three bodies, which preaches the dharma?"
The Master said, "I'm always close to this."
The monk later asked Caoshan [i.e., Caoshan Benzhi 曹山本寂 (840-901)],
"Dongshan said, 'I'm always close to this.' What does that mean?"
Shan said, "If you want my head, cut it off and take it."
The monk again asked Xuefeng [i.e., Xuefeng Yicun 雪峰義存 (822-908)]. Feng struck him in the mouth with his staff and said, "I've been to Dongshan."

24. Painted Cakes *Gabyō* 畫餅   265

[24:6]

畫餅といふ道取、かつて見來せるともがらすくなし、知及せるものまたく
あらず。なにとしてか恁麼しる。從來の一枚・二枚の臭皮袋を勘過する
に、疑著におよばず、親覲におよばず、ただ鄰談に側耳せずして不管なる
がごとし。

In the past, there have been few who saw the words "painted cake,"
and no one at all who really knew them. How do I know this? Previously, when I examined one or two stinking skin bags, they were unable
even to question it, unable personally to attend to it; they seemed uncon-
cerned, as if not bending an ear to the neighbors' talk.[11]

[24:7]

畫餅といふは、しるべし、父母所生の面目あり、父母未生の面目あり。米
麵をもちいて作法せしむる正當恁麼、かならずしも生・不生にあらざれど
も、現成道成の時節なり、去來の見聞に拘牽せらるると參學すべからず。
餅を畫する丹臒は、山水を畫する丹臒とひとしかるべし。いはゆる、山水
を畫するには青丹をもちいる、畫餅を畫するには米麵をもちいる。恁麼な
るゆえに、その所用おなじ、功夫ひとしきなり。

"A painted cake," we should realize, has a face born of father and
mother, and has a face before your father and mother were born.[12] Precisely when it is being made using rice flour, while it is not necessarily "born" or "not born," its realization is the moment that the way is
attained; and we should not study it constrained by our perception of
coming and going.[13] The pigments for painting cakes should be the same

---

11 **stinking skin bags** (*shū hitai* 臭皮袋): A common term for the body, especially of
humans; often used by Dōgen in reference especially to Chan monks. For the meaning
of the metaphor and other examples of its usage, see Supplementary Notes, s.v. "Bag of
skin."

12 **face born of father and mother** (*bumo shoshō no menmoku* 父母所生の面目); **face
before your father and mother were born** (*bumo mishō no menmoku* 父母未生の面
目): I.e., phenomenal and ultimate identities respectively. The phrase "before your father
and mother were born" (*bumo mishō* 父母未生; also read *fubo mishō*) is a classic Zen expression for the true self, sometimes understood as "before your father and mother gave
birth"; see Supplementary Notes, s.v. "Before your father and mother were born." The
use of this metaphor here likely reflects Weishan's challenge to Xiangyan to say a word
"from the time before your father and mother were born." (See Supplementary Notes,
s.v. "A painted cake can't satisfy hunger.") Other versions of the story give somewhat
different phrasing; for example, Dōgen's *sainji Shōbōgenzō* 眞字正法眼藏 (DZZ.5:134,
case 17) has:

吾今問汝、汝生下爲嬰兒時、未辦東西南北、當此之時、與吾説看。

Now, I ask you: When you were an infant just born, before you could distinguish
north, south, east, and west — try saying something for me from just this time.

13 **Precisely when it is being made using rice flour** (*beimen o mochiite sahō
seshimuru shōtō inmo* 米麵をもちいて作法せしむる正當恁麼): Taking *shōtō inmo* 正
當恁麼 ("just such") as the common *shōtō inmo ji* 正當恁麼時 ("at just such a time").

as the pigments for painting mountains and waters.[14] That is, we use blue cinnabar to paint mountains and waters, and we use rice flour to paint painted cakes. Such being the case, what is used is the same and the work is identical.

[24:8] {1:270}
しかあればすなはち、いま道著する畫餅といふは、一切の糊餅・菜餅・乳餅・焼餅・糍餅等、みなこれ畫圖より現成するなり。しるべし、畫等、餅等、法等なり。このゆえに、いま現成するところの諸餅、ともに畫餅なり。このほかに畫餅をもとむるには、つひにいまだ相逢せず、未拈出なり。一時現なりといへども、一時不現なり。しかあれども、老少の相にあらず、去來の跡にあらざるなり。しかある這頭に、畫餅國土あらはれ、成立するなり。

This being so, the "painted cake" spoken of here means that all the pastry cakes, vegetable cakes, milk cakes, roasted cakes, steamed cakes, and so forth — all of them appear from paintings. We should realize that the paintings are equal, the cakes are equal, the dharmas are equal.[15] For this reason, the cakes appearing here are all "painted cakes." When we seek painted cakes other than these, we will never meet them, never bring them out.[16] While they may be a simultaneous occurrence, they are

---

Some read *beimen* 米麵 ("rice flour") as "rice and wheat"; however it is read, note that, here and below, the "painted cake" is painted with the ingredients of the cake.

its realization is the moment that the way is attained (*genjō dōjō no jisetsu nari* 現成道成の時節なり): A tentative translation of a phrase somewhat difficult to parse, taking *genjō* 現成 ("realization") as the grammatical subject and reading *dōjō* 道成 as "attainment of the way" in accordance with its use below, in the first line of the verse in section 11. The exact sense of this sentence is subject to interpretation, but one reading might be something like, "whatever cake is or is not produced from the ingredients, the making of the cake is the realization of Buddhist practice."

14 **pigments** (*tankaku* 丹雘): More literally, "cinnabar and ochre," used as a generic term for the colors employed in painting. The compound "mountains and waters" is a standard term for "landscape."

15 **the paintings are equal, the cakes are equal, the dharmas are equal** (*ga tō, byō tō, hōtō* 畫等、餅等、法等): A common rhetorical pattern that Dōgen will repeat below, section 18. It can be seen, for example, in a saying by Mazu Daoyi 馬祖道一 (709-788) (e.g., at *Jingde chuandeng lu* 景德傳燈錄, T.2076.51:440a12-13):

> 名等義等一切諸法皆等、純一無雜。
>
> The names are equal, the meanings are equal, and all the dharmas are equal, pure and unadulterated.

Dōgen quotes this line in his *Fushukuhanpō* 赴粥飯法 (DZZ.6:46) and uses a variant of the pattern in his "Shōbōgenzō shinjin gakudō" 正法眼藏身心學道 (DZZ.1:49):

> 語等なり、心等なり、法等なり。
>
> The words are equal, the minds are equal, the dharmas are equal.

16 **we will never meet them, never bring them out** (*tsui ni imada sōhō sezu, minenshutsu nari* つひにいまだ相逢せず、未拈出なり): Borrowing the fixed expression,

24. Painted Cakes *Gabyō* 畫餅   267

a simultaneous non-occurrence.[17] Nevertheless, it is not [that they show] signs of old age or youth, it is not [that they leave] traces of coming and going. Here, in such a place, the land of the "painted cake" appears and is established.

[24:9]

不充飢といふは、飢は十二時使にあらざれども、畫餅に相見する便宜あらず、畫餅を喫著するにつひに飢をやむる功なし。飢に相待せらるる餅なし、餅に相待せらるる餅あらざるがゆえに、活計つたはれず、家風つたはれず。飢も一條拄杖なり、横擔竪擔、千變萬化なり。餅も一身心現なり、青黄赤白、長短方圓なり。

"Doesn't satisfy hunger" means that, while "hunger" is not employed by the twelve times, there is no opportune time to meet the "painted cake"; and that, when we consume the "painted cake," it does not in the end have the power to end our "hunger."[18] Since there is no cake relative to "hunger," and there is no hunger relative to "hunger," no [such] livelihood is transmitted, no house style transmitted.[19] "Hunger" is a single staff; shouldered horizontally, shouldered vertically, it is a thousand changes and a myriad transformations. "Cake" is the single occurrence of body and mind; it is blue, yellow, red, and white; long, short, square, and round.[20]

"meeting without bringing it out" (*sōhō funenshutsu* 相逢不拈出); here, probably meaning simply that there are no other painted cakes.

17   **while they may be a simultaneous occurrence, they are a simultaneous non-occurrence** (*ichiji gen nari to iedomo, ichiji fugen nari* 一時現なりといへども、一時不現なり): Probably, meaning that the cakes and the paintings occur and do not occur together.

18   **employed by the twelve times** (*jūni ji shi* 十二時使): The notion of employing and being employed by the twelve times (into which the day was traditionally divided) occurs frequently in the *Shōbōgenzō*; it comes from a popular saying attributed to the famous Tang-dynasty Chan master Zhaozhou Congshen 趙州從諗 (778-897); see Supplementary Notes, s.v. "Employ the twelve times."

19   **Since there is no cake relative to "hunger," and there is no hunger relative to "hunger," no [such] livelihood is transmitted, no house style transmitted** (*ki ni sōtai seraruru byō nashi, byō ni sōtai seraruru byō arazaru ga yue ni, kakkei tsutawarezu, kafū tsutawarezu* 飢に相待せらるる餅なし、餅に相待せらるる餅あらざるがゆえに、活計つたはれず、家風つたはれず): Perhaps meaning that, since "cake" and "hunger" are not related to each other, there is no Buddhist tradition of eating painted cakes to satisfy hunger. The first two phrases here could also be parsed, "There is no cake relative to hunger; and because there is no hunger relative to hunger . . . ."

20   **single occurrence of body and mind** (*ichi shinjin gen* 一身心現): Or "occurrence of a single body and mind." See Supplementary Notes, s.v. "Body and mind."

blue, yellow, red, and white; long, short, square, and round (*sei ō shaku byaku, chō tan hō en* 青黄赤白、長短方圓): A fixed set, appearing often in Buddhist literature, for the variety of things in the world.

268 DŌGEN'S *SHŌBŌGENZŌ* VOLUME II

[24:10]

いま山水を畫するには、青緑丹臒をもちい、奇巖怪石をもちい、七寳四寳
をもちいる。餅を畫する經營もまたかくのごとし。人を畫するには、四大
五蘊をもちいる。佛を畫するには、泥龕土塊をもちいるのみにあらず、三
十二相をももちいる、一莖草をもちいる、三祇百劫の熏修をももちいる。
かくのごとくして、壹軸の畫佛を圖しきたれるがゆえに、一切諸佛はみな
畫佛なり、一切畫佛は、みな諸佛なり。畫佛と畫餅と搩點すべし。いづれ
か石烏龜、いづれか鐵拄杖なる、いづれか色法、いづれか心法なると、審
細に功夫參究すべきなり。恁麼功夫するとき、生死去來はことごとく畫圖
なり、無上菩提すなはち畫圖なり。おほよそ法界虚空、いづれも畫圖にあ
らざるなし。

Now, when we paint mountains and waters, we use blue patina and
cinnabar and ochre, we use weird cliffs and strange rocks, we use the
seven treasures or four treasures.[21] The task of painting a cake is also
like this. In painting a person, we use the four elements and five aggregates.[22] In painting a buddha, we use not only a clay shrine and dirt
clod: we use the thirty-two marks; we use one blade of grass; we use the
inculcation of three *asaṃkhyeya* and one hundred kalpas.[23] In this way,

---

21 **blue patina and cinnabar and ochre** (*seiroku tankaku* 青緑丹臒): The term *seiroku*
青緑 (translated here "blue patina") is thought to be synonymous with *rokushō* 緑青
(literally, "greenish blue," referring to the patina forming on bronze and copper used as a
pigment); the expression *seiroku sansui* 清緑山水 indicates a colored landscape painting
(as opposed to a black ink landscape).

weird cliffs and strange rocks (*kigan kyōseki* 奇巖怪石): A fixed idiom for the bizarre
natural forms in Chinese landscape painting.

seven treasures or four treasures (*shippō shihō* 七寳四寳): "The seven treasures"
(*shippō* or *shichihō* 七寳; S. *sapta-ratna*) is a standard term in Buddhist literature for
various lists of precious substances; one common version gives gold, silver, beryl, crystal, agate, ruby, and cornelian. Mount Sumeru, at the center of the world, is sometimes
said to be made of the seven treasures. "The four treasures" (*shihō* 四寳) is a somewhat
less common list consisting of gold, silver, beryl, and crystal. Interestingly, in our context of painting here, the same expression can refer to the four implements used in calli-
graphy: brush, ink, paper, and inkstone.

22 **four elements and five aggregates** (*shidai goun* 四大五蘊): I.e., the four primary
forms of matter (S. *mahābhūta*) — earth, water, fire, and wind — of which the physical
world is composed; and the five "heaps" (S. *skandha*) — form, sensation, cognition, formations, and consciousness — into which the psychophysical organism can be analyzed.
See Supplementary Notes, s.v. "Four elements and five aggregates."

23 **clay shrine and dirt clod** (*deigan dokai* 泥龕土塊): I.e., the materials of the Buddhist icon. Perhaps alluding to the conversations of Chan Master Zhaozhou Congshen 趙
州從諗. See *Jingde chuandeng lu* 景德傳燈錄, T.2076.51:277c3:

僧問、如何是佛。師云、殿裏底。僧云、殿裏者豈不是泥龕塑像。師云、是。

A monk asked, "What is a buddha?"
The Master said, "What's in the hall."
The monk said, "What's in the hall — that's nothing but a molded image in a clay
shrine."

24. Painted Cakes *Gabyō* 畫餅 269

because we have been drawing the painted buddha on a single scroll, all the buddhas are painted buddhas, and all the painted buddhas are the buddhas. We should examine the painted buddha and the painted cake. Which is the black stone tortoise, and which is the iron staff?[24] Which is a form dharma and which is a mind dharma?[25] We should work away at investigating this in detail. When we work away at it like this, birth and death, coming and going, are all paintings; unsurpassed bodhi itself is a painting. Overall, the dharma realm and empty space are nothing but paintings.

* * * * *

[24:11] {1:271}
古佛言、道成白雪千扁去、畫得青山數軸來。

An old buddha has said,[26]

The way attained, white snow flies off in a thousand flakes;
The painting done, blue mountains come forth in multiple scrolls.

The Master said, "Right."

And see *Zongmen wuku* 宗門武庫, T.1998.47:951c06:

有僧問、如何是佛。云、土塊。
A monk asked, "What is a buddha?"
He said, "A dirt clod."

thirty-two marks (*sanjūni sō* 三十二相): The extraordinary physical characteristics ascribed to the body of a buddha in Buddhist literature.

one blade of grass (*ikkyō sō* 一莖草): Likely reflecting a well-known Zen trope, invoked elsewhere in the *Shōbōgenzō*, that equates a single blade of grass with the sixteen-foot body of the buddha; see Supplementary Notes, s.v. "One blade of grass."

three *asaṃkhyeya* and one hundred kalpas (*sangi hyakkō* 三祇百劫): The length of time it takes in some accounts to become a buddha; three incalculable (*asaṃkhyeya*) æons to master the six (or ten) perfections of the bodhisattva, and a hundred additional æons to develop the thirty-two marks of a buddha's body.

24　**black stone tortoise** (*seki uki* 石烏龜); **iron staff** (*tetsu shujō* 鐵拄杖): The former is a stone image of a black tortoise used as an auspicious decoration and sometimes used in Zen texts as a symbol of something free from deluded discrimination; the latter is the walking stick of the traveling Buddhist monk, often carried by the Zen master when he "ascends to the hall" (*jōdō* 上堂) for a formal lecture. (See Supplementary Notes, s.v. "Staff.") Why the two appear together here is uncertain.

25　**form dharma** (*shiki hō* 色法); **mind dharma** (*shinpō* 心法): Standard terms for physical and mental phenomena respectively; or for the first of the five aggregates and the remaining four, respectively.

26　**old buddha** (*kobutsu* 古佛): The source of this verse, given in Chinese, has not been identified.

270 DŌGEN'S *SHŌBŌGENZŌ* VOLUME II

[24:12]

これ大悟話なり、辨道功夫の現成せし道底なり。しかあれば、得道の正當恁麼時は、青山白雪を數軸となく畫圖しきたれるなり。一動一靜、しかしながら畫圖にあらざるなし。われらがいまの功夫、ただ畫よりえたるなり。十號・三明、これ一軸の畫なり。根・力・覺・道、これ一軸の畫なり。もし畫は實にあらずといはば、萬法みな實にあらず。萬法みな實にあらずば、佛法も實にあらず。佛法もし實なるには、畫餅すなはち實なるべし。

This is the talk of great awakening, a saying revealing concentrated effort in pursuit of the way. Thus, at the very moment of gaining the way, the blue mountains and white clouds have been painted in what he calls "multiple scrolls."[27] One moving, one still, yet all of it nothing but a painting.[28] Our present concentrated effort has come solely from a painting. The ten epithets and three knowledges — these are a single scroll of painting; the faculties, powers, awakening, and path — these are a single scroll of painting.[29] If we say that paintings are not real, then all the myriad dharmas are not real; if all the myriad dharmas are not real, then the buddha dharma is also not real. If the buddha dharma is real, then the "painted cake" must be real.

* * * * *

---

27 **what he calls "multiple scrolls"** (*sūjiku to naku* 數軸となく): Following the reading of MSS that give *sūjiku to nazuku* 數軸となづく.

28 **One moving, one still** (*ichidō ichijō* 一動一靜): Or "each movement, each stillness." The translation assumes "clouds" and "mountains" respectively as the antecedents.

29 **ten epithets and three knowledges** (*jūgō sanmyō* 十號・三明): (a) Ten titles by which a buddha is known, and (b) the three paranormal knowledges possessed by a buddha.

a) Ten epithets: (1) *tathāgata* (*nyorai* 如來; "thus come"), (2) *arhat* (*ōgu* 應供; "worthy"), (3) *samyak-saṃbuddha* (*shōtōgaku* 正等覺 or *shōhenchi* 正遍知; "perfectly awakened"), (4) *vidyā-caraṇa-saṃpanna* (*myōgyō enman* 明行圓滿; "perfectly endowed with wisdom and conduct"), (5) *sugata* (*zenzei* 善逝; "well gone"), (6) *lokavid* (*seken ge* 世間解; "knower of the world"), (7) *anuttara* (*mujō shi* 無上士; "unsurpassed"), (8) *puruṣadamya-sārathi* (*jōgo jōbu* 調御丈夫; "tamer of people"); (9) *śāstā-devamanuṣyāṇām* (*tennin shi* 天人師; "teacher of devas and humans"); *bhagavān* (*seson* 世尊; "world-honored").

b) Three knowledges: (1) *divya-cakṣus* (*tengen* 天眼; "the deva eye"), (2) *pūrva-nivāsānusmṛti* (*shukumyō chi* 宿命智; "recollection of former lives"), (3) *āsrava-kṣaya-jñāna* (*rojin tsū* 漏盡通; "knowledge of the elimination of the contaminants").

faculties, powers, awakening, and path (*kon riki kaku dō* 根・力・覺・道): Four of the groups of virtues that make up the traditional list of the thirty-seven factors of bodhi (*sanjūshichi hon bodai bunpō* 三十七品菩提分法; S. *saptatriṃśad-bodhi-pakṣikā-dharmāḥ*; for Dōgen's discussion of which, see "Shōbōgenzō sanjūshichi hon bodai bunpō" 正法眼藏三十七品菩提分法): (1) the five faculties (*kon* 根; S. *indriya*); (2) the five powers (*riki* 力; S. *balāni*); (3) the seven factors of awakening (*kakushi* 覺支; S. *bodhyaṅga*); and (d) the eightfold path (*dō* 道; S. *mārga*).

24. Painted Cakes *Gabyō* 畫餅

271

[24:13]

雲門匡眞大師、ちなみに僧とふ、いかにあらんかこれ超佛越祖之談。師い
はく、 糊餅。

Great Master Kuangzheng of Yunmen was once asked by a monk,
"What is the talk that *transcends the buddhas and surpasses the ancestors?*"[30]

The Master said, "Pastry cakes."

[24:14]

この道取、しづかに功夫すべし。糊餅すでに現成するには、超佛越祖の談
を説著する祖師あり、聞著せざる鐵漢あり、聽得する學人あるべし、現成
する道著あり。いま糊餅の展事投機、かならずこれ畫餅の二枚三枚なり。
超佛越祖の談あり、入佛入魔の分あり。

This saying, we should work on quietly. Where "pastry cakes" are fully realized, there will be ancestral masters who speak of "*talk that transcends the buddhas and surpasses the ancestors,*" men of iron who do not
hear it, and students who listen to it; and they have sayings that realize
it.[31] *Divulging the matter and achieving accord* using "pastry cakes" here
is certainly one or two "painted cakes."[32] They have the "*talk that transcends the buddhas and surpasses the ancestors*"; they have the status of
entering into buddha and entering into Māra.[33]

* * * * *

---

30 **Great Master Kuangzheng of Yunmen** (*Unmon Kyōshin daishi* 雲門匡眞大師):
I.e., Yunmen Wenyan 雲門文偃 (864–949). "Great Master Kuangzheng" is a posthumous title; "Yunmen" is the name of a mountain in the Shaozhou 韶州 area of Guangdong Province. This dialogue, given here mostly in Japanese, is found in several sources;
see, e.g., *Yunmen Kuangzhen chanshi guanglu* 雲門匡眞禪師廣録, T.1988.47:548b5-6;
Biyan lu 碧巖録, T.2003.48:204b13-14, case 77.

31 **men of iron who do not hear it** (*monjaku sezaru tekkan* 聞著せざる鐵漢): "Man
of iron" (*tekkan* 鐵漢) is a common Zen term, occurring frequently in Dōgen's writings,
for the solid practitioner; see Supplementary Notes, s.v. "Man of iron." Some manuscript
witnesses give here the less surprising *monjaku seru* 聞著せる ("have heard it").

32 **Divulging the matter and achieving accord using "pastry cakes" here** (*ima kobyō
no tenji tōki* いま糊餅の展事投機): "Divulging the matter and achieving accord" is a fixed
idiom, common in Zen texts, used especially for the relationship between master and disciple; see Supplementary Notes, s.v. "Divulging the matter and achieving accord."

33 **status of entering into buddha and entering into Māra** (*nyūbutsu nyūma no
bun* 入佛入魔の分): I.e., advanced spiritual abilities, taking *bun* 分 here as *mibun* 身分
(one's "place," or "lot"). To "enter into buddha and Māra" is a common image in Zen
texts, as in the saying, "You can enter into buddha (*nyūbutsu* 入佛), but you can't enter
into Māra (*nyūma* 入魔). (See, e.g., Dahui Zonggao's 大慧宗杲 *Zongmen wuku* 宗門
武庫, T.1998B.47:950a15.)

272 DŌGEN'S *SHŌBŌGENZŌ* VOLUME II

[24:15] {1:272}

先師道、脩竹芭蕉入畫圖。

My former master said, "The tall bamboo and the banana plant enter the picture."[34]

[24:16]

この道取は、長短を超越せるものの、ともに畫圖の參學ある道取なり。

This saying is a saying in which one who has transcended and surpassed the long and the short studies the picture of both.

[24:17]

脩竹は長竹なり。陰陽の運なりといへども、陰陽をして運ならしむるに、脩竹の年月あり。その年月陰陽、はかることうべからざるなり。大聖は陰陽を覷見すといへども、大聖、陰陽を測度することあたはず。陰陽ともに法等なり、測度等なり、道等なるがゆえに。いま外道・二乘等の心目にかかはる陰陽にはあらず。これは脩竹の陰陽なり。脩竹の歩暦なり、脩竹の世界なり。脩竹の眷屬として十方諸佛あり。しるべし、天地乾坤は脩竹の根莖枝葉なり。このゆえに、天地乾坤をして長久ならしむ、大海須彌・盡十方界をして堅牢ならしむ、拄杖・竹篦をして一老・一不老ならしむ。

"Tall bamboo" is long bamboo.[35] While it may be the movement of yin and yang, what makes the yin and yang move are the years and months of the "tall bamboo."[36] Those years and months, the yin and yang, cannot be calculated. The great sage may observe the yin and yang, but the great sage cannot measure the yin and yang; for with both yin and yang, the dharmas are equal, the measurements are equal, the ways are equal.[37] They are not the yin and yang now seen by the mind and eye of the other paths and the two vehicles; they are the yin and yang of the "tall bamboo."[38] They are the transit of the "tall bamboo"; they are the

---

34 **My former master** (*senshi* 先師): I.e., Tiantong Rujing 天童如淨 (1162-1227). His words occur at *Rujing chanshi yulu* 如淨禪師語錄, T.2002A.48:126c24-25.

35 **"Tall bamboo" is long bamboo** (*shūchiku wa chōchiku nari* 脩竹は長竹なり): Dōgen is here simply explaining the Chinese term.

36 **While it may be the movement of yin and yang** (*onyō no un nari to iedomo* 陰陽の運なりといへども): I.e., although the length of the bamboo is a result of the processes of yin and yang.

37 **great sage** (*daishō* 大聖): May refer either (a) to a buddha or other advanced Buddhist adept, or (b) to a sagely figure of Chinese tradition.

the dharmas are equal, the measurements are equal, the ways are equal (*hō tō nari, shikitaku tō nari, dō tō naru* 法等なり、測度等なり、道等なる): Repeating the rhetorical pattern seen above, section 8.

38 **mind and eye of the other paths and the two vehicles** (*gedō nijō tō no shin moku* 外道二乘等の心目): I.e., the perceptual faculties of the members of non-Buddhist religions and non-Mahāyāna Buddhist traditions.

24. Painted Cakes *Gabyō* 畫餅 273

world of the "tall bamboo."[39] As attendants of the "tall bamboo," there are the buddhas of the ten directions. We should realize that heaven and earth are the "roots, stalks, branches, and leaves" of the "tall bamboo."[40] Therefore, they make heaven and earth long endure; they stabilize the great oceans and Sumeru, and all the worlds in the ten directions; they make the staff and the bamboo stick "one old, one not old."[41]

[24:18]

芭蕉は、地水火風空・心意識智慧を根莖枝葉・華果光色とせるゆえに、秋風を帶して秋風にやぶる。のこる一塵なし、淨潔といひぬべし。眼裏に筋骨なし、色裏に膠繋あらず、當處の解脱あり。なほ速疾に拘牽せられば、須臾利那等の論におよばず。この力量を擧して、地水火風を活計ならしめ、心意識智を大死ならしむ。かるがゆえに、この家業に春秋冬夏を調度として受業しきたる。

"The banana plant" takes *earth, water, fire, wind, and space; mind, mentation, consciousness, and wisdom* as its "*roots, stalks, branches, and leaves, flowers and fruit, lustrous and colored*"; therefore, it wears the autumn wind and is broken by the autumn wind.[42] Not a single dust mote remains; we can say it is pure. In the eye, there are no sinews or

---

39 **transit of the "tall bamboo"** (*shūchiku no horeki* 脩竹の歩暦): Using an astrological term for the progress of a body through the celestial houses.

40 **"roots, stalks, branches, and leaves"** (*kon kyō shi yō* 根莖枝葉): Recalling a verse from the *Lotus Sūtra*, repeated in the following section; see Note 42, below.

41 **great oceans and Sumeru** (*daikai Shumi* 大海須彌): I.e., Mount Sumeru, the mountain at the center of a Buddhist world system. "The great oceans" (*daikai* 大海) refers to the rings of seas surrounding Sumeru.

they make the staff and the bamboo stick "one old, one not old" (*shujō shippei o shite ichi rō ichi furō narashimu* 拄杖・竹篦をして一老・一不老ならしむ): "Staff" (*shujō* 拄杖) and "bamboo stick" (*shippei* 竹篦) refer to implements carried by the Zen master: a walking staff and a curved stick held when teaching. The expression "one old, one not old" likely reflects a verse by Dongshan Liangjie 洞山良价 (*Dongshan Wupen chanshi yulu* 洞山悟本禪師語録, T.1986A.47:510a19-20; quoted by Dōgen in his *Eihei kōroku* 永平廣録, DZZ.3:226, no. 351):

> 道無心合人、人無心合道。欲識箇中意、一老一不老。
> The way, without mind, accords with the person;
> The person, without mind, accords with the way.
> If you want to know the point in this,
> It's one old, one not old.

42 **earth, water, fire, wind, and space; mind, mentation, consciousness, and wisdom** (*chi sui ka fū kū shin i shiki chie* 地水火風空・心意識智慧): I.e., the physical and mental realms. The first five terms (*chi sui ka fū kū* 地水火風空) represent the five elements of Buddhist physics; the next three terms (*shin i shiki* 心意識) are a common expression for mental functions; the last item (*chie* 智慧) is the standard compound expression for "wisdom" (though, for linguistic symmetry, it might be that we are supposed to read it here as separate words, "knowledge" and "wisdom").

274   DŌGEN'S *SHŌBŌGENZŌ* VOLUME II

bones; in the colors, there is no adhesive: there is liberation on the spot.[43] Since it is restricted to being quick, it is not a question of moments or *kṣana*.[44] Taking up this power, it makes a livelihood of earth, water, fire, and wind; it makes the great death of mind, mentation, consciousness, and wisdom.[45] Thus, in this family enterprise, the work has been taken on with spring, autumn, winter, and summer as the implements.

[24:19] {1:273}

いま脩竹・芭蕉の全消息、これ畫圖なり。これによりて竹聲を聞著して大悟せんものは、龍蛇ともに畫圖なるべし、凡聖の情量と疑著すべからず。那竿得恁麼長なり、這竿得恁麼短なり。這竿得恁麼長なり、那竿得恁麼短なり。これみな畫圖なるがゆゑに、長短の圖、かならず相符するなり。長畫あれば、短畫なきにあらず。この道理、あきらかに參究すべし。ただまさに盡界・盡法は畫圖なるがゆゑに、人法は畫より現じ、佛祖は畫より成ずるなり。

Now, as for the whole situation of the "tall bamboo" and "banana plant," they are a picture. Based on this, those who have a great awakening by hearing the sound of bamboo, whether dragons or snakes, must be pictures.[46] We should not doubt this with the sentiments of common peo-

---

"roots, stalks, branches, and leaves, flowers and fruit, lustrous and colored" (*kon kyō shi yō ke ka kō shiki* 根莖枝葉・華果光色): From a verse in the *Lotus Sūtra* describing the varied plants of the world watered by the same rain; see Supplementary Notes.

43   **in the colors, there is no adhesive** (*shikiri ni kōchi arazu* 色裏に膠黐あらず): The term *kōchi* 膠黐 refers to the bonding agent in pigments (in Kawamura's text, the element 黐 is written with radical 130). The choice of "color" for *shiki* 色 here obscures its use to render *rūpa*, the object of the "eye" (*gen* 眼) with which it is being paired.

there is liberation on the spot (*tōsho no gedatsu ari* 當處の解脱あり): It is not obvious what is liberated from what. Perhaps the banana plant is liberated, or the "eye" and "colors" are both liberated.

44   **Since it is restricted to being quick** (*sokushitsu ni kōken serareba* 速疾に拘牽せられば): Some editions read here "since it is not restricted in its quickness" (*sokushitsu ni kōken serarezareba* 速疾に拘牽せられざれば).

moments or *kṣana* (*shuyu setsuna* 須臾刹那): The term *kṣana* is used in Buddhist texts for the shortest unit of time. The term *shuyu* 須臾 is used for Sanskrit *muhūrta*, a very short period of time, sometimes reckoned as 216,000 *kṣana*, or one thirtieth part of a day.

45   **Taking up this power** (*kono rikiryō o koshite* この力量を舉して): Both the agent of the verb and the antecedent of the pronoun are unexpressed. The translation assumes that the "banana plant" takes up the power of liberation, but one might also understand that we take up the power of the "banana plant."

46   **those who have a great awakening by hearing the sound of bamboo** (*chikushō o monjaku shite daigo sen mono* 竹聲を聞著して大悟せんもの): Likely an allusion to the story, alluded to above, Note 6, of the awakening of Xiangyan Zhixian 香嚴智閑, who gained an understanding upon hearing the sound of a bit of debris striking a bamboo stalk.

dragons or snakes (*ryūda* 龍蛇): Also read *ryōda*, *ryōja*, and *ryūja*. Used generically for reptilian creatures, and sometimes used for great men ("a dragon of a snake"); in the

24. Painted Cakes *Gabyō* 畫餅 275

ple and sages.[47] It is "*that stem is that long*"; it is "*this stem is this short*"; it is "*this stem is this long*"; it is "*that stem is that short*."[48] Because they are both pictures, inevitably they match long and short pictures. It is not that, when there are long pictures, there are no short pictures. We should clearly study this principle. Truly, because all the worlds and all the dharmas are a picture, persons and dharmas appear from the picture; buddhas and ancestors are realized from the picture.

[24:20]

しかあればすなはち、畫餅にあらざれば充飢の藥なし、畫飢にあらざれば人に相逢せず、畫充にあらざれば刀量あらざるなり。おほよそ、飢に充し、不飢に充し、飢を充せず、不飢を充せざること、畫飢にあらざれば不得なり、不道なるなり。しばらく這箇は畫餅なることを參學すべし。この宗旨を參學するとき、いささか轉物物轉の功德を、身心に究盡するなり。この功德、いまだ現前せざるがごときは、學道の力量、いまだ現成せざるなり。この功德を現成せしむる、證畫現成なり。

This being so, if it is not a "painted cake," it has no cure that "satisfies hunger"; if it is not painted hunger, it never encounters a person; if it is not painted satisfaction, it has no efficacy. In general, satisfying hunger, satisfying non-hunger, not satisfying hunger, not satisfying non-hunger — if they are not painted hunger, they are not attained, they are not spoken of. We should study for a while the fact that this is a

---

context here, likely "the great and the small" — i.e., akin to "common people and sages" (*bonshō* 凡聖). Perhaps, reflecting the expression "dragon head, snake tail" (*ryūtō dabi* 龍頭蛇尾), used in reference to those who pretend to be better than they are.

47 **common people and sages** (*bonshō* 凡聖): I.e., ordinary people and advanced adepts on the Buddhist path.

48 **"that stem is that long"** (*na kan toku inmo chō* 那竿得恁麼長): Reference to the culm of the bamboo; after a saying of Cuiwei Wuxue 翠微無學 (dates unknown) included in Dōgen's *shinji Shōbōgenzō* 眞字正法眼藏 (DZZ.5:162, case 71) and treated elsewhere in his writings. Here is the version from the *Jingde chuandeng lu* 景德傳燈錄 (T.2076.51:318c4-7):

問、如何是西來的的意。翠微曰、待無人即向汝説。師良久曰。無人也請師説。翠微下禪床引師入竹園。師又曰、無人也請和尚説。翠微指竹曰、遮竿得恁麼長、那竿得恁麼短。

[Yunmen Wenyan 雲門文偃] asked, "What is the clear intention of [Bodhidharma's] coming from the west?"
Cuiwei said, "Once no one's around, I'll tell you."
The Master [i.e., Wenyan] waited a while and said, "No one's around; I beg the Master to tell me."
Cuiwei got down from his meditation seat and led the Master into the bamboo garden. The Master said again, "No one's around; I beg the Reverend to tell me."
Cuiwei pointed at the bamboo and said, "This stem is this long; that stem is that short."

painted cake.[49] When we study the essential point of this, we exhaustively investigate with body and mind a little of the virtue of turning things and things turning.[50] Where this virtue is not yet manifest, the power of studying the way is not yet realized. To bring about the realization of this virtue is the realization that verifies the painting.

正法眼藏畫餅第二十四
Treasury of the True Dharma Eye
Painted Cakes
Number 24

[Ryūmonji MS:]

爾時仁治三年壬寅十一月初五日、在于觀音導利興聖寶林寺示衆
Presented to the assembly at Kannon Dōri Kōshō Hōrin Monastery; fifth day, eleventh month of the senior water year of the tiger, the third year of Ninji [28 November 1242] [51]

[Tōunji MS:]

仁治壬寅十一月初七日、在于興聖客司書寫之。懷奘
Copied this in the guest office at Kōshō; seventh day, eleventh month of the senior water year of the tiger, in Ninji [30 November 1242]. Ejō

---

49 **this is a painted cake** (*shako wa gabyō naru* 這箇は畫餅なる): The pronoun "this" (*shako* 這箇) here has no obvious antecedent; perhaps, a reference to both our hunger and its satisfaction.

50 **turning things and things turning** (*tenmotsu motten* 轉物物轉): Expressions best known from the Chinese *Śūraṅgama-sūtra* (*Shoulengyan jin* 首楞嚴經, T.945.19:111c25-28):

一切衆生從無始來迷己爲物。失於本心爲物所轉。故於是中觀大觀小。若能轉物則同如來。身心圓明、不動道場、於一毛端遍能含受十方國土。

Living beings from beginningless time have all been deluded by things. They lose their original mind due to being turned by things. Therefore, they see here the large and see the small. If they could turn the things, they would be the same as a tathāgata. Their bodies and minds would be perfect and bright; without moving from the place of awakening, in the tip of a single hair, they could fully include the lands of the ten directions.

51 The Tōunji 洞雲寺 MS shares an identical colophon.

TREASURY OF THE TRUE DHARMA EYE

NUMBER 25

Sound of the Stream, Form of the Mountain
Keisei sanshoku

溪聲山色

Sound of the Stream, Form of the Mountain

Keisei sanshoku

INTRODUCTION

This text was composed in the spring of 1240, during the summer retreat at Kōshōji. It is thus among the earliest chapters of the *Shōbōgenzō*, written before the period 1241-1244, during which the bulk of the collection is dated. It occurs as number 25 in both the seventy-five and sixty-chapter editions and as number 9 in the Honzan edition.

The work takes its title from a verse by the famed Song-dynasty poet official Su Shi 蘇軾, known as Su Dongpo 蘇東坡 (1036-1101), that celebrates an experience on Mount Lu 盧山 in which the poet heard the sound of a stream as the preaching of a buddha and the form of the mountain as the body of a buddha. The title theme, then, is the natural world as the manifestation of the dharma body of the buddha and the expression of the buddha's teaching. Dōgen would return to these two elements of Su Dongpo's verse in later texts of the *Shōbōgenzō* — e.g., in the celebrated "Mountains and Waters Sūtra" ("Sansui kyō" 山水經), written in the autumn of 1240, and "The Insentient Preach the Dharma" ("Mujō seppō" 無情説法), from 1243.

After commenting on Su Dongpo's verse, Dōgen makes brief remarks on several thematically related passages dealing with the natural world: the famous stories of Xiangyan Zhixian's 香嚴智閑 spiritual awakening at the sound of a tile striking a bamboo, and of Lingyun Zhiqin's 靈雲志勤 resolving thirty years of practice upon seeing peach trees in bloom; as well as two Zen dialogues on the topic of the phrase "the mountains, rivers, and the whole earth" (*senga daichi* 山河大地).

The "Keisei sanshoku," however, is not merely a poetic appreciation of the spiritual value of the natural world. Surprisingly enough, after the material on the title theme (which occupies less than half the total work), the remainder of the text is taken up with matters ethical. In a lament about the moral state of Japanese Buddhism in his own day and an extended criticism of clerics who seek fame and profit through Buddhism, Dōgen warns his readers against "the dogs that lick the dry bone"

25. Sound of the Stream, Form of the Mountain *Keisei sanshoku* 溪聲山色 279

of worldly fortune, "the dogs that bark at good people," "the dogs" like those who tried out of jealousy to poison the first Chan ancestor, Bodhidharma. He calls on his readers to repent of their transgressions and pray for help from the buddhas and ancestors, to arouse the pure aspiration of the bodhisattva for unsurpassed, perfect bodhi, and "to walk the path of prior sages." In the end, Dōgen concludes, it is only when we have this right attitude toward Buddhist practice that we hear "the eighty-four thousand verses" of the mountain stream.

正法眼藏第二十五

Treasury of the True Dharma Eye
Number 25

溪聲山色

Sound of the Stream, Form of the Mountain

[25:1] {1:274}

阿耨菩提に傳道授業の佛祖おほし、粉骨の先蹤即不無なり。斷臂の祖宗ま
なぶべし、掩泥の毫髮もたがふることなかれ。各各の脱殻うるに、從來の
知見解會に拘牽せられず、曠劫未明の事、たちまちに現前す。恁麼時の而
今は、吾も不知なり、誰も不識なり、汝も不期なり、佛眼も覰不見なり。
人慮あに測度せんや。

In *anuttara-bodhi*, the buddhas and ancestors who transmitted the way
and handed on the work are many; and the traces of predecessors who
pulverized their bones are not lacking.[1] We should learn from the ancestor who cut off his arm; do not differ so much as a hair covering the
mud.[2] As each is able to slough off the husk, we are not restrained by our
previous knowledge and understandings, and matters unclear for vast
kalpas suddenly appear before us.[3] The present of such a time, I do not

---

1   **In *anuttara-bodhi*, the buddhas and ancestors who transmitted the way and
handed on the work are many** (*anoku bodai ni dendō jugō no busso ooshi* 阿耨菩提
に傳道授業の佛祖おほし): The expression *anoku bodai* transliterates the Sanskrit for
"unsurpassed awakening" (*anuttara-bodhi*), the spiritual state of the buddhas. The unusual phrase "transmitted the way and handed on the work" is the result of splitting two
familiar compound terms: "transmit and hand on" (*denju* 傳授) "the work of the way"
(*dōgō* 道業).

the traces of predecessors who pulverized their bones (*funkotsu no senshō* 粉骨の先
蹤): I.e., historical examples of ascesis; from the common expression "to pulverize the
bones and shatter the body" (*funkotsu saishin* 粉骨碎身).

2   **the ancestor who cut off his arm** (*danpi no soshū* 斷臂の祖宗): Reference to the
famous tradition that the monk who was to become the Second Ancestor cut off his arm
and presented it to the First Ancestor, Bodhidharma, as a token of his commitment; see
Supplementary Notes, s.v. "Cut off an arm."

do not differ so much as a hair covering the mud (*endei no gōhatsu mo tagauru koto
nakare* 掩泥の毫髮もたがふることなかれ): Word play combining the idiom "differ a
hair's breadth" and the famous legend that Buddha Śākyamuni in a previous life as
Bodhisattva Māṇava (*Judō* 儒童) let down his hair for Buddha Dīpaṅkara (*Nentōbutsu*
燃燈佛) to step on.

3   **As each is able to slough off the husk** (*kyakukyaku no datsukoku uru ni* 各各の脱

25. Sound of the Stream, Form of the Mountain *Keisei sanshoku* 溪聲山色   281

know, no one recognizes, you do not expect, the eye of the buddha looks at without seeing. How could human thinking fathom it?

[25:2]

大宋國に、東坡居士蘇軾とてありしは、字は子瞻といふ。筆海の眞龍なりぬべし、佛海の龍象を學す。重淵にも游泳す、曾雲にも昇降す。あるとき、盧山にいたれりしちなみに、溪水の夜流する聲をきくに悟道す。偈をつくりて、　常總禪師に呈するにいはく、溪聲便是廣長舌、山色無非清淨身、夜來八萬四千偈、他日如何擧似人。

In the Land of the Great Song, lived Su Shi, the layman Dongpo, who was styled Zizhan.[4] He must have been a real dragon in the ocean of the brush, who studied the dragon elephants in the ocean of the buddha.[5] He swam in deep pools; he climbed and dived through the layered clouds.[6] Once, when he had gone to Mount Lu, he awakened to the way upon hearing the sound of the evening current of a valley stream.[7] Composing a gāthā, he presented it to Chan Master Changzong:[8]

The sound of the stream is his long, broad tongue;
The mountain form, his immaculate body.
This evening's eighty-four thousand gāthās —
How will I tell them tomorrow?

殻うるに): "To slough off the husk" (*datsukoku* 脱殻) seems to be synonymous with the more familiar "to slough off" (*datsuraku* 脱落); see Supplementary Notes, s.v. "Slough off." The subject of this sentence and the antecedent of "each" here are unclear; the translation takes both in the first person, but one could also read it as the third person (i.e., the buddhas and ancestors).

4 **Su Shi, the layman Dongpo** (*Tōba kōji Soshoku* 東坡居士蘇軾): The famed author, calligrapher, and government official Su Shi 蘇軾 (1037-1101).

5 **a real dragon in the ocean of the brush** (*hikkai no shinryū* 筆海の眞龍); **dragon elephants in the ocean of the buddha** (*bukkai no ryūzō* 佛海の龍象): I.e., a giant of the literary world; the masters of the Buddhist world. The term *ryūzō* 龍象 (translated here "dragon elephants") often represents *mahānāga* or *hastināga*, a "great elephant" (both *ryū* 龍 and *zō* 象 being used to translate Sanskrit *nāga*); but the compound term is also regularly taken to mean "dragons and elephants" and used, as here, in reference to superior religious practitioners.

6 **He swam in deep pools; he climbed and dived through the layered clouds** (*jūen ni mo yūei su, sōun ni mo shōkō su* 重淵にも游泳す、曾雲にも昇降す): Continuing the dragon imagery. The term *sōun* 曾雲 is taken as equivalent to *sōun* 層雲.

7 **Mount Lu** (*Rozan* 盧山): The famous mountain in present-day Jiangxi, site of many Buddhist monasteries, including Donglinsi 東林寺, the residence of Su Dongpo's teacher, Zhaojue Chanzong 照覺常總.

8 **Chan Master Changzong** (*Jōsō zenji* 常總禪師): I.e., Donglin Changzong 東林常總 (1025-1091); his honorific title was Chan Master Zhaojue 照覺禪師. Su Dongpo's verse offering to him appears (in a slightly different version) at *Jiatai pudeng lu* 嘉泰普燈錄, ZZ.137:318b7-9.

DŌGEN'S *SHŌBŌGENZŌ* VOLUME II

[25:3] {1:275}

この偈を総禪師に呈するに、　総禪師、然之す。総は照覺常總禪師なり、総は黄龍慧南禪師の法嗣なり、南は慈明楚圓禪師の法嗣なり。

When this gāthā was presented to Chan Master Zong, Chan Master Zong accepted it. Zong was Chan Master Zhaojue Changzong. Zong was the dharma heir of Chan Master Huanglong Huinan; Nan was the dharma heir of Chan Master Ciming Chuyuan.[9]

[25:4]

居士、あるとき佛印禪師了元和尚と相見するに、佛印さづくるに法衣・佛戒等をもてす。居士、つねに法衣を搭して修道しき。居士、佛印にたてまつるに無價の玉帶をもてす。ときの人いはく、凡俗所及の儀にあらずと。

At one time, when the layman was meeting with Reverend Liaoyuan, Chan Master Foyin, Foyin presented him with a dharma robe and the buddha precepts.[10] The layman always put on the dharma robe to practice the way. The layman offered Foyin a priceless jeweled belt.[11] People of the time said it was not behavior that could be reached by the worldly.

[25:5]

しかあれば、　聞溪悟道の因縁、さらにこれ晩流の潤益なからんや。あはれむべし、いくめぐりか現身説法の化儀にもれたるがごとくなる。なにとしてかさらに山色を見、　溪聲をきく。一句なりとやせん、半句なりとやせん、八萬四千偈なりとやせん。うらむべし、山水にかくれたる聲色あること。またよろこぶべし、山水にあらはるる時節因縁あること。舌相も懈倦なし、身色あに存没あらんや。しかあれども、あらはるるときをや、ちかしとならふ、かくれたるときをや、ちかしとならはん。一枚なりとやせん、半枚なりとやせん。從來の春秋は、山水を見聞せざりけり、夜來の時節は、山水を見聞することわづかなり。いま學道の菩薩も、山流水不流より學入の門を開すべし。

9　**Chan Master Huanglong Huinan** (*Ōryū Enan zenji* 黄龍慧南禪師): 1002-1069; his honorific title was Chan Master Pujue 普覺禪師; considered the founder of the Huanglong 黄龍 branch of the Linji 臨濟 lineage.

Chan Master Ciming Chuyuan (*Jimyō Soen zenji* 慈明楚圓禪師): I.e., Shishuang Chuyuan 石霜楚圓 (986-1039); Chan Master Ciming 慈明禪師 was his honorific title.

10　**Reverend Liaoyuan, Chan Master Foyin** (*Butsuin zenji Ryōgen oshō* 佛印禪師了元和尚): I.e., Juelao Liaoyuan 覺老了元 (1032-1098); Chan Master Foyin is a posthumous title. The account of Su Dongpo's interaction with him is found at *Liandeng huiyao* 聯燈會要, ZZ.136:907b10ff; this passage mentions the presentation of the robe but not of the "buddha precepts" (*butsukai* 佛戒) — which here probably refers to the bodhisattva precepts (*bosatsu kai* 菩薩戒) given to a lay person.

11　**priceless jeweled belt** (*muge no gyokutai* 無價の玉帶): According the *Liandeng huiyao* 聯燈會要 account, Su Dongpo forfeited his jeweled belt when he was unable to respond to a challenge from Liaoyuan.

25. Sound of the Stream, Form of the Mountain *Keisei sanshoku* 渓聲山色 283

Thus, might not the episode of *hearing the stream and awakening to the way* be of benefit as well to later types?[12] What a pity that, for so many times, we seem to have missed the teaching method of *"manifesting a body to preach the dharma."*[13] How does he further see the form of the mountain and hear the sound of the stream? Is it one verse? Is it a half verse? Is it eighty-four thousand gāthās? We should regret that there are sounds and forms hidden in the mountains and waters; again, we should rejoice that there are times and circumstances when they appear in the mountains and waters.[14] The mark of the tongue does not weary; how could the form of the body persist and expire?[15] Nevertheless, should we learn that, when they appear, they are close, or should we learn that, when they are hidden, they are close? Are they one piece? Are they a half piece? For the preceding springs and autumns, he had not seen or heard the mountains and waters; on the occasion of "this evening," he sees and hears a little of the mountains and waters. Bodhisattvas who study the way today should also open the gate that enters the study from *the mountain flows; the water does not flow.*[16]

---

12 **benefit as well to later types** (*sara ni kore banru no junyaku* さらにこれ晩流の潤益): "Later types" (*banru* 晩流) is likely akin to "latecomers" (*banshin* 晩進), or "later students" (*bangaku* 晩學) — i.e., those of us today. The translation loses what may be an intentional play with the waters of Dongpo's poem, since this phrase could be rendered more literally, "moisten" (*junyaku* 潤益) "later streams" (*banru* 晩流). Such play seems to continue in the following sentence with the verb rendered "have missed" (*moretaru* もれたる), which has the primary sense "to have leaked out."

13 **for so many times, we seem to have missed the teaching method of "manifesting a body to preach the dharma"** (*ikumeguri ka genshin seppō no kegi ni moretaru ga gotoku naru* いくめぐりか現身説法の化儀にもれたるがごとくなる): The subject here is unexpressed; it could also be taken as "he" ("Su Dongpo") or as "they" ("later types"). The sense would seem to be that we have gone through many lifetimes without encountering the preaching of the manifested buddha body. See Supplementary Notes, s.v. "Manifesting a body to preach the dharma."

14 **there are times and circumstances when they appear in the mountains and waters** (*sansui ni arawaruru jisetsu innen aru* 山水にあらはるる時節因縁ある): "Times and circumstances" here translates the fixed phrase *jisetsu innen* 時節因縁, more often rendered herein as "conditions of the time." For the derivation of the phrase, see Supplementary Notes, s.v. "If you wish to know the meaning of 'buddha nature,' you should observe the conditions of the time."

15 **The mark of the tongue does not weary** (*zessō mo geken nashi* 舌相も懈倦なし): A large tongue (*kōchō zetsu* 廣長舌; S. *prabhūta-jihvā*) is one of the thirty-two marks (*sō* 相; S. *lakṣaṇa*) of a buddha's body; as in the use of "long, broad tongue" (*kōchō zetsu* 廣長舌), in Su Dongpo's verse (section 2, above), the Buddha's "tongue" is regularly used metonymically for his preaching of the dharma.

16 **the mountain flows; the water does not flow** (*san ryū sui furyū* 山流水不流): A variant of the well-known line from a verse attributed to the sixth-century figure Fu Dashi 傅大士 (497-569); see Supplementary Notes, s.v. "Water doesn't flow." Dōgen uses the image of the flowing mountain again in his "Shōbōgenzō sansuikyō" 正法眼藏山水經.

284　DŌGEN'S *SHŌBŌGENZŌ* VOLUME II

[25:6]

この居士の悟道せし夜は、そのさきの日、　総禪師と無情説法話を参問せしなり。禪師の言下に飜身の儀いまだしといへども、　溪聲のきこゆるところは、逆水の波浪たかく天をうつものなり。しかあれば、いま溪聲の、居士をおどろかす、溪聲なりとやせん、照覺の流瀉なりとやせん。うたがふらくは、照覺の無情説法の語、ひびきいまだやまず、ひそかに溪流のよるの聲にみだれいる。たれかこれ一升なりと辦肯せん、一海なりと潮宗せん。畢竟じていはば、居士の悟道するか、山水の悟道するか。たれの明眼あらんか、長舌相・清淨身を急著眼せざらん。

On the day before the evening when this layman awakened to the way, he had asked Chan master Zong about the saying, "*the insentient preach the dharma*."[17] Although, under the words of the Chan master, he did not yet exhibit the behavior of flipping the body, when he heard the sound of the stream, the waves of water reversing struck the heavens on high.[18] Therefore, where the sound of the stream startled the layman, should we take it as the sound of the stream, or should we take it as the pouring forth of Chaojue?[19] What I wonder is whether Chaojue's words on "insentient beings preach the dharma" may still be echoing, secretly mixed into the evening voice of the valley stream. Who could confirm this as one quart, or merge the currents as one ocean?[20] Ultimately speaking, did the layman awaken to the way, or did the mountains and water awaken to the way? Who with clear eyes would not sharply fix their eye on the mark of the "*long tongue*" and the "*immaculate body*"?

* * * * *

17　**"the insentient preach the dharma"** (*mujō seppō* 無情説法): An expression best known in Zen literature from the teachings of Nanyang Huizhong 南陽慧忠 (d. 775). Dōgen discusses the saying at length in his "Shōbōgenzō mujō seppō" 正法眼藏無情説法.

18　**the behavior of flipping the body** (*honshin no gi* 翻身の儀): An act of understanding, a "conversion," as in the idiom "flipping the body in the stream of words" (*gomyakuri honshin* 語脈裏翻身). (Also written 飜身.)

19　**the pouring forth of Chaojue** (*Shōkaku no ryūsha* 照覺の流瀉): Or "Chaojue's overflow," another watery image in a standard metaphor for fulsome teaching.

20　**Who could confirm this as one quart, or merge the currents as one ocean?** (*tare ka kore isshō nari to benkō sen, ikkai nari to chōsō sen* たれかこれ一升なりと辦肯せん、一海なりと潮宗せん): I.e., who could calculate its dimensions, small or large? "Quart" (*shō* 升) translates a measure of volume, varying with time and place, equal to one-tenth peck (*tō* 斗). To "merge the currents" is a loose translation for a common idiom *chōsō* 潮宗 (more often written 朝宗) for rivers flowing together into the sea, from the image of courtiers gathering at court.

25. Sound of the Stream, Form of the Mountain *Keisei sanshoku* 溪聲山色 285

[25:7] {1:276}

又香嚴智閑禪師、かつて大潙大圓禪師の會に學道せしとき、大潙いはく、なんぢ聡明博解なり、章疏のなかこり記持せず、父母未生以前にあたりて、わがために一句を道取しきたるべし。香嚴、いはんことをもとむること數番すれども不得なり。ふかく身心をうらみ、年來たくはふるところの書籍を披尋するに、なほ茫然なり。つひに火をもちて、年來のあつむる書をやきていはく、画にかけるもちひは、うゑをふさぐにたらず。われちかふ、此生に佛法を會せんことをのぞまじ。ただ行粥飯僧とならん、といひて、行粥飯して年月をふるなり。行粥飯僧といふは、衆僧に粥飯を行益するなり。このくにの陪饌伇送のごときなり。

Again, once, when Chan Master Xiangyan Zhixian was studying the way in the community of Chan Master Dayuan of Dawei, Dawei said, "You are intelligent and learned.[21] Without something memorized from the commentaries, say a line for me as you were before your father and mother were born."[22]

Xiangyan repeatedly sought for something to say but could not get it. Deeply regretting his body and mind, he searched through the volumes he had collected over the years but was still stumped. Finally, setting fire to the books he had collected over the years, he said, "A painted cake does not satisfy hunger. I vow that I shall not seek to understand the buddha dharma in this life. I shall simply become a meal-server monk."

So saying, he spent the years and months providing the gruel and rice. "Meal-server monk" refers to the one who provides gruel and rice to the assembled monks; it is like the meal attendant in this land.[23]

---

21 **Chan Master Xiangyan Zhixian** (*Kyōgen Chikan zenji* 香嚴智閑禪師): Also written 香嚴, d. 898; his honorific title was Chan Master Xideng 襲燈禪師.

Chan Master Dayuan of Dawei (*Daii Daien zenji* 大潙大圓禪師): I.e., Weishan Lingyou 潙山靈祐 (also sometimes read Guishan Lingyou), known as Dawei 大潙 (771-853); Dayuan 大圓 is his honorific title. The following passage is a Japanese retelling of a famous story found in several sources, including Dōgen's *shinji Shōbōgenzō* 眞字正法眼藏 (DZZ.5:134, case 17); see Supplementary Notes, s.v. "A painted cake can't satisfy hunger."

22 **"before your father and mother were born"** (*bumo mishō izen* 父母未生以前): Also read *fubo mishō izen*. A classic Zen expression for the true self; sometimes understood as "before your father and mother gave birth." See Supplementary Notes, s.v. "Before your father and mother were born."

23 **"Meal-server monk" refers to the one who provides gruel and rice to the assembled monks; it is like the meal attendant in this land** (*gyō shukuhan sō to iu wa, shusō ni shukuhan o gyōyaku suru nari. kono kuni no baisen ekisō no gotoki nari* 行粥飯僧といふは、衆僧に粥飯を行益するなり。このくにの陪饌伇送のごときなり): Dōgen here steps back from his story to explain the Chinese term *xing zhoufan seng* 行粥飯僧 to his Japanese readers. "Gruel and rice" (*shukuhan* 粥飯) is a standard term for monastic meals, from the customary diet of gruel for breakfast and rice for lunch. The "meal attendant" (*baisen ekisō* [or *yakusō*] 陪饌伇送) provided table service to nobility and high ranking clerics.

[25:8]

かくのごとくして大潙にまうす、智閑は身心昏昧にして道不得なり、和尚わがためにいふべし。大潙のいはく、われ、なんぢがためにいはんことを辞せず、おそらくは、のちになんぢわれをうらみん。

Thus, he said to Dawei, "Zhixian, confused in body and mind, cannot say anything. The Reverend should say something for me."

Dawei said, "I don't refuse to say something for you, but you would likely resent me later."

[25:9]

かくて年月をふるに、大證國師の蹤跡をたづねて、武當山にいりて、國師の庵のあとに、くさをむすびて爲庵す。竹をうゑてともとしけり。あるとき、道路を併淨するちなみに、かはらほどばしりて、竹にあたりてひびきをなすをきくに、豁然として大悟す。沐浴し、潔齋して、大潙山にむかひて燒香禮拜して、大潙にむかひてまうす、大潙大和尚、むかしわがためにとくことあらば、いかでかいまこの事あらん。恩のふかきこと、父母よりもすぐれたり。つひに偈をつくりていはく、一撃亡所知、更不自修治、動容揚古路、不堕悄然機、處處無蹤跡、聲色外威儀、諸方達道者、咸言上上機。この偈を大潙に呈す。大潙いはく、此子徹也。

Having spent the years and months in this way, following the traces of the National Teacher Dacheng, he entered Mount Wudang, where he bound the grasses to fashion a hut at the site of the National Teacher's hut.[24] He planted bamboo to keep him company. Once, when he was clearing a path, a piece of tile flew up and hit against a bamboo; upon hearing the sound, he suddenly had a great awakening.

Bathing and purifying himself, he faced Mount Dawei, offered incense, made bows, and said to Dawei, "Most Reverend Dawei, if long ago you had explained it to me, how could this have happened? The depth of your kindness is greater than that of a parent."

Then, he composed a gāthā that said,

One hit, and I lost what I know;
I won't be training myself again.
Action and rest promote the old path;
I won't be sinking into worry.
Without traces wherever I go;
Deportment beyond sound and form.
Masters of the way in all quarters
Will call this the highest faculty.

---

24 **following the traces of the National Teacher Dacheng** (*Daishō kokushi no shōseki o tazunete* 大證國師の蹤跡をたづねて): The reference is to Nanyang Huizhong 南陽慧忠, disciple of the Sixth Ancestor, who is supposed to have stayed in a hermitage on Mount Wudang 武當山, in present-day Hubei.

25. Sound of the Stream, Form of the Mountain *Keisei sanshoku* 溪聲山色 287

He presented this gāthā to Dawei. Dawei said, "This child has penetrated it."

* * * * *

[25:10] {1:277}

又、靈雲志勤禪師は、三十年の辦道なり。あるとき游山するに、山脚に休息して、はるかに人里を望見す。ときに春なり。桃華のさかりなるをみて、忽然として悟道す。偈をつくりて大潙に呈するにいはく、三十年來尋劍客、幾回葉落又抽枝、自從一見桃華後、直至如今更不疑。大潙いはく、從緣入者、永不退失。すなはち許可するなり。

Again, Chan Master Lingyun Zhiqin pursued the way for thirty years.[25] Once, while traveling in the mountains, resting at the foot of a mountain, he looked out at a village in the distance. The time was spring, and, seeing the peach blossoms in bloom, he suddenly awakened to the way. Composing a gāthā, he presented it to Dawei.

> *Thirty years a passenger seeking the sword.*[26]
> *How many times have the leaves fallen and the branches budded?*
> *After once seeing the peach blossoms,*
> *I'm like this now, without further doubts.*

Dawei said, *"Those who enter from objects never regress or lose it."*[27]

This was his acknowledgement.

[25:11]

いづれの入者か從緣せざらん、いづれの入者か退失あらん、ひとり勤をいふにあらず。つひに大潙に嗣法す。山色の清淨身にあらざらん、いかでか恁麼ならん。

Which of "those who enter" does not do so "from objects"? Which of "those who enter" "reverts or loses it"? This is not just said about Qin. Subsequently, he inherited the dharma of Dawei. Were the "mountain form" not the "immaculate body," how could this be?

---

25 **Chan Master Lingyun Zhiqin** (*Reiun Shigon zenji* 靈雲志勤禪師): A disciple of Dawei 大潙, dates unknown. His poem on seeing the peach blossoms occurs in a number of sources (see, e.g., Dahui's 大慧 *Zhengfayanzang* 正法眼藏, ZZ.118:36b14-17), including Dōgen's own *shinji Shōbōgenzō* 眞字正法眼藏 (DZZ.5:206, case 155). See Supplementary Notes, s.v. "Peach blossoms."

26 **Thirty years a passenger seeking the sword** (*sanjū nen rai jin ken kyaku* 三十年來尋劍客): Allusion to the story, from the *Lüshi Chunqiu* 呂氏春秋 ("Master Lü's Spring and Autumn Annals"; KR.3j0009.015-22a-b), of the stupid man of Chu 楚 who dropped his sword from a boat and marked the spot by notching the side of the boat.

27 **"Those who enter from objects"** (*jū en nyū sha* 從緣入者): Dōgen switches to Chinese for this quotation. "Objects" (*en* 緣) refers to objects of perception, such as the blossoms.

288 DŌGEN'S *SHŌBŌGENZŌ* VOLUME II

* * * * *

[25:12]
長沙景岑禪師に、ある僧とふ、いかにしてか山河大地を轉じて自己に歸せしめん。師いはく、いかにしてか自己を轉じて山河大地に歸せしめん。

Chan Master Changsha Jingcen was asked by a monk, "How does one turn the mountains, rivers, and the whole earth back to the self?"[28]

The Master said, "How does one turn the self back to the mountains, rivers, and the whole earth?"

[25:13] {1:278}
いまの道取は、自己のおのづから自己にてある、自己たとひ山河大地といふとも、さらに所歸に導礙すべきにあらず。

This saying means that the self is naturally the self, that while "the self" may be "the mountains, rivers, and the whole earth," it should not be obstructed by "returning."[29]

* * * * *

[25:14]
瑯琊の廣照大師慧覺和尚は、南嶽の遠孫なり。あるとき、教家の講師子璿とふ、清淨本然、云何忽生山河大地。かくのごとくとふに、和尚しめすにいはく、清淨本然、云何忽生山河大地。

Reverend Huijue, Great Master Huangzhao of Langye, was a distant descendant of Nanyue.[30] Once Zixuan, a lecturer from a teaching house,

---

28 **Chan Master Changsha Jingcen** (*Chōsha Keishin zenji* 長沙景岑禪師): Dates unknown; a disciple of Nanquan Puyuan 南泉普願 (748-835). Japanese version of a conversation that occurs in a number of sources, including Dōgen's *shinji Shōbōgenzō* 眞字正法眼藏, DZZ.5:132-133, case 16.

29 **it should not be obstructed by "returning"** (*sara ni shoki ni gaige su beki ni arazu* さらに所歸に導礙すべきにあらず): Perhaps, meaning that "the self" is already "the mountains, rivers, and the whole earth" and need not be "turned back" to them. Dōgen sometimes uses the predicate *gaige* 導礙 ("to obstruct"), equivalent to the somewhat more common *keige* 罣礙, in the sense "to delimit," "to define."

30 **Reverend Huijue, Great Master Huangzhao of Langye** (*Rōya no Kōshō daishi Ekaku oshō* 瑯琊の廣照大師慧覺和尚): I.e., Langye Huijue 瑯琊慧覺, dates unknown. "Great Master Huangzhao" is his posthumous title. Mount Langye is located in present-day Anhui province. This anecdote appears in several sources (e.g., *Jiatai pudeng lu* 嘉泰普燈錄, ZZ.137:75b18-76a2), including Dōgen's *shinji Shōbōgenzō* 眞字正法眼藏 (DZZ.5:128, case 6).

distant descendant of Nanyue (*Nangaku no onson nari* 南嶽の遠孫なり): I.e., in the lineage of Nanyue Huairang 南嶽懷讓 (677-744).

25. Sound of the Stream, Form of the Mountain *Keisei sanshoku* 溪聲山色 289

asked him, "*How does what has purity as its original state suddenly produce the mountains, rivers, and the whole earth?*"[31]

Thus asked, the Reverend responded, "*How does what has purity as its original state suddenly produce the mountains, rivers, and the whole earth?*"

[25:15]

ここにしりぬ、清淨本然なる山河大地を、山河大地とあやまるべきにあらず。しかるを、經師、かつてゆめにもきかざれば、山河大地を山河大地としらざるなり。

Here, we know that we should not confuse the mountains, rivers, and the whole earth that "have purity as their original state" with the mountains, rivers, and the whole earth. Nevertheless, since the sūtra master has never heard of them even in his dreams, he does not know the mountains, rivers, and the whole earth as the mountains, rivers, and the whole earth.

* * * * *

[25:16]

しるべし、山色溪聲にあらざれば、拈華も開演せず、得髓も依位せざるべし。溪聲山色の功德によりて、大地有情同時成道し、見明星悟道する諸佛あるなり。かくのごとくなる皮袋、これ求法の志氣甚深なりし先哲なり。その先蹤、いまの人、かならず參取すべし。いまも、名利にかかはらざらん眞實の參學は、かくのごときの志氣をたつべきなり。遠方の近來は、まことに佛法を求覓する人まれなり。なきにはあらず、難遇なるなり。たまたま出家兒となり、離俗せるににたるも、佛道をもて名利のかけはしとするのみおほし。あはれむべし、かなしむべし、この光陰をおしまず、むなしく黑暗業に賣買すること。いづれのときかこれ出離得道の期ならん。たとひ正師にあふとも、眞龍を愛せざらん。かくのごとくのたぐひ、先佛これを可憐憫者といふ。その先世に惡因あるによりてしかあるなり。生をうくるに爲法求法のこころざしなきによりて、眞法をみるとき眞龍をあやしみ、正法にあふとき正法にいとふるなり。この身心骨肉、かつて從法而生ならざるによりて、法と不相應なり、法と不受用なり。祖宗師資、かくのごとく相承してひさしくなりぬ。菩提心は、むかしのゆめをとくがごとし。あはれむべし、寶山にうまれながら寶財をしらず、寶財をみず、いはんや法財をえんや。もし菩提心をおこしてのち、六趣四生に輪轉すといへども、その輪轉の因緣、みな菩提の行願となるなり。しかあれば、從來の光陰はたとひむなしくすごすといふとも、今生のいまだすぎざるあひだに、いそぎて發願すべし。

---

31 **Zixuan** (*Shisen* 子璿): I.e., Changshui Zixuan 長水子璿 (d. 1038), a scholar of the *Śūraṅgama-sūtra* (*Shoulengyan jing* 首楞嚴經; T.945), the text from which his question here comes.

"How does what has purity as its original state suddenly produce the mountains, rivers, and the whole earth?" (*shōjō honnen, un ga kotsu shō senga daichi* 清淨本然、云何忽生山河大地): A line from the *Shoulengyan jing* 首楞嚴經 (T.945.19:119c17), where the topic is the *tathāgata-garbha* (*nyorai zō* 如來藏).

290 DŌGEN'S *SHŌBŌGENZŌ* VOLUME II

We should realize that, were it not for the "mountain form" and "stream sound," "holding up a flower" would not expound [the dharma]; "getting the marrow" would not be "in place."[32] Because of the virtues of the "stream sound" and "mountain form," "*the whole earth and sentient beings simultaneously attain the way*," and there are buddhas who *see the dawn star and awaken to the way*.[33] Bags of skin such as these are the prior wise men whose resolve to seek the dharma was extremely deep.[34] Their traces, people of today should study without fail. Even today, the true study that has nothing to do with fame or profit should establish such resolve.

In the recent times of a remote quarter, people who truly seek the buddha dharma are rare.[35] It is not that there are none; it is that they are difficult to meet. There are many who happen to become renunciants and seem to be apart from the secular, but they just treat the way of the

---

32 **"holding up a flower" would not expound [the dharma]; "getting the marrow" would not be "in place"** (*nenge mo kaien sezu, tokuzui mo ei sezaru beshi* 拈華も開演せず、得髓も依位せざるべし): I.e., the transmission of the ancestors would not occur. "Holding up a flower" (*nenge* 拈華) alludes to the famous legend of Buddha Śākyamuni's silently holding up a flower to expound the dharma and transmit the "treasury of the true dharma eye" to the First Ancestor, Mahākāśyapa; see Supplementary Notes, s.v. "Hold up a flower." "Getting the marrow" (*tokuzui* 得髓) refers to the well-known story of Bodhidharma's test of his four disciples, of whom Huike demonstrated that he had "gotten the marrow" by bowing and standing "in place" (*e i ni ryū* 依位而立); see Supplementary Notes, s.v. "skin, flesh, bones, and marrow."

33 **"the whole earth and sentient beings simultaneously attain the way"** (*daichi ujō dōji jōdō* 大地有情同時成道); **see the dawn star and awaken to the way** (*ken myōjō godō* 見明星道): References to the Buddha's awakening under the bodhi tree. The expression, which appears in several of Dōgen's texts, is from a line that he will quote in his "Shōbōgenzō hotsu bodai shin" 正法眼藏發菩提心 (DZZ.2:164; also quoted at *Eihei kōroku* 永平廣錄, DZZ.3:28, no. 37):

> 釋迦牟尼佛言、明星出現時、我與大地有情、同時成道。

> Buddha Śākyamuni said, "When the dawn star appeared, I, together with the whole earth and sentient beings, simultaneously attained the way."

Although the passage appears in Chan texts from this period (see, e.g, *Jianzhong Jingguo xudeng lu* 建中靖國續燈錄, ZZ.136:36b17-18), it has not been located in any extant sūtra. The translation here follows the usual reading of *daichi ujō* 大地有情 as a compound subject; the phrase could also be read, "sentient beings of the whole earth."

34 **Bags of skin such as these** (*kaku no gotoku naru hitai* かくのごとくなる皮袋): It is unclear just who is being called here a "bag of skin" (a common term for the body and, by extension, a person); possibly all those mentioned so far who studied "the mountain form and stream sound." See Supplementary Notes, s.v. "Bag of skin."

35 **In the recent times of a remote quarter** (*enpō no kinrai* 遠方の近來): I.e., at a time and place (like Dōgen's Japan) so distant from the India of the Buddha and the China of the Chan ancestors. The English loses the play with the glyphs *en* 遠 and *kin* 近 ("far" and "near").

25. Sound of the Stream, Form of the Mountain *Keisei sanshoku* 溪聲山色 291

buddhas as a ladder to fame and profit.[36] It is pitiful, it is lamentable, that, without regretting the years and months, they trade at their dark deeds in vain.[37] When can they expect to get free and gain the way? Even if they were to meet a true master, they would not love the real dragon.[38] Such types, the former buddha called "the pitiful."[39] They are like this because they have evil causes in their former lives. While receiving birth, because they have no resolve to seek the dharma for the sake of the dharma, when they see the real dharma, they doubt the real dragon; when they meet the true dharma, they are despised by the true dharma. Because their bodies and minds, bones and flesh, have never been *born from the dharma*, they are not in accord with the dharma, do not make use of them as the dharma.[40]

The ancestral masters and disciples have been inheriting this sort of thing for a long time. It is as if they speak of the thought of bodhi as an old dream.[41] What a pity that, while they are born on a mountain of jewels, they do not know the jewels, do not see the jewels, let alone

---

36 **a ladder to fame and profit** (*myōri no kakehashi* 名利のかけはし): Or "a bridge to fame and profit."

37 **they trade at their dark deeds in vain** (*munashiku koku'angō ni maimai suru* むなしく黒暗業に賣買する): I.e., they go about vainly producing bad karma. Taking *koku'angō* 黒暗業 as equivalent to *kokugō* 黒業 ("black karma").

38 **Would not love the real dragon** (*shinryū o ai sezaran* 眞龍を愛せざらん): Allusion to the ancient Chinese story of the Duke of She 楚葉公, who loved the image of the dragon but was terrified of the real thing; the *locus classicus* is *Xinxu* 新序, Zashi 雜事 (KR.3a0008.005.14a).

39 **Such types, the former buddha called "the pitiful"** (*kaku no gotoku no tagui, senbutsu kore o karenminsha to iu* かくのごとくのたぐひ、先佛これを可憐憫者という ふ): Or "the former buddhas." The term *senbutsu* 先佛, like the somewhat more common *zenbutsu* 前佛 seen below, typically refers to the buddhas of the past; the translation here treats it as an unusual form of reference to Buddha Śākyamuni (perhaps in contrast to the future Buddha Maitreya), in a variation of the commonly encountered phrase "the Tathāgata called them 'the pitiful'" (*nyorai setsu i karenminsha* 如來説爲可憐憫者). Some readers have taken "the former buddha" as indicating Dōgen's teacher, Tiantong Rujing 天童如淨 (1162-1227), to whom he frequently refers as "my former master, the Old Buddha" (*senshi kobutsu* 先師古佛); the expression, however, does not occur in Rujing's recorded sayings.

40 **born from the dharma** (*jū hō ni shō* 從法而生): A phrase used to describe the birth of the advanced bodhisattva.

do not make use of them as the dharma (*hō to fujuyū nari* 法と不受用なり): Some would read this "make use of the dharma," but the particle *to* と here would seem to require that we supply a direct object — most likely, "body and minds, bones and flesh."

41 **the thought of bodhi** (*bodai shin* 菩提心): I.e., *bodhi-citta*; the bodhisattva's aspiration to attain the unsurpassed perfect awakening of a buddha; see Supplementary Notes, s.v. "Bring forth the mind."

292 DŌGEN'S *SHŌBŌGENZŌ* VOLUME II

get the riches of the dharma.[42] After we have produced the thought of bodhi, though we may turn round in the six destinies and four births, the causes and conditions of that turning all become the practice of the vow of bodhi.[43] Hence, though we may have spent our previous years and months in vain, while this life is not yet exhausted, we should forthwith make a vow.[44]

[25:17] {1:279}

ねがはくは、われと一切衆生と、今生より乃至生生をつくして、正法をきくことあらん。きくことあらんとき、正法を疑著せじ、不信なるべからず。まさに正法にあはんとき、世法をすてて佛法を受持せん。つひに大地有情、ともに成道することをえん。

> I pray that, together with all living beings, from this life through life after life to come, I shall hear the true dharma; that whenever I hear it, I shall not doubt it and fail to believe in it; that when I encounter the true dharma, casting aside the worldly dharma, I shall receive and keep the buddha dharma, and finally attain the way together with the whole earth and sentient beings.

[25:18]

かくのごとく發願せば、おのづから正發心の因縁ならん。この心術、懈倦することなかれ。

---

42 **a mountain of jewels** (*hōsen* 寶山): Perhaps reflecting the simile, familiar from the *Dazhidu lun* 大智度論 (T.1509.25:a7-12), of faith as like hands: just as one without hands can enter a mountain of jewels but be unable to take any of them, so one without faith cannot gain anything from entering "the jeweled mountain of the buddha dharma" (*fofa baoshan* 佛法寶山).

43 **the six destinies and four births** (*rokushu shishō* 六趣四生): I.e., the "six paths" (*rokudō* 六道) of rebirth in saṃsāra and the four ways in which sentient beings are born in saṃsāra; See Supplementary Notes, s.v. "Six paths," and "Four births."

44 **though we may have spent our previous years and months in vain** (*jūrai no kōin wa tatoi munashiku sugosu to iutomo* 從來の光陰はたとひむなしくすごすといふとも): A Japanese rendering of a Chinese phrase, "to pass your years and months in vain" (*xu du guangyin* 虛度光陰), well known from the *Cantong qi* 參同契, of Shitou Xiqian 石頭希遷 (700-791), *Jingde chuandeng lu* 景德傳燈錄, T.2076.51:459b20-21. The term *kōin* 光陰 (literally, "light and shade") refers to the sun and moon as metonyms for passing time; variously understood as "years and months," "days and months," and "days and nights."

we should forthwith make a vow (*isogite hotsugan su beshi* いそぎて發願すべし): The vow introduced here, together with that found below, in section 25, forms the content of a text known as the *Hotsu ganmon* 發願文 (DZZ.7:223). The manuscript, said to be in Dōgen's own hand, bears a colophon dated the twelfth month of 1247 in Kamakura, where Dōgen resided during the autumn and winter of that year.

25. Sound of the Stream, Form of the Mountain *Keisei sanshoku* 溪聲山色 293

When we make a vow in this way, it will naturally be the cause and condition of correctly bringing forth the mind.[45] This mental attitude is not to be neglected.[46]

[25:19]

又、この日本國は、海外の遠方なり。人のこころ至愚なり。むかしよりいまだ聖人うまれず、生知うまれず、いはんや學道の實士まれなり。道心をしらざるともがらに、道心をおしふるときは、忠言の逆耳するによりて、自己をかへりみず、他人をうらむ。おほよそ菩提心の行願には、菩提心の發・未發、行道・不行道を世人にしられんことをおもはざるべし、しられざらんといとなむべし、いはんやみづから口稱せんや。いまの人は、實をもとむることまれなるによりて、身に行なく、こころにさとりなくとも、他人のほむることありて、行解相應せりといはむ人をもとむるがごとし。迷中有迷、すなはちこれなり。この邪念、すみやかに抛捨すべし。

Again, this Land of Japan is a remote quarter beyond the ocean. The minds of the people are exceedingly stupid. From ancient times, no sages have been born here, no innately wise have been born here; needless to say, real gentlemen who study the way are rare. When a person teaches the mind of the way to those who do not know the mind of the way, since sincere words offend the ear, they resent the person instead of reflecting on themselves.[47]

In general, in the vow of the thought of bodhi, one should not think to inform the worldly of whether one has or has not brought forth the thought of bodhi, whether one is or is not practicing the way. We should conduct ourselves so as not to inform them, how much less should we voice it ourselves. Because it is rare for them to seek the real thing, people today, though their bodies lack practice and their minds lack insight, when they get praise from another, seem to look for the people who will tell them that their practice and understanding are in accord. *Delusion within delusion* — this is it.[48] These false thoughts, we should quickly cast away.

---

45   **bringing forth the mind** (*hosshin* 發心): I.e., arousing the thought of bodhi; see above, Note 41.

46   **mental attitude** (*shinjutsu* 心術): More literally, "mental art"; a term appearing several times in Dōgen's writings in the sense of one's "mindset."

47   **sincere words offend the ear** (*chūgen no gyaku ni suru* 忠言の逆耳する): A Japanese version of the Chinese saying, "sincere words offend the ear but benefit conduct" (*zhongyan ni yu er li yu xing* 忠言逆於耳利於行).

48   **Delusion within delusion — this is it** (*meichū u mei, sunawachi kore nari* 迷中有迷、すなはちこれなり): I.e., this is a prime example of the saying "delusion within delusion." Kawamura's text here follows the seventy-five-chapter compilation; the sixty-chapter manuscripts give the more common "further delusion within delusion" (*meichū u mei* 迷中又迷).

DŌGEN'S *SHŌBŌGENZŌ* VOLUME II

[25:20] {1:280}

學道のとき、見聞することかたきは、正法の心術なり。その心術は、佛佛相傳しきたれるものなり。これを佛光明とも、佛心とも相傳するなり。如來在世より今日にいたるまで、名利をもとむるを學道の用心とするににたるともがらおほかり。しかありしも、正師のおしへにあひて、ひるがへして正法をもとむれば、おのづから得道す。いま學道には、かくのごとくのやまふのあらんとしるべきなり。たとへば、初心始學にもあれ、久修練行にもあれ、傳道授業の機をうることもあり、機をえざることもあり、慕古してならふ機あるべし、訕謗してならはざる魔もあらん。兩頭ともに愛すべからず、うらむべからず。いかにしてかうれへなからん、うらみざらん。いはく、三毒を三毒としれるともがらまれなるによりて、うらみざるなり。いはんや、はじめて佛道を欣求せしときのこころざしをわすれざるべし。いはく、はじめて發心するときは、他人のために法をもとめず、名利をなげすてきたる。名利をもとむるにあらず、ただひとすぢに得道をこころざす、かつて國王大臣の恭敬・供養をまつこと、期せざるものなり。しかあるに、いまかくのごとくの因緣あり、本期にあらず、所求にあらず、人天の繫縛にかかはらんことを期せざるところなり。しかあるを、おろかなる人は、たとひ道心ありといへども、はやく本志をわすれて、あやまりて人天の供養をまちて、佛法の功德いたれりとよろこぶ。國王・大臣の歸依、しきりなれば、わがみちの、　　　　見成とおもへり。これは學道の一魔なり。あはれむこころをわするべからずといふとも、よろこぶことなかるべし。みずや、ほとけ、のたまはく、如來現在、猶多怨嫉の金言あることを。愚の賢をしらず、小畜の大聖をあたむこと、理、かくのごとし。

What is difficult to see and hear when we study the way is the mental attitude of the true dharma. This mental attitude is what buddha after buddha has transmitted. It is transmitted as both the radiance of the buddha and as the buddha mind.[49] From the lifetime of the Tathāgata till today, there have been many who appear to take the search for fame and profit as a concern in studying the way. Nevertheless, on encountering the teachings of a true master, if they reverse themselves and seek the true dharma, they will naturally gain the way. We should realize that there is likely this kind of sickness in the study of the way now.[50]

For example, whether they be beginners starting the study, or trained practitioners of long practice, one may get those with the potential to transmit the dharma and hand on the work, or one may not get them.[51]

---

49 **the radiance of the buddha** (*butsu kōmyō* 佛光明): I.e. the light emanating from a buddha; the nimbus surrounding a buddha's body.

50 **there is likely this kind of sickness** (*kaku no gotoku no yamau no aran* かくのごとくのやまふのあらん): Reading the verb *yamau* やもう ("to be ill") as functioning like the noun *yamai* やまい ("illness").

51 **one may get those with the potential to transmit the dharma and hand on the work** (*dendō jugō no ki o uru koto mo ari* 傳道授業の機をうることもあり): The term *ki* 機 here likely indicates "spiritual faculties," and the phrase *ki o uru* 機をうる should probably be taken as "to get a disciple with such faculties."

25. Sound of the Stream, Form of the Mountain *Keisei sanshoku* 溪聲山色 295

There should be some who "admire the ancients" and learn; there are likely also demons who disparage [the dharma] and will not learn. We should neither love nor resent either one. How can we not deplore them, not resent them? Because those who know the three poisons as the three poisons are rare, we do not resent them.[52]

Not to mention that we should not forget our aspiration at the time we first embarked on the joyful quest for the way of the buddhas. At the time we first bring forth the mind [of bodhi], we do not seek the dharma for the sake of other people; we have discarded fame and profit. Without seeking fame or profit, we aspire only single-mindedly to gain the way and never anticipate respect or offerings from the king of the land or his great ministers. Still, now there are such causes and conditions.[53] They are not our original anticipation; they are not what we seek: to get caught up in the bonds of humans and devas is not what we anticipate.

Yet foolish people, even if they have the mind of the way, quickly forgetting their original resolve and mistakenly expecting the offerings of humans and devas, rejoice that the merit of the buddha dharma has reached them.[54] When the refuge of the king of the land and his great ministers is frequent, they think it is an expression of their way. This is one [type of] demon studying the way. Though we should not forget the mind of compassion, this is not something in which to rejoice. Have you not seen the golden words spoken by the buddha, "*even in the lifetime of the Tathāgata, there are many who are hateful and jealous*"?[55] The principle that the stupid does not know the wise, the little beast hates the great sage, is like this.

---

52 **Because those who know the three poisons as the three poisons are rare, we do not resent them** (*sandoku o sandoku to shireru tomogara mare naru ni yorite, uramizaru nari* 三毒を三毒としれるともがらまれなるによりて、うらみざるなり): Though not entirely clear, the argument here seems to be that, to the extent that we recognize that "those who know the three poisons as the three poisons are rare," we will not resent those "demons who slander the dharma." The "three poisons" are greed (*ton* 貪; S. *rāga*), anger (*shin* 瞋; S. *dveṣa*), and delusion (*chi* 癡; S. *moha*).

53 **now there are such causes and conditions** (*ima kaku no gotoku no innen ari* いまかくのごとくの因縁あり): I.e., we now find ourselves in circumstances where we may receive respect and offerings from the powerful.

54 **the merit of the buddha dharma has reached them** (*buppō no kudoku itareri* 佛法の功德いたれり): I.e., they are benefiting from their merit as Buddhist renunciants.

55 **"even in the lifetime of the Tathāgata, there are many who are hateful and jealous"** (*nyorai genzai, yū ta onshitsu* 如來現在、猶多怨嫉): From the *Lotus Sūtra* (*Miaofa lianhua jing* 妙法蓮華經, T.262.9:31b20-21).

[25:21] {1:281}

又、西天の祖師、おほく外道・二乗・國王等のためにやぶられたるを。これ外道の、すぐれたるにあらず、祖師に、遠慮なきにあらず。初祖西來よりのち、嵩山に掛錫するに、梁武もしらず、魏主もしらず。ときに兩箇のいぬあり、いはゆる、菩提流支三藏と光統律師となり。虚名邪利の、正人にふさがれんことをおそりて、あふぎて天日をくらまさんと擬するがごとくなりき。在世の達多よりもなほほはなはだし。あはれむべし、なんぢが深愛する名利は、祖師これを糞穢よりもいとふなり。かくのごとくの道理、佛法の力量の究竟せざるにはあらず、良人をほゆるいぬありとしるべし。ほゆるいぬをわづらふことなかれ、うらむることなかれ。引導の發願すべし、汝是畜生、發菩提心と施設すべし。先哲いはく、これはこれ人面畜生なり。又、歸依供養する魔類もあるべきなり。前佛いはく、不親近國王・王子・大臣・官長・婆羅門・居士。まことに佛道を學習せん人、わすれざるべき行儀なり。菩薩初學の功徳、すすむにしたがふてかさなるべし。

Again, many of the ancestral masters of Sindh in the West were destroyed by followers of other paths or the two vehicles or kings of the land — though it is not the case that the other paths were superior, or that the ancestral masters lacked circumspection.[56] After the First Ancestor came from the west, he hung up his staff at Mount Song.[57] Wu of Liang did not know him; the ruler of Wei did not know him.[58] At that time, there were two dogs, named Tripiṭaka Bodhiruci and Vinaya Mas-

---

56 **many of the ancestral masters of Sindh in the West were destroyed by followers of other paths or the two vehicles or kings of the land** (*Saiten no soshi, ooku gedō nijō kokuō tō no tame ni yaburaretaru o* 西天の祖師、おほく外道・二乗・國王等のためにやぶられたるを): The final accusative particle *o* を here suggests that Dōgen expects us to supply something like another "have you not seen?" (*mizu ya* みずや) at the beginning of this sentence. "Other paths" translates *gedō* 外道, followers of non-Buddhist religions (S. *tīrthika*); "the two vehicles" (*nijō* 二乗) refers to non-Mahāyāna Buddhists. See Supplementary Notes, s.v. "Three vehicles." While Dōgen may be exaggerating to say that "many" of the figures in the traditional list of the Indian ancestors of Zen suffered violent ends, the list does include the Fifteenth Ancestor, Kāṇadeva (*Kanadaiba* 迦那提婆), who is said to have died at the hands of his opponents among the non-Buddhist teachers; and the Twenty-fourth Ancestor, Siṃha (*Shishi* 獅子), who was beheaded by the king of Kaśmīra.

57 **After the First Ancestor came from the west, he hung up his staff at Mount Song** (*shoso seirai yori nochi, Sūzan ni kashaku suru* 初祖西來よりのち、嵩山に掛錫する): Reference to the tradition that Bodhidharma resided at Shaolin 少林, on Mount Song 嵩山, in present-day Henan province. To "hang up one's staff" (*kashaku* 掛錫) is a standard term for a monk's residence at a monastery; see Supplementary Notes, s.v. "Staff."

58 **Wu of Liang** (*Ryō Bu* 梁武); **the ruler of Wei** (*Gi shu* 魏主): I.e., the rulers of the two kingdoms into which China was divided at the time. Dōgen recounts the story of Bodhidharma's arrival in China in his "Shōbōgenzō gyōji" 正法眼藏行持, part 2. That story includes a famous interview with Emperor Wu 武, and Dōgen's statement here that the two emperors "did not know him" may allude to Emperor Wu's question in that interview, "Who are you?" and Bodhidharma's famous answer, "I don't know."

25. Sound of the Stream, Form of the Mountain *Keisei sanshoku* 溪聲山色 297

ter Guangtong.[59] Fearing that their empty fame and false profit would be obstructed by a true person, they were as if looking up and thinking to darken the sun in the sky.[60] They were worse than Datta, when [the Buddha] was in the world.[61]

How pitiful: the fame and profit you so deeply love, the Ancestral Master hates more than dung and filth. The reason for this sort of thing is not that the power of the buddha dharma is not complete; we should realize that there are dogs that bark at good people. Do not be bothered by barking dogs; do not resent them. We should make a vow to guide them; we should declare to them, "*You are beasts, but you should bring forth the mind of bodhi.*"[62] A prior wise man has said, "These are beasts with human faces."[63] Again, there must also be a class of demons that takes refuge and makes offerings.[64] The former buddha said, "*He does not approach kings of the land, princes, great ministers, officials, brahmans, or laymen.*"[65] Truly this is a practice not to be forgotten by those who

59 **Tripiṭaka Bodhiruci** (*Bodairushi sanzō* 菩提流支三藏); **Vinaya Master Guang-tong** (*Kōzu risshi* 光統律師): Bodhiruci (d. 527) was a monk from north India active as a translator in the Northern Wei capital of Loyang; Vinaya Master Guangtong was the monk Huiguang 慧光 (468-537), a contemporary of Bodhiruci, who worked with him and wrote important commentaries on the vinaya and other texts.

60 **they were as if looking up and thinking to darken the sun in the sky** (*augite tenjitsu o kuramasan to gi suru ga gotoku nariki* あふぎて天日をくらまさんと擬するがごとくなりき): Reference to the story that these two monks conspired to poison Bodhidharma (as told, e.g., at *Jingde chuandeng lu* 景德傳燈錄, T.2076.51:220a23-29).

61 **Datta, when [the Buddha] was in the world** (*zaise no Datta* 在世の達多): I.e., Devadatta, during Buddha Śākyamuni's lifetime. Gautama's cousin, Devadatta plotted to kill the Buddha and take over his community.

62 **"You are beasts, but you should bring forth the mind of bodhi"** (*nyo ze chikushō, hotsu bodai shin* 汝是畜生、發菩提心): From the *Fanwang jing* 梵網經, T.1484.24:1009a27-29:

若見牛馬猪羊一切畜生、應心念口言．汝是畜生發菩提心。而菩薩入一切處山林川野、皆使一切衆生發菩提心。

If he sees an ox, a horse, a pig, a sheep, or any beast, he should think to himself and say out loud, "You are beasts, but you should bring forth the mind of bodhi." Thus, the bodhisattva goes everywhere — the mountains, forests, rivers, and fields — and causes all living beings to bring forth the mind of bodhi.

63 **A prior wise man has said** (*sentetsu iwaku* 先哲いはく): A well-known expression, though Dōgen's source for it is unidentified.

64 **a class of demons that takes refuge and makes offerings** (*kie kuyō suru marui* 歸依供養する魔類): It is unclear whether these demons go for refuge and make offerings to the Buddhist saṃgha in general or to the "dogs" in particular. Though the connection with the next sentence is not explicit, it would seem that the list given there of those to be avoided identifies the members of this class of demons.

65 **The former buddha said, "He does not approach kings of the land, princes, great ministers, officials, brahmans, or laymen"** (*senbutsu iwaku, fushinkin kokuō*

298 DŌGEN'S *SHŌBŌGENZŌ* VOLUME II

would study the way of the buddhas. The merit of the initial practice of the bodhisattva will accumulate as one progresses.

[25:22] {1:282}

又むかしより、天帝きたりて行者の志氣を試驗し、あるひは魔波旬きたりて行者の修道をさまたぐることあり。これみな、名利の志氣はなれざるとき、この事ありき。大慈大悲のふかく、廣度衆生の願の老大なるには、これらの障導あらざるなり。修行の力量、おのづから國土をうることあり、世運の達せるに相似せることあり。かくのごとくの時節、さらにかれを辨肯すべきなり、かれに瞌睡することなかれ。愚人、これをよろこぶ、たとへば癡犬の枯骨をねぶるがごとし。賢聖、これをいとふ、たとへば世人の糞穢をおづるににたり。

Again, since ancient times, the Deva Lord has come to test the resolve of a practitioner, or Māra-pāpīyān has come to block a practitioner's training in the way.[66] These things always happened when [the practitioner] was not free from the ambition for fame and profit; where his great kindness and great compassion were deep and his vow to deliver living beings everywhere was mature, these obstacles did not occur. The power of practice sometimes naturally gains a country, sometimes resembles the achievement of worldly fortune. At such times, we should further confirm that [case]; do not doze through that.[67] Stupid people's celebrating this is like a stupid dog licking a dry bone.[68] The worthy sages hate this, as the worldly fear dung and filth.

ōji daijin kanchō baramon kōji 前佛いはく、不親近國王・王子・大臣・官長・婆羅門・居士): A slightly variant version of the advice for bodhisattvas given by Buddha Śākyamuni to Bodhisattva Mañjuśrī in the *Lotus Sūtra* (*Miaofa lianhua jing* 妙法蓮華經, T.262.9:37a21-22); the list in the sūtra ends not with "laymen" but with *nirgrantha* (*nikenshi* 尼揵子), non-Buddhist ascetics, such as the Jains.

66 **Deva Lord** (*Tentai* 天帝); **Māra-pāpīyān** (*Mahajun* 魔波旬): I.e., the deva Śakra (*Taishaku Ten* 帝釋天), or Indra, lord of the gods, who resides in Tuṣita Heaven on Mount Sumeru, and who often appears in Buddhist stories to test the sincerity of the characters; and the Deva Māra, the Evil One, in the sixth heaven of the desire realm, who seeks to interfere with the conduct of the Buddhist life. It is unclear why, in the sentence following, Dōgen limits the actions of Śakra and Māra to cases where the motives of the practitioner are questionable, since in fact the two devas do appear in the narratives of model Buddhists — as, e.g., Śakra's test of the famous Bodhisattva Sadāprarudita (*Jōtai bosatsu* 常啼菩薩), or, indeed, Māra's attack on Prince Siddhārtha himself, on the night that the prince became Buddha Śākyamuni.

67 **we should further confirm that** (*sara ni kare o benkō su beki nari* さらにかれを辨肯すべきなり): Ordinarily, one would be tempted to read this, "we should further confirm him" (i.e., one who "gains a country" or achieves what looks like "worldly fortune" through "the power of practice"); but the following *kare ni kassui su* かれに瞌睡す ("doze through that") would seem to require that we take *kare* かれ, not as the third person pronoun but as "that" [case or matter].

68 **a stupid dog licking a dry bone** (*chiken no kokotsu o neburu* 癡犬の枯骨をねぶる): Perhaps reflecting a simile found in the *Nirvāṇa Sūtra* (*Da banniepan jing* 大般涅槃

25. Sound of the Stream, Form of the Mountain *Keisei sanshoku* 溪聲山色 299

[25:23]

おほよそ初心の情量は、佛道をはからふことあたはず、測量すといへども、あたらざるなり。初心に測量モずといへども、究竟に究盡なきにあらず。徹地の堂奥は、初心の淺識にあらず。ただまさに先聖の道をふまんことを行履すべし。このとき、尋師訪道するに、梯山航海あるなり。導師をたづね、知識をねがふには、從天降下なり、從地涌出なり。その接渠のところに、有情に道取せしめ、無情に道取せしむるに、身處にきき、心處にきく。若將耳聽は家常の茶飯なりといへども、眼處聞聲、これ何必不必なり。見佛にも、自佛・他佛をもみ、大佛・小佛をみる。大佛にもおどろきおそれざれ、小佛にもあやしみわづらはざれ。いはゆる大佛・小佛を、しばらく山色溪聲と認ずるものなり。これに廣長舌あり、八萬偈あり、舉似迥脱なり、見徹獨抜なり。このゆえに、俗いはく、彌高彌堅なり。先佛いはく、彌天彌綸なり。春松の操あり、秋菊の秀ある、即是なるのみなり。

In sum, the sentiments of the beginner cannot gauge the way of the buddhas; one may measure it but will not get it right. Even though, as a beginner, one fails to measure it, it is not that ultimately it is not exhaustively investigated. The fully penetrated interior of the hall is not the shallow consciousness of the beginner.[69] One should just observe the practice of walking the path of prior sages. At this time, in *seeking out teachers and inquiring about the way*, one *ladders up mountains and boats over seas*.[70] As one visits guides and inquires of wise friends, they *descend from the heavens, they well up from the earth*.[71] Where they engage him, they make sentient beings speak, they make insentient beings

---

經, T.374.12:496b8-9) that the bodhisattva who takes pleasure in the objects of the five senses is like "a dog gnawing on a dry bone" (*quan nie kugu* 犬嚙枯骨).

69 **The fully penetrated interior of the hall** (*tetchi no dōō* 徹地の堂奥): The translation takes the term *tetchi* 徹地, which Dōgen uses elsewhere in the sense to "penetrate to the ground," as an adjective here; the "interior of the hall" is a common expression for the "inner sanctum" of Zen.

70 **ladders up mountains and boats over seas** (*teizan kōkai* 梯山航海): A fixed expression for the student's quest, sometimes in reverse order (*kōkai teizan* 航海梯山).

71 **visits guides and inquires of wise friends** (*dōshi o tazune, chishiki o negau* 導師をたづね、知識をねがふ): I.e., seeks out teachers. "Wise friend" (*chishiki* 知識, or, as below, *zenchishiki* 善知識), is a standard term throughout Buddhism for a spiritual advisor.

they descend from the heavens, they well up from the earth (*jūten kōge nari, jūchi yushutsu nari* 從天降下なり、從地涌出なり): Two fixed phrases often found together in Zen texts; since he quotes just below from the same passage, Dōgen likely had as his source here a teaching of Yunju Daoying 雲居道膺 (d. 902) (*Liandeng huiyao* 聯燈會要, ZZ.136:797a6):

從天降下則貧寒、從地涌出則富貴。

Descending from heaven, they're impoverished;
Welling up from the earth, they're privileged.

The latter phrase (also written *jūchi yōshutsu* 從地踊出) is the title of the chapter of the *Lotus Sūtra* in which a huge legion of bodhisattvas dedicated to maintaining the sūtra emerge from the earth (*Miaofa lianhua jing* 妙法蓮華經, T.262.9:39c18).

300   DŌGEN'S *SHŌBŌGENZŌ* VOLUME II

speak; and one hears them with the body and hears them with the mind. "*Using the ears to hear*" is everyday tea and rice, but "*when the eyes hear the voices,*" this is "*why is it necessary? It's not necessary.*"[72]

In seeing the buddha as well, one sees both one's own buddha and the buddha of others, sees a great buddha and a small buddha. Do not be surprised or frightened by the great buddha; do not be suspicious of or troubled by the small buddha. The "great buddha and small buddha" here are what we are for now recognizing as "the mountain form and stream sound." In them are "his long broad tongue" and the "eighty thousand gāthās"; "to tell" them is "far off and free"; to see through them is "*alone and removed.*"[73] Therefore, the secular say, "*ever higher, ever harder.*"[74] A former buddha said, "*it fills the heavens; it fills everywhere.*"[75] That

---

72   **"Using the ears to hear"** (*nyaku shō ni chō* 若將耳聽); **"when the eyes hear the voices"** (*gensho mon shō* 眼處聞聲: From a verse by Dongshan Liangjie 洞山良价 (807-869) that Dōgen discusses in his "Shōbōgenzō mujō seppō" 正法眼藏無情説法. The verse occurs, e.g., at *Jingde chuandeng lu* 景德傳燈録, T.2076.51:321c10-11:

也太奇、也太奇、無情説法不思議、若將耳聽終難會、眼處聞聲方得知。

How strange! How strange!
The insentient preaching the dharma is inconceivable.
If we use our ears to hear it, it's hard in the end to understand;
Only when our eyes hear the voices do we know it.

everyday tea and rice (*kajō no sahan* 家常の茶飯): Japanese version of a fairly common expression, in both Zen texts and Dōgen's writings, for the "daily fare" of the home, or "normal practice"; see Supplementary Notes.

"why is it necessary? It's not necessary" (*ka hitsu fu hitsu* 何必不必): Or "What's the need? There's no need." A fixed pattern; it is unclear if Dōgen had a particular example of its use in mind. Perhaps, to be taken here as indicating the indeterminacy or transcendent quality of what is said by the voices heard by the eyes.

73   **"to tell" them is "far off and free"; to see through them is "alone and removed"** (*koji kyōdatsu nari, kentetsu dokubatsu nari* 舉似迴脱なり、見徹獨拔なり): A loose translation: *kyōdatsu dokubatsu* 迴脱獨拔 (usually written 迥脱獨拔), meaning something like "distantly liberated, extricated in solitude," comes from a saying of Yunju Daoying 雲居道膺 (*Liandeng huiyao* 聯燈會要, ZZ.136:797a8):

一言迴脱獨拔當時、言語不要多、多即無用處。

When a single word is distantly liberated, extricated in solitude, one doesn't need many words; many are useless.

Dōgen also draws on this passage in his "Shōbōgenzō gyōbutsu iigi" 正法眼藏行佛威儀. "To tell" (*koji* 舉似) here would seem to refer back to the last line of Su Dongpo's poem:

他日如何舉似人

How will I tell them tomorrow?

74   **"ever higher, ever harder"** (*mikō miken* 彌高彌堅): Said of Confucius' teachings by his student Yan Hui 顔回 in the *Lunyu* 論語 9 (Zi Han 子罕; KR.1h0005.005.4b).

75   **"it fills the heavens; it fills everywhere"** (*miten mirin* 彌天彌綸): Both these phrases occur throughout the Buddhist canon (the latter, sometimes written 彌淪), and it is not clear whether Dōgen had a particular source in mind — or, indeed, whether his "former

25. Sound of the Stream, Form of the Mountain *Keisei sanshoku* 渓聲山色 301

the spring pine has constancy, and the autumn chrysanthemum has elegance, is nothing but precisely this.

[25:24] {1:283}

善知識この田地にいたらんとき、人天の大師なるべし。いまだこの田地に
いたらず、みだりに爲人の儀を存せん、人天の大賊なり。春松しらず、秋
菊みざらん。なにの草料かあらん、いかが根源を截斷せん。

When the wise friend reaches this field, he will be a great teacher of humans and devas.[76] One who arbitrarily adopts a demeanor for the sake of others without having reached this field, is a great thief of humans and devas. He does not know the spring pine; he does not see the autumn chrysanthemum. What fodder could he have? How could he cut off the root source?[77]

[25:25]

又、心も肉も、懈怠にもあり、不信にもあらんには、誠心をもはらして、
前佛に懺悔すべし。恁麼するとき、前佛懺悔の功德力、われをすくひて清
淨ならしむ。この功德、よく無礙の淨信・精進を生長せしむるなり。淨信
一現するとき、自他おなじく轉ぜらるるなり。その利益、あまねく情・非
情にかぶらしむ。その大旨は、願は、われたとひ過去の惡業おほくかさな
りて、障道の因緣ありとも、佛道によりて得道せりし諸佛諸祖、われをあ
はれみて、業累を解脱せしめ、學道さはりなからしめ、その功德法門、あ
まねく無盡法界に充満彌綸せざらん、あはれみをわれに分布すべし。佛祖
の往昔は吾等なり、吾等が當來は佛祖ならん。佛祖を仰觀すれば一佛祖な
り、發心を觀想するにも一發心なるべし。あはれみを七通八達せんに、得
便宜なり、落便宜なり。

Again, both the mind and flesh may flag, may lose faith; in such cases, with sincere mind, one should repent before the buddha. At such times, the power of the merit of repenting before the buddha will save us and

---

buddha" (*senbutsu* 先佛) here refers to Buddha Śākyamuni or to a Chan ancestor. The translation obscures the parallel with Yan Hui's remark, with the graph *mi* 彌 functioning in the former case as an adverb ("ever more") and in the latter as a verb ("to fill").

76 **When the wise friend reaches this field** (*zenchishiki kono denchi ni itaran toki* 善知識この田地にいたらんとき): The agricultural term *denchi* (also read *denji*; "paddy field") is often used in Zen texts for a realm of discourse or state of mind; occurs with some frequency in the *Shōbōgenzō*.

77 **What fodder could he have?** (*nani no sōryō ka aran* なにの草料かあらん); **How could he cut off the root source?** (*ikaga kongen o setsudan sen* いかが根源を截斷せん): Two classical vegetative images, no doubt meant to accompany the preceding pine and chrysanthemum: the former introduces the "fodder" (*sōryō* 草料) regularly used in reference to the subject of Zen discussion — somewhat as we might say "food for thought"; the latter alludes to a line in the *Zhengdao ge* 證道歌, attributed to the early Chan figure Yongjia Xuanjue 永嘉玄覺 (d. 723) (T.2014:48.395c21-22):

直截根源佛所印。

Directly cutting off the root source — this is sealed by the Buddha.

302 DŌGEN'S *SHŌBŌGENZŌ* VOLUME II

make us pure. This merit will grow a pure faith and vigor without obstacles. When pure faith once appears, self and other are equally turned by it. Its benefits cover the sentient and the insentient everywhere. The gist is [as follows]:

> I pray that, although I have accumulated evil deeds in the past and have causes and conditions that obstruct the way, the buddhas and ancestors who have gained the way through the way of the buddhas, taking pity on me, will liberate me from the bonds of my deeds and remove my hindrances to studying the way; that their merit and dharma gates will fill and pervade everywhere the inexhaustible dharma realm, and that they will share their compassion with me.[78]

The buddhas and ancestors were us in the past; we will be buddhas and ancestors in the future. When we look up at the buddhas and ancestors, it is one buddha and ancestor; and when we contemplate their bringing forth the mind [of bodhi], it is one bringing forth of the mind.[79] As they extend their compassion through seven passes and eight arrivals, we gain an advantage, we *lose the advantage*.[80]

[25:26] {1:284}

このゆえに、龍牙のいはく、昔生未了今須了、此生度取累生身、古佛未悟同今者、悟了今人即古人。しづかにこの因縁を参究すべし、これ證佛の承當なり。

Therefore, Longya said,[81]

78　**their merit and dharma gates will fill and pervade everywhere the inexhaustible dharma realm** (*sono kudoku hōmon, amaneku mujin hokkai ni jūman mirin sezaran* その功徳法門、あまねく無盡法界に充満彌綸せざらん): Reading *sezaran* as *seran*, in keeping with most editions.

79　**one buddha and ancestor** (*ichi busso* 一佛祖); **one bringing forth of the mind** (*ichi hosshin* 一發心): Likely reflecting the previous sentence: we are (at least potentially) one with the buddhas and ancestors, and their bringing forth of the thought of bodhi is no different from our own.

80　**As they extend their compassion through seven passes and eight arrivals, we gain an advantage, we lose the advantage** (*awaremi o shittsū hattatsu sen ni, toku bengi nari, raku bengi nari* あはれみを七通八達せんに、得便宜なり、落便宜なり): Dōgen has here made a transitive verb of the expression "seven passes and eight arrivals" (*shittsū hattatsu* 七通八達), commonly used in the sense of "complete understanding," or "total mastery," but here more likely expressing expansion throughout space. "To gain an advantage" (*toku bengi* 得便宜) and "to lose the advantage" (*raku bengi* 落便宜) are fixed expressions, often occurring together in the context of the give and take of Zen repartee; sometimes read here to mean that one benefits from the compassion of the buddhas and ancestors without intentionally or consciously taking advantage of it.

81　**Longya** (*Ryūge* 龍牙): I.e., Longya Judon 龍牙居遁 (835-923), disciple of Dongshan Liangjie 洞山良价. His verse can be found at *Chanmen zhuzushi jisong* 禪門諸祖師偈頌, ZZ.116:923b12-13.

25. Sound of the Stream, Form of the Mountain *Keisei sanshoku* 溪聲山色 303

What in past lives we have not finished, now we should finish.
In this life, we can deliver the bodies of accumulated lives.
When the old buddhas were not yet awakened, they were the same as those now.
Once awakened, people now will be the people of old.

We should quietly investigate this case; it is what is assented to as the verification of buddhahood.[82]

[25:27]

かくのごとく懺悔すれば、かならず佛祖の冥助あるなり。心念身儀發露白佛すべし、發露のちから、罪根をして銷殞せしむるなり。これ一色の正修行なり、正信心なり、正信身なり。正修行のとき、溪聲溪色・山色山聲、ともに八萬四千偈を、をしまざるなり。自己もし名利身心を不惜すれば、溪山また恁麼の不惜あり。たとひ溪聲山色、八萬四千偈を現成せしめ、現成せしめざることは、夜來なりとも、溪山の、溪山を擧似する盡力未便ならんは、たれかなんぢを溪聲山色と見聞せん。

When one repents in this way, one will invariably have the unseen aid of the buddhas and ancestors. We should expose and announce to the buddha the thoughts of our minds and the conduct of our bodies: the power of exposure causes the roots of our offenses to be destroyed. This is right practice of a single color; it is the mind of right faith; it is the body of right faith.[83]

When we have right practice, "*the sound of the stream*" *and the form of the stream*, "*the form of the mountain*" *and the sound of the mountain* — none begrudge the "eighty-four thousand gāthās." When self does not begrudge the body and mind of fame and profit, the stream and mountain are also ungrudging in this way.[84] "This evening" may be one in which the "*sound of the stream*" *and* "*the form of the mountain*" manifest or do not manifest the "eighty-four thousand gāthās"; but, were the stream and the mountain to *exhaust their strength without success* in "telling them"

---

82 **this case** (*kono innen* この因縁): The referent of "case" (usually used in reference to a story, or episode) is not obvious here; perhaps, the case in which we are like the buddhas before their awakening, and they are like us after our awakening.

what is assented to as the verification of buddhahood (*shōbutsu no jōtō* 證佛の承當): A tentative translation of a phrase variously interpreted but perhaps meaning simply, "how buddhahood is understood"; it might also be read "what verified buddhas assent to."

83 **right practice of a single color** (*isshiki no shō shugyō* 一色の正修行): The term *isshiki* 一色 ("one color") here likely has the sense "pure" (i.e., "unmixed"), a usage akin to the phrase *isshiki shi bendō* 一色之辨道 ("pursuit of the way of a single color") found elsewhere in Dōgen's writings.

84 **the body and mind of fame and profit** (*myōri shinjin* 名利身心): A combination not encountered elsewhere in Dōgen writings, it could also be interpreted as "fame and profit, body and mind." See Supplementary Notes, s.v. "Body and mind."

DŌGEN'S *SHŌBŌGENZŌ* VOLUME II

of the stream and mountain, who would see and hear you as the sound of the stream and form of the mountain?[85]

正法眼藏渓聲山色第二十五
Treasury of the True Dharma Eye
Sound of the Stream, Form of the Mountain
Number 25

[Ryūmonji MS:]

爾時延應庚子結制後五日、在觀音導利興聖寶林寺示衆
Presented to the assembly at Kannon Dōri Kōshō Hōrin Monastery; the fifth day following the binding of the rule, senior metal year of the rat, in En'ō [13 May 1240][86]

[Tōunji MS:]

寛元癸卯結制前佛誕生日、在同寺侍司書寫之。懐奘
Copied at the acolyte's office of the same monastery; on the birthday of the Buddha, before the binding of the rule, junior water year of the rabbit, in Kangen [28 April 1243]. Ejō

---

85   **were the stream and the mountain to exhaust their strength without success in "telling them" of the stream and mountain, who would see and hear you as the sound of the stream and form of the mountain?** (*keisan no, keisan o koji suru jinriki miben naran wa, tare ka nanji o keisei sanshoku to kenmon sen* 溪山の、溪山を擧似する盡力未便ならんは、たれかなんぢを溪聲山色と見聞せん): A rather convoluted sentence apparently meaning that we experience the sound of the stream and the form of the mountain because the stream and mountain tell us about them. "Tell them" (*koji* 擧似) is again drawn from the final line of Su Dongpo's verse; "you" translates *nanji* なんぢ, a form of the second person used by a commentator to address the speakers in a passage, here presumably used for the stream and mountain.

86   The Tōunji 洞雲寺 MS shares an identical colophon.

binding of the rule (*kessei* 結制): I.e., the opening of the summer retreat (*ango* 安居).

TREASURY OF THE TRUE DHARMA EYE

NUMBER 26

Beyond the Buddha
Butsu kōjō ji

佛向上事

Beyond the Buddha

Butsu kōjō ji

INTRODUCTION

This work was produced at Kōshōji, in April 1242, near the beginning of a period of intense productivity during which, if we are to believe their colophons, Dōgen was composing a *Shōbōgenzō* chapter on an average of one per week. "Butsu kōjō ji" represents number 26 in both the seventy-five and sixty-chapter compilations of the *Shōbōgenzō* and number 28 in the Honzan edition. This chapter is not to be confused with another work (translated below as Variant Text 3) with the same title but quite different content.

As its title suggests, the present text deals with the notion that the way of the Zen masters transcends the traditional categories of Buddhism — a notion famously expressed in the sayings of the ninth-century master Dongshan Liangjie 洞山良价, founder of Dōgen's Sōtō lineage, that there is "something beyond the buddha" (*butsu kōjō ji* 佛向上事) or "someone beyond the buddha" (*butsu kōjō nin* 佛向上人). In his essay, Dōgen offers his comments on nine examples of sayings, by Dongshan and others, that use the term *kōjō* 向上 (variously rendered here "beyond," "above," or "higher").

307

正法眼藏第二十六
Treasury of the True Dharma Eye
Number 26

佛向上事
Beyond the Buddha

[26:1] {1:285}

高祖筠州洞山悟本大師は、潭州雲巌山無住大師の親嫡嗣なり、如來より三
十八位の祖向上なり、自己より向上三十八位の祖なり。

The Eminent Ancestor, Great Master Wuben of Mount Dong, in Yun-zhou, was the close legitimate heir of Great Master Wuzhu of Mount Yunyan, in Tanzhou; from the Tathāgata, he is the thirty-eighth beyond the ancestors; he is the ancestor of the thirty-eight beyond him.[1]

---

1 **The Eminent Ancestor, Great Master Wuben of Mount Dong, in Yunzhou** (*Kōso Inshū Tōzan Gohon daishi* 高祖筠州洞山悟本大師): I.e., Dongshan Liangjie 洞山良价 (807-869), a disciple of Yunyan Tansheng 雲巌曇晟 (782-841); his biography appears at *Jingde chuandeng lu* 景德傳燈録, T.2076.51:321b20. "Great Master Wuben" (*Gohon daishi* 悟本大師) is a posthumous title; "Eminent Ancestor" (*kōso* 高祖) is an honorific recognizing Dongshan as founder of the Caodong (*Sōtō* 曹洞) lineage. Yunzhou (*Inshū* 筠州) is in present-day Jiangxi, the site of Mount Dong.

close legitimate heir (*shin tekishi* 親嫡嗣): An unusual expression, not encountered elsewhere in Dōgen's writings, perhaps meaning "immediate descendant."

Great Master Wuzhu of Mount Yunyan, in Tanzhou (*Tanshū Unganzan Mujū daishi* 潭州雲巌山無住大師): I.e., Dongshan's master, Yunyan Tansheng 雲巌曇晟, disciple of Yaoshan Weiyan 藥山惟儼 (751-834). "Great Master Wuzhu" (*Mujū daishi* 無住大師) is a posthumous title. Tanzhou is in present-day Hunan, the site of Mount Yunyan.

from the Tathāgata, he is the thirty-eighth beyond the ancestors; he is the ancestor of the thirty-eight beyond him (*nyorai yori sanjūhachi i no so kōjō nari, jiko yori kōjō sanjūhachi i no so nari* 如來より三十八位の祖向上なり、自己より向上三十八位の祖なり): A tentative translation of an odd locution, presumably meaning that Dong-shan represents the thirty-eighth generation of Zen ancestors after Buddha Śākyamuni, all of whom have transcended their status as ancestors. The phrase "beyond the ances-tors" (*so kōjō* 祖向上) is a construction, found elsewhere in Zen writings, paralleling the more common "beyond the buddha" (*butsu kōjō* 佛向上) of our title; see Supplementary Notes, s.v. "Beyond the buddha." The interpretation of the second phrase here is tenta-tive: it is sometimes read, "[The Tathāgata] is the ancestor thirty-eighth beyond him," and might also be parsed, "The thirty-eighth ancestor beyond himself."

DŌGEN'S *SHŌBŌGENZŌ* VOLUME II

[26:2]

大師、有時示衆云、體得佛向上事、方有些子語話分。僧便問、如何是語
話。大師云、語話時闍黎不聞。僧曰、和尚還聞否。大師云、待我不語話時
即聞。

> On one occasion, the Great Master addressed the assembly, saying,
> "When you've experienced what's beyond the buddha, then you're in
> a position to talk a bit."[2]
>
> A monk asked, "What is this talk?"
>
> The Great Master said, "When talking, the Ācārya doesn't hear it."[3]
>
> The monk said, "Then does the Reverend hear it?"
>
> The Great Master said, "Once I'm not talking; then I hear it."[4]

[26:3]

いまいふところの佛向上事の道、大師その本祖なり。自餘の佛祖は、大師
の道を參學しきたり、佛向上事を體得するなり。まさにしるべし、佛向上
事は、在因にあらず果滿にあらず。しかあれども、語話時の不聞を體得
し、參徹することあるなり。佛向上にいたらざれば、佛向上を體得する
ことなし。語話にあらざれば、佛向上事を體得せず。相顯にあらず、相隱
にあらず、相與にあらず、相奪にあらず。このゆえに、語話現成のとき、
これ佛向上事なり。佛向上事現成のとき、闍黎不聞なり。闍黎不聞といふ
は、佛向上事自不聞なり、語話時闍黎不聞なり。しるべし、語話それ聞に
染汚せず、不聞に染汚せず。このゆえに、聞・不聞に不相干なり。

The Great Master is the original ancestor of the saying, "what's beyond the buddha," being discussed here.[5] Other buddhas and ancestors
have been studying the words of the Great Master and have "experienced
what's beyond the buddha."[6] We should realize that "what's beyond the

---

2   **On one occasion, the Great Master addressed the assembly** (*daishi, uji jishu* 大師、有時示衆): An anecdote found in the *Jingde chuandeng lu* 景德傳燈
錄 (T.2076.51:322b29-c3); as well as Dōgen's *shinji Shōbōgenzō* 眞字正法眼藏
(DZZ.5:132, case 12).

"position" (*bun* 分): I.e., "status," "qualifications."

3   **"When talking, the Ācārya doesn't hear it"** (*gowa ji jari fumon* 語話時闍黎不聞):
"Ācārya" (*jari* 闍黎; also written 闍梨), a transliteration of a Sanskrit term for "teacher,"
or "preceptor," is regularly used in direct address to a monk. The subject of "talk" here
is unexpressed; hence, the translation could be read, "when you're talking" or "when
I'm talking."

4   **"Once I'm not talking; then I hear it"** (*tai ga fugowa ji soku mon* 待我不語話
時即聞): The subject of the verb "hear" is unexpressed; hence, an alternative translation
could be, "once I'm not talking, then you'll hear it."

5   **the original ancestor of the saying, "what's beyond the buddha"** (*butsu kōjōji
no dō, daishi sono honso nari* 佛向上事の道、大師その本祖なり): I.e., Dongshan orig-
inated the saying, "what's beyond the buddha."

6   **"experienced what's beyond the buddha"** (*butsu kōjōji o taitoku suru* 佛向上事を
體得する): Dōgen here simply puts Dongshan's words above into Japanese grammar.

26. Beyond the Buddha *Butsu kōjō ji* 佛向上事

buddha" is not remaining at the cause, is not fulfilling the effect.[7] Nevertheless, there is the experience, and the mastery, of "not hearing" "when I'm talking." When we do not reach "beyond the buddha," we do not have the "experience of beyond the buddha"; when we are "not talking," we do not "experience what's beyond the buddha." They do not reveal each other; they do not conceal each other.[8] They do not give to each other; they do not take from each other. Therefore, when "talking" occurs, this is "what's beyond the buddha." When "what's beyond the buddha" occurs, "the Ācārya doesn't hear it." To say that "the Ācārya doesn't hear it" is "*what's beyond the buddha" itself "doesn't hear it,*" is "*when I'm talking, the Ācārya doesn't hear it.*" We should realize that "talking" is not defiled by "hearing," not defiled by "not hearing." Therefore, "hearing" and "not hearing" are not concerned with each other.

[26:4] {1:286}

不聞裏藏闍黎なり、語話裏藏闍黎なりとも、逢人・不逢人、恁麼・不恁麼なり。闍黎語話時、すなはち闍黎不聞なり。その不聞たらくの宗旨は、舌骨に罣礙せられて不聞なり、耳裏に罣礙せられて不聞なり、眼睛に照穿せられて不聞なり、身心に塞却せられて不聞なり。しかあるゆゑに不聞なり。これらを拈じてさらに語話とすべからず、不聞すなはち語話なるにあらず、語話時不聞なるのみなり。高祖道の語話時闍黎不聞は、語話の道頭道尾は、如藤倚藤なりとも、語話纏語話なるべし、語話に罣礙せらる。

While "*the Ācārya" is concealed within "not hearing,*" and "*the Ācārya" is concealed within "talking,*" they are meeting someone and not meeting someone, are like this and not like this.[9] When the Ācārya is talking, "the Ācārya doesn't hear it." The essential point of his not hearing is that he is obstructed by the tongue and "doesn't hear it"; he

---

7 **remaining at the cause** (*zai'in* 在因); **fulfilling the effect** (*kaman* 果滿): I.e., Buddhist practice and its fruition.

8 **They do not reveal each other; they do not conceal each other** (*sōken ni arazu, sōon ni arazu* 相顯にあらず、相隱にあらず): Here and in the following sentence, the point would seem to be that "talking" and "what's beyond the buddha" are not two separate concepts.

9 **"the Ācārya" is concealed within "not hearing," and "the Ācārya" is concealed within "talking"** (*fumonri zō jari nari, gowari zō jari nari* 不聞裏藏闍黎なり、語話裏藏闍黎なり): Generally taken to mean that there is no Ācārya apart from the two states of "not hearing" and "talking."

they are meeting someone and not meeting someone, are like this and not like this (*hōnin fuhōnin, inmo fuinmo nari* 逢人・不逢人、恁麼・不恁麼なり): The grammatical subject is unstated; the translation takes it as the two "concealments" of the preceding clause. On this reading, the point would seem to be that the two states of "talking" and "not hearing" in which the Ācārya is "concealed" are analogous respectively to "meeting" and "not meeting," "like this" and "not like this" — expressing, perhaps, the relative and absolute perspectives repectively. (See, e.g., *Shōbōgenzō keiteki* 正法眼藏啓迪 2:602.)

DŌGEN'S *SHŌBŌGENZŌ* VOLUME II

is obstructed by the ear and "doesn't hear it"; he is illumined by the eye and "doesn't hear it"; he is blocked by body and mind and "doesn't hear it."[10] Because of this, he "doesn't hear it." We should not go on to take these as "talking": it is not the case that "not hearing" is "talking"; it is just that "when talking, he doesn't hear it." In these words by the Eminent Ancestor — "*When talking, the Ācārya doesn't hear it*" — while the head and tail of "talking" are like vines relying on vines, "talking" should entwine "talking" and be obstructed by "talking."[11]

[26:5]

僧いはく、和尚還聞否。いはゆるは、和尚を擧して聞語話と擬するにあらず、擧聞さらに和尚にあらず、語話にあらざるがゆえに。しかあれども、いま僧の擬議するところは、語話時に即聞を參學すべしやいなやの咨參するなり。たとへば、語話すなはち語話なりやと聞取せんと擬し、還聞これ還聞なりやと聞取せんと擬するなり。しかもかくのごとくいふとも、なんぢが舌頭にあらず。

The monk said, "*Then does the Reverend hear it?*" What this is saying is not taking up "the Reverend" and trying to "hear" the "talking"; for the "hearing" he takes up is by no means "the Reverend" or the "talking."[12] Rather, what the monk is considering here is instruction on whether or not he should study "then I hear it" in "when I'm talking."[13]

---

10 **obstructed by the tongue** (*zekkotsu ni gaige serarete* 舌骨に导礙せられて): The term *zekkotsu* 舌骨 ("tongue bone") literally refers to the hyoid at the base of the tongue. Dōgen regularly uses the expression "to be obstructed" (*gaige seraru* 导礙せらる; also *keige seraru* 罣礙せらる) in the sense "to be defined by," "to be identified with."

illumined by the eye (*ganzei ni shōsen serarete* 眼睛に照穿せられて): The exact sense of the term *shōsen* 照穿 (literally, "illumine and pierce"), is unclear; it does not occur elsewhere in Dōgen's writings and is not common in the Chinese Chan texts.

11 **while the head and tail of "talking" are like vines relying on vines** (*gowa no dōzu dōbi wa, nyo tō i tō nari tomo* 語話の道頭道尾は、如藤倚藤なりとも): Perhaps meaning something like, "we can describe the 'talking' in Dongshan's saying as 'like vines relying on vines,' but [we can also say] . . . ." "Like vines relying on vines" (*nyo tō i tō* 如藤倚藤) represents a variant of a common saying; see Supplementary Notes, s.v. "Like vines relying on a tree."

"talking" should entwine "talking" (*gowa ten gowa* 語話纏語話): Recalling a saying of Dōgen's master, Tiantong Rujing 天童如淨 (1162-1227) quoted elsewhere in the *Shōbōgenzō*; see Supplementary Notes, s.v. "The bottle gourd vine entwines the bottle gourd."

12 **the "hearing" he takes up is by no means "the Reverend" or the "talking"** (*komon sara ni oshō ni arazu, gowa ni arazaru* 擧聞さらに和尚にあらず、語話にあらざる): I.e., the monk's question about hearing does not concern the subject ("the Reverend") or the object (the "talking") of hearing.

13 **should study "then I hear it" in "when I'm talking"** (*gowa ji ni sokumon o sangaku su beshi* 語話時に即聞を參學すべし): I.e., should understand the "hearing" and "talking" as concurrent (or, perhaps, as not different).

26. Beyond the Buddha *Butsu kōjō ji* 佛向上事　　311

For example, he is thinking to hear whether the "talking" is "talking"; he is thinking to hear whether "hearing it" is "hearing it."[14] Still, while we may say this, it isn't your tongue.[15]

[26:6] {1:287}

洞山高祖道の待我不語話時即聞、あきらかに參究すべし。いはゆる、語話のとき、さらに即聞あらず。即聞の現成は、不語話のときなるべし。いたづらに不語話のときをさしおきて、不語話をまつにはあらざるなり。即聞のとき、語話を傍觀とするにあらず、眞箇に傍觀なるがゆえに。即聞のとき、語話さりて一邊の那裏に存取せるにあらず。語話のとき、即聞したしく語話の眼睛裏に藏身して霹靂するにあらず。しかあればすなはち、たとひ闍黎にても、語話時は不聞なり。たとひ我にても、不語話時即聞なる、これ方有些子語話分なり、これ體得佛向上事なり。たとへば、語話時即聞を體得するなり。このゆえに、待我不語話時即聞なり。しかありといへども、佛向上事は、七佛已前事にあらず、七佛向上事なり。

We should clearly study the words of the eminent ancestor of Mount Dong, *"Once I'm not talking, then I hear it."* It says that, at the time he is "talking," there is no "then I hear it"; the occurrence of "then I hear it" is when he is "not talking." It is not that he sets aside the time when he is "not talking" and waits in vain for "not talking."[16] It is not that he treats "talking" as an onlooker at the time of "then I hear it"; for it is truly an onlooker.[17] It is not that, at the time of "then I hear it," "talking" has gone off to stay over there to one side.[18] It is not that, when "I'm talking," "then I hear it" is a clap of thunder hiding itself within the

---

14　**he is thinking to hear whether "hearing it" is "hearing it"** (*genmon kore genmon nari ya to monshu sen to gi suru nari* 還聞これ還聞なりやと聞取せんと擬するなり): The translation "hearing it" here loses Dōgen's use of the neologism *genmon* 還聞 from the monk's question, *gen mon hi* 還聞否 (*mata kiku ya ina ya* また聞くやいなや; "then, do [you] hear it?"). Dōgen will repeat this type of word play below with the term *sokumon* 即聞 ("then [I'll] hear it").

15　**it isn't your tongue** (*nanji ga zettō ni arazu* なんぢが舌頭にあらず): Generally taken to mean "it [i.e., the real issue here] is beyond what you [i.e., the monk] can express."

16　**It is not that he sets aside the time when he is "not talking" and waits in vain for "not talking"** (*itazura ni fugowa no toki o sashiokite, fugowa o matsu ni wa arazaru nari* いたづらに不語話のときをさしおきて、不語話をまつにはあらざるなり): Perhaps to be understood in the sense that he is not positing a separate time of "not talking" when he will hear it.

17　**for it is truly an onlooker** (*shinko ni bōkan naru ga yue ni* 眞箇に傍觀なるがゆえに): The grammatical subject is unstated; most readers take it as "talking." While Dōgen usually uses "onlooker" (*bōkan* 傍觀) in reference to a mere bystander, "truly an onlooker" may suggest the thing in itself, without reference to another. (See, e.g., *Shōbōgenzō keiteki* 正法眼藏啓迪 2:615.)

18　**"talking" has gone off to stay over there to one side** (*gowa sarite ippen no nari ni zonshu seru* 語話さりて一邊の那裏に存取せる): I.e., the moment of his "hearing it" has left "talking" behind.

eye of "talking."[19] This being the case, whether in regard to the Ācārya, who does not hear it when I talk, or in regard to the I of "*Once I'm not talking; then I hear it*," this is "*then you're in a position to talk a bit*"; this is "*when you've experienced what's beyond the buddha*." For example, it is to experience "*when I talk, then I hear it*." Hence, it is "*Once I'm not talking; then I hear it*." So it may be, but "what's beyond the buddha" is not what is prior to the seven buddhas; it is what is beyond the seven buddhas.[20]

* * * * *

[26:7]

高祖悟本大師、示衆云、須知有佛向上人。時有僧問、如何是佛向上人。大師云、非佛。雲門云、名不得狀不得、所以言非。保福云、佛非。法眼云、方便呼爲佛。

> The Eminent Ancestor, Great Master Wuben, addressed the assembly, saying, "You should know that there's someone beyond the buddha."[21]
>
> At that time, a monk asked, "What is this 'someone beyond the buddha'?"
>
> The Great Master said, "Not the buddha."
>
> Yunmen said, "He can't get its name, he can't get its state; so, he says it's 'not.'"
>
> Baofu said, "Buddha is 'not.'"
>
> Fayan said, "As an expedient, he's called 'the buddha.'"

[26:8]

おほよそ佛祖の向上に佛祖なるは、高祖洞山なり。そのゆえは、餘外の佛面祖面おほしといへども、いまだ佛向上の道は、夢也未見なり。德山・臨濟等には、爲説すとも承當すべからず。巖頭・雪峰等は、粉碎其身すとも喫拳すべからず。高祖道の體得佛向上事、方有些子語話分、および須知有

---

19   **a clap of thunder hiding itself within the eye of "talking"** (*shitashiku gowa no ganzeiri ni zōshin shite byakuryaku suru* したしく語話の眼睛裏に藏身して霹靂する): I.e., his "hearing it" is already latent within his talking. For the meanings of "eye" (*ganzei* 眼睛) in Zen texts, see Supplementary Notes, s.v. "Eye."

20   **the seven buddhas** (*shichi butsu* 七佛): I.e., the series of buddhas of the past ending with Buddha Śākyamuni; see Supplementary Notes, s.v. "Seven buddhas."

21   **The Eminent Ancestor, Great Master Wuben, addressed the assembly** (*Kōso Gohon daishi, jishu* 高祖悟本大師、示衆): The exchange between Dongshan and the monk, together with the comment of Yunmen Wenyen 雲門文偃 (864-949), resembles a discussion of "what's beyond the buddha" (as opposed to "someone beyond the buddha") in Dōgen's *shinji Shōbōgenzō* 眞字正法眼藏 (DZZ.5:162, case 72), perhaps taken from the *Zhengfayanzang* 正法眼藏 of Dahui Zonggao 大慧宗杲 (1089-1163) (ZZ.118:11b9-10). For a likely source of the version given here, see Supplementary Notes, s.v. "Beyond the buddha."

26. Beyond the Buddha *Butsu kōjō ji* 佛向上事 313

佛向上人等は、ただ一二三四五の三阿僧祇・百大劫の修證のみにては證究
すべからず。まさに玄路の參學あるもの、その分あるべし。

The buddha and ancestor who is beyond the buddhas and ancestors is
the Eminent Ancestor Dongshan. The reason is that, though there may
be many other buddha faces and ancestor faces, the saying "beyond the
buddha," they have not seen even in their dreams. The likes of Deshan
or Linji, though we teach it to them, would not accede to it; the likes of
Yantou or Xuefeng, though they pulverize their bodies, would not taste
the fist.[22] The sayings of the Eminent Ancestor, such as *"when you've
experienced what's beyond the buddha, then you're in a position to talk a
bit,"* or *"you should know that there's someone beyond the buddha,"* will
not be thoroughly verified merely in practice and verification over one,
two, three, four, or five threefold *asaṃkhyeya* and one hundred great
kalpas.[23] Truly, only those who have the study of the dark road are in
that position.[24]

[26:9] {1:288}

すべからく佛向上人ありとしるべし。いはゆるは、弄精魂の活計なり。し
かありといへども、古佛を擧してしり、拳頭を擧起してしる。すでに恁麼
見得するがごときは、有佛向上人をしり、無佛向上人をしる。而今の示衆
は、佛向上人となるべしとにあらず、佛向上人と相見すべしとにあらず、
ただしばらく佛向上人ありとしるべしとなり。この關棙子を使得するがご
ときは、まさに有佛向上人を不知するなり、無佛向上人を不知するなり。
その佛向上人、これ非佛なり。いかならんか非佛、と疑著せられんとき、

---

22 **Deshan or Linji** (*Tokusan Rinzai* 德山・臨濟); **Yantou or Xuefeng** (*Gantō Seppō*
巖頭・雪峰): I.e., Deshan Xuanjian 德山宣鑑 (780-865) or Linji Yixuan 臨濟義玄 (d.
866); Yantou Quanhuo 巖頭全豁 (828-887) or Xuefeng Yicun 雪峰義存 (822-908), two
disciples of Deshan. Linji and Deshan are singled out for criticism in several texts of the
Shōbōgenzō.

though they pulverize their bodies, would not taste the fist (*funsai goshin sutomo
kikken su bekarazu* 粉碎其身すとも喫拳すべからず): I.e., however hard they train, they
would not get the point. The expression 'taste the fist' (*kikken* 喫拳) does not occur
elsewhere in the *Shōbōgenzō*; see Supplementary Notes, s.v. "Fist."

23 **practice and verification over one, two, three, four, or five threefold *asaṃkhyeya*
and one hundred great kalpas** (*ichi ni san shi go no san asōgi hyaku daikō no shushō* 一
二三四五の三阿僧祇・百大劫の修證): I.e., many bodhisattva careers. "Three *asaṃkhy-
eya* [incalculably long æons] and a hundred great æons" is a common Buddhist reference
to the time required for a bodhisattva to complete the path to buddhahood. In versions of
the fifty-two-stage path with which Dōgen would have been most familiar, completion
of the three *asaṃkhyeya* would bring the bodhisattva to the stage of "virtual awakening"
(*tōkaku* 等覺); the final hundred great kalpas would then be devoted to developing the
thirty-two marks and eighty auspicious signs of a buddha body.

24 **dark road** (*genro* 玄路): While this term occurs with some frequency in Buddhist literature, Dōgen likely has in mind here its association with Dongshan's teachings, where
it figures as one of the "three roads" (*sanro* 三路) through which he instructed people;
see Supplementary Notes, s.v. "Dongshan's three roads."

314　　　DŌGEN'S *SHŌBŌGENZŌ* VOLUME II

思量すべし、ほとけより以前なるゆえに非佛といはず、佛よりのちなるゆ
えに非佛といはず、佛をこゆるゆえに非佛なるにあらず、ただひとへに佛
向上なるゆえに非佛なり。その非佛といふは、脱落佛面目なるゆえにい
ふ、脱落佛身心なるゆえにいふ。

We should know that there's "someone beyond the buddha." This refers to the way of life that plays with the spirit.[25] Be that as it may, we
know it by taking up an old buddha; we know it by raising up a fist.[26] To
have seen it in this way is to know "*there's someone beyond the buddha,*" to know *there's no one beyond the buddha.*[27] The address to the assembly here does not mean that we should become "someone beyond the
buddha," or that we should encounter "someone beyond the buddha": it
means simply that, for the moment, we should know that there is "someone beyond the buddha." One who can use this pivot surely does not
know "*there's someone beyond the buddha,*" does not know "*there's no
one beyond the buddha.*"[28] This "someone beyond the buddha" is "not
a buddha."[29] When wondering what this "not a buddha" is, we should

---

25　**the way of life that plays with the spirit** (*rō seikon no kakkei* 弄精魂の活計): To
"play with the spirit" (*rō seikon* 弄精魂) occurs with some frequency in Zen literature,
often in the pejorative sense of what we might call "fiddling with the mind." Dōgen,
however, also uses the expression in a positive sense — particularly in "Shōbōgenzō
udonge" 正法眼藏優曇華 (DZZ.2:171):

> 拈華を弄精魂といふ。弄精魂とは、祇管打坐、脱落身心なり。佛となり祖とな
> るを、弄精魂といふ、著衣喫飯を、弄精魂といふなり。おほよそ佛祖極則の
> 事、かならず弄精魂なり。

> "Holding up the flower" is called "playing with the spirit." "Playing with the spirit"
> means "just sitting, sloughing off body and mind." Becoming a buddha, becoming
> an ancestor, is called "playing with the spirit"; putting on robes and eating rice is
> called "playing with the spirit." In general, the matter of the ultimate standard of the
> buddhas and ancestors is invariably "playing with the spirit."

26　**taking up an old buddha** (*kobutsu o ko shite* 古佛を舉して); **raising up a fist** (*kentō
o koki shite* 拳頭を舉起して): Both verbs may refer to taking up an object (the buddhas
and ancestors, respectively) for study; alternatively, the second verb may refer to the
physical act of raising a fist (i.e., performing as an ancestor). See Supplementary Notes,
s.v. "Old buddha," "Fist."

27　**"there's someone beyond the buddha"** (*u butsu kōjō nin* 有佛向上人); **there's no one
beyond the buddha** (*mu butsu kōjō nin* 無佛向上人): Dōgen is here repeating, and then
modifying, Dongshan's words, but the Chinese phrases can also be (and by some readers are)
parsed, "someone beyond an existent buddha (*ubutsu* 有佛); someone beyond a nonexistent
buddha (*mubutsu* 無佛)." (See, e.g., *Shōbōgenzō keiteki* 正法眼藏啓迪 2:624.)

28　**use this pivot** (*kono kanreisu o shitoku suru* この關棙子を使得する): I.e., master
this crucial point; see Supplementary Notes, s.v., "Pivot."

does not know (*fuchi suru* 不知する): Perhaps, meaning that one who is "beyond the
buddha" is not cognizant of being or not being "someone beyond the buddha."

29　**is "not a buddha"** (*hi butsu nari* 非佛なり): Or "is 'not the buddha,'" or "is 'a
non-buddha.'"

26. Beyond the Buddha *Butsu kōjō ji* 佛向上事 315

think, it is not called "not a buddha" because it is prior to the buddha; it is not called "not a buddha" because it is subsequent to the buddha; it is not that it is "not a buddha" because it transcends the buddha: it is "not a buddha" solely because it is "beyond the buddha." It is called "not a buddha" because it is the face of the buddha sloughed off, because it is the body and mind of the buddha sloughed off.

* * * * *

[26:10]

東京淨因枯木禪師〈嗣芙蓉、諱、法成〉示衆云、知有佛祖向上事、方有説話分。諸禪德、且道、那箇是佛祖向上事。有箇人家兒子、六根不具、七識不全、是大闡提、無佛種性。逢佛殺佛、逢祖殺祖。天堂收不得、地獄攝無門。大衆還識此人麼。良久曰、對面不仙陀、睡多饒寱語。

Chan Master Kumu, of Jingyin in Dongjing (successor to Furong; monastic name, Facheng), addressed the assembly saying, "When you know there's something beyond the buddhas and ancestors, then you're in a position to talk.[30] Chan worthies, tell me, what is this something beyond the buddhas and ancestors? There's a child of this family whose six organs are lacking and seven consciousnesses are incomplete.[31] He's a great icchantika, without the nature of the seed of buddhahood.[32] When he meets a buddha, he kills the buddha; when he meets an ancestor, he kills the ancestor.[33] The halls of heaven can't contain him; hell has no door to admit him. Members of the great assembly, do you know this person?"

---

30 **Chan Master Kumu, of Jingyin in Dongjing (successor to Furong; monastic name, Facheng)** (*Tonkin Jōin Koboku zenji* [*shi Fuyō, ki, hōjō*] 東京淨因枯木禪師〈嗣芙蓉、諱、法成〉): (Parentheses are in the original.) I.e., Kumu Facheng 枯木法成 (1071-1128), disciple of the important Caotong master Furong Daokai 芙蓉道楷 (1043-1118). The name Jingyin derives from the Jingyin Chan Cloister 淨因禪院, in Dongjing 東京 (in modern Henan), where Daokai was abbot. His words can be found at *Liandeng huiyao* 聯燈會要, ZZ.136:920b15-921a1; and *Jiatai pudeng lu* 嘉泰普燈錄, ZZ.137:105b12-16.

31 **six organs** (*rokkon* 六根); **seven consciousnesses** (*shichishiki* 七識): I.e., the six sense organs and the corresponding six sense consciousnesses plus the *manas* (*i* 意), the cognitive function posited in some Buddhist systems that synthesizes the six sense consciousnesses and experiences them as belonging to a self.

32 *icchantika* (*sendai* 闡提): I.e., one incapable of achieving buddhahood.

the nature of the seed of buddhahood (*butsu shushō* 佛種性): A fairly common Buddhist term for the potential to become a buddha; equivalent to "buddha nature" (*busshō* 佛性).

33 **When he meets a buddha, he kills the buddha; when he meets an ancestor, he kills the ancestor** (*hō butsu satsu butsu, hō so sasso* 逢佛殺佛、逢祖殺祖): An expression best known from the saying attributed to Linji Yixuan 臨濟義玄; see Supplementary Notes, s.v. "Kill the buddha."

316 DŌGEN'S *SHŌBŌGENZŌ* VOLUME II

After a while, he said, "Face-to-face, he's no saindhava; a lot of sleep and plenty of talking in his sleep."[34]

[26:11] {1:289}

いはゆる六根不具といふは、眼睛被人換却木槵子了也、鼻孔被人換却竹筒了也、髑髏被人借作屎杓了也。作麼生是換却底道理。このゆえに、六根不具なり。不具の六根なるがゆえに、爐鞴裏を透過して金佛となれり、大海裏を透過して泥佛となれり、火焔裏を透過して木佛となれり。

To say that "his six organs are lacking" means *he has had his eyes switched by someone for soapberry seeds, he has had his nose switched by someone for a bamboo tube, he has had his skull borrowed by someone to make a shit dipper.*[35] *What is the principle behind this switching?*

---

34 **"Face-to-face, he's no *saindhava*"** (*taimen fu senda* 對面不仙陀): I.e., "in person, he's not very quick." The grammatical subject of this description is variously interpreted: the translation here takes it as "the child" being described by Kumu; this would seem to be Dōgen's reading in section 12, below; but it could be, and often is, taken as the assembly that has failed to respond to Kumu's challenge — i.e., "the ones facing me are no *saindhava*." The term *saindhava* is shorthand here for "one who could correctly interpret the word *saindhava*," a Sanskrit word, meaning "of the Sindh," with multivalent references; the wise can understand the correct referent from the context. (See the traditional source and Dōgen's commentary in "Shōbōgenzō ō saku sendaba" 正法眼藏王索仙陀婆.)

35 **he has had his eyes switched by someone for soapberry seeds** (*ganzei hi nin kankyaku mokukansu ryō ya* 眼睛被人換却木槵子了也): From here through the sentence "What is the principle behind this switching?" Dōgen shifts to Chinese, as if quoting some (unidentified) text. The soapberry seed is used for Buddhist prayer beads (*juzu* 珠數); for uses of "eyes," see Supplementary Notes, s.v. "Eye." Dōgen has a very similar line in his "Shōbōgenzō jippō" 正法眼藏十方 (DZZ.2:95), probably after a saying of Chan Master Yunmen Wenyan 雲門文偃 (*Yunmen yulu* 雲門語錄, T.1988.47:544a11-12):

若説佛説祖、佛意祖意大似將木槵子換却爾眼睛相似。

If we talk of the buddhas and talk of the ancestors, the intention of the buddhas and the intention of the ancestors resemble switching soapberry seeds for your eyes.

he has had his nose switched by someone for a bamboo tube (*bikū hi nin kankyaku chikutō ryō ya* 鼻孔被人換却竹筒了也): A tube made of bamboo used for inhaling medicinal vapors is one of the items permitted a monk. A similar juxtaposition of the soapberry seed and bamboo tube occurs in Dōgen's *Eihei kōroku* 永平廣錄, DZZ.3:88, no. 143:

職由瞿曇眼睛在山僧手裏如木患子、山僧鼻孔在瞿曇手裏如竹筒兒。

Hence, Gautama's eyes are in this mountain monk's hand, like soapberry seeds; this mountain monk's nose is in Gautama's hand, like a bamboo tube.

For more on the metaphorical uses of the word "nose," see Supplementary Notes, s.v. "Nose."

he has had his skull borrowed by someone to make a shit dipper (*dokuro hi nin sha sa shishaku ryō ya* 髑髏被人借作屎杓了也): Reference to the dipper used in emptying a privy; likely reflecting the words of Zhaozhou Congshen 趙州從諗 (778-897), reported by Dōgen in his "Shōbōgenzō hakujushi" 正法眼藏柏樹子 (DZZ.1:438):

三年、五年、二十年、三十年せんに、道をえずといはば、老僧が頸をとりて、杓につくりて小便をくむべし。

26. Beyond the Buddha *Butsu kōjō ji* 佛向上事   317

Because of it, his six organs are lacking. Because he lacks the six organs, he has passed through the forge and become a golden buddha, he has passed through the great ocean and become a clay buddha, he has passed through the flames and become a wooden buddha.[36]

[26:12]

七識不全といふは、破木杓なり。殺佛すといへども逢佛す、逢佛せるゆえに殺佛す。天堂にいらんと擬すれば、天堂すなはち崩壊す。地獄にむかへば、地獄たちまちに破裂す。このゆえに、對面すれば破顔す、さらに仙陀なし。睡多なるにも寐語おほし。しるべし、この道理は、擧山市地兩知己、玉石全身百雜碎なり。枯木禪師の示衆、しづかに參究功夫すべし、卒爾にすることなかれ。

To say that "his seven consciousnesses are incomplete" means he is a broken wooden dipper.[37] Though he "kills the buddha," he "meets the buddha"; he kills the buddha because he meets the buddha. If he thinks to enter "the halls of heaven," the halls of heaven will crumble; if he heads for "hell," hell will immediately rupture. Hence, "face-to-face," he breaks into a smile; there is no further "*saindhava*."[38] While he "sleeps a lot," he still "talks in his sleep" a lot. We should realize that the principle here is that *all the mountains and the entire earth both know themselves; the entire body of the jewels and stones are a hundred fragments.*[39] We

---

If, in three years, or five years, or twenty years, or thirty years, you haven't attained the way, you can take this old monk's head, make it into a ladle, and scoop piss with it.

No exact source for Dōgen's report has been identified in the records of Zhaozhou.

36 **passed through the forge and become a golden buddha** (*rohairi o tōka shite konbutsu to nareri* 爐鞴裏を透過して金佛となれり): The term *rohai* 爐鞴 refers to bellows and, by extension, a forge. Dōgen's sentence derives from the popular saying attributed to Zhaozhou Congshen 趙州從諗:

金佛不度爐。木佛不度火。泥佛不度水。眞佛内裏坐。

The golden buddha can't pass the forge; the wooden buddha can't pass the flames; the clay buddha can't pass the water. The real buddha sits within.

37 **a broken wooden dipper** (*ha mokushaku* 破木杓): A common expression in Chan texts for something worthless; sometimes used (as perhaps here) in an ironic positive sense.

38 **breaks into a smile** (*hagan su* 破顔す): Perhaps meant to evoke the famous smile of Mahākāśyapa when Buddha Śākyamuni held up a flower on Vulture Peak; see Supplementary Notes, s.v. "Break into a smile."

39 **all the mountains and the entire earth both know themselves; the entire body of the jewels and stones are a hundred fragments** (*kozan sōchi ryō chi ki, gyokuseki zenshin hyaku zassui* 擧山市地兩知己、玉石全身百雜碎): These lines are given in Chinese, as if a quotation, but no source has been identified. For the idiom "a hundred fragments" (*hyaku zassui* 百雜碎), see Supplementary Notes, s.v. "A hundred fragments." The exact sense here is subject to interpretation. It may be that the "knowing themselves" of the first clause is "the principle" of "sleeping a lot," while the "hundred fragments" of the second clause refers to "talking in his sleep."

318 DŌGEN'S *SHŌBŌGENZŌ* VOLUME II

should quietly work at investigating Chan Master Kumu's address to the assembly; do not treat it hastily.

* * * * *

[26:13] {1:290}

雲居山弘覺大師、參高祖洞山。山間、闍黎名什麼。雲居曰、道膺。高祖又間、向上更道。雲居曰、向上道即不名道膺。洞山道、吾在雲巖時祇對無異也。

> *Great Master Hongjue of Mount Yunju went to study with the Eminent Ancestor Dongshan.*[40] *Shan asked, "What is the Ācārya's name?"*
>
> *Yunju said, "Daoying."*
>
> *The Eminent Ancestor asked again, "Say something beyond that."*
>
> *Yunju said, "If I say something beyond that, I'm not named Daoying."*
>
> *Dongshan said, "When I was at Yunyan, my answer was no different."*[41]

[26:14]

いま師資の道、かならず審細にすべし。いはゆる向上不名道膺は、道膺の向上なり。適來の道膺に、向上の不名道膺あることを參學すべし。向上不名道膺の道理現成するよりこのかた、眞箇道膺なり。しかあれども、向上にも道膺なるべし、といふことなかれ。たとひ高祖道の向上更道をきかんとき、領話を呈するに、向上更名道膺と道著すとも、すなはち向上道なるべし。なにとしてかしかいふ。いはく、道膺たちまちに頂顙に跳入して藏身するなり。藏身すといへども、露影なり。

The words here by master and disciple, we should definitely examine in detail. The saying, "*If I say something beyond that, I'm not named Daoying*" is "beyond" Daoying. We should study the fact that, in the previous Daoying, there is a "not named Daoying" "beyond." With the appearance of the principle that he is "not named Daoying beyond," he is the true Daoying. Nevertheless, do not say that even "beyond" he must be Daoying. Even if, upon hearing the Eminent Ancestor's words, "*say something beyond that,*" he had presented his understanding by saying, "*beyond that, I'm named Daoying,*" this would be a "saying beyond." Why do we say this? Because Daoying leaps immediately into the crown

---

40 **Great Master Hongjue of Mount Yunju** (*Ungozan Gukaku daishi* 雲居山弘覺大師): I.e., Yunju Daoying 雲居道膺 (d. 902), disciple of Dongshan Liangjie 洞山良价 (referred to here as "Eminent Ancestor Dongshan" [*kōso Tōzan* 高祖洞山]). "Great Master Hongjue" 弘覺大師 is a posthumous title conferred by Emperor Zhaozong 昭宗; Daoying lived on Mount Yunju 雲居山 (in present-day Jiangxi Province) for thirty years. This conversation can be found at *Jingde chuandeng lu* 景德傳燈錄, T.2076.51:334c20-22.

41 **"When I was at Yunyan"** (*go zai Ungan ji* 吾在雲巖時): Reference to the mountain name of Dongshan's teacher Yunyan Tansheng 雲巖曇晟.

26. Beyond the Buddha *Butsu kōjō ji* 佛向上事 319

of his head and hides his body.[42] Though he may hide his body, he exposes his shadow.[43]

* * * * *

[26:15]

曹山本寂禪師、參高祖洞山。山問、闍黎名什麼。曹山云、本寂。高祖云、向
上更道。曹山曰、不道。高祖云、爲甚麼不道。師云、不名本寂。高祖然之。

Chan Master Benji of Caoshan went to study with the Eminent Ancestor Dongshan.[44] Dongshan asked him, "What is the Ācārya's name?"

Caoshan said, "Benji."

The Eminent Ancestor said, "Say something beyond that."

Caoshan said, "I won't say."

The Eminent Ancestor said, "Why won't you say?"

The Master said, "I'm not named Benji."

The Eminent Ancestor approved of this.

[26:16]

いはく、向上に道なきにあらず、これ不道なり。爲甚麼不道、いはゆる不
名本寂なり。しかあれば、向上の道は不道なり、向上の不道は不名なり、
不名の本寂は、向上の道なり。このゆえに、本寂不名なり。しかあれば、
非本寂あり、脱落の不名あり、脱落の本寂あり。

What this says is, not that he has nothing to say beyond that, but that he "won't say" it. "*Why won't he say it?*" Because he is "*not named Benji.*" Therefore, saying something "beyond" is "I won't say"; his "I won't say" something "beyond" is his "I'm not named"; the Benji "not named" is his saying something "beyond."[45] Therefore, "Benji" is "not named." In this way, there is a non-Benji; there is the "not named" sloughed off; there is a "Benji" sloughed off.

---

42 **Daoying leaps immediately into the crown of his head and hides his body** (*Dōyō tachimachi ni chōnei ni chōnyū shite zōshin suru* 道膺たちまちに頂顙に跳入して藏身する): Likely meaning that Daoying is completely identified with what is "not named Daoying." See Supplementary Notes, s.v. "Crown of the head."

43 **Though he may hide his body, he exposes his shadow** (*zōshin su to iedomo, royō nari* 藏身すといへども、露影なり): (Also read *roei* 露影.) From the Chinese expression "to hide the body and expose the shadow" (*cangsheng luying* 藏身露影); i.e., to conceal the meaning in the words.

44 **Chan Master Benji of Caoshan** (*Sōzan Honjaku zenji* 曹山本寂禪師): I.e., Caoshan Benji 曹山本寂 (840-901), disciple of Dongshan Liangjie 洞山良价. This conversation with his master can be found at *Jingde chuandeng lu* 景德傳燈錄, T.2076.51:336a7-9.

45 **saying something "beyond" is "I won't say"** (*kōjō no dō wa fudō nari* 向上の道は不道なり): I.e., Caoshan's refusal to describe what he is beyond his identity as Benji is his act of "saying something beyond" his name — what he goes on to characterize as "I'm not named Benji."

320 DŌGEN'S *SHŌBŌGENZŌ* VOLUME II

* * * * *

[26:17] {1:291}

盤山寶積禪師云、向上一路、千聖不傳。

Chan Master Baoji of Panshan said, "The one road beyond — even a thousand sages don't transmit it."[46]

[26:18]

いはくの向上一路は、ひとり盤山の道なり。向上事といはず、向上人といはず、向上一路といふなり。その宗旨は、千聖、競頭して出來すといへども、向上一路は不傳なり。不傳といふは、千聖は不傳の分を保護するなり。かくのごとくも學すべし。さらに又いふべきところあり、いはゆる千聖・千賢はなきにあらず、たとひ賢聖なりとも、向上一路は賢聖の境界にあらず、と。

"The one road beyond" is a saying only of Panshan. He does not say, "what's beyond"; he does not say, "someone beyond": he says, "the one road beyond." The essential point is that, though "a thousand sages" may compete to appear, "the one road beyond," they "don't transmit."[47] To say, they "don't transmit it," means the thousand sages preserve their position of not transmitting it.[48] We should study it in this way. And there is something further to say about it: it is not that there are not a thousand sages and a thousand worthies; though they may be worthies and sages, "the one road beyond" is not the realm of the worthies and sages.[49]

* * * * *

---

46   **Chan Master Baoji of Panshan** (*Banzan Hōshaku zenji* 盤山寶積禪師): Baoji 寶積 (dates unknown), a disciple of Mazu Daoyi 馬祖道一 (709-788), taught on Mount Pan 盤山 in Youzhou 幽州 in present-day Hobei province. His saying occurs at *Jingde chuandeng lu* 景德傳燈錄, T.2076.51:253b13.

47   **"the one road beyond," they "don't transmit"** (*kōjō ichiro wa fuden nari* 向上一路は不傳なり): Or "the one road beyond is not transmitted."

48   **the thousand sages preserve their position of not transmitting it** (*senshō wa fuden no bun o hogo suru* 千聖は不傳の分を保護する): As above, Note 2, the term "position" (*bun* 分) here means one's "status," or "standing."

49   **"the one road beyond" is not the realm of the worthies and sages** (*kōjō ichiro wa kenshō no kyōkai ni arazu* 向上一路は賢聖の境界にあらず): I.e., "the one road beyond" is beyond the advanced Buddhist adepts. The term *kenshō* 賢聖, elsewhere rendered as "worthy sage," is standard Buddhist language for the *bhadra* and ārya stages, respectively, of the Buddhist path; see below, section 29.

26. Beyond the Buddha *Butsu kōjō ji* 佛向上事 321

[26:19]

智門山光祚禪師、因僧問、如何是佛向上事。師云、拄杖頭上挑日月。

Chan Master Guangzuo of Mount Zhimen was once asked by a monk, "What is 'what's beyond the buddha'?"[50]

The Master said, "The head of the staff hoists the sun and moon."

[26:20]

いはく、拄杖の、日月に罣礙せらるる、これ佛向上事なり。日月の、拄杖を參學するとき、盡乾坤くらし、これ佛向上事なり。日月是拄杖とにあらず。拄杖頭上とは、全拄杖上なり。

That "the staff" is obstructed by "the sun and moon" — this is "what's beyond the buddha." When we study "the staff" of "the sun and moon," all of heaven and earth is dark — this is "what's beyond the buddha." It does not mean that "the sun and moon" are "the staff." "The head of the staff" means "above the entire staff."[51]

* * * * *

[26:21]

石頭無際大師の會に、天皇寺の道悟禪師とふ、如何是佛法大意。師云、不得不知。道悟云、向上更有轉處也無、師云、長空不礙白雲飛。

In the assembly of Great Master Wuji of Shitou, Chan Master Daowu of the Tianhuang Monastery asked, "What is the basic meaning of the buddha dharma?"[52]

The Master answered, "Unattainable, unknowable."[53]

---

50 **Chan Master Guangzuo of Mount Zhimen** (*Chimonzan Kōso zenji* 智門山光祚禪師): Guangzuo (dates unknown) was a disciple of Xianglin Chengyuan 香林澄遠 (908-987), in the lineage of Yunmen 雲門. His Zhimen Monastery 智門寺 was in Suizhou 隨州, in present-day Hubei. This exchange with a monk can be found at *Tiansheng guangdeng lu* 天聖廣燈錄, ZZ.135:818b2-3.

51 **"The head of the staff" means "above the entire staff"** (*shujō tōjō to wa, zen shujō jō nari* 拄杖頭上とは、全拄杖上なり): Or, perhaps, "the head of the staff means the entire staff is above." The sentence plays with the sense of the term *tōjō* 頭上 as both "head" and "overhead." See Supplementary Notes, s.v. "Staff."

52 **Great Master Wuji of Shitou** (*Sekitō Musai daishi* 石頭無際大師): I.e., Shitou Xiqian 石頭希遷 (700-790); "Great Master Wuji" is a posthumous title.

Chan Master Daowu of the Tianhuang Monastery (*Tennōji no Dōgo zenji* 天皇寺の道悟禪師): I.e., Shitou's disciple Tianhuang Daowu 天皇道悟 (748-807). This exchange can be found at *Jingde chuandeng lu* 景德傳燈錄, T.2076.51:309c3-5; and *shinji Shōbōgenzō* 眞字正法眼藏, DZZ.5:222, case 191.

53 **"Unattainable, unknowable"** (*futoku fuchi* 不得不知): The translation here follows the usual interpretation of this ambiguous phrase. The four characters might also be read in various other ways: e.g., "one cannot fail to know it"; "since I haven't got it, I don't know it"; etc.

322 DŌGEN'S *SHŌBŌGENZŌ* VOLUME II

Daowu said, "Beyond this, is there some further turning point?"[54]

The Master said, "The vast sky doesn't obstruct the flight of the white clouds."

[26:22] {1:292}

いはく、石頭は曹溪の二世なり。天皇寺の道悟和尚は、藥山の師弟なり。あるときとふ、いかならんか佛法大意。この間は、初心晩學の所堪にあらざるなり。大意をきかば、大意を會取しつべき時節にいふなり。

Shitou was the second generation after Caoxi; Reverend Daowu of Tianhuang Monastery was the younger fellow disciple of Yaoshan.[55] On one occasion, he asked, "*What is the basic meaning of the buddha dharma?*" This question is not something of which the beginner or the late student is capable.[56] If he asked about "the basic meaning," he did so at a time when he must have understood "the basic meaning."

[26:23]

石頭いはく、不得不知。しるべし、佛法は初一念にも大意あり、究竟位にも大意あり。その大意は不得なり。發心・修行・取證はなきにあらず、不得なり。その大意は不知なり。修證は無にあらず、修證は有にあらず、不知なり、不得なり。又その大意は、不得不知なり。聖諦・修證なきにあらず、不得不知なり。聖諦・修證あるにあらず、不得不知なり。

Shitou said, "Unattainable, unknowable." We should realize that "the buddha dharma" has a "basic meaning" in the first thought and has a "basic meaning" in the ultimate stage.[57] That basic meaning is "unattainable": it is not that it lacks bringing forth the thought [of bodhi], cultivating the practice, and acquiring the verification; they are "unattainable."

---

54 **"Beyond this, is there some further turning point?"** (*kōjō kō u tenjo ya mu* 向上更有轉處也無): I.e., "Do you have something to say that will go beyond this?" The term *tenjo* 轉處 here should doubtless be taken as *tenshin sho* 轉心處, the point at which the Zen student moves to a higher spiritual level.

55 **Shitou was the second generation after Caoxi** (*Sekitō wa Sōkei no nise nari* 石頭は曹溪の二世なり): Shitou was the disciple of Qingyuan Xingsi 青原行思 (d. 740), a disciple of the Sixth Ancestor, Huineng 慧能 of Caoxi 曹溪.

Reverend Daowu of Tianhuang Monastery was the younger fellow disciple of Yaoshan (*Tennōji no Dōgo oshō wa, Yakusan no sutei nari* 天皇寺の道悟和尚は、藥山の師弟なり): A reference to Yaoshan Weiyan 藥山惟儼, who also studied under Shitou. Daowu is said to have lived 748-807; Weiyan's dates, while sometimes given as 745-828, are more likely 751-834 — making him the younger of the two.

56 **the beginner or the late student** (*shoshin bangaku* 初心晩學): A standard expression, appearing often in Dōgen's writings, for the inexperienced practitioner; see Supplementary Notes, s.v. "Beginner's mind."

57 **the first thought** (*sho ichinen* 初一念); **the ultimate stage** (*kukyō i* 究竟位): I.e., the entire path of the bodhisattva, from the initial aspiration for bodhi to the attainment of buddhahood.

26. Beyond the Buddha *Butsu kōjō ji* 佛向上事 323

That basic meaning is "unknowable": it is not that it lacks practice and verification; it is not that it has practice and verification; they are "unknowable"; they are "unattainable."[58] And their "basic meaning" is "unattainable, unknowable." It is not that it lacks the sacred truths, practice and verification; they are "unattainable, unknowable."[59] It is not that it has the sacred truths, practice and verification; they are "unattainable, unknowable."

[26:24]

道悟いはく、向上更有轉處也無。いはゆるは、轉處もし現成することあらば、向上現成す。轉處といふは、方便なり。方便といふは、諸佛なり、諸祖なり。これを道取するに、更有たるべし。たとひ更有なりとも、更無をもらすべきにあらず、道取あるべし。

Daowu said, "Beyond this, is there some further turning point?" What he is saying is that, if the "turning point" is manifest, "beyond" is manifest. "Turning point" means an expedient.[60] An expedient means the buddhas, the ancestors. In saying this, there should be "something further." Even if there is "something further," "nothing further" should not be omitted, should be said.

---

58 **it is not that it lacks practice and verification** (*shushō wa mu ni arazu* 修證は無にあらず): Allusion to the words of Nanyue Huairang 南嶽懷讓 (677-744), recorded in the *shinji Shōbōgenzō* 眞字正法眼藏 (DZZ.5:178, case 101) and often cited by Dōgen; see Supplementary Notes, s.v. "What thing is it that comes like this?"

59 **the sacred truths** (*shōtai* 聖諦): Presumably, the four sacred truths of the buddha dharma; possibly reflecting another remark of Nanyue in conversation with the Sixth Ancestor, Huineng 慧能 (see, e.g., *Jingde chuandeng lu* 景德傳燈錄, T.2076.51:240a19-21):

後聞曹谿法席乃往參禮。問曰。當何所務即不落階級。祖曰。汝曾作什麼。師曰。聖諦亦不爲。祖曰。落何階級。曰聖諦尚不爲。何階級之有。祖深器之。

Later, upon hearing of the dharma seat at Caoxi, he [i.e., Nanyue] went and paid his respects. He asked, "What business would avoid falling down the stages?"
The Ancestor said, "How do you understand it?"
The Master said, "Don't do even the sacred truths."
The Ancestor said, "What stage will you fall to?"
He said, "If you don't do even the sacred truths, what stages are there?" The Ancestor deeply respected him.

60 **"Turning point" means an expedient** (*tenjo to iu wa, hōben nari* 轉處といふは、方便なり): I.e., in asking for a turning point, Daowu is seeking an expedient teaching (*hōben* 方便; S. *upāya*) from Shitou.

[26:25]

長空不礙白雲飛は、石頭の道なり。長空さらに長空を不礙なり。長空これ
長空飛を不礙なりといへども、さらに白雲みづから白雲を不礙なり。白雲
飛不礙なり、白雲飛さらに長空飛を礙せず。他に不礙なるは、自にも不礙
なり。面面の不礙を要するにはあらず、各各の不礙を存するにあらず、こ
のゆえに不礙なり。長空不礙白雲飛の性相を擧拈するなり。正當恁麼時、
この參學眼を揚眉して、佛來をも覷見し、祖來をも相見す、自來をも相見
し、他來をも相見す。これを問一答十の道理とせり。いまいふ問一答十
は、問一もその人なるべし、答十もその人なるべし。

"*The vast sky doesn't obstruct the flight of the white clouds*" are the
words of Shitou. "The vast sky," moreover, does not obstruct "the vast
sky." While "the vast sky" may not obstruct "the flight" of "the vast
sky," "the white clouds," moreover, do not themselves obstruct "the
white clouds." "*The flight of the white clouds*" *is unobstructed*; "the
flight of the white clouds," moreover, does not obstruct the flight of "the
vast sky." Being unobstructed by the other, they are unobstructed by
themselves.[61] It is not that each requires the non-obstruction of the other;
it is not that each possesses the non-obstruction of the other: therefore,
they are "unobstructed."[62] They take up the nature and marks of "*the vast
sky does not obstruct the flight of the white clouds*." Precisely at such a
time, raising the eyebrows of the eye of study, we spy the coming of the
buddhas, we see the coming of the patriarchs, we see the coming of ourselves, we see the coming of the other. This has been taken as the principle of asking one and answering ten.[63] In the asking one and answering
ten here, the one asking one must be that person, and the one answering
ten must be that person.[64]

---

61 **Being unobstructed by the other, they are unobstructed by themselves** (*ta ni fuge
naru wa, ji ni mo fuge nari* 他に不礙なるは、自にも不礙なり): A tentative translation
of a sentence in which the grammatical subject is unclear; here and in the following
sentence, the translation takes the subject to be "the vast sky" and "the white clouds." It
is also possible to take this sentence as an abstract statement: "that which is unobstructed
by another is unobstructed by itself" (i.e., has no identity apart from what it is not).

62 **It is not that each requires the non-obstruction of the other** (*menmen no fuge
o yō suru ni wa arazu* 面面の不礙を要するにはあらず): Again, a tentative translation,
taking the meaning to be that "the vast sky" and "the white clouds" are "unobstructed" in
the sense that they are beyond the issue of obstruction or non-obstruction.

63 **This has been taken as the principle of asking one and answering ten** (*kore o
mon ichi tō jū no dōri to seri* これを問一答十の道理とせり): "To ask one question and
get ten answers" is a common expression for getting a very full response; here, no doubt,
said in praise of Shitou's answer to Daowu's question.

64 **the one asking one must be that person** (*mon ichi mo sono hito naru beshi* 問一も
その人なるべし): I.e., the questioner, Daowu [as well as the answerer, Shitou], must be
qualified. The term *sono hito* ("that person") occurs several times in the *Shōbōgenzō*, in
the sense a "real person," "a person with real understanding."

26. Beyond the Buddha *Butsu kōjō ji* 佛向上事   325

* * * * *

[26:26] {1:293}

黄檗云、夫出家人、須知有從上來事分。且如四祖下牛頭法融大師、横説豎
説、猶未知向上關楝子。有此眼腦、方辨得邪正宗黨。

Huangbo said,[65]

Those who have left home should know that they are allotted what has come down to them.[66] *Now, take Great Master Farong of Niutou, under the Fourth Ancestor: while he could teach horizontally and teach vertically, he still didn't know the higher pivot.*[67] *Only when we have this eye and brain, can we distinguish true and false lineage groups.*

[26:27]

黄檗恁麼道の從上來事は、從上佛佛祖祖、正傳しきたる事なり。これを正法
眼藏涅槃妙心といふ。自己にありといふとも須知なるべし、自己にありとい
へども猶未知なり。佛佛正傳せざるは、夢也未見なり。黄檗は百丈の法子と
して百丈よりもすぐれ、馬祖の法孫として、馬祖よりもすぐれたり。おほよ
そ祖宗三・四世のあひだ、黄檗に齊肩なるなし。ひとり黄檗のみありて、牛
頭の兩角なきことをあきらめたり。自餘の佛祖、いまだしらざるなり。

This "what has come down" that Huangbo speaks of like this is what has been directly transmitted down through buddha after buddha and ancestor after ancestor. This is called "*the treasury of the true dharma eye, the wondrous mind of nirvāṇa.*"[68] Though it may be in oneself, we

---

65   **Huangbo** (*Ōbaku* 黄檗): I.e., Huangbo Xiyun 黄檗希運 (dates unknown), famed disciple of Baizhang Huaihai 百丈懷海 (749-814). His words here can be found at *Jing-de chuandeng lu* 景德傳燈錄, T.2076.51:266c4-7.

66   **"Those who have left home"** (*shukke nin* 出家人): I.e., those who have entered the Buddhist order.

"they are allotted what has come down to them" (*u jūjō rai ji bun* 有從上來事分): Taking *bun* 分 here in the sense "one's lot in life," "one's station or duties in life." Others take it as "understanding" or "the ability to understand."

67   **Great Master Farong of Niutou** (*Gozu Hōyū daishi* 牛頭法融大師): I.e., Niutou Farong 牛頭法融 (594-657), disciple of the Fourth Ancestor, Daoxin 道信, and founder of the so-called "Oxhead" (Niutou 牛頭) lineage of early Chan, considered by the descendants of the Sixth Ancestor to be a collateral line.

teach horizontally and teach vertically (*ōsetsu jusetsu* 横説豎説): I.e., speak with facility.

higher pivot (*kōjō kanreisu* 向上關楝子): Or, to preserve the lexical continuity of *kōjō* 向上, "pivot beyond"; see above, Note 28. Versions of this expression occur elsewhere in the *Shōbōgenzō*. See Supplementary Notes, s.v. "Pivot."

68   **"the treasury of the true dharma eye, the wondrous mind of nirvāṇa"** (*shōbō-genzō nehan myōshin* 正法眼藏涅槃妙心): Reference to the words of Buddha Śākyamuni describing what he was transmitting on Vulture Peak to the First Ancestor, Mahākāśyapa; the essence of the Buddhist teaching, handed down through the lineage of the buddhas and ancestors; see Supplementary Notes, s.v. "Treasury of the true dharma eye."

"should know" it; though it is in oneself, he "still didn't know" it. Those who have not received the direct transmission of buddha after buddha have never seen it even in their dreams. Huangbo, as the dharma child of Baizhang, was superior to Baizhang; and, as the dharma grandchild of Mazu, was superior to Mazu.[69] For three or four generations of the ancestors, there was no one of equal stature to Huangbo. Only with Huangbo alone was Niutou shown not to have a pair of horns.[70] Other buddhas and ancestors did not yet realize it.

[26:28]
牛頭山の法融禪師は、四祖下の尊宿なり。横説竪説、まことに經師論師に比するには、西來東地のあひだ、不爲不足なりといへども、うらむらくはいまだ向上の關棙子をしらざるなることを、向上の關棙子を道取せざることを。もし從上來の關棙子をしらざらんは、いかでか佛法の邪正を辨會することあらん、ただこれ學言語の漢なるのみなり。しかあれば、向上の關棙子をしること、向上の關棙子を修行すること、向上の關棙子を證すること、庸流のおよぶところにあらざるなり。眞箇の功夫あるところには、かならず現成するなり。

Chan Master Farong of Mount Niutou was a venerable under the Fourth Ancestor.[71] "He could teach vertically and teach horizontally"; indeed, if we compare him with the sūtra masters and treatise masters, within the Land of the East and coming from the west, we cannot regard him as wanting.[72] Nevertheless, what is regrettable is the fact that he still did not know "the higher pivot," the fact that he did not speak of "the higher pivot." If one does not know the pivot that has "come down," how could he distinguish the "true and false" in the buddha dharma? He is just a fellow who studies words. This being the case, to know "the higher pivot," to practice "the higher pivot," to verify "the higher pivot" — these are not something that mediocre types can reach. They always occur where there is true concentrated effort.

---

69 **the dharma grandchild of Mazu** (*Baso no hōson* 馬祖の法孫): Reference to Mazu Daoyi 馬祖道一, teacher of Huangbo's master, Baizhang Huaihai 百丈懷海.

70 **was Niutou shown not to have a pair of horns** (*Gozu no ryōkaku naki koto o akirametari* 牛頭の兩角なきことをあきらめたり): Dōgen is punning here on Farong's mountain name, which means "Oxhead."

71 **Mount Niutou** (*Gozusan* 牛頭山): A mountain in the Jiangning 江寧 District of present-day Jiangsu Province; site of Farong's Hongjuesi 弘覺寺.

72 **the sūtra masters and treatise masters** (*kyōji ronji* 經師論師): I.e., specialists in the interpretation of the sūtras and treatises; scholastics. A dismissive term commonly found in Dōgen's works.

within the Land of the East and coming from the west (*seirai Tōchi no aida* 西來東地のあひだ): I.e., of China and India respectively. Kawamura's text here is faithful to the manuscript tradition, while most modern editions follow the Honzan printing in amending the phrase to the more familiar *Saiten Tōchi no aida* 西天東地のあひだ ("within Sindh in the West and the Land of the East"). See Supplementary Notes, s.v. "Coming from the west."

26. Beyond the Buddha *Butsu kōjō ji* 佛向上事   327

[26:29] {1:294}

いはゆる佛向上事といふは、佛にいたりて、すすみてさらに佛をみるなり。衆生の、佛をみるにおなじきなり。しかあればすなはち、見佛もし衆生の見佛とひとしきは、見佛にあらず。見佛もし衆生の見佛のごとくなるは、見佛錯なり。いはんや佛向上事ならんや。しるべし、黄檗道の向上事は、いまの杜撰のともがら、領覧におよばざらん。ただまさに法道もし法融におよばざるあり、法道おのづから法融にひとしきありとも、法融に法兄弟なるべし。いかでか向上の關棙子をしらん。自餘の十聖三賢等、いかにも向上の關棙子をしらざるなり。いはんや向上の關棙子を開閉せんやや。この宗旨は、參學の眼目なり。もし向上の關棙子をしるを、佛向上人とするなり、佛向上事を體得せるなり。

"What's beyond the buddha" means, having reached [the status of] the buddha, to go on further to see the buddha. It is the same as living beings seeing the buddha: that is, if seeing the buddha is equivalent to living beings seeing the buddha, then it is not seeing the buddha; if seeing the buddha is like living beings seeing the buddha, seeing the buddha is a mistake.[73] How much more is this the case with "what's beyond the buddha." We should realize that Huangbo's saying of "what's beyond" is beyond the grasp of the illiterates of today.[74] There may be those whose dharma words do not reach those of Farong, and there may be those whose dharma words are equal to Farong's; but they are younger and older dharma brothers of Farong. How could they know "the higher pivot?" And certainly others, like the ten sages and three worthies do not know "the higher pivot," much less can they open and close "the higher pivot."[75] This essential point is the eye of study. To know "the higher pivot" is to be considered "someone beyond the buddha," to have "experienced what's beyond the buddha."

---

73 **It is the same as living beings seeing the buddha** (*shujō no, butsu o miru ni onajiki nari* 衆生の、佛をみるにおなじきなり): The Kawamura text follows most witnesses here; other editions adopt the Rurikōji 瑠璃光寺 manuscript in reading *onajikarazu nari* おなじからずなり ("it is not the same"). The point here would seem to be that, just as living beings cannot truly see the buddha, so those who have not themselves gone "beyond" cannot really grasp what is "beyond the buddha."

74 **illiterates** (*zusan* 杜撰): Literally, "Du composition"; used in pejorative reference to a literary work that, like those of Du, is ignorant of classical precedents. (Du is most often identified as the Song-dynasty poet Du Mo 杜默; for alternative theories, see Mochizuki:14477.122.) Dōgen regularly uses the term to refer to those in the Chan tradition who are ignorant of the tradition.

75 **the ten sages and three worthies** (*jisshō sanken* 十聖三賢): Also read *jisshō sangen*. A common Buddhist technical term in reference to those on the traditional path of the bodhisattva: the ten stages, or "grounds" (*chi* 地; S. *bhūmi*), of the "sage," or "noble" (S. ārya) — i.e., those on the advanced levels of the path — and the three types of "worthy" (S. *bhadra*) — i.e., those on the level just preceding the ārya.

328 DŌGEN'S *SHŌBŌGENZŌ* VOLUME II

正法眼藏佛向上事第二十六
Treasury of the True Dharma Eye
Beyond the Buddha
Number 26

[Ryūmonji MS:]

爾時仁治三年壬寅三月二十三日、在觀音導利興聖寶林寺示衆
*Presented to the assembly at Kannon Dōri Kōshō Hōrin Monastery;
twenty-third day, third month of the senior water year of the tiger, the
third year of Ninji [24 April 1242][76]*

[Tōunji MS:]

正元元年己未夏安居日、以未再治御草本、在永平寺書寫之。懷奘
*Copied this from an unrevised holograph at Eihei Monastery; on a day
of the summer retreat, in the junior earth year of the snake, the first
year of Shōgen [1259]. Ejō[77]*

---

76 The Tōunji 洞雲寺 MS shares an identical colophon.

77 **day of the summer retreat** (*ge ango no hi* 夏安居日): Dates of the summer retreat
vary; a common practice put it from the fifteenth of the fourth lunar month through the
fifteenth of the seventh month; in 1259, this would have corresponded to 8 May through
5 August.

TREASURY OF THE TRUE DHARMA EYE

NUMBER 27

Talking of a Dream within a Dream
Muchū setsu mu

夢中説夢

Talking of a Dream within a Dream

Muchū setsu mu

INTRODUCTION

This essay was composed at Kōshōji in the autumn of 1242. It represents number 27 in both the seventy-five and sixty-chapter *Shōbōgenzō* compilations and number 38 in the Honzan edition.

The title theme of the essay is a common motif in the literature of the Mahāyāna — that everything, including Buddhism itself, is "empty" of the ontological status we ordinarily attribute to it. It exists like objects in a dream. Buddhism talks of this dream while itself being this dream. For Dōgen, this does not mean that what Buddhism talks of is a delusion from which we need to awaken. Do not, he says, think of dreams here as inferior to the waking state: dreaming and awakening are both real. There is "talking of a dream," he says, that is prior to our dreams: it is the buddha's turning of the dharma wheel, from which arise Mount Sumeru and the great oceans. This is the dream talking of itself.

Dōgen ends his essay with comments on a passage from the *Lotus Sūtra*, in which those who hear the dharma are promised auspicious dreams of themselves becoming buddhas, preaching the dharma to their devotees for countless kalpas. This is no mere parable, Dōgen says: the dream of becoming a buddha is the reality of the buddha dharma.

正法眼藏第二十七
Treasury of the True Dharma Eye
Number 27

夢中説夢
Talking of a Dream within a Dream

[27:1] {1:295}

諸佛諸祖出興之道、それ朕兆已前なるゆえに、舊窠の所論にあらず。これ
によりて、佛祖邊、佛向上等の功德あり。時節にかかはれざるがゆえに、
壽者命者、なほ長遠にあらず、頓息にあらず、はるかに凡界の測度にあら
ざるべし。法輪轉、また朕兆已前の規矩なり。このゆえに、大功不賞、千
古榜樣なり。これを夢中説夢す。證中見證なるがゆえに、夢中説夢なり。

The way on which the buddhas and ancestors arise is prior to any portent; therefore, it is not something discussed in old dens.[1] Consequently,
they have virtues in the vicinity of the buddhas and ancestors, beyond
the buddha, and so on.[2] Because they have nothing to do with times,
their lives are neither long nor short, and are far beyond the calculations
of the ordinary world.[3] Their turning of the dharma wheel is also a rule
prior to any portent. For this reason, it is *"great virtue unpraised, a mod-*

---

1 **prior to any portent** (*chinchō izen* 朕兆已前): I.e., before the first indications of
something coming into existence; a variant of such common expressions in Zen texts as
chinchō mibō 朕兆未萠 ("before the germination of any portent"), *chinchō mishō* 朕兆
未生 ("before the birth of any portent"), etc.

something discussed in old dens (*kyūka no shoron* 舊窠の所論): "Old den" (or "old
nest," "old burrow"; *kyūka* 舊窠) is regularly used in Zen literature for old or habitual
ways of thinking, "tired" concepts or clichés; here, perhaps, scholastic treatments of the
Buddhist path.

2 **they have virtues in the vicinity of the buddhas and ancestors, beyond the buddha, and so on** (*busso hen, butsu kōjō tō no kudoku ari* 佛祖邊、佛向上等の功德あり):
Perhaps to be understood, "they have the virtues proper to the buddhas and ancestors, as
well as those that transcend even the buddhas." "Beyond the buddha" (*butsu kōjō* 佛向
上) is a very common expression in Zen texts and the theme of Dōgen's "Shōbōgenzō
butsu kōjō ji" 正法眼藏佛向上事. "The vicinity of the buddhas and ancestors" (*busso
hen* 佛祖邊) is less common and seems to occur most often in a dismissive sense for
what is limited to the buddhas and ancestors. See Supplementary Notes, s.v. "Beyond
the buddha."

3 **lives** (*jusha myōsha* 壽者命者): Two standard Buddhist terms for living beings,
though here seemingly used in the abstact sense of "lifespan." This usage occurs elsewhere in the *Shōbōgenzō*.

332　　　DŌGEN'S *SHŌBŌGENZŌ* VOLUME II

el for a thousand ages."[4] Of this, we "*talk of a dream within a dream.*"[5]
Because it is *experiencing verification within verification*, it is "*talking
of a dream within a dream.*"

[27:2]

この夢中説夢處、これ佛祖國なり、佛祖會なり。佛國・佛會、祖道・祖席
は、證上而證、夢中説夢なり。この道取・説取にあひながら、佛會にあら
ずとすべからず、これ佛轉法輪なり。この法輪、十方八面なるがゆえに、
大海・須彌、國土・諸法現成せり。これすなはち、諸夢已前の夢中説夢な
り。遍界の彌露は夢なり、この夢、すなはち明明なる百草なり。擬著せん
とする正當なり、紛紜なる正當なり。このとき、夢草・中草・説草等な
り。これを參學するに、根莖枝葉・華果光色、ともに大夢なり。夢然なり
とあやまるべからず。

The place where there is "*talking of a dream within a dream*" is the
land of the buddhas and ancestors, the community of the buddhas and
ancestors. The buddha land, the buddha community, the ancestral path,
the ancestral seat — these are *verifying on top of verification*, "*talking
of a dream within a dream.*"[6] While we are encountering these words,
this talk, we should not take it as not the buddha community: it is the
buddha's turning the dharma wheel. It is because this dharma wheel is
the ten directions and eight faces that *the great oceans and Sumeru, the*

4　**"great virtue unpraised, a model for a thousand ages"** (*daikō fushō, senko bōyō*
大功不賞、千古榜樣): Quoting Tiantong Rujing 天童如淨 (1162-1227), at *Rujing heshang yulu* 如淨和尚語錄, T.2002A.48:123a21.

5　**Of this, we "talk of a dream within a dream"** (*kore o muchū setsu mu su* これを夢
中説夢す): An odd locution, in which the entire phrase, "talk of a dream within a dream"
is treated as a transitive verb; perhaps to be understood, "We talk of this as a dream
within a dream." "Talking of a dream within a dream" (*muchū setsu mu* 夢中説夢) is a
common image in Zen, drawn from the literature of the Mahāyāna. A classic example of
its use is a passage in the *Great Perfection of Wisdom Sūtra (Da bore boluomiduo jing*
大般若波羅蜜多經, T.220.7:1084b10-14):

復次善勇猛、如人夢中説夢、所見種種自性、如是所説夢境自性、都無所有。何
以故。善勇猛、夢尚非有。況有夢境自性可説。如是般若波羅蜜多。雖假説有種
種自性、而此般若波羅蜜多、實無自性可得宣説。

Again, Suvikrāntavikramī, it is like a person talking of a dream within a dream: the
various self-natures that are seen, like the self-natures of the dream objects talked
about, are all without existence. Why is this? Suvikrāntavikramī, dreams are non-ex-
istent. How could there be self-natures of dream objects to be talked about? It is like
this prajñā-pāramitā: although it talks provisionally of various self-natures, in this
prajñā-pāramitā, there really are no self-natures to be expounded.

6　**verifying on top of verification** (*shōjō ni shō* 證上而證): I.e. further to verify verification.

27. Talking of a Dream within a Dream *Muchū setsu mu* 夢中説夢 333

lands and the dharmas have appeared.[7] This is the *"talking of a dream within a dream"* that is prior to dreams.[8]

Full exposure in the realms everywhere is the "dream"; this "dream" is the hundred grasses, perfectly clear.[9] It is precisely our trying to figure it out, precisely our confusion.[10] At this time, it is "dream" grasses, "within" grasses, "talking" grasses, and so on.[11] When we study this, "the roots, stalks, branches, and leaves, flowers and fruit, lustrous and colored," are all the great dream.[12] We should not mistake it as being dreamlike.[13]

---

7 **ten directions and eight faces** (*jippō hachimen* 十方八面): I.e., the eight cardinal and ordinal compass points ("eight faces") plus the zenith and nadir ("ten directions").

great oceans and Sumeru (*daikai Shumi* 大海・須彌): I.e., Mount Sumeru, the central mountain of a Buddhist world system, and the seas surrounding it.

lands and the dharmas (*kokudo shohō* 國土・諸法): A somewhat unusual combination, perhaps referring to the many lands and teachings of the buddhas. Some MS witnesses read "the lands and buddhas" (*kokudo shobutsu* 國土諸佛) or "the lands and directions" (*kokudo shohō* 國土諸方).

8 **prior to dreams** (*shomu izen* 諸夢已然): Echoing the phrase "prior to any portent" (*chinchō izen* 朕兆已前) of section 1.

9 **Full exposure in the realms everywhere** (*henkai no miro* 遍界の彌露): Perhaps combining two common Zen expressions: "in the realms everywhere, it has never been hidden" (*henkai fu zō zō* 遍界不曾藏), and "wanting to hide and fully exposed" (*yokuin miro* 欲隱彌露).

the hundred grasses, perfectly clear (*meimei naru hyakusō* 明明なる百草): The "hundred grasses" (*hyakusō* 百草) is a common expression for "all phenomena." Here, an allusion to the well-known Zen saying cited several times by Dōgen and recorded in his *shinji Shōbōgenzō* 眞字正法眼藏 (DZZ.5:168, case 88); see Supplementary Notes, s.v. "Perfectly clear, the tips of the hundred grasses."

10 **precisely our trying to figure it out** (*gijaku sen to suru shōtō* 擬著せんとする正當): Some witnesses give the more common homonym *gijaku* 疑著 ("have doubts about") here.

11 **"dream" grasses, "within" grasses, "talking" grasses** (*musō chūsō sessō* 夢草・中草・説草): Dōgen has here simply added "grasses" to each of the elements of the phrase "talking of a dream within a dream." In the absence of Kawamura's punctuation, the line could be read "grasses talking of grasses within dream grasses."

12 **"roots, stalks, branches, and leaves, flowers and fruit, lustrous and colored"** (*kon kyō shi yō ke ka kō shiki* 根莖枝葉・華果光色): From a verse in the *Lotus Sūtra* describing the varied plants of the world watered by the same rain; see Supplementary Notes.

13 **dreamlike** (*bōzen* 夢然): I.e., "indistinct"; also "absent," "vacant" (*bōzen* 茫然).

334 DŌGEN'S *SHŌBŌGENZŌ* VOLUME II

[27:3] {1:296}
しかあれば、佛道をならはざらんと擬する人は、この夢中説夢にあひなが
ら、いたづらに、あるまじき夢草の、あるにもあらぬをあらしむるをいふ
ならん、とおもひ、まどひにまどひをかさぬるがごとくにあらん、とおも
へり。しかにはあらず。たとひ迷中又迷といふとも、まどひのうへのまど
ひと道取せられゆく道取の通霄の路、まさに功夫参究すべし。

Thus, people who think not to study the way of the buddhas, upon
encountering this "*talk of a dream within a dream*," vainly think that
it means that a dubious dream grass gives existence to what does not
exist, and think that it is like adding delusion onto delusion.[14] Not so.
Though it may be called *further delusion within delusion*, we should
make concentrated effort and study the road through the clouds on which
the words "delusion on top of delusion" are spoken.[15]

[27:4]
夢中説夢は諸佛なり、諸佛は風雨水火なり。この名號を受持し、かの名號
を受持す。夢中説夢は古佛なり。乘此寶乘、直至道場なり。直至道場は、
乘此寶乘中なり。夢曲夢直、把定放行逞風流なり。正當恁麼の法輪、ある
いは大法輪界を轉ずること、無量無邊なり。あるいは一微塵にも轉ず、塵
中に消息不休なり。この道理、いづれの恁麼事を轉法するにも、怨家笑點
頭なり。いづれの處所も、恁麼事を轉法するゆえに、轉風流なり。このゆ
えに、盡地みな驀地の無端なる法輪なり。遍界みな不昧の因果なり、諸佛
の無上なり。しるべし、諸佛化道、および説法蘊、ともに無端に建化し、
無端に住位せり。去來の端をもとむることなかれ。盡從遮裏去なり、盡從
遮裏來なり。このゆえに、葛藤をうゑて葛藤をまつふ、無上菩提の性相な
り。菩提の無端なるがごとく、衆生無端なり、無上なり。籠籠無端なりと
いへども、解脱無端なり。公案見成は、放儞三十棒、これ見成の夢中説夢
なり。

"*Talking of a dream within a dream*" is the buddhas; the buddhas are
wind and rain, water and fire. It receives and keeps this title; it receives

---

14 **dubious dream grass** (*arumajiki musō* あるまじき夢草): I.e., a dream grass unlikely really to exist. The term "dream grass" (*musō* 夢草), while of course reflecting the
discussion, in the preceding section, of the "dream" as "the hundred grasses," is also the
name (usually read *bōsō*; C. *mengcao*) of a magic grass, described in the *Dongming ji* 洞
冥記 (KR.310097.003-1b), that, when carried on the person, promotes dreams and their
interpretation.

15 **further delusion within delusion** (*meichū u mei* 迷中又迷), a fixed form found also
in the "Shōbōgenzō genjō kōan" 正法眼藏現成公案 and seen as well in the *Dahui Pujue
chanshi yulu* 大慧普覺禪師語録 (T.1998A.47:893a21).

road through the clouds (*tsūshō no ro* 通霄の路): Japanese rendering of the Chinese
expression *tong xiaolu* 通霄路, used in Song-dynasty Chan texts for a "higher" way, beyond the standard understandings of Buddhist practice. The term *shō* 霄, translated here
as "clouds," can also refer to, and is probably more often interpreted as, the "heavens,"
or "firmament" (or sometimes the "night"). The term occurs elsewhere in the *Shōbōgenzō*, in the "Dōtoku" 道得 and "Mujō seppō" 無情説法 chapters.

27. Talking of a Dream within a Dream *Muchū setsu mu* 夢中説夢   335

and keeps that title.[16] "*Talking of a dream within a dream*" is the old bud-dha.[17] It is "*mounting this jeweled vehicle and arriving straightaway at the place of awakening.*"[18] "*Arriving straightaway at the place of awakening*" is within "*mounting this jeweled vehicle.*" Whether the "*dream*" is roundabout, or the "*dream*" is straightaway, it is "*holding fast and letting go, full of style.*"[19]

Precisely such a dharma wheel sometimes turns the world of the great dharma wheel, incalculable and limitless; and sometimes turns in a single infinitesimal dust mote, its movements unceasing within the dust.[20]

16 **It receives and keeps this title; it receives and keeps that title** (*kono myōgō o juji shi, kano myōgō o juji su* この名號を受持し、かの名號を受持す): The subject is unex-pressed. Perhaps to be understood, "talking of a dream in a dream" is known by the titles "wind and rain, water and fire" and "the buddhas."

17 **the old buddha** (*kobutsu* 古佛): Or "the old buddhas," though, given the imme-diately following quotation of Buddha Śākyamuni, the reference here may be to that particular "old buddha."

18 **"mounting this jeweled vehicle and arriving straightaway at the place of awak-ening"** (*jō shi hōjō, jikishi dōjō* 乘此寶乘、直至道場): Quoting Buddha Śākyamuni in the *Lotus Sūtra* (*Miaofa lianhua jing* 妙法蓮華經, T.262.9:15a13-14), in which he offers the one vehicle leading to buddhahood to all his followers.

19 **Whether the "dream" is roundabout, or the "dream" is straightaway** (*mu kyoku mu choku* 夢曲夢直): Presumably, picking up the preceding quotation, "arriving straight-away at the place of awakening."

"holding fast and letting go, full of style" (*hajō hōgyō ei fūryū* 把定放行逞風流): Elsewhere read *tei fūryū* 逞風流; taking 逞 as 盈. In reference to Zen teaching styles; after a verse by Tiantong Rujing 天童如淨 (*Rujing chanshi yulu* 如淨禪師語錄, T.2002A.48:122c18):

放行把住逞風流。

Letting go and holding on, full of style.

20 **turns the world of the great dharma wheel** (*dai hōrin kai o tenzuru* 大法輪界を轉ずる): The expression "the world of the great dharma wheel" is rather odd; and it may be that the clause should be parsed, "Precisely such a dharma wheel is sometimes the great dharma wheel that turns the world."

turns in a single infinitesimal dust mote (*ichi mijin ni mo tenzu* 一微塵にも轉ず): A concept found in many Zen texts, drawn from a passage in the *Śūraṅgama-sūtra* (*Shou-lengyan jing* 首楞嚴經, T.945.19:121a6-7):

於一毛端現寶王刹。坐微塵裏轉大法輪。

Manifest the land of the Jewel King on the tip of a hair; turn the great dharma wheel seated in an infinitesimal dust mote.

Dōgen borrows the sūtra passage in his *Tenzo kyōkun* 典座教訓 (DZZ.6:6-8):

莫以凡眼觀。莫以凡情念。拈一莖草建寶王刹、入一微塵轉大法輪。

Do not look at it with the ordinary eye; do not think of it with the ordinary sentiment. Take up a single blade of grass and build the land of the Jewel King; enter a single infinitesimal dust mote and turn the great dharma wheel.

See also *Eiheiji chiji shingi* 永平寺知事清規 (DZZ.6:162):

336 DŌGEN'S *SHŌBŌGENZŌ* VOLUME II

This principle is, however it turns the dharma of such a thing, "*enemies laugh and nod their heads.*"[21] Wherever it is, because it turns the dharma of such a thing, it is turning in style.[22]

Therefore, all the earth is entirely a beginningless dharma wheel at full speed; the realms everywhere are all cause and effect not obscured, the buddhas unsurpassed.[23] We should realize that the buddhas' propagation of the way and their preaching of the aggregate of dharmas are both established beginninglessly, abide beginninglessly. Do not seek the beginning of their comings and goings. It is "*they all go from here*"; it is *they all come from here.*[24] Therefore, planting tangled vines, and entwining tangled vines, are the nature and marks of unsurpassed bodhi.[25]

夫拈一莖草建寶王利、拈一微塵轉。

Take up a single blade of grass and build the land of the Jewel King; take up a single infinitesimal dust mote and turn the great dharma wheel.

21 **however it turns the dharma of such a thing, "enemies laugh and nod their heads"** (*izure no inmo ji o tenbō suru ni mo, onke shō tentō* いづれの恁麼事を轉法するにも、怨家笑點頭): "Enemies laugh and nod their heads" (*enke shō tentō* 怨家笑點頭) represents the line in Rujing's verse immediately following that quoted above: "Holding tight and letting go, full of style." "Such a thing" recalls the famous saying attributed to Yunju Daoying 雲居道膺 (d. 902); see Supplementary Notes, s.v. "Such a person." The translation "turns the dharma of such a thing" attempts to replicate the double accusative resulting from the use of *tenbō* 轉法 ("turn the dharma") as a transitive verb.

22 **it is turning in style** (*ten fūryū nari* 轉風流なり): Modifying Rujing's "full of style" (*ei fūryū* 逞風流) quoted above.

23 **beginningless dharma wheel at full speed** (*makuchi no mutan naru hōrin* 驀地の無端なる法輪): "Beginningless" translates *mutan* 無端, a word meaning "without origin," "without limits," "without reason," etc. "At full speed" translates *makuchi* 驀地, an adverb, much favored in Zen writing, for "suddenly," "precipitously," "headlong," etc.

cause and effect not obscured (*fumai no inga* 不昧の因果): Recalling the famous words of Baizhang Huaihai 百丈懷海 (749-814) that the person of great practice "is not in the dark about" cause and effect. (See, e.g., *Liandeng huiyao* 聯燈會要, ZZ.136:495a9-b2; *shinji Shōbōgenzō* 眞字正法眼藏, DZZ.5:178, case 102. Dōgen treats the story at length in his "Shōbōgenzō dai shugyō" 正法眼藏大修行.)

24 **it is "they all go from here"; it is they all come from here** (*jin jū shari ko nari, jin jū shari rai nari* 盡從這裏去なり、盡從這裏來なり): Recalling the words of Shitou Xiqian 石頭希遷 (700-790) on where to find the Buddhist teachings; see, e.g., *shinji Shōbōgenzō* 眞字正法眼藏 (DZZ.5:152, case 53):

青原謂石頭云、人人盡道、曹溪有消息。頭云、有人不道曹溪有消息。師曰、大藏小藏、從何得。頭曰、盡從這裏去、諸事総不闕。

Qingyuan [Xingsi] said to Shitou, "People all say that Caoxi has the news."
Tou said, "There's someone who doesn't say that Caoxi has the news."
The Master said, "Then, where can you get the great treasury and small treasury?"
Tou said, "They all go from here, without losing anything."

25 **tangled vines** (*kattō* 葛藤): Literally, "arrowroot and wisteria," twining plants commonly used as a metaphor for "entanglements," or "complications," especially of

27. Talking of a Dream within a Dream *Muchū setsu mu* 夢中説夢   337

Just as bodhi is beginningless, so living beings are beginningless, are unsurpassed. Although the cages and nets are beginningless, liberation is beginningless.[26] "The kōan is realized" is *sparing you the thirty blows*"; this is the realized "*talking of a dream within a dream.*"[27]

[27:5] {1:297}

しかあればすなはち、無根樹・不陰陽地・喚不響谷、すなはち見成の夢中説夢なり。これ人天の境界にあらず、凡夫の測度にあらず。夢の菩提なる、たれか疑著せん、疑著の所管にあらざるがゆえに。認著するたれかあらん、認著の所轉にあらざるがゆえに。この無上菩提、これ無上菩提なるがゆえに、夢これを夢といふ。中夢あり、夢説あり、説夢あり、夢中あるなり。夢中にあらざれば説夢なし、説夢にあらざれば夢中なし。説夢にあらざれば諸佛なし、夢中にあらざれば諸佛出世し轉妙法輪することなし。その法輪は、唯佛なり與佛なり、夢中説夢なり。ただまさに夢中説夢に、無上菩提衆の諸佛諸祖あるのみなり。さらに法身向上事、すなはち夢中説夢なり。ここに唯佛與佛の奉觀あり。頭目髓腦・身肉手足を愛惜することあたはず、愛惜せられざるがゆえに、賣金須是買金人なるを、玄之玄といひ、妙之妙といひ、證之證といひ、頭上安頭ともいふなり。これすなはち佛の行履なり。これを參學するに、頭をいふには、人の頂上とおもふのみなり。さらに毘盧の頂上とおもはず、いはんや明明百草頭とおもはんや、いはんや頭顬をしらず。

This being so, the "*tree without roots,*" the "*ground without shade or sunlight,*" and the "*valley where calls don't echo*" — these are the realized "*talking of a dream within a dream.*"[28] This is not the realm

---

language; see Supplementary Notes, s.v. "Tangled vines."

26 **cages and nets** (*rōra* 籠籮): Variant (more often written 籠羅) of the more common *rarō* 羅籠 (or 籮籠), a classic metaphor for entrapment, or bondage; see Supplementary Notes, s.v. "Nets and cages."

27 **"The kōan is realized" is "sparing you the thirty blows"** (*kōan genjō wa, hō ni sanjū bō* 公案見成は、放儞三十棒): From the famous saying attributed to the Tang-dynasty figure Daoming 道明 (dates unknown) (*Jingde chuandeng lu* 景德傳燈錄, T.2076.51:291b17):

師見僧來云、見成公案放汝三十棒。

The Master, seeing a monk approaching, said, "Yours is a settled case, but I spare you the thirty blows."

See Supplementary Notes, s.v. "Realized kōan."

this is the realized "talking of a dream within a dream" (*kore genjō no muchū setsu mu nari* これ見成の夢中説夢なり): Or, "this is the 'talking of a dream within a dream' of realization."

28 **the "tree without roots," the "ground without shade or sunlight," and the "valley where calls don't echo"** (*mu kon ju fu onyō chi kan fukyō koku* 無根樹・不陰陽地・喚不響谷): Allusion to the well-known tale of the seven wise maidens (see, e.g., *Zongmen liandeng huiyao* 宗門聯燈會要, ZZ.136:444a8-16), on which Dōgen comments in his *Eihei kōroku* 永平廣錄, DZZ.3:42-44, no. 64. A group of seven princesses visits a charnel field and, seeing the corpses there, gains understanding of the Buddhist teachings. The king of the devas, Śakra, then offers them a boon:

DŌGEN'S *SHŌBŌGENZŌ* VOLUME II

of humans and devas, not the calculations of common people. That the dream is bodhi — who could doubt it? For it is not governed by doubt. Who could acknowledge it? For it is not turned by acknowledgment. Because this unsurpassed bodhi is unsurpassed bodhi, dreams are called dreams. There is the dream of "within"; there is the dream "talking"; there is "talking of a dream"; there is "within a dream." Were it not "within a dream," there would be no "talking of a dream"; were it not "talking of a dream," there would be no "within a dream." Were it not "talking of a dream," there would be no buddhas; were it not "within a dream," the buddhas would not appear in the world and turn the wondrous dharma wheel. That dharma wheel is "only buddhas," is "with buddhas," is "*talking of a dream within a dream.*"[29] Truly it is only in "*talking of a dream within a dream*" that there exist the buddhas and ancestors of the assembly of unsurpassed bodhi.[30]

Furthermore, what is beyond the dharma body — this is "*talking of a dream within a dream.*" Herein, there are "only buddhas with buddhas" paying their respects. Unable to regret "head and eyes, marrow and brains, body and flesh, hands and feet" — because they are not to be regretted — "*a seller of gold must be a buyer of gold*"; this is called the

---

女曰、我家四事七珍悉皆具足。唯祗要三般物。第一要無根樹子一株。第二要無陰陽地一片。第三要叫不響山谷一處。帝釋曰、一切所須我悉有之、三般物者實無。欲與聖姉同去白佛。於是同往見佛、乃問斯事。佛言、　憍尸迦、我諸弟子大阿羅漢、悉皆不解此義。唯有諸大菩薩、乃知斯事。

The women said, "Our household is fully provided with the four necessities [food, clothing, furnishings, and medicines] and the seven precious substances. We want only three things: first, we want a tree without roots; second, we want a piece of ground without shade or sunlight; third, we want a valley where calls don't echo."

Lord Śakra said, "I have everything you could require, but these three things, I do not have. I will go together with the noble sisters to consult the Buddha."

Thereupon, they went together to see the Buddha and asked him about this matter. The Buddha said, "Kauśika [i.e., Śakra], none of my disciples, the great arhats, understand the meaning of this. Only the great bodhisattvas know about this matter."

29 **That dharma wheel is "only buddhas," is "with buddhas"** (*sono hōrin wa, yui butsu nari yo butsu nari* その法輪は、唯佛なり與佛なり): Playing off a line, often cited by Dōgen, in Kumārajīva's translation of the *Lotus Sūtra*; see Supplementary Notes, s.v. "Only buddhas with buddhas can exhaustively investigate the real marks of the dharmas."

30 **the buddhas and ancestors of the assembly of unsurpassed bodhi** (*mujō bodai shu no shobutsu shoso* 無上菩提衆の諸佛諸祖): An unusual expression, akin to the phrase in "Shōbōgenzō *Hokke* ten *Hokke*" 正法眼藏法華轉法華:

十方三世一切諸佛、阿耨多羅三藐三菩提衆

All buddhas of the ten directions and three times, the assembly of *anuttara-samyak-saṃbodhi.*

Similarly, in his "Shōbōgenzō kenbutsu" 正法眼藏見佛, Dōgen speaks of "the assembly of all who have verified bodhi" (*issai shō bodai shu* 一切證菩提衆).

27. Talking of a Dream within a Dream *Muchū setsu mu* 夢中説夢   339

"mystery of mysteries," called "marvel of marvels," called "verification of verifications," called *putting a head on top of your head.*"[31] This is the conduct of a buddha. In studying it, we think only that the "head" is the top of the head of a human; we do not think further of atop the head of Vairocana, much less do we think of "perfectly clear, the heads of the hundred grasses," much less do we know the head itself.[32]

[27:6]

むかしより頭上安頭の一句、つたにれきたれり。愚人これをききて、剰法をいましむる言語とおもふ。あるべからず、といはんとては、いかでか頭上安頭することあらん、といふを、よのつねのならひとせり。まことにそれあやまらざるか。説と現成する、凡聖ともにもちいるに相違あらず。このゆえに、凡聖ともに夢中説夢なる、きのふにても生ずべし、今日にても長ずべし。しるべし、きのふの夢中説夢は、夢中説夢を夢中説夢と認じきたる、如今の夢中説夢は、夢中説夢を夢中説夢と参ずる、すなはちこれ値佛の慶快なり。かなしむべし、佛祖明明百草の夢あきらかなること、

---

31 **Unable to regret "head and eyes, marrow and brains, body and flesh, hands and feet"** (*zu moku zui nō shin niku shu soku o aijaku suru koto atawazu* 頭目髓腦・身肉手足を愛惜することあたはず): From the line in the *Lotus Sūtra* (*Miaofa lianhua jing* 妙法蓮華經, T.262.9:34b27-28) describing Buddha Śākyamuni in a previous life as a king who gave away all his possessions:

心無恪惜象馬七珍國城妻子奴婢僕從頭目髓腦身肉手足不惜軀命。

In my mind, not begrudging elephants or horses, the seven precious substances, lands and cities, wife and children, slaves and servants, head and eyes, marrow and brains, body and flesh, hands and feet, not regretting my physical life.

"a seller of gold must be a buyer of gold" (*mai kin shu ze mai kin nin* 賣金須是買金人): Dōgen's source for this saying is uncertain. It does occur in Chinese sources (see, e.g., *Xu chuangdeng lu* 續傳燈錄, T.2077.51:595a22), along with the more common saying, "a seller of gold must encounter a buyer of gold" (*mai jin xu yu mai jin ren* 賣金須遇買金人).

"mystery of mysteries," called "marvel of marvels," called "verification of verifications" (*gen shi gen to ii, myō shi myō to ii, shō shi shō to ii* 玄之玄といひ、妙之妙といひ、證之證といひ): A play with the famous line of the *Daode jing* 道德經 (KR.5c0046.000.001a), "mystery upon mystery, the gateway to the marvels" (*xuan shi you xuan zhongmiao shi men* 玄之又玄衆妙之門).

"putting a head on top of your head" (*zujō an zu* 頭上安頭): A common expression in Zen texts for the mistake of adding something superfluous, of saying something unnecessary, or imagining or seeking something one already has; see Supplementary Notes, s.v. "Putting a head on top of your head."

32 **atop of the head of Vairocana** (*Biru no chōjō* 毘盧の頂上): From the popular Zen saying, "to tread atop the head of Vairocana" (*tō Biru chōjō gyō* 踏毘盧頂上行) — i.e., walk on the dharma body of the buddha.

"perfectly clear, the heads of the hundred grasses" (*meimei hyaku sōtō* 明明百草頭): Playing here with *hyaku sōtō* 百草頭 ("tips of the hundred grasses"). See above, Note 9.

head itself (*zunii* 頭聻): Exact sense is uncertain; perhaps what the head really is, or what the word *zu* 頭 ("head") really means.

340　DŌGEN'S *SHŌBŌGENZŌ* VOLUME II

百千の日月よりもあきらかなりといへども、生盲のみざること、あはれむ
べし。いはゆる頭上安頭といふその頭は、すなはち百草頭なり、千種頭な
り、萬般頭なり、通身頭なり、全界不曾藏頭なり、盡十方界頭なり、一句
合頭なり、百尺竿頭なり。安も上も頭頭なると參ずべし、究すべし。

The line, "putting a head on top of your head," has been handed down
from long ago. Stupid people hearing it, think it is words warning against
something superfluous. When one wants to say that something is not necessary, it has become a familiar custom to say, "why put a head on top of your
head?" Actually, is this not mistaken? When it appears as "talking," there
is no difference in its use by the common person and the sage; therefore,
that both the common person and the sage are "*talking of a dream within a
dream*" must be something born yesterday, something that grows today.[33]

We should realize that yesterday's "*talking of a dream within a dream*"
has recognized "*talking of a dream within a dream*" as "*talking of a
dream within a dream*; and the present "*talking of a dream within a
dream*" studies "*talking of a dream within a dream*" as "*talking of a
dream within a dream*" — and this is the blessing and comfort of encountering the buddha. How sad! Though the clarity of the buddhas' and
ancestors' dreams of "perfectly clear the hundred grasses" is clearer than
a hundred thousand suns and moons, it is pitiful that the congenitally
blind do not see it. The "head" spoken of in saying "*putting a head on
top of your head*" is the head of the hundred grasses, is the head of a
thousand types, is the head of ten thousand kinds, is the head of the body
throughout, is the head of the whole world never hidden, is the head of
all the worlds in the ten directions, is the head of "one line in accord,"
is the head of a hundred-foot pole.[34] We should also study, should also
master, "putting" and "on top of" as "heads."

33　**When it appears as "talking"** (*setsu to genjō suru* 説と現成する): Some versions
of the text read here "when it appears as 'talking of a dream within a dream'" (*muchū
setsu mu to genjō suru* 夢中説夢と現成する). Presumably, the sense is, "when it comes
to the case of 'talking' [as in 'talking of a dream within a dream']."

must be something born yesterday, something that grows today (*kinō nite mo shō
zu beshi, kyō nite mo chō zu beshi* きのふにても生ずべし、今日にても長ずべし):
Perhaps meaning something like, "yesterday's ordinary understanding of 'talking of a
dream within a dream' is today's Buddhist understanding of the phrase."

34　**head of the hundred grasses** (*hyaku sōtō* 百草頭): Dōgen begins here a list of
expressions including the glyph *tō* (or *zu*) 頭 ("head"); in some of these cases — as in
this expression (for which, see above, Note 9), or "one phrase in accord," and "head of
a hundred-foot pole" — the glyph occurs in the original Chinese; in the others, Dōgen
has created neologisms.

head of a thousand types (*senshutō* 千種頭); **head of ten thousand kinds** (*banpantō*
萬般頭): From the fixed expression, "a thousand types and ten thousand kinds" (*senshu
banpan* 千種萬般).

27. Talking of a Dream within a Dream *Muchū setsu mu* 夢中説夢   341

[27:7] {1:298}

しかあればすなはち、一切諸佛及諸佛阿耨多羅三藐三菩提、皆從此經出
も、頭上安頭しきたれる夢中説夢なり。此經、すなはち夢中説夢するに、
阿耨菩提の佛を出興せしむ。菩提の諸佛、さらに此經をとく、さだまれる
夢中説夢なり。夢因くらからざれば、夢果不昧なり。ただまさに一槌千
當・萬當なり、千槌・萬槌は一當・半當なり。かくのごとくなるによ
て、恁麼事なる夢中説夢あり、恁麼人なる夢中説夢あり、不恁麼事なる夢
中説夢あり、不恁麼人なる夢中説夢ありとしるべし。しるべし、しられき
たる道理、顯赫なり。いはゆるひめもすの夢中説夢、すなはち夢中説夢な
り。

Thus, "*all the buddhas and the buddhas' anuttara-samyak-saṃbodhi
issue from this sūtra*" is also "*talking of a dream within a dream*" that
has been "*putting a head on top of a head.*"[35] "This sūtra," in "*talking
of a dream within a dream,*" causes the buddhas of *anuttara-bodhi* to
arise. That the buddhas of bodhi then go on to preach "this sūtra" is
certainly "*talking of a dream within a dream.*" When the dream cause
is not obscure, the dream effect is not obscure.[36] It is truly a case of one
hammer and a thousand hits, ten thousand hits; of a thousand hammers,

---

head of the body throughout (*tsūshintō* 通身頭): The expression *tsūshin* 通身, which
occurs regularly in Dōgen's writings, reflects the saying of Daowu Yuanzhi 道吾圓智
(769-835) regarding the thousand-armed, thousand-eyed Bodhisattva Avalokiteśvara
(*senju sengen Kannon* 千手千眼觀音) that "his body throughout is hands and eyes." See
Supplementary Notes, s.v. "His body throughout is hands and eyes."

head of the whole world never hidden (*zenkai fuzōzō tō* 全界不曾藏頭): Variant of
"in the realms everywhere, it has never been hidden" (*henkai fu zō zō* 遍界不曾藏); see
above, Note 9.

head of all the worlds in the ten directions (*jin jippō kai tō* 盡十方界頭): Adding a
"head" to the common expression for "everywhere throughout the universe."

head of "one line in accord" (*ikku gattō* 一句合頭): From a saying of Chuanzi Decheng
船子德誠:

一句合頭語、萬劫繫驢橛。

Words of a single line in accord; a donkey's hitching post for myriad kalpas.

head of a hundred-foot pole (*hyakushaku kantō* 百尺竿頭): A common expression in
Zen literature for the extreme limit of religious practice, as in the saying, "proceed one
step beyond the tip of a hundred-foot pole" (*hyakushaku kantō shin ippo* 百尺竿頭進一
步).

35 **"all the buddhas and the buddhas' *anuttara-samyak-saṃbodhi* issue from this
sūtra"** (*issai shobutsu kyū shobutsu anokutarasamyakusanbodai, kai jū shi kyō shutsu*
一切諸佛及諸佛阿耨多羅三藐三菩提、皆從此經出): From the *Diamond Sūtra* (*Jin-
gang jing* 金剛經, T.235.8:749b23-24).

36 **When the dream cause is not obscure, the dream effect is not obscure** (*muin
kurakarazareba, muka fumai nari* 夢因くらからざれば、夢果不昧なり): Likely an allusion to the saying of Baizhang introduced above, Note 23.

342　DŌGEN'S *SHŌBŌGENZŌ* VOLUME II

ten thousand hammers, and one hit, half a hit.[37] On the basis of this, we should realize that there is the "*talking of a dream within a dream*" that is "such a thing"; there is the "*talking of a dream within a dream*" that is "such a person"; there is the "*talking of a dream within a dream*" that is not "such a thing"; there is the "*talking of a dream within a dream*" that is not "such a person."[38] We should recognize that the principle we have been learning here is obvious: our "*talking of a dream within a dream*" all day long is itself "*talking of a dream within a dream.*"

[27:8] {1:299}
このゆえに古佛いはく、我今爲汝夢中説夢、三世佛也夢中説夢、六代祖師也夢中説夢。

Therefore, an old buddha has said, "*Now, for you, I'm talking of a dream within a dream. The buddhas of the three times talk of a dream within a dream; the ancestral masters of the six generations talk of a dream within a dream.*"[39]

[27:9]
この道、あきらめ學すべし。いはゆる、拈華瞬目、すなはち夢中説夢なり、禮拜得髓、すなはち夢中説夢なり。

We should clarify and study these words. *Holding up a flower and blinking the eyes is "talking of a dream within a dream"; making a bow and getting the marrow is "talking of a dream within a dream."*[40]

[27:10]
おほよそ、道得一句、不會不識、夢中説夢なり。千手千眼、用許多作麼な

37　**one hammer and a thousand hits, ten thousand hits** (*ittsui sentō bantō* 一槌千當・萬當): A play on the more common expression, "one hammer and two hits" (*ittsui ryōtō* 一槌兩當; i.e., "two birds with one stone").

38　**"talking of a dream within a dream" that is "such a thing"** (*inmo ji naru muchū setsu mu* 恁麼事なる夢中説夢): This and the following three phrases reflect the saying of Daoying 道膺 cited above, Note 21.

39　**an old buddha has said** (*kobutsu iwaku* 古佛いはく): This apparent quotation does not seem to correspond to any extant Chinese source, though there are several examples of the phrase, "the buddhas of the three times talk of dreams; the ancestral masters of the six generations talk of dreams" (*sanshi zhufo shuo meng liudai zushi shuo meng* 三世諸佛説夢六代祖師説夢) (see, e.g., *Mingjue chanshi yulu* 明覺禪師語錄, T.1996.47:693a15; *Dahui Pujue chanshi yulu* 大慧普覺禪師語錄, T.1998A.47:897a26-27).

40　**Holding up a flower and blinking the eyes** (*nenge shunmoku* 拈華瞬目); **making a bow and getting the marrow** (*raihai tokuzui* 禮拜得髓): References to the two most famous examples of the transmission of Zen: Buddha Śākyamuni's holding up a flower and transmitting his dharma to Mahākāśyapa; and Huike's bowing before Bodhidharma and receiving recognition that he had "gotten the marrow" of the Indian ancestor's teaching. See Supplementary Notes, s.v. "Holding up a flower and blinking the eyes" and "Skin, flesh, bones, and marrow."

27. Talking of a Dream within a Dream *Muchū setsu mu* 夢中説夢   343

るがゆえに、見色見聲、聞色聞聲の功德具足せり。現身なる夢中説夢あ
り、説夢説法蘊なる夢中説夢あり。把定・放行なる夢中説夢なり。直指は
説夢なり、的當は説夢なり。把定しても放行しても、平常の秤子を擧すべ
し。擧得するに、かならず目鋪機鋪あらはれて、夢中説夢しいづるなり。
鋪鋪を論ぜず平にいたらざれば、平の見成なし。平をうるに、平をみるな
り。すでに平をうるところ、物によらず、秤によらず、機によらず。空に
かかれりといへども、平をえざれば平をみず、と參究すべし。みづから
空にかかれるがごとく、物を接取して空に遊化せしむる、夢中説夢あり。
空裏に平を現身す、平は秤子の大道なり、空をかけ、物をかく。たとひ空
なりとも、たとひ色なりとも、平にあふ、夢中説夢あり。解脱の夢中説夢
にあらずといふことなし。夢これ盡大地なり、盡大地は平なり。このゆえ
に、廻頭轉腦の無窮盡、すなはち夢裏證夢する信受奉行なり。

In sum, *saying a single line, not understanding, and not knowing*, are
"talking of a dream within a dream."[41] Because the thousand arms and
thousand eyes are "how does he use so many?" they are endowed with
the virtues of seeing forms and seeing sounds, hearing forms and hearing
sounds.[42] There is the *"talking of a dream within a dream"* that is the
manifest body; there is the *"talking of a dream within a dream"* in which
talking of the dream is talking of the aggregate of dharmas.[43]

---

41 **saying a single line, not understanding, and not knowing** (*dōtoku ikku, fue
fushiki* 道得一句、不會不識): "To say a single line" is a fixed expression for a profound utterance. "Not understanding" here may reflect the words of the Sixth Ancestor, Huineng 慧能, "I don't understand the buddha dharma" (*ga fue buppō* 我不會佛
法) (see, e.g., *shinji Shōbōgenzō* 眞字正法眼藏, DZZ.5:158, case 59). "Not knowing" is
perhaps most familiar from the famous response, "I don't know," by the First Ancestor,
Bodhidharma to the question, "who are you?" (see, e.g., *Jingde chuandeng lu* 景德傳燈
錄, T.2076.51:219a29).

42 **Because the thousand arms and thousand eyes are "how does he use so many?"**
(*senjusengen yō kota somo* 千手千眼用許多作麼): Allusion to the conversation, introduced above (Note 34) regarding Bodhisattva Avalokiteśvara, who is represented as having a thousand arms, each with an eye in the palm of its hand. The question is,

大悲菩薩、用許多手眼作麼

The bodhisattva of great compassion, how does he use so many hands and eyes?

Dōgen devotes much of the "Shōbōgenzō Kannon" 正法眼藏觀音 to this conversation.

seeing forms and seeing sounds (*ken shiki ken shō* 見色見聲): The synesthesia here may
reflect a play on the bodhisattva's name, *Kannon* 觀音 (literally, "Viewer of Sound").

43 **manifest body** (*genshin* 現身): Although also used in reference to one's "present
body," in the context here, more likely an allusion to the famous thirty-two bodies manifested by Bodhisattva Avalokiteśvara, as described in the *Pumen* 普門 chapter of the
Lotus Sūtra, which begins (at *Miaofa lianhua jing* 妙法蓮華經, T.262.9:57a22-23):

佛告無盡意菩薩、善男子、若有國土衆生應以佛身得度者、觀世音菩薩、即現佛
身而爲説法。

The Buddha said to Bodhisattva Akṣayamati, "Good man, if there are in the land
living beings who ought to attain deliverance by a buddha body, Bodhisattva
Avalokiteśvara manifests a buddha body and preaches the dharma to them."

344 DŌGEN'S *SHŌBŌGENZŌ* VOLUME II

It is the "*talking of a dream within a dream*" that is "holding fast and letting go."[44] Pointing directly is "talking of a dream"; hitting the mark is "talking of a dream."[45] Whether holding fast or letting go, we should study the ordinary scale.[46] When we study it, invariably, the [ability to] "*eyeball a pennyweight and estimate a tael*" will appear, and "*talking of a dream within a dream*" will emerge.[47] Regardless of the pennyweight and tael, if it does not achieve balance, we have no realization of balance. When it does achieve balance, we see the balance. Where it has achieved balance, it does not depend on the things, it does not depend on the scale, it does not depend on the mechanism. Though it may be hanging in emptiness, we should investigate that, if it does not achieve balance, we do not see the balance.[48]

There is "*talking of a dream within a dream*" that, as if itself hanging in emptiness, takes in things and sets them wandering in emptiness. Within emptiness, it manifests the body of balance; balance is the great way of the scale.[49] It weighs emptiness; it weighs things. Whether it be empti-

---

"talking of a dream within a dream" in which talking of the dream is talking of the aggregate of dharmas (*setsu mu setsu hōun naru muchū setsu mu* 説夢説法蘊なる夢中説夢): A tentative rendering of a phrase difficult to parse. Taken together with the preceding clause, the sense would seem to be that "talking of a dream within a dream" may refer to the buddha doing the talking or to the collection of his talks.

44 **"holding fast and letting go"** (*hajō hōgyō* 把定放行): See above, Note 19.

45 **Pointing directly** (*jikishi* 直指); **hitting the mark** (*tekitō* 的當): Common references to Chan statements.

46 **the ordinary scale** (*byōjō no hyōsu* 平常の秤子): A play with the glyph *byō* 平 (or *hei*), which has the sense of "average" or "ordinary" (as in the famous saying, "the ordinary mind is the way" [*byōjō shin ze dō* 平常心是道]) and as "equal," "level," or "in balance" (as in the balance scale; *hyōsu* 秤子). The translation will use "balance" for this glyph throughout this passage, but the reader may well wish to keep the sense of "the ordinary" in mind.

47 **"eyeball a pennyweight and estimate a tael"** (*moku shu ki ryō* 目銖機鋪): Variant of "eyeball and estimate a pennyweight and tael" (*moku ki shu ryō* 目機銖兩). The ability to reckon at a glance the weights of *liang* 鋪 (or 兩; "tael") and *zhu* 銖 ("pennyweight"; 1/24 *liang*); by extension, insight into things. Sometimes included as one of the so-called "three phrases" (*sanju* 三句) of Yunmen 雲門; see Supplementary Notes, s.v. "Yunmen's three phrases."

48 **hanging in emptiness** (*kū ni kakareri* 空にかかれり): One is tempted to take *kū* 空 here as the "space" in which the balance scale is suspended; but note that, below, Dōgen will interpret the glyph as "emptiness" (S. *śūnyatā*), in juxtaposition with "form" (*shiki* 色; S. *rūpa*), as in the famous line from the *Heart Sūtra* (see Supplementary Notes, s.v. "Form is itself emptiness; emptiness is itself form"). It may well be that, here and throughout the following passage, Dōgen wants us to read the glyph with both meanings.

49 **it manifests the body of balance** (*byō o genshin su* 平を現身す): No doubt, the "manifest body" (*genshin* 現身) appearing above in this section, here used as a transitive verb, perhaps to be understood as a causative: "make balance a manifest body."

27. Talking of a Dream within a Dream *Muchū setsu mu* 夢中説夢   345

ness or form, there is "*talking of a dream within a dream*" that encounters balance. There is nothing that is not the "*talking of a dream within a dream*" of liberation.[50] The "dream" is all the whole earth; all the whole earth is in balance. Therefore, our inexhaustible turning the head and spinning the brain are the faithful acceptance and reverent practice of "*talking of a dream within a dream*."[51]

* * * * * *

[27:11] {1:300}

釋迦牟尼佛言、諸佛身金色、百福相莊嚴。聞法爲人説、常有是好夢。又夢作國王、捨宮殿眷屬及上妙五欲、行詣於道場、在菩提樹下、而處師子座、求道過七日、得諸佛之智。成無上道竟、起而轉法輪、爲四衆説法、逕千萬億劫、説無漏妙法、度無量衆生。後當入涅槃、如烟盡燈滅。若後惡世中、説是第一法。是人得大利、如上諸功德。

Buddha Śākyamuni said,[52]

The bodies of the buddhas of golden hue,
Adorned with hundreds of fortuitous marks.
Hearing the dharma, they preach it to people,
Who always have these auspicious dreams.
They also dream of becoming the king of a country,
Who abandons his palace and his entourage,
And the most marvelous pleasures of the five senses,
And, going to the place of awakening,
There, beneath the bodhi tree,

---

50   **"talking of a dream within a dream" of liberation** (*gedatsu no muchū setsu mu* 解脱の夢中説夢): The sense is ambiguous but probably best understood as "liberated 'talking of a dream within a dream.'"

51   **turning the head and spinning the brain** (*kaitō tennō* 廻頭轉腦): (Also written 回頭轉腦.) A fixed expression associated especially with a saying of the famous Tang-dynasty monk Shitou Xiqian 石頭希遷 (see, e.g., *shinji Shōbōgenzō* 眞字正法眼藏, DZZ.5:274, case 299):

從生至死、只是這箇。更回頭轉惱作什麼。

From birth to death, it's just this. Why turn your head and spin your brain?

faithful acceptance and reverent practice (*shinju bugyō* 信受奉行): A fixed expression for the pious audience's response to the Buddhist teachings.

52   **Buddha Śākyamuni** (*Shakamuni butsu* 釋迦牟尼佛): From the *Lotus Sūtra* (*Miaofa lianhua jing* 妙法蓮華經, T.262.9:39c6-17). The original sūtra passage is describing the auspicious dreams of devotees of the *Lotus Sūtra*, not the dreams of "the buddhas," as it might seem from Dōgen's passage. His quotation begins with the object of the devotees' vision, as is clear from the lines of the sūtra (39c5) just preceding:

深入禪定見十方佛。

Entering into meditation,
They see the buddhas of the ten directions.

DŌGEN'S *SHŌBŌGENZŌ* VOLUME II

Then sits upon the lion throne
And, seeking the way for seven days,
Attains the wisdom of the buddhas.
Having attained the unsurpassed way,
They arise and turn the dharma wheel,
Preaching the dharma for the fourfold assembly,
During thousands of myriads of koṭis of kalpas,
Preaching the wondrous dharma, free from taint,
And delivering incalculable living beings,
Thereafter, they enter into nirvāṇa,
Like a burning lamp extinguished.
If, during the latter evil age,
One preaches this foremost dharma,
The benefits attained by these people,
Will resemble the merits described above.

[27:12]
而今の佛説を參學して、諸佛の佛會を究盡すべし。これ譬喩にあらず。諸佛の妙法は、ただ唯佛與佛なるゆえに、夢・覺の諸法、ともに實相なり。覺中の發心・修行・菩提・涅槃あり、夢裏の發心・修行・菩提・涅槃あり。夢・覺おのおの實相なり、大小せず、勝劣せず。

Studying this preaching of the Buddha, we should exhaustively investigate the buddha community of the buddhas.[53] This is not a parable.[54] Because it is just "*only buddhas with buddhas*," in the wondrous dharma of the buddhas, the dharmas of both dreaming and awakening are "the real mark."[55] There is bringing forth the mind [of bodhi], practice, bodhi, and nirvāṇa while awake; there is bringing forth the mind, practice, bodhi, and nirvāṇa within dreams. Dreaming and awakening, each is "the real mark":

---

53 **exhaustively investigate** (*gūjin* 究盡): A common enough verb but here no doubt meant to evoke the famous line from the *Lotus* to which Dōgen will allude in the sentence following; see Supplementary Notes, s.v. "Only buddhas with buddhas can exhaustively investigate the real marks of the dharmas."

buddha community of the buddhas (*shobutsu no butsue* 諸佛の佛會): I.e., an assembly of buddhas or the followers of buddhas; here, perhaps, the congregation on Vulture Peak that was the site of the preaching of the *Lotus Sūtra*.

54 **This is not a parable** (*kore hiyu ni arazu* これ譬喩にあらず): Or, perhaps, "not a metaphor." I.e., the sūtra's description of dreams is not merely a figure of speech. The *Lotus Sūtra*, of course, is famous for its many parables.

55 **"only buddhas with buddhas"** (*yui butsu yo butsu* 唯佛與佛): See Note 53, above.

dreaming and awakening (*mukaku* 夢覺): The term "awakening" (*kaku* 覺) here can refer to both the waking state (as opposed to dreaming) and to bodhi (as opposed to ignorance).

"the real mark" (*jissō* 實相): See Note 53, above.

27. Talking of a Dream within a Dream *Muchū setsu mu* 夢中説夢

they are not great and small; they are not superior and inferior.

[27:13]

しかあるを、又夢作國王等の前後の道著を見聞する古今おもはくは、説是
第一法のちからによりて、夜夢のかくのごとくなると錯會せり。かくのご
とく會取するは、いまだ佛説を曉了せざるなり。夢覺もとより如一なり、
實相なり。佛法は、たとひ譬喩なりとも、實相なるべし。すでに譬喩にあ
らず、夢作、これ佛法の眞實なり。釋迦牟尼佛および一切の諸佛諸祖、み
な夢中に發心・修行し、成等正覺するなり。しかあるゆえに、而今の裟婆
世界の一化の佛道、すなはち夢作なり。七日といふは、得佛智の量なり。
轉法輪・度衆生、すでに逕千萬億劫といふ、夢中の消息たどるべからず。

Nonetheless, people past and present who have seen or heard the passage, "*They also dream of becoming the king of a country,*" mistakenly understand that, as a result of the power of "preaching this foremost dharma," their dreams at night will be like this. Those who understand it like this have not yet fully comprehended the buddha's preaching. Dreaming and waking are fundamentally one, are "the real mark." The buddha dharma, even when a parable, must be "the real mark." And since it is not a parable, the "dream of becoming" is the reality of the buddha dharma. Buddha Śākyamuni and all the buddhas and ancestors bring forth the mind, practice, and attain complete awakening "within a dream." Because this is so, the way of the buddhas propagated throughout [Śākyamuni's] entire ministry in the present Sahā world is a "dream of becoming." "Seven days" is the measure for attaining the wisdom of a buddha. To say that their "turning the dharma wheel" and "delivering living beings" are already "during thousands of myriads of *koṭis* of kalpas" means that events "within a dream" cannot be traced.

[27:14] {1:301}

諸佛身金色、百福相莊嚴、聞法爲人説、常有是好夢、といふ。あきらかに
しりぬ、好夢は諸佛なり、と證明せらるるなり。常有の如來道あり、百年
の夢のみにあらず。爲人説は、現身なり、聞法は、眼處聞聲なり、心處聞
聲なり、舊窠處聞聲なり、空劫已前聞聲なり。

He says,

The bodies of the buddhas of golden hue,
Adorned with hundreds of fortuitous marks.
Hearing the dharma, they preach it to people;
They always have these auspicious dreams.

348   DŌGEN'S *SHŌBŌGENZŌ* VOLUME II

Clearly here the fact that the "auspicious dreams" are "the buddhas" is verified. There is a way of the tathāgatas that "always has": it is not merely a hundred years of dreaming.[56] "Preaching it to people" is the manifest body; "hearing the dharma" is "the eye hears the voices," is the mind hears the voices, is the old dens hear the voices, is before the kalpa of emptiness hears the voices.[57]

[27:15]
諸佛身金色、百福相莊嚴、といふ、好夢は諸佛身なりといふこと、直至如今更不疑なり。覺中に佛化やまざる道理ありといへども、佛祖現成の道理、かならず夢作夢中なり。莫謗佛法の參學すべし。莫謗法の參學するき、而今の如來道、たちまちに現成するなり。

He says,

> The bodies of the buddhas of golden hue,
> Adorned with hundreds of fortuitous marks.

The fact that the "auspicious dreams" are "the bodies of the buddhas" is "*I'm like this now, without further doubts.*"[58] Although there may be a

---

56 **There is a way of the tathāgatas that "always has"** (*jō u no nyorai dō ari* 常有の如來道あり): Playing with the predicate of the sūtra phrase "they always have these auspicious dreams." The sentence could also be read "there is a way of the tathāgatas that always exists."

a hundred years of dreaming (*hyakunen no mu* 百年の夢): Or "a hundred-year dream." I.e., the dreaming of a human lifespan.

57 **"the eye hears the voices"** (*gensho mon shō* 眼處聞聲): Perhaps echoing the synesthesia introduced in section 10, above. The language likely reflects a verse by Dongshan Liangjie 洞山良价 (807-869) (see, e.g., *shinji Shōbōgenzō* 眞字正法眼藏, DZZ.5:204, case 148; discussed at "Shōbōgenzō mujō seppō" 正法眼藏無情説法):

> 也太奇、也太奇、無情説法不思議、若將耳聽終難會、眼處聞聲方得知。
> How strange! How strange!
> The insentient preaching the dharma is inconceivable.
> If we use our ears to hear it, it's hard in the end to understand;
> Only when our eyes hear the voices do we know it.

the old dens (*kyūsōsho* 舊窠處): See above, Note 1.

before the kalpa of emptiness (*kūgō izen* 空劫已前): An expression occurring regularly in Zen texts in reference to a state before even the kalpa before the emergence of the world; see Supplementary Notes, s.v. "Before the kalpa of emptiness."

58 **"I'm like this now, without further doubts"** (*jikishi nyo kon kō fu gi* 直至如今更不疑): From the verse by Lingyun Zhiqin 靈雲志勤 (dates unknown), included in Dōgen's *shinji Shōbōgenzō* 眞字正法眼藏 (DZZ.5:206, case. 155):

> 三十年來尋劍客、幾回葉落又抽枝、自從一見桃華後、直至如今更不疑。
> Thirty years the passenger seeking the sword.
> How many times have the leaves fallen and the branches budded?
> After once seeing the peach blossoms,
> I'm like this now, without further doubts.

See Supplementary Notes, s.v. "Peach blossoms."

27. Talking of a Dream within a Dream *Muchū setsu mu* 夢中説夢

principle that, in awakening, the buddhas' propagation never ceases, the principle realized by the buddhas and ancestors is inevitably "*talking of a dream within a dream.*" We should study "*do not denigrate the buddha dharma.*" When we study "*do not denigrate the dharma,*" the present way of the tathāgatas is immediately realized.

正法眼藏夢中説夢第二十七

Treasury of the True Dharma Eye
Talking of a Dream within a Dream
Number 27

[Ryūmonji MS:]

爾時仁治三年壬寅秋九月二十一日、在雍州宇治郡觀音導利興聖寶林精舍示衆
Presented to the assembly at Kannon Dōri Kōshō Hōrin Vihāra, Uji District, Yōshū; twenty-first day, ninth month, autumn of the senior water year of the tiger, the third year of Ninji [16 October 1242][59]

[Tōunji MS:]

寬元元年癸卯三月廿三日、書寫畢。侍者懷奘
Kangen [13 April 1243]. Acolyte Ejō

---

59 The Tōunji 洞雲寺 MS shares an identical colophon.

TREASURY OF THE TRUE DHARMA EYE

NUMBER 28

Making a Bow and Getting the Marrow
Raihai tokuzui

禮拜得髓

Making a Bow and Getting the Marrow

Raihai tokuzui

INTRODUCTION

This work is dated in spring of 1240 at Kōshōji. Thus, it represents one of the earlier chapters, written before its author began work on his essays in earnest. It occurs as number 28 in the seventy-five-chapter *Shōbōgenzō* but is not included in the sixty-chapter compilation; instead, it is found as number 8 of fascicle 1 in the twenty-eight-text *Himitsu Shōbōgenzō* collection, in a version twice as long. Though the *Himitsu* text bears a colophon dated in the winter of 1240, some months after that of the seventy-five-chapter Shōbōgenzō text, we should probably not assume that its additional material was added to the original version; more likely, the *Himitsu* text represents a draft from which the additional material was removed in the editing of the seventy-five-chapter *Shōbōgenzō* version. This additional material is incorporated in the ninety-five-chapter Honzan edition of the *Shōbōgenzō*, where the text appears as number 8, and is included in all modern printed editions of this chapter. The translation below accords with the Kawamura text in treating this material as an addendum following the first colophon.

The title of the chapter is taken from a well-known story, in which the First Ancestor, Bodhidharma, asks four disciples to state their understanding of Buddhism. After each does so, the ancestor characterizes their degree of understanding. To the first, he says, "You've gotten my skin"; to the second, "You've gotten my flesh"; to the third, "You've gotten my bones." The fourth disciple, Huike 慧可, who would become Bodhidharma's successor, makes no reply but simply makes a bow to the ancestor. Bodhidharma says, "You've gotten my marrow."

Dōgen often alludes to this story and treats it in some detail in the "Kattō" chapter of the *Shōbōgenzō*; but here, he is concerned less with the story itself than with the broader issue of paying obeisance to a teacher — or, as he says in the opening line of our text, finding a spiritual guide. On our side, so to speak, the key is the sincerity of our commitment; on the other side, the question is only whether or not the teacher has gained the way. These points are made early on in the essay, the remainder of which is then devoted to a critique of the common assumption that women are not qualified to be teachers.

In the appended material from the *Himitsu* text, Dōgen pursues the issue of gender, in a remarkable attack on male Buddhist attitudes toward women — including monks who cater to rich women, monks who see women only as objects of lust, monks who vow never to look upon women, monks who denigrate women for having bad karma in their past lives. The essay concludes with an extended, stinging rebuke of the practice, common in Dōgen's Japan, of designating certain Buddhist sites as off-limits to women — a practice dismissed here as "laughable" and "stupid." It is probably fair to say that the "Raihai tokuzui" represents one of the strongest statements against gender prejudice in premodern Buddhist literature.

正法眼藏第二十八

Treasury of the True Dharma Eye
Number 28

禮拜得髓

Making a Bow and Getting the Marrow

[28:1] {1:302}

修行阿耨多羅三藐三菩提の時節には、導師をうること、もともかたし。その導師は、男女等の相にあらず、大丈夫なるべし、恁麼人なるべし。古今人にあらず、野狐精にして善知識ならん。これ得髓の面目なり、導利なるべし。不昧因果なり、儞我渠なるべし。

When one practices *anuttara-samyak-saṃbodhi*, the most difficult thing is to find a guide. Without taking the form of either male or female, the guide should be a great person, should be such a person.[1] It might be a wise friend who is a fox spirit, not a person in past or present.[2] It will be a face that has "gotten the marrow," one who is a guide and benefactor; it will be one who is *not in the dark about cause and effect,*" one who is *you or I or someone else.*[3]

---

1 **great person** (*daijōbu* 大丈夫): In ordinary parlance, a brave or strong male; used in Buddhism to translate *mahā-puruṣa* ("great person"); one of the epithets of a buddha.

such a person (*inmo nin* 恁麼人): No doubt an allusion to the well-known saying attributed to the ninth-century master Yunju Daoying 雲居道膺; see Supplementary Notes, s.v. "Such a person."

2 **wise friend who is a fox spirit** (*yakozei ni shite zenchishiki* 野狐精にして善知識): A "wise friend" is standard Buddhist usage for a teacher; the "fox spirit" here introduces the story of Baizhang Huaihai 百丈懷海 (749-814) and the fox to which Dōgen alludes just below; it also points ahead to the reference to the god Śakra and the fox in section 6 and the remark by the nun Moshan Liaoran 末山了然 in section 12.

not a person in past or present (*kokon nin* 古今人): I.e., not an historical human figure.

3 **"not in the dark about cause and effect"** (*fumai inga* 不昧因果): Allusion to the famous tale of Baizhang Huaihai 百丈懷海 and the teacher who was reborn as a fox for five hundred lifetimes as a consequence of saying that the person of great practice "does not fall into cause and effect" (*furaku inga* 不落因果). The expression "not in the dark about cause and effect" represents Baizhang's own description of the person of great practice — his teaching of which liberated the fox. (See, e.g., *Liandeng huiyao* 聯燈會要, ZZ.136:495a9-b2; *shinji Shōbōgenzō* 眞字正法眼藏, DZZ.5:178, case 102. Dōgen treats the story at length in his "Shōbōgenzō dai shugyō" 正法眼藏大修行.)

28. Making a Bow and Getting the Marrow *Raihai tokuzui* 禮拜得髓 355

[28:2]

すでに導師を相逢せんよりこのかたは、萬縁をなげすてて、寸陰をすごさず、精進辦道すべし。有心にても修行し、無心にても修行し、半心にても修行すべし。しかあるを、頭燃をはらひ、翹足を學すべし。かくのごとくすれば、訕謗の魔儻におかされず。斷臂得髓の祖、さらに他にあらず、脱落身心の師、すでに自なりき。

Once we have encountered a guide, we should cast off the myriad involvements and, without spending an inch of shadow, devote ourselves vigorously to pursuing the way.[4] We should practice with mind, practice without mind, practice with half a mind.[5] Thus, we should brush the fire from our heads and study standing on one leg.[6] When we do this, we will not be assaulted by the abusive minions of Māra.[7] The ancestor who cut off his arm and got the marrow is not someone else; the master who sloughs off body and mind is ourselves.[8]

---

4 **cast off the myriad involvements** (*ban'en o nagesutete* 萬縁をなげすてて): Reminiscent of the fixed phrase encountered in Dōgen's meditation manuals; see, e.g., "Shōbōgenzō zazen gi" 正法眼藏坐禪儀:

諸縁を放捨し、萬事を休息すべし。

Cast aside all involvements and discontinue the myriad affairs.

an inch of shadow (*sun'in* 寸陰): A literary expression for "a moment of time," occurring often in Dōgen's writings.

5 **practice with mind** (*ushin nite mo shugyō shi* 有心にても修行し): The contrasting pair *ushin* 有心 and *mushin* 無心 can indicate (a) "conscious" and "unconscious," (b) "discriminating consciousness" and "nondiscriminating consciousness," or (c) "intention" and "nonintention." "Half a mind" (*hanshin* 半心) is Dōgen's playful third alternative.

6 **brush the fire from our heads** (*zunen o harau* 頭燃をはらふ): A standard metaphor for the urgency of practice, occurring several times in the *Shōbōgenzō*.

standing on one leg (*gyōsoku o gaku su* 翹足を學す): In ordinary parlance, the expression *gyōsoku* 翹足 might indicate "standing on tiptoe," hence "anxiously await"; in Buddhist usage, it is a term for the ascetic practice of standing for long periods with one leg raised. In his "Shōbōgenzō zanmai ō zanmai" 正法眼藏三昧王三昧, Dōgen quotes a passage from the *Dajidu lun* 大智度論 (T.1509.25:111b23), in which the practice is attributed to non-Buddhist ascetics; but, elsewhere, Buddha Śākyamuni himself reports that, in a previous life, he stood on one leg for seven days while chanting hymns of praise to Buddha Tiṣya (Fusha 弗沙) (see, e.g., *Zhuanji baiyuan jing* 撰集百緣經, T.200.4:253c20-254a2). In his *Gakudō yōjin shū* 學道用心集 (DZZ.5:14), Dōgen celebrates this practice in a passage somewhat akin to ours here:

恐怖時光之太速、所以行道救頭燃。顧眄身命不牢、所以精進慣翹足

Fearing the speed of the passing time, we practice the way to save ourselves from the fire on our heads. Reflecting on the insecurity of our lives, we exert ourselves to train in the practice of standing on one leg.

7 **the abusive minions of Māra** (*senbō no matō* 訕謗の魔儻): I.e., the demon army of Māra, the Evil One, lord of the sixth heaven of the realm of desire, who seeks to obstruct Buddhist practice.

8 **The ancestor who cut off his arm and got the marrow** (*danpi tokuzui no so* 斷臂

356   DŌGEN'S *SHŌBŌGENZŌ* VOLUME II

[28:3]

髓をうること、法をつたふること、必定して至誠により、信心によるな
り。誠信、ほかよりきたるあとなし、内よりいづる方なし。ただまさに法
をおもくし、身をかろくするなり。世をのがれ、道をすみかとするなり。
いささかも身をかへりみること法よりもおもきには、法つたはれず、道う
ることなし。その法をおもくする志氣、ひとつにあらず、他の教訓をまた
ずといへども、しばらく一二を擧拈すべし。

Getting the marrow and receiving transmission of the dharma always
depend upon utmost sincerity, upon the believing mind. There are no
traces of sincere faith coming from elsewhere, nor are there directions
to which it departs from within. It is simply giving weight to the dharma
while taking ourselves lightly. It is to flee the world and regard the way
as our abode. If regard for ourselves is even slightly weightier than the
dharma, the dharma will not be passed on to us nor will we gain the way.
There is not just one instance of the determination to give weight to the
dharma; and, although we need not rely on the instructions of others, we
should take up one or two [examples here].

[28:4] {1:303}

いはく、法をおもくするは、たとひ露柱なりとも、たとひ燈籠なりとも、
たとひ諸佛なりとも、たとひ野干なりとも、鬼神なりとも、男女なりと
も、大法を保任し、吾髓を汝得せるあらば、身心を牀座にして、無量劫に
も奉事するなり。身心はうることやすし、世界に稲麻竹葦のごとし、法は
あふことまれなり。

To give weight to the dharma means "to make one's body and mind a
couch" and serve for innumerable kalpas whatever maintains the great
dharma and has "you've gotten" "my marrow" — whether it be a pillar,
or a lantern, or the buddhas, or a fox, or a spirit, or a man or a woman.[9]

得髓の祖): I.e., the Second Ancestor Huike 慧可, who became a disciple of Bodhidharma after cutting off his arm as a token of his commitment, and of whom Bodhidharma
subsequently said that he had "gotten my marrow." See Supplementary Notes, s.v. "Cut
off an arm" and "Skin, flesh, bones, and marrow."

the master who sloughs off body and mind (*datsuraku shinjin no shi* 脱落身心の師):
To "slough off body and mind" is a fixed phrase (also occurring in reverse order: *shinjin datsuraku* 身心脱落) that Dōgen attributes to his master, Tiantong Rujing 天童如淨
(1162–1227); see Supplementary Notes, s.v. "Body and mind sloughed off."

9   **make one's body and mind a couch** (*shinjin o shōza ni shite* 身心を牀座にし
て): Likely an allusion to the passage in the "Devadatta" chapter of the *Lotus Sūtra*, in
which Buddha Śākyamuni in a previous life was a king who served as a menial for a
seer (Devadatta in a previous life) who promised to teach him the *Lotus Sūtra*. The king
"picked his fruit, drew his water, gathered his firewood, and prepared his meals, going
so far as to make his body a couch" (*i shin ji i shōza* 以身而爲床座) (*Miaofa lianhua jing*
妙法蓮華經, T.262.9:34c5-6).

has "you've gotten" "my marrow" (*gozui o nyo toku seru* 吾髓を汝得せる): I.e., has

28. Making a Bow and Getting the Marrow *Raihai tokuzui* 禮拜得髓   357

Getting a body and mind is easy, "like rice, hemp, bamboo, and reeds" in the world; to encounter the dharma is rare.[10]

[28:5]

釋迦牟尼佛のいはく、無上菩提を演説する師にあはんには、種姓を觀ずることなかれ、容顏をみることなかれ、非をきらふことなかれ、行をかんがふることなかれ。ただ般若を尊重するがゆえに、日日に百千兩の金を食せしむべし。天食をおくりて供養すべし、天華を散じて供養すべし。日日三時禮拜し恭敬して、さらに患悩の心を生ぜしむることなかれ。かくのごとくすれば、菩提の道、かならずところあり。發心よりこのかた、かくのごとく修行して、今日は阿耨多羅三藐三菩提をえたるなり。

Buddha Śākyamuni said,[11]

When you meet teachers who expound unsurpassed bodhi, you must not consider their caste; you must not look at their facial features; you must not scorn their faults; you must not consider their conduct. Simply because we respect and value prajñā, we should let them eat [offerings worth] a hundred thousand taels of gold each day. We should make offerings by presenting heavenly food, make offerings by scattering heavenly flowers. Paying obeisance and venerating them three times a day, do not give rise to thoughts of vexation. When we behave like this, the way of bodhi will surely appear. Having practiced like this ever since I brought forth the mind, I have today attained *anuttara-samyak-saṃbodhi*.[12]

[28:6]

しかあれば、若樹・若石も、とかまことねがひ、若田・若里も、とかましともとむべし。露柱に問取し、牆壁をしても參究すべし。むかし、野干を師として禮拜問法する天帝釋あり、大菩薩の稱、つたはれり、依業の尊卑によらず。

---

got the essence of the teaching handed down by the buddhas and ancestors. Dōgen plays here with the phrase "you've gotten my marrow," said by Bodhidharma to Huike 慧可.

10   **"like rice, hemp, bamboo, and reeds" in the world** (*sekai ni tō ma chiku i no gotoshi* 世界に稲麻竹葦のごとし): I.e., [sentient beings are] profuse in the world; a simile used in Kumārajīva's translation of the *Lotus Sūtra*. See Supplementary Notes.

11   **Buddha Śākyamuni said** (*Shakamuni butsu no iwaku* 釋迦牟尼佛のいはく): A textual source for this passage in Japanese has not been identified. It has been suggested that some of it at least may have been inspired by a passage found in the *Fanwang jing* 梵網經 (T.1484.24:1005b22-28), which speaks of how a disciple should honor the teacher.

12   **ever since I brought forth the mind** (*hosshin yori kono kata* 發心よりこのかた): "To bring forth the mind" (*hosshin* 發心) refers to the initial resolve of the bodhisattva to achieve *anuttara-samyak-saṃbodhi*; an abbreviated form of *hotsu bodai shin* 發菩提心 ("to bring forth the mind of bodhi"; S. *bodhi-cittotpāda*). See Supplementary Notes, s.v. "Bring forth the mind."

358 DŌGEN'S *SHŌBŌGENZŌ* VOLUME II

Thus, we should request to be taught "whether by trees or by rocks"; we should seek to be taught "whether in fields or in villages."[13] We should "ask the pillars" and investigate the fences and walls.[14] Long ago, there was the case of Deva Lord Śakra, who, taking a fox as his teacher, paid it obeisance and asked it about the dharma.[15] It became known as a great bodhisattva, without regard to the status of its secondary karma.[16]

[28:7] {1:304}

しかあるに、不聞佛法の愚痴のたぐひおもはくは、われは大比丘なり、年少の得法を拜すべからず、われは久修練行なり、得法の晩學を拜すべからず、われは師號に署せり、師號なきを拜すべからず、われは法務司なり、得法の餘僧を拜すべからず、われは僧正司なり、得法の俗男・俗女を拜すべからず、われは三賢十聖なり、得法せりとも、比丘尼等を禮拜すべからず、われは帝胤なり、得法なりとも、臣家・相門を拜すべからずといふ。かくのごとくの癡人、いたづらに父國をはなれて、他國の道路に跉跰することによりて、佛道を見聞せざるなり。

---

13 **"whether by trees or by rocks"** (*nyaku ju nyaku seki* 若樹・若石): Allusion to a well-known story, found in the *Nirvāṇa Sūtra*, of the "boy of the Himalayas" (Śākyamuni in a previous life) who wrote a Buddhist teaching on trees and rocks; see Supplementary Notes, s.v. "Whether on trees or on rocks."

"whether in fields or in villages" (*nyaku den nyaku ri* 若田・若里): Another common allusion (often found together with the preceding "trees and rocks"), to a passage in the *Lotus Sūtra*, in which Buddha Śākyamuni exhorts his followers to go forth and preach what they have heard from him; see Supplementary Notes.

14 **"ask the pillars"** (*rochū ni monshu shi* 露柱に問取し): Allusion to a well-known saying of the famous Tang-dynasty Chan master Shitou Xiqian 石頭希遷 (700-790), included in Dōgen's *shinji Shōbōgenzō* 眞字正法眼藏 (DZZ.5:148, case 41); see Supplementary Notes, s.v. "Pillars and lanterns."

investigate the fences and walls (*shō heki o shitemo sankyū su* 牆壁をしても參究す): "Fences and walls," often together with "tiles and pebbles" (*shō heki ga ryaku* 牆壁瓦礫), are regularly used to represent an inanimate world that is nevertheless spiritually "alive" with significance — as, for example, the phenomenal expression of the buddha mind (*busshin* 佛心). See Supplementary Notes, s.v. "Fences, walls, tiles, and pebbles."

15 **Deva Lord Śakra** (*Ten Taishaku* 天帝釋): I.e., Indra, king of the devas in Tuṣita Heaven, who, upon hearing a fox trapped in a well calling out to the buddhas of the ten directions, descended from his heaven to ask him for teachings. The story is told in the *Weicengyu yinyuan jing* 未曾有因緣經 (T.745.17:576c21ff). In his "Shōbōgenzō kie buppōsōbō" 正法眼藏歸依佛法僧寶 (DZZ.2:383), Dōgen quotes this story from Zhanran's 湛然 (711-782) *Zhiguan fuxing zhuan honjue* 止觀輔行傳弘決 (T.1912.46:272a25ff).

16 **It became known as a great bodhisattva, without regard to the status of its secondary karma** (*dai bosatsu no shō, tsutawareri, egō no sonpi ni yorazu* 大菩薩の稱、つたはれり、依業の尊卑によらず): The grammatical subject is unexpressed; the translation takes it as the "fox"; but some would read it as the deva Śakra. "Secondary karma" (*egō* 依業) refers to what is more often called "secondary recompense" (*ehō* 依報): the circumstances into which one is born as a result of past deeds — here, no doubt, the lowly circumstances of the fox.

28. Making a Bow and Getting the Marrow *Raihai tokuzui* 禮拜得髓   359

However, those imbeciles who do not listen to the buddha dharma say, I am a great bhikṣu and should not bow before a younger one who has gained the dharma;[17] I am trained in long practice and should not bow before a later student who has gained the dharma; I have been assigned the title "master" and should not bow before one who lacks the title "master"; I hold the office of dharma affairs and should not bow before other monks who have gained the dharma;[18] I hold the office of saṃgha rectification and should not bow before lay men and lay women who have gained the dharma;[19] I am of the three worthies and ten sages and should not pay obeisance to a *bhikṣuṇī*, even if she has gained the dharma;[20] I belong to the imperial lineage and should not bow before the houses of officials or the families of ministers, even if they have gained the dharma.

Fools such as these neither see nor hear the way of the buddhas because they have vainly left the land of their father to wander the roads of another land.[21]

* * * * *

---

17   **great bhikṣu** (*dai biku* 大比丘): A term that may refer either to a fully ordained monk, as opposed to a novice (*shami* 沙彌; S. *śrāmaṇera*); or, as likely in this case, to a monk of senior standing.

a younger one who has gained the dharma (*nenshō no tokuhō* 年少の得法): While not a particularly common term in Dōgen's vocabulary, the term *tokuhō* 得法 ("attain, or acquire, the dharma") receives special attention in this essay; it implies "understanding the truth of the buddha dharma."

18   **office of dharma affairs** (*hōmu shi* 法務司): The exact office is uncertain; in the case of early Japan, the term *hōmu* 法務 can refer simply to the monk in charge of a ritual event, an administrative officer in a monastery, or an ecclesiastical official of the government saṃgha bureau (*sōkō* 僧綱).

19   **Office of Saṃgha Rectification** (*sōjō shi* 僧正司): The term *sōjō* 僧正 was used in both China and Japan for the head ecclesiastical official of the saṃgha bureau; some see the term *sōjō shi* 僧正司 here as referring to an administrator at a regional level.

20   **three worthies and ten sages** (*sanken jisshō* 三賢十聖): A common Buddhist technical term in reference to the traditional path of the bodhisattva: the ten stages, or "grounds" (*chi* 地; S. *bhūmi*), of the "sage," or "noble" (S. ārya) — i.e., those on the advanced levels of the path — and the three types of "worthy" (S. *bhadra*) — i.e., those on the levels just preceding the ārya.

21   **left the land of their father** (*fukoku o nanarete* 父國をはなれて): Allusion to the famous parable, in the *Lotus Sūtra* (*Miaofa lianhua jing* 妙法蓮華經, T.262.9:16b7-19a12), of the son who runs away from his wealthy father's land and wanders for years in abject poverty. Eventually, he returns and is restored to his rightful estate.

360 DŌGEN'S *SHŌBŌGENZŌ* VOLUME II

[28:8]

むかし、唐朝趙州眞際大師、こころをおこして發足行脚せしちなみにいふ、たとひ七歳なりとも、われよりも勝ならば、われかれにとふべし。たとひ百歳なりとも、われよりも劣ならば、われ、かれををしふべし。

Long ago, under the Tang dynasty, Zhaozhou, Great Master Zhenji, upon arousing the aspiration [for awakening] and setting out on a pilgrimage, said, "Even if they are seven years old, if they are superior to me, I will ask them; even if they are a hundred years old, if they are inferior to me, I will teach them."[22]

[28:9]

七歳に問法せんとき、老漢、禮拜すべきなり。奇夷の志氣なり、古佛の心術なり。得道得法の比丘尼、出世せるとき、求法參學の比丘僧、その會に投じて禮拜問法するは、參學の勝躅なり。たとへば、渇に飲にあふがごとくなるべし。

When asking a seven-year-old about the dharma, the old man should pay obeisance.[23] It is a determination strange and elusive; it is the mindset of an old buddha.[24] When a *bhikṣuṇī* who has gained the way and gained the dharma has appeared in the world, for a member of the bhikṣu saṃgha seeking the dharma and studying to join her community, pay obeisance, and ask about the dharma is a wonderful example of study.[25] It is like a thirsty person finding a drink.

* * * * *

22 **Zhaozhou, Great Master Zhenji** (*Jōshū Shinsai daishi* 趙州眞際大師): I.e., Zhaozhou Congshen 趙州從諗 (778-897). "Great Master Zhenji" 眞際大師 is a posthumous title. "Zhaozhou" 趙州 refers to the province, in present-day Hebei, where Congshen spent many years, at Guanyin Cloister 觀音院. His biography appears at *Jingde chuandeng lu* 景德傳燈錄, T.2076.51:276c-278b; *Song gaoseng zhuan* 宋高僧傳, T.2061.50:775c6ff; *Zhaozhou Zhenji chanshi yulu bing xingzhuang* 趙州眞際禪師語錄并行狀, in *Guzunsu yulu* 古尊宿語錄, ZZ.118:152c11ff; etc. His pilgrimage and vow to learn even from a seven-year-old child occurs in various sources (see, e.g., *Guzunsu yulu* 古尊宿語錄, ZZ.118:152c17-d13). Dōgen also praises this vow in his "Shōbōgenzō hakujushi" 正法眼藏柏樹子 and "Gyōji" 行持.

23 **the old man should pay obeisance** (*rōkan raihai su beki nari* 老漢禮拜すべきなり): This could well be a reference to any "old man" or to Zhaozhou, who in some accounts was already sixty years old at the time of his pilgrimage.

24 **a determination strange and elusive** (*kii no shiki* 奇夷の志氣): Variant of the idiom "rare and elusive" (*kii* 希夷), said of the *dao* 道 at *Daode jing* 道德經 14 (KR.5c0046.000.004a).

the mindset of an old buddha (*kobutsu no shinjutsu* 古佛の心術): "Old buddha" could be a reference to (a) the buddhas of the past, (b) awakened masters of the Zen tradition, or (c) Zhaozhou, who was known as "Zhaozhou, the old buddha." See Supplementary Notes, s.v. "Old buddha."

25 **appeared in the world** (*shusse* 出世): I.e., has become established as a teacher.

28. Making a Bow and Getting the Marrow *Raihai tokuzui* 禮拜得髓 361

[28:10]

震旦國の志閑禪師は、臨濟下の尊宿なり。臨濟ちなみに師のきたるをみて、とりとどむるに、師いはく、 領也。臨濟はなちていはく、 且放儞一頓。これより臨濟の子となれり。

Chan Master Zhixian in the Land of Cīnasthāna was a venerable under Linji.[26] Once, when Linji saw the Master coming, he grabbed hold of him, whereupon the Master said, "Collared."[27]

Linji released him, saying, "*Well, I'll spare you a blow.*"[28]

From this time, he became Linji's "child."

[28:11]

臨濟をはなれて末山にいたるに、末山とふ、近離甚處。師いはく、 路口。末山いはく、 なんぢなんぞ蓋却しきたらざる。師、無語。すなはち禮拜して師資の禮をまうく。

When he left Linji and went to Moshan, Moshan asked him, "*Where did you just come from?*"[29]

The Master replied, "The mouth of the road."[30]

Moshan said, "Why did you come without shutting it?"

The Master was without words; paying obeisance, he gave the bow of a disciple to a master.

---

26 **Chan Master Zhixian** (*Shikan zenji* 志閑禪師): I.e., Guanxi Zhixian 灌溪志閑 (d. 895).

Land of Cīnasthāna (*Shintan koku* 震旦國): I.e., "China," represented here by a Sanskrit name transliterated by the Chinese *zhendan* 震旦.

Linji (*Rinzai* 臨濟): I.e., the famed Linji Yixuan 臨濟義玄 (d. 866).

27 **"Collared"** (*ryō ya* 領也): Or "understood." Word play with the term *ryō* 領, which means to understand but has the primary sense "neck," "collar"; hence, "to have by the collar," "to lead about," "to control," etc.

28 **"I'll spare you a blow"** (*hō ni itton* 放儞一頓): I.e., "you deserve a blow, but I'll let you off." The term *ton* 頓 can serve as a counter for both blows and meals; some readers would take *itton* 一頓 to refer here not to a blow but to a meal and would read Linji's remark as "I'll spare you one meal" — i.e., will let you stay overnight.

29 **Moshan** (*Massan* 末山): I.e., Moshan Liaoran 末山了然 (dates unknown), a *bhikṣuṇī* heir of Gaoan Dayu 高安大愚 (dates unknown). "Moshan" is the name of a mountain in present-day Jiangxi province. The story of Zhixian's encounter with Moshan is found in various sources (see, e.g., *Jingde chuandeng lu* 景德傳燈錄, T.2076.51:289a1-9; Dōgen also tells it in his *Eiheiji chiji shingi* 永平寺知事清規, DZZ.6:118.)

30 **"mouth of the road"** (*rokō* 路口): I.e., the start (or intersection) of the road, but Moshan puns on the literal sense of *kō* 口 as "mouth."

[28:12] {1:305}

師、かへりて末山にとふ、いかならんかこれ末山。末山いはく、不露頂。師いわく、 いかならんかこれ山中人。末山いはく、 非男女等相。師いはく、 なんぢなんぞ變ぜざる。末山いはく、 これ野狐精にあらず、なにをか變ぜん。師、禮拜す。つひに發心して、園頭をつとむること始終三年なり。

The Master in return put a question to Moshan, "What is Moshan?"

Moshan said, "It doesn't show its peak."[31]

The Master said, "What sort of person is on the mountain?"

Moshan said, "One without marks such as male or female."

The Master said, "Why don't you change yourself?"[32]

Moshan replied, "I'm not a fox spirit. What would I change?"

The Master bowed.

Eventually, of his own accord, he served as a monastery gardener for fully three years.

[28:13]

のちに出世せりし時、衆にしめしていはく、 われ臨濟爺爺のところにして半杓を得しき、末山孃孃のところにして半杓を得しき。ともに一杓につくりて、喫しおはりて、直至如今飽餉餉なり。

Later, when he had appeared in the world, he said to the assembly,

At Papa Linji's place, I got half a ladle; at Mama Moshan's place, I got half a ladle.[33] After putting them together into one ladle and drinking from it, *I've been completely full right up till now.*[34]

---

31 **"It doesn't show its peak"** (*furo chō* 不露頂): Generally taken to mean that Moshan is so high that its peak cannot be seen. It has been suggested that there is a play here with the *uṣṇīṣa*, the protuberance on a buddha's head referred to as the "unseen head mark" (*muken chōsō* 無見頂相).

32 **"Why don't you change yourself?"** (*nanji nanzo henzezaru* なんぢなんぞ變ぜざる): The conversation here is replaying the famous exchange about gender identity in the *Vimalakīrti Sūtra* (*Weimoji suoshuo jing* 維摩詰所説經, T.475.14:548b22-c9) between the Buddha's disciple Śāriputra and an unnamed devī. The exchange begins,

舍利弗言、汝何以不轉女身。天曰、我從十二年來、求女人相了不可得。當何所轉。

Śāriputra said, "Why don't you transform your female body?"

The devī said, "For twelve years, I've been searching for the mark of the female, without ever finding it. So, what am I to transform?"

33 **he said to the assembly** (*shu ni shimeshite iwaku* 衆にしめしていはく): The saying appears (with some variation) in several sources (see, e.g., *Foguo chanshi yulu* 佛國禪師語錄, T.2551.80:266a16-18).

34 **"I've been completely full right up till now"** (*jikishi nyokon hōshōshō* 直至如今飽餉餉): Dōgen switches here to Chinese. "Right up till now" (*jikishi nyokon* 直至如今) is a common fixed expression. "Completely full" is a loose translation for *hōshōshō* 飽

28. Making a Bow and Getting the Marrow *Raihai tokuzui* 禮拜得髓 363

[28:14]

いまこの道をききて、昔日のあとを慕古するに、末山は高安大愚の神足なり、命脈ちからありて志閑の嬢となる。臨濟は黄檗運師の嫡嗣なり、功夫ちからありて志閑の爺となる。爺とは、ちち、といふなり。嬢とは、母、といふなり。志閑禪師の、末山尼了然を禮拜求法する、志氣の勝躅なり、晩學の慣節なり、撃關破節といふべし。

When, hearing these words here, we admire the ancients in the traces of yesterday, Moshan was a superior disciple of Gaoan Dayu, with a vital artery strong enough to make her Zhixian's mom; Linji was the legitimate heir of Master Yun of Huangbo, with a practice strong enough to make him Zhixian's dad.[35] *Ye* means "father"; *niang* means "mother."[36] That Chan Master Zhixian paid obeisance to and sought the dharma from the nun Liaoran of Moshan is an excellent trace of his determination, is integrity to be emulated by later students.[37] It should be called assaulting the barriers and breaking down the sections.[38]

* * * * *

餉餉 ("satiated and stuffed"). Some reports of Zhixian's words give the variant "full and not hungry right up till now" (*jikishi nyokon hō fuki* 直至如今飽不飢).

35 **admire the ancients** (*boko* 慕古): One of Dōgen's favorite terms for the love of and respect for the tradition.

superior disciple (*jinsoku* 神足): A casual translation of a term, regularly indicating an outstanding student, that more literally means "spiritual foot" (from *ṛddhi-pāda*) and is used in reference to paranormal powers.

vital artery (*meimyaku* 命脈): I.e., the "bloodline" of her spiritual lineage.

Master Yun of Huangbo (*Ōbaku Un shi* 黄檗運師): I.e., Linji's teacher, Huangbo Xiyun 黄檗希運 (dates unknown).

36 *Ye* **means "father"**; *niang* **means "mother"** (*ya to wa chichi to iu nari, jō to wa haha to iu nari* 爺とはちちといふなり、嬢とは母といふなり): Dōgen is here explaining the colloquial Chinese of Zhixian's "mom" and "dad" to his Japanese audience.

37 **an excellent trace** (*shōchoku* 勝躅): I.e., an outstanding historical example.

38 **assaulting the barriers and breaking down the sections** (*gyakukan hasetsu* 撃關破節): Generally taken to mean "eliminating all obstacles to spiritual passage"; likely synonymous with *tōkan hasetsu* 透關破節 ("passing through the barriers and breaking down the sections") used elsewhere in the *Shōbōgenzō*.

364 DŌGEN'S *SHŌBŌGENZŌ* VOLUME II

[28:15]

妙信尼は仰山の弟子なり。仰山ときに廨院主を選するに、仰山あまねく勤
舊・前資等にとふ、たれ人かその仁なる。問答往來するに、仰山つひにい
はく、信淮子、これ女流なりといへども、大丈夫の志氣あり。まさに廨院
主とするにたへたり。衆みな應諾す。妙信つひに廨院主に充す。ときに仰
山の會下にある龍象うらみず。まことに非細の職にあらざれども、選にあ
たらん自己としては、自愛しつべし。

The nun Miaoxin was a disciple of Yangshan.[39] When Yangshan was
choosing a director of the office for secular affairs, he asked widely
among the retired senior and junior officers who the person should be.[40]
After an exchange of questions and answers, Yangshan said in the end,
"Xin, the disciple from Huai, though she may be female, has the determination of a great person.[41] She's certainly qualified to serve as the
director of the office for secular affairs."

All in the assembly agreed; and, in the end, Miaoxin was appointed
director of the office for secular affairs. At the time, the "dragon elephants" in Yangshan's assembly did not resent it.[42] Although this was
not really a non-trivial position, the one appointed to it would naturally
have cared for it.[43]

[28:16] {1:306}

充職して廨院にあるとき、蜀僧十七人ありて、儻をむすびて尋師訪道する
に、仰山にのぼらんとして、薄暮に廨院に宿す。歇息する夜話に、曹溪高
祖の風幡話を擧す。十七人おのおのいふこと、みな道不是なり。ときに廨
院主、かべのほかにありてききていはく、十七頭瞎驢、おしむべし、いく
ばくの草鞋をかつひやす。佛法也未夢見在。

---

39 **The nun Miaoxin** (*Myōshin ni* 妙信尼): Dōgen's source of information on this nun,
who is otherwise unknown, has not been identified.

Yangshan (*Kyōzan* 仰山): I.e., Yangshan Huiji 仰山慧寂 (803-887), disciple of Weishan
Lingyou 潙山靈祐 (771-853).

40 **office for secular affairs** (*kaiin* 廨院): A term meaning simply "public office," in a
monastic context, it refers to the office responsible for collecting rent for monastic land,
acquiring food for the monks, arranging lodgings for visitors, overseeing offerings for
the monastery, dealing with secular authorities, and other such tasks.

41 **"Xin, the disciple from Huai"** (*Shin Waisu* 信淮子): Presumably, a reference to the
Huai River region, from present-day Honan, through Anhui, into Jiangsu.

great person (*daijōbu* 大丈夫): Retaining the Buddhist sense of this term used in section
1, above, though here, it might better be read "a real man."

42 **"dragon elephants"** (*ryūzō* 龍象): A term for superior religious practitioners. Although originally used in reference to great elephants, it is often interpreted as "dragons
and elephants."

43 **a non-trivial position** (*hisai no shoku* 非細の職): I.e., one of the major monastic offices, such as the six stewards (*roku chiji* 六知事) and six prefects (*roku chōshu* 六頭首).

28. Making a Bow and Getting the Marrow *Raihai tokuzui* 禮拜得髓   365

After she had taken up her position, once, when she was in the office for secular affairs, there were seventeen monks from Shu, who had banded together to seek out a teacher and inquire about the way.[44] Thinking to climb Yangshan, they had taken lodgings at dusk in the office for secular affairs. During the evening talk while they were staying, someone brought up the Eminent Ancestor Caoxi's wind and banner story.[45] What every one of the seventeen monks had to say said it wrong. At that time, the Director of the Office for Secular Affairs, who could hear from the other side of the wall, said, "Seventeen blind donkeys.[46] How sad! How many pairs of straw sandals have they wasted?[47] *The buddha dharma, they've never seen even in their dreams.*"

[28:17]

ときに行者ありて、廨院主の、僧を不肯するをききて、十七僧にかたるに、十七僧ともに廨院主の不肯するをうらみず、おのれが道不得をはぢて、すなはち威儀を具し、焼香禮拜して請問す。

At that time there was a postulant who, hearing the Director of the Office for Secular Affairs's disapproval of the monks, told the seventeen monks.[48] None of the seventeen monks resented the disapproval of the Director of the Office for Secular Affairs. Ashamed that they could not say it, they straightaway donned proper attire and, offering incense and making bows, requested instruction.[49]

---

44   **Shu** (*Shoku* 蜀): I.e., the region of southwestern China corresponding roughly to present-day Sichuan.

45   **the Eminent Ancestor Caoxi's wind and banner story** (*Sōkei kōso no fūban wa* 曹溪高祖の風幡話): I.e., the famous tale of the Sixth Ancestor, Huineng 慧能, who, on hearing two monks arguing over whether, when the temple banners moved, it was the banners or the wind that was moving, said to them, "It's your minds that are moving." The story is found in various sources (see, e.g., *Jingde chuandeng lu* 景德傳燈錄, T.2076.51:235c3-6); Dōgen records it in his *shinji Shōbōgenzō* 眞字正法眼藏 (DZZ.5:202, case 146) and discusses it in "Shōbōgenzō inmo" 正法眼藏恁麼 (DZZ.1:207-208).

46   **"blind donkeys"** (*katsuro* 瞎驢): The term can also mean "one-eyed donkey."

47   **"How many pairs of straw sandals have they wasted?"** (*ikubaku no sōai o ka tsuiyasu* いくばくの草鞋をかつひやす): I.e., the sandals of itinerant monks worn out by their peregrinations in search of the teachings.

48   **postulant** (*anja* 行者): A lay candidate for ordination living in a monastery and working as a servant or assistant to the monastic officers.

49   **they could not say it** (*dō futoku* 道不得): I.e., were unable to say what should have been said about the wind and banner; a fixed expression for an inadequate statement, the negative of *dōtoku* 道得 ("a saying").

donned proper attire (*iigi o gu shi* 威儀を具し): Literally, "to equip oneself with dignified manner," the expression refers to adopting the monk's formal habit and ritual etiquette.

[28:18]

廨院主いはく、近前來。十七僧近前するあゆみいまだやまざるに、廨院主いはく、不是風動、不是幡動、不是心動。かくのごとく爲道するに、十七僧ともに有省なり。禮謝して師資の儀をなす。すみやかに西蜀にかへる。つひに仰山にのぼらず。まことにこれ三賢十聖のおよぶところにあらず、佛祖嫡嫡の道業なり。

The Director of the Office for Secular Affairs said, "Come forward!"

As the seventeen monks were still coming forward, the Director of the Office for Secular Affairs said, *"It's not the wind moving; it's not the flag moving; it's not the mind moving."*

Instructed in this way, all seventeen monks had an insight. Bowing in thanks, they adopted the deportment of disciples to a teacher. They quickly returned to the Western Shu and, in the end, never climbed Yangshan.[50] Truly this is not something that could be reached by the three worthies and ten sages; it is the work of the way of successor after successor of buddhas and ancestors.[51]

* * * * *

[28:19]

しかあれば、いまも住持および半座の職むなしからんときは、比丘尼の得法せらんを請すべし。比丘の高年宿老なりとも、得法せざらん、なにの要かあらん。爲衆の主人、かならず明眼によるべし。

Thus, today too, when the position of abbot or co-seat falls vacant, a *bhikṣuṇī* who has gained the dharma should be asked.[52] What would be the use of a bhikṣu, even an elder of advanced years, if he has not gained the dharma? The leaders of the community should always be based on their clear eye.

[28:20] {1:307}

しかあるに、村人の身心に沈溺せらんは、かたくなにして、世俗にもわらひぬべきことおほし。いはんや佛法には、いふにたらず。又女人および師姑等の、傳法の師僧を拜不肯ならんと擬するもありぬべし。これはしることなく、學せざるゆえに、畜生にはちかく、佛祖にはとほきなり。

However, often they are obstinate and sunk in the body and mind of a villager who would be laughed at even in the secular world; how much

---

50 **Western Shu** (*Seishoku* 西蜀): A name sometimes used for the ancient kingdom in Shu.

51 **work of the way** (*dōgō* 道業): I.e., training in the way of the buddhas.

52 **co-seat** (*hanza* 半座): The office of head monk (*shuso* 首座), who "shares the seat" of the abbot when he (or she) substitutes as lecturer.

28. Making a Bow and Getting the Marrow *Raihai tokuzui* 禮拜得髓 367

less are they deserving of mention in the buddha dharma.[53] Again, there will also be those who do not approve of women and senior nuns paying obeisance to teachers who transmit the dharma.[54] Because they know nothing and do not study, they are close to beasts and far from the buddhas and ancestors.

[28:21]

一向に佛法に身心を投ぜんことを、ふかくたくはふるこころとせるは、佛法かならず人をあはれむことあるなり。おろかなる人天、なほまことを感ずるおもひあり。諸佛の正法、いかでかまことに感應するあはれみなからん。土石沙礫にも、誠感の至神はあるなり。

The buddha dharma will invariably have compassion for the person who harbors a deep commitment to throw body and mind exclusively into the buddha dharma. Even foolish humans and devas have a turn of mind that is moved by sincerity. How could the true dharma of the buddhas lack the compassion that responds sympathetically to sincerity? Even earth, stones, sand, and pebbles have a spirit moved by sincerity.

[28:22]

見在大宋國の寺院に、比丘尼の掛搭せるが、もし得法の聲あれば、官家より尼寺の住持に補すべき詔をたまふには、即寺にて上堂す。住持以下衆僧みな上參して、立地聽法するに、問話も比丘僧なり。これ古來の規矩なり。得法せらんは、すなはち一箇の眞箇なる古佛にてあれば、むかしのたれにて相見すべからず。かれ、われをみるに、新條の特地に相接す。われ、かれをみるに、今日須入今日の相待なるべし。たとへば、正法眼藏を傳持せらん比丘尼は、四果支佛および三賢十聖もきたりて禮拜問法せんに、比丘尼、この禮拜をうくべし。男兒なにをもてか貴ならん。虛空は虛空なり、四大は四大なり、五蘊は五蘊なり、女流も又かくのごとし。得道はいづれも得道す。ただし、いづれも得法を敬重すべし。男女を論ずることなかれ。これ佛道極妙の法則なり。

53　**sunk in the body and mind of a villager** (*sonjin no shinjin ni chindeki seran* 村人の身心に沈溺せらん): Probably to be understood as "possessed of a simple villager's body and mind"; some have suggested the sense "holding the simple villager's view of body and mind." The unexpressed subject here is the community "leaders" (*shujin* 主人) of the previous sentence.

54　**there will also be those who do not approve of women and senior nuns paying obeisance to teachers who transmit the dharma** (*nyonin oyobi shiko ra no, denbō no shisō o hai fukō naran to gi suru mo arinu beshi* 女人および師姑等の、傳法の師僧を拜不肯ならんと擬するもありぬべし): A sentence the reading of which is subject to disagreement. The translation here follows Kawamura's punctuation, which treats the first particle *no* as a grammatical subject marker; others prefer to take it as a genitive, yielding a sentence like, "There will also be those who do not approve of paying obeisance to teachers who transmit the dharma who are women and senior nuns." While this latter reading seems to make somewhat more sense in the context here, it is less likely as a sentence. "Senior nuns" here translates *shiko* 師姑, a polite term for a *bhikṣuṇī*; the *Himitsu Shōbōgenzō* text gives the homophorous "elder sisters and aunts" (*shiko tō* 姉姑).

368 DŌGEN'S *SHŌBŌGENZŌ* VOLUME II

At the present time, in the Land of the Great Song, if a *bhikṣuṇī* registered at a monastery has a reputation for having gained the dharma, upon receiving an invitation from the court to fill the post of abbot of a nunnery, she will hold convocations at that monastery.[55] The monks of the assembly, from the abbot down, will all attend, and when they stand and listen to the dharma, the question words will come from the bhikṣu saṃgha.[56] This has been the rule since ancient times. Anyone who has gained the dharma is one true old buddha and, therefore, should not be encountered as whoever he or she was in the past.[57] When the person sees us, he or she engages us specifically in the new situation; when we see the person, it should be a relationship in which *today takes on today*.[58]

For example, in the case of a *bhikṣuṇī* who has received transmission and keeps the treasury of the true dharma eye, when those possessed of the fourth fruit, the *pratyeka-buddhas*, or those among the three worthies and ten sages come to pay obeisance and ask about the dharma, the *bhikṣuṇī* should accept the obeisance.[59] What is so exalted about a male?

55 **Hold convocations at that monastery** (*sokuji nite jōdō su* 即寺にて上堂す): I.e., address the formal assemblies in the dharma hall (*hattō* 法堂) of the monastery where she is registered.

56 **stand and listen to the dharma** (*ritchi chōhō* 立地聴法): A fixed phrase for the practice of standing during a formal dharma talk by a teacher.

question words (*monna* 問話): The questions posed to an abbot during a formal convocation.

57 **Anyone who has gained the dharma is one true old buddha** (*tokuhō seran wa sunawachi ikko no shinko naru kobutsu* 得法せらんはすなはち一箇の眞箇なる古佛): A striking claim that the honorific term "old buddha," usually reserved for the seven buddhas of the past and the most revered masters of the Zen lineage, can be applied to anyone who has "gained the dharma" — including *bhikṣuṇīs*. See Supplementary Notes, s.v. "Old buddha."

58 **he or she engages us specifically in the new situation** (*shinjō no tokuchi ni sōsetsu su* 新條の特地に相接す): Dōgen uses here a version of the phrase *shinjō tokuchi* 新條 特地 ("a new instance in particular") that occurs several times in the *Shōbōgenzō*. The element *chi* 地 in *tokuchi* should be taken as an adverbial marker.

a relationship in which today takes on today (*konnichi shu nyū konnichi* 今日須入今日): Generally taken to mean a relationship based on the present. Dōgen uses the unusual expression "takes on today" in his "Shōbōgenzō Kannon" 正法眼藏觀音: "inexplicably it takes on today" (*mutan shu nyū konnichi* 無端須入今日). While the predicate *shu nyū* 須入 is regularly read here as the deontic predicate "should enter," the translation takes it in the sense "to employ," "to make use of."

59 **those possessed of the fourth fruit, the *pratyeka-buddhas*, or those among the three worthies and ten sages** (*shika shibutsu oyobi sanken jisshō* 四果支佛および三賢十聖): I.e., those on the three vehicles of *śrāvaka*, *pratyeka-buddha*, and bodhisattva. "The fourth fruit" (*shika* 四果) refers to the last of the four levels of attainment on the path leading to the state of the arhat (stream-entrant, once-returner, nonreturner, and

28. Making a Bow and Getting the Marrow *Raihai tokuzui* 禮拜得髓   369

Empty space is empty space; the four elements are the four elements; the five aggregates are the five aggregates.[60] The female is also like this. In gaining the way, all gain the way. All should hold in esteem one who has gained the dharma. Do not make an issue of whether it is man or woman. This is a most wondrous law of the way of the buddhas.

* * * * *

[28:23] {1:308}
又、宋朝に居士といふは、未出家の士夫なり。庵居して夫婦そなはれるもあり、また孤獨潔白なるもあり。なほ塵勞稠林といひぬべし。しかあれども、あきらむるところあるは、雲衲霞袂あつまりて禮拜請益すること、出家の宗匠におなじ。たとひ女人なりとも、畜生なりとも、またしかあるべし。

Again, in the Song dynasty, "layman" means a gentleman who has not left home.[61] Some reside in hermitages with their wives; some are solitary and pure.[62] We can say they are still in the thicket of afflictions.[63] Nevertheless, when they have some clarity, those robed in clouds and sleeved in mist gather to pay obeisance and request benefit, just as they

---

arhat); the term may also be read as "the four fruits" and refer to the *śrāvaka* path as a whole, but see Dōgen's use below, section 28. The term *shibutsu* 支佛 is an abbreviation of *byakushibutsu* 辟支佛, a transliteration of the Sanskrit *pratyeka-buddha*, interpreted either as "awakened alone" (*dokkaku* 獨覺) or "awakened to conditions" (*engaku* 緣覺).

60   **four elements** (*shidai* 四大): Earth, water, fire, and wind; the addition of space to this list yields the five elements (*godai* 五大); the further addition of consciousness gives the six elements (*rokudai* 六大). See Supplementary Notes, s.v. "Four elements and five aggregates."

five aggregates (*goun* 五蘊): The factors comprising the psychophysical organism: form, sensation, perception, formations, and consciousness. See Supplementary Notes, s.v. "Four elements and five aggregates."

61   **"layman" means a gentleman who has not left home** (*koji to iu wa, mishukke no shifu nari* 居士といふは、未出家の士夫なり): The term *koji* 居士 (literally, something like "resident gentleman") usually refers to a householder who is an active participant in the Buddhist institution, typically one expected to keep the five lay precepts: not to kill, steal, engage in sexual misconduct, lie, or drink intoxicants. The female counterpart is known as *nyo koji* 女居士. "To leave home" (*shukke* 出家; S. *pravajya*; "to go forth") is a standard term for abandoning the householder status and entering the Buddhist renunciant order.

62   **solitary and pure** (*kodoku keppaku* 孤獨潔白): I.e., are single and chaste.

63   **the thicket of afflictions** (*jinro chūrin* 塵勞稠林): Read literally, the rather mixed metaphor of "the dense grove of dust and toil"; a term regularly used for the ordinary condition of beings in saṃsāra, subject to the afflictions (*bonnō* 煩惱; S. *kleśa*). See Supplementary Notes, s.v. "Dust."

370 DŌGEN'S *SHŌBŌGENZŌ* VOLUME II

would with a master who had left home.[64] And so it should be whether it be a woman, whether it be a beast.

[28:24]
佛法の道理いまだゆめにもみざらんは、たとひ百歳なる老比丘なりとも、得法の男女におよぶべきにあらず、うやまふべからず、ただ賓主の禮のみなり。

One who has not yet seen the truth of the buddha dharma even in his dreams, though he be an old bhikṣu of a hundred years, cannot reach the status of a man or woman who has gained the dharma.[65] We should not venerate him but merely treat him according to the etiquette of guest and host.

[28:25]
佛法を修行し、佛法を道取せんは、たとひ七歳の女流なりとも、すなはち四衆の導師なり、衆生の慈父なり。たとへば龍女成佛のごとし。供養恭敬せんこと、諸佛如來にひとしかるべし。これすなはち佛道の古儀なり。しらず、單傳せざらんは、あはれむべし。

Those who practice the buddha dharma and speak the buddha dharma, though females of but seven years, are guides for the fourfold saṃgha and compassionate fathers for all living beings.[66] They are like the dragon girl who attained buddhahood.[67] The offerings and homage to them should be the same as those to the buddhas, the tathāgatas. This is an ancient rule in the way of the buddhas. Those who do not know it and have not received its unique transmission are to be pitied.

---

64 **robed in clouds and sleeved in mist** (*unnō kabei* 雲衲霞袂): A literary expression for the itinerant monk; akin to the more common "clouds and water" (*unsui* 雲水).

pay obeisance and request benefit (*raihai shin'eki* 禮拜請益): I.e., pay respects and ask for instruction.

65 **One who has not yet seen the truth of the buddha dharma even in his dreams** (*buppō no dōri imada yume ni mo mizaran* 佛法の道理いまだゆめにもみざらん): A Japanese variant of the remark, in section 16 above, by Moshan about the seventeen monks from Shu.

an old bhikṣu of a hundred years (*hyakusai naru rō biku* 百歳なる老比丘): Recalling the vow of Zhaozhou in section 8 above.

66 **though females of but seven years** (*tatoi shichisai no nyoryū nari tomo* たとひ七歳の女流なりとも): Again, recalling Zhaozhou's vow in section 8 above.

fourfold saṃgha (*shishu* 四衆): A term that can refer to (a) bhikṣu, *bhikṣuṇī*, *upāsaka* and *upāsikā* (monks, nuns, lay men and women); or to (b) bhikṣu, *bhikṣuṇī*, *śrāmaṇera* and *śrāmaṇerikā* (fully ordained monks, fully ordained nuns, novice monks, and novice nuns).

67 **the dragon girl who attained buddhahood** (*ryūnyo jōbutsu* 龍女成佛): Reference to the well-known story in the *Lotus Sūtra* (*Miaofa lianhua jing* 妙法蓮華經, T.262.9:35b13-c26) of the eight-year-old daughter of the Dragon King, who transforms herself into a man and immediately attains buddhahood.

28. Making a Bow and Getting the Marrow *Raihai tokuzui* 禮拜得髓   371

正法眼藏禮拜得髓第二十八

Treasury of the True Dharma Eye
Making a Bow and Getting the Marrow
Number 28

[Ryūmonji MS:]

延應庚子清明日記、觀音導利興聖寶林寺

*Written at the Kannon Dōri Kōshō Hōrin Monastery; on the day of Sei-
mei, in the senior metal year of the rat, in En'ō [7 April 1240]*[68]

Appendix

[28:26]

又、和漢の古今に、帝にして女人あり。その國土、みなこの帝王の所領な
り、人、みなその臣となる。これは、人をうやまふにあらず、位をうやま
ふなり。比丘尼も又その人をうやまふことは、むかしよりなし、ひとへに
得法をうやまふなり。

Furthermore, throughout past and present in both Wa and Kan, there
have been women who held the rank of emperor.[69] The land was all con-
trolled by these emperors, and the people all became their subjects. They
were not venerated as individuals; they were venerated for their rank.
Bhikṣuṇīs as well, from ancient times were not venerated as individuals;
it is solely their having gained the dharma that has been venerated.

[28:27] {1:309}

又、阿羅漢となれる比丘尼あるには、四果にしたがふ功德みなきたる。功
德なほしたがふ、人天たれか四果の功德よりもすぐれん。三界の諸天、み
なおよぶ處にあらず、しかしながらすつるものとなる、諸天みなうやまふ
處なり。況や如來の正法を傳來し、菩薩の大心をおこさん、たれのうやま
はざるかあらん。これをうやまはざらんは、おのれがをかしなり。おのれ
が無上菩提をうやまはざれば、謗法の愚痴なり。

---

68 **Seimei** 清明: Literally "clear and bright," a festival on the fifth of the twenty-four
seasonal periods into which the traditional solar calendar was divided. It is celebrated
on the fifteenth day after the spring equinox, corresponding in 1240 to the seventh day
of April.

69 **Wa and Kan** 和漢: I.e., Japan and China. Dōgen's use of "throughout past and
present" (*kokon* 古今) here must be taken in the sense "thoughout history," since neither
China nor Japan had female emperors in his day. In Japan, between the years 592 and
770, no less than seven women reigned as emperors, while China was briefly ruled by
the famous Wu Zetian 武則天 (r. 690-705).

372   DŌGEN'S *SHŌBŌGENZŌ* VOLUME II

Also, when there is a *bhikṣuṇī* who has become an arhat, all the virtues that accompany the fourth fruit will come to her. These virtues surely accompany it; and who among humans or devas surpasses the virtues of the fourth fruit?[70] It is not something reached by the devas of the three realms; those who abandon everything are venerated by all the devas.[71] How much more in the case of those who have received the transmission of the true dharma of the tathāgatas and aroused the great mind of the bodhisattva — who would not venerate them? Those who fail to venerate them are themselves at fault; one who fails to venerate unsurpassed bodhi is an imbecile who denigrates the dharma.

[28:28]

又、わが國には、帝者のむすめ、或は大臣のむすめの、后宮に準ずるあり、また皇后の院號せるあり。これら、かみをそれるあり、かみをそれざるあり。しかあるに、貪名愛利の比丘僧に似たる僧侶、この家門にわしるに、かうべをはきものにうたずと云ことなし。なほ主從よりも劣なり、況やまた奴僕となりて、としをふるもおほし。あはれなるかな、小國邊地にうまれぬるに、如是の邪風ともしらざることは。天竺・唐土にはいまだなし、我が國にのみあり、悲しむべし。あながちに鬢髮をそりて、如來の正法をやぶる、深重の罪業と云べし。これひとへに夢幻空華の世途をわするるによりて、女人の奴僕と繋縛せられたること、かなしむべし。いたづらなる世途のため、なほかくの如す。無上菩提のため、なんぞ得法のうやまふべきをうやまはざらん。これは、法をおもくするこころざしあさく、法をもとむるこころざしあまねからざるゆえなり。

Again, in our land, there are daughters of emperors or daughters of ministers of state who have served as imperial consorts, as well as empresses who took the title "cloistered."[72] Some have shaved their heads, and others do not shave their heads. Clergy resembling members of the bhikṣu saṃgha who are greedy for fame and love profit run to their houses and never fail to knock their heads at their footwear.[73] They are more

---

70   **These virtues surely accompany it** (*kudoku nao shitagau* 功徳なほしたがふ): Taking *nao* なほ in the sense *tashika* たしか.

71   **the three realms** (*sangai* 三界): I.e, the threefold world system of saṃsāra; see Supplementary Notes, s.v. "Three realms."

those who abandon everything (*shikashi nagara sutsuru mono to naru* しかしながらすつるものとなる): Presumably, a reference to the arhats, who forsake the world of rebirth and enter nirvāṇa. Some would read this phrase "those who are completely abandoned."

72   **empresses who took the title "cloistered"** (*kōgō no ingō seru* 皇后の院號せる): The title "cloistered" (*in* 院) was given to members of the imperial family retired from court into a Buddhist cloister.

73   **Clergy resembling members of the bhikṣu saṃgha** (*biku sō ni nitaru sōryo* 比丘僧ににたる僧侶): Likely a sarcastic reference to clergy unworthy of the bhikṣu saṃgha.

never fail to knock their heads at their footwear (*kōbe o hakimono ni utazu to iu koto*

28. Making a Bow and Getting the Marrow *Raihai tokuzui* 禮拜得髓   373

degraded than a vassal with his master. Not to mention that there are many who spend years as their servants. How pathetic it is that, having been born in a small country and peripheral land, they do not realize that this is a corrupt custom.[74] It never existed in Sindhu or the Land of the Tang but only in our land.[75] It is deplorable. Willfully to shave one's head and then destroy the true dharma of the tathāgatas must be considered a profoundly serious offense. It is deplorable that, solely because they have forgotten the paths of this world are dreams, illusions, sky flowers, they are bound as the servants of women.[76] They are like this for the sake of the worthless paths of this world.[77] Why do they not for the sake of unsurpassed bodhi venerate those who should be venerated for having gained the dharma? It is because their determination to take the dharma seriously is shallow and their determination to seek the dharma is not all-encompassing.

[28:29] {1:310}

すでにたからをむさぼるとき、女人のたからにてあれば、うべからずとおもはず、法をもとめんときは、このこころざしにはすぐるべし。もししからば、草木牆壁も正法をほどこし、天地・萬法も正法をあたふるなり。かならずしるべき道理なり。眞善知識にあふといへども、いまだこの志氣をたてて法をもとめざるときは、法水のうるほひ、かうぶらざるなり。審細に功夫すべし。

When they covet riches, they do not think that, because they are a woman's riches, they should not accept them. When they seek the dharma, this attitude should be even stronger. If it is, then grass, trees, fences, and walls will bestow the true dharma; heaven and earth and the myriad dharmas will likewise provide the true dharma.[78] This is a truth we should certainly understand. When we do not seek the dharma with this attitude, we will not receive any moisture from the waters of the dharma,

---

nashi かうべをはきものにうたずといふことなし): i.e., kowtow at the women's feet.

74   **a small country and peripheral land** (*shōkoku henji* 小國邊地): I.e., an insignificant country on the borders of the Buddhist world; a common characterization of Japan by Japanese Buddhist authors of Dōgen's day.

75   **the Land of the Tang** (*Tōdo* 唐土): I e., China, referred to here by its most powerful dynasty (618-907).

76   **sky flowers** (*kūge* 空華): S. *khapuṣpa*; spots appearing to the diseased eye; a standard metaphor in Buddhist texts for what is mere appearance without objective reality; see Supplementary Notes, s.v. "Clouded eyes and sky flowers."

77   **paths of this world** (*seito* 世途): I.e. worldly livelihoods; the ways we make our way in the world.

78   **heaven and earth and the myriad dharmas** (*tenchi manbō* 天地・萬法): Following Kawamura's punctuation, without which, the phrase could read "the myriad dharmas of heaven and earth."

374 DŌGEN'S *SHŌBŌGENZŌ* VOLUME II

even though we encounter a true wise friend.[79] We should carefully work on this.

[28:30]

又、いま至愚のはなはだしき人おもふことは、女流は貪婬所對の境界にてあり、とおもふこころをあらためずして、これをみる。佛子如是あるべからず。婬所對の境となりぬべし、とていむことあらば、一切男子も又いむべきか。染汚の因縁となることは、男も境となる、女も境縁となる。非男非女も境縁となる、夢幻空華も境縁となる。あるいは水影を縁として非梵行あることありき、あるいは天日を縁として非梵行ありき。神も境となる、鬼も境となる。その縁、かぞへつくすべからず、八萬四千の境界ありと云ふ、これみなすつべきか、みるべからざるか。

Again, today some people, stupid in the extreme, look at females without revising their sense that they are the objects of lust.[80] A child of the Buddha should not be like this.[81] If we despise them because they become the objects of lust, should we also despise all males? In becoming an occasion of defilement, males may become the objects, females may become the objects; those neither male nor female may become the objects; dreams, illusions, and sky flowers may become the objects.[82] There have been impure acts committed with a reflection in the water as the object; there have been impure acts with the sun in the heaven as the object.[83] Spirits may become the objects; demons may become the objects.[84] These objects cannot be counted. It is said there are eighty-four thousand objects. Should we discard them all? Should we not look at them?

---

79 **moisture from the waters of the dharma** (*hōsui no uruoi* 法水のうるほひ): I.e., benefit from the Buddhist teachings; a standard metaphor.

80 **the objects of lust** (*ton'in shotai no kyōkai* 貪婬所對の境界): Literally, "the perceptual object that is taken by lust as its object."

81 **child of the Buddha** (*busshi* 佛子): I.e., a Buddhist; the progenitor imagined here is no doubt Buddha Śākyamuni, often depicted as the father of his followers — especially, perhaps, of the bodhisattvas among his followers, who sometimes describe themselves as members of the "buddha clan" (S. *buddha-gotra*).

82 **neither male nor female** (*hinan hinyo* 非男非女): Used in reference to eunuchs (*ōmon* 黄門) and hermaphrodites (*nigyō* 二形).

83 **impure acts** (*hibongyō* 非梵行): A term representing a combination of transliteration and translation of the Sanskrit *abrahmacarya* (not the practice of chastity). It is unclear what, if any, sources Dōgen may have had in mind here.

84 **Spirits may become the objects; demons may become the objects** (*shin mo kyō to naru, ki mo kyō to naru* 神も境となる、鬼も境となる): Taking *shin* 神 and *ki* 鬼 as good and evil spirits. The *Fanwang jing* 梵網經 (T.1484.24:1004b27-28) prohibits sexual acts with female animals, devas, demons, and spirits (*chusheng nü zhutian guishen nü* 畜生女諸天鬼神女).

28. Making a Bow and Getting the Marrow *Raihai tokuzui* 禮拜得髓　375

[28:31]

律云、男二所、女三所、おなじくこれ波羅夷不共住。

In the vinaya, it is said, with a man, two places; with a woman, three places: these are all *pārājika*, requiring expulsion.[85]

[28:32]

しかあれば、婬所對の境になりぬべしとてきらはば、一切の男子と女人と、たがひにあいきらうて、更に得度の期あるべからず。この道理、子細に撿點すべし。

Thus, if we despise those who become the objects of lust, all men and women will despise each other, and there will be no prospect of deliverance.[86] This truth, we should examine in detail.

[28:33]

又、外道も妻なきあり。妻なしといへども、佛法に入らざれば、邪見の外道なり。佛弟子も、在家の二衆は夫婦あり。夫婦あれども、佛弟子なれば、人中・天上にも、かたをひとしくする餘類なし。

Again, there are followers of other paths who do not have wives.[87] Though they may not have wives, since they have not entered the buddha dharma, they are still followers of other paths with false views. Among disciples of the Buddha as well, the two classes of householders have husbands and wives.[88] Though they have husbands and wives, since they are disciples of the Buddha, there are no other types among humans and devas who can stand shoulder to shoulder with them.

---

85 **In the vinaya** (*ritsu* 律): A summary of the rule (found, for example, in the *Sifen lü* 四分律, T.1428.22:571c17-23), that a monk is guilty of a *pārājika* offense if he inserts his penis into the anus, vagina, or mouth of a woman, or into the anus or mouth of a man.

***pārājika*, requiring expulsion** (*harai fugūjū* 波羅夷不共住): The most serious category of offense, requiring that the guilty party be expelled from the saṃgha.

86 **no prospect of deliverance** (*tokudo no ki aru bekarazu* 得度の期あるべからず): Given the context here, the term *tokudo* 得度 ("deliverance") might also be taken in the sense "ordination" into the monastic community.

87 **followers of other paths** (*gedō* 外道): I.e., members of non-Buddhist traditions (S. *tīrthika*); in the South Asian context, most often referring to Hindus and Jains; in East Asia, used as well for Daoism and Confucianism.

88 **the two classes of householders** (*zaike no nishu* 在家の二衆): I.e. lay men (*ubasoku* 優婆塞; S. *upāsaka*) and lay women (*ubai* 優婆; S. *upāsikā*).

376 DŌGEN'S *SHŌBŌGENZŌ* VOLUME II

[28:34] {1:311}

又、唐國にも、愚痴僧ありて、願志を立するにいはく、 生生世世、ながく
女人をみることなからん。この願、なにの法にかよる。世法によるか、佛
法によるか、外道の法によるか、天魔の法によるか。女人なにのとがかあ
る、男子なにの德かある。惡人は、男子も惡人なるあり、善人は、女人も
善人なるあり。聞法をねがひ、出離をもとむること、かならず男子・女人
によらず。もし未斷惑のときは、男子・女人おなじく未斷惑なり。斷惑證
理のときは、男子・女人、簡別さらにあらず。又、ながく女人をみじと願
せば、衆生無邊誓願度のときも、女人をばすつべきか。捨てば菩薩にあら
ず、佛慈悲と云はんや。ただこれ聲聞の酒にゑふことふかきによりて、酔
狂の言語なり。人天、これをまことと信ずべからず。

Again, in the Land of the Tang, there was an ignorant monk who made
a vow saying, "In life after life, through age after age, may I never look
upon a woman."[89] On what dharma is this vow based?[90] Is it based on
the worldly dharma? Is it based on the buddha dharma? Is it based on
the dharma of an other path? Is it based on the dharma of the Deva
Māra? What fault do women have? What virtue do men have? Among
bad people, there are men who are bad people; among good people, there
are women who are good people. Desiring to hear the dharma and seeking emancipation certainly do not depend on whether one is a man or
a woman. When they have not cut off their delusions, men and women
alike have not cut off their delusions; when they have cut off their delusions and verified the principle, between men and women there is no
distinction. Furthermore, if you vow never to look upon a woman, are
you to exclude women when [you say] "*living beings are limitless, I vow
to deliver them*"?[91] If you exclude them, you are not a bodhisattva; do
you call this the compassion of the buddhas? These are just the drunken
words of someone deeply intoxicated by the wine of the *śrāvaka*.[92] Humans and devas should not believe in this as true.

---

89   **there was an ignorant monk** (*guchi sō arite* 愚痴僧ありて): Or, perhaps, "there
are (or have been) ignorant monks." The most likely target here seems to be the famous
Huayan scholar Chengguan 澄觀, who made ten vows, of which the third is "my eyes
shall not look upon a woman" (*mu bushi nüren* 目不視女人) (*Song Gaoseng zhuan* 宋高
僧傳, T.2061.5:737c15).

90   **On what dharma is this vow based?** (*kono gan, nani no hō ni ka yoru* この願、
なにの法にかよる): The term *hō* 法 ("dharma") can be taken as "teaching" or "rule" or
"norm."

91   **"living beings are limitless, I vow to deliver them"** (*shujō muhen seigan do* 衆生
無邊誓願度): The first of the four great vows (*shi guseigan* 四弘誓願) of the bodhisattva.

92   **the wine of the *śrāvaka*** (*shōmon no shu* 聲聞の酒): I.e., the teachings for those on
the *śrāvaka* vehicle, which does not involve the bodhisattva vow to deliver beings.

28. Making a Bow and Getting the Marrow *Raihai tokuzui* 禮拜得髓 377

[28:35]

又、むかし犯罪ありしとてきらはば、一切、菩薩をもきらふべし。もし、のちに犯罪ありぬべし、とてきらはば、一切發心の菩薩をもきらふべし。如此きらはば、一切みなすてん、なにによりてか佛法現成せん。如是のことばは、佛法を知らざる癡人の狂言なり、かなしむべし。もしなんぢが願の如くにあらば、釋尊、および在世の諸菩薩、みな犯罪在りけるか、又なんぢよりも菩提心もあさかりけるか、しづかに觀察すべし。付法藏の祖師、および佛在世の菩薩、この願なくば、佛法にならふべき處やある、と參學すべきなり。もし汝ぢが願のごとくにあらば、女人を濟度せざるのみにあらず、得法の女人、世にいでて、人天のために説法せんときも、來りてきくべからざるか。もし來りてきかずは、菩薩にあらず、すなはち外道なり。

Again, if you despise them as having committed offenses in the past, then you should also despise bodhisattvas.[93] If you despise them as likely subsequently to commit offenses, then you should also despise all the bodhisattvas who have brought forth the mind [of bodhi]. If you are like this, you will be forsaking everyone. How then will the buddha dharma be realized? Words like these are the crazed talk of a fool who does not understand the buddha dharma.[94] How sad. According to your vow, would Śākya, the Honored One, as well the bodhisattvas during his lifetime all have committed offenses?[95] And would their aspiration for bodhi have been shallower than yours? You should quietly examine this. If the ancestral masters who succeed to the treasury of the dharma and the bodhisattvas during the lifetime of the Buddha did not make this vow, you should study whether it has something to be learned in the buddha dharma.[96] According to your vow, not only would you not save women, but when a woman who has gained the way emerges in the world to

---

93 **if you despise them as having committed offenses in the past** (*mukashi bonzai arishi tote kirawaba* むかし犯罪ありしとてきらはば): Though not explicitly stated, the object here is surely "women," who were often thought to have been born in their unhappy estate by reason of bad karma in past lives. As the sentence goes on to point out, of course all living beings, including advanced bodhisattvas, have committed countless bad deeds in their past lives.

94 **Words like these** (*kaku no gotoki no kotoba* 如是のことば): I.e., words like the vow never to look upon a woman.

95 **According to your vow** (*moshi nanji ga gan no gotoku ni araba* もしなんぢが願の如くにあらば): Up to this point in his discussion of the vow not to look upon women, Dōgen may have been speaking in general terms, but here he explicitly addresses his questions to the "ignorant monk" who made the vow. Since, of course, Śākyamuni and his bodhisattva disciples are depicted in scripture as teaching women, they would be violating that monk's vow.

96 **whether it has something to be learned in the buddha dharma** (*buppō ni narau beki tokoro ya aru* 佛法にならふべき處やある): A tentative translation of a phrase that might also be read "whether they [i.e., the ancestral masters and bodhisattvas] have something to be learned in the buddha dharma."

preach the dharma for humans and devas, are you not supposed to come to hear her? Should you not come to hear her, you are not a bodhisattva; you are in fact a follower of an other path.

[28:36] {1:312}
今大宋國をみるに、久修練行に似たる僧侶の、いたづらに海沙をかぞへて、生死海に流浪せざるあり。女人にてあるとも、參尋知識し、辦道功夫して、人天の導師にてあるあり。餅をうらず、餅をすてし老婆等あり。あはれむべし、男兒の比丘僧にてあれども、いたづらに教海のいさごをかぞへて、佛法は夢にもいまだみざること。

When we look at the Land of the Great Song today, there are clergy who seem trained in long practice who drift about in the ocean of birth and death while vainly counting the sands of the ocean.[97] Meanwhile, there are those who, although women, inquire of wise friends, make concentrated efforts to pursue the way, and are guides to humans and devas.[98] There are those like the old woman who discarded her cake without selling it.[99] How pitiful it is that a male, while a member of the bhikṣu saṃgha, would vainly count the sands in the ocean of the teachings and never see the buddha dharma even in his dreams.

[28:37]
およそ境をみては、あきらむることをならふべし。おぢてにぐるとのみならふは、小乘聲聞の教行なり。東をすてて西にかくれんとすれば、西にも境界なきにあらず。たとへにげぬるとおもふとあきらめざるにも、遠にても境なり、近にても境なり。なほこれ解脱の分にあらず、遠練はいよいよ深かるべし。

In sum, when we see an object, we should learn to see it clearly.[100] If we learn only to fear and escape it, this is the teaching and practice of the śrāvaka of the Small Vehicle. If we try to abandon the east and hide in

---

97 **drift about in the ocean of birth and death** (*shoji kai ni rurō sezaru* 生死海に流浪せざる): Reading *rurō seru* 流浪せる.

vainly counting the sands of the ocean (*itazura ni kaisha o kazoete* いたづらに海沙をかぞへて): To "count grains of sand" is a common metaphor for scholastic attention to the words in Buddhist books. See Supplementary Notes, s.v. "Counting sand."

98 **inquire of wise friends** (*sanjin chishiki shi* 參尋知識し): I.e., study with Buddhist teachers, the Chinese verb-object construction being treated as itself a verb.

99 **the old woman who discarded her cake without selling it** (*mochii o urazu, mochii o suteshi rōba* 餅をうらず、餅をすてし老婆): Allusion to the story of the old woman selling cakes who refused to sell her cakes to the learned monk Deshan Xuanjian 德山宣鑑 (or 宣鑒, 780-865) when he failed to answer her question on the dharma. Dōgen treats this story in his "Shōbōgenzō shin fukatoku" 正法眼藏心不可得, where he does not, in fact, seem to think much of the old woman.

100 **when we see an object** (*kyō o mite wa* 境をみては): Though never made explicit, clearly throughout this section, the word "object" (*kyō* 境, *kyōkai* 境界) refers to the "objects of lust" (*ton'in shotai no kyōkai* 貪婬所對の境界) introduced in section 31, above.

28. Making a Bow and Getting the Marrow *Raihai tokuzui* 禮拜得髓   379

the west, the west will also not be without objects. Even if we think we have escaped them, when we have not clearly understood them, they are objects, even if distant, objects, even if close. This is still not a factor in liberation.[101] [Attachment to] the distant objects will only grow deeper.[102]

* * * * *

[28:38]

又、日本國に、ひとつのわらひごとあり。いわゆる、或は結界の地と稱し、あるいは大乘の道場と稱して、比丘尼・女人等を來入せしめず。邪風ひさしくつたはれて、人、わきまふることなし。稽古の人、あらためず、博達の士も、かんがふることなし。或は權者の所爲と稱し、あるいは古先の遺風と號して、更に論ずることなき、笑はば人の腸も斷じぬべし。權者とはなに者ぞ、賢人か聖人か、神か鬼か、十聖か三賢か、等覺か妙覺か。又、ふるきをあらためざるべくは、生死流轉をばすつべからざるか。

Again, there is something laughable in the Land of Japan: called "places of fixed realms," or called "practice places of the Great Vehicle," they do not permit *bhikṣuṇīs* or other women to enter.[103] This corrupt custom has been handed down over a long time, and no one ever discerns it as such. Those who investigate the ancient do not correct it; gentlemen of broad mastery have given it no thought. It is said to be something established by avatars, or it is called the heritage of the old forebears.[104] That no one has gone on to take issue with this makes a person laugh till he could bust his gut. Who are these avatars? Are they worthies; are they sages?[105] Are they spirits; are they demons? Are they the ten sages; are they the three worthies? Are they the virtually awakened? Are they the wondrously awakened?[106] Furthermore, if we should not correct what

---

101 **a factor in liberation** (*gedatsu no bun* 解脱の分): Reading as a variant of the standard Buddhist term *gedatsu bun* 解脱分 ("having to do with, or being conducive to liberation"; S. *mokṣa-bhāgīya*).

102 **distant objects** (*onren* 遠練): Reading *ren* 練 as *kyō* 境.

103 **"places of fixed realms"** (*kekkai no chi* 結界の地): Sacred precincts, considered ritually pure and off-limits to certain types of people and objects. The term *kekkai* 結界 ("binding the boundary"; S. *sīmā-bandha*) is applied broadly to various sacred spaces; those specifically prohibiting women are known as *nyonin kekkai* 女人結界.

104 **avatars** (*gonza* 權者): (Also read *gonja*.) Temporary manifestations of spiritual beings, like the buddhas and bodhisattvas; better known as *gongen* 權現 ("expedient appearance") or *gonge* 權化 ("expedient transformation").

105 **Are they worthies; are they sages?** (*kennin ka shōnin ka* 賢人か聖人か): Here, presumably, the worthies and sages of Chinese tradition, as opposed to the "ten sages" (*jisshō* 十聖) and "three worthies" (*sanken* 三賢) on the stages of the bodhisattva path, given just below.

106 **virtually awakened** (*tōgaku* 等覺); **wondrously awakened** (*myōkaku* 妙覺): The final two stages of the bodhisattva path according to the fifty-two-stage schema common

380 DŌGEN'S *SHŌBŌGENZŌ* VOLUME II

is old, should we then not abandon our drifting about through birth and death?

[28:39] {1:313}

況や大師釋尊、これ無上正等覺なり。あきらむべきは、ことごとくあきら
む、おこのふべきは、ことごとくこれをおこのふ、解脱すべきは、みな解
脱せり。いまのたれか、ほとりにもおよばん。しかあるに、在世の佛會
に、みな比丘・比丘尼・優婆塞・優婆夷等の四衆あり、八部あり、三十七
部あり、八萬四千部あり。みなこれ佛界を結せること、あらたなる佛會な
り。いづれの會か比丘尼なき、女人なき、男子なき、八部なき。如來在世
の佛會よりもすぐれて清淨ならん結界をば、われらねがふべきにあらず、
天魔界なるがゆえに。佛會の法儀は、自界他方、三世千佛、ことなること
なし。ことなる法あらんは、佛會にあらずと知るべし。

Need we mention that the great teacher Śākya, the Honored One, is
one who has attained unsurpassed, perfect awakening: all that he should
understand he has understood; all that he should do, he has done; all that
from which he should be liberated, he has been liberated from. Who
today comes close to him? Nevertheless, in the assembly of the Buddha
during his lifetime, there were the four classes: bhikṣu, *bhikṣuṇī*, *upāsaka*, and *upāsikā*; there was the group of eight; there was the group of
thirty-seven; there was the group of eighty-four thousand.[107] The realm
of the buddha fixed by all these is the obvious buddha assembly. In which
assembly are there no *bhikṣuṇīs*, no women, no men, no eight classes?
We ought not hope for a restricted realm of purity superior to the buddha
assembly during the lifetime of the Tathāgata; for this would be a realm
of the Deva Māra. The dharma conventions of a buddha assembly do not
differ, whether in our own realm or other quarters or among the thousand

---

in East Asian Buddhism; the latter represents the supreme perfect bodhi of a buddha; the
former, the stage just preceding that.

107 **group of eight** (*hachibu* 八部): A standard list of mythical beings often appearing
in the audience for the buddhas' sermons in Mahāyāna literature: devas (*ten* 天; heavenly
beings, inhabiting the upper reaches of Mount Sumeru and the celestial realms), *nāgas*
(*ryū* 龍; great serpents living in the clouds or bodies of water and associated with rain),
yakṣas (*yasha* 夜叉; flesh-eating flying demons), gandharvas (*kendatsuba* 乾闥婆; spirit
musicians who subsist on scents), *asuras* (*ashura* 阿修羅; demigods, or titans, who war
with the gods), garuḍas (*karura* 迦樓羅; mythical birds that feed on *nāgas*), *kiṃnaras*
(*kinnara* 緊那羅; heavenly musicians, sometimes described as part god, part human, part
animal), and *mahoragas* (*magoraga* 摩睺羅迦; giant python-like snakes).

group of thirty-seven (*sanjūshichibu* 三十七部): Perhaps a reference to "the thirty-sev-
en honored ones" (the five buddhas and thirty-two attendant bodhisattvas) of the Dia-
mond-realm maṇḍala. Some have suggested that this is a reference to "the thirty-seven
factors of awakening" (*sanjūshichi dōhon* 三十七道本), but this traditional list of Buddhist virtues would hardly make sense here.

group of eighty-four thousand (*hachiman shisenbu* 八萬四千部): I.e., all the myriad
beings taught by the buddhas.

28. Making a Bow and Getting the Marrow *Raihai tokuzui* 禮拜得髓　381

buddhas of the three times.[108] If it has a different rule, we can be sure it is not a buddha assembly.

[28:40]
いはゆる四果は極位なり。大乗にても小乗にても、極位の功徳は差別せず。然あるに、比丘尼の、四果を證するおほし。三界のうちにも、十方の佛土にも、いづれの界にかいたらざらん。たれかこの行履をふさぐことあらん。又、妙覺は無上位なり。女人すでに作佛す、諸法いづれのものか究盡せられざらん。たれかこれをふさぎて、いたらしめざらんと擬せん。すでに遍照於十方の功徳あり、界畔いかがせん。又、天女をもふさぎていたらしめざるか、神女をもふさぎていたらしめざるか。天女・神女も、いまだ斷惑の類にあらず、なほこれ流轉の衆生なり。犯罪あるときはあり、なきときはなし。人女・畜女も、罪あるときはあり、罪なきときはなし。天のみち、神のみち、ふさがん人はたれぞ。すでに三世の佛會に參詣す、佛所に參學す。佛所・佛會にことならん、たれか佛法と信受せん。ただこれ狂惑世間人の至愚也。野干の、窟穴を人にうばはれざらんとをしむよりも、おろかなり。

"The fourth fruit" is the ultimate level. Whether in the Great Vehicle or the Small Vehicle, the virtues of the ultimate level are not distinguished.[109] Yet there are many *bhikṣuṇīs* who have realized the fourth fruit. Whether in the three realms, whether in the buddha lands of the ten directions, what realm do they not reach? Who would block their conduct? Again, wondrous awakening is the unsurpassed level. Women have become buddhas, so which of the dharmas have they not exhaustively investigated?[110] Who would think to obstruct them and prevent them from proceeding? Since they have the virtue of "*universally il-*

108　**the thousand buddhas of the three times** (*sanze senbutsu* 三世千佛): Reference to the tradition that there are a thousand buddhas in each of the three kalpas of past, present, and future.

109　**the virtues of the ultimate level are not distinguished** (*gokui no kudoku wa sabetsu sezu* 極位の功徳は差別せず): A rather surprising claim that runs counter to most Mahāyāna literature, which emphasizes that the qualities developed on the bodhisattva path to the unsurpassed, perfect awakening of a buddha far surpass those attained by the *śrāvaka* path to the fourth fruit of the arhat — a distinction that Dōgen himself usually takes for granted in his frequent dismissals of the Small Vehicle (as, e.g., in section 35 above). The treatment of the arhat as equal to a buddha is also found in the "Shōbōgenzō arakan" 正法眼藏阿羅漢 chapter.

110　**Women have become buddhas** (*nyonin sude ni sabutsu su* 女人すでに作佛す): Or "since women become buddhas." "Becoming a buddha" (*sabutsu* 作佛) is equivalent to attaining "wondrous awakening" (*myōkaku* 妙覺) and is, by standard Buddhist definition, the mastery of all dharmas (i.e., Buddhist teachings and practices). The claim that women become buddhas is a controversial one that goes counter to much Buddhist literature; Dōgen likely has in mind here the famous case of the dragon king's daughter referred to above, section 25 (though she attained buddhahood only after transforming herself into a male).

382 DŌGEN'S *SHŌBŌGENZŌ* VOLUME II

lumining the ten directions," what could their boundary be?[111] Again, would a devī be blocked and not permitted to proceed? Would a goddess be blocked and not permitted to proceed? The devī and the goddess, not yet being types that have cut off the afflictions, are still living beings that drift about. When they have offenses, they have them; when they do not, they do not. Human females and animal females as well, when they have offenses, have them; when they have no offenses, have none. Who would block the paths of the devas and the paths of the gods? Since they take part in the assemblies of the buddhas of the three times, they study at the places of the buddhas.[112] Whatever differs from the places of the buddhas and the assemblies of the buddhas — who would believe it to be the buddha dharma? This is the extreme of stupidity that only "*deceives the people of the world*."[113] It is more stupid than the little fox that fears someone will seize its den.

[28:41] {1:314}

又、佛弟子の位は、菩薩にもあれ、たとひ聲聞にもあれ、第一比丘、第二比丘尼、第三優婆塞、第四優婆夷、かくのごとし。この位、天上・人間ともにしれり、ひさしくきこえたり。しかあるを、佛弟子第二の位は、轉輪聖王よりもすぐれ、釋提桓因よりもすぐるべし、いたらざるところあるべからず。いはんや小國邊土の國王・大臣の位にならぶべきにあらず。いま、比丘尼いるべからず、と云道場をみるに、田夫・野人・農夫・樵翁みだれ入る。況や國王・大臣・百官・宰相、たれか入らんあらん。田夫等と比丘尼と、學道を論じ、得位を論ぜんに、勝劣つひにいかん。たとひ世法にて論ずとも、たとひ佛法にて論ずとも、比丘尼のいたらん處へ、田夫・野人あへていたるべからず。錯亂のはなはだしき、小國、はじめてこのあとをのこす。あはれむべし、三界慈父の長子、小國にきたりて、ふさぎていたらしめざる處あり。

---

111 **"universally illuminating the ten directions"** (*henshō o jippō* 遍照於十方): A standard description of a buddha, often used in reference to a buddha's all-pervading dharma body. Dōgen may well be recalling here the verse spoken by the dragon girl in praise of buddhahood in the *Lotus Sūtra* (*Miaofa lianhua jing* 妙法蓮華經, T.262.9:35b28):

深達罪福相、遍照於十方。

Deeply mastering the marks of good and evil karma,
Universally illuminating the ten directions.

112 **Since they take part in the assemblies of the buddhas of the three times** (*sude ni sanze no butsue ni sankei su* すでに三世の佛會に參詣す): The subject here is unexpressed; it could be taken either as the devas and gods, or as the females of these species, or as females more broadly.

113 **This is the extreme of stupidity that only "deceives the people of the world"** (*tada kore kyōwaku seken nin no shigu nari* ただこれ狂惑世間人の至愚也). Reading *kyōwaku* 誑惑 ("deception") for *kyōwaku* 狂惑. The antecedent of "this" is most likely the general concept and practice of setting up of zones off-limits to women. The phrase "to deceive people of the world" comes from the *Lotus Sūtra* (*Miaofa lianhua jing* 妙法蓮華經, T.262.9:36c5), in an attack by the sūtra's opponents on its authors for creating a scripture that teaches the doctrines of the other paths.

28. Making a Bow and Getting the Marrow *Raihai tokuzui* 禮拜得髓　　383

Again, the ranks of the disciples of the buddha, be they bodhisattvas or *śrāvakas*, are as follows: first, bhikṣu; second, *bhikṣuṇī*; third, *upāsaka*; fourth, *upāsikā*. These ranks are known in the heavens and among the humans and have long been heard. Thus, the second rank of the disciples of the buddha must be superior to the wheel-turning sage king, superior to Śakrodevānām Indra; there should not be any place she cannot go.[114] How much less then should she be lined up in the ranks of the kings and great ministers of a small country and peripheral land. When we look at the practice places now where *bhikṣuṇīs* are not permitted to enter, all manner of country hicks and rustic clods, peasant farmers and old wood-cutters enter at will. And, needless to say, who among the kings, great ministers, hundred officials, and prime ministers does not enter?[115] Considering the country hicks and the *bhikṣuṇīs* in terms of their study of the way or their attainment of rank, who in the end would be the superior? Whether we consider them in terms of secular norms or consider them in terms of the buddha dharma, country hicks and rustic clods should not be able to go where the *bhikṣuṇīs* cannot. This is confusion in the extreme: our small country is the first to leave this trace.[116] How sad, that the eldest offspring of the compassionate father to the three realms, on coming to a small country, find places where they are prevented from entering.[117]

[28:42]

又、かの結界と稱する處にすめるやから、十惡をおそるることなし、十重つぶさにをかす。ただ造罪界として、不造罪人をきらふか。況や逆罪をおもきこととす。結界の地にすめるもの、逆罪もつくりぬべし。かくのごとくの魔界は、まさにやぶるべし。佛化を學すべし、佛界にいるべし、まさに佛恩を報ずるにてあらん。如是の古先、なんぢ結界の旨趣をしれりやいなや。たれよりか相承せりし、たれが印をかかうぶれる。

114　**wheel-turning sage king** (*tenrin jōō* 轉輪聖王): The *cakravartin*, the ideal Buddhist ruler, who rules by the force of his righteousness.

Śakrodevānāṃ Indra (*Shakudaikan'in* 釋提桓因): I.e., the god Indra, or Śakra, who rules over Tuṣita Heaven.

115　**who . . . does not enter?** (*tare ka iran aran* たれか入らんあらん): reading *irazaru aran* 入らざるあらん, after Ōkubo 1:256.

116　**our small country is the first to leave this trace** (*shōkoku, hajimete kono ato o nokosu* 小國、はじめてこのあとをのこす): I.e., Japan is the first Buddhist country in which one finds signs of this practice.

117　**the eldest offspring of the compassionate father to the three realms** (*sangai jifu no chōshi* 三界慈父の長子): I.e., the most senior followers of Buddha Śākyamuni. The term *chōshi* 長子, while usually used in reference to the first-born male, can refer to either gender. "Father to the three realms" (*sangai jifu* 三界慈父) recalls the famous "burning house" parable of the *Lotus Sūtra*; see Supplementary Notes, s.v. "Three realms," and "Burning house."

384   DŌGEN'S *SHŌBŌGENZŌ* VOLUME II

Again, the sort of fellows who live in those places called "fixed realms" have no fear of the ten evils and violate every one of the ten grave precepts.[118] Do they simply take it as a realm for commission of evil and reject those people who do not commit evil? Worse still of course are the heinous offenses, which are regarded as the most serious.[119] Those living in "places of fixed realms" may also have committed the heinous offenses. We should destroy such a realm of Māra. We should study the instruction of the Buddha; we should enter the realm of the Buddha. This is how we repay the benevolence of the Buddha. You "old forebears," have you understood the significance of a "fixed realm." From whom have you inherited this? Whose seal have you been granted?[120]

[28:43] {1:315}

いはゆる、この諸佛所結の大界にいるものは、諸佛も衆生も、大地も虚空も、繋縛を解脱し、諸佛の妙法に歸源するなり。しかあれば即ち、この界をひとたびふむ衆生、しかしながら佛功德をかうぶるなり。不違越の功德あり、得清淨の功德あり。一方を結するとき、すなはち法界みな結せられ、一重を結するとき、法界みな結せらるるなり。あるいは水を以て結する界あり、あるいは心を以て結界することあり、あるいは空を以て結界することあり。かならず相承相傳ありて知るべきこと在り。

Whatever enters this great realm fixed by the buddhas — whether buddhas or living beings, the whole earth or empty space — is liberated

---

118 **the ten evils** (*jūaku* 十惡): S. *daśākuśala*. One standard list: (1) killing, (2) stealing, (3) sexual misconduct, (4) lying, (5) fine talk, (6) slander, (7) treachery, (8) covetousness, (9) anger, and (10) false views. This list is sometimes divided into the three types of karma: body (1-3), speech (4-7), and mind (8-10).

the ten grave precepts (*jūjū* 十重): Likely the set of precepts for bodhisattvas found in the *Fanwang jing* 梵網經: (1) not to kill, (2) not to steal, (3) not to engage in sexual misconduct, (4) not to lie, (5) not to sell intoxicants, (6) not to speak of the faults of saṃgha members, (7) not to praise oneself and defame others, (8) not to be stingy, (9) not to become angry, and (10) not to denigrate the three treasures (of buddha, dharma, and saṃgha).

119 **the heinous offenses** (*gyakuzai* 逆罪): Most commonly, a set of five deeds said to lead to rebirth in the *avīci* hell: (1) patricide, (2) matricide, (3) killing an arhat, (4) shedding the blood of a buddha, and (5) causing a schism within the saṃgha. Another, less common list, sometimes called the "fundamental grave offenses" (*konpon jūzai* 根本重罪) (see *Da sazhe niqianzi suoshuo jing* 大薩遮尼乾子所説經, T.272.9:336b1-12) includes acts that were, in fact, quite common in the contentious Japanese Buddhist world of Dōgen's day: (1) destroying monasteries, burning scriptures, and looting the property of the saṃgha or its members; (2) denigrating any of the three vehicles (of *śrāvaka*, *pratyeka-buddha*, and bodhisattva); (3) beating, tormenting, forcibly laicizing, or killing members of the saṃgha; (4) committing any of the common set of five heinous offenses; (5) denying the karmic consequences of committing offenses and therefore engaging in the ten evils or encouraging others to do so.

120 **Whose seal have you been granted?** (*tare ga in o ka kōbureru* たれが印をかうぶれる): I.e., who gave you the authority to establish your "fixed realms"?

28. Making a Bow and Getting the Marrow *Raihai tokuzui* 禮拜得髓　　385

from bondage and returns to the source in the wondrous dharma of the buddhas.[121] Therefore, living beings who once set foot in this realm all receive the virtues of a buddha: they have the virtue of not deviating; they have the virtue of attaining purity.[122] When one area is fixed, the dharma realms are all fixed; when one level is fixed, the dharma realms are all fixed.[123] There are realms fixed by water; there is the fixing of realms by mind; there is the fixing of realms by space.[124] Invariably, they have a succession and transmission through which they can be known.

[28:44]

況や結界のとき、灑甘露の後ち、歸命の禮、をはり、乃至淨界等の後ち、頌に云、茲界遍法界、無爲結清淨。

What is more, at the time of fixing the realm, after the sprinkling of the ambrosia, after the prostrations are finished, and so on, through the purification of the realm, there is a verse saying,

This realm and the dharma realms everywhere
Are unconditioned and fixed as pure.[125]

121　**this great realm fixed by the buddhas** (*kono shobutsu shoketsu no daikai* この諸佛所結の大界): While here presumably denoting the entire dharma realm, the term "great realm" (*daikai* 大界) has a technical sense in Buddhist monastic literature that refers to the range, from a single monastery to a geographical area, within which the saṃgha members are considered a single ritual community.

122　**the virtue of not deviating** (*fuiotsu no kudoku* 不違越の功德); **the virtue of attaining purity** (*toku shōjō no kudoku* 得清淨の功德): The virtues, respectively, of being in accord with the buddha dharma and being free from spiritual defilements. The former term is used in reference both to intellectual agreement and ethical compliance; the latter term is well known as a reason given in the *Lotus Sūtra* (*Miaofa lianhua jing* 妙法蓮華經, T.262.9:7a23-25) for buddhas to appear in the world:

諸佛世尊、欲令衆生開佛知見、使得清淨故、出現於世。

The buddhas, the world-honored ones, appear in the world because they wish to cause living beings to open the knowledge and insight of a buddha and thereby attain purity.

123　**when one level is fixed** (*ichijū o kessuru toki* 一重を結するとき): Likely a reference to the levels marking off concentric sacred spaces, from the immediate ritual space, through the surrounding vicinity, to the larger saṃgha district.

124　**realms fixed by water** (*mizu o motte kessuru kai* 水を以て結する界): Presumably, a reference to the practice of purifying the sacred precincts with the "ambrosia" (*kanro* 甘露) mentioned in the following section.

the fixing of realms by space (*kū o mote kekkai suru koto* 空をもて結界すること): Or, conceivably, "the fixing of realms by emptiness."

125　**the sprinkling of the ambrosia** (*sha kanro* 灑甘露): Literally, "sweet dew," the term *kanro* 甘露 was used to translate the Sanskrit *amṛta* ("deathless"), used for the nectar of the gods; here, it denotes the scented water used to purify a ritual space.

and so on, through the purification of the realm (*naishi jōkai tō* 乃至淨界等): The exact sense of *jōkai* 淨界 ("purification of the realm") here is uncertain; it might refer to

386 DŌGEN'S *SHŌBŌGENZŌ* VOLUME II

[28:45]

この旨趣、いま、ひごろ結界と稱する古先老人、知れりやいなや。おもふに、なんだち、結の中に遍法界の結せらるること、しるべからざるなり。しりぬ、なんぢ聲聞のさけにゑふて、小界を大事とおもふなり。願くは、ひごろの迷酔すみやかにさめて、諸佛の大界の、遍界に違越すべからざる、濟度攝受に一切衆生みな化をかうぶらん功德を、禮拜恭敬すべし。たれかこれを得道髓といはざらん。

Have you "old forebears" and elders who always speak of "fixed realms" understood the meaning of this? I suspect you cannot understand that, in the ritual fixing, "the dharma realms everywhere" are fixed.[126] We know that, drunk on the wine of the *śrāvaka*, you think your little realm is a great matter.[127] May you quickly awaken from your long intoxication; and, [recognizing that] the great realm of the buddhas must not deviate from the realms everywhere, you should pay obeisance and venerate the virtue that, in delivering them and gathering them in, bestows conversion on all living beings. Who would not say that this is "getting the marrow of the way."[128]

正法眼藏禮拜得髓
Treasury of the True Dharma Eye
Making a Bow and Getting the Marrow

[*Himitsu* MS:]

仁治元年庚子冬節前日、書於興聖寺
Written at Kōshō Monastery; the day before winter solstice, senior metal year of the rat, the first year of Ninji [14 December 1240][129]

---

the completion of the entire ritual of purification or to the final rite in that ritual.

This realm and the dharma realms everywhere are unconditioned and fixed as pure (*shikai hen hokkai, mui ketsu shōjō* 茲界遍法界、無爲結清淨): A tentative translation. Dōgen's source for this verse is uncertain.

126 **in the ritual fixing, "the dharma realms everywhere" are fixed** (*ketsu no naka ni hokkai no kesseraruru koto* 結の中に法界の結せらるること): I.e., when a sacred precinct is marked off, it is the entire universe that is marked off.

127 **you think your little realm is a great matter** (*shōkai o daiji to omou* 小界を大事とおもふ): Dōgen is here playing on "the small realm" (*shōkai* 小界) of the ritual space and "the small vehicle" (*shōjō* 小乘) of the *śrāvaka*, in contrast to "the great matter" (*daiji* 大事), "the great realm" (*daikai* 大界), and the "great vehicle" (*daijō* 大乘).

128 **"getting the marrow of the way"** (*tokudōzui* 得道髓): Combining into one the two terms *tokudō* 得道 ("to gain the way") and *tokuzui* 得髓 ("to get the marrow").

129 Copyist unknown.

winter solstice (*tōsetsu* 冬節): The last day of the intercalary tenth month.

TREASURY OF THE TRUE DHARMA EYE
NUMBER 29

The Mountains and Waters Sūtra
Sansui kyō
山水經

The Mountains and Waters Sūtra

Sansui kyō

INTRODUCTION

The "Sansui kyō" represents one of the earlier chapters of the *Shōbō-genzō*. According to its colophon, it was composed at Kōshōji in the autumn of 1240, the year in which Dōgen seems to have begun work in earnest on the essays that would make up his *Shōbōgenzō*. This was a time when he was at the height of his literary powers, and "The Mountains and Waters Sūtra" is widely appreciated as one of the most elegant of his essays. Number 14 in the Honzan edition and number 29 in the seventy-five-chapter *Shōbōgenzō*, this text is not included in the sixty-chapter compilation; instead, it is found in the twenty-eight-text *Himitsu Shōbōgenzō* collection as number 3 of fascicle 2.

Several months before he wrote the "Sansui kyō," Dōgen composed another chapter of the *Shōbōgenzō* entitled "Keisei sanshoku" 溪聲山色 ("Sound of the Stream, Form of the Mountain"), inspired by a verse by the famed Song-dynasty poet Su Dongpo 蘇東坡:

The sound of the stream is his long, broad tongue;
The mountain, his immaculate body.
This evening's eighty-four thousand verses —
How will I tell them tomorrow?

In the "Sansui kyō," Dōgen returned to the theme of this poem, to explore in detail the meaning of mountains and rivers as the very body and speech of the buddha. As he says in his opening lines, the natural landscape that surrounds us here and now is the expression of the ancient buddhas. In the "Sansui kyō," the mountains and waters are at once preaching a sūtra that reveals the dharma and themselves putting that dharma into practice — themselves, as Dōgen says in his final line, becoming wise men and sages.

正法眼藏第二十九

Treasury of the True Dharma Eye
Number 29

山水經

The Mountains and Waters Sūtra

[29:1] {1:316}

而今の山水は、古佛の道現成なり。ともに法位に住して、究盡の功德を成ぜり。空劫已前の消息なるがゆえに、而今の活計なり。朕兆未萠の自己なるがゆえに、現成の透脱なり。山の諸功德、高廣なるをもて、乘雲の道德、かならず山より通達す。順風の妙功、さだめて山より透脱するなり。

These mountains and waters of the present are the statements of the old buddhas.[1] Each, abiding in its dharma position, fulfills exhaustive virtues.[2] Because they are the circumstances before the kalpa of emptiness, they are the livelihood of the present; because they are the self before the germination of any portent, they are liberation in realization.[3] The

---

1 **statements of the old buddhas** (*kobutsu no dō genjō* 古佛の道現成): I.e., "the expression of Buddhist teachings." The term *dō genjō* 道現成 ("realization of the words"), translated here as "statements," occurs several times in the *Shōbōgenzō*, typically, in reference to the sayings of Buddhist masters — so, e.g., the opening line of "Shōbōgenzō bukkyō" 正法眼藏佛教 (DZZ.1:380):

> 諸佛の道現成、これ佛教なり。
>
> The statements of the buddhas — these are the teachings of the buddhas.

The term *kobutsu* 古佛, "old (or ancient) buddha," is regularly used in Zen texts both in reference to the buddhas of the past and as an honorific for past masters of the tradition. See Supplementary Notes, s.v. "Old buddha."

2 **Each, abiding in its dharma position** (*tomo ni hōi ni jūshite* ともに法位に住して): Typically understood to mean, "each, just as it is." "The mountains just as mountains, the waters just as waters." (*Shōbōgenzō monge* 正法眼藏聞解, SCZ.2:218.) The expression "to abide in its dharma position" (*jū hōi* 住法位) reflects a traditional reading of a phrase in Kumārajīva's translation of the *Lotus Sūtra*; see Supplementary Notes, s.v. "Dharmas abide in their dharma positions."

3 **circumstances before the kalpa of emptiness** (*kūgō izen no shōsoku* 空劫已前の消息): The expression *kūgō izen* 空劫已前 occurs regularly in Zen texts in reference to a state before even the kalpa before the emergence of the world; see Supplementary Notes, s.v. "Before the kalpa of emptiness."

the livelihood of the present (*nikon no kakkei* 而今の活計): The term *kakkei* 活計 is regularly used in Zen texts for one's "means of living" or "occupation," etc.; frequently encountered in Dōgen's writing.

390 DŌGEN'S *SHŌBŌGENZŌ* VOLUME II

virtues of the mountains being high and broad, the spiritual power of riding the clouds is always penetrated from the mountains, and the subtle skill of following the wind is invariably liberated from the mountains.[4]

* * * * *

[29:2]

大陽山楷和尚、示衆云、青山常運歩、石女夜生兒。

Reverend Kai of Mount Dayang addressed the assembly, saying, "The blue mountains are always walking.[5] The stone woman gives birth to a child in the night."[6]

---

the self before the germination of any portent (*chinchō mibō no jiko* 朕兆未萌の自己): The expression *chinchō mibō* 朕兆未萌 (or variants such as *chinchō mishō* 朕兆未生, *chinchō mibun* 朕兆未分, etc.) occurs regularly in Zen texts in reference to that which precedes being. The term, while drawing on early Daoist imagery, seems closely akin to the more Buddhist *kūgō izen* 空劫已前.

liberation in realization (*genjō no tōdatsu* 現成の透脱): Or, perhaps, "realized liberation." A tentative rendering of an expression subject to various interpretations. The translation here takes the original to mean that the mountains and waters are "liberated in their occurrence" as mountains and waters.

4 **The virtues of the mountains being high and broad** (*yama no sho kudoku, kōkō naru o mote* 山の諸功德、高廣なるをもて): Likely intended to invoke the sense both that mountains are "high and broad" and that the mountain's virtues extend everywhere vertically and horizontally.

the spiritual power of riding the clouds (*jōun no dōtoku* 乗雲の道德); **the subtle skill of following the wind** (*junpū no myōkō* 順風の妙功): "Spiritual power" is a loose translation for *dōtoku* 道德, more literally, "the virtue of the way"; in this and the parallel *myōkō* 妙功 ("subtle skill"), Dōgen is playing with the two glyphs of the mountains' "virtues" (*kudoku* 功德). Both these phrases refer to the power of flight widely attributed to the spiritual adept in Chinese, especially Daoist, texts. In Buddhism, such power is one of the "spiritual bases" (*jinsoku* 神足; S. *ṛddhi-pāda*) in the standard list of the six paranormal spiritual powers (*jinzū* 神通; S. *abhijñā*); see Supplementary Notes, s.v. "Spiritual powers."

penetrated from the mountains (*yama yori tsūdatsu su* 山より通達す); **liberated from the mountains** (*yama yori tōdatsu suru nari* 山より透脱するなり): The exact sense of the particle *yori* より ("from") here is unclear; in the context, perhaps "on the basis of," "in dependence on."

5 **Reverend Kai of Mount Dayang** (*Taiyōzan Kai oshō* 大陽山楷和尚): I.e., Furong Daokai 芙蓉道楷 (1043-1118), a significant figure in the Caotong lineage. Mount Dayang 大陽山 is located in Yingzhou 郢州 in present-day Hubei province. Daokai's saying can be found at *Jiatai pudeng lu* 嘉泰普燈錄, ZZ.137:18b11. Dōgen invokes this saying again in his *Eihei kōroku* 永平廣錄 (DZZ.3:18, no. 23).

6 **"The stone woman"** (*sekinyo* 石女): An idiomatic expression for a "barren woman" (S. *vandhyā*), whose child (*sekinyo ji* 石女兒; S. *vandhyā-putra*) is used in Buddhist logic to represent that which is logically impossible. Dōgen will play below with the metaphor of stone.

29. The Mountains and Waters Sūtra *Sansui kyō* 山水經 391

[29:3]

山は、そなはるべき功德の虧闕することなし。このゆえに常安住なり、常運歩なり。その運歩の功德、まさに審細に參學すべし。山の運歩は、人の運歩のごとくなるべきがゆえに、人間の行歩におなじくみえざればとて、山の運歩をうたがふことなかれ。

The mountains lack none of their proper virtues; hence, they are always at rest and always walking. That virtue of walking, we should study in detail. Since the walking of the mountains should be like that of people, do not doubt the mountains' walk simply because it may not appear to be like the stride of humans.

[29:4] {1:317}

いま佛祖の説道、すでに運歩を指示す、これその得本なり。常運歩の示衆を究辨すべし。運歩のゆえに常なり。青山の運歩は、其疾如風よりもすみやかなれども、山中人は不覺不知なり。山中とは、世界裏の華開なり。山外人は不覺不知なり。山をみる眼目あらざる人は、不覺不知、不見不聞、這箇道理なり。もし山の運歩を疑著するは、自己の運歩をも、いまだしらざるなり。自己の運歩なきにはあらず、自己の運歩いまだしられざるなり、あきらめざるなり。自己の運歩をしらんがごとき、まさに青山の運歩をもしるべきなり。

The saying of the buddha and ancestor here has pointed out walking, and this has got the root.[7] We should thoroughly investigate his address to the assembly on "always walking." It is "always" because it is "walking." Although the walking of the blue mountains is faster than "*its speed like the wind*," those in the mountains do not perceive it, do not know it.[8] To be "in the mountains" is the "*flower opening within the*

---

7 **The saying of the buddha and ancestor here** (*ima busso no setsudō* いま佛祖の説道): I.e., the words of Daokai above.

this has got the root (*kore sono tokuhon nari* これその得本なり): As in the common Zen expression, "Just get the root and don't worry about the branches" (*dan de ben mo chou mo* 但得本莫愁末).

8 **faster than "its speed like the wind"** (*go shitsu nyo fū yori mo sumiyaka* 其疾如風よりもすみやか): An awkward effort to retain the fixed phrase "its speed like the wind" (*go shitsu nyo fū* 其疾如風), taken from the passage in the "Parable" chapter of the *Lotus Sūtra* describing the white oxen that pull the great carts (representing the buddha vehicle) given by the father to his children after they escaped from the burning house (representing saṃsāra) (*Miaofa lianhua jing* 妙法蓮華經, T.262.9:12c23):

行步平正、其疾如風。

Its gait even, its speed like the wind.

See Supplementary Notes, s.v. "Burning house."

do not perceive it, do not know it (*fukaku fuchi* 不覺不知): While this expression is common enough in Buddhist writing, given his allusion here to the burning house parable of the *Lotus Sūtra*, Dōgen may well have had in mind the line in the sūtra describing the father's recognition that his children are oblivious to the fire (*Miaofa lianhua jing* 妙

392   DŌGEN'S *SHŌBŌGENZŌ* VOLUME II

world."[9] Those outside the mountains *do not perceive it, do not know it.* Those without eyes to see the mountains, *do not perceive, do not know, do not see, do not hear this truth.*[10] To doubt the walking of the mountains means that one does not yet know the walking of the self.[11] It is not that the self has no walking but that the walking of the self is not yet known, not yet clarified. Those who would know the walking of the self, should also know the walking of the blue mountains.

[29:5]
青山すでに有情にあらず、非情にあらず。自己すでに有情にあらず、非情にあらず。いま青山の運歩を疑著せんこと、うべからず。いく法界を量局として、青山を照鑑すべしとしらず。青山の運歩、および自己の運歩、あきらかに撿點すべきなり。退歩歩退、ともに撿點あるべし。未朕兆の正當時、および空王那畔より、進歩退歩に運歩しばらくもやまざること、撿點すべし。

Given that the blue mountains are neither sentient nor insentient, that the self is neither sentient nor insentient, we cannot have doubts here about the blue mountains' walking. We do not know what measure of dharma realms it would take to discern the blue mountains. We should clearly examine the walking of the blue mountains and the walking of the self. There should be an examination of both stepping back and back stepping.[12] We should examine the fact that, since the very time before

---

法蓮華經, T.262.9:12b21-22):

而諸子等、於火宅内、樂著嬉戲、不覺不知、不驚不怖。

But my children, enjoying themselves in play within the burning house, do not perceive it, do not know it, are not alarmed, are not afraid.

See Supplementary Notes, s.v. "Burning house."

9   **"flower opening within the world"** (*sekai ri no ke kai* 世界裏の華開): An allusion to the final line of the dharma transmission verse attributed to Bodhidharma's master, Prajñātāra. See Supplementary Notes, s.v. "A flower opens, and the world arises."

10   **do not perceive, do not know, do not see, do not hear this truth** (*fukaku fuchi, fuken fumon, shako dōri nari* 不覺不知、不見不聞、這箇道理なり): Dōgen has here shifted to Chinese syntax. The string of four negative verbs represents a variant of the common expression "see, hear, perceive, and know" (*ken mon kaku chi* 見聞覺知), used to mean roughly "experience." The expression *shako dōri* 這箇道理, rendered here rather ponderously as "this truth," can also mean simply, "why (or how) this is so."

11   **the walking of the self** (*jiko no unpo* 自己の運歩): Here and below, this expression could also be rendered less metaphysically as "one's own walking."

12   **stepping back and back stepping** (*taiho hotai* 退歩歩退): An awkward attempt to capture something of Dōgen's play with the common term *taiho* 退歩, widely used in Zen texts both in its literal sense, "to step back" (as, for example, in a ritual) and in a figurative sense, "to reflect," "to look within," as in the expression "try stepping back" (*taiho kan* 退歩看); in this latter sense, akin to, and sometimes combined with, *henshō* 返照, "reflection," a common term for contemplative introspection. The variant *hotai* is not attested elsewhere in Dōgen's corpus, and its oddity has led to speculation that this

29. The Mountains and Waters Sūtra *Sansui kyō* 山水經   393

the germination of any portent, since that side of King of Emptiness, walking by stepping forward and stepping back has never ceased even for a moment.[13]

[29:6]

運歩、もし休することあらば、佛祖不出現なり。運歩、もし究極あらば、佛法不到今日ならん。進歩いまだやまず、退歩いまだやまず。進歩のとき、退歩に乖向せず、退歩のとき、進歩を乖向せず。この功徳を、山流とし、流山とす。

If walking had ever rested, the buddhas and ancestors would never have appeared; if walking had a limit, *the buddha dharma would never have reached us today.*[14] Stepping forward has never ceased; stepping back has never ceased. At the time of stepping forward, this does not oppose stepping back; at the time of stepping back, this does not oppose stepping forward. This virtue we take as the mountain flowing, as the flowing mountain.

[29:7]

青山も運歩を參究し、東山も水上行を參學するがゆえに、この參學は山の參學なり。山の身心をあらためず、やまの面目ながら、廻途參學しきたれり。

Because the blue mountains investigate walking, and the East Mountain studies "walking on the water," this study is the mountains' own study.[15] The mountains, without altering their own body and mind, with

---

expression is an error for "stepping forward and back" (*shinpo taiho* 進歩退歩), which appears in the next sentence; see Supplementary Notes, s.v. "Stepping forward and stepping back." The reversal of terms here is repeated at the end of the next section in the expression "the mountain flowing, the flowing mountain" (*sanryū ryūzan* 山流流山).

13   **that side of King of Emptiness** (*Kūō nahan* 空王那畔): An unusual expression, found only here and in the "Hotsu bodai shin" 發菩提心 chapter; presumably derived from the common Zen saying, "that side of King Majestic Voice" (*Ion'ō nahan* 威音王那畔), used in reference to what precedes all differentiation; see Supplementary Notes, s.v. "Before King of Emptiness."

14   **the buddha dharma would never have reached us today** (*buppō futō konnichi* 佛法不到今日): Dōgen has here slipped into Chinese syntax, possibly reflecting a remark of the monk Baoen Xuanze 報恩玄則, cited by Dōgen in his *shinji Shōbōgenzō* 眞字正法眼藏 (DZZ.5:192, case 122):

佛法若如是不到今日

If the buddha dharma were like this, it would never have reached today.

A similar linguistic pattern occurs frequently throughout the *Shōbōgenzō*: "if the buddha dharma (or 'the way of the buddhas') were like this, it would never have reached today"; or "if X were the case, the buddha dharma would never have reached today."

15   **the East Mountain studies "walking on the water"** (*Tōzan mo suijō kō o sangaku suru* 東山も水上行を參學する): From a saying of Yunmen Wenyen 雲門文偃 (864-949) that will be introduced below, section 13.

394   DŌGEN'S *SHŌBŌGENZŌ* VOLUME II

their own mountain countenance, have been studying [themselves] on the road back.[16]

[29:8] {1:318}

青山は運歩不得なり、東山水上行不得なる、と、山を誹謗することなかれ。低下の見處のいやしきゆえに、青山運歩の句をあやしむなり。小聞のつたなきによりて、流山の語をおどろくなり。いま流水の言も、七通八達せずといへども、小見小聞に沈溺せるのみなり。

Do not slander mountains by saying that the blue mountains cannot walk, nor the East Mountain walk on the water. It is because of the baseness of a lowly point of view that one doubts the phrase "the blue mountains walk"; because of the crudeness of limited experience, we are surprised by the words "flowing mountain."[17] Without having thoroughly mastered even the term "flowing water," we are simply sunk in small views and limited experience.[18]

[29:9]

しかあれば、所積の功德を擧せるを形名とし、命脈とせり。運歩あり、流行あり。山の山兒を生ずる時節あり、山の佛祖となる道理によりて、佛祖かくのごとく出現せるなり。

---

16   **studying [themselves] on the road back** (*kaito sangaku* 廻途参學): A tentative translation. The term *kaito* (also read *eto* and more often written 回途), has received various interpretations. While it is sometimes understood as a reference to the monk's "circuit," or peregrinations, in search of the dharma, the translation takes it as a reference to the bodhisattva's return to the world to save beings. While the word does not appear elsewhere in the *Shōbōgenzō*, it does occur in the *Eihei kōroku* 永平廣錄 (DZZ.3:206, no. 316), in a saying found in a number of Zen texts:

陌巷不騎金色馬、廻途却著破襴衫。

In the narrow alley, one doesn't ride a golden horse;
On the road back, one still wears tattered robes.

17   **lowly point of view** (*teige no kenjo* 低下の見處): The term *teige* 低下 is sometimes taken here in reference to lowly types, but the word is usually used for the condition or action of "decline" or "deterioration"; it does not seem to be a common pejorative in Dōgen's vocabulary.

18   **thoroughly mastered** (*shittsū hattatsu* 七通八達): A loose translation of an expression that plays with the term *tsūdatsu* 通達 ("to penetrate," "to master"); more literally, "seven passes and eight arrivals," or perhaps "seven penetrations and eight masteries." A common expression in Dōgen's writings and earlier Chan texts for "thorough understanding," "complete mastery."

small views and limited experience (*shōken shōmon* 小見小聞): Literally "small seeing, small hearing." Here, as in the expressions translated just above as "point of view" (*kenjo* 見處), and "limited experience" (*shōmon* 小聞), Dōgen is playing with the term *kenmon* 見聞: "seeing and hearing"; hence, "perception" or "experience."

29. The Mountains and Waters Sūtra *Sansui kyō* 山水經   395

Thus, the taking up of its accumulated virtues represents the shape and name, the vital artery [of the mountain].[19] There is its "walking"; there is its "flowing"; there is a time when the mountain gives birth to a mountain child.[20] From the principle that the mountains become buddhas and ancestors, the buddhas and ancestors have appeared like this.

[29:10]

たとひ草木・土石・牆壁の見成する眼睛あらんときも、疑著にあらず、動著にあらず、全現成にあらず。たとひ七寶莊嚴なりと見取せらるる時節現成すとも、實歸にあらず。たとひ諸佛行道の境界と見現成あるも、あながちの愛處にあらず。たとひ諸佛不思議の功德と見現成の頂顆をうとも、如實これのみにあらず。各各の見成は、各各の依正なり。これらを佛祖の道業とするにあらず、一偶の管見なり。

Even when we have the eyes [to see mountains as] the appearance of grass and trees, earth and stone, fences and walls, this is nothing to doubt, nothing to be moved by: it is not the complete appearance [of the mountains].[21] Even when an occasion occurs in which [the mountains] are seen as adorned with the seven treasures, this is still not the real refuge.[22] Even when they appear to us as the realm of the buddhas' practice of the way, this is not necessarily something to be desired. Even when we attain the crowning appearance of the vision of [the mountains as] the inconceivable virtues of the buddhas, their reality is not just this. Each of these appearances is a particular secondary and primary recompense; they are not to be taken as the work of the way of the buddhas and ancestors; they are narrow, one-sided views.[23]

---

19   **the taking up of its accumulated virtues** (*shoseki no kudoku o koseru o* 所積の功德を擧せるを): Likely indicating the various virtues of mountains (such as walking and flowing) taken up for comment by the past masters under discussion here.

20   **there is a time when the mountain gives birth to a mountain child** (*yama no sanji o shō zuru jisetsu ari* 山の山兒を生ずる時節あり): This might be taken to mean simply that the mountain reproduces itself in each time; but, given the following sentence, the "mountain child" (*sanji* 山兒) seems more likely to be the "buddhas and ancestors."

21   **grass and trees, earth and stone, fences and walls** (*sōmoku doseki shōheki* 草木・土石・牆壁): Terms regularly used to represent the insentient phenomenal world, often treated in Zen as expressions of the dharma or identified with the buddha mind. See Supplementary Notes, s.v. "Fences, walls, tiles, and pebbles."

22   **adorned with the seven treasures** (*shippō shōgon* 七寶莊嚴): The seven treasures (S. *sapta-ratna*) are variously listed in Buddhist texts; a popular version is that of the *Lotus Sūtra* (T.262.9:21b20-21): gold, silver, beryl, moonstone, agate, pearl, and cornelian.

23   **secondary and primary recompense** (*eshō* 依正): A standard Buddhist term for the results of past karma reflected respectively in the circumstances into which one is born and the mental and physical makeup of the person; see Supplementary Notes, s.v. "Secondary and primary recompense."

The four views of the mountain given here seem to correspond to part of a list appearing

396 DŌGEN'S *SHŌBŌGENZŌ* VOLUME II

[29:11]

轉境轉心は大聖の所呵なり、説心説性は佛祖の所不肯なり。見心見性は外
道の活計なり、滯言滯句は解脱の道著にあらず。かくのごとくの境界を透
脱せるあり、いはゆる青山常運歩なり、東山水上行なり。審細に參究すべ
し。

Turning the object and turning the mind is something criticized by the
great sages; *talking of the mind and talking of the nature* is something not
condoned by the buddhas and ancestors; *seeing the mind and seeing the
nature* is the livelihood of other paths.[24] *Clogged by words and clogged*

---

in the *Xiangfa jueyi jing* 像法決疑經 (T.2870.8:1337a5-a15):

> 今日座中無央數衆各見不同 ．．． 或見此處沙羅林地悉是土沙草木石壁。或見
> 此處金銀七寶清淨莊嚴。或見此處乃是三世諸佛所行之處。或見此處即是不可思
> 議諸佛境界眞實法體。
>
> Among the countless numbers in the assembly today, each has a different view. . . .
> Some may see this place as a sāla grove and everything as earth and sand, grass and
> trees, rocks and walls. Others may see this place as the immaculate splendor of gold,
> silver, and the [other] seven treasures. Others may see this place as the place of the
> practice of all the buddhas in the three times. Still others may see this place as the
> true dharma body, the inconceivable realm of the buddhas.

work of the way of the buddhas and ancestors (*busso no dōgō* 佛祖の道業): The term
dōgō 道業, translated here as "work of the way," usually refers to training on the way of
the buddhas; here, however, given the contrast with *eshō* 依正, it may indicate "karma,"
not as action, but as the fruits of action.

narrow, one-sided views (*ichigū no kanken* 一偶の管見). Reading *gū* 偶 ("even," "ac-
cidental") as *gū* 隅 ("corner," "nook") after the Honzan edition.

24 **Turning the object and turning the mind** (*tenkyō tenshin* 轉境轉心): An uncommon expression, without obvious source. The verb *ten* 轉 ("to turn") can be taken in the
sense "to teach" (as in *ten Hokke* 轉法華, "to teach the *Lotus*"); but this phrase is often
interpreted as the view that mind and its object "turn" and are "turned" by each other.
Possibly reflecting a usage seen in a conversation of Changsha Jingcen 長沙景岑 (dates
unknown), recorded in Dōgen's *shinji Shōbōgenzō* 眞字正法眼藏 (DZZ.5: 132-133, case
16) and discussed in his "Shōbōgenzō keisei sanshoku" 正法眼藏溪聲山色:

> 因僧問、作麼生轉得山河大地歸自己去。師曰、作麼生轉得自己歸山河大地去。
>
> A monk asked, "How does one turn the mountains, rivers, and the whole earth back
> to the self?"
> The Master said, "How does one turn the self back to the mountains, rivers, and the
> whole earth?"

the great sages (*daishō* 大聖): Or "the Great Sage." An honorific used in reference to
buddhas, bodhisattvas, and arhats; sometimes understood here as referring specifically
to Buddha Śākyamuni.

talking of the mind and talking of the nature (*sesshin sesshō* 説心説性): An expression found frequently in Zen texts, perhaps best known from a saying of Dongshan
Liangjie 洞山良价 (807-869):

> 裏面有人説心説性
>
> Inside [this cloister], there's someone talking of the mind and talking of the nature.

In striking contrast to his remark here, in his "Shōbōgenzō sesshin sesshō" 正法眼藏

29. The Mountains and Waters Sūtra *Sansui kyō* 山水經   397

by phrases is not the speech of liberation.[25] There are [words] that have transcended such realms: they are "*the blue mountains always walking*"; they are "*the East Mountain walking on the water*."[26] We should give them detailed investigation.

[29:12]

石女夜生兒は、石女の生兒するときを夜といふ。おほよそ、男石・女石あり、非男女石あり。これよく天を補し、地を補す。天石あり、地石あり。俗のいふところなりといへども、人のしるところまれなるなり。生兒の道理しるべし。生兒のときは、親子亞化するか。兒の親となるを、生兒現成と參學するのみならんや、親の兒となるときを、生兒現成の修證なりと參學すべし、究徹すべし。

"*The stone woman gives birth to a child in the night.*"[27] This means that the time when "*a stone woman gives birth to a child*" is "*the night.*" There are male stones, female stones, and stones neither male nor female. They repair the heavens, and they repair the earth.[28] There are stones of heaven, and there are stones of earth. Though this is something said in the secular world, it is something rarely understood. We should understand the principle of this "*giving birth to a child.*" At the time of

---

説心説性, Dōgen praises such talk as "the great origin of the way of the buddhas" and attacks the famous Chan master Dahui Zonggao 大慧宗杲 (1089-1163) for being dismissive of it.

seeing the mind and seeing the nature (*kenshin kenshō* 見心見性): Not a common combination, though of course Zen tradition was famous for claiming that one could "see one's nature and attain buddhahood" (*kenshō jōbutsu* 見性成佛), a saying attributed to no less than Bodhidharma himself; see Supplementary Notes, s.v. "Pointing directly at the person's mind, seeing the nature and attaining buddhahood." In his "Shōbōgenzō shizen biku" 正法眼藏四禪比丘, however, Dōgen strongly criticizes this claim, saying, "Where among the seven buddhas and twenty-eight Indian ancestors does one find it said that the buddha dharma is just seeing the nature?"

the livelihood of other paths (*gedō no kakkei* 外道の活計): I.e., the pursuit of non-Buddhist (S. *tīrthika*) religions.

25   **Clogged by words and clogged by phrases** (*taigon taiku* 滯言滯句): The translation retains the verb-object parallel with the preceding phrases; in other contexts, the terms might also be understood as "stagnant words and stagnant phrases."

26   "**the East Mountain walking on the water**" (*Tōzan suijō kō* 東山水上行): Again, anticipating the saying to be quoted below, section 13.

27   "**The stone woman gives birth to a child in the night**" (*sekinyo ya shōji* 石女夜生兒): Dōgen here returns to Daokai's passage quoted above, section 2.

28   **They repair the heavens, and they repair the earth** (*ten o fushi, chi o fusu* 天を補し、地を補す): Some commentators see this as an allusion to the ancient Chinese story of Nü Wa's 女媧 melting rocks of five colors to mend cracks in the sky (*Huainanzi* 淮南子, Lanming xun 覽冥訓, KR.3j0010.006-9b).

398 DŌGEN'S *SHŌBŌGENZŌ* VOLUME II

birth, do parent and child instruct together?[29] We should not only study the child becoming the parent as the realization of "giving birth to a child"; we should study, we should completely master [the understanding that] the time when the parent becomes the child is the practice and verification of the realization of "giving birth to a child."[30]

[29:13] {1:319}

雲門匡眞大師いはく、東山水上行。

Great Master Kuangzhen of Yunmen said, "*The East Mountain walks on the water.*"[31]

[29:14]

この道現成の宗旨は、諸山は東山なり、一切の東山は水上行なり。このゆえに、九山迷盧等の現成せり、修證せり。これを東山といふ。しかあれども、雲門いかでか東山の皮肉骨髓、修證活計に透脱ならん。

The essential point of this statement is that the various mountains are "the East Mountain," and all the East Mountains are "walking on the water." Therefore, Mount Sumeru and the nine mountains have appeared,

---

29 **do parent and child instruct together** (*shinshi heika suru ka* 親子竝化するか): An expression variously interpreted, depending on how the predicate *heika* 竝化 is understood here. Some would take it as "lined up together"; others as "born together"; still others as "become two." This translation takes it as playful allusion to the saying, "two honored ones do not instruct together" (*er zun bubinghua* 二尊不竝化) — i.e., two buddhas do not propagate the dharma simultaneously. (Hence, perhaps, the implied question, "are both parent and child to be taken as buddhas?") This use occurs in Zen literature in the story of Venerable Duan's 端長老 visit to Liangshan Yuanguan 梁山緣觀 (dates unknown); see, e.g., *Jingde chuandeng lu* 景德傳燈錄, T.2076.51:406c21-23:

有僧問、二尊不竝化、爲什麼兩人居方丈。師曰、一亦非師。

A monk asked, "Two honored ones do not instruct together. So why are you both in the abbot's quarters?"
The Master [Yuanguan] said, "One of us isn't a teacher."

30 **the child becoming the parent . . . the parent becomes the child** (*ji no shin to naru . . . shin no ji to naru* 兒の親となる . . . 親の兒となる): A sentence subject to various interpretations. A common reading would take the former phrase as a reference to the practitioner awakening to buddhahood, while the latter phrase indicates the expression of awakening (or buddhahood) in practice.

31 **Great Master Kuangzhen of Yunmen** (*Unmon Kyōshin daishi* 雲門匡眞大師): I.e., Yunmen Wenyan 雲門文偃, founder of the Yunmen house of Chan. His saying can be found in the *Yunmen yulu* 雲門語錄 (T.1988.47:145c19):

問、如何是諸佛出身處。師云、東山水上行。

[Someone] asked, "What is the place where the buddhas leave the body?"
The Master [Yunmen] said, "The East Mountain walks on the water."

The "East Mountain" (*Tōzan* 東山) here may refer to the mountain on which Yunmen resided and from which he got his name, located in southern Shaoxing 紹興 district, Zhejiang province.

29. The Mountains and Waters Sūtra *Sansui kyō* 山水經   399

have practiced and verified [the buddha dharma].[32] This is called "the East Mountain." Nevertheless, how could Yunmen be liberated in the skin, flesh, bones, and marrow of the East Mountain and its livelihood of practice and verification?[33]

[29:15]

いま現在大宋國に、杜撰のやから一類あり、いまは群をなせり。小實の撃不能なるところなり。かれらいはく、いまの東山水上行話、および南泉の鎌子話ごときは、無理會話なり。その意旨は、もろもろの念慮にかかはれる語話は、佛祖の禪話にあらず、無理會話、これ佛祖の語話なり。かるがゆえに、黄蘗の行棒、および臨濟の擧喝、これら理會およびがたく、念慮にかかはれず。これを朕兆未萌已前の大悟とするなり。先德の方便、おほく葛藤斷句をもちいるといふは、無理會なり。

At the present time in the Land of the Great Song, there is a certain bunch of illiterates who have formed such a pack that they cannot be struck down by the few real ones [34] They maintain that [words] like this *talk of "the East Mountain walking on the water,"* or Nanquan's talk of

---

32   **Mount Sumeru and the nine mountains** (*kūsen meiro* 九山迷盧): The central mountain and the eight concentric ranges that together make up a Buddhist world system. The nine *cakravāla* are variously named; a common list is found in the *Abhidharma-ma-koṣa* (*Apidamo jushe lun* 阿毘達磨倶舍論, T.1558.29:57b2).

33   **how could Yunmen be liberated in the skin, flesh, bones, and marrow of the East Mountain and its livelihood of practice and verification?** (*Unmon ikade ka Tōzan no hi niku kotsu zui, shushō kakkei ni tōdatsu naran* 雲門いかでか東山の皮肉骨髓、修證活計に透脱ならん): Usually taken as a criticism of Yunmen's failure fully to understand the East Mountain, though some would read it as a statement of the inseparability of Yunmen and the mountain. The compound *tōdatsu* 透脱 regularly occurs in Dōgen's writing as a transitive verb meaning "to pass beyond," "to transcend," etc.; here (and in section 33, below), it takes the particle *ni* に, presumably to be read as a locative marker.

skin, flesh, bones, and marrow (*hi niku kotsu zui* 皮肉骨髓): An expression, occurring very often throughout the *Shōbōgenzō*, indicating the essence or truth or entirety of something or someone. From the famous story, included in the *shinji Shōbōgenzō* 眞字正法眼藏 (DZZ.5:230, case 201), of Bodhidharma's testing of four disciples, to whom he said of each in turn that he (or, in one case, she) had gotten his skin, flesh, bones, and marrow. See Supplementary Notes.

34   **illiterates** (*zuzan* 杜撰): Literally, "Du composition," used in pejorative reference to a literary work that, like those of Du, is ignorant of classical precedents. (Du is most often identified as the Song-dynasty poet Du Mo 杜默; for alternative theories, see Morohashi 14477.122.) Dōgen regularly uses the term to refer to those in the Zen tradition who are ignorant of the tradition.

the few real ones (*shōjitsu* 小實): I.e., the few authentic teachers, as in the saying, "A lot of false ones aren't like a few real ones" (*duoxu buru xiaoshi* 多虛不如小實).

400 DŌGEN'S *SHŌBŌGENZŌ* VOLUME II

his "sickle," is irrational talk.[35] Their point is that any speech that involves thinking is not the Zen talk of the buddhas and ancestors; irrational talk — this is the speech of the buddhas and ancestors. Consequently, [they hold that] Huangbo's using his staff and Linji's raising his roar are beyond rational understanding and do not involve thinking; and they take these as the great awakening preceding the time before the germination of any portent.[36] That the expedient means of the prior worthies often employ tangle-cutting phrases is [because they are] irrational.[37]

[29:16]

かくのごとくいふやから、かつていまだ正師をみず、參學眼なし。いふにたらざる小獣子なり。宋土、ちかく二三百年よりこのかた、かくのごとくの魔子・六群禿子おほし。あはれむべし、佛祖の大道の廢するなり。これらが所解、なほ小乗聲聞におよばず、外道よりもおろかなり。俗にあらず、僧にあらず、人にあらず、天にあらず、學佛道の畜生よりもおろかなり。禿子がいふ無理會話、なんぢのみ無理會なり、佛祖はしかあらず。なんぢに理會せられざるはとて、佛祖の理會路を參學せざるべからず。たとひ畢竟無理會なるべくば、なんぢがいまいふ理會もあたるべからず。しかのごときのたぐひ、宋朝の諸方におほし、まのあたり見聞せしところなり。あはれむべし、かれら、念慮の、語句なることをしらず、語句の、念慮を透脱することをしらず。在宋のとき、かれらをわらふに、かれら所陳なし、無語なりしのみなり。かれらがいまの無理會の邪計なるのみなり。たれかなんぢにをしふる。天眞の師範なしといへども、自然の外道兒なり。

---

35 **Nanquan's talk of his "sickle"** (*Nansen no rensu wa* 南泉の鎌子話): Reference to a conversation involving Nanquan Puyuan 南泉普願 (748-835), recorded in several Zen sources, as well as Dōgen's *shinji Shōbōgenzō* 眞字正法眼藏 (DZZ.5:206, case 154):

池州南泉山願禪師、一日、在山作務、有僧過問師、南泉路向什麼處去。師拈起鎌子云、我這茅鎌子、三十文錢買得。僧曰、不問茅鎌子三十文錢買、南泉路向什麼處去。師云、我如今使得正快。

Chan Master Yuan of Mount Nanquan in Chizhou was working one day in the mountains. A monk passing by asked the Master, "Where does the Nanquan road go?"
The Master picked up his sickle and said, "I bought this sickle for thirty cash."
The monk said, "I'm not asking about buying a sickle for thirty cash. Where does the Nanquan road go?"
The Master said, "When I use it like this, it's really sharp."

36 **Huangbo's using his staff and Linji's raising his roar** (*Ōbaku no gyōbō, oyobi Rinzai no kokatsu* 黄檗の行棒、および臨濟の舉喝): Reference to the famous teaching techniques of "beating and shouting" (*bōkatsu* 棒喝) associated respectively with Huangbo Xiyun 黄檗希運 (dates unknown) and his disciple Linji Yixuan 臨濟義玄 (d. 866).

37 **expedient means of the prior worthies** (*sentoku no hōben* 先德の方便): I.e., the teaching techniques of the former masters.

tangle-cutting phrases (*kattō dan ku* 葛藤斷句): Literally, "phrases that cut through arrowroot and wisteria." As a compound, *kattō* (elsewhere, rendered "tangled vines") has the colloquial sense of an "entanglement," a "complexity," "complication," or "difficulty." Zen texts typically, as here, treat the term as referring to (especially intellectual) obstacles to be cut through by practice. See Supplementary Notes, s.v. "Tangled vines."

29. The Mountains and Waters Sūtra *Sansui kyō* 山水經 401

Those who talk in this way have never met a true master and lack the eye of study; they are little simpletons not worth mentioning. In the Song, for the last two or three hundred years, there have been many such sons of Māra and shavelings of the gang of six.[38] What a pity that the great way of the buddhas and ancestors is abandoned. Their understanding is inferior to that of the *śrāvakas* of the Small Vehicle, dumber than that even of the other paths. They are not laymen; they are not monks. They are not humans; they are not devas. They are dumber than beasts studying the way of the buddhas. What you shavelings call "irrational talk" is irrational only to you, not to the buddhas and ancestors. That you do not understand it rationally is no reason not to study the path understood rationally by the buddhas and ancestors. Even granted that [Zen sayings] were in the end irrational, this rational understanding of yours would then also be wrong.[39] Such types are common throughout all quarters of the state of Song; I saw them with my own eyes. They are to be pitied: they do not know that thoughts are words; they do not know that words transcend thoughts.[40] When I was in the Song, I made fun of them, but they never had an explanation, never a word to say for themselves, just this false notion of theirs about irrationality. Who could have taught you this? Though you may have no natural teacher, you are children of an other path of spontaneity.[41]

---

38 **sons of Māra and shavelings of the gang of six** (*mashi rokugun tokushi* 魔子・六群禿子): The sons (and daughters) of Māra, the Evil One (S. Māra-pāpīyān) are regularly blamed for obstructing the dharma; a standard Buddhist term of reproach. The term appears elsewhere in the *Shōbōgenzō* in pejorative reference to what Dōgen considers heretical types, in contrast to "sons of the buddha" (*busshi* 佛子). "Monks of the gang of six" (*rokugun biku* 六群比丘; S. *saḍvargika-bhikṣu*) are a notorious group of lawless monks among the followers of Buddha Śākyamuni; the label derives from vinaya texts, where it is emblematic of bad behaviors and bad attitudes on the part of monks. "Shaveling" (*tokushi* 禿子), literally, "baldy," is a rude term for a tonsured Buddhist cleric.

39 **Even granted that [Zen sayings] were in the end irrational, this rational understanding of yours would then also be wrong** (*tatoi hikyō murie naru bekuba, nanji ga ima iu rie mo ataru bekarazu* たとひ畢竟無理會なるべくば、なんぢがいまいふ理會もあたるべからず): I.e., the assertion that the sayings are incomprehensible to reason represents a certain comprehension of them and, hence, by definition misunderstands them. An interesting example of Dōgen's hoisting an opponent with his own petard and of his directly addressing the opponent with the familiar second person pronoun (a practice not unusual in Zen commentary).

40 **they do not know that thoughts are words; they do not know that words transcend thoughts** (*karera, nenryo no, goku naru koto o shirazu, goku no, nenryo o tōdatsu suru koto o shirazu* かれら、念慮の、語句なることをしらず、語句の、念慮を透脱することをしらず): An intriguing statement subject to various interpretations. It is unclear whether Dōgen is here referring specifically to the sayings of the Chan masters or he is making a general claim about the relationship between thought and language.

41 **Though you may have no natural teacher, you are children of an other path of**

402 DŌGEN'S *SHŌBŌGENZŌ* VOLUME II

[29:17] {1:320}

しるべし、この東山水上行は、佛祖の骨髓なり。諸水は東山の脚下に現成せり。このゆえに、諸山、くもにのり、天をあゆむ。諸水の頂頗は諸山なり。向上・直下の行歩、ともに水上なり。諸山の脚尖、よく諸水を行歩し、諸水を趨出せしむるゆえに、運歩七縱八横なり、修證即不無なり。

We should realize that this "East Mountain walking on the water" is the very "bones and marrow" of the buddhas and ancestors. The waters are appearing at the feet of the East Mountain, and therefore the mountains mount the clouds and stride through the heavens. The mountains are the peaks of the waters, and in both ascending and descending their walk is "on the water." The tips of the mountains' feet walk across the waters, setting them dancing. Therefore, their walking is seven high and eight across; it is "it's not that it lacks practice and verification."[42]

* * * * *

[29:18]

水は強弱にあらず、濕乾にあらず、動靜にあらず、冷暖にあらず、有無にあらず、迷悟にあらざるなり。こりては金剛よりもかたし、たれかこれをやぶらん。融じては乳水よりもやはらかなり、たれかこれをやぶらん。

Water is neither strong nor weak, neither wet nor dry, neither moving nor still, neither cold nor hot, neither being nor non-being, neither delusion nor awakening. Frozen, it is harder than diamond; who could break it? Melted, it is softer than milk; who could break it?

---

spontaneity (*tenshin no shihan nashi to iedomo, jinen no gedōji nari* 天眞の師範なしといへども、自然の外道兒なり): The translation obscures Dōgen's play here with the terms *tenshin* 天眞 and *jinen* 自然 (rendered somewhat problematically as "natural" and "spontaneity" respectively), near synonyms used in reference to what Buddhists consider the false view that things arise, not from causes and conditions, but from themselves of their own accord — what we might call a doctrine of "autogenesis" or "accidentalism." The sentence could be interpreted to mean, "though you may have no teacher of spontaneity, you are spontaneously children of an other path." The Honzan text has *gedō ken* 外道見 ("view of an other path") for *gedō ji* 外道兒 ("children of an other path").

42 **seven high and eight across** (*shichijū hachio* 七縱八横): I.e., unimpeded anywhere; literally, "seven vertical; eight horizontal," a fixed expression.

"it's not that it lacks practice and verification" (*shushō soku fu mu* 修證即不無): I.e., it is "nondefiling" (*fuzenna*) spiritual practice. From the dialogue, recorded in the *shinji Shōbōgenzō* 眞字正法眼藏 (DZZ.5:178, case 101) and often alluded to by Dōgen, between the Sixth Ancestor, Huineng 慧能, and his disciple Nanyue Huairang 南嶽懷讓 (677-744); see Supplemental Notes, s.v. "Practice and verification," and "Not defiled."

29. The Mountains and Waters Sūtra *Sansui kyō* 山水經   403

[29:19]

しかあればすなはち、現成所有の功徳をあやしむことあたはず、しばらく十
方の水を十方にして著眼看すべき時節を參學すべし。人天の、水をみるとき
のみの參學にあらず、水の、水をみる參學あり。水の、水を修證するがゆえ
に、水の、水を道著する參究あり。自己の、自己に相逢する通路を現成せし
むべし、他己の、他己を參徹する活路を進退すべし、跳出すべし。

This being the case, we cannot doubt the many virtues realized [by wa-
ter]. We should study for a bit the occasions when we look at the water
of the ten directions in the ten directions.[43] This is not a study only of the
time when humans or devas see water: there is a study of water seeing
water. Water practices and verifies water; hence, there is an investigation
of water speaking water. We should bring to realization the way through
on which the self encounters the self; we should advance and retreat
along, we should spring forth from, the way out on which the other studies and fully comprehends the other.[44]

[29:20] {1:321}

おほよそ山水をみること、種類にしたがひて不同あり。いはゆる水をみる
に、瓔珞とみるものあり。しかあれども、瓔珞を水とみるにはあらず。われ
らがなにとみるかたちを、かれが水とすらん。かれが瓔珞は、われ水と
みる。水を妙華とみるあり。しかあれど、華を水ともちいるにあらず。鬼
は、水をもて猛火とみる、濃血とみる。龍魚は、宮殿とみる、樓臺とみ
る。あるひは七寶摩尼珠とみる、あるひは樹林牆壁とみる、あるひは清淨
解脱の法性とみる、あるひは眞實人體とみる、あるひは身相心性とみる。
人間、これを水とみる、殺活の因緣なり。

In general, then, the seeing of mountains and waters differs according
to the type of being.[45] In seeing water, there are beings that see it as a
jeweled necklace. This does not mean, however, that they see a jeweled
necklace as water. How, then, do we see what they consider water? Their

---

43   **the occasions when we look at the water of the ten directions in the ten directions** (*jippō no mizu o jippō ni shite jakugankan su beki jisetsu* 十方の水を十方にして
著眼看すべき時節): Judging from what follows below, this can probably be taken to
mean more simply "the various ways in which water is seen."

44   **the way through** (*tsūro* 通路); **the way out** (*katsuro* 活路): The translation seeks
to retain something of the play with these two terms for "road" that occur with some
frequency in Dōgen's writing. The former suggests a "route" or "passageway" to some
destination; the latter (while sometimes interpreted in Dōgen as "living, or vital, path")
has the common meaning of "life-saving path" — i.e., an "outlet" from a life-threatening
situation or an "avenue" of survival.

45   **differs according to the type of being** (*shurui ni shitagaite fudō ari* 種類にした
がひて不同あり): Dōgen draws here on the Buddhist teaching, found especially in Yo-
gācāra literature, known as "the four views of water" (*issui shiken* 一水四見): devas see
water as jeweled ground, humans as water, pretas ("hungry ghosts") as pus and blood,
fish as a dwelling. (See, e.g., Xuanzang's 玄奘 translation of the *She dasheng lun shi* 攝
大乘論釋, T.1598.31:402c-16-19.)

404 DŌGEN'S *SHŌBŌGENZŌ* VOLUME II

jeweled necklace is what we see as water. Some see water as marvelous flowers, though this does not mean that they use flowers as water. Ghosts see water as raging flames or see it as pus and blood. Dragons and fish see it as a palace or see it as a tower. Some see it as the *maṇi* jewel and the seven treasures, or see it as woods and walls, or see it as the pure, liberated dharma nature, or see it as the true human body, or see it as the physical marks and mental nature.[46] Humans see these as water. They are the causes and conditions that kill it and give it life.[47]

[29:21]

すでに隨類の所見不同なり、しばらくこれを疑著すべし。一境をみるに諸見しなじななりとやせん、諸象を一境なりと誤錯せりとやせん、功夫の頂顀にさらに功夫すべし。しかあればすなはち、修證辨道も一般・兩般なるべからず、究竟の境界も千種萬般なるべきなり。

So, what is seen is different according to the type [of being that sees it]. Now, we should question this a bit. Is it that there are various ways of seeing one object? Or is it that we have mistaken various images for one object? At the peak of our concentrated effort on this, we should concentrate still more. Therefore, our practice and verification, our pursuit of the way, must also be not merely of one or two kinds, and the ultimate realm must also have a thousand types and ten thousand kinds.

[29:22]

さらにこの宗旨を憶想するに、諸類の水たとひおほしといへども、本水なきがごとし、諸類の水なきがごとし。しかあれども、隨類の諸水、それ心によらず、身によらず、業より生ぜず。依自にあらず、依他にあらず、依

---

46 *maṇi* **jewel and the seven treasures** (*shippō mani ju* 七寶摩尼珠): "The *maṇi* jewel" (*mani ju* 摩尼珠) here likely refers to the *cinta-maṇi*, or "wish-fulfilling gem" (*nyoi ju* 如意珠), said to be the property of the dragon king. This gem often appears in lists of the seven treasures (see above, Note 22); hence the combination here might best be understood as "the *maṇi* jewel and the [other] seven treasures."

true human body (*shinjitsu nintai* 眞實人體): A fairly common Zen expression used to identify the individual with the dharma realm. Appears in the *shinji Shōbōgenzō* 眞字正法眼藏 (DZZ.5:196, case 131) and several times in Dōgen's writings; see Supplementary Notes, s.v. "True human body."

physical marks and mental nature (*shinsō shinshō* 身相心性): An unusual combination, not found elsewhere in Dōgen's writings, that plays with the two compounds, *shinjin* 身心 ("body and mind") and *sōshō* 相性 ("marks and nature"); while it might be understood simply as "body and mind," given the context, it may well invoke the auspicious marks (*sō* 相) of the buddha body and awakened nature (*shō* 性) of the buddha mind. See Supplementary Notes, s.v. "Body and mind."

47 **they are the causes and conditions that kill it and give it life** (*sekkatsu no innen nari* 殺活の因緣なり): A rather obscure remark, in which neither the grammatical subject nor the object is expressed; generally taken to mean that water comes into and goes out of existence depending on the various ways of seeing given here.

29. The Mountains and Waters Sūtra *Sansui kyō* 山水經 405

水の透脱あり。しかあれば、水は地・水・火・風・空・識等にあらず、水
は青・黄・赤・白・黒等にあらず、色・聲・香・味・觸・法等にあらざれ
ども、地水火風空等の水、おのづから現成せり。

If we reflect further on this point, although we may say there is water
of the various types, it would seem there is no original water, no water
of various types. Nevertheless, the various waters in accordance with the
types [of beings] do not depend on their minds, do not depend on their
bodies; they do not arise from their karma; they are not dependent on
self; they are not dependent on other. They have a transcendence dependent on water.[48] Therefore, water is not [the water of] earth, water, fire,
wind, space, or consciousness; it is not blue, yellow, red, white, or black;
it is not form, sound, smell, taste, touch, or dharma.[49] Nevertheless, the
waters of earth, water, fire, wind, space, and the rest, have appeared of
their own accord.

[29:23]

かくのごとくなれば、而今の國土・宮殿、なにものの能成・所成とあきら
めいはんことかたかるべし。空輪・風輪にかかれると道著する、わがまこ
とにあらず、他のまことにあらず、小見の測度を擬議するなり。かかれる
ところなくば住すべからず、とおもふによりて、この道著するなり。

This being the case, it becomes difficult to explain by what and of
what the present land and palace are made. To say that they rest on the
wheel of space and the wheel of wind is true neither for oneself nor for
others; it is just considering the speculations of small views and is said
only out of fear that, without some place of support, they could not abide
anywhere.[50]

---

48 **They have a transcendence dependent on water** (*esui no tōdatsu ari* 依水の透脱
あり): Usually taken to mean that water just as itself transcends itself.

49 **earth, water, fire, wind, space, or consciousness** (*chi sui ka fū kū shiki* 地・水・
火・風・空・識): I.e., the six "elements" (*roku dai* 六大) of Buddhist physics. See Supplementary Notes, s.v. "Four elements and five aggregates."

blue, yellow, red, white, or black (*shō ō shaku byaku koku* 青・黄・赤・白・黒): I.e.,
the five primary colors (*go shiki* 五色) according to Buddhist usage; water is associated
with the color white.

form, sound, smell, taste, touch, or dharma (*shiki shō kō mi soku hō* 色・聲・香・
味・觸・法): I.e., the six sense objects recognized in Buddhist epistemology; the last (*hō*
法) represents the object of the mental sense organ (S. *manas* 意).

50 **the wheel of space and the wheel of wind** (*kūrin fūrin* 空輪・風輪): I.e., two of
the four disks, or wheels (S. *maṇḍala*), beneath the earth in Buddhist cosmology: in
descending order, wind, water, metal, and space.

406 DŌGEN'S *SHŌBŌGENZŌ* VOLUME II

[29:24] {1:322}
佛言、一切諸法、畢竟解脱、無有所住。

A buddha has said, "All dharmas are ultimately liberated; they have no abode."[51]

[29:25]
しるべし、解脱にして繋縛なしといへども、諸法住位せり。しかあるに、人間の水をみるに、流注してとどまらざるとみる一途あり。その流に多般あり、これ人見の一端なり。いはゆる地を流通し、空を流通し、上方に流通し、下方に流通す。一曲にもながれ、九淵にもながる。のぼりて雲をなし、くだりてふちをなす。

We should realize that, although they may be liberated, without any bonds, "the dharmas abide in their positions."[52] However, when humans look at water, they have the one way that sees it only as flowing without rest. This flow takes many forms, of which the human view is but one. [Water] flows over the earth; it flows across the sky; it flows up; it flows down. It flows around bends and into deep abysses. It mounts up to form clouds; it descends to form pools.

[29:26]
文子曰、水之道、上天爲雨露、下地爲江河。

The *Wenzi* says, "The way of water, ascending to heaven, becomes rain and dew; descending to earth, becomes rivers and streams."[53]

[29:27]
いま俗のいふところ、なほかくのごとし。佛祖の兒孫と称せんともがら、俗よりもくらからんは、もともはづべし。いはく、水の道は、水の所知覺にあらざれども、水よく現行す。水の不知覺にあらざれども、水よく現行するなり。

---

51 **"All dharmas are ultimately liberated; they have no abode"** (*issai shohō, hikkyō gedatsu, mu u shojū* 一切諸法、畢竟解脱、無有所住): An exact source of this saying has not been identified. It is sometimes suggested that the quotation represents a paraphrase of the final words of the Fourth Ancestor, "All dharmas in their entirety are liberated" (*issai shohō shikkai gedatsu* 一切諸法悉皆解脱), quoted in Dōgen's "Shōbōgenzō gyōji" 正法眼藏行持 (DZZ.1:186). One can also find similar phrases in the sūtras: see, e.g., *Da baoji jing* 大寶積經, T.310.11:21c23; 499a28-29.

52 **"the dharmas abide in their positions"** (*shohō jūi seri* 諸法住位せり): For this usage, see above, Note 2. Dōgen seems here to be identifying this phrase with the statement in the quotation, "they have no abode."

53 **The *Wenzi*** (*Monshi* 文子): The early Daoist classic, later known as the *Tong xuan zhen jing* 通玄眞經, attributed to a Master Wen 文子, supposed to have been a follower of Laozi. The quotation reflects a line in Book 1, Daoyuan 道元 (KR.5c0118.001.7b).

29. The Mountains and Waters Sūtra *Sansui kyō* 山水經 407

Such is said even by a layman; it would be shameful indeed if those who call themselves descendants of the buddhas and ancestors were more ignorant than a layman. It says that, although "the way of water" is not perceived by water, water actually functions [as water]; although "the way of water" is not unperceived by water, water actually functions [as water].

[29:28] {1:323}

上天爲雨露、といふ。しるべし、水は、いくそばくの上天・上方へものぼりて雨露をなすなり。雨露は、世界にしたかふてしなじなり。水のいたらざるところあるといふは、小乘聲聞教なり、あるひは外道の邪教なり。水は火焔裏にもいたるなり、心念・思量・分別裏にもいたるなり、覺知・佛性裏にもいたるなり。

"*Ascending to heaven, it becomes rain and dew.*" We should realize that water climbs to so many heavens and heights and becomes rain and dew. "Rain and dew" are of various kinds, in accordance with the various worlds. To say that there are places to which water does not reach is the *śrāvaka* teaching of the Small Vehicle or the false teaching of other paths. Water extends into flames; it extends into thought, reasoning, and discrimination; it extends into perception and the buddha nature.

[29:29]

下地爲江河。しるべし、水の下地するとき、江河をなすなり。江河の精、よく賢人となる。いま凡愚・庸流のおもはくは、水はかならず江河・海川にあるとおもへり。しかにはあらで、水のなかに江海をなせり。しかあれば、江海ならぬところにも水はあり。水の下地するとき、江海の功をなすのみなり。

"*Descending to earth, it becomes rivers and streams.*" We should realize that, when water descends to earth, it becomes rivers and streams. The spirits of rivers and streams become worthies. Common fools and mediocre types think that water is always in rivers, streams, and seas; but this is not so: it makes rivers and seas within water. Therefore, water is in places that are not rivers and seas; it is just that, when water "descends to earth," it works as rivers and seas.

[29:30]

また水の、江海をなしつるところなれば、世界あるべからず、佛土あるべからず、と學すべからず。一滴のなかにも、無量の佛國土現成なり。しかあれば、佛土のなかに水あるにあらず、水裏に佛土あるにあらず。水の所在、すでに三際にかかはれず、法界にかかはれず。しかもかくのごとくなりといへども、水現成の公案なり。

Moreover, we should not study that, when water has become rivers and seas, there is then no world and no buddha land [within water]: incalculable buddha lands are realized even within a single drop of water.

408 DŌGEN'S *SHŌBŌGENZŌ* VOLUME II

Consequently, it is not that water exists within the buddha land, nor that the buddha land exists within water: the locus of water's existence has nothing to do with the three junctures, nothing to do with the dharma realm.[54] Nevertheless, though it may be like this, it is the koan of the realization of water.

[29:31]

佛祖のいたるところには、水かならずいたる。水のいたるところ、佛祖かならず現成するなり。これによりて、佛祖かならず水を拈じて身心とし、思量とせり。

Wherever the buddhas and ancestors are, water is always there; wherever water is, there the buddhas and ancestors always appear. Therefore, the buddhas and ancestors have always taken up water as their body and mind, as their thinking.

[29:32]

しかあればすなはち、水はかみにのぼらずといふは、内外の典籍にあらず。水之道は、上下・縦横に通達するなり。しかあるに、佛經のなかに、火風は上にのぼり、地水は下にくだる。この上下は、參學するところなり。いはゆる、佛道の上下を參學するなり。いはゆる、地水のゆくところを下とするなり、下を地水のゆくところとするにあらず。火風のゆくところは上なり。法界かならずしも上下四維の量にかかはるべからざれども、四大・五大・六大等の行處によりて、しばらく方隅法界を建立するのみなり。無想天は、かみ、阿鼻獄は、しも、とせるにあらず。阿鼻も盡法界なり、無想も盡法界なり。

Thus, [the idea] that water does not climb up is to be found in neither the inner nor outer texts.[55] "The way of water" penetrates everywhere, above and below, vertically and horizontally. Still, in the sūtras of the buddhas, fire and wind go up, while earth and water go down. But this "up" and "down" bears some study — the study of the "up" and "down" of the way of the buddhas. That is, where earth and water go is considered "down"; but "down" here does not mean some place to which earth and water go. Where fire and wind go is "up." While the dharma realm is not necessarily connected with measures of up and down or the four directions, simply on the basis of the movements of the four, five, or six elements, we provisionally set up a dharma realm with directions.[56] It is not that the heaven of non-conception is above and the *avīci* hell is

---

54 **three junctures** (*sansai* 三際): I.e., "the three times" (*sansei* 三世), or periods, of past, present, and future.

55 **found in neither the inner nor outer texts** (*naige no tenseki ni arazu* 内外の典籍にあらず): I.e., occurs in neither Buddhist nor non-Buddhist texts.

56 **the four, five, or six elements** (*shidai godai rokudai* 四大・五大・六大): For the six elements, see above, Note 49; the set of five elements omits consciousness; the four elements, space.

29. The Mountains and Waters Sūtra *Sansui kyō* 山水經　　　409

below: *avīci* is the entire dharma realm; the heaven of non-conception is the entire dharma realm.[57]

[29:33] {1:324}

しかあるに、龍魚の、水を宮殿とみるとき、人の、宮殿をみるがごとくなるべし、さらにながれゆくと知見すべからず。もし傍觀ありて、なんぢが宮殿は流水なりと爲説せんときは、われらがいま山流の道著を聞著するがごとく、龍魚たちまちに驚疑すべきなり。さらに宮殿・樓閣の欄階・露柱は、かくのごとくの説著あると保任することもあらん。この料理、しづかにおもひきたり、おもひもてゆくべし。この邊表に透脱を學せざれば、凡夫の身心を解脱せるにあらず、佛祖の國土を究盡せるにあらず、凡夫の國土を究盡せるにあらず、凡夫の宮殿を究盡せるにあらず。

Nevertheless, when dragons and fish see water as a palace, it must be just as when humans see palaces: they would not know it as flowing. And, if some onlooker were to explain to them, "your palace is flowing water," they would surely be just as amazed as we are now to hear it said that mountains flow. Still, there might also be some who would accept such an explanation of the railings, stairs, and pillars of palaces and pavilions. We should be calmly considering, over and over, how to handle this. If we do not study liberation in these confines, we have not liberated ourselves from the body and mind of the common person, we have not exhaustively investigated the land of the buddhas and ancestors, we have not exhaustively investigated the land of the common person, we have not exhaustively investigated the palace of the common person.[58]

[29:34]

いま人間には、海のこころ、江のこころを、ふかく水と知見せりといへども、龍魚等、いかなるものをもて水と知見し、水と使用すと、いまだしらず。おろかに、わが水と知見するを、いづれのたぐひも水にもちいるらん、と認ずることなかれ。

Although humans may have fully known the heart of the seas and the heart of the rivers, as water, just what kind of thing dragons, fish, and other beings know as water and use as water we do not yet know. Do not foolishly assume that every type of being must use as water what we know as water.

57　**the heaven of non-conception** (*musō ten* 無想天); **the *avīci* hell** (*abi goku* 阿鼻獄): I.e., the zenith and nadir of the world. The heaven of non-conception (S. *asaṃjñika*) represents the highest of the heavens associated with the four dhyānas (*shizen ten* 四禪天); *avīci* ("without interval"; *mugen* 無間) is the lowest of the hot hells, where suffering is "uninterrupted."

58　**liberation in these confines** (*kono henpyō ni tōdatsu* この邊表に透脱): Presumably, freedom from fixed categories based on particular perspectives. For this usage of *tōdatsu* 透脱, see above, Note 33.

410 DŌGEN'S *SHŌBŌGENZŌ* VOLUME II

[29:35]

いま學佛のともがら、水をならはんとき、ひとすぢに人間のみにはとどこ
ほるべからず、すすみて佛道のみづを參學すべし。佛祖のもちいるところ
の水は、われらこれをなにとか所見すると參學すべきなり。佛祖の屋裏、
また水ありや水なしやと參學すべきなり。

When those studying Buddhism now seek to learn about water, they
should not stick solely to the human; they should go on to study the
water of the way of the buddhas. We should study how we see the water
used by the buddhas and ancestors; we should study whether within the
house of the buddhas and ancestors there is or is not water.[59]

* * * * *

[29:36] {1:325}

山は、超古超今より大聖の所居なり。賢人・聖人、ともに山を堂奥とせ
り、山を身心とせり。賢人・聖人によりて、山は現成せるなり。おほよ
そ、山は、いくそばくの大聖・大賢いりあつまれるらんとおぼゆれども、
山は、いりぬるよりこのかたは、一人にあふ一人もなきなり、ただ山の活
計の現成するのみなり。さらにいりきたりつる蹤跡、なほのこらず。世間
にて山をのぞむ時節と、山中にて山にあふ時節と、頂顴・眼睛、はるかに
ことなり。不流の憶想、および不流の知見も、龍魚の知見と一齊なるべか
らず。人天の、自界にところをうる、他類これを疑著し、あるひは疑著に
およばず。

From beyond the past and beyond the present, mountains have been
the dwelling place of the great sages.[60] Worthies and sages have all made
the mountains their inner sanctum, their body and mind.[61] And through
these worthies and sages the mountains have appeared. However many
great sages and great worthies we suppose have assembled in the mountains, ever since they entered the mountains no one has met a single one
of them; it is only the expression of the mountain way of life. No traces
of their having entered remains. The crown and eyes are completely different when one is in the world gazing off at the mountains and when one

---

59 **the house of the buddhas and ancestors** (*busso no okuri* 佛祖の屋裏): A common expression in Dōgen's writing (also written 屋裡), it can imply both the "house," or
tradition of the masters, and the "chambers," or innermost dwelling place of the masters.
See Supplementary Notes, s.v. "Buddhas and ancestors."

60 **From beyond the past and beyond the present** (*chōko chōkon yori* 超古超今よ
り): Likely synonymous with the more common "beyond past and present" (*chōkokon*
超古今), "timeless" or "for all time."

61 **inner sanctum** (*dōō* 堂奥): The interior of the abbot's quarters, used metaphorically
for the innermost recesses of the tradition; very common in Dōgen's writings, where it
seems virtually synonymous with *okuri* 屋裏.

29. The Mountains and Waters Sūtra *Sansui kyō* 山水經 　　411

is in the mountains meeting the mountains.[62] Our concept of not-flowing and our knowledge of not-flowing must not be the same as the dragon's knowledge. Humans and devas take their places in their own worlds, and other beings may question this or they may not question it.

[29:37]

しかあれば、山流の句を佛祖に學すべし、驚疑にまかすべからず。拈一は これ流なり、拈一はこれ不流なり、一回は流なり、一回は不流なり。この 參究なきがごときは、如來正法輪にあらず。

Therefore, without giving way to our surprise and doubt, we should study the words "mountains flow" with the buddhas and ancestors. Taking up one, it is flowing; taking up one, it is not flowing. At one turn, it is flowing; at one turn, not flowing.[63] If our study is not like this, it is not the true dharma wheel of the tathāgatas.[64]

[29:38]

古佛いはく、欲得不招無間業、莫謗如來正法輪。

An old buddha has said,

> "If you don't wish to incur unremitting karma,
> Don't denigrate the true dharma wheel of the Tathāgata."[65]

62　**crown and eyes** (*chōnei ganzei* 頂顆・眼睛): Two terms, common in Dōgen's writing, for the true identity of someone or something. See Supplementary Notes, s.v. "Crown of the head," "Eye." The reference here could be either to the mountains or to those who enter the mountains (or both)

63　**Taking up one** (*nen ichi* 拈一); **At one turn** (*ikkai* 一回): Presumably, both these terms refer to our study. The verb *nen* 拈 is regularly used for the act of "taking up" a topic for consideration; "at one turn" here is likely equivalent to "at one time," but note the possible play on the "dharma wheel" (*hōrin* 法輪; i.e., teachings) in the following sentence.

64　**the true dharma wheel of the tathāgatas** (*nyorai shōbōrin* 如來正法輪): A common expression in Buddhist literature for the true teachings of the buddhas.

65　**An old buddha** (*kobutsu* 古佛): From the *Zhengdao ge* 證道歌 (T.2014.48:396b27), traditionally attributed to the early eighth-century Chan figure Yongjia Xuanjue 永嘉玄 覺 (d. 723).

"unremitting karma" (*muken gō* 無間業): Deeds the consequences of which lead to *avīci*, the hell of incessant (S. *ānantarya*) suffering (or, by some accounts, lead immediately to *avīci*). The standard list of such deeds (matricide, patricide, killing an arhat, wounding a tathāgata, and damaging the saṃgha) does not explicitly include denigration of the dharma (though one might well read this into the last member).

412 DŌGEN'S *SHŌBŌGENZŌ* VOLUME II

[29:39]

この道を、皮肉骨髄に銘すべし、身心依正に銘すべし、空に銘すべし、色に銘すべし。若樹・若石に銘せり、若田・若里に銘せり。

These words, we should engrave on our skin, flesh, bones, and marrow, should engrave on our body and mind, our secondary and primary recompense, should engrave on emptiness, should engrave on form.[66] They are engraved "*whether on trees or on rocks*," engraved "*whether in fields or in villages*."[67]

[29:40] {1:326}

おほよそ、山は國界に屬せりといへども、山を愛する人に屬するなり。山かならず主を愛するとき、聖賢・高德、やまにいるなり。聖賢、やまにすむとき、やま、これに屬するがゆえに、樹石鬱茂なり、禽獸靈秀なり。これ聖賢の德をかうぶらしむるゆえなり。しるべし、山は賢をこのむ實あり、聖をこのむ實あり。

Although we may say that mountains belong to the land, actually, they belong to those who love the mountains. When the mountains inevitably love their owners, the sages and worthies, and the eminently virtuous enter the mountains. And when the sages and worthies live in the mountains, because the mountains belong to them, trees and rocks flourish and abound, and the birds and beasts take on a supernatural excellence. This is because the sages and worthies have covered them with their virtue. We should realize that the mountains actually take delight in the worthy, actually take delight in the sage.

---

66 **skin, flesh, bones, and marrow** (*hi niku kotsu zui* 皮肉骨髄): See above, Note 33.

our body and mind, our secondary and primary recompense (*shinjin eshō* 身心依正): A combination found several times in Dōgen's writings but only infrequently elsewhere. See Supplementary Notes, s.v. "Body and mind," and "Secondary and primary recompense."

should engrave on emptiness, should engrave on form (*kū ni mei su beshi, shiki ni mei su beshi* 空に銘すべし、色に銘すべし): Doubtless alluding to the famous formula of the *Heart Sūtra*; see Supplementary Notes, s.v. "Form is itself emptiness; emptiness is itself form."

67 **engraved "whether on trees or on rocks," engraved "whether in fields or in villages"** (*nyaku ju nyaku seki ni mei seri, nyaku den nyaku ri ni mei seri* 若樹・若石に銘せり、若田・若里に銘せり): A combination of two scriptural allusions found together elsewhere in the *Shōbōgenzō*. "Whether on trees or on rocks" (*nyaku ju nyaku seki* 若樹若石) refers to the tale in the *Nirvāṇa Sūtra* of Śākyamuni in a previous life, as the "boy of the Himalayas," who wrote a Buddhist teaching on trees and rocks; see Supplementary Notes. "Whether in fields or in villages" (*nyaku den nyaku ri* 若田若里) derives from a passage in the *Lotus Sūtra*, in which Śākyamuni encourages his followers to preach the dharma in fields and villages; see Supplementary Notes.

29. The Mountains and Waters Sūtra *Sansui kyō* 山水經 413

[29:41]

帝者おほく山に幸して、賢人を拜し、大聖を拜問するは、古今の勝躅なり。このとき、師禮をもてうやまふ、民間の法に準ずることなし。聖化のおよぶところ、またく山賢を強爲することなし。山の、人間をはなれたること、しりぬべし。崆峒・華封のそのかみ、黃帝これを拜請するに、膝行して叩頭して、廣成にとふしなり。釋迦牟尼佛、かつて父王の宮をいでて山へいれり。しかあれども、父王、やまをうらみず。父王、やまにありて太子をおしふるともがらを、あやしまず。十二年の修道、おほく山にあり。法王の運啓も在山なり。まことに輪王、なほ山を強爲せず。

It is an excellent example in past and present that many emperors have gone to the mountains to pay homage to the worthies and seek instruction from great sages. At such times, they respected them as teachers and honored them without standing on social forms. For the reach of the imperial influence has no authority over the worthies of the mountains: it should be recognized that the mountains are beyond the human. At the time of Kongtong and the Hua Guard, when the Yellow Emperor made his visit, he went on his knees, prostrated himself, and begged instruction from Guang Chengzi.[68] Again, Buddha Śākyamuni left the palace of his father the king and went into the mountains. Yet his father the king felt no resentment toward the mountains; his father the king felt no distrust of those in the mountains who instructed the prince. The twelve years of practicing the way were largely spent in the mountains, and it was in the mountains that the Dharma King's felicitous opening occurred.[69] Truly, even a wheel-turning king does not wield authority over the mountains.[70]

[29:42]

しるべし、山は人間のさかひにあらず、上天のさかひにあらず。人慮の測度をもて、山を知見すべからず。もし人間の流に比準せずば、たれか山流、山不流等を疑著せん。

---

68 **At the time of Kongtong and the Hua Guard** (*Kōtō Kahō no sono kami* 崆峒・華封のそのかみ): Dōgen seems to be running together two stories from the ancient Daoist classic the *Zhuangzi* 莊子, one dealing with the Yellow Emperor's interview with Guang Chengzi 廣成子 of Mount Kongtong (Zaiyou 在宥, KR.5c0126.011.8a); the other, with Emperor Yao's instruction by the Hua Guard (Tiandi 天地, KR.5c0126.012.5a-7a). The same combination occurs in the *Eihei kōroku* 永平廣錄 (DZZ.4:170).

69 **The twelve years of practicing the way** (*jūni nen no shudō* 十二年の修道): Presumably, based on the tradition (found, e.g., in the *Jingde chuandeng lu* 景德傳燈錄, T.2076.51:205b12-24), that Gautama left home at age nineteen and achieved awakening at age thirty — a tradition found in the section on Śākyamuni in "Shōbōgenzō gyōji" 正法眼藏行持. The more common version of the Buddha's life has him leaving his father's palace at age twenty-nine and awakening under the bodhi tree at age thirty-five.

Dharma King's felicitous opening (*hōō no unkei* 法王の運啓): I.e., the opening of Śākyamuni's buddhahood.

70 **wheel-turning king** (*rinnō* 輪王): The ideal monarch of Indian tradition; S. *cakravartin*.

414 DŌGEN'S *SHŌBŌGENZŌ* VOLUME II

We should understand that the mountains are not within the boundaries of the human, not within the boundaries of the heavens. They are not to be known with the calculations of human thinking. If only we did not compare them with flowing among humans, who would have any doubts about such things as the mountains' flowing or not flowing?

[29:43]

あるひはむかしよりの賢人・聖人、ままに水にすむもあり。水にすむとき、魚をつるあり、人をつるあり、道をつるあり。これともに、古來、水中の風流なり。さらにすすみて、自己をつるあるべし、釣をつるあるべし、釣につらるるあるべし、道につらるるあるべし。

Again, since ancient times, the worthies and the sages have sometimes lived by the water. When they live by the water, they hook fish. Or they hook people, or they hook the way. These are all ancient traditions of being in the water. And going further, there should be hooking oneself; there should be hooking the hook; there should be being hooked by the hook; there should be being hooked by the way.

[29:44] {1:327}

むかし德誠和尚、たちまちに藥山をはなれて江心にすみし、すなはち華亭江の賢聖をえたるなり。魚をつらざらんや、人をつらざらんや、水をつらざらんや、みづからをつらざらんや。人の、德誠をみることをうるは、德誠なり。德誠の、人を接するは、人にあふなり。

Long ago, when Reverend Decheng suddenly left Yaoshan and went to live on the river, he got the worthy sage of the Huating River.[71] Is this not hooking a fish? Is it not hooking a person? Is it not hooking water? Is it not hooking himself? That the person got to see Decheng is Decheng; Decheng's engaging the person is his meeting the person.[72]

---

71 **Reverend Decheng** (*Tokujō oshō* 德誠和尚): I.e., Chuanzi ("the Boatman") Decheng 船子德誠 (dates unknown), a disciple of Yaoshan Weiyan 藥山惟儼 (751-834). After studying with Yaoshan for thirty years, he became a boatman on the Huating River 華亭江 (in Jiangsu). There he met Jiashan Shanhui 夾山善會 (805-881). After transmitting the dharma to Shanhui by throwing him in the river, Decheng tipped over his boat and vanished into the water. Dōgen records this well-known story in his *shinji Shōbōgenzō* 眞字正法眼藏 (DZZ.5:168-172, case 90).

worthy sage (*kenshō* 賢聖): I.e., Shanhui 善會. The epithet *kenshō* 賢聖 here should probably be taken as the compound term (also read *kensei*) for a wise and virtuous person.

72 **That the person got to see Decheng is Decheng** (*hito no, Tokujō o miru koto o uru wa, Tokujō nari* 人の、德誠をみることをうるは、德誠なり): May be taken to mean, "the reason that Jiashan was able to meet Decheng is that Jiashan was himself Decheng." The subsequent sentence suggests, "Decheng's instructing Jiashan was Jiashan encountering himself."

29. The Mountains and Waters Sūtra *Sansui kyō* 山水經 415

[29:45]

世界に水ありといふのみにあらず、水界に世界あり。水中の、かくのごと
くあるのみにあらず、雲中にも有情世界あり、風中にも有情世界あり、火
中にも有情世界あり、地中にも有情世界あり、法界中にも有情世界あり、
一茎草中にも有情世界あり、一拄杖中にも有情世界あり。有情世界あるが
ごときは、そのところ、かならず佛祖世界あり。かくのごとくの道理、よ
くよく參學すべし。

It is not the case simply that there is water in the world; within the
world of water there is a world. And this is true not only within water:
within clouds as well there is a world of sentient beings; within wind
there is a world of sentient beings; within fire there is a world of sentient beings; within earth there is a world of sentient beings. Within the
dharma realm there is a world of sentient beings; within a single blade
of grass there is a world of sentient beings; within a single staff there
is a world of sentient beings. And wherever there is a world of sentient
beings, there, invariably, is the world of the buddhas and ancestors. The
reason this is so, we should study very carefully.

[29:46]

しかあれば、水はこれ眞龍の宮なり、流落にあらず。流のみなりと認ずる
は、流のことば、水を謗ずるなり。たとへば、非流と強爲するがゆえに。
水は水の如是實相のみなり、水是水功德なり、流にあらず。一水の流を參
究し、不流を參究するに、萬法の究盡、たちまちに現成するなり。山も實
にかくるる山あり、澤にかくるる山あり、空にかくるる山あり、山にかく
るる山あり。藏に藏山する參學あり。

Thus, water is the palace of the real dragon; it is not flowing away.[73] If
we regard it only as flowing, the word "flowing" is an insult to water: for
it is like imposing "not flowing." Water is nothing but "such real marks"
of water; *water is the virtues of water*: it is not flowing.[74] In the investigation of the flowing or the not-flowing of a single [drop of] water, the
exhaustive investigation of the myriad dharmas is instantly realized.

---

73   **real dragon** (*shinryū* 眞龍): In contrast to the carved dragon; from the well-known
Chinese story of the Duke of She 楚葉公, famous for his love of carved dragons, who
was one day visited by a real dragon and frightened out of his wits. The *locus classicus*
of the story is *Xinxu* 新序, *Zashi* 雜事 5.137.

74   **"such real marks" of water** (*mizu no nyoze jissō* 水の如是實相): "Such real marks"
or "the real marks of suchness" (*nyoze jissō* 如是實相) is a fixed expression indicating
what something really is. The words here likely reflect a passage in the *Lotus Sūtra* often
invoked in the *Shōbōgenzō*; see Supplementary Notes, s.v. "Only buddhas with buddhas
can exhaustively investigate the real marks of the dharmas."

water is the virtues of water (*sui ze sui kudoku nari* 水是水功德なり): Dōgen here
switches to Chinese, as if quoting some (unidentified) source; perhaps, meaning something like, "water is the sum total of the qualities of water."

416 DŌGEN'S *SHŌBŌGENZŌ* VOLUME II

Among mountains as well, there are mountains hidden in treasures; there are mountains hidden in marshes, mountains hidden in the sky; there are mountains hidden in mountains.[75] There is a study of mountains hidden in hiddenness.[76]

[29:47]
古佛云、山是山、水是水。

An old buddha has said, "Mountains are mountains, waters are waters."[77]

[29:48]
この道取は、やま、これやま、といふにあらず、山これやま、といふなり。しかあれば、山を参究すべし。山を参窮すれば、山に功夫なり。かくのごとく、山水おのづから、賢をなし、聖をなすなり。

These words do not say that mountains are mountains; they say that mountains are mountains. Therefore, we should thoroughly investigate these mountains. When we thoroughly investigate the mountains, this is the mountain training.[78] In this way, mountains and waters themselves make worthies and make sages.

---

75 **mountains hidden in treasures** (*takara ni kakururu yama* 寶にかくるる山): It is not clear whether Dōgen had in mind specific examples of hidden mountains in this sentence. Here, he may have been thinking of Mount Sumeru, each of the four sides of which is said to be composed of a different precious substance: gold, silver, *vaiḍūrya* (beryl), and *sphaṭika* (crystal). (See, e.g., *Apidamo jushe lun* 阿毘達磨倶舍論, T.1558.29:57b14-15.)

mountains hidden in marshes (*sawa ni kakururu yama* 澤にかくるる山): Reminiscent of a line in the *Zhuangzi* 莊子 (Dazongshi 大宗師, KR.5c0126.006.4a) that is quoted in a number of Zen texts: "Hide the boat in the gully; hide the mountain in the marsh" (*zang zhou yu he, zang shan yu ze* 藏舟於壑、藏山於澤). (The original text is better read "hide the fishnet [*shan*] 汕 in the marsh.")

mountains hidden in the sky (*sora ni kakururu yama* 空にかくるる山): Or "mountains hidden in emptiness" (*kū* 空).

76 **study of mountains hidden in hiddenness** (*zō ni zōsan suru sangaku* 藏に藏山する參學): Or, perhaps, "study of hiding mountains in hiddenness," if we read the unusual form *zōsan suru* 藏山する as a verb-object construction.

77 **"Mountains are mountains, waters are waters"** (*san ze san, sui ze sui* 山是山、水是水): A phrase occurring often in Zen literature. Most often associated with a saying of Yunmen Wenyan 雲門文偃 (*Yunmen yulu* 雲門語錄, T.1988.47:547c11-12):

諸和尚子、莫妄想。天是天地是地。山是山水是水。僧是僧俗是俗。

Reverends, do not have deluded notions. Heaven is heaven, earth is earth; mountains are mountains, waters are waters; monks are monks, laymen are laymen.

78 **this is the mountain training** (*yama ni kufū nari* 山に功夫なり): Depending on how one wishes to read the particle *ni* に here, this might be understood as "concentrated effort in (*ni okite* におきて) the mountains," "concentrated effort by (*ni yorite* によりて) the mountains," or "concentrated effort as (*nite* にて) the mountains."

29. The Mountains and Waters Sūtra *Sansui kyō* 山水經

{1:328}

正法眼藏山水經第二十九
Treasury of the True Dharma Eye
The Mountains and Waters Sūtra
Number 29

[Ryūmonji MS:]

爾時仁治元年庚子十月十八日于時、在觀音導利興聖寶林寺示衆
Presented to the assembly at Kannon Dōri Kōshō Hōrin Monastery;
eighteenth day, tenth month of the senior metal year of the rat, the first
year of Ninji [3 November 1240][79]

[*Himitsu* MS:]

寬元元年甲辰六月三日申時、在越州吉田縣吉峰寺侍司寮書寫之。慧上
Copied this at the acolyte's office, Kippō Monastery, Yoshida District, Esshū;
third day, sixth month of the senior wood year of the dragon, the first
year of Kangen [21 June 1243]. Ejō[80]

---

79 The *Himitsu* 秘密 MS shares an identical colophon.

80 This colophon is found only in the *Himitsu* 秘密 MS.

Ejō 慧上: Written with a homonym for Ejō 懷奘, a practice also found in the *Himitsu* 秘密 MS of the "Mitsugo" 密語 chapter.

TREASURY OF THE TRUE DHARMA EYE
NUMBER 30

Sūtra Reading
Kankin
看經

Sūtra Reading

Kankin

INTRODUCTION

This essay was composed at Kōshōji in the autumn of 1241. It represents number 30 in both the seventy-five and sixty-chapter compilations of the *Shōbōgenzō* and number 21 in the Honzan edition.

The title theme of the essay, *kankin* 看經, refers to the practices both of reading and reciting scripture. Dōgen divides his essay on the theme into two quite different parts. In the first, he quotes and comments on nine sayings on sūtra reading from the Chinese Chan literature (plus a tenth saying at the conclusion); in the second part, he provides detailed instruction on how to perform sūtra reading ceremonies. The text represents, then, an unusual combination of kōan commentary and ritual manual, bringing together in one work two of Dōgen's favorite genres.

正法眼藏第三十

Treasury of the True Dharma Eye
Number 30

看經

Sūtra Reading

[30:1] {1:329}

阿耨多羅三藐三菩提の修證、あるひは知識をもちい、あるひは經卷をもち
いる。知識といふは、全自己の佛祖なり。經卷といふは、全自己の經卷な
り。全佛祖の自己、全經卷の自己なるがゆえに、かくのごとくなり。自己
と稱すといへども、我・儞の拘牽にあらず、これ活眼睛なり、活拳頭な
り。

The practice and verification of *anuttara-samyak-saṃbodhi* sometimes
employs wise friends, sometimes employs sūtra scrolls.[1] "Wise friends"
are the buddhas and ancestors of one's whole self; "sūtra scrolls" are the
sūtra scrolls of one's whole self.[2] This is so because the self of the whole
of the buddhas and ancestors is the self of the whole of the sūtra scrolls.
Although it may be called the "self," it has nothing to do with "I" and
"you"; it is the living eye; it is the living fist.[3]

---

1   ***anuttara-samyak-saṃbodhi*** (*anokutara sanmyaku sanbodai* 阿耨多羅三藐三菩
提): "Unsurpassed, perfect awakening."

sometimes employs wise friends, sometimes employs sūtra scrolls (*arui wa chishiki
o mochii, arui wa kyōkan o mochiiru* あるひは知識をもちい、あるひは經卷をもちい
る): From a fixed expression, occurring often in the *Shōbōgenzō*, for the two sources of
Buddhist learning; see Supplementary Notes, s.v. "Whether from a wise friend, whether
from a sūtra scroll."

2   **the buddhas and ancestors of one's whole self** (*zen jiko no busso* 全自己の佛祖):
A tentative translation. The expression *zen jiko* 全自己, rendered here "one's whole self,"
does not occur elsewhere in Dōgen's writing and is not attested in the extant Buddhist
literature of his day. This translation follows the traditional reading, but the passage
might also be parsed, "'Wise friends' are all the buddhas and ancestors of one's own self;
'sūtra scrolls' are all the sūtra scrolls of one's own self. This is so because the self of all
the buddhas and ancestors is the self of all the sūtra scrolls."

3   **living eye** (*katsu ganzei* 活眼睛); **living fist** (*katsu kentō* 活拳頭): Both "eye" and
"fist" are regularly used as synechdoches for the true person — the former, in reference
to the insight of the awakened; the latter, to the power of the Zen master. See Supplementary Notes, s.v. "Eye," "Fist." The expression "living eye" (more often, simply *katsugan*
活眼) is common in the Zen literature and occurs several times in Dōgen's writing; "living fist," on the other hand, is unusual and is not found elsewhere in the *Shōbōgenzō*.

422 DŌGEN'S *SHŌBŌGENZŌ* VOLUME II

[30:2]

しかあれども、念經・看經・誦經・書經・受經・持經あり、ともに佛祖の
修證なり。しかあるに、佛經にあふ事、たやすきにあらず。於無量國中、
乃至名字不可得聞なり、於佛祖中、乃至名字不可得聞なり、於命脈中、乃
至名字不可得聞なり。佛祖にあらざれば、經卷を見聞・讀誦・解義せず。
佛祖參學より、かつがつ經卷を參學するなり。このとき、耳處・眼處・
舌處・鼻處・身心塵處・到處・聞處・話處の聞・持・受・説經等の現成あ
り。爲求名聞故説外道論議の輩、佛經を修行すべからず。そのゆえは、經
卷は若樹・若石の傳持あり、若田・若里の流布あり。塵刹の演出あり、虛
空の開講あり。

Nevertheless, there is thinking on sūtras, reading sūtras, reciting sūtras,
copying sūtras, receiving sūtras, and keeping sūtras — all of which are
the practice and verification of the buddhas and ancestors. To come into
contact with the sūtras of the buddhas, however, is not easy. "*In incalculable lands, even the name cannot be heard.*"[4] *Among the buddhas
and ancestors, even the name cannot be heard; within their vital artery,
even the name cannot be heard.*[5] If one is not a buddha and ancestor, one
does not see or hear, read or recite, or elucidate the meaning of the sūtra
scrolls. It is from the study of the buddhas and ancestors that one eventually comes to study something of the sūtra scrolls.[6] At this time, there appear the hearing, keeping, receiving and preaching of the sūtras, through
the sphere of the ear, sphere of the eye, sphere of the tongue, sphere of
the nose, spheres of the objects of body and mind, the sphere of everywhere; and the sphere of hearing and the sphere of speaking.[7] The types

---

4　**"In incalculable lands, even the name cannot be heard"** (*o muryō koku chū, naishi myōji fukatokumon* 於無量國中、乃至名字不可得聞): From the *Lotus Sūtra* (*Miaofa
lianhua jing* 妙法蓮華經, T.262.9:38c21-21):

　　文殊師利、是法華經、於無量國中、乃至名字不可得聞、何況得見受持讀誦。

　　Mañjuśrī, this *Lotus Sūtra*, in incalculable lands, even its name cannot be heard,
　　much less can one see, receive or keep, read or recite it.

5　**Among the buddhas and ancestors** (*o busso chū* 於佛祖中); **within their vital
artery** (*o meimyaku chū* 於命脈中): Dōgen's variations, also in Chinese, on the preceding sūtra passage. "Vital artery" (*meimyaku* 命脈) refers to the lineage, or "blood line,"
of the buddhas and ancestors. Presumably, the sense of the sentence is that, even within
the lineage, there are those oblivious of the sūtras — likely, an oblique reference to those
who would treat the Zen tradition as a "separate transmission outside the teachings" (*kyō
ge betsu den* 教外別傳). See Supplementary Notes, s.v. "A separate transmission outside
the teachings."

6　**from the study of the buddhas and ancestors** (*busso sangaku yori* 佛祖參學よ
り): Ambiguous: can mean either "one's study *of* (or *with*) the buddhas and ancestors,"
or "the study *by* the buddhas and ancestors."

7　**sphere of the ear** (*nisho* 耳處): Dōgen begins here a list of "spheres" (*sho* 處)
derived from, and then playing with, the traditional Buddhist doctrine of the "twelve
spheres" (or "bases"; *jūni sho* 十二處; S. *dvādaśāyatana*) — i.e., the six sense organs
(*rokkon* 六根; S. *ṣaḍ-indriya*) and their objects (*rokkyō* 六境, or *rokujin* 六塵; S. *ṣaḍ-*

30. Sūtra Reading *Kankin* 看經 423

who, "*because they seek name and fame, preach the doctrines of other paths*," would not undertake the practice of the sūtras of the buddhas.[8] Therefore, with regard to the sūtra scrolls, there is the transmission and maintaining of "*whether on trees or on rocks*"; there is the propagation of "*whether in fields or in villages*."[9] There are revelations of *kṣetra* like dust motes, and there are the lectures of empty space.[10]

---

viṣaya). Dōgen's list introduces the first four organs, then summarizes the remainder with "the spheres of the objects of body and mind" (*shinjin jinsho* 身心塵處); he then includes the playful "sphere of everywhere" (*tōsho* 到處), an ordinary term for "every place"; and ends with the "spheres" of "hearing" and "speaking" (*monsho washo* 聞處話處), ordinary Chinese constructions meaning "what is heard" and "what is said."

8 **"because they seek name and fame, preach the doctrines of other paths"** (*i gu myōmon ko setsu gedō rongi* 爲求名聞故説外道論議): Ironically, derived from a passage in the *Lotus Sūtra* (*Miaofa lianhua jing* 妙法蓮華經, T.262.9:36c3-6), in which other Buddhists are quoted as disparaging those who preach the sūtra:

此諸比丘等、爲貪利養故、説外道論議。自作此經典、誑惑世間人。爲求名聞故、分別於是經。

These bhikṣus, because they are greedy for profit and support, preach the doctrines of other paths. They themselves fabricate this sūtra, deceiving and confusing the worldly. Because they seek name and fame, they draw false distinctions in this sūtra.

would not undertake the practice of the sūtras of the buddhas (*bukkyō o shugyō su bekarazu* 佛經を修行すべからず): Or "should not undertake the practice of the sūtras of the buddhas."

9 **"whether on trees or on rocks"** (*nyaku ju nyaku seki* 若樹・若石); **"whether in fields or in villages"** (*nyaku den nyaku ri* 若田・若里): A combination of two scriptural allusions found together elsewhere in the *Shōbōgenzō*. "Whether on trees or on rocks" refers to the tale in the *Nirvāṇa Sūtra* of Śākyamuni in a previous life as the "boy of the Himalayas" who wrote a Buddhist teaching on trees and rocks; see Supplementary Notes. "Whether in fields or in villages" derives from a passage in the *Lotus Sūtra*, in which Śākyamuni encourages his followers to preach the dharma in fields and villages; see Supplementary Notes.

10 **revelations of *kṣetra* like dust motes** (*jinsetsu no enshutsu* 塵利の演出): Likely an allusion to a well-known passage in the *Avataṃsaka-sūtra* (*Huayan jing* 華嚴經, T.279.10:273b15-18):

如有大經卷　量等三千界
在於一塵内　一切塵悉然
有一聰慧人　淨眼悉明見
破塵出經卷　普饒益衆生

Suppose that there was a great sūtra scroll,
Equal in size to three thousand worlds,
Existing within a single dust mote,
And that all motes of dust, without exception, were like that.
And suppose there was a sharp-witted person who,
Being pure of eye, clearly saw it all,
And breaking open the motes of dust, revealed the sūtra scrolls,
Widely and abundantly benefiting living beings.

lectures of empty space (*kokū no kaikō* 虚空の開講): Allusion to a conversation

424 DŌGEN'S *SHŌBŌGENZŌ* VOLUME II

* * * * *

[30:3] {1:330}

藥山曩祖弘道大師、久不陞堂。院主白云、大衆久思和尚慈誨。山云、打鐘著。院主打鐘。大衆才集。山陞堂、良久便下座歸方丈。院主隨後白云、和尚適來聽許爲衆説法、如何不垂一言。山云、經有經師、論有論師、爭怪得老僧。

The Ancient Ancestor of Yaoshan, Great Master Hongdao, had not as-cended the dharma hall in a long time.[11] The head of cloister spoke to him saying, "The monks of the great assembly have long pined for the Reverend's compassionate instruction."[12]

Yaoshan said, "Ring the bell."

The head of cloister rang the bell, and the great assembly gathered accordingly. Yaoshan ascended the dharma hall; after a long while, he got down from the lecture seat and returned to the abbot's quarters.

The head of cloister followed behind him and said, "A while ago the Reverend agreed to preach the dharma for the assembly. Why did you not offer a single word?"

Yaoshan said, "For sūtras, there are sūtra masters; for treatises, there are treatise masters. How can you doubt this old monk?"

[30:4]

曩祖の慈誨するところは、拳頭有拳頭師、眼睛有眼睛師なり。しかあれども、しばらく曩祖に拜問すべし、爭怪得和尚はなきにあらず、いぶかし、和尚是什麼師。

The "compassionate instruction" given by the Ancient Ancestor is "For fists, there are fist masters; for eyes, there are eye masters." Still, for a bit, we should bow and inquire of the ancient ancestor, "'*How can you doubt the Reverend?*' is not wrong, but I do wonder, of what is the Reverend a master?"

* * * * *

recorded in Dōgen's *shinji Shōbōgenzō* 眞字正法眼藏 (DZZ.5:126, case 4) and in his "Empty Space" chapter ("Shōbōgenzō kokū" 正法眼藏虚空, DZZ.2:211); see Supplementary Notes, s.v. "Prelate Liang."

11 **The Ancient Ancestor of Yaoshan, Great Master Hongdao** (*Yakusan nōso Gudō daishi* 藥山曩祖弘道大師): I.e., Yaoshan Weiyan 藥山惟儼 (751-834). "Great Master Hongdao" (*Gudō daishi* 弘道大師) is a posthumous title; "ancient ancestor" (*nōso* 曩祖) is an honorific. This anecdote occurs in a number of sources; see, e.g., *Jingde chuandeng lu* 景德傳燈録 (T.2076.51:311c19-22).

12 **head of cloister** (*inju* 院主): The chief administrator of the monastery.

30. Sūtra Reading *Kankin* 看經 425

[30:5]

韶州曹溪山大鑑高祖會下、誦法華經曽法達來參。高祖爲法達説偈云、心迷
法華轉、心悟轉法華、誦久不明己、與義作讐家、無念念即正、有念念成
邪、有無倶不計、長御白牛車。

> In the assembly of the Eminent Ancestor Dajian of Mount Caoxi in
> Shaozhou, a monk named Fada, who specialized in reciting the *Lotus
> Sūtra*, had come to study.[13] The Eminent Ancestor recited a gāthā for
> Fada:
>
> > When the mind is deluded, the *Lotus* turns it;
> > When the mind is awakened, it turns the *Lotus*.[14]
> > Reciting for long without clarifying the self
> > Makes an enemy of the meaning.
> > Having no thought, thought is right;
> > Having thought, thought becomes wrong.[15]
> > Without reckoning with either having or not having,
> > We ride forever on the white ox cart.[16]

[30:6] {1:331}

しかあれば、心迷は法華に轉せられ、心悟は法華を轉ず。さらに迷悟を跳
出する時は、法華の法華を轉ずるなり。

> Thus, when the mind is deluded, it is turned by the *Lotus*; when the
> mind is awakened, it turns the *Lotus*. And further, when it springs forth
> from delusion and awakening, the *Lotus* turns the *Lotus*.

---

13 **the Eminent Ancestor Dajian of Mount Caoxi in Shaozhou** (*Sōshū Sōkeizan
Daikan kōso* 韶州曹溪山大鑑高祖): I.e., the Sixth Ancestor, Caoxi Huineng 曹溪慧能.
His verse appears in the biography of Fada in several Chan sources (see, e.g., *Jingde
chuandeng lu* 景德傳燈錄, T.2076.51:238a24-27).

14 **the *Lotus* turns it** (*Hokke ten* 法華轉); **it turns the *Lotus*** (*ten Hokke* 轉法華): The
verse takes advantage of the use of the verb "to turn," or "revolve" (*ten* 轉), in reference
to turning the spindles on which a sūtra is rolled (or the pages, if the sūtra is folded in
accordion fashion or bound into a book); it also means, by extension, "to read a sūtra"
(*dokkyō* 讀經).

15 **Having no thought, thought is right** (*munen nen soku shō* 無念念即正): Here and
below, the translation fails to capture the semantic range, crucial to this discussion, of
the term *nen* 念, rendered here "thought" but also used for "memorizing," "contemplating," and "reciting" texts. Hence, the expression "no thought" (*munen* 無念), famous as
a description of the Sixth Ancestor's teaching on meditation, can here also imply "no
recitation" of the *Lotus*.

16 **white ox cart** (*byakugosha* 白牛車): Reference to the one, buddha vehicle, as presented in the famous parable of the burning house in the *Lotus Sūtra*, in which a father
lures his children from a burning house with the offer of goat, deer, and ox carts, and
then, once they are safely outside, presents them with great carts pulled by swift white
oxen; see Supplementary Notes, s.v. "Burning house."

DŌGEN'S *SHŌBŌGENZŌ* VOLUME II

[30:7]

法達まさに偈をききて、踊躍歡喜、以偈讚曰、經誦三千部、曹溪一句亡、未明出世旨、寧歇累生狂、羊鹿牛權設、初中後善揚、誰知火宅內、元是法中王。

Fada, upon hearing the gāthā, *jumped for joy and praised it with a gāthā of his own.*[17]

Three thousand recitations of the sūtra,
Died with a single line by Caoxi.[18]
If the meaning of the advent is not yet clear,
How can we stop the madness of repeated births?[19]
The goat, deer, and ox, provisionally set up,
Are proclaimed good in the beginning, middle, and end.[20]
Who knew that inside the burning house
Was the king among dharmas from the start?[21]

---

17 **jumped for joy and praised it with a gāthā** (*yuyaku kangi, i ge san etsu* 踊躍歡喜、以偈讚曰): This phrase and the following verse are quoted from Fada's biography (e.g., at *Jingde chuandeng lu* 景德傳燈錄, T.2076.51:238b13-18).

18 **Three thousand recitations of the sūtra** (*kyōju sanzen bu* 經誦三千部): Earlier in the biography, Fada tells Huineng, "I have already recited the *Lotus Sūtra* as many as three thousand times" (*nen hokkekyō i kyū senzen bu* 念法華經已及三千部) (T.2076.51:237c24).

19 **meaning of the advent** (*shusse shi* 出世旨): I.e., the meaning of the buddhas' "appearance in the world," which, according to the *Lotus Sūtra*, is to guide living beings to buddhahood. See Supplementary Notes, s.v. "Buddhas, the world-honored ones, appear in the world for the reason of one great matter alone."

20 **The goat, deer, and ox, provisionally set up** (*yō roku go gonsetsu* 羊鹿牛權設): Reference again to the parable of the burning house in the *Lotus Sūtra*, where the three vehicles (*śrāvaka*, *pratyeka-buddha*, and bodhisattva) of Buddhism, are likened respectively to goat, deer, and ox carts, which are not real but only provisionally offered by the father to lure his children from danger. See Supplementary Notes, s.v. "Burning house," "Three vehicles."

proclaimed good in the beginning, middle, and end (*shochūgo zen'yō* 初中後善揚): An allusion to a passage of the *Lotus Sūtra*, as a description of the true dharma (*shōbō* 正法); see Supplementary Notes, s.v. "Good in the beginning, middle, and end."

21 **inside the burning house was the king among dharmas from the start** (*kataku nai, gen ze hotchū ō* 火宅內、元是法中王): Reflecting Huineng's teaching to Fada in the latter's biography (*Jingde chuandeng lu* 景德傳燈錄, T.2076.51:2386-7) that it is because people do not realize they are already seated in the white ox cart that they seek the three carts outside. "King among dharmas" (*hotchū ō* 法中王) refers to the ultimate teachings of Buddhism — in this case, the one, buddha vehicle. See Supplementary Notes, s.v. "Burning house."

30. Sūtra Reading *Kankin* 看經　　　427

[30:8]

そのとき、高祖曰、汝今後、方可名爲念經僧也。

At that time, *the Eminent Ancestor said, "From now on, you may be called a monk who thinks on the sūtra."*[22]

[30:9]

しるべし、佛道に念經僧あることを。曹溪古佛の直指なり。この念經僧の念は、有念・無念等にあらず、有無倶不計なり。ただそれ從劫至劫手不擇卷、從晝至夜無不念時なるのみなり。從經至經無不經なるのみなり。

We should realize that, in the way of the buddhas, there are "monks who think on the sūtras" — this is directly pointed out by the Old Buddha Caoxi. The "thought" of the monk who thinks on the sūtras" has nothing to do with having thought or not having thought: *we do not reckon with having or not having.* It is just, *"from kalpa to kalpa, never releasing a scroll from your hand; from day to night, never a moment not thinking on it."*[23] It is just, *from sūtra to sūtra, never not a sūtra.*

* * * * *

[30:10] {1:332}

第二十七祖、東印度般若多羅尊者。因東印度國王、請尊者齋次、國王乃問、諸人盡轉經、唯尊者爲甚不轉。祖曰、貧道出息不隨衆緣、入息不居蘊界、常轉如是經、百千萬億卷、非但一卷兩卷。

The Twenty-seventh Ancestor, Venerable Prajñātāra of eastern India, was once invited to a maigre feast by a king of eastern India.[24] *On that occasion, the king inquired of him, "Everyone turns the sūtras; why is it that only you, Venerable One, do not turn them?"*

The Ancestor said, "When this humble wayfarer breathes out, he does not follow along with conditions; when he breathes in, he does not

---

22　**the Eminent Ancestor** (*kōso* 高祖): Quoting Huineng in Fada's biography (*Jingde chuandeng lu* 景德傳燈錄, T.2076.51:233b19).

"a monk who thinks on the sūtra" (*nenkin* sō 念經僧): Or "a monk who recites the sūtra"; see above, Note 15.

23　**"from kalpa to kalpa, never releasing a scroll from your hand; from day to night, never a moment not thinking on it"** (*jū kō shi kō shu fujaku kan, ju chū shi ya mu funen ji* 從劫至劫手不擇卷、從晝至夜無不念時): Quoting Huineng from Fada's biography (*Jingde chuandeng lu* 景德傳燈錄, T.2076.51:238b12-13). Taking *shaku* 擇 ("to select") as *shaku* 釋 ("to release"), after the Chinese text. The sentence following this is Dōgen's variation on the pattern "from X to X, never not."

24　**Twenty-seventh Ancestor** (*dai nijūshichi so* 第二十七祖): An anecdote found in several sources (see, e.g., *Hongzhi chanshi guanglu* 宏智禪師廣錄, T.2001.48:18c12-15) and cited by Dōgen in "Shōbōgenzō bukkyō" 正法眼藏佛經 and *Eihei kōroku* 永平廣錄 (DZZ.3:16, no. 20).

428 DŌGEN'S *SHŌBŌGENZŌ* VOLUME II

settle down in the aggregates and constituents.[25] *Perpetually turning such a sūtra is hundreds of thousands of myriads of koṭis of scrolls, not merely one scroll or two scrolls.*"[26]

[30:11]

般若多羅尊者は、天竺國東印度の種草なり。迦葉尊者より第二十七世の正嫡なり。佛家の調度、ことごとく正傳せり。頂顟・眼睛、拳頭・鼻孔・拄杖・鉢盂、衣法・骨髓等を住持せり。我等が曩祖なり、我等は雲孫なり。今尊者の渾力道は、出息の衆縁に不隨なるのみにあらず、衆縁も出息に不隨なり。衆縁たとひ頂顟・眼睛にてもあれ、衆縁たとひ渾身にてもあれ、衆縁たとひ渾心にてもあれ、擔來擔去又擔來、ただ不隨衆縁なるのみなり。不隨は渾隨なり、このゆえに築著磕著なり。出息これ衆縁なりといへども、不隨衆縁なり。無量劫來、いまだ入息・出息の消息をしらざれども、而今まさにはじめてしるべき時節到來なるがゆえに、不居蘊界をきく、不隨衆縁をきく。衆縁はじめて入息等を參究する時節なり。この時節、かつてさきにあらず、さらにのちにあるべからず、ただ而今のみにあるなり。

Venerable Prajñātāra was a native of eastern India in the Land of Sindhu. He was the direct descendant in the twenty-seventh generation after Venerable Kāśyapa. He directly transmitted all of the implements belonging to the house of the buddhas, maintaining the crown of the head, the eyes, the fist, the nostrils, the staff, the bowl, the robe and dharma, the bones and marrow, and the like. He is our ancient ancestor; we are his distant descendants. In the Venerable's forceful words here, it is not only that "breathing out" does not "follow along" with "conditions"; "conditions," too, do not "follow along" with "breathing out." Even supposing that the "conditions" are the crown of the head and the eyes, even supposing that the "conditions" are the entire body, even supposing that the conditions are the entire mind, "*bearing the load coming, bearing the load going, bearing the load coming again*" is nothing but "*not following along with conditions.*"[27] "Not to follow along" is completely to follow along. It is, therefore, hitting and banging.[28] Although "breathing

---

25 **aggregates and constituents** (*unkai* 蘊界): I.e., the five "heaps" (S. *skandha*) (form, sensation, perception, formations, and consciousness) into which the psychophysical organism can be analyzed; and the eighteen "constituents" (S. *dhātu*), of cognition: the six sense organs, their objects, and the corresponding consciousnesses. But see below, Note 30, for Dōgen's reading of this compound.

26 **Perpetually turning such a sūtra** (*jōten nyoze kyō* 常轉如是經): The expression "such a sūtra" (*nyoze kyō* 如是經) may be taken either as "the sūtra of inhaling and exhaling" or as "the sūtra of suchness."

27 **"bearing the load coming, bearing the load going, bearing the load coming again"** (*tanrai tanko yū tanrai* 擔來擔去又擔來): Quoting Rujing 如淨 (1162-1227), Dōgen's Chinese teacher; see Supplementary Notes, s.v. "Bearing the load coming, bearing the load going, bearing the load coming again."

28 **hitting and banging** (*chikujaku katsujaku* 築著磕著): A common expression in

30. Sūtra Reading *Kankin* 看經

out" may be "conditions," it is "not following along with conditions." The circumstances of "breathing in" and "breathing out" have remained unknown from innumerable kalpas past to the present; but now at this very moment, finally, because the time to know them has come, we hear of "*not settling down in aggregates and constituents*" and "*not following along with conditions.*"[29] It is time, finally, for the "conditions" to investigate "breathing in," and the rest. This time is not before; it is not after: it is just now.

[30:12] {1:333}

蘊界、といふは、五蘊なり。いはゆる色・受・想・行・識をいふ。この五蘊に不居なるは、五蘊いまだ到來せざる世界なるがゆえなり。この関棙子を拈ぜるゆえに、所轉の経、ただ一巻・両巻にあらず、常轉轉百千萬億巻なり。百千萬億巻は、しばらく多の一端をあぐといへども、多の量のみにあらざるなり。一息出の不居蘊界を、百千萬億巻　の量とせり。しかあれども、有漏・無漏智の所測にあらず、有漏・無漏法の界にあらず。このゆえに、有智の知の測量にあらず、有知の智の卜度にあらず、無智の知の商量にあらず、無知の智の所到にあらず。佛佛祖祖の修證、皮肉骨髓、眼睛・拳頭、頂顎・鼻孔、拄杖・拂子、蹲跳造次なり。

"Aggregates and constituents" means the five aggregates: form, sensation, perception, formations, and consciousness.[30] "Not settling down" in these five aggregates is the realm in which the five aggregates have not yet arrived. Because he takes up this pivot, the sūtras being turned are not merely one scroll or two scrolls: they are "*hundreds of thousands of myriads of koṭis of scrolls,*" "*perpetually turned.*" While "hundreds of thousands of myriads of *koṭis* of scrolls" may be taken as giving a large numerical unit, it is not just a large measure. The "*not settling down in the aggregates and constituents*" of a single "breathing out" is measured as "hundreds of thousands of myriads of *koṭis* of scrolls." However, it is not what is calcuated by contaminated or uncontaminated wisdom; it is not the realm of contaminated or uncontaminated dharmas.[31] Therefore, it is not gauged through the knowledge of those with wisdom; it is not

---

Chan texts, variously interpreted as "hitting with a whack" or "knocking together." See Supplementary Notes, s.v. "Hitting and banging."

29　**the time to know them has come** (*shiru beki jisetsu tōrai naru* しるべき時節到來なる): "When the time comes" (*jisetsu tōrai* 時節到來) is a fixed expression, occurring often in Zen texts, for the moment of opportunity.

30　**"Aggregates and constituents" means the five aggregates** (*unkai, to iu wa, goun nari* 蘊界、といふは、五蘊なり): Dōgen here seems to be interpreting the term *unkai* 蘊界 ("aggregates and constituents") as the "realm" (*kai* 界) of the "aggregates" (*un* 蘊).

31　**contaminated or uncontaminated wisdom** (*uro muro chi* 有漏・無漏智): "Contaminated wisdom" (*uro chi* 有漏智; S. *sāsrava-jñāna*) and "uncontaminated wisdom" (*muro chi* 無漏智; S. *anāsrava-jñāna*) refer respectively to knowledge defiled or undefiled by the mental "afflictions" (*bonnō* 煩惱; S. *kleśa*); the former is characteristic of

430 DŌGEN'S *SHŌBŌGENZŌ* VOLUME II

divined through the wisdom of those with knowledge; it is not figured out through the knowledge of those without wisdom; it is not arrived at through the wisdom of those without knowledge. It is the practice and verification; the skin, flesh, bones, and marrow; the eyes, the fist, the crown of the head, the nostrils, the staff, the whisk, and the quick, leaping acts of buddha after buddha and ancestor after ancestor.[32]

* * * * *

[30:13]

趙州觀音院眞際大師、因有婆子、施淨財請大師轉大藏經。師下禪床、遶一帀、向使者云、轉藏已畢。使者廻擧似婆子。婆子曰、比來請轉一藏、如何和尚只轉半藏。

Great Master Zhenji of Guanyin Cloister in Zhaozhou once received a donation of pure assets from an old woman, who requested that the Great Master turn the great treasury of sūtras.[33] The Master got down from his meditation seat, circumambulated it once around, and said to her representative, "I've finished turning the treasury."

The representative went back and reported this to the old woman. The old woman said, "A while ago I asked to have the entire treasury turned. Why did the Reverend only turn half the treasury?"

[30:14]

あきらかにしりぬ、轉一藏・半藏は、婆子經三卷なり、轉藏已畢は、趙州經一藏なり。おほよそ轉大藏經のていたらくは、禪床をめぐる趙州あり、禪床ありて趙州をめぐる、趙州をめぐる趙州あり、禪床をめぐる禪床あり。しかあれども、一切の轉藏は、遶禪床のみにあらず、禪床遶のみにあらず。

Obviously, "turning the entire treasury" or "half the treasury" is the old woman's sūtra in three scrolls, whereas "I've finished turning the treasury" is the entire treasury of Zhaozhou's sūtras.[34] In sum, the reality

---

the spiritual "commoner" (*bonbu* 凡夫; S. *pṛthagjana*); the latter, of the spiritual "noble" (*shō* 聖; S. *ārya*), or "sage."

32 **quick, leaping acts** (*botchō zōji* 踔跳造次): A tentative translation of an unusual expression; perhaps somewhat akin to English "fits and starts." The term *botchō* 踔跳 means "to spring" or "to jump"; akin to the more common *chōshutsu* 跳出 ("to spring forth"). *Zōji* 造次 can refer to something "quick," or "fleeting," as well as to something done "hastily" or "casually."

33 **Great Master Zhenji of Guanyin Cloister in Zhaozhou** (*Jōshū Kannon'in Shinsai daishi* 趙州觀音院眞際大師): I.e., Zhaozhou Congshen 趙州從諗 (778-897). This story is found in the *Dahui Pujue chanshi yulu* 大慧普覺禪師語錄 (T.1998A.47:849b11-15), as well as Dōgen's *shinji Shōbōgenzō* 眞字正法眼藏 (DZZ.5:164, case 74).

34 **the old woman's sūtra in three scrolls** (*basu kyō sankan* 婆子經三卷); **the entire treasury of Zhaozhou's sūtras** (*Jōshū kyō ichizō* 趙州經一藏): These could also be

30. Sūtra Reading *Kankin* 看經   431

of turning the great treasury of sūtras is that there is Zhaozhou's going around the meditation seat; there is the meditation seat, which goes around Zhazhou; there is Zhaozhou going around Zhaozhou; and there is the meditation seat going around the meditation seat. However, the complete turning of the treasury is not only circumambulating the meditation seat, nor is it only the meditation seat circumambulating.

* * * * *

[30:15] {1:334}

益州大隋山神照大師、法諱法眞、嗣長慶寺大安禪師。因有婆子、施淨財請師轉大藏經。師下禪床一帀、向使者曰、大藏經已畢。使者歸擧似婆子。婆子云、比來請轉一藏、如何和尚只轉半藏。

Great Master Shenzhao of Mount Dasui in Yizhou, whose dharma name was Fazhen, was heir to Chan Master Daan of Changqing Monastery.[35] Once, there was an old woman who made a donation of pure assets and requested that the Master turn the great treasury of sūtras. The Master got down from his meditation seat, walked around it once, and said to her representative, "I've finished turning the great treasury of sūtras."

The representative returned and reported this to the old woman. The old woman said, "Just now I asked to have the entire treasury turned. Why did the Reverend only turn half the treasury?"

[30:16]

今、大隋の、禪床をめぐると學することなかれ、禪床の、大隋をめぐると學する事なかれ。拳頭・眼睛の團圞のみにあらず、作一圓相せる打一圓相なり。しかあれども、婆子それ有眼なりや、未具眼なりや。只轉半藏、たとひ道取を拳頭より正傳すとも、婆子さらにいふべし、比來請轉大藏經、如何和尚只管弄精魂。あやまりてちかくのごとく道取せましかば、具眼睛の婆子なるべし。

Do not study here that Dasui goes around the meditation seat; do not study that the meditation seat goes around Dasui. This is not only the ball of the fist or the eye; it is drawing a full circle made of a full circle.[36]

---

rendered as sūtra titles: "*The Old Woman Sūtra*, in three scrolls"; "*The Zhaozhou Sūtra*, in an entire treasury."

35   **Great Master Shenzhao of Mount Dasui in Yizhou** (*Ekishū Daizuizan Shinshō daishi* 益州大隋山神照大師): I.e., Dasui Fazhen 大隋法眞 (834-919); his teacher, "Chan Master Daan," is Changqing Daan 長慶大安 (793-883). This episode, almost identical to the preceding story quoted here, can be found in the *Liandeng huiyao* 聯燈會要, ZZ.136:593b10-14.

36   **drawing a full circle made of a full circle** (*sa ichiensō seru ta ichiensō* 作一圓相せる打一圓相): Or "drawing a full circle that made a full circle." A somewhat odd

432   DŌGEN'S *SHŌBŌGENZŌ* VOLUME II

Still, did the old woman have the eye, or was she not yet equipped with the eye? Even if "only turn half the treasury" was a statement directly transmitted from a fist, the old woman should have gone on to say, "*Just now I asked to have the great treasury of sūtras turned. Why did the Reverend just play with the spirit?*"[37] Even if it was mistaken, if she had made a statement like that, she would have been an old woman equipped with the eye.

* * * * *

[30:17]
高祖洞山悟本大師、因有官人、設齋施淨財、請師看轉大藏經。大師下禪床、向官人揖。官人揖大師。引官人俱遶禪床一帀、向官人揖。良久向官人云、會麼。官人云、不會。大師云、我與汝看轉大藏經、如何不會。

The Eminent Ancestor, Great Master Wuben of Dongshan, once [dealt with] an official who sponsored a meal, made a donation of pure assets, and asked the Master to read and turn the great treasury of sūtras.[38] *The Great Master got down from his meditation seat, faced the official, and bowed with hands clasped. The official bowed to the great master. Leading the official, the Master circumambulated the meditation seat with him, once around. He then faced the official and bowed. After a while, still facing the official, he said, "Do you understand?"*

The official said, "I don't understand."

The Great Master said, "I just read and turned the great treasury of sūtras for you.[39] *Why don't you understand?"*

---

expression that may mean Dasui's words described the circle he had made by circling the seat. "Full circle" translates *ichiensō* 一圓相, the circle made by the Zen teacher, either on paper or simply in the air, as a symbol of perfection.

37 **"just play with the spirit"** (*shikan rō seikon* 只管弄精魂): The term *rō seikon* 弄精魂 is a fixed expression, occurring with some frequency in Zen literature, often in the pejorative sense of what we might call "fiddling with the mind."

38 **The Eminent Ancestor, Great Master Wuben of Dongshan** (*kōso Tōzan Gohon daishi* 高祖洞山悟本大師): I.e., Dongshan Liangjie 洞山良价 (807-869). This story appears in *Dongshan dashi yulu* 洞山大師語錄 (T.1986A.47:509c1-4) and in the biography of Dongshan in *Wujia yulu* 五家語錄 (ZZ.119:902a17-19).

read and turn the great treasury of sūtras (*kanten daizōkyō* 看轉大藏經): I.e., perform a recitation of the canon. The term *kanten* 看轉 is synonymous with *tendoku* 轉讀 ("revolving reading"), often used in reference to an abbreviated ritual pass through the books of the canon.

39 **"I just read and turned the great treasury of sūtras for you"** (*ga yo nyo kanten daizōkyō* 我與汝看轉大藏經): Or "you and I just read and turned the great treasury of sūtras."

30. Sūtra Reading *Kankin* 看經

[30:18] {1:335}

それ我與汝看轉大藏經、あきらかなり。遶禪床を看轉大藏經と學するにあらず、看轉大藏經を遶禪床と會せざるなり。しかありといへども、高祖の慈誨を聽取すべし。

That statement, "*I just read and turned the great treasury of sūtras for you*," is clear. We do not study this to mean that "circumambulating the meditation seat" is "reading and turning the great treasury of sūtras"; we do not understand "reading and turning the great treasury of sūtras" as "circumabulating the meditation seat." While this may be so, we should listen to the compassionate instruction of the Eminent Ancestor.

[30:19]

この因緣、先師古佛、天童山に住せりしとき、高麗國の施主、入山施財、大衆看經、請先師陞座のとき、擧するところなり。擧しおはりて、先師すなはち拂子をもておほきに圓相をつくる事一帀していはく、天童今日與汝看轉大藏經。便擲下拂子、下座。

This episode was raised when my former master, the Old Buddha, was abbot of Mount Tiantong, and a donor from the Land of Goryeo visited the monastery, *made a donation, had the assembly read the sūtras, and requested my former master to mount the seat.*[40] After raising it, my former master swung his whisk once around in a big circle and said, "*Today, Tiantong read and turned the great treasury of the sūtras for you.*" *Then he threw down his whisk and got down from the seat.*

[30:20]

いま先師の道處を看轉すべし、餘者に比準すべからず。しかありといふとも、看轉大藏經には、一隻眼をもちいるとやせん、半隻眼をもちいるとやせん。高祖の道處と先師の道處と、用眼睛、用舌頭、いくばくをかもちいきたれる。究辨看。

We should now "read and turn" what my former master said; we should not compare him with others.[41] While this may be so, in "reading and turning the great treasury of the sūtras" does he use one eye, or does he use half an eye? In what the Eminent Ancestor said and what my former master said, how many eyes were used and how many tongues? Try examining it thoroughly.

※ ※ ※ ※ ※

---

40 **my former master, the Old Buddha** (*senshi kobutsu* 先師古佛): I.e., Tiantong Rujing 天童如淨. The source of this anecdote is unknown and may represent Dōgen's memory of an event that took place at Tiantong during his study there with Rujing, 1225-1227.

mount the seat (*shinzo* 陞座): I.e., give a lecture from the altar.

41 **we should not compare him with others** (*yosha ni hijun su bekarazu* 餘者に比準すべからず): Here, perhaps, meaning "we should not make comparisons of his words with those of Dongshan."

434 DŌGEN'S *SHŌBŌGENZŌ* VOLUME II

[30:21] {1:336}

曩祖藥山弘道大師、尋常不許人看經。一日將經自看。因僧問、和尚尋常不
許人看經、爲甚麼却自看。師云、我只要遮眼。僧云、某甲學和尚得麼。師
云、儞若看、牛皮也須穿。

> The Ancient Ancestor, Great Master Hongdao of Yaoshan, ordinarily
> did not permit people to read sūtras.[42] One day he was himself holding
> a sūtra and reading it. A monk asked, "The Reverend ordinarily doesn't
> permit people to read sūtras; why, then, are you yourself reading one?"
>
> The Master said, "I just need to shield my eyes."[43]
>
> The monk said, "And may I imitate the Reverend?"
>
> The Master said, "If you were to read it, it would even pierce oxhide."[44]

[30:22]

いま我要遮眼の道は、遮眼の自道處なり。遮眼は打失眼睛なり、打失經な
り、渾眼遮なり、渾遮眼なり。遮眼は、遮中開眼なり、遮裏活眼なり、眼
裏活遮なり、眼皮上更添一枚皮なり、遮裏拈眼なり、眼自拈遮なり。しか
あれば、眼睛經にあらざれば、遮眼の功徳いまだあらざるなり。牛皮也須
穿は、全牛皮なり、全皮牛なり、拈牛作皮なり。このゆえに、皮肉骨髓・
頭角鼻孔を、牛牸の活計とせり。學和尚のとき、牛爲眼睛なるを遮眼と
す、眼睛爲牛なり。

The saying here, "*I need to shield my eyes*," is said by the "shielded
eyes" themselves. "Shielding the eyes" is "losing the eyes"; it is losing
the sūtras; it is the entire eye shielding; it is the entire shielded eye.[45]
"Shielding the eyes" is the opened eye within the "shielding"; it is the
living eye in the "shielding"; it is the living shielding in the eye; it is *adding another lid to the eyelid*; it is taking up the eye in the "shielding"; it
is the eye itself taking up the "shielding."[46] Thus, if it is not an eye sūtra,
there is no merit in "shielding the eyes."

---

42 **The Ancient Ancestor, Great Master Hongdao of Yaoshan** (*nōso Yakusan Gudō
daishi* 曩祖藥山弘道大師): I.e., Yaoshan Weiyan 藥山惟儼. This story can be found in
the *Jingde chuandeng lu* 景德傳燈錄 (T.2076.51:312b5-8), the *Liandeng huiyao* 聯燈會
要 (ZZ.136:740a8-10), and elsewhere.

43 **"shield my eyes"** (*shagen* 遮眼): In ordinary parlance, to protect the eyes from the
sun or dust; here, perhaps, to protect against the "dust" (*jin* 塵) of the defiling objects of
the senses. See Supplementary Notes, s.v. "Dust."

44 **"it would even pierce oxhide "** (*ni nyaku kan, gohi ya shu sen* 儞若看、牛皮也須
穿): I.e., even leather would not shield your eyes.

45 **"losing the eyes"** (*tashitsu ganzei* 打失眼睛): A fixed expression in Zen texts;
here, perhaps an allusion to a verse by Tiantong Rujing 天童如淨, in celebration of the
Buddha's awakening; see Supplementary Notes, s.v. "Eye."

46 **"adding another lid to the eyelid"** (*ganpi jō kō ten ichimai hi* 眼皮上更添一枚
皮): Perhaps reflecting the common use of the eyelid as an example of something too
close to be seen.

30. Sūtra Reading *Kankin* 看經   435

"*It would even pierce oxhide*" is "the hide of the whole ox"; it is the ox of the whole hide; it is taking up the ox and making the hide.[47] Therefore, the skin, flesh, bones, and marrow, the horns on the head and the nose represent the livelihood of the cow.[48] When we "imitate the Reverend," we take the ox forming the eyes as "shielding the eye"; it is the eyes forming the ox.

* * * * *

[30:23]

冶父道川禪師云、億千供佛福無邊、爭似常將古教看、白紙上邊書墨字、請君開眼目前觀。

Chan Master Yefu Daochuan said,[49]

Limitless the merit of millions of thousands of offerings to the buddhas;
How could it compare with the regular reading of the old teachings?
Characters written in black ink on white paper;
Gentlemen, please, open your eyes and look at what's in front of you.

---

47 **"the hide of the whole ox"** (*zengyūhi* 全牛皮): "The whole ox" appears often in Zen texts, especially in recollection of the famous words of Cook Ding (Pao ding 庖丁), in Book 3 of the *Zhuangzi* 莊子 (Yangshengzhu 養生主, KR.5c0126.003.3a):

始臣之解牛之時、所見無非牛者。三年之後、未嘗見全牛也。方今之時、臣以神遇、而不以目。

When I first began to cut up an ox, what I saw was nothing but the ox. After three years, I no longer saw the whole ox. Now, I approach it with the spirit and don't look at it with my eyes.

48 **skin, flesh, bones, and marrow** (*hi niku kotsu zui* 皮肉骨髓): Dōgen is likely expanding here on the "hide" of the whole ox. This expression occurs very often throughout the *Shōbōgenzō*, in reference to the essence or truth or entirety of something or someone. From the famous story, found in the *shinji Shōbōgenzō* 眞字正法眼藏 (DZZ.5:230, case 201), of Bodhidharma's testing of four disciples, to whom he said of each in turn that he (or, in one case, she) had gotten his skin, flesh, bones, and marrow. See Supplementary Notes.

49 **Chan Master Yefu Daochuan** (*Yabu Dōsen zenji* 冶父道川禪師): Twelfth-century figure (dates unknown) in the Linji lineage, who became abbot of the Shiji Chan Cloister 實際禪院 on Mount Yefu 冶父山 in 1163; known for his verse commentary on the *Diamond Sūtra*, from which Dōgen is quoting here (*Chuan lao Jinggang jing zhu* 川老金剛經註, ZZ.38:730b15-17). The comment is on a passage of the *Diamond Sūtra* claiming that the merit for reading, reciting, receiving, and keeping the sūtra is far greater than making offerings to countless buddhas.

DŌGEN'S *SHŌBŌGENZŌ* VOLUME II

[30:24] {1:337}

しるべし、古佛を供ずると古教をみると、福德齊肩なるべし、福德超過なるべし。古教といふは、白紙の上に墨字を書せる、たれかこれを古教としらん。當恁麼の道理を參究すべし。

We should realize that making offerings to the old buddhas and looking at the old teachings must be of equal merit, must transcend merit. "The old teachings" are letters of black ink written on white paper, but who knows them as "the old teachings"? We should investigate such a principle.

* * * * *

[30:25]

雲居山弘覺大師、因有一僧、在房内念經。大師隔窓問云、闍梨念底、是什麼經。僧對日、維摩經。師云、不問儞維摩經、念底是什麼經。此僧從此得入。

[In the community of] Great Master Hongjue of Mount Yunju, there was a monk thinking on a sūtra in his room.[50] From the other side of the window, the Great Master said, "The Ācārya's thinking — what sūtra is it?"

The monk replied, "The Vimalakīrti Sūtra."

The Master said, "I didn't ask you about the Vimalakīrti Sūtra. The thinking — what sūtra is it?"

From this, the monk gained an entry.

[30:26]

大師道の念底是什麼經は、一條の念底、年代深遠なり、不欲擧似於念なり。路にしては死蛇にあふ、このゆえに什麼經の問著現成せり。人にあふては錯擧せず、このゆえに維摩經なり。おほよそ看經は、盡佛祖を把拈しあつめて、眼睛として看經するなり。正當恁麼時、たちまちに佛祖作佛し、説法し、説佛し、佛作するなり。この看經の時節にあらざれば、佛祖の頂顎・面目いまだあらざるなり。

In the words of the Great Master, "*The thinking — what sūtra is it?*" the single line of "thinking" is "*the age is so remote,*" is "*I wouldn't want to tell*" the thinking.[51] On the road, he came across a dead snake, and

---

50 **Great Master Hongjue of Mount Yunju** (*Ungozan Gukaku daishi* 雲居山弘覺大師): I.e., Yunju Daoying (d. 902). "Great Master Hongjue" is a posthumous title conferred by the Emperor Zhaozong 昭宗. This story can be found in the *Jingde chuandeng lu* 景德傳燈錄, T.2076.51:335b23-25.

thinking on a sūtra (*nenkin* 念經): I.e., "reading (or contemplating) a sūtra." The semantic range of *nen* 念, as both "reading" and "thinking," is crucial to the dialogue here.

51 **is "the age is so remote," is "I wouldn't want to tell" the thinking** (*nendai jinnon nari, fu yoku ko ji o nen nari* 年代深遠なり、不欲擧似於念なり): After a re-

30. Sūtra Reading *Kankin* 看經   437

therefore his question, "what sūtra?" appears; meeting someone, he does not make a mistake, and therefore it is "the *Vimalakīrti Sūtra*."[52]

In sum, sūtra reading is grasping and gathering the buddhas and ancestors in their entirety, and reading the sūtras with them as the eyes. At this very moment, the buddhas and ancestors immediately become buddhas, preach the dharma, preach the buddhas, and work as buddhas.[53] If it is not the time of this sūtra reading, there are not yet any heads or faces of the buddhas and ancestors.

---

mark by Yangshan Huiji 仰山慧寂 (803-887), when asked whether anyone else besides Linji 臨濟 received transmission from Huangbo 黃檗 (see, e.g., *Linji yulu* 臨濟語錄, T.1985.47:5a10-12; *Tiansheng guangdeng lu* 天聖廣燈錄, ZZ.135:684b6-8):

> 仰云、有。祇是年代深遠、不欲舉似和尚。

> Yang said, "There was. But the age is so remote that I wouldn't want to tell it to the Reverend."

52 **On the road, he came across a dead snake** (*michi ni shite wa shija ni au* 路にしては死蛇にあう): Likely alluding to a story about Chinglin Shiqian 青林師虔 (d. 904) that appears as case 59 in the *Congrong lu* 從容錄 (T.2004.48:264a26-b4) and is recorded in Dōgen's *shinji Shōbōgenzō* 眞字正法眼藏 (DZZ.5:232, case 204):

> 後洞山師虔禪師＜嗣洞山、號青林＞、因僧問、學人徑往時如何。師云、死蛇當大路。勸子莫當頭。僧云、當頭時如何。師曰、亦喪子命根。僧曰、不當頭時如何。師曰、亦無迴避處。僧曰、正當恁麼時如何。師曰、却失也。僧曰、未審向甚麼處去也。師曰、草深無覓處。僧曰、和尚也須隄防始得。師撫掌云、一等是箇毒氣。

> Dongshan's follower Shiqian (succeeded Dongshan, named Chinglin) was once asked by a monk, "What about when a student takes a side path?"
> The Master said, "There's a dead snake on the great road. I urge you not to confront it."
> The monk said, "What if I do confront it?"
> Lin said, "You lose your life."
> The monk said, "What if I don't confront it?"
> Lin said, "There's still no place to avoid it."
> The monk said, "So, at this very moment, what?"
> Lin said, "You're lost."
> The monk said, "I don't understand where to go."
> Lin said, "The grass is deep and there's nowhere to find it."
> The monk said, "The Reverend should also take care."
> Lin clapped his hands and said, "This is the same poison."

53 **At this very moment** (*shōtō inmo ji* 正當恁麼時): Perhaps reflecting the same phrase in the dead snake tale noted just above.

become buddhas, preach the dharma, preach the buddhas, and work as buddhas (*sabutsu shi, seppō shi, setsubutsu shi, bussa suru* 作佛し、說法し、説佛し、佛作する): Dōgen moves here, from the familiar *sabutsu* 作佛 ("become a buddha") and *seppō* 説法 ("preach the dharma"), through the novel *setsubutsu* 説佛 ("preach the buddhas"), to the playful neologism *bassa* 佛作 (weakly translated as "work as buddhas"), which if read according to the verb-object construction of the other expressions in the list, would have to be rendered something like "buddha a becoming."

438　DŌGEN'S *SHŌBŌGENZŌ* VOLUME II

* * * * *

[30:27]

現在佛祖の會に、看經の儀則それ多般あり。いはゆる、施主入山請大衆看經、或は常轉僧看經、或は僧衆自發心看經等なり。このほか、大衆爲亡僧看經あり。

In present day assemblies of the buddhas and ancestors, there are many types of ceremonial procedures for sūtra reading: *sūtra reading in which the donor visits the monastery and makes a request of the great assembly*; or *sūtra reading in which the monks are requested to engage in perpetual turning*; or *sūtra reading initiated by monks of the assembly of their own accord*; and so on. In addition, there is *sūtra reading performed by the great assembly on behalf of a deceased monk*.

[30:28]

施主入山請僧看經は、當日の粥時より、堂司、あらかじめ看經牌を僧堂前、および諸寮にかく。粥罷に拜席を聖僧前にしく。とき、いたりて、僧堂前鐘を三會うつ、或は一會うつ。住持人の指揮にしたがふなり。鐘聲罷に、首座・大衆、搭袈裟、入雲堂、就被位正面而坐。つぎに、住持人入堂し、向聖僧問訊燒香罷、依位而坐。つぎに、童行をして經を行ぜしむ。この經、さきより庫院にととのへ安排しまうけて、ときいたりて供達するなり。經は、或は經函ながら行じ、或は盤子に安じて行ず。大衆、すでに經を請して、すなはちひらきよむ。このとき、知客、いまし施主をひきて雲堂にいる。施主、まさに雲堂前にて手爐をとりて、ささげて入堂す。手爐は院門の公界にあり。あらかじめ裝香して、行者をして雲堂前にまうけて、施主まさに入堂せんとするとき、めしによりて施主にわたす。手爐をめす事は、知客、これをめすなり。入堂するときは、知客、さき、施主、のち、雲堂の前門の南頰よりいる。施主、聖僧前にいたりて、燒一片香、拜三拜あり。拜のあひだ、手爐をもちながら拜するなり。拜のあひだ、知客は拜席の北に、おもてを南にして、すこしき施主にむかひて、叉手してたつ。施主の拜、をはりて、施主、みぎに轉身して、住持人にむかひて、手爐をささげて曲躬し揖す。住持人は椅子にいながら、經をささげて合掌して揖をうく。施主、つぎに北にむかひて揖す。揖、をはりて、首座のまへにより巡堂す。巡堂のあひだ、知客、さきにひけり。巡堂一帀して、聖僧前にいたりて、なほ聖僧にむかひて、手爐をささげて揖す。このとき、知客は雲堂の門限のうちに、拜席のみなみに、面をきたにして叉手してたてり。施主、揖聖僧、をはりて、知客にしたかひて雲堂前にいでて、巡堂前一帀して、なほ雲堂内にいりて、聖僧にむかひて拜三拜す。拜、をはりて、交椅につきて看經を證明す。交椅は、聖僧のひだりの柱のほとりに、南にむかひてこれをたつ。或は南柱のほとりに、北にむかひてもたつ。施主すでに座につきぬれば、知客、すべからく施主にむかひて揖してのち、くらいにつく。或は施主巡堂のあひだ、梵音あり。梵音の座、或は聖僧のみぎ、或は聖僧のひだり、便宜にしたがふ。

For *sūtra reading in which the donor visits the monastery and makes a request of the monks*, on the appointed day following gruel time, in advance, the hall manager hangs up the "sūtra reading" placards in front of

30. Sūtra Reading *Kankin* 看經   439

the saṃgha hall and in the various quarters. After breakfast, a prostration mat is laid out in front of the Sacred Monk.[54] When the appointed time arrives, three sequences are rung on the bell in front of the saṃgha hall — or one sequence, according to the directions of the abbot. After the bell-ringing, *the head seat and the monks of the great assembly don their kāṣāya, enter the cloud hall, take their assigned places, face forward, and sit.*[55] Next, the abbot enters the hall, *faces the Sacred Monk, bows with joined palms, burns incense, and when finished, sits at his or her place.*

Then, the young postulants are made to distribute the sūtras. These sūtras are prepared and lined up ahead of time in the administration cloister and delivered for distribution when the time comes. The sūtras are either distributed while still in their sūtra boxes or are placed on stands and distributed. The monks of the great assembly, having received the sūtras, immediately open and read them.

At this point, the guest prefect at once leads the donor into the cloud hall. The donor takes the hand-held censer in the front of the cloud hall, and carries it raised up into the hall. The hand-held censer is the common property of the cloister.[56] It is filled with incense in advance and provided in the front of the cloud hall by a postulant.[57] When the donor is just about to enter the hall, it is handed to the donor upon request; this request for the hand-held censer is made by the guest prefect.[58] When entering the hall, the guest prefect goes first and the donor follows after. They enter through the south side of the front door of the cloud hall. The donor goes before the Sacred Monk, burns a pinch of incense, and makes three prostrations, holding the hand-held censer during the prostrations. During the prostrations, the guest prefect stands with folded hands to the north of the prostration mat, looking south and slightly facing the donor.[59]

---

54   **Sacred Monk** (*shōsō* 聖僧): I.e., Bodhisattva Mañjuśrī, a statue of which is installed in an altar in the saṃgha hall of a Zen monastery.

55   **cloud hall** (*undō* 雲堂): I.e., the saṃgha hall. In this and the following sentence, Dōgen slips in and out of Chinese.

56   **carries it raised up** (*sasagete* ささげて): I.e., raised with both hands above eye level.

common property of the cloister (*inmon no kugai* 院門の公界): I.e., belongs to the administration cloister (*kuin* 庫院) and lent to the donor for use in the ritual. For other meanings of the glyphs 公界 (*kugai*), see Supplementary Notes, s.v. "Public realm."

57   **in the front of the cloud hall** (*undō zen* 雲堂前): Probably indicating the outer hall (*gaidō* 外堂) of the saṃgha hall.

58   **upon request** (*meshi ni yorite* めしによりて): Probably, when the donor is requested by the guest prefect to enter the hall.

59   **looking south and slightly facing the donor** (*omote o minami ni shite, sukoshiki*

440　　　DŌGEN'S *SHŌBŌGENZŌ* VOLUME II

When finished making prostrations, the donor turns to the right, faces the abbot, raises up the hand-held censer, and bends forward, bowing with hands clasped. The abbot, remaining in the chair, receives the bow by raising up a sūtra and bowing with palms together. The donor next faces north and bows with hands clasped. Having bowed, he or she passes in front of the head seat and tours the hall. During the touring of the hall, the guest prefect goes first, taking the lead. Touring the hall once around, and returning in front of the Sacred Monk, [the donor] faces the Sacred Monk again, raises up the hand-held censer, and bows with hands clasped. At this time, the guest prefect stands with folded hands inside the threshold of the cloud hall, to the south of the prostration mat, facing north. When finished bowing to the Sacred Monk, following the lead of the guest prefect, the donor exits to the front of the cloud hall, tours the front of the hall once around, again enters the cloud hall, faces the Sacred Monk, and makes three prostrations.

When finished making prostrations, [the donor] sits in a folding chair and bears witness to the sūtra reading. The folding chair is set up next to the pillar to the left of the Sacred Monk, facing south. Or, it is set up next to the south pillar, facing north. When the donor is seated, the guest prefect should face the donor, bow with hands clasped, and then take his or her own place. In some cases, while the donor is touring the hall, there is musical chanting.[60] Seats for musical chanting are either to the right of the Sacred Monk or to the left of the Sacred Monk, according to convenience.

[30:29] {1:339}

手爐には、沈香・箋香等の名香をさしはさみ、たくなり。この香は、施主みづから辨備するなり。

The hand-held censer is filled with precious incense, such as aloes wood incense or *jian* incense, and lit.[61] The incense is personally provided by the donor.

---

seshu ni mukaite おもてを南にして、すこしき施主にむかひて): If the guest prefect is standing north of the donor facing south, the sense of "slightly facing the donor" is unclear; perhaps indicating that the guest prefect stands somewhat closer to the altar, facing the donor at an angle.

60　**musical chanting** (*bonnon* 梵音): Literally, "brahmanical sounds"; melodic chanting, sometimes accompanied by musical instruments. The "seats" mentioned here are likely for the chanters (and/or perhaps for musicians).

61　**precious incense, such as aloes wood incense or *jian* incense** (*jinkō senkō tō no meikō* 沈香・箋香等の名香): The exact referent of the term *senkō* 箋香 here is unclear. While in some contexts it may mean simply "stick incense," here the glyph *jian* 箋 more likely refers to a particular substance. It is identified in one Song-dynasty source (Fan Chengda's 范成大, *Guihai yuheng zhi* 桂海虞衡志, *zhi xiang* 志香) as the product of a

30. Sūtra Reading *Kankin* 看經   441

[30:30]

施主巡堂のときは、衆僧、合掌す。

When the donor tours the hall, the monks of the assembly join their palms.

[30:31]

つぎに看經錢を俵す。錢の多少は、施主の心にしたがふ。或は綿、或は扇等の物子、これを俵す。施主みづから俵す、あるいは知事、これを俵す、或は行者、これを俵す。俵する法は、僧のまへにこれをおくなり、僧の手にいれず。衆僧は、俵錢をまへに俵するとき、おのおの合掌してうくるなり。俵錢、或は當日の齋時にこれを俵す。もし齋時に俵するがごときは、首座施食ののち、さらに打槌一下して、首座、施財す。

Next, the sūtra-reading money is distributed. The amount of money follows the wishes of the donor. In some cases, goods, such as cloth or fans are distributed. The donor personally makes the distribution, or a steward makes the distribution, or a postulant makes the distribution. The procedure for distribution is to place the item in front of the monk, not to put it directly into the monk's hands. When the allotment of money is distributed in front of them, the monks of the assembly each receive it with palms joined. Allotments of money, alternatively, may be distributed at the main meal time on the day [of the sūtra reading]. If the distribution is at the main mealtime, after the head seat's "Food Offering" is finished, the block is struck with the mallet once again, and the head seat does "Giving Wealth."[62]

---

fragrant tree of Hainan; it is often read as equivalent to *zhan* 栴 and taken as referring to a fragrant tree said in Chinese sources to grow in northern Vietnam. Dōgen uses these same two terms for incense in his "Shōbōgenzō darani" 正法眼藏陀羅尼.

62 **head seat's "Food Offering"** (*shuso sejiki* 首座施食): I.e., the head seat's chanting of the "Gāthā of Food Offering" (*Sejiki ge* 施食偈):

三德六味、施佛及僧、法界有情、普同供養。

This food of three virtues and six flavors
Is given to the Buddha and his saṃgha.
May sentient beings throughout the dharma realm
Be equally nourished by this offering

the block is struck with the mallet once again (*sara ni tatsui ichige shite* さらに打槌一下して): Reference to the percussion instrument known as the "mallet and block" (*tsuichin* 槌砧) used to signal stages in the formal meal service in the saṃgha hall; an octagonal wooden pillar, standing on the floor, the top of which is struck by a wooden mallet. The block is struck before the chanting of the "Gāthā of Food Offering."

the head seat does "Giving Wealth" (*shuso sezai su* 首座施財す): I.e., the head seat chants the "Gāthā of Giving Wealth" (*sezai no ge* 施財の偈):

財法二施、功德無量、檀波羅蜜、具足圓滿。

The two gifts, of wealth and dharma,
Are incalculable in their merit.

442 DŌGEN'S *SHŌBŌGENZŌ* VOLUME II

[30:32] {1:340}
施主回向の旨趣を紙片にかきて、聖僧の左の柱に貼せり。

The aim of the donor's dedication of merit is written on a sheet of paper, which is pasted to the pillar to the left of the Sacred Monk.[63]

[30:33]
雲堂裏看經のとき、揚聲してよまず、低聲によむ。或は經卷をひらきて、文字をみるのみなり。句讀におよばず、看經するのみなり。

When sūtra reading takes place inside the cloud hall, one does not raise the voice to read, but reads in a low voice. Or, one may open the sūtra scroll and just look at the words. One simply reads the sūtra without punctuating it.

[30:34]
かくのごとくの看經、おほくは金剛般若經・法華經普門品・安樂行品・金光明經等を、いく百千卷となく、常住にまうけおけり。毎僧一卷を行ずるなり。看經、をはりぬれば、もとの盤、もしは凾をもちて、座のまへをすぐれば、大衆おのおの經を安ず。とるとき、おくとき、ともに合掌するなり。とるときは、まづ合掌して、のちにとる。おくときは、まづ經を安じて、のちに合掌す。そののち、おのおの合掌して、低聲に回向するなり。

For this kind of sūtra reading, some hundreds or thousands of scrolls are kept ready in the administrative wing — generally, the *Diamond Prajñā Sūtra*, the "Universal Gate Chapter" and "Pleasant Practice Chapter" of the *Lotus Sūtra*, the *Golden Light Sūtra*, and so on.[64] One scroll is distributed to each monk. When the sūtra reading is finished, the

---

The *dāna-pāramitā*
Is fulfilled and perfected.

63 **The aim of the donor's dedication of merit** (*seshu ekō no shishu* 施主回向の旨趣): A verse for the dedication of merit (*ekōmon* 回向文) typically states how the merit was generated, to whom the merit is dedicated, and what the donor hopes to receive in return, as expressed in a formal prayer at the end of the verse. This last is the "aim" (*shishu* 旨趣) of the dedication.

64 **administrative wing** (*jōjū* 常住): Literally, "ever abiding," the term is used for the permanent property of the monastery, here extended to the administration hall (*kudō* 庫堂) and nearby adjoining administrative offices, in which lived and worked the monastic officers (*kusu* 庫司) in charge of such property.

the *Diamond Wisdom Sūtra*, the "Universal Gate Chapter" and "Pleasant Practice Chapter" of the *Lotus Sūtra*, the *Golden Light Sūtra* (*Kongō hannya kyō Hokke kyō Fumon bon Anrakugyō hon Konkyōmyō kyō* 金剛般若經・法華經普門品・安樂行品・金光明經): Some of the most popular texts for chanting: Kumārajīva's translation of the *Vajracchedikā-prajñā-pāramitā-sūtra* (*Jingang bore boluomi jing* 金剛般若波羅蜜經, T.235); Kumārajīva's translation of the *Saddharma-puṇḍarīka-sūtra* (*Miaofa lianhua jing* 妙法蓮華經, T.262), chapters 25 and 14; and Dharmakṣema's translation of the *Suvarṇa-prabhāsottama-sūtra* (*Jin guangming jing* 金光明經, T.663).

30. Sūtra Reading *Kankin* 看經   443

original stands or boxes are carried around, and as it passes it front of his seat, each monk of the great assembly deposits the sūtra. Both when taking and when depositing it, one puts palms together. When taking it, one first puts palms together and then takes it; when depositing it, one first puts it down and then puts palms together. After that, each one puts palms together and recites the dedication of merit in a low voice.

[30:35]

もし常住公界の看經には、都監寺僧、燒香・禮拜・巡堂・俵錢、みな施主のごとし。手爐をささぐる事も、施主のごとし。もし衆僧の中に施主となりて、大衆の看經を請するも、俗施主のごとし。燒香・禮拜・巡堂・俵錢等あり。知客これをひく事、俗施主のごとくなるべし。

In the event that sūtra reading is held in a common area in the administrative wing, the monk serving as prior burns incense, makes bows, tours the hall, and distributes money — all in the same way as a donor. The raising up of the hand-held censer, too, is the same as with a donor. If there is someone within the assembly of monks who, as a donor, requests that the monks of the great assembly read sūtras, [the procedure] is the same as for a lay donor, with the burning of incense, bows, hall touring, distribution of money, and so on. The procedure of the guest prefect leading [the donor] should be the same as for a lay donor.

[30:36]

聖節の看經といふ事あり。かれは、今上の聖誕の、假令もし正月十五日なれば、先十二月十五日より、聖節の看經、はじまる。今日上堂なし。佛殿の釋迦佛のまへ、連床を二行にしく。いはゆる、東西にあひむかへて、おのおの南北行にしく。東西牀のまへに檯盤をたつ。そのうへに經を安ず。金剛般若經・仁王經・法華經・最勝王經・金光明經等なり。堂裏の僧を一日に幾僧と請して、齋前に點心をおこなふ。或は麵一椀、羹一杯を毎僧に行ず。或は饅頭六七箇、羹一分、毎僧に行ずるなり。饅頭、これも椀にもれり、はしをそへたり、かひをそへず。おこなふときは、看經の座につきながら、座をうごかずしておこなふ。點心は、經を安せる檯盤に安排せり、さらに棹子をきたせることなし。行點心のあひだ、經は檯盤に安ぜり。點心、おこなひ、をはりぬれば、僧おのおの座をたちて、漱口して、かへりて座につく。すなはち看經す。粥罷より齋時にいたるまで看經す。齋時三下鼓響に、座をたつ。今日の看經は、齋時をかぎりとせり。

There is a service called the imperial holiday sūtra reading. If, for example, the current emperor's birthday is the fifteenth day of the first month, then the imperial holiday sūtra reading begins from the fifteenth day of the preceeding twelfth month. On this day, there is no convocation.[65] In the buddha hall, two rows of long seating platforms are set up in front of Buddha Śākyamuni. That is to say, they are set up in rows that

---

65 **convocation** (*jōdō* 上堂): I.e., abbot's formal teaching to the assembled community in the dharma hall.

444 DŌGEN'S *SHŌBŌGENZŌ* VOLUME II

run from south to north, and face each other east and west. Stands are placed between the east and west platforms, and on them are placed the sūtras: the *Diamond Prajñā Sūtra, Benevolent Kings Sūtra, Lotus Sūtra, Most Excellent King Sūtra,* or *Golden Light Sūtra,* and so on.[66]

Several monks are invited each day from the inner hall saṃgha, and a snack is provided before the midday meal. Sometimes, each monk is given a bowl of noodles and a cup of soup. Or, each monk is given six or seven steamed dumplings and a portion of soup. The steamed dumplings are also piled in a bowl; chopsticks are provided but a spoon is not provided. When performing the rite, the monks take their sūtra-reading seats and perform without moving from their seats. The snacks are lined up on the stands where the sūtras are placed, and no additional tables are brought in. While the snacks are being served, the sūtras remain on the stands. When snack service is finished, the monks rise from their seats, rinse their mouths, return, and take their seats. Then they do the sūtra reading. The sūtra reading continues from the close of morning gruel to the time of the main meal. With the sound of the drum struck three times to signal the time of the main meal, [the monks] stand up from their seats. The day's sūtra reading is brought to an end at the main meal time.

[30:37] {1:341}

はじむる日より、建祝聖道場の牌を、佛殿の正面の東の簷頭にかく、黄牌なり。また佛殿のうちの正面の東の柱に、祝聖の旨趣を、障子牌にかきてかく、これ黄牌なり。住持人の名字は、紅紙、あるひは白紙にかく。その二字を小片紙にかきて、牌面の年月日の下頭に貼せり。かくのごとく看經して、その御降誕の日にいたるに、住持人上堂し、祝聖するなり。これ古來の例なり、いまにふりざるところなり。

From the opening day on, an "establishing practice place for imperial prayers" placard is hung under the eaves on the east side of the front of the buddha hall. It is a horizontal placard. Also, the aim of the imperial prayers is written on a screen placard, a horizontal placard, hung on the east pillar in front of the altar inside the buddha hall. The abbbot's name is written on red paper or white paper. The two Chinese characters of the

---

66 *Diamond Prajñā Sūtra, Benevolent Kings Sūtra, Lotus Sūtra, Most Excellent Kings Sūtra,* or *Golden Light Sūtra* (*Kongō hannya kyō Ninnō kyō Hokke kyō Saishō ō kyō Konkōmyō kyō* 金剛般若經・仁王經・法華經・最勝王經・金光明經): Sūtras most often recited for protection of the nation; hence, particularly auspicious for the celebration of the emperor's birthday. For the *Diamond, Lotus,* and *Golden Light Sūtras,* see above, Note 64. The *Most Excellent Kings Sūtra* (*Zuishengwang jing* 最勝王經) is an abbreviated title for Yijing's 義浄 translation of the *Golden Light Sūtra* (*Jin guangming zuishengwang jing* 金光明最勝王經, T.665). The *Benevolent Kings Sūtra* (*Renwang jing* 仁王經) is a scripture, traditionally thought to be a translation by Kumārajīva (T.245, and again by Amoghavajra, T.246), but now considered to have been originally composed in Chinese.

30. Sūtra Reading *Kankin* 看經 445

name are written on a small sheet cf paper that is glued to the front of the placard beneath the year, month, and day. Sūtra reading in this manner is continued up until the imperial birthday, when the abbot ascends to the dharma hall and performs prayers for the emperor. This has been the custom from ancient times, and even now it is not out of fashion.

[30:38]

また、僧のみづから發心して看經するあり。寺院もとより公界の看經堂あり。かの堂につきて看經するなり。その儀、いま清規のごとし。

Again, there is sūtra reading that monks engage in of their own accord. Monasteries have always had communal sūtra reading halls. Sūtra reading is done in those halls. The ritual procedures are as given in current rules of purity.[67]

* * * * *

[30:39]

高祖藥山弘道大師、問高沙彌云、汝從看經得、從請益得。高沙彌云、不從看經得、亦不從請益得。師云、大有人不看經、不請益、爲什麼不得。高沙彌云、不道他無、只是他不肯承當。

The Eminent Ancestor, Great Master Hongdao of Yaoshan, asked Śrāmaṇera Gao, "Do you get it from reading sūtras, or do you get it from seeking instruction [from a master]?"[68]

Śrāmaṇera Gao said, "I don't get it from reading sūtras, and I don't get it from seeking instruction."

The Master said, "Lots of people don't read sūtras and don't seek instruction. Why don't they get it?"

Śrāmaṇera Gao said, "I don't say they don't have it. It's just that they don't accept it."

---

67 **current rules of purity** (*ima shingi* いま清規). Almost certainly a reference to the *Chanyuan qinggui* 禪苑清規, compiled in 1103, a set of organizational and procedural guidelines that circulated widely in Song China and was used by Dōgen and other Zen masters to promote Song-style monastic practice in Japan. Many chapters of Dōgen's *Shōbōgenzō* contain quotations of and commentaries on passages from this text.

68 **The Eminent Ancestor, Great Master Hongdao of Yaoshan** (*kōso Yakusan Gudō daishi* 高祖藥山弘道大師): I.e., Yaoshan Weiyan 藥山惟儼. This story appears in the biography of Śrāmaṇera Gao (*Gao shami* 高沙彌) found in the *Jingde chuandeng lu* 景德傳燈錄 (T.2076.51:315c14-17).

[30:40] {1:342}

佛祖の屋裏に承當あり、不承當ありといへとも、看經・請益は、家常の調
度なり。

Although, within the house of the buddhas and ancestors, there is "accepting it" and there is "not accepting it," sūtra reading and seeking instruction are everyday implements.

正法眼藏看經第三十
Treasury of the True Dharma Eye
Sūtra Reading
Number 30

[Ryūmonji MS:]

天文丁未桃月十九日、挍了
Proofed nineteenth day, peach month, junior fire year of the sheep, Tenbun [9 April 1547][69]

[Tōunji MS:]

爾時仁治二年辛丑秋九月十五日、在雍州宇治郡興聖寶林寺示衆
Presented to the assembly at Kōshō Hōrin Monastery, Uji District, Yōshū; fifteenth day, ninth month, autumn of the junior wood year of the ox, the second year of Ninji [21 October 1241]

寬元三年乙巳七月八日、在越州吉田縣大佛寺侍司書寫之。懷奘
Transcribed in the acolyte's office, Daibutsu Monastery, Yoshida District, Esshū; eighth day, seventh month of the junior wood year of the snake, the third year of Kangen [1 August 1245]. Ejō

---

69   By Tessō Hōken 喆凾芳賢 (d. 1551), copyist of the Ryūmonji 龍門寺 MS. This manuscript lacks the usual colophon by Dōgen.

peach month (*tōgetsu* 桃月): I.e., the third month of the lunar calendar.

The Sōtō Zen Text Project *Shōbōgenzō*

Volume I
The Seventy-five-Chapter Compilation, Part 1

1. The Realized Kōan *Genjō kōan* 現成公案
2. Mahā-prajñā-pāramitā *Maka hannya haramitsu* 摩訶般若波羅蜜
3. Buddha Nature *Busshō* 佛性
4. Studying the Way with Body and Mind *Shinjin gakudō* 身心學道
5. This Mind Itself Is the Buddha *Soku shin ze butsu* 即心是佛
6. Deportment of the Practicing Buddha *Gyōbutsu iigi* 行佛威儀
7. One Bright Pearl *Ikka myōju* 一顆明珠
8. The Mind Cannot Be Got *Shin fukatoku* 心不可得
9. The Old Buddha Mind *Kobutsushin* 古佛心
10. Great Awakening *Daigo* 大悟
11. Principles of Seated Meditation *Zazen gi* 坐禪儀
12. Needle of Seated Meditation *Zazen shin* 坐禪箴
13. Ocean Seal Samādhi *Kaiin zanmai* 海印三昧
14. Sky Flowers *Kūge* 空華
15. Radiance *Kōmyō* 光明

Volume II
The Seventy-five-Chapter Compilation, Part 2

16A. Sustained Practice, Part 1 *Gyōji jō* 行持上
16B. Sustained Practice, Part 2 *Gyōji ge* 行持下
17. Such *Inmo* 恁麼
18. Avalokiteśvara *Kannon* 觀音
19. The Old Mirror *Kokyō* 古鏡
20. Sometimes *Uji* 有時
21. Prediction *Juki* 授記
22. Full Function *Zenki* 全機
23. The Moon *Tsuki* 都機
24. Painted Cake *Gabyō* 畫餅
25. Sound of the Stream, Form of the Mountain *Keisei sanshoku* 谿聲山色
26. Beyond the Buddha *Butsu kōjō ji* 佛向上事
27. Talking of a Dream within a Dream *Muchū setsumu* 夢中説夢
28. Making a Bow and Getting the Marrow *Raihai tokuzui* 禮拜得髓
29. The Mountains and Waters Sūtra *Sensui kyō* 山水經
30. Sūtra Reading *Kankin* 看經

Volume III
The Seventy-five-Chapter Compilation, Part 3

31. Do No Evil *Shoaku makusa* 諸惡莫作
32. Transmitting the Robe *Den'e* 傳衣
33. Sayings *Dōtoku* 道得
34. The Teachings of the Buddhas *Bukkyō* 佛教
35. Spiritual Powers *Jinzū* 神通
36. The Arhat *Arakan* 阿羅漢

37. Spring and Autumn *Shunjū* 春秋
38. Tangled Vines *Kattō* 葛藤
39. The Inheritance Certificate *Shisho* 嗣書
40. The Cypress Tree *Hakujushi* 柏樹子
41. The Three Realms Are Only Mind *Sangai yui shin* 三界唯心
42. Talking of the Mind, Talking of the Nature *Sesshin sesshō* 説心説性
43. The Real Marks of the Dharmas *Shohō jissō* 諸法實相
44. The Way of the Buddhas *Butsudō* 佛道
45. Secret Words *Mitsugo* 密語

Volume IV
The Seventy-five-Chapter Compilation, Part 4

46. The Insentient Preach the Dharma *Mujō seppō* 無情説法
47. Sūtras of the Buddhas *Bukkyō* 佛經
48. Dharma Nature *Hosshō* 法性
49. Dhāraṇī *Darani* 陀羅尼
50. Washing the Face *Senmen* 洗面
51. Face-to-Face Conferral *Menju* 面授
52. Buddhas and Ancestors *Busso* 佛祖
53. Plum Blossoms *Baika* 梅華
54. Washing and Purifying *Senjō* 洗淨
55. The Ten Directions *Jippō* 十方
56. Seeing Buddha *Kenbutsu* 見佛
57. Extensive Study *Henzan* 遍參
58. The Eye *Ganzei* 眼睛
59. Everyday Matters *Kajō* 家常
60. The Thirty-seven Factors of Bodhi *Sanjūshichi hon bodai bunpō* 三十七品菩提分法

Volume V
The Seventy-five-Chapter Compilation, Part 5

61. Song of the Dragon *Ryūgin* 龍吟
62. The Intention of the Ancestral Master's Coming from the West
     Soshi seirai i 祖師西來意
63. Bringing Forth the Mind of Bodhi *Hotsu bodai shin* 發菩提心
64. The Udumbara Blossom *Udonge* 優曇華
65. The Entire Body of the Tathāgata *Nyorai zenshin* 如來全身
66. The King of Samādhis Samādhi *Zanmai ō zanmai* 三昧王三昧
67. Turning the Dharma Wheel *Ten hōrin* 轉法輪
68. Great Practice *Dai shugyō* 大修行
69. The Samādhi of Self Verification *Jishō zanmai* 自證三昧
70. Empty Space *Kokū* 虛空
71. The Pātra Bowl *Hou* 鉢盂
72. The Retreat *Ango* 安居
73. Reading Other Minds *Tashin tsū* 他心通
74. The King Requests Saindhava *Ō saku sendaba* 王索仙陀婆
75. Leaving Home *Shukke* 出家

Volume VI
The Twelve-Chapter Compilation

T1. The Merit of Leaving Home *Shukke kudoku* 出家功德
T2. Receiving the Precepts *Jukai* 受戒
T3. The Merit of the Kāṣāya *Kesa kudoku* 袈裟功德
T4. Bringing Forth the Mind of Bodhi *Hotsu bodai shin* 發菩提心
T5. Offerings to the Buddhas *Kuyō shobutsu* 供養諸佛
T6. Refuge in the Treasures of Buddha, Dharma, and Saṃgha
    Kie buppōsōbō 歸依佛法僧寶
T7. Deep Faith in Cause and Effect *Jinshin inga* 深信因果
T8. Karma of the Three Times *Sanjigō* 三時業
T9. Four Horses *Shime* 四馬
T10. The Bhikṣu of the Fourth Dhyāna *Shizen biku* 四禪比丘
T11. One Hundred Eight Gateways to the Illumination of the Dharma
    Ippyakuhachi hōmyōmon 一百八法明門
T12. The Eight Understandings of the Great Person *Hachi dainin gaku* 八大人覺

Volume VII
Supplementary Chapters, Variant Texts

Supplementary Chapters

S1. Talk on Pursuing the Way *Bendōwa* 辨道話
S2. Procedures for the Hall of Gathered Clouds *Jūundō shiki* 重雲堂式
S3. The *Lotus* Turns the *Lotus Hokke ten Hokke* 法華轉法華
S4. The Mind Cannot Be Got *Shin fukatoku* 心不可得
S5. The Four Attractions of the Bodhisattva *Bodaisatta shishōbō* 菩提薩埵四攝法
S6. Instructions to the Administration Cloister *Ji kuin mon* 示庫院文
S7. Only Buddhas with Buddhas *Yui butsu yo butsu* 唯佛與佛
S8. Birth and Death *Shōji* 生死
S9. The Way of the Buddhas *Butsudō* 佛道 (*Dōshin* 道心)

Variant Texts

V1. Talk on Pursuing the Way *Bendōwa* 辨道話
V2. The Inheritance Certificate *Shisho* 嗣書
V3. Beyond the Buddha *Butsu kōjō ji* 佛句上事
V4. Washing the Face *Senmen* 洗面
V5. Extensive Study *Henzan* 遍參
V6. Great Awakening *Daigo* 大悟
V7. Karma of the Three Times *Sanji gō* 三時業

Volume VIII

Introduction
Appendices
Supplementary Notes
Works Cited